Near Eastern Royalty and Rome, 100-30 BC

During the first century BC the royalty of the Near and Middle East figured prominently in the great transition from the Seleucid and Ptolomaic empires, by way of the brief Pontic and Armenian empires, to the triumphant Parthian and Roman empires. Richard D. Sullivan provides, through narrative and citations, a context for the frequent references to eastern kings and queens by Caesar, Cicero, Strabo, Josephus, Tacitus, Appian, Dio, and others. He also discusses related inscriptions, coins, and papyri.

Sullivan focuses on the personnel of the many dynasties that ruled the Near and Middle East, from Thrace through Asia Minor and the Levant to Egypt, then eastward to Armenia, Mesopotamia, and Parthia. He studies such famous figures as Mithradates Eupator, Cleopatra, and Herod the Great, as well as others now obscure. To 'locate' them properly, he provides a narrative history of each dynasty and draws them together in a coherent account of Eastern royal governance and its accommodations with Rome and Parthia during the period of Rome's transition from Republic to Empire.

RICHARD D. SULLIVAN (1936–1988) was Professor of Classics and History at the University of Saskatchewan for several years. From 1980 until his death he was Adjunct Professor of History at Simon Fraser University. He wrote many articles in Greek and Roman history and published two books, *Ancient Coins of the Graeco-Roman World: The Nickle Numismatic Papers* (Waterloo, Ont. 1984, with W. Heckel) and *The Story of Ramses* (New York 1986).

PHOENIX

Journal of the Classical Association of Canada
Revue de la Société canadienne des études classiques
Supplementary Volume XXIV
Tome supplémentaire XXIV

RICHARD D. SULLIVAN

Near Eastern Royalty and Rome, 100–30 BC

UNIVERSITY OF TORONTO PRESS
Toronto Buffalo London

Toronto Buffalo London
Printed in Canada
ISBN 0-8020-2682-6

Canadian Cataloguing in Publication Data

Sullivan, Richard D., 1936–1988
Near Eastern royalty and Rome, 100–30 BC

(Phoenix. Supplementary volume; 24 = Phoenix.
Tome supplémentaire ISSN 0079-1784; 24)
Bibliography: p.
Includes index.
ISBN 0-8020-2682-6

1. Middle East – History – To 622. 2. Rome – History – Republic, 265–30 B.C. 3. Middle East – Kings and rulers. 4. Royal houses – Middle East – History. I. Title. II. Series: Phoenix. Supplementary volume (Toronto, Ont.); 24.

DS62.23.S85 1989 939'.4 C89-094277-3

This book has been published with
the help of a grant from
the Canadian Federation for the Humanities,
using funds provided by the Social Sciences and
Humanities Research Council of Canada.

NOTE

On 12 July 1988 my husband, Richard D. Sullivan, died in Vancouver at the age of fifty-two. Death took him swiftly, shielding him from the knowledge that he would not see the publication of this book, which had been the focus of his research for several years. At the time of his death, the manuscript of the book had been accepted for publication and was in its final form. He had completed a reworking of the text, selected the illustrations, drawn the stemmata, and arranged for the preparation of the maps. My contribution has been small: entering corrections on the manuscript, checking page proofs, preparing an index. The index was made ready principally by Mrs Lyn Rae, whom I thank for her generous help. Errors that may have entered the text during these final stages of preparation I accept as my own. Since the dedication was written long before my husband's death, I have left it in place, without claiming any credit for the book. If this volume wins praise, let it be his alone.

αἱ δὲ τεαὶ ζῶουσιν ἀηδόνες, ᾗσιν ὁ πάντων
ἁρπακτὴς ᾿Αίδης οὐκ ἐπὶ χεῖρα βαλεῖ.

Shirley Darcus Sullivan
Department of Classics
University of British Columbia

January 1989

TO SHIRLEY,

WITHOUT WHOM NOT

CONTENTS

LIST OF MAPS, ILLUSTRATIONS, STEMMATA xiii

ACKNOWLEDGMENTS xv

ABBREVIATIONS xvii

MAPS xxii

Introduction 1

PART I: THE FIRST GENERATION OF CONFLICT, 100-70 BC 7

1. The Historical and Geographical Position of the Late Hellenistic Dynasties 9

I. The Hellenistic Background 9

II. Kings 12

III. Intermarriage 14

IV. Dynastic Politics 16

V. Historical Geography 17

VI. Rome; Parthia 20

2. Asia Minor and the Mithradatic Wars 25

§1. Thrace 25

§2. Bithynia 30

§3. Pontus 35

§4. Galatia 48

§5. Cappadocia 51

3. The Levant 59
§6. Commagene 59
§7. Emesa 62
§8. Seleucid Syria 65
§9. Palestine, the Nabataeans, Judaea 69

4. Egypt 81
§10. The Ptolemies of Egypt 81

5. Dynasties beyond the Euphrates, 100-69 BC 96
§11. Armenia 96
§12. Trans-Euphrates Dynasties, I 105
§13. Parthia 112

ILLUSTRATIONS 122

PART II: THE EAST IN THE GENERATION OF ACTIUM, 69-30 BC 143

6. Asia Minor in the Generation before Actium 145
§14. Thrace: The Odrysian-Astaean Dynasty 145
§15. Pontus 151
§16. Galatia 163
§17. Cappadocia 174
§18. Cilicia. The Tarcondimotids 185

7. The Levant 193
§19. Commagene 193
§20. Emesa 198
§21. The Last Seleucids 202
§22. Palestine, the Nabataeans, Judaea 205

8. Egypt 229
§23. The Last Ptolemies 229

9. Dynasties beyond the Euphrates 280
§24. Armenia 280
§25. Trans-Euphrates Dynasties, II 291
§26. Parthia 300

PART III: THE ROYAL EAST 319

10. The Eastern Dynastic Network 321

11. Epilogue 329

NOTES 335

SELECTED BIBLIOGRAPHY 473

INDEX 495

STEMMATA

MAPS, ILLUSTRATIONS, STEMMATA

Maps

1. The Middle East from Greece to the Indus River xxii–xxiii
2. Thrace and Asia Minor xxiv
3. Mesopotamia xxv
4. Armenia and N. Mesopotamia xxvi
5. Egypt and the Levant xxvii

Illustrations

Nicomedes II of Bithynia 122
Mithradates VI Eupator of Pontus 122
Anatolian Plateau in Ancient Galatia 123
Ariobarzanes I of Cappadocia 124
Possibly Queen Laodice of Commagene 124
View from a volcanic-cone habitation near Göreme (Cappadocia) 125
Antiochus I of Commagene with 'Armenian' tiara 126
Cleopatra Thea and Antiochus VIII Grypus 126
Rock-cut structures at Petra, the Nabataean capital 127
Ptolemy XII Auletes 128
Tigranes the Great of Armenia 128
View eastward from Nemrud Dagh 129
Hatra: ruins of the Great Palace 129
Queen Dynamis of Bosporus 130
Polemo I of Pontus 130
The ruins at Susa, *circa* 1920 131
Mithradates II of Parthia 131

Tarcondimotus I of Cilicia 132
Archelaus I of Cappadocia 132
Temple at Elaeussa-Sebaste, Cilicia 133
Emesa: unknown member of Royal Family 134
Commagene: Colossi atop Nemrud Dagh 135
Jerusalem. Mt Moriah's 'Dome of the Rock' 136
Cleopatra VII; Antony on reverse 137
Antony as triumvir; Cleopatra on reverse 137
Cleopatra VII holding Ptolemy XV 138
Cleopatra as Isis: temple at Denderah 139
Artavasdes I of Atropatene 140
Phraates III of Parthia 141
Orodes II of Parthia 141
Pacorus I of Parthia 141
The ruins of the Nabataean city of Humayma 142

Stemmata

1. Thrace
2. Pontus
3. Galatia
4. Cappadocia
5. Commagene
6. Emesa
7. Ptolemies and Seleucids
8. Judaea
9. Armenia; Atropatene
10. Parthia

ACKNOWLEDGMENTS

No study like this one can progress without the work of numerous scholars. Its debt to previous generations of them appears throughout the notes and bibliography. Thanking those who, over the years, have commented on aspects of the preparation of this volume, but who thus assume no liability for my errors, is a pleasure. Professor Mortimer H. Chambers directed my dissertation on an aspect of the subject. Further suggestions came, in North America, from Professors E. Badian, G.W. Bowersock, T.S. Brown, R. Hewsen, P.M. Swan, and S. Vryonis. At Oxford, comments were offered by Professor Fergus Millar, Dr Stephen Mitchell, Dr John Rea, Dr Sue Sherwin-White, and Sir Ronald Syme. Mr Eric Gray of Christ Church improved the book fundamentally. The late Dr Colin Kraay made his vast numismatic knowledge unstintingly available. In London, suggestions came from Professor A.D.H. Bivar, Professor M.A.R. Colledge, the late Professor Eric Turner, and Mr G.K. Jenkins of the British Museum; in Europe, from Professor Dr F.K. Dörner, the late Dr Otto Mørkholm, Dr Elmar Schwertheim, Prince Cyril Toumanoff, and Dr Jörg Wagner. For permission to reproduce illustrations of various figures and coins and certain of the stemmata, I thank the British Museum, the Damascus Museum, the Heberden Coin Room at the Ashmolean Museum, and Walter de Gruyter and Co.

The book benefited immeasurably from my being allowed access to the facilities of the Ashmolean Museum in Oxford as Permanent Reader, and from support by the Social Sciences and Humanities Research Council of Canada. It has been published with the help of a grant from the Canadian Federation for the Humanities, using funds provided by the Social Sciences and Humanities Research Council of Canada. Resources at the University of Saskatchewan, Simon Fraser University, the University of British Columbia, Harvard University, and the University of California at Berkeley and Los

Angeles also facilitated the study. To Mr Robert Smith and Mrs Marianne Favero, who diligently entered the first version of the book onto the computer, and to Mr Luke Dallabona, who drew the maps, I give my thanks. Mr Philip Amos read the manuscript carefully, to its benefit. To all who helped with this project I express my deep appreciation.

Richard D. Sullivan
June 1988

ABBREVIATIONS

Most abbreviations used in this book are as in *L'année philologique*. Others appear below.

AE	*L'année épigraphique* (1888–present)
ANRW	*Aufstieg und Niedergang der römischen Welt*, ed. H. Temporini and W. Haase (Berlin 1972–present)
ANSMN	*American Numismatic Society, Museum Notes* [also *ANSMusN*]
Archiv	*Archiv für Papyrusforschung*
BASP	*Bulletin of the American Society of Papyrologists*
BGU	*Berliner griechische Urkunden* (*Aegyptische Urkunden aus den königlichen Museen zu Berlin*, 1895–present)
BMC	*Catalogue of the Greek Coins in the British Museum* (identified by regional names). The following are used herein, all published in London: B.V. Head and P. Gardner, *Thrace*, 1877; P. Gardner, *Seleucid Kings of Syria*, 1878; R.S. Poole, *The Ptolemies, Kings of Egypt*, 1883; W. Wroth, *Pontus and Paphlagonia*, 1889; G.F. Hill, *Lycia, Pamphylia, and Pisidia*, 1897; W. Wroth, *Galatia, Cappadocia, and Syria*, 1899; G.F. Hill, *Lycaonia, Isauria, and Cilicia*, 1900; W. Wroth, *Parthia*, 1903; G.F. Hill, *Arabia, Mesopotamia, and Persia*, 1922. These must now be supplemented with *SNG* and other sources.
Broughton	See *MRR*, below.
CAH	*The Cambridge Ancient History*, esp. Vols. IX-XI (Cambridge 1932 to 1936; new editions in preparation)
CHRESTOMATHIE	See *Grundzüge*, below.
CIG	*Corpus Inscriptionum Graecarum*

CIL	*Corpus Inscriptionum Latinarum* I-XVI (Berlin 1862 ff., ed. Th. Mommsen and others)
CIRB	B. Latyschev, *Corpus Inscriptionum Regni Bosporani* (Moscow-Leningrad 1965)
EPRO	*Études préliminaires aux religions orientales dans l'empire romain* (Leiden: Brill)
ESAR	T. Frank, ed., *An Economic Survey of Ancient Rome*, I-V (Baltimore 1933-1940)
Festschrift Dörner	S. Şahin, E. Schwertheim, and J. Wagner, eds., *Studien zur Religion und Kultur Kleinasiens: Festschrift für F.K. Dörner zum 65. Geburstag*, I-II (Leiden 1978; = *EPRO* 66)
FGrH	F. Jacoby, *Die Fragmente der griechischen Historiker*, 13 vols. (Berlin 1923-1958) [also *FGrHist*]
FHG	C. Müller, *Fragmenta Historicorum Graecorum*, 1-5 (Paris 1841-1870)
Grundzüge	L. Mitteis and U. Wilcken, *Grundzüge und Chrestomathie der Papyruskunde* (Leipzig 1912)
Head, *HN*²	B.V. Head, *Historia Numorum. A Manual of Greek Numismatics*, 2nd ed. (Oxford 1911)
IG	*Inscriptiones Graecae*
I.G.Bulg.	G. Mihailov, *Inscriptiones Graecae, Bulgaria Repertae* I, 2nd ed. (Sophia 1970) [also *IGBR*]
IGCH	M. Thompson, O. Mørkholm, and C. Kraay, *Inventory of Greek Coin Hoards* (New York 1973)
IGLS	L. Jalabert, R. Mouterde, and others, *Inscriptions grecques et latines de la Syrie*, I-XIII (Paris 1929-1982) [also *IGLSyr*]
IGRR	R. Cagnat and others, *Inscriptiones Graecae ad Res Romanas Pertinentes*, I, III, IV (Paris 1906-1927)
IGSK	*Inschriften griechischer Städte aus Kleinasien* (Bonn)
ILLRP	A. Degrassi, *Inscriptiones Latinae Liberae Rei Publicae*, I (Firenze 1957)
ILS	H. Dessau, *Inscriptiones Latinae Selectae*, I-III (Berlin 1892-1916)
IMiletus	A. Rehm, *Die Inschriften: Milet* III (Berlin 1914)
IOSPE	B. Latyschev, *Inscriptiones antiquae orae septentrionalis Ponti Euxini Graecae et Latinae*, 2nd ed. (Petersburg 1916)
IPriene	F. Hiller von Gaetringen, *Die Inschriften von Priene* (Berlin 1906)
JHS	*Journal of Hellenic Studies*
Jones, *Cities*²	A.H.M. Jones, *The Cities of the Eastern Roman Provinces*, 2nd ed. (Oxford 1971)

JRS	*Journal of Roman Studies*
MAMA	*Monumenta Asiae Minoris Antiqua*, I-VIII (Manchester 1928-1962)
MélBeyr	*Mélanges de la Faculté Orientale de l'Université Saint-Joseph* (Beyrouth, Liban) [also abbreviated *MUB*]
MélBidez	*Mélanges Bidez* (Bruxelles 1934; Univ. Libre de Bruxelles, Annuaire de l'institut de philologie et d'histoire orientales)
MRR	T.R.S. Broughton, *The Magistrates of the Roman Republic*, I-II with Supplements (Lancaster, Pa., and New York 1951-1952, 1960, and 1986)
NNM	*Numismatic Notes and Monographs* (American Numismatic Society, New York)
OGIS	W. Dittenberger, *Orientis Graeci Inscriptiones Selectae*, I and II (Leipzig 1903 and 1905)
PEQ	*Palestine Exploration Quarterly*
PIR^2	E. Groag, with A. Stein and L. Petersen, *Prosopographia Imperii Romani*, 2nd ed. (Berlin 1933–present). By 1987, it had reached letters N-O (Pars V, fasc. 3). This book and its stemmata use the numbers from the first edition of this work for the letters from M to Z.
PIR	H. Dessau and others, *Prosopographia Imperii Romani* (Berlin 1897-1898)
P. Lond.	F. Kenyon and H. Bell, *Greek Papyri in the British Museum* (London 1893-1917)
P. Mich.	C. Edgar and others, *Papyri in the University of Michigan Collection* (Ann Arbor 1931-1947)
PP	W. Peremans, E. van 't Dack, and others, *Prosopographia Ptolemaica* (Louvain 1950 onward), esp. Vol. VI (1968)
RE	Pauly-Wissowa-Kroll, *Real-Encyclopädie der classischen Altertumswissenschaft*
REArm	*Revue des Études arméniennes*
Recueil I^2	W. Waddington, E. Babelon, and Th. Reinach, *Recueil général des monnaies grecques*, 2nd ed. (Paris 1925), Vol. I
SB	*Sammelbuch griechischer Urkunden aus Ägypten* (see Bibliography, under Preisigke, F.)
Schürer	E. Schürer (revised by G. Vermes and F. Millar), *History of the Jewish People in the Age of Jesus Christ (175 B.C.–A.D. 135)*, I-III.1 (Edinburgh 1973-1986)
SDB	*Dictionnaire de la Bible, Suppl.* VII (Paris 1966)
SEG	*Supplementum Epigraphicum Graecum*

SEHHW	M.I. Rostovtzeff, *The Social and Economic History of the Hellenistic World*, I-III (Oxford 1941)
SEHRE	M.I. Rostovtzeff, *The Social and Economic History of the Roman Empire*, 2nd ed., rev. P.M. Fraser (Oxford 1957)
SIG[3]	W. Dittenberger, *Sylloge Inscriptionum Graecarum*, I-IV, 3rd ed. (Leipzig 1915-1924)
Smallwood, *Jews*	E.M. Smallwood, *The Jews under Roman Rule* (Leiden 1976; corr. repr. 1981)
Sylloge[3]	See SIG[3], above.
TAM	*Tituli Asiae Minoris*
TAVO B V 6	E. Olshausen and J. Wagner, 'Asia Minor and Black Sea Area: The Epoch of Mithradates the Great (121-63 B.C.),' *Tübinger Atlas des Vorderen Orients* B V 6 (Wiesbaden 1981)
TAVO B V 7	J. Wagner, 'Eastern Mediterranean and Mesopotamia. The Reorganization of the Orient from Pompey to Augustus (67 B.C.–14 A.D.),' *Tübinger Atlas des Vorderen Orients* B V 7 (Wiesbaden 1982)
Wilcken, *Chrest.*	U. Wilken, *Grundzüge und Chrestomathie der Papyruskunde*, 2 vols. (Leipzig and Berlin 1912)
ZfN	*Zeitschrift für Numismatik* [also abbreviated *ZNum*]

Maps

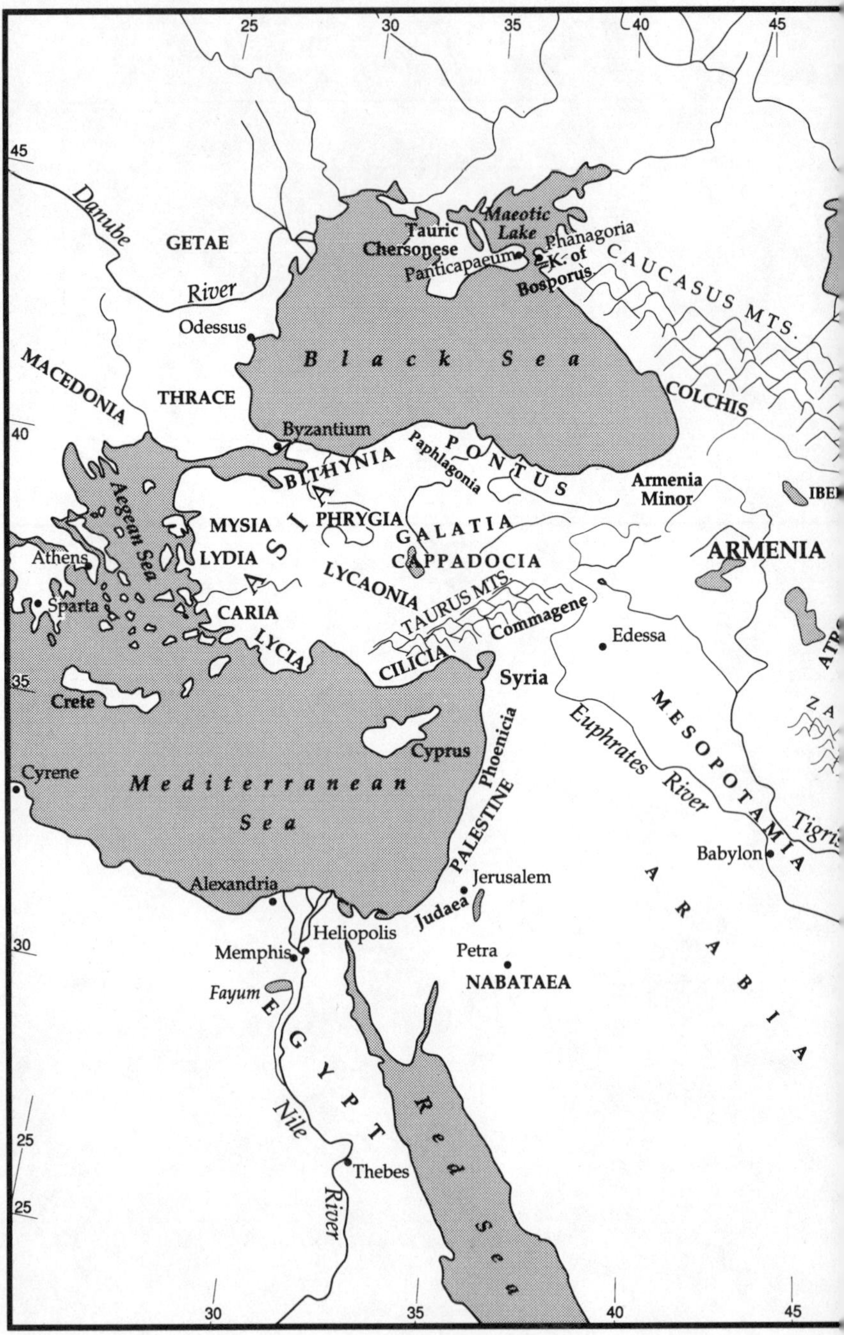

GETAE
Danube
River
Odessus
Black Sea
Tauric Chersonese
Maeotic Lake
Phanagoria
Panticapaeum
K. of Bosporus
CAUCASUS MTS.
MACEDONIA
THRACE
Byzantium
COLCHIS
BITHYNIA
Paphlagonia
PONTUS
Armenia Minor
ARMENIA
Aegean Sea
MYSIA
PHRYGIA
GALATIA
ASIA
Athens
LYDIA
CAPPADOCIA
Sparta
LYCAONIA
CARIA
TAURUS MTS.
Commagene
LYCIA
CILICIA
Edessa
Crete
Syria
MESOPOTAMIA
Euphrates River
Cyprus
Phoenicia
Cyrene
Mediterranean Sea
PALESTINE
Tigris
Babylon
Jerusalem
Alexandria
Judaea
ARABIA
Heliopolis
Memphis
Petra
NABATAEA
Fayum
EGYPT
Nile River
Thebes
Red Sea

The Middle East from Greece to the Indus River
0 Kilometres 500
0 Miles 300
Map Area
N
Jaxartes R.
Aral Sea
Oxus River
MASSAGETAE
SOGDIANA
BACTRIA
DAHAE
HYRCANIA
BURZ MTS.
ARTHIA
KUSHANS
PUNJAB
Salt Desert
MTS.
Aspadana
ARACHOSIA
Persepolis
Carmana
SAKASTAN
PERSIS
Indus River
GEDROSIA
Arabian Sea
Sea
stan Gulf
55
60
65
70
45
40
35
30
25
50

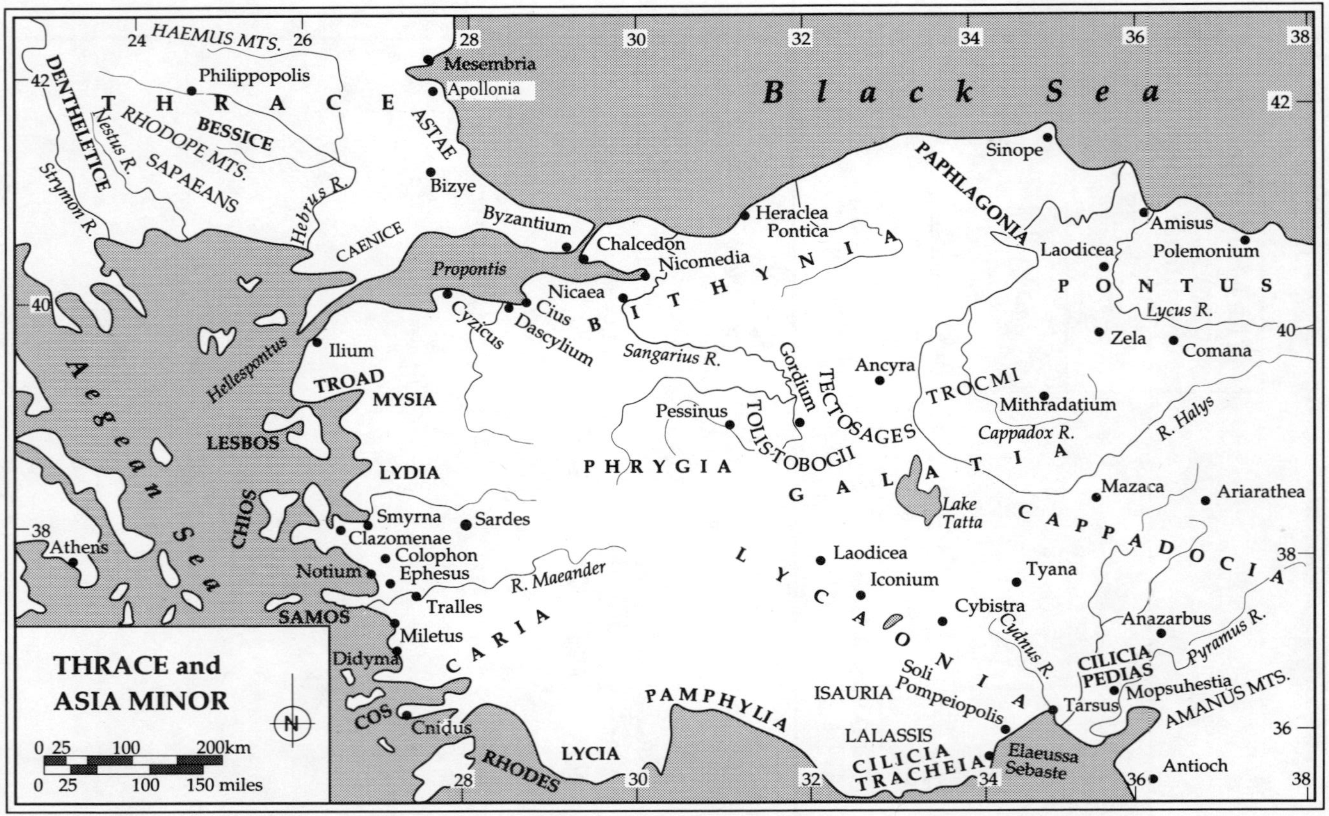

THRACE and ASIA MINOR
0 25 100 200km
0 25 100 150 miles
Black Sea
Aegean Sea
Propontis
Hellespontus
THRACE
HAEMUS MTS.
RHODOPE MTS.
DENTHELETICE
BESSICE
SAPAEANS
ASTAE
CAENICE
Strymon R.
Nestus R.
Hebrus R.
Philippopolis
Mesembria
Apollonia
Bizye
Byzantium
Chalcedon
Nicomedia
Nicaea
Cius
Cyzicus
Dascylium
Heraclea Pontica
Sinope
PAPHLAGONIA
BITHYNIA
Sangarius R.
Gordium
Ancyra
Pessinus
TECTOSAGES
TOLISTOBOGII
TROCMI
GALATIA
PHRYGIA
Mithradatium
Cappadox R.
R. Halys
Amisus
Laodicea
Polemonium
PONTUS
Lycus R.
Zela
Comana
Ilium
TROAD
MYSIA
LESBOS
LYDIA
CHIOS
Smyrna
Sardes
Clazomenae
Colophon
Notium
Ephesus
R. Maeander
Tralles
SAMOS
Miletus
Didyma
CARIA
COS
Cnidus
RHODES
LYCIA
PAMPHYLIA
Athens
Lake Tatta
Mazaca
Ariarathea
CAPPADOCIA
LYCAONIA
Laodicea
Iconium
Tyana
Cybistra
Cydnus R.
Anazarbus
Pyramus R.
CILICIA PEDIAS
Mopsuhestia
AMANUS MTS.
Tarsus
Soli Pompeiopolis
ISAURIA
LALASSIS
CILICIA TRACHEIA
Elaeussa Sebaste
Antioch

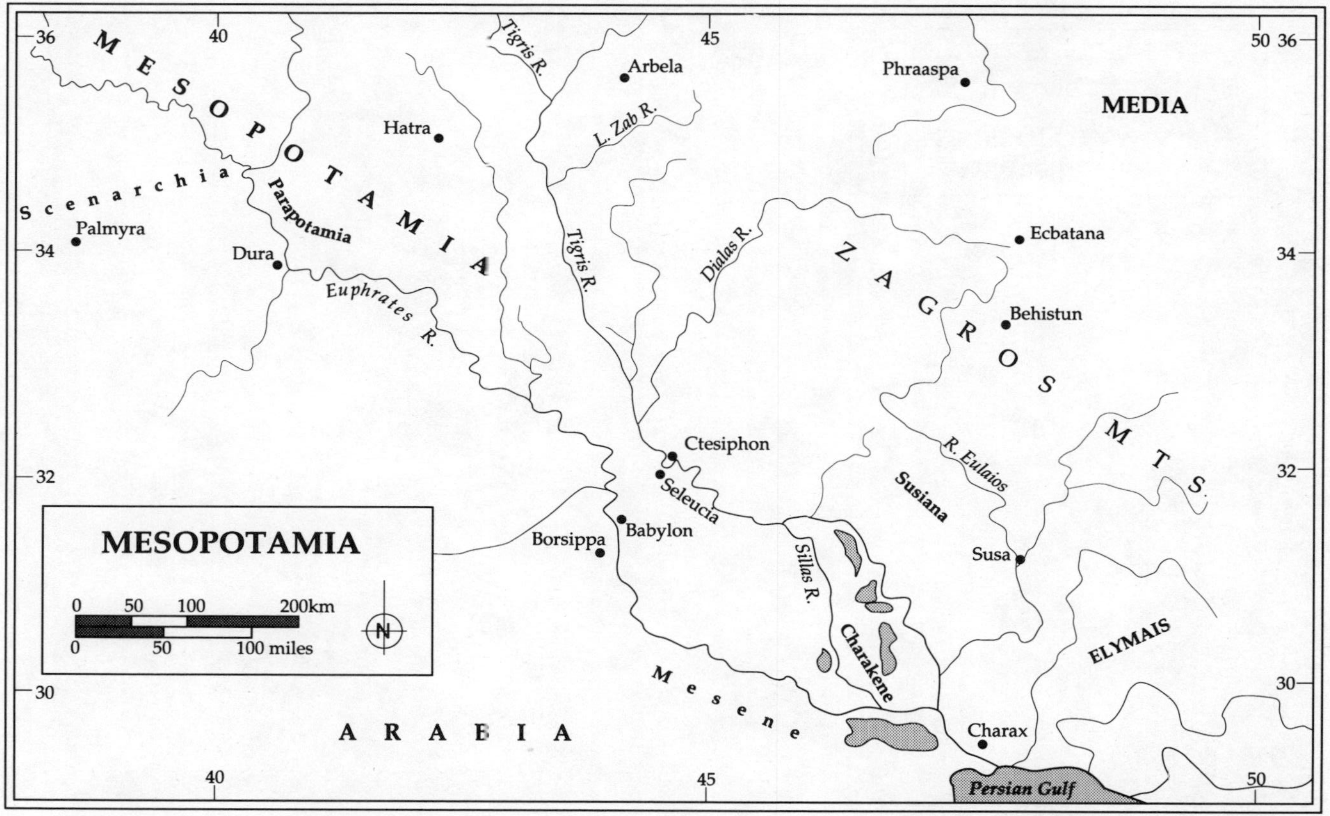
MESOPOTAMIA
0
50
100
200km
0
50
100 miles
N
MESOPOTAMIA
Scenarchia
Parapotamia
MEDIA
ZAGROS MTS.
Susiana
Charakene
ELYMAIS
Mesene
ARABIA
Palmyra
Dura
Hatra
Arbela
Phraaspa
Ecbatana
Behistun
Ctesiphon
Seleucia
Babylon
Borsippa
Susa
Charax
Persian Gulf
Euphrates R.
Tigris R.
Tigris R.
L. Zab R.
Dialas R.
R. Eulaios
Sillas R.
36
40
45
50
34
32
30

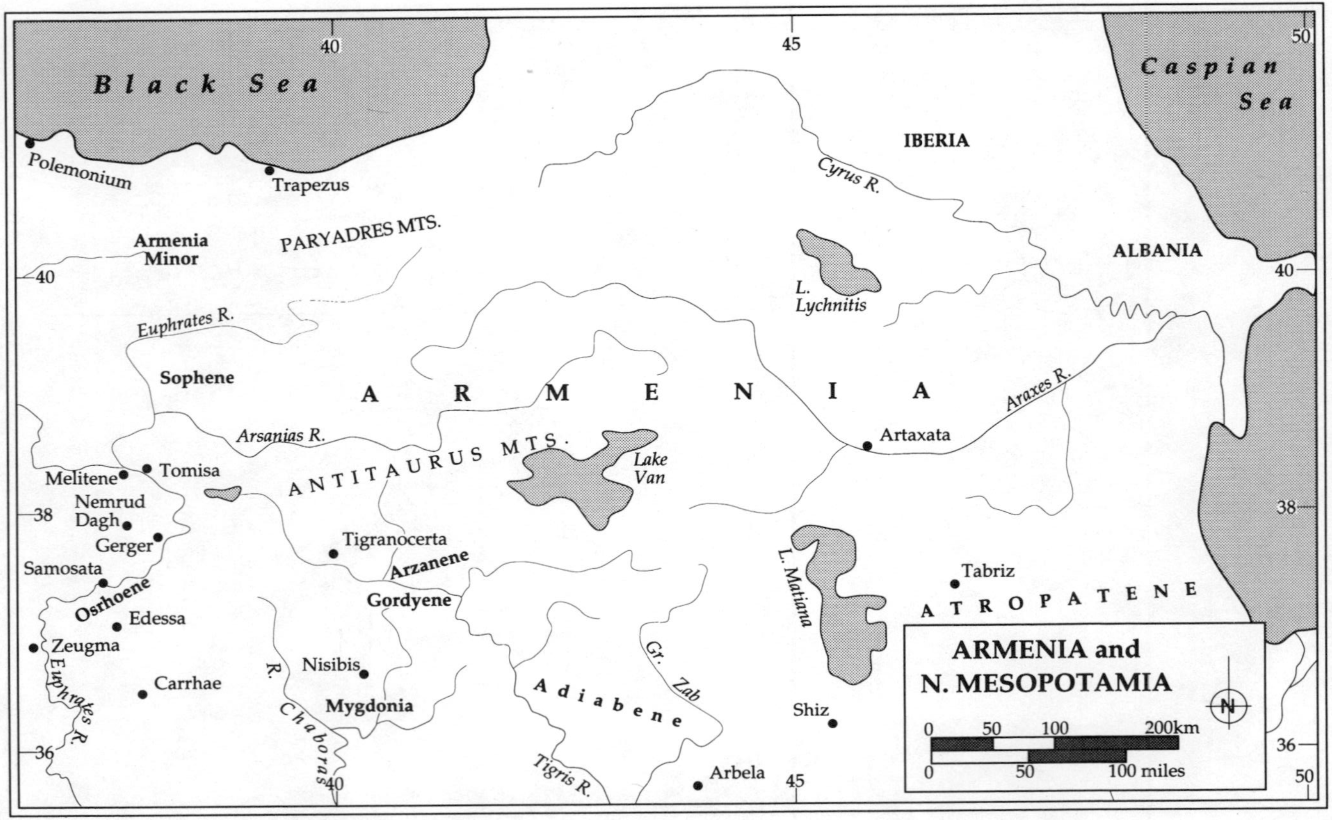
ARMENIA and
N. MESOPOTAMIA
Black Sea
Caspian Sea
IBERIA
ALBANIA
ARMENIA
ATROPATENE
Armenia Minor
PARYADRES MTS.
ANTITAURUS MTS.
Sophene
Arzanene
Gordyene
Osrhoene
Mygdonia
Adiabene
Polemonium
Trapezus
Melitene
Tomisa
Nemrud Dagh
Gerger
Samosata
Edessa
Zeugma
Carrhae
Tigranocerta
Nisibis
Artaxata
Tabriz
Shiz
Arbela
Cyrus R.
Araxes R.
Euphrates R.
Arsanias R.
Chaboras R.
Gr. Zab
Tigris R.
L. Lychnitis
Lake Van
L. Matiana
0 50 100 200km
0 50 100 miles
N
40
45
50
38
36

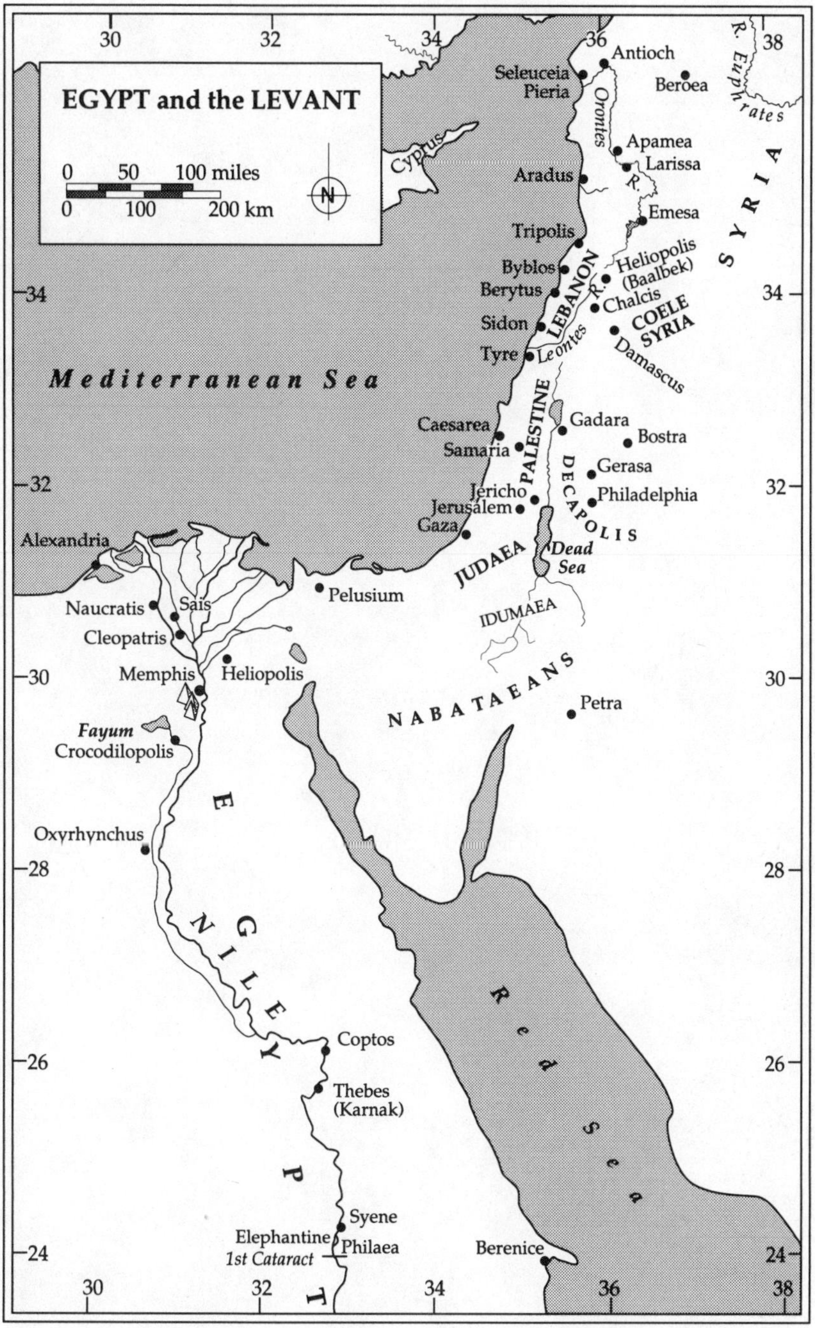
EGYPT and the LEVANT
0 50 100 miles
0 100 200 km
N
Mediterranean Sea
Cyprus
Antioch
Seleuceia Pieria
Beroea
R. Euphrates
Orontes R.
Apamea
Larissa
Aradus
Emesa
SYRIA
Tripolis
Byblos
Berytus
Heliopolis (Baalbek)
Chalcis
LEBANON
COELE SYRIA
Sidon
Tyre
Leontes R.
Damascus
PALESTINE
Gadara
Caesarea
Samaria
Bostra
DECAPOLIS
Gerasa
Jericho
Jerusalem
Philadelphia
Gaza
Alexandria
JUDAEA
Dead Sea
IDUMAEA
Pelusium
Naucratis
Sais
Cleopatris
Memphis
Heliopolis
NABATAEANS
Petra
Fayum
Crocodilopolis
EGYPT
NILE
Oxyrhynchus
Red Sea
Coptos
Thebes (Karnak)
Syene
Elephantine
Philaea
1st Cataract
Berenice
30
32
34
36
38
24
26
28

Near Eastern Royalty and Rome, 100–30 BC

INTRODUCTION

After a period of relative neglect, the history of the Greek, Iranian, Arab, and Jewish worlds during late Hellenistic and early Imperial times has been the subject of a number of studies (see Selected Bibliography). The work of Altheim and Stiehl, Bowersock, Braund, Cimma, Colledge, Gagé, Gruen, Hoben, Olshausen, Pani, Schürer (revised by Vermes and Millar), Sherwin-White, Smallwood, and others has begun to fill the vacancy caused by the gradual outdating of *CAH*, Magie, Rostovtzeff, and other authorities in the field. The contributions of numismatic, epigraphical, papyrological, archaeological, and historical studies in recent decades have put much of the field on a new footing, and the results of these studies are entering the literature.

P.C. Sands dealt thematically with a portion of the present topic in his Thirlwall Prize Essay of 1906, *The Client Princes of the Roman Empire under the Republic* (publ. Cambridge 1908). That curious title reflects the difficulties of the subject, and, as yet, no study has attempted a systematic treatment of the Late Hellenistic dynasties themselves, though the accumulation of evidence concerning the several hundred known royal individuals from 190 BC to AD 100 has been enormous. The present book attempts to furnish a narrative guide to the 'tangled histories' (J.B. Ward-Perkins) of the Eastern dynasties from 100 BC to 30 BC, examining two generations of these rulers, not as 'clients' (see Ch. 1) but as representatives of centuries-old royal systems firmly controlling the East. In this period, these rulers dealt with one of the ancient world's most momentous series of events: the collapse of the Seleucid and Ptolemaic empires, the efflorescence of the Pontic empire of Mithradates Eupator and the Armenian one of Tigranes, and the replacement of all four of these by the empires of Rome and Parthia. Though the roots of this transformation go back, and the consequences ahead, for centuries, the seventy years within which it occurred (100-30 BC) can be studied separately.

The period immediately preceding that focused upon in this book belongs to Hellenistic history, as do the kings and queens treated here. In the Near East, the last two centuries before Christ constituted a time of transition, with Rome a distant element before 190 but an active diplomatic agent by 100, on the threshold of serious military and political intervention. The evolution of Roman policy after Magnesia and Apamea included military activity in Galatia and by governors of the new territory in Macedonia, drawn eastward against Thracians. Only with the acquisition of the Attalid Kingdom in 133 BC did the new era open, and then slowly. Also in the second century, the Parthians rapidly eroded any remaining Seleucid authority east of the Euphrates.

While the present study treats some events of the period 133-100 BC, it does so in detail only for those beginning in 100 and after. During the six years after 101 BC, events took place that had profound consequences in the Near East. To review them, one would need in the following pages to consult the discussions on the conquests of Didius; the visit of Marius; the Bithynian attempt on Cappadocia; the election of Ariobarzanes; the aggressive acts against Cappadocia by Eupator; his son's reign there; the campaign of Sulla; his meeting with the Parthian representative; the formation of the new Pontic Empire; the release of Tigranes; his marriage alliance with Eupator; the inception of the Armenian Empire; the sole rule of Grypus; the Seleucid juncture with Commagene; the fratricidal warfare among the Seleucid sons of Grypus; the conquests of Jannaeus; the watershed reign of Cleopatra III; the bequest of Cyrene; the overtures to Rome by Mithradates II of Parthia. A glance at the index will locate any of these. The opening pages of the first thirteen sections of the book set the contexts for each.

The rationale for ending the study with 30 BC can be given more succinctly. Actium and the deaths of Cleopatra and Antony closed one era and opened another. Hellenistic history is usually considered to have ended here, and the transition from Roman republic to empire did create markedly different conditions for the dynasties west of the Euphrates than prevailed before. However, the changes came slowly, and at the death of Cleopatra most of the Near East up to the Euphrates, and all of it beyond, remained loyal. The closing pages of the last thirteen sections of the book provide an account of the consequences of Actium for each dynasty.

Full explanation must sometimes involve treatment of events occurring a few years before 100 BC or a few years after 30 BC. These limits can be altered slightly for many dynasties. However, the basic themes of the book require that these seventy years serve as the focal period.

The break in treatment at the end of one generation, that is, at 70/69 BC, accords in major respects with the book's themes, especially given the direct consequences for Pontus, Armenia, Syria, and Rome of the battle at Tigranocerta in 69, with its indirect consequences for Egypt, Judaea, Commagene, Emesa, and many of the kingdoms beyond the Euphrates, including Parthia. The ramifications of this break are studied in the closing pages of the first thirteen sections and the opening pages of the last thirteen sections. In or soon after 70 BC occurred the removal of Tigranes as an international force, and the consequent collapse of the Seleucids, despite the last attempts of Antiochus XIII and Philip II to rule. Also then or soon after came the eclipse of Mithradates Eupator in Pontus, the advent of Deiotarus I in Galatia, the rise of the Astaean-Odrysian dynasty in Thrace, the succession of Ariobarzanes II as the new Cappadocian dynasty took hold, the emergence of Emesa under Sampsigeramus I, the transfer of power from Alexandra Salome to her two contentious sons, the reign of Aretas III the Nabataean, the first Roman contacts by Ptolemy Auletes of Egypt (the father of Cleopatra), the new dynasty of Tarcondimotus in Cilicia, the appearance of Antiochus I in Commagene, and the succession of Phraates III in Parthia. In the period 100 to 30 BC, no other division suits the historical facts as well as this one at 70/69 does, though of course it fits some dynasties better than others.

In 100 BC, much lay ahead. During the following two centuries, dynasties west of the Euphrates co-operated for the most part with the growing power of Rome, to the point of their own absorption, when a brief struggle might occur (Pergamon, Syria, Egypt, Judaea, Thrace, Commagene) or might not (Bithynia, Galatia, Cappadocia, Pontus). Even in the peaceful cases, alternative claimants (Bithynia) or an imputation of trouble under the surface (Cappadocia after Archelaus) or an arranged abdication (Polemo II in Pontus) could mar the happy event.

This book examines the kings, queens, princes, and princesses ruling the Near East, and studies the approach of Rome or Parthia. It follows the evidence, sometimes ample (as for Egypt, Judaea, or Parthia) but often meagre (Sophene and Adiabene). Some dynasties cannot be systematically included (e.g., Paphlagonia); on the other hand, some minor figures (e.g., the rulers of Chalcis) require discussion because of their relative contribution to the larger dynastic movements around them. Occasionally, as for Egypt, seemingly disproportionate treatment reflects both the abundant evidence and the region's importance to the book's themes. The span of discussion extends to previous developments in any dynasty as necessary – for instance, the early machinations of Eupator regarding Ariarathid Cappadocia, since the effects of his activity endured.

Parts of two basic questions are examined here: how the distant state of Rome took control of a dozen kingdoms up to the Euphrates in the three centuries following the victory it and its allies achieved at Magnesia, and how Parthia came to form the *de facto* limit to Roman expansion east of the Euphrates. Some accounts of this vast process have retrojected its conclusion to its stages, underestimating the contribution of kings or queens and their adherents, as well as of the individual Romans or Parthians who dealt with them. The long and painful progress of Rome to more than nominal control of this entire region involved quite as much diplomatic as military skill, especially after 100 BC. The basic *modus vivendi* with the Parthian Empire was achieved about the time this study ends, soon after Actium.

This book presents these main themes with citation of ancient sources and selective reference to the most useful modern studies. Documentation has been more comprehensive than is usual, because of the fragmentary nature of the sources. To reach a responsible assessment of a king's or queen's reign may require evidence from coins, inscriptions, papyri, parchments, statues, monuments, or buildings, in addition to the usual literary authorities and scattered fragments of lost works. The notes suggest, for interested readers, the main avenues into this vast body of material. However, the text confines itself to the dynasts' external policies, their marital and state alliances, and the outcome of their multifaceted struggle to maintain the kingdoms that they inherited or created. Numerous other questions have necessarily gone untreated. The study does not attempt source-criticism and cannot usually argue disputed points: these aspects of the task have been reserved to a series of articles and monographs, or have been done by others, as cited. Questions dealt with in detail here do *not* include how the dynasties worked; what their methods of landholding were; how they dealt with finance, military control, or lower levels of political authority. These would require extensive separate treatment. There is also herein no systematic treatment of the composition and personnel of the dynasties' administrations; their numismatic and sculptural programs for promoting domestic loyalty (most spectacular for Antiochus of Commagene, but discernible elsewhere); their routine business with adjoining states; the domestic considerations behind Roman, Parthian, Pontic, and Armenian military or political activity; their religious practices (notable in Egypt, Judaea, Commagene, and to a lesser degree virtually everywhere).

The basic contention here is that the royal system worked well: kings and queens ruled with full authority in the East before Actium (and for the most part after, though that requires separate study). Rome and Parthia operated perforce through the existing social structure in the centuries of constructing their empires. Most of the kingdoms entered into alliance with one or, in some cases, both of them, as well as with one another. The terms on which the parties constructed these agreements were those consequent on being 'friends and allies.' The alliances remained what they purported to be, expressions of intended co-operation among sovereign states. Those kings allied to Rome controlled realms explicitly outside Roman territorial claims, into which no Roman rights extended. The kings raised and spent revenues on their own authority, coined as they wished (see Ch. 1), and retained the ancient right of kings to supremacy in judicial, religious, and military matters. Their armed forces were organized along traditional local lines. Except for unusual circumstances, as in Judaea after Pompey and elsewhere during the career of Antony, they paid no regular tribute or levies to Rome. The main restriction imposed by the alliance was what it usually is between sovereign allies: consultation on foreign policy if military conflict was involved, and mutual obligations in defence.

In the last analysis, resort to force potentially underlay the arrangements, as when Pompey met Antiochus I of Commagene and 'fought him into friendship,' or the Parthian 'King of Kings' invaded rebellious Atropatene. Ultimately, Rome (but not Parthia) was working against the interests of the kings, though it rewarded them later and co-opted their descendants into its own senatorial nobility. Nevertheless, during the centuries when kings ruled, they did so in their own right and they ruled well. By studying in detail the individuals, their family interconnections, and their dealings with other dynasts as well as with Rome or Parthia, this book seeks to reveal facets of a crucial period of Near Eastern history as Greek control gradually yielded to Roman or Iranian.

In this book the arrangement is both chronological and geographical, since the themes pursued fall naturally into two periods, both clearly reflected in regional dynastic politics. Detail is provided as appropriate to the dynasty under discussion, with consequent minor repetition for clarity. A progressive account of the kingdoms' positions emerges as examination of individual dynasties proceeds. The goal is full depiction of each kingdom by the end of Part II, with a treatment of its relation to its neighbours as well as to Rome and Parthia.

Citations of journals are as in *L'année philologique*, of ancient sources as in the *Oxford Classical Dictionary*, 2nd ed. (1970), and of modern scholars by abbreviation of the full references in the Selected Bibliography. The notes present materials in the order in which they appear in the text. The sources for a statement or argument appear in the order of their importance to it.

Orthography presents unusual problems, with Roman, Greek, Egyptian, Jewish, Arabic, and Iranian proper names on virtually every page. The practice has been to use a familiar form wherever available: hence, Cleopatra rather than Kleopatra, and Herod rather than Herodes. Some Iranian names appear in native spelling, such as Mithradates rather than Mithridates.

Others, however, are clearer if given the Greek spelling: Tigranes rather than Tigran. In the last analysis, clarity has become the only indispensable consideration. Alexander Jannaeus appears as Jannaeus since no one else does. A Ptolemaic sovereign usually receives his irreverent Alexandrian nickname – Auletes rather than Ptolemy Theos Philopator Philadelphos.

PART I

The First Generation of Conflict, 100-70 BC

1

The Historical and Geographical Position of the Late Hellenistic Dynasties

I. The Hellenistic Background

Thousands of years before the period examined in this book, the lands discussed here had already been settled by civilized peoples, as their distant descendants were fully aware. The invention of writing probably occurred here during the fourth millennium, in Mesopotamia, and soon after, in Egypt. The cities that arose were among the earliest anywhere. The ancient empires of the Sumerians, Babylonians, and Egyptians set a high standard for their successors, which the Assyrians and then the Persians tried to meet. In Asia Minor and Upper Mesopotamia, the Indo-European Hittites appeared after 2000 BC, as did other groups now imperfectly known (the Luwians, Mitanni, and Hurrians). About the time of the Trojan War a new group entered, the Phrygians.

Traces of all this past history endured into the first century, especially in religion (mankind's most conservative institution), in personal or geographical names, and in some linguistic elements. Some of these traces are reflected in this study. It is not surprising, for instance, to find Tigranes the Great employing a tiara that may derive from one belonging to the ancient Anatolian goddess Anahita. As another example, Cleopatra describes herself with formulae derived from Pharaonic high antiquity. Parthians considered themselves descended from the Achaemenid Persians. Armenians regarded their ancestry as including the ancient Kings of Urartu. And so on.

Some previous religions survived intact. The kingdoms of Pontus and Cappadocia practised Mazdaism, and Commagene featured both Ahura-mazda and Mithraism in its syncretistic pantheon. Cults from very early times were revived, such as that of the gods of Uruk in Mesopotamia. Zoroastrianism remained strong among the Parthian successors of the Achaemenids.

Linguistic survivals were more subtle, but indisputably occurred, for instance by a process called 'allography.' A Sumerian or Akkadian term, often abbreviated, might be written down even when the Hittite or Greek equivalent was to be pronounced. This process was similar to what occurs when we read 'e.g.' but say 'for example' rather than *exempli gratia*, or when we see 'etc.' but say 'and so forth' rather than *et cetera*. By this and other processes, a fund of knowledge regarding the previous civilizations survived, and the Seleucids made an effort at reviving much of this knowledge in Babylonia. They probably encouraged the making of copies of poems, hymns, omens, ritual texts, syllabaries, chronicles, and works on national history, such as the *Babyloniaca* of Berossus (*FGrH* 680), which all appeared during the time of the late Seleucids.

After Persia under Darius the Great completed its conquest of most of Asia Minor, the Levant, and Egypt by the early fifth century before Christ, it became the empire to which Near Eastern kings later traced their pedigrees. Not only did the Parthians claim descent from the Achaemenid Persians, but so did the royal lines in Pontus and Commagene. Distinguished lineage counted highly in the Near East.

The Persian attempts on Greece from 492 to 479 BC created a resentment that Alexander allayed between 334 and 323 by conquering Persia and the lands it had held. His 'Successors' (*Diadochoi*) tried to carve up and hold this vast domain, and in so doing set the stage for the movements traced in this book.

Alexander's conquests reached all the way to India, but left parts of Asia Minor free. The Persian satrapies there survived in new forms after his conquest of Persia itself. Dynasties arose by the early third century in Bithynia, Pontus, and Cappadocia, and a century later in Armenia. These maintained themselves until the first century before Christ. The Galatians moved into Asia Minor and took up permanent residence in what had been Phrygia.

The vast Persian hinterland out to the Indus received a new system of organization from the Seleucids, partly modelled on the Persian one of satrapies, but employing subdivisions called 'eparchies.' It was this type of subdivision that later gave rise to many of the smaller kingdoms discussed in this book, most of them recognizable by a termination in '-ene' (Commagene, Atropatene, Gordyene, and so on).

The rivalry between the Seleucids of Syria and the Ptolemies of Egypt kept the question of control of Asia Minor largely unsettled during the third century BC. There the Seleucids held parts of Lydia, Phrygia, Caria, and Cilicia, especially in Campestris; the Ptolemies controlled much of the seaboard from Halicarnassus northward, including the islands.

11 Late Hellenistic Dynasties

Soon after 250 BC, Bactria seceded to form its own line of rulers, and the Parthians appeared in the north of the Iranian plateau to begin their own rise to empire. Seleucid attempts to deal with this rise of Parthia, especially by Seleucus II and Antiochus III, IV, and VII, ultimately failed. Parthia grew steadily over nearly five hundred years, and gave way in the third century AD to the similarly successful Sassanids.

When Antiochus III lost the battle of Magnesia to Rome and its Eastern allies, and then reached the Peace of Apamea in 188 BC, Rome gained title to what he had possessed in Asia Minor north of the Taurus. That was not a large proportion of Asia Minor. Excluded were the kingdoms of the Attalids in Pergamon, as well as those of Bithynia, Pontus, Cappadocia, and perhaps Paphlagonia. Many small native principalities ruled on, as they had throughout Seleucid times. Galatia maintained its independence, though usually as an ally of Rome.

The defeat of Antiochus III brought other consequences in its wake. The eparchy of Commagene became independent. So did Judaea, and smaller states followed. The weakening Seleucids attempted to hold their empire, but the rising empires of Pontus, Armenia, and Parthia proved too strong. From the west, the Roman Republic had been moving steadily towards Asia Minor and the Levant since just after the end of the Second Punic War in 201 BC. After Apamea in 188, Rome ended Macedonian independence in 168 at Pydna, and Greek independence at Corinth in 146, though Thrace remained. Upon taking up the Attalid Kingdom of Pergamon in 133, Rome advanced to the position where the great contest for the Near East could begin. Under King Mithradates I, Parthia had just formed an opposing empire. Between these empires lay the twenty-three kingdoms studied here.

During the seventy years following 100 BC, several kingdoms west of the Euphrates fell at the behest of Rome (Bithynia, Syria, Egypt, Cyrene; Galatia soon to follow). Others retained their independence, with varying degrees of alliance to Rome. Pontus became subject to Rome when Mithradates and Pharnaces II were conquered, but regained its king when Antony recognized Polemo I. Cappadocia went straight through the first century before Christ as a kingdom, the dynasty of the Ariarathids yielding to that of Ariobarzanes and it in turn to Archelaus. Commagene continued its relatively new royal traditions throughout the period, falling under the domination of Tigranes for some seventeen years but recovering its freedom when Rome conquered him. Emesa and the Tarcondimotid portion of Cilicia rose out of previous obscurity to the status of small kingdoms. Judaea endured a period of severe internal struggle under the last Hasmonaeans, but by 37 BC came under the domination of Herod, who provided stability in exchange for a government more severe than many wished. The Nabataeans grew, if anything, stronger, with well over a century remaining after Actium before a portion of their territory entered the Roman provincial system. Egypt experienced the rule of its last Ptolemies, with an increasing tempo of intervention by Rome until finally Actium led to the death of Cleopatra and to the loss of Egyptian independence.

Across the Euphrates, Armenia provided the ancient world with one of its endless examples of bathos when Tigranes rose from the status of captive to that of emperor and then fell back to that of king, with events subsequently leading to his son's capture by Antony and murder by Cleopatra. This series of events created a hatred for Rome among Armenians, which Tacitus finds persisting fifty years later. Atropatene moved from ally of Parthia to ally of Rome late in this period; an exiled king fled to Octavian and prepared for an attempt to rule Armenia through his dynasty, but this policy yielded to the power and proximity of the Arsacids of Parthia. Finally, Parthia itself achieved a remarkable chapter in the historical record of these seventy years, encountering Roman representatives directly for the first time, arranging friendship and alliance, watching the fall of Mithradates Eupator and Tigranes, defeating Crassus, and avoiding serious trouble from Antony. After years of manoeuvre Parthia came to a position of equality and respect with regard to Rome.

A word on the nature of Near Eastern kingship might clarify what was to come.

II. Kings

From the inception of its recorded history, the Near East structured its societies along aristocratic lines, usually culminating in rule by kings or chieftains. The *lugal*, *ensi*, Pharaoh, *shar kishshati*, *tabarna*, *phylarch*, ethnarch, or *basileus* stood at the head of a government carefully constructed on an ascending scale of personal worth. The majority of the population obeyed, willingly or not. The precise systems varied with location and period, but except for the tetrarchs of the immigrant Galatians all of the Near East employed forms of monarchical rule. The present study treats the major figures who became recognized kings or queens, most of them by heredity, though a few became the first royal members of their lines (Polemo, Deiotarus, Tarcondimotus, and Sampsigeramus).

The great empires of high antiquity left their mark long after their passing, with dynasties claiming distant succession to the Assyrians, Persians, Hittites, or Pharaohs, as examples herein will demonstrate. Styles of dress or iconography persisted for centuries following the loss of imperial power, as for instance in the 'strange afterglow' of Hittite civilization along the Euphrates, or the distant origins of that crown worn by Armenian sovereigns.

The geographical extent of kingship in the Near East amounted to a very high proportion of its land area. All of the Seleucid Empire and the regions adjoining it on the north (Bithynia, Paphlagonia, Galatia, Pontus, Bosporus, Armenia) utilized royal control, except for Galatia, which also later adopted it (§ 16). The vast areas of Seleucid rule east of the Euphrates had kings. The Ptolemaic Empire did as well. Only the Arab lands instead used tribal chiefs, whom the Greeks dubbed *phylarchs*, and some of these rose to be kings, as we shall see.

The sheer numbers of those who ruled in the East demonstrate the depth of royalist sentiment there. The stemmata appended to this book record more than three hundred kings, queens, princes, or princesses active during the two centuries following 100 BC. Untold numbers of aristocrats, commanders, viceroys, satraps, governors, and nobles supported this extensive structure, hoping to ascend through it to higher station. Another avenue upward lay in the various national priesthoods; in the case of Archelaus and his grandfather this avenue even led to the thrones of Cappadocia (§ 17) and Egypt (§ 23).

The extent and depth of royal control during the first century before Christ can be underestimated through hindsight. Scholars mindful of the great power exercised by the Roman and Parthian empires after the late first century risk imputing to both a greater measure of control earlier in the century than in fact they had. The risk is especially great with the Roman Empire. The tendency to retroject its later influence has led some to describe its relations with kings in the same terms when treating the period around 100 BC as when dealing with conditions a century later.

The range of terms employed for Near Eastern rulers may obscure their precise functions, but the various forms of the word 'king' conveyed a clear meaning. ('It is not easy to tell whether, except in the case of *basileus* and *rex*, one deals with titles or with epithets.') This book terms kings 'recognized,' not 'created,' by the nascent imperial powers, since local credentials determined acceptance. Entirely indefensible at any period is the habit, adopted since P.C. Sands wrote, of terming monarchs 'client-kings' or 'clients' (*clientela* was a term rarely used for kingdoms by the Romans, though Cicero at least once slips into it – *Fam.* 15.4.15). Worse is the anachronistic 'vassals.' Such terms as 'puppet' or 'marionette' demonstrate a woeful misunderstanding of the relationship kings bore to their allies, whether Roman, Pontic, or Parthian. Scholars ask rhetorically whether kings can be what their titles imply if they can be interfered with in various ways, forgetting that the experience of a few individuals recognized for vacant thrones did not alter the institution of kingship, any more than irregularities of tenure among consuls altered the consulship. As Antony noted with Herod, a king is a king, not subject to review or limit from without (§ 22).[1]

Even late in the century, kingship constituted a powerful and authentic institution. Kings succeeded from the legitimate lines, in accordance with Eastern practice. Once installed, a king controlled his realm, its citizens' lives, the judicial affairs of the kingdom, its finance, army, administration, taxes, and territory. No tribute normally went to Rome, though exactions by Pompey and Antony are recorded, and Roman commanders always welcomed contributions 'from friends' (*ab amicis*: e.g., *BAlex.* 70) who ruled in the East. Mommsen's notion that kings allied to Rome could not mint gold coins has been argued to be wrong. Only in foreign policy was the kings' power limited, as expected of any alliance: they supplied troops and had common enemies with their ally. Otherwise, the kings enjoyed a lifetime of rule if their subjects remained quiet, and retained the ancient right of passing on the kingdom to their heirs. Whether or not Rome began to interfere with this after Actium, it did not regularly do so before that, even when it had conquered a king (Tigranes; Eupator; Aristobulus II of Judaea; Antiochus I of Commagene). Ordinarily, the Greek and Latin formulae for 'friend and ally' seem sincerely meant on both sides (e.g., Cic. *Ver.* 2.4.30.68). Ancients distinguished clearly between subject and allied territories (e.g., Dio 38.10.1).[2]

Despite their importance in antiquity, most of the figures treated here languish now in obscurity. The lives of a few (Mithradates Eupator, Cleopatra, and Herod) are known in some detail, but for most only traces remain. Use of common throne-names, such as Ptolemy, Antiochus, Ariarathes, Arsaces, and a host of others has left a bewildering tangle of individuals whose contributions must be assessed. The arrangement followed in this book allows rapid identification without interrupting its central arguments.

III. Intermarriage

Millennia of dynastic intermarriage characterized the ancient East. The stability of its great empires derived in part from the practice of uniting royal families by marriage, resulting in a 'pool' of acceptable claimants for every vacant throne. No greater pre-condition for legitimacy of rule existed than proper descent. Intermarriage linked the major states during the period studied here as it had for centuries: Seleucids wed Parthians or Ptolemies or Commagenians; Tigranes of Armenia received a daughter of Mithradates Eupator of Pontus and supplied one to Mithradates II of Parthia; a princess from Atropatene became the mother of royalty in Emesa and Commagene; Thracians married into the dynasties of Pontus and Bosporus. The Hellenistic practice merely continued that of its predecessors and was itself continued far into 'Roman' times. Ultimately, the scions of royal lines survived incorporation by Rome to become governors and consuls, lending the same stability to the region as that provided by their ancestors. Early in the second century after Christ, a descendant of the kings of Commagene, the Roman consul 'King' Philopappus, ranked at the top of Athenian society and left an extant monument there, glorying in his descent from the Seleucids. The 'Eastern dynastic network' survived in a new form, west of the Euphrates, but continued unchanged beyond – in Asiatic Iberia, Armenia, Atropatene, and the many constituents of the Parthian Empire.

The flexibility of the royal system explains important events or policies. Romans' and Parthians' ready understanding of it allowed them early, continuing roles as arbiters. For example, despairing of her prospects for further rule in Syria, Cleopatra Selene sought in Rome to obtain for her sons her native Egypt. To gain control of Judaea, Herod turned to Rome, and his opponent Antigonus, to Parthia, each claiming the throne on grounds of family connection. Herod acknowledged his claim to be the weaker and had to win by force of arms the throne for which Rome 'recognized' him.

The loyalty commanded by the royal system among the populace at large is difficult to assess. The choice made to remain under kings in Cappadocia early in the first century BC or in Commagene more than one hundred years later hardly came from the mass of the population, whose consent had been neither given nor sought in previous dynastic evolutions. A certain level of domestic agreement doubtless underlay the smooth workings of a royal society, as random instances reveal, but for the most part kings ruled and subjects obeyed. The firm control of society by combined royalty and aristocracy progressively lessened in direct relation to distance from the population centres of the state, to judge from attested conditions in Egypt and Judaea. A more rural pattern prevailed in the Iranian lands, from Pontus and Cappadocia eastward.

What may seem a distortion – the separate study of kings, queens, their close adherents in the aristocracy, and a few priests – in fact represents the bias of antiquity, outside the democratic Greek states. In the Near East, society tended towards a highly-favoured aristocracy supported by gradations of service, down to slave labour. The merchants, craftsmen, farmers, labourers, soldiers, and ordinary families upon whom the system rested lie outside this study because the aristocratic state seldom left a record of those individuals, but it carefully documented its nobility. The data available on them more than constitute a subject of study.[3]

IV. Dynastic Politics

A fully articulated system governed the interrelations among royal states during Hellenistic times. Principles openly espoused included territorial claims based on conquest. This practice normally went unquestioned, and when it operated to advantage, Rome later followed it also. Thus the Syrian territory conquered by Tigranes formed a portion of his empire for some seventeen years. When Lucullus conquered him in distant battle, the effects included, in Pompey's eyes, Roman possession of Syria. Returning it to the former Seleucid claimants would have given them 'the rewards of another's work,' which he declined to do.

No serious questioning of this principle occurred during the first century. Possession and legitimate tenure sometimes constituted one and the same thing. A leader able to conquer and hold a region ruled it until conquered in turn. The dispossessed naturally failed to acquiesce, but unless reinstated by their own and their allies' efforts they had no other primary recourse. In this way, an empire accrued to Tigranes and later, except for his own kingdom, fell away. Parthia grew to dominate the vast region east of the Euphrates. Rome acquired claims to some of Asia Minor above the Taurus after it and its allies won the battle of Magnesia, followed by a treaty at Apamea in 188. They were, however, still fighting for quiet tenure more than a century later, just as their Seleucid predecessors had been compelled to do. Jews, Ptolemies, and Nabataean Arabs incessantly manoeuvred for territory adjoining their respective holdings.[4]

A second principle, dependent on that of territorial claims based on conquest, governed dynastic succession. The right to pass on a kingdom to heirs within the family was considered implicit. Only a question of legitimacy or an armed interposition would disrupt succession. Once duly installed, a king or queen exercised undisputed authority if originating from the 'legitimate' ruling line. Otherwise, even if he or she were nominated by a power such as Rome, lack of this qualification could preclude effective rule. Such preclusion occurred repeatedly in the first century after Christ when Rome installed a series of outside kings in Armenia, utilizing descendants of related houses in the Judaean-Cappadocian line, or nominees from Atropatene. The Armenians promptly rejected all but Zeno-Artaxias of Pontus, whose adoption since boyhood of Armenian culture allowed him a successful reign. In general, nothing superseded claims 'by right of descent and relationship,' as recognized by Romans also.[5]

The third implicit principle, succession across dynastic boundaries because of interrelationship, worked well for centuries in the Hellenistic world. It allowed queens from Pontus to exercise authority in Bosporus, as Dynamis did, and in Cappadocia, as Laodice did. Their children inherited full local legitimacy. Ptolemaic queens in Syria, a Seleucid in Commagene, Commagenian and Armenian queens in Parthia, a Pontic queen in Armenia, all provide instances herein of this principle. Since the queen usually journeyed to her husband's realm, most 'foreign' sovereigns were women, but that practice need not be invariable, as the husbands of Queen Berenice IV of Egypt demonstrate, drawn to her court from the nobility of Pontus or from the deposed Seleucids.

Attempts to import kings from abroad seldom succeeded, even when from a nearby dynasty. Ariarathes IX could be maintained in Cappadocia only by the repeated intervention of his father, Mithradates Eupator of Pontus. Archelaus I of Cappadocia experienced no effective opposition because he derived from a line of priests in Pontus in close contact for decades with the Cappadocian royal line. Polemo I enjoyed no local claims in Bosporus beyond those supplied through his wife, Dynamis of Pontus, and died fighting there. By and large, the difficulties attendant on introducing an outside king precluded it. Rome was forced to try in Armenia after the demise of its Artaxiad line, but failed; Parthia, long intermarried with that line, succeeded.

V. Historical Geography

The area here studied can be termed 'the East' only from the viewpoint of Greeks and Romans, who named it for the 'rising' sun east of them ('Orient' from Latin or 'Anatolia' from Greek). To Parthians this region lay in the west and to its own inhabitants it lay in the centre. For convenience the classical habit can suffice, in the absence of a universally recognized central longitude in antiquity. Nature has chosen 'natural' zones only as caused by earth's rotation along its axis (tropics; arctic and antarctic circles), leaving humans to divide 'east' and 'west' according to where they stand.

Detailed geographical discussion arises throughout the sections, as appropriate, but the historical geography of this vast region requires mention here.[6] The area's position 'between two empires' evolved precisely during the period under examination as the Seleucid Empire gave way, first to that of Tigranes, and then to the nascent one of Rome, while Parthia in these years made good its claim to control beyond the Euphrates. The span between Rome and Parthia, containing Thrace, Asia Minor, the Levant, and Egypt, exhibits a compelling geographical and historical unity. The Thracian kingdoms joined the network of dynastic intermarriage eastward. Though part of the country nominally lay within the Roman orbit by late in the second century before Christ, some 150 years of further fighting showed the unreliability of this claim. Lying beyond the lofty mountains of northern Greece, delimited by the Strymon, Oescus, and Danube rivers and cushioned by the territories of such formidable tribes as the Dentheletae, Thrace continued its intense tribal development during the last century before Christ. The process of unification under fewer, more powerful dynastic houses continued through this period and culminated in the decades after Actium.

Across the Hellespont, Roman provincial territory existed by late in the second century BC, after Rome's assumption of the former Attalid kingdom as 'Asia' (see § 1). Not until more than half a century later came acquisition of the adjacent Kingdom of Bithynia, about 74 BC. The Aegean seaboard developed its cities on an accelerated basis with Roman favour after removal of the threat presented by Mithradates Eupator. The rugged lands of northern Asia Minor, especially Pontus, Galatia, and Armenia Minor, continued under royal dominion, with a gradual but comparatively insignificant development of towns and cities. Cappadocia in particular remained notoriously poor in cities. For a brief period after the defeat of Pharnaces II, Rome ruled Pontus as a province, but much of it returned to royal control with Antony's recognition of Polemo I as king there.

The Galatians, a Celtic people intrusive to the central plateau of Asia Minor, remained distinct there linguistically for at least seven centuries, though they adopted an increasing admixture of Greek among the upper classes. Their division into tetrarchies under chiefs on a tribal basis rather than under kings long delayed their unification. This was briefly accomplished by Deiotarus, who rose to kingship in the mid-first century, as did Brogitarus. King Amyntas, who succeeded them both, became the last full ruler of Galatia. The future did not favour this development, with Galatia incorporated into the Roman Empire soon after Actium, by 25 BC. A member of the dynastic line ruled on in Paphlagonia some twenty years more. The Hellenization of the nobility continued under Roman dominion, with vast estates controlled by men able to call themselves both 'first of the Greeks' and 'descendant of kings' on into the second century AD.

The rugged southern portion of Asia Minor, in Cilicia Tracheia and Lycaonia, relied on kings throughout this period and for more than a century afterward, though the work of Amyntas helped pacify some territories. The fierce tribes locked in the mountains proved at first intractable to outside rulers, but a series of kings added the region to their other holdings and ruled successfully there (Archelaus I and II; Polemo I and II; Antiochus IV; and King Alexander).

The gentler land of Cilicia Pedias supported numerous small rulers as well, and after expulsion of the Seleucids it did see the rise of one royal dynasty, that of Tarcondimotus. In the Amanus range, tribesmen proved nearly as difficult as those in Tracheia to control from without; they favoured the milder Parthians over the Romans, but independence over both.

The great plateau of Cappadocia sustained a unified and prosperous populace under a long succession of kings. The change of dynasty under Ariobarzanes I early in the first century succeeded despite the miseries Mithradates Eupator caused him. The highly organized Cappadocians proved able to withstand Pontic invasions and intrigue, but the extortionate interest charged their kings by such Roman lenders as Pompey bled the kingdom, which was *inanis* by the time of Cicero. The intrinsic wealth of the country reasserted itself under Archelaus for half a century, then passed to the Romans when Tiberius made it a province.

South of Cappadocia, Commagene also enjoyed great prosperity, making its king later 'richest of all' those allied to Rome. Its wide range of products nearly matched that of Cappadocia, with the addition of deep iron deposits, which made it the land 'where iron is born' (*ubi ferrum nascitur*). The thriving populace, part Iranian and part Greek, enjoyed the ancient world's most thoroughly syncretistic religion, well expressed by the great monuments of Antiochus I in the mid-first century. Unhappily, the wealth attracted such besiegers as Mark Antony and King Herod, but a bribe satisfied them. Suspicion of intrigue with Parthia, to which the dynasty bore marital ties, endured for the following century, and eventually led Vespasian to incorporate the kingdom.[7]

Lying south of Asia Minor, the Levant displayed in places the same mountainous terrain, in parts of Syria and Lebanon, but in general presented a contrast of rich, fertile land near the coast and in the river valleys, progressively slipping towards desert in the east. The mixture of population was one of the most extensive in the ancient world, with Arabs, Jews, Iranians, Greeks – descendants of earlier Babylonian, Assyrian, Sumerian, and other stocks – all intermingled in a polyglot society difficult for an outside power to conquer or govern. (No accident that the Tower of Babel story arose here.) Rapid collapse of the Seleucid Empire left a vacuum into which Rome rushed, in Syria, where the key to its Eastern empire lay. The rising state of Judaea attained control over minor dynasts who had emerged in the area as the Seleucids declined. Some dynasties, such as that in Chalcis, remained into the reign of Herod, and Emesa established its new kingdom on so strong a footing that it may have survived even beyond Herod's dynasty in the late first century AD.

The history of Egypt belonged as much to the Near East as to Africa. In the first century, Egypt looked northward and eastward consistently, especially when Cleopatra succeeded her father, Ptolemy Auletes, and fixed her heart on a renewal and expansion of Ptolemaic rule in those lands. Her grand attempt with Antony to control Egypt, Cyprus, Lebanon, parts of Arabia and Palestine, and a portion of Cilicia, with her sons ruling much of the remainder of the royal East, collapsed at Actium.

Beyond the Euphrates lay the vast steppes, mountain ranges, and deserts of the Parthian Empire. By common consent, but not without repeated military testing of the idea, the Euphrates came to constitute the boundary between the two empires. Parthian reliance on cavalry, adequately supported by the Iranian grasslands, worked to the disadvantage of Rome, which had brought to high development the art of warfare on foot but relied on allies for its cavalry. The legions always predominated over these allied *alae*, which made the military task beyond the Euphrates one of great difficulty, compounded by the sheer vastness that lay under Parthian suzerainty.

The ethnographical complexity of the Parthian Empire defies almost all generalizations but this one. Historically, that produced numerous satrapies and kingdoms under overall Parthian leadership, using their title 'King of Kings' with its full range of implications. These kings ruled their own dynasties, with full freedom of internal policy and action. They raised and commanded their own armies, issued their own coinages, passed on their kingdoms to family members, and intermarried. The system pre-dated both the Parthian and the Roman empires; it followed Persian and Seleucid usage in recognizing local sovereignties. The nature of dynasties includes expansion, but intermarriage regularized this and imperial control limited it.

VI. Rome; Parthia

In 100 BC, the future 'two greatest empires' (*duo imperia summa Romanorum Parthorumque*, Pliny *HN* 5.88) had far to go before getting their claims mutually recognized and before settling the contest over Asia Minor, the Levant, and Armenia. Extensive manoeuvre and warfare lay between their first official meeting, on the Euphrates in Cappadocia, and the resolution of the Armenian question by Nero, Vologaeses, and Tiridates more than one and a half centuries later.[8]

The tacit assumption by some modern writers that Rome could have taken control of all Asia Minor much earlier than it did rests on four further postulates: that Roman generals in the East could have consistently operated with the military effectiveness of Lucullus or the diplomatic and military skills of Pompey; that the Roman Senate had the will in 100 BC or soon afterwards to commit itself as heavily to this task as it later did with Pompey; that kings might have been dispensed with in the decades after Pompey; and finally, in that case, that the monarchs of the East would not have presented a more unified opposition to the Roman advance than they did. Surmises of this kind bring little profit, and can be shown to be baseless; to speak as if they required no proof distorts the slow, unsystematic, partly circumstantial process by which Rome did attain hegemony in the East.

No Roman statesman, however skilled in warfare and political settlement, would have been likely to weaken substantially the powerful Mithradates Eupator early in his career, assisted as he was by his vigorous son-in-law Tigranes the Great and by the recurring crises in Cappadocia. For the Roman state to have organized a more effective approach to the East prior to 89 would have required a different outlook and the absence of such severe problems of its own as the Italian War. When the first major resistance to Mithradates came, it was not a considered act of Roman policy but a response by field-commanders. Pompey's command made differences in Eastern political alignments, but it left major portions of the later empire still ruled by kings – not for convenience but as a matter of social and political necessity. While the Roman Republic collapsed, generals discovered personal gain in Eastern wars, as Caesar did with Auletes or Deiotarus (*BAlex.* 34), or Pompey with Ariobarzanes III. But Pompey or Caesar rushing from Arabia to Galatia or from Egypt to Pontus settled little, directly. Behind them remained severe domestic disputes, often exacerbated by the Roman intervention, as in Pompey's substitution of a new system for the old in Galatia, or Caesar's favouring of the party of Cleopatra in Egypt, or Antony's promoting eclipse of the Hasmonaeans in Judaea. Only after protracted local conflict carried on by the kings did these policies bear fruit in strengthening favoured dynasties. After Pompey, the adventures of Caesar and then Antony in the East bore as much relation to the Roman civil wars as they did to empire; even after Actium most of the East remained royal. The kings had not resisted in concert at any point but might have at several. A combination of Parthia, Armenia, Pontus, Cappadocia, and Commagene could have been most dangerous.

Such concerted resistance did not occur, west of the Euphrates. One of the most remarkable aspects of the long process by which kings were gradually replaced here is that the ancient dynastic habit of identifying allies and enemies among themselves did not lead to consistent and unified opposition to Rome. Factors in this were the empires of Pontus and Parthia, each of which could seem a greater local danger than Rome, especially in the western kingdoms where the Iranian constituent of the population thinned. Near the Euphrates, adherence to Parthia rather than Rome, if a choice had to be made, was more common; strong elements in Commagene, Cilicia, Judaea, and perhaps Cappadocia inclined this way. Beyond the Euphrates, Atropatene wavered between the two powers but finally chose Parthia, with more than gentle encouragement from that direction. Armenia tended likewise, and even Iberia attempted only a brief espousal of the Roman effort locally. In all cases, self-interest dictated independence guaranteed by strong alliances as the primary policy. To local ears, 'king' sounded a fairer name than either 'governor' or 'satrap,' if the choice existed. Rome became the eventual victor in Asia Minor partly because Parthia chose not to contest it seriously, beyond the brief expeditions in 51 and 40-38; the Euphrates sufficed as a boundary, leaving Parthia free to deal with its own troublesome East.

Paradoxically, the period when Rome was most unstable, during the civil wars that accompanied the transition from republic to empire, saw its successful efforts against the kings of the East. The most extensive battles of the first century in the East tended to be those involving Rome – the wars against Eupator; the battle of Tigranocerta; Pharsalus; Philippi. The importance of the kings in this phase is reaffirmed by the level of conflict necessary to replace or rearrange them. Their domestic powers underlay the importance placed by Romans on the 'bequests' of territory to Rome. Without the ostensible will of the individual king, no bequest was deemed worth taking up, given the conflict that would ensue; solemn discussions in the Roman Senate as to the intentions of a royal testator remind us of the respect in which Romans held the system of hereditary rule by kings. Roman cupidity dictated replacement of kings here and there – especially after the Mithradatic Wars 'blocked Asia's revenues' (Cic. *Leg. Agr.* 2.30.83). The publicans had to be restrained from extending revenue contracts into sacred territory at Ilium and elsewhere; some were murdered. However, Rome benefited from the presence of kings and the social stability it offered.

One basis of the eventual Roman triumph in Asia Minor lay in that stability of the dynasties, and of the populations they ruled. These societies were not, however, static. This point cannot be made too carefully, for it is open to misstatement. At first glance, the East presents an aspect of uniformity and even rigidity: kingdoms cover its landscape, all structured on an aristocracy. Kings and nobles together control the military, finance, priesthoods, foreign policy, and other ingredients of a prosperous royal state. But a closer look at the kingdoms and their kings or queens, one by one, begins to reveal surprising diversity. This in turn reflects their populace. As Strabo notes (13.629), local societies 'merged into one another' and could confuse Romans.

Records from Egypt (especially the papyri), from Dura, and from elsewhere show the ethnographic and onomastic diversity that renders imprecise most general statements about the East. What later became the Roman Empire in the East was, about 100 BC, a number of things: the empires of the Seleucids, the Ptolemies, Mithradates Eupator, and soon

Tigranes. Independent states included Judaea, the Nabataeans, Commagene, the kingdoms of northern Asia Minor, and those in Mesopotamia (§ 12). Beyond lay the Parthian Empire, building rapidly to its full status. Beneath this lay another stratum, since 'empire' ranks among the loosest of political terms, covering a wide variety of relations and arrangements. The intense local feeling of the East, its bewildering social complexities, the easy syncretism with which it mixed religious and cultural elements, its tolerance of diversity, the wide spectrum of attitudes, the sharp class divergences, all combine to dilute the force of both 'Empire' and *Koine* when applied to the larger region. As the detailed examination herein repeatedly demonstrates, the composition of the populations of these kingdoms varied, and so did relations between king and people. For example, 'national' traditions could not be the same in Egypt, where due regard both to Pharaonic and to Ptolemaic usages must prevail, as they were in Commagene, where the 'gods throned together' and the 'twin roots' of kingship celebrated a detailed admixture of Iranian and Greek doctrines or historical figures, back to Ahuramazda and Zeus on the divine scale and to Darius and Alexander on the human. This kind of rich cultural heritage underlying the political arrangements rendered progress towards larger control a slow but rewarding business. A society based on common ancestors and a 'substrate' of ancient religious convictions or cultural elements presents difficulties for an outside power that would conquer and hold it. Rome earns respect not for military might, nor for sturdy Italian overcoming esurient Greek (as in some perennial mythologies), but for perseverance and manipulation of local leaders.[9]

Roman partisan recording of such lengthy processes as its audacious attempts to rule the Iranians of Armenia leads the incautious even now to assume that Romans somehow 'rightfully' conceived their designs on that remote land, despite its own traditions, culture, and history. So we find *Armenia capta* and *supplex Arsacides* dutifully repeated, Parthian attention to their long-standing interests there characterized by such phrases as 'the renewal of Parthian interference' (*CAH* X, Ch. XXII.ii), and the establishment of an Arsacid dynasty considered a Roman victory! Tiridates rode happily home with more than a million sesterces after an expense-paid sojourn in Rome at a cost to it of 800,000 sesterces a day (Dio 63.2.2), plus the expense of rebuilding of Artaxata. No need for Tiridates to anticipate Charlemagne and put on his Armenian crown himself when Nero was willing to pay so handsomely for the privilege.

Alexander had conquered the Near East virtually overnight, and he immediately began the work of consolidation that his successors completed, however erratically. By contrast, nearly a century passed after the Battle of

Magnesia in 190/189 BC, which led to hegemony in part of Asia Minor but not effective control there, before a Roman statesman stood on a bank of the Euphrates, and then more as visitor than conqueror. Three full centuries lay between Magnesia and the last Roman incorporations of territory up to the Euphrates, after the reigns of Kings Antiochus IV of Commagene, Alexander in Cilicia, and Agrippa II of Judaea. Arabia did not join the provincial system until AD 106. This long span betokens not comparative weakness on the part of Rome, but rather two strengths: that of the Graeco-Iranian-Semitic royal East, and that of Rome itself in utilizing it. Kings remained essential to this process, down to Actium, when, as Augustus himself notes (*RG* 27.3), kings still ruled 'the major part' of the territory claimed by Rome east of Greece. They also ruled all lands beyond the Euphrates.

Centuries must pass before one ethnic group can replace another, and such replacement neither occurred nor was attempted in the Roman East, even with its colonies. Greek, Iranian, and Semitic languages and cultures persisted through the Roman Empire and into the Byzantine, Sassanian, and Arab states that emerged after it. That empire consisted largely of fiscal ties, leaving its major traces in buildings or other amenities of the towns, and the roads between them. The Greek emphasis on cities furnished the focus of the Eastern Roman Empire. The rural populations proceeded as in centuries past, now raising produce and taxes for a different power. The Byzantine heirs of Rome, diplomatically terming themselves – in *Greek* – 'the Romans,' ruled a Greek Empire. The final echo of the centuries in which the 'Greek East' formed part of the Roman Empire sounded in the fifteenth century, when Turks named the region about ancient Iconia (now Konya) 'the Sultanate of Roum.'

This study concentrates on the kings and queens, their work, their attitudes, and their interrelations: it looks up to descry Rome approaching but attempts no full treatment of Roman policies. The substantial authority that ancient kings enjoyed persisted down to Actium, and in most cases beyond. Throughout the period here studied, the kings bore the relationship to Rome or Parthia that they said they did: that of 'friends and allies.'

2

Asia Minor and the Mithradatic Wars

In a full generation of warfare against Mithradates Eupator, Rome began sustained intervention in the affairs of Asia and the Levant. The period from 100 to 70 BC demonstrates three main processes at work. *First*, the dynastic system – expansionist in nature but pursuing rational evolution through such devices as intermarriage and nationalistic requirements for 'legitimate' rule – had governed the East for centuries and continued to do so. *Second*, portions of the region lay under challenge from without as the decline of the Seleucids drew Rome into Asia Minor to oppose Mithradates and Tigranes. The succession of Parthia to Seleucid lands east of the Euphrates, begun by Mithradates I, became complete under Mithradates II. Consequences of the Seleucid eclipse now also affected the Judaeans, Nabataeans, and Ptolemies. *Third*, the period contains the first deliberate annexations of dynastic territory by Rome in the East after its acquisition of the Attalid territories in 133 BC. Cyrene and Bithynia became Roman, ostensibly by bequest; Egypt itself was rumoured a testamentary gift of Ptolemy XI, and before that of Ptolemy VIII Physcon in 155, though this never came into effect. The dynasties had begun their adaptation to new distributions of power – or had seen it begun for them.

§ 1. Thrace

By the opening of the last century before Christ, Thrace had still not achieved dynastic unification, though conditions moved slowly towards that end. Despite the pessimistic prediction of Herodotus that unity would always elude this powerful collection of tribes, the Odrysians had brought precisely that unity to pass in the late fifth century and again briefly in the early second. They were to be instrumental in doing so again, though by 100 BC there were few indications that this would result in one of the most important dynasties of the East at the time of Augustus, with significant ramifications in the Bosporus for some three centuries beyond that.[1]

The Thracians inhabited a distinctive area of considerable extent, bounded by Macedonia, the Danube, the Black Sea, the Propontis, and the Aegean. A large population, renowned for its wealth and its warriors, made Thracian tribes valuable allies or fearsome antagonists in late Hellenistic warfare. Much of the interior flourished agriculturally and a number of prosperous Greek colonies dotted the coastline. The country lay by no means out of touch with the surrounding Greek world, culturally or politically, and even by the second century the extensive intermarriage that characterized the Eastern dynasties had reached Thrace too. 'Thracian' names long appeared among the populations of northwest Asia Minor.[2]

Yet despite the warlike nature of the population, one geographic fact left Thrace unusually vulnerable to external manipulation: its position as a crossroads, both east-west and north-south. The Celtic invasions of the early third century had passed through, leaving permanent traces. The Roman wars against Macedonia in the second century had necessarily involved Thracians, as had the evolutions of late Attalid history; the coming Mithradatic Wars were to do so again. Lying on the only land route from Europe to Asia, Thrace could not but participate in the great events associated with the conquest of Greece in one direction and replacement of the Seleucid Empire by the Roman in the other as Rome took up its new holdings in 'Asia.' This activity had its civil and religious sides too, measured for instance by proxeny and other decrees at Delphi and by Roman dedications at Delos known from at least as early as 171 BC.

North to south, Thrace also suffered from a vulnerability that in late Hellenistic times could be masked by the warlike and expansionist nature of the populace. The Carpathians and the Danube constituted protective ramparts more comforting than real, but Thracians and their relatives in the Kingdom of Bosporus were to enjoy relatively quiet tenure of this important region before Thrace became a Roman province in AD 46. At its peak, we hear of 'the 150 cities of Thrace' – probably no more reliable than Homer's '100 cities of Crete' although in both cases the remark reflects ancient perceptions of prosperity. The endless succession of Germanic, Ural-Altaic (Huns; Avars), and Slavic invaders began in earnest late in the second century after Christ, followed by such dramatic events in Thrace as the defeat of Valens at Hadrianople in 378. Not until late Byzantine times did the Bulgars and then the Turks settle the question of who would possess the land once known as Thrace.[3]

Rome and Thrace

About 100 BC, the chief problems facing the Thracian tribes externally lay to the west, in Macedonia, now a Roman province, and to the east, in Asia Minor, where Mithradates VI Eupator of Pontus aspired to wider dominion and soon involved Thracians directly in his conflict with Rome.

Difficulties between Thracians and Romans in the area of Macedonia had, in the more than half a century since the defeat of Perseus at Pydna in 168, mainly involved skirmishing along the northern and eastern boundaries of the new province, with a series of battles after 119. Tribes like the Scordisci – 'formerly savage and ferocious' – probably occupied a peripheral position even among the Thracians; their conflicts minimally involved the dominant royal houses. They did defeat a Roman force under C. Porcius Cato, consul for 114 BC, which M. Minucius Rufus avenged a few years later. None the less, aside from building a road along part of the southern coast of Thrace and annexing some territory adjoining it, probably as far as the Chersonese, Romans preferred to rely on diplomacy and alliance with the existing royalty. Their main anxiety in the East concerned suppression of piracy far to the south, until Mithradates came to the fore. However, they began to cultivate ties in Asia Minor, as for instance at Aphrodisias. We also read in a decree from 129 BC that the people of Pergamon (or nearby Elea) hope for 'our friendship and alliance with the Romans to remain for all time' following Roman assumption of Asia. The island of Astypalaea near Cos renewed a military alliance with Rome in 105.

The *SC de agro Pergameno* demonstrates a rising level of involvement by Rome in the area one hundred miles south of Thrace. As conquerors of Antiochus III, Romans might claim parts of Thrace just as he had, though the mere claim would carry even less weight than it had for him. Inscriptional evidence shows Romans at the end of the second century relying in a part of Thrace on title conferred by the victory of Didius at the Caenic Chersonese. In the inscription, the boundaries have yet to be determined, but this should be done 'as quickly as possible.' The reasons are to collect revenues and to assist Roman friends and allies there, presumably the Odrysians and Astaeans.[4]

Mostis

Among Thracian dynasts of the second century BC, most are now mere names: Seuthes, Teres, Barsabas, Byses, Dyegilus. The best-known of them derived from the Sapaean and the Odrysian lines, the latter having intermarried with the Astaeans of the eastern maritime region. But others, however obscure now, engaged fully in the evolutions then transforming the East. A certain King Mostis, known only from his coinage, ruled for at least thirty-eight years in a region corresponding roughly with Bessice in southeastern Thrace, adjacent on the west to the territory of the Astaeans. If in fact he ruled the Bessi, their many decades of opposition to Rome might have begun with his reign, and the iconography of his coins has been said to show him to be an adherent of Mithradates Eupator, among the 'friends of the Pontic King' known to have offered their support in Thrace. The armed presence of Sulla in Thrace in 86 BC appears to fall after the termination of this coinage. Whether or not he contended with the Bessi, he did enjoy the assistance of their enemies in the neighbouring Odrysian kingdom. The notice by Granius Licinianus of Sulla's victory over the Dentheletae omits any mention of the Bessi, but Marcus Terentius Varro Lucullus in 72 definitely conquered them. About 60 BC they contended 'in a great battle' with C. Octavius, and in 55 their offer to support a Roman force fell afoul of the continued hostility of the Odrysian-Astaean King. Ultimately they must have come under Odrysian dominance, though retaining their own identity.[5]

Of the other large tribes initially unincorporated by the Sapaeans or Odrysians even less is known. Among them stood the people occupying the rugged valley of the Upper Strymon and above, and thus nearest of the Thracians to Rome. Whether or not they had joined in the Thracian alliance with Perseus, they presumably could not escape involvement in the long series of skirmishes with Romans over effective control of Eastern Macedonia. Under the collective name of the Dentheletae they receive mention as one of the groups 'who were troubling Macedonia' and who surrendered to Sulla. Once allied to Rome they proved 'always loyal.' The long series of raids on Macedonia by Thracians, and of Roman battles with Thracians for twenty years following 92 BC, included the Dardani, whom Sulla had also defeated, and no doubt the Bessi, but apparently not the Dentheletae.[6]

Cotys VI

In the period covered by this chapter (100-70 BC), three kings are known from the two major dynasties. These are Cotys VI of the Sapaean line, Cotys III of the Odrysian-Astaean house, and Sadalas I, his son. Of the first named, practically nothing is known. An Athenian inscription honours 'King Rhescuporis, son of Cotys.' The absence of royal title for the father may reflect a period of eclipse for the Sapaean line, recently revived or refounded.

Even the son, later an adherent of Pompey and then of Brutus, appears in one notice as 'dynast,' not king.

In a restored inscription, the Sapaean king Abrupolis may already be termed a Roman ally by c. 170 BC. The Rhoemetalces mentioned in 80 BC on an inscription from Thasos might have been from this family, to judge from the later use of that name among its kings (§ 14) and the proximity of Sapaean lands to Thasos. The Sapaean territory, though relatively small, lay in the region south of that controlled by the Bessi, an area accessible to Romans and potentially of considerable value to them. Sapaeans had certainly become reliable allies by the mid-first century before Christ, and in spite of twice choosing the vanquished party they survived to form the nucleus of the united Thracian dynasty after Actium (§ 14).[7]

Cotys III; Sadalas I

The Odrysian-Astaean line has left an only slightly more informative record. Despite their alliance in 168 BC with Perseus, the Odrysians under Cotys II had long since made their peace with Rome. The Roman victories over Thracians in 108, 104, and 100 BC probably involved Bessi rather than Astaeans or Odrysians. But during the governorship of Gaius Sentius in Macedonia, when he suffered at least one defeat at Thracian hands as well as an attempted coup aimed at restoration of the Macedonian monarchy, there emerges obscurely onto the stage of history 'Cotys, King of the Thracians.' This man, the blandishments of Mithradates Eupator notwithstanding, had apparently resolved that the safer course would be to stand with Rome. He not only assisted materially in preventing a Macedonian rebellion, but perhaps also concluded an alliance, for it must be Sadalas I, his son, who sent aid to Sulla at Chaeronea in 87/86, as an inscription records.[8]

This policy of support for Rome long before the success or failure of Mithradates had been determined involved considerable risk, but the strong internal opposition of the Thracian tribes of the interior to those of the coast forced the choice. The Odrysians and Astaeans were too accessible to Rome for comfort should they choose to resist; events of the past half-century had revealed this when such cities as Abdera had appealed to Rome in a boundary dispute with Cotys II, or Byzantium had concluded its own treaty. Mesembria, on the coast north of the Astaean capital, billeted Roman troops in the Third Mithradatic War and even received a Roman prefect in 71 BC. Whether or not the Odrysians and the Astaeans had yet united their two houses during the reign of Cotys III, they did so later in the first century, and the further amalgamation of these with the Sapaean line created a formidable counterweight to the Bessi, Dardani, and others. The open and steady adherence of the coastal dynasties to Rome during the Mithradatic Wars contrasted with the equally strong support rendered the Pontic King by his allies in the Thracian interior. Though Thracians later showed themselves entirely capable of feigning alliances in order to wait on events, with two brothers joining opposing camps so that one would be sure of victory and of an opportunity to save the other (§ 14), the issues bulked too large in the period of these wars for such temporizing. The later severe split in Thrace during the reigns of Augustus and Tiberius demonstrates the abiding and implacable rivalries from which the country never ceased to suffer. Like Cilicia, it constituted a region on which the imposition of Roman provincial status came late, after considerable dynastic manoeuvring. Herodotus had not been far wrong.[9]

§ 2. Bithynia

The Kingdom of Bithynia, the first land to be encountered by travellers proceeding eastward from Thrace across the Bosporus, grew out of a vigorous combination of Thracian settlers and Greek coastal cities, with which it was especially well endowed. For the most part, these failed to maintain their independence of the Bithynian kings, though at times Dascylium, Cius, Cierus, and Tieium succeeded. Chalcedon enjoyed freedom, though not uninterruptedly. Heraclea Pontica resisted the Bithynians, but lost most of its territory to them. The mountainous character of much of Bithynia was relieved by valleys running inland from its long coastline, which extended along the Propontis through the Bosporus to the Euxine. These valleys formed fertile plains receiving ample water, especially the Regio Tarsica (Ak Ova) and others lying along the River Sangarius, which ran near the southern boundary before turning north to cross the kingdom and empty into the Euxine; in Strabo's day it was navigable. The kingdom abounded in timber, fish, grain, and fruit. Major commercial and military routes traversed it.

Nicomedes III

As early as 169 BC, King Prusias II of Bithynia sent an embassy to Rome, seeking a role as negotiator in Rome's conflict with Perseus. He visited Rome himself in 167/166. Bithynia, however, faced a curtailed future. The reign of Nicomedes III (127-95 BC) witnessed the severe weakening of Bithynia and its dynasty; that of Nicomedes IV (95-74), his son, terminated Bithynian independence. By the opening of the last century before Christ, the position of this kingdom had become virtually untenable. Adjacent to it across the

Bosporus lay Thrace, part of it allied to Rome and part to Pontus. To the west lay the new Roman province of Asia, with the Attalid domains safely secured and the provincial apparatus under construction during the reign of Nicomedes III. South of Bithynia, Phrygia Maior came under Roman control but not without a challenge from Mithradates Eupator; to the southeast the Galatian tribes in their diversity vacillated as the two major antagonists closed in battle near them during the Mithradatic Wars (§ 4). East of Bithynia, Paphlagonia presented the temptation for an ill-conceived partition between Nicomedes III, whose political judgment was not of a high order, and Mithradates. Beyond it loomed the formidable King of Pontus himself. Finally, as if not already overextended, Nicomedes rashly involved himself first in an invasion of Cappadocia, and then in a forlorn dynastic attempt to control it.[10]

The Paphlagonian partition sprang from a number of factors. Like Mithradates, Nicomedes probably at first felt little apprehension that Romans would deal forcefully with challenges in the East. His refusal to assist Romans in the Cimbrian wars received no effective rebuke. There was little to warn him, about 104-101, that a period of strong Roman intervention in Eastern affairs lay not many years ahead, and on the other hand he could readily see for himself the danger presented by the ambitions of Mithradates. The invitation to divide Paphlagonia with him doubtless appeared to be one way of blocking the westward advance of Mithradates towards Bithynia itself, and of converting the Pontic monarch into an ally. The objection that he might in this way merely strengthen a potential adversary would, if offered by his advisers, have foundered on the realization that Mithradates could easily engulf Paphlagonia unassisted, should the need arise. Bithynia had no forces capable of standing against those of Pontus, as Nicomedes later showed that he realized when asked by Rome to proceed against Mithradates.

However, by taking control of Paphlagonia, Nicomedes risked antagonizing Rome, which had a standing treaty with its dynasty and which soon ordered that he and Mithradates evacuate the country. The senatorial legation conveying these instructions met not with an outright refusal but with an interesting attempt to convince Romans that Nicomedes was merely returning the kingdom 'to its rightful king.' What in fact he had done was to alter the name of one of his sons to Pylaemenes, the Paphlagonian royal name. Whether Romans saw through this device or not, the occupation did last at least until 96, and probably longer.[11]

A more serious adventure for Nicomedes lay in his attempt to control Cappadocia. Emboldened by its dynastic troubles as the Ariarathid house fought its way into oblivion, he seized upon the questionable status of the incumbents after the death of Ariarathes VI (125-111 BC) and invaded the country as being 'vacant at the death of its king.' This event occurred during the regency of Laodice, widow of Ariarathes and sister of Mithradates Eupator, with Ariarathes VII (111–c. 100), her son. Mithradates could hardly brook a Bithynian conquest of Cappadocia, and prepared to 'rescue' his sister, only to see her marry the invader! Dismay turning to rage, he drove the pair from Cappadocia but retained his nephew on the throne, sending the infamous Gordius, who had murdered Ariarathes VI, to keep control of the kingdom (§ 5). Since Nicomedes and Laodice supported the rule of her son, this arrangement might have satisfied everyone had Ariarathes VII not fallen out with Gordius, and thus with Mithradates, who treacherously despatched him and put forward his own son, duly furnished with a Cappadocian name and an arguable Cappadocian ancestry, as King Ariarathes (IX). Nicomedes and Laodice supported instead the claims of another son of hers by Ariarathes VI, and he did rule briefly as King Ariarathes (VIII) too, supported by the Cappadocian aristocracy. At his predictable expulsion by Mithradates, followed by his death, Rome finally entered the lists, for Laodice put forward yet a third, probably spurious, son and appealed to Rome for assistance in his preferment. So, for his part, did Mithradates. The Senate in Rome, perplexed by the multiplicity of claimants and their pedigrees, chose rather to regard the dynasty of the Ariarathids as extinct.

Little understanding the disposition of royal subjects in Asia Minor, and accustomed rather to dealing with city-states along the Hellenized seaboard, the Senate grandly decided that both Cappadocia and Paphlagonia should be 'free': 'each people received freedom.' However arguable the right of Rome – as conqueror of Antiochus III, heir of the Attalids, and ally of both dynasties – to set these kingdoms free, the inhabitants of both promptly stated their preference for royal rule. The Cappadocians founded a new dynasty, that of Ariobarzanes I (§ 5). The Paphlagonians, their own native dynasty in eclipse, declined the risk-filled benefits of 'freedom' – knowing that Mithradates would define that for himself – and apparently acquiesced in the continued rule of Nicomedes through 'Pylaemenes,' his son. They sought protection not only against the further advance of Mithradates, but also against their unpredictable Galatian neighbours to the south (§ 4). When Mithradates, partly furnished with Galatian allies, fought Rome and invaded Paphlagonia about 89, the Bithynians were still there.[12]

Though freed for the moment from any Roman reprisals for his refusal to vacate Paphlagonia, Nicomedes did have a chronic problem: financial difficulties at Roman hands. He had long deplored the influence of Roman money-lenders in his kingdom. Their virtual enslavement of Bithynian debtors in fact prompted a senatorial enactment against the practice when it involved free men from allied states. However, the associated export of capital continued to plague Bithynia. Combined with the expenses of the two military adventures of Nicomedes in Paphlagonia and in Cappadocia and with his many benefactions to Greek states, this export virtually guaranteed to his successor a kingdom dangerously weakened financially. Nicomedes III bought his title *Euergetes* ('Benefactor'), as well as honours for himself and Laodice, at the expense of his subjects and his heirs.[13]

Nicomedes IV

Nicomedes IV, cautiously surnamed *Philopator* ('Father-Loving'), succeeded his father about 94 BC. Some suspicion that poison lodged in the deceased (*mortuo, incertum an veneno*) detracted from the glory attending this accession. His reign was later beset not only by outside challenges, but also by imputations of depravity. Some of these grew serious enough that Julius Caesar had to endure ribald references to his visit at the King's court in 81/80 BC.

However, the boy had been raised carefully for the succession, with honours arranged for him in Delos, and Socrates 'Chrestos,' his younger brother, sequestered lest he challenge the crown, as he did anyway. To consolidate his position dynastically, Nicomedes married a sister of his father; her name has not survived and she apparently died soon, 'by disease or deceit' – perhaps a sacrifice to the desired stability of the royal house. An equally attractive match brought him the Cappadocian princess Nysa, sister of the recent kings Ariarathes VII and VIII and daughter of his father's second wife, Laodice, sister of Mithradates Eupator. Presumably he had learned from the ill-considered invasion of Nicomedes III into Cappadocia that no welcome for aggressive intentions on his part would be extended by the new king, Ariobarzanes I, still less by partisans of the pretender Ariarathes IX, son of Eupator. But the close tie now with both dynasties through Nysa appeared to Nicomedes IV some warrant for the safety of his reign.[14]

It was not to be. Mithradates coveted not only Cappadocia, but also Bithynia. A useful and apparently willing dynastic agent existed: Socrates, brother of Nicomedes. An imputation of illegitimacy which was lodged against him in antiquity did not, if it came to the ears of Mithradates, deter him from putting Socrates forward as a rival to Nicomedes IV, allegedly by first sending him to Rome. On what grounds such an appeal could be expected to prevail must now be unclear, unless through an accusation of incompetence against the depraved Nicomedes, and the trip cannot be regarded with certainty as historical. If it did occur it failed: 'in vain he set out for Rome, seeking a kingdom.' Mithradates found it expedient in Bithynia, as in Paphlagonia and Cappadocia, to employ force; with an army he soon installed Socrates and sent Nicomedes flying to join the Cappadocian Ariobarzanes, in Rome imploring assistance.[15]

The Senate there decided to restore both monarchs at once, by force of arms if necessary. For Nicomedes, the subsequent operations exacerbated an already unhappy economic position. Not only did he inherit financial problems from his father, but he had borrowed heavily since; now he found himself forced to agree that he pay the cost of his own restoration, estimated as 'large sums.' Finding that he could not, he had to accede reluctantly to the demands of the Roman commissioners Manius Aquillius and Gaius Cassius, that he – as well as Ariobarzanes – invade Pontus. Surprising military and financial success attended the venture, mainly because Mithradates chose not yet to fight.[16]

When he did contend, it was impressive. His attempts to remove Nicomedes by assassination and then by the agency of Socrates had failed, but Mithradates could perform the task himself. He arranged for the murder of the ineffective Socrates, either to mitigate senatorial opposition to his machinations in Bithynia or to facilitate the establishment of his own direct control there. Both motives can be inferred from the rapid oscillations of his policy between conciliation and warfare during these years. To be sure, he went through the form of a protest first, though he suspected a deliberate Roman provocation in the attack by Nicomedes and Ariobarzanes. Only after failing to obtain restitution did he retaliate (§ 3).

Against all odds, Nicomedes survived the first two Mithradatic wars, assisting the Roman war effort as far as he could but more often assisted himself by Roman forces and by their Galatian allies. He probably even took up a portion of Paphlagonia to rule, as his father had tried to before him. Authorship of a letter to Aphrodisias ascribed to Nicomedes has been questioned, but in any case good relations with the Greek cities appear likely. He did not live to see the Third Mithradatic War begin in spring 73, since he died in the last months of 74 BC. The dynasty of Bithynia died with him.[17]

After producing eight kings over a span of more than two centuries, the royal house was said this time to lack a male heir. But the possibility of a real or spurious one, on the model of that 'third son' of Ariarathes VI (§ 5), was suggested. In fact, the purported letter of Mithradates Eupator to the current Parthian monarch, Sinatruces, accuses the Romans and their Bithynian sympathizers of taking the kingdom by deceit, alleging that a true son of the royal couple existed. A daughter also survived, another Nysa, whom Caesar later defended in the Senate at Rome. But it could hardly be lost on the Romans that direct possession of this kingdom worked more to their advantage than yet another dangerously weak ruler would. Nicomedes himself had already given them twenty years' cause for concern. The contiguity of Bithynia with Paphlagonia and Phrygia, its proximity to Roman holdings in Asia and to staunch Roman allies in Galatia, and its advantages for campaigns eastward by land and sea against Pontus, all constituted factors in favour of accepting from Nicomedes IV a posthumous 'bequest.' Whether authentic or invented lurks too deep for recovery now, as it probably did at the time; so do the circumstances of his death. However, it is noteworthy that controversy about the bequest existed at the time, and that 'numerous' Bithynians, of anti-royal sentiment, were called upon to testify against the legitimacy of the proposed successor to Nicomedes IV. Mithradates, in his subsequent invasion of Bithynia, probably sought to install this claimant, given his previous methods (involving Socrates, Gordius, Ariarathes IX, and others elsewhere) and the tolerance of the 'Eastern dynastic network' for rulers from collateral lines, if this lad was not a true scion.[18]

Whatever the case, a bequest was deemed to have been made and the Senate duly accepted it. One ancient notice may show indecision in taking up the new territory, with Ariobarzanes I of Cappadocia serving briefly as caretaker. But if this did occur, it was the last application of dynastic rule in Bithynia, where the second major Roman retrenchment of Anatolian royal control now occurred successfully.[19]

§ 3. Pontus

The traditional area of the Kingdom of Pontus occupied the southeastern coast of the Black Sea (Pontus Euxinus; hence the kingdom's name) and extended south to include the mountain ranges known collectively as the Paryadres, which ran parallel to the sea. As increased by Mithradates Eupator, the kingdom came to include a vast region stretching from beyond Amastris on the Euxine in the west to Colchis in the Caucasus, and to the Tauric Chersonese (the Crimea) in the north. To varying degrees, Pontic influence encompassed the entire coast of the Euxine under Eupator. In Asia Minor, Pontic dominance extended southward to include the lower Halys, its headwaters, the Lycus and Iris rivers, and some of the upper Euphrates, most of which lay in the traditional territory of Armenia Minor.

Despite its ruggedness, Pontus enjoyed a degree of fertility adequate to support its large, rural Iranian population. Fruits, nuts, olives, and grains contributed to its relative prosperity; so did pasture lands and a variety of minerals or metals. Timber for the kingdom's ships grew abundantly on the mountains. Communications utilizing the river valleys and the sea offset the restrictions imposed by the dearth of major east-west roads, except for the one running from Amisus.

The organization of Pontus reflected its physical conditions, with the nobility controlling a large percentage of the land, and the temple-estates occupying another rich portion. The tasks of a Pontic monarch always included the necessity for retaining the co-operation of these powerful elements of the state.

Mithradates VI Eupator

The opening years of the last century before Christ witnessed developments without precedent in the dynastic history of the East, and many of these were precipitated by the policies of Mithradates VI Eupator Dionysus (120-63 BC). His dynasty believed itself descended from the Seven Persians, and asserted that it held Pontus by right of a grant from Darius himself. Although not required to wade through slaughter to his throne, since the murder of his father was accomplished by others, he soon demonstrated himself capable of doing so to keep it, and despatched both his ambitious mother, the Seleucid Laodice, and his brother, Mithradates Chrestos. Then ensued a career that would take Pontus from relative obscurity to the hegemony of an empire reaching from the Crimea to the Aegean; it was already connected commercially with the Mediterranean, as illustrated for instance by the remark of Polybius regarding expensive 'Pontic [Black Sea] smoked fish' imported to Rome. This expansion by Mithradates brought him straight into conflict with Rome, which extended its sphere of active concern steadily eastward during his reign, partly in reaction to his own policies. The spreading shock waves of this collision engulfed Armenia, where Tigranes the Great, son-in-law of Mithradates, built and then lost a significant empire in these years, in the process encompassing the demise of the Seleucids in Syria. The wider ramifications of the conflict initiated Roman contact with its future antagonist, Parthia, for the first time; the great Arsacid Mithradates II left to his successors a legacy of formal allied status with Rome conjoined with a policy of watchful opportunism. At the southern fringes of the Near East, the internecine struggles of the Seleucid heirs of Antiochus VIII Grypus after his death in 96 permitted the rise to new prominence of the Judaeans and the Nabataean Arabs. The Ptolemies, still rent by discord after the death of the violent Cleopatra III in 101, did manage to weather these tumultuous years down to 69 BC, but at the cost of Cyrene and of their remaining influence in Syria, with the loss of Cyprus soon to follow. The blow that Tigranes administered to their last representative in Syria, Cleopatra Selene, barely preceded his own enforced withdrawal to meet the Roman challenge to his homeland. Pontus stood in the forefront of these events, which, within a generation, transformed large portions of the ancient Near East.

Expansion towards Empire

Mithradates initiated much of this expansion towards empire first by consolidating his inherited holdings to the north and northeast, then by systematically extending them over 'the kings around the Phasis up to the regions beyond the Caucasus.' Pharnaces I preceded him in the north by a treaty with the Crimean city of Chersonese. In the years to come this portion of his empire, reaching along the eastern coast of the Black Sea and into the Crimea, proved unreliable when Mithradates needed assistance from it, but posed no direct threat to his kingdom, in part because of his later efforts to organize the region along traditional dynastic lines (see below). Probably about 114 BC, at the age of seventeen or eighteen Mithradates began this work. By 105 he had achieved his aims there and felt secure enough to turn to the areas of Asia Minor lying near the frontiers claimed now by Rome, and thus to risk military confrontation, though he tried to avoid it. At some point, probably in this initial period of his reign, Mithradates also forged a prudent alliance with Parthia, if Memnon is correct.[20]

In Anatolia, he began with Armenia Minor, Paphlagonia, and Cappadocia. By this time Phrygia Maior, to which Mithradates had an inherited claim, had been for more than a decade converted into Roman territory. Although there was as yet no overt conflict over Phrygia Maior, the resentment of Mithradates endured and contributed to his growing conviction that in Rome lay his primary foe. The increasingly Hellenized empire he began to create from the Iranian core of his ancestral kingdom could spread, in his youthful imagination, over all of Asia Minor; to an old man, after a reign of some fifty-seven years, this empire still beckoned. Mithradates Eupator never gave up.

The incorporation of Armenia Minor constituted a second important step towards the realization of his dream. This region, which because of its location was to assume in the next two centuries an importance disproportionate to its size, was 'always ruled by dynasts.' The incumbent, Antipater, held not only Armenia Minor itself, but portions of the Euxine coast that he had gained, especially Trapezus and Pharnacia. If Mithradates was to control the Black Sea, he needed the coastal cities from Colchis (where he later installed his son, as coins confirm) to the Hellespont. But the co-operation of the dynast of Armenia Minor could by no means be taken for granted; the independent-minded rulers here, 'sometimes friendly to the other Armenians, sometimes keeping to themselves,' pursued a policy geared to the cycles of strength or weakness among the larger kingdoms surrounding them: Pontus, Cappadocia, and Armenia. In the present instance Mithradates probably achieved a compromise, leaving Antipater and his family in place but forcing him to surrender the coast 'up to Colchis and Armenia Minor.' A later measure in part designed to ensure the loyalty of Antipater to this new arrangement was the marriage of Cleopatra, daughter of Mithradates, to the formidable Tigranes of Armenia, whose holdings joined Armenia Minor to the east, along the headwaters of the Euphrates.[21]

The partition of Paphlagonia with the co-operation of Nicomedes III of Bithynia (§ 2) lay, though questionably, within the dynastic rights of Mithradates, who could claim at least a portion of the kingdom by descent from Mithradates V Euergetes, who had received it by inheritance. But the treaty of the Paphlagonian dynasty with Rome allowed a potential challenge to this claim, since it partly conflicted with the legitimate rights of the native dynasty. The tenure by Nicomedes of his portion was subject to challenge on the same grounds, since the king he put forward apparently bore no closer relation to the royal house there than his hastily adopted dynastic name, Pylaemenes. As with all matters of this nature, what lay at its base was a question less of claims than of power, and for the next fifteen years the local preponderance of that favoured Mithradates.[22]

The First Cappadocian Interventions

The largest theatre of operations for Mithradates, Cappadocia, occupied him virtually for the rest of his reign. An associated problem he had with Galatia received no solution during these early years but by the same token presented no serious difficulty until Deiotarus I achieved unification of the tribes (§ 4). Only in Cappadocia did Eupator encounter a dynasty with sufficient strength, cohesiveness, stability, and proximity to constitute a threat to his nascent empire, especially in light of its standing treaty of friendship and alliance with Rome. His efforts at subverting this dynasty of the Ariarathids were to be so successful that he ended it, but the basic problem remained and eventually involved him in conflicts far wider than he had expected.

The pretext for intervention in Cappadocian affairs originated not with Mithradates but with his father. Mithradates V had taken advantage of a temporary weakness in the dynasty when Ariarathes VI acceded as a child, with his mother, Nysa, as regent. Threats and even an invasion failed, but he gained a foothold in the kingdom when Laodice, his daughter, became the new monarch's queen. By 111 BC, this connection provided Mithradates Eupator with the excuse he required for openly assuming control of Cappadocia. The death of Ariarathes VI at that time, probably through the agency of Gordius, acting for Mithradates, left Laodice as regent. Her independence of mind soon deprived Mithradates of any expectation of *de facto* rule there, and the unforeseen, unwise invasion by Nicomedes III gave him every warrant for intervention on behalf of his sister. Laodice neatly removed this pretext by marrying the invader. Mithradates drove them both from the kingdom, asserting that his nephew, the young Ariarathes VII, son of Laodice and Ariarathes VI, should enjoy his lawful rule, unimpeded by the overambitious Bithynian. This situation might have been stabilized had the youth been of amenable disposition, but he soon proved himself his mother's son when Gordius, the reputed assassin of his father, sought with the help of Mithradates to resume his position of influence in Cappadocia, and may even have aimed at the throne.[23]

Ariarathes VII, rightly suspicious of this man, sought to move against him but precipitated an invasion by Mithradates and perished at his hands, in 101 or 100 BC. Mithradates installed his own son, citing distant dynastic claims and giving him the Cappadocian royal name Ariarathes (IX); Gordius remained as regent. This plan seems more inadvisable than it was, since a faction in the nobility of Cappadocia supported rule from Pontus as a counterweight to increasing Roman influence. This group remained a not inconsiderable force, at least until Cicero's visit half a century later (§ 17).

Another factor remained the continuing determination of Laodice and Nicomedes. They put forward a more legitimate claimant, Ariarathes VIII, the second son of Ariarathes VI. He achieved perhaps two years' rule, against the steady opposition of Mithradates, Gordius, and Ariarathes IX, whose coins show him claiming an uninterrupted period of rule from his second to his fifth regnal years (about 99 to 96). The dual monarchy, if there was one, probably fell at the beginning of this period. The absence of extant coins for the first regnal year of Ariarathes IX may reflect the internal struggle. In any case, Ariarathes VIII soon found exile and death, leaving no further incumbent from the Ariarathid house.[24]

That is not to say that Laodice and Nicomedes had finished. They introduced a possibly spurious third son of Ariarathes VI. He required support from the outside for his preferment, and for the first time Rome entered significantly into the dispute. Laodice went there in person to solicit aid for her 'son.' Mithradates, not yet ready for open opposition to Rome, sent an embassy there to argue the case for Ariarathes IX, charging Nicomedes with repeated violation of the Pontic borders. At this point occurred the pronouncement that Cappadocia should be free. The designs of Mithradates and Nicomedes on Paphlagonia were also to be blocked by a similar declaration, which both monarchs ignored. The ancient but improbable view discerned in this second decision some compensation to Mithradates for the first, forgetting that he too lost territory deemed rightfully his, in Paphlagonia, if the declaration stood. So Mithradates emerged from these negotiations doubly dissatisfied, and had no intention of letting matters rest, even when a portion of the Cappadocian nobility elected Ariobarzanes to found the first new dynasty there in nearly three centuries.[25]

Mithradates and Rome

By now, about 96 BC, conditions in Rome varied from those Mithradates had relied upon previously. No longer did Jugurtha, Cimbri, and Teutones distract Romans, though approaching domestic strife threatened even greater dangers. An increasing tempo of political, military, and economic activity in Thrace and Asia brought Rome ever closer to the sphere Mithradates regarded as his own. Though not yet ready to risk serious conflict with Rome, he had been testing the waters repeatedly and had so far discovered little to deter him from the grand design that had emerged in his thinking. To be sure, Marius may have already appeared, about 98 (possibly earning a statue at Delos), and delivered his pompous aphorism that Mithradates should either equal Rome or obey it. Whether or not laughter accompanied rehearsals of this remark henceforward in his banquet halls, Mithradates exhibited no intention of heeding it until forced to by three wars over the coming thirty-five years.

Hence his adoption of a policy that became almost a habit, the repeated ejection of Ariobarzanes I from his kingdom. Usually the task was carried out for him by Tigranes, his son-in-law, freeing Mithradates for activity on other fronts. Without question these expulsions appeared to Romans an offence against their treaty arrangements with the Cappadocian house, since the Senate had already rejected the arguments of Mithradates for the legitimacy of his son's rule. Certainly after Sulla's mission to assist Ariobarzanes, the neighbouring kingdoms had in effect received formal notice that Rome intended to support its ally, though there might linger doubts as to the efficacy and duration of such aid, as Rome drifted into domestic war. Mithradates had ignored the warning of Marius, whose ostensible reasons for appearing in the East had nothing to do with Mithradates and who probably did not represent Rome in any official way at the time of his remarks. However, ignoring the wishes of Rome after Sulla's action required either stronger arguments or steadier nerve.[26]

Down to the outbreak of the First Mithradatic War, the policy of the Pontic monarch did involve keeping diplomatic channels open and avoiding provocations sufficiently serious to bring war. Mithradates withdrew, for instance, from his Cappadocian intervention in 97 or 96 when the Senate told him to, while embassies determined which claimant had the legitimate right to rule. When Sulla arrived there was fighting, but Mithradates apparently left that to others. The continued occupation of Paphlagonia against Roman wishes might have constituted a provocation, but he could logically assume that Nicomedes would bear some of the blame and that, if required to by military developments, both could simply withdraw. Not until the 'Asiatic vespers' of 89/88 BC, when he ordered wholesale massacre of Romans resident in Asia, did Mithradates take any step that must lead ineluctably to war. Whether his interventions in Cappadocia and elsewhere constituted a carefully graduated scale of incitements or whether he thought that they bore reasonable prospects of success cannot now be discerned. The construction of his empire took precedence over ridding Asia Minor of its intrusive Italian element, whom he presumed to constitute only one aspect of his task. The rapid adjustment in his thinking required by the Roman response in the first war left him a more cautious ruler but did not weaken his resolve.[27]

As relations between Mithradates and Rome degenerated in the last two or three years before the outbreak of war, his policy bore risks but cannot be called reckless. After the change of ruler in Bithynia in 94 BC, with the weak newcomer duly recognized by Rome, prudence might have dissuaded Mithradates from his expulsion of Nicomedes IV in 91 or 90. But the occupation roughly coincided with the outbreak of the Italian War, and Mithradates could regard it as a test of Rome's ability to protect its allies. Presumably he viewed the Cappadocian situation similarly, and could not in any case leave its control out of his plans; accordingly he once more expelled Ariobarzanes and installed Ariarathes IX, his own son. One reconstruction of the dynastic coinage the young man issued there places his 'year 12' and 'year 13' in 89 and 88 BC. These occur after a hiatus, in the extant corpus, covering the years 95 to 90; Ariarathes IX regarded these as among his regnal years, but he may not have been in a position to issue a coinage then, thus reflecting the temporary success of Ariobarzanes I, who was supported by Rome. The evidence provided by missing coins cannot, of course, inspire confident deductions. But it would neatly synchronize the newly re-established control of Cappadocia by Mithradates with the inception of open warfare in the First Mithradatic War, which occurred in 89 or 88. If open warfare began in 89, it shows that the policy of Mithradates was more sensibly based than if he had taken steps tantamount to a declaration of war only in 88, when the tides of the Italian War had turned in Rome's favour.

Mithradates had laid his plans carefully for twenty years and would scarcely have allowed the opportunity of a major war in Italy to slip. By now he was ready, with extensive preparations completed. The news of that war must have seemed to him a clarion call to empire.[28]

Dynastic Activity

In his plans Mithradates had consistently employed what might be called the 'dynastic principle.' He placed close relatives in the royal houses of the Near East. He used his extensive circle of relatives and offspring to administer conquered territory. He supported dynasts not related to him but with claims elsewhere, relying on their gratitude and co-operation; an instance of this was his installation of Socrates Chrestos in Bithynia.

The relatives lodged in other dynasties constituted a formidable array. Laodice, his sister, once Queen of Cappadocia, became Queen of Bithynia, though hardly in the pursuit of Mithradates's interests. The rulers of Cappadocia, between about 115 and 89 BC, included a brother-in-law, two nephews, and a son of Mithradates; a subsequent queen there was his daughter Athenais (see below). After 94, the Queen of Bithynia was his niece, Nysa, daughter of Laodice. Probably by 90 his daughter Cleopatra had brought Tigranes the Great of Armenia into the family, a most useful connection as events were to prove. A later attempt at marrying his daughter Mithradatis to the future Ptolemy XII of Egypt, and his daughter Nysa to the brother of this man, Ptolemy of Cyprus, failed to proceed beyond the betrothal stage for reasons outside his control (§ 10). However, daughters installed in the Crimea and 'Scythia' did probably serve their purpose, though towards the end of his life Mithradates had to replenish the supply.[29]

Control of conquered territory through relatives appealed to Mithradates but failed on the whole to promote his abiding interests. Ariarathes IX did not enjoy success in Cappadocia beyond the initial five years and the brief restoration, though his claimed tenure descended to 'year 15' (86 BC). The appointment of Machares, son of Mithradates, to rule the Crimea succeeded initially but eventually foundered on the treacherous reluctance of the young king to support the war effort vigorously or, later, to resist the attractions of an alliance with Lucullus against his own father. In Thrace, the forces commanded by his son Arcathias presumably aimed at detaching territory from the adherents of Rome and making it over to allied kings there, such as the ruler of the Bessi (§ 1); by the time Arcathias met his death, this operation had threatened Macedonia itself. Another important general of Mithradates, Archelaus, was probably among his sons too; like Machares, he betrayed his father. But the report that the descendants of this man were to include a king of Egypt (§ 23) and the founder of Cappadocia's last dynasty (§ 17) must have gladdened the shade of the philodynastic Mithradates.

Other sons found employment throughout the nascent empire as it developed. One homonymous son of Mithradates commanded a force sent to oppose Fimbria in Bithynia. Another son, Mithradates Philopator Philadelphos, is the man who controlled Colchis for him, as coins confirm, with a strong garrison evident at Vani. Numerous progeny gave Eupator an abundant supply of potential dynasts, and he also incorporated more distant relatives into the system; for instance, he placed Philopoemen, father of his wife Monime, over Ephesus. Even a 'childhood companion' of his, Dorylaus, joined the cause by commanding a relief-force sent into Greece. Late in his reign another son, Pharnaces II, was being groomed for the succession, and we hear of others.[30]

The advantage of this system was that Mithradates could call forth allied forces from widely diverse regions, enjoying the support at times of Thracians, Cappadocians, Galatians, Armenians, and even contingents 'from Scythia.' The disadvantage was that few of these proved reliable as the years of warfare wore on and Mithradates began to draw increasingly vigorous responses from Rome. A long and doleful roll-call of defectors marks the course of the three wars and their aftermath: Machares, Archelaus, Diocles, a member of the royal house named Phoenix, and Pharnaces. Even Dorylaus, who had been made priest at Comana, betrayed Mithradates; so did his cousin Lagetas. Two other notable members of this family, Moaphernes and the maternal grandfather of Strabo, went over to the Romans or tried to. Two more met death at the hands of Mithradates. His insistence on loyalty led him to offer an astonishing forty talents for the collaborator Chaeremon of Nysa and his two sons if brought in alive, or half of that if dead.[31]

The inability of Mithradates to retain the loyalty of his followers in the long run sprang from an assortment of causes. His description of the Romans as 'the common enemy of mankind' did meet initially with considerable agreement, but constituted a negative basis for empire. More serious was the dawning realization among many of the Greeks, especially those in the west of Asia Minor, that the yoke of Mithradates would bear heavily. He had little patience for dealing with city-states. Even his local accommodations often missed the point, as for instance when he assumed the eponymous archonship in Athens. His instinct was to structure his empire along satrapal lines, with a governor for each city responsible to himself. This weakened the local tendency to regard Rome as an overriding danger, especially in those cities that Rome, as conqueror of Antiochus III, had declared 'free.' Some, such as Aphrodisias and Nysa, joined the Roman cause as early as 88/87. Others followed belatedly. The case of Ephesus can represent many: the rule of Mithradates soon became intolerable and the city shifted from its initial support to open opposition, 'declaring war against Mithradates on behalf of the hegemony of the Romans.' After the first war, Sulla pointed out at Ephesus the comparative advantage of Roman rule and rewarded with freedom cities that had resisted Mithradates, such as Stratoniceia in Caria. For city-states, hegemony by a republic presented a more flexible system than did satrapal control by a king.

Even kings came to realize that the aims of Mithradates failed to coincide with their own. Already the type of empire enjoyed by Mithradates II of Parthia, 'King of Kings,' was approaching Asia Minor when Tigranes took up that title after the Parthian's death about 86 BC. Syria, Cilicia, Commagene, and at times Cappadocia came under the sway of the new Armenian King of Kings. The prospect of an empire of Mithradates Eupator on the same model provoked little enthusiasm among the kings who would have to acknowledge him their overlord, but so powerful was the concept that Eupator probably assumed this grandest of titles. Queen Dynamis, his granddaughter, used it in speaking of him long afterwards, though according only 'Great King' to her father, Pharnaces II, son and successor of Mithradates. Pharnaces too called himself 'King of Kings' – until Caesar came, saw, and persuaded him of its inappropriateness.[32]

The Mithradatic Wars

Mithradates relied in the first war on the awe he provoked among the Greeks of the East, who 'called him God, Father, Saviour of Asia, Euhius, Nysus, Bacchus, Liber.' A gem from 80 BC of him as Dionysus shows the persistence of this attitude, and such tributes are found even after his death. Despite his popularity, the defeat of Mithradates stemmed from his own mistakes of administration, coupled with the growing effectiveness of the Roman forces sent to oppose him. These forces in turn relied heavily on allied assistance, which was forthcoming not through adherence to the interests of the distant Republic, but rather because its methods appeared more likely to offer a reasonable measure of local autonomy.

The ultimate success of Rome in achieving hegemony in Asia Minor despite the challenge of Mithradates reflects not so much military as diplomatic prowess. An ascending scale of formal contact marks the period of the Mithradatic Wars. Beginning with the casual visit of Marius and with the series of senatorial pronouncements on related dynastic affairs, Rome increased its involvement in response to the expanding empire of Mithradates. Sulla supported Ariobarzanes and employed military force in the process. A special commission under Manius Aquillius, assisted by Gaius

Cassius, governor of Asia, and by allied forces from Galatia and Phrygia, effected the removal of Socrates from Bithynia and of Ariarathes IX from Cappadocia. Mithradates had not yet determined to resist. The possibly apocryphal story of his previous journey incognito through Bithynia and Asia at least demonstrates the care he was believed to take with what would now be called 'military intelligence.' Activity on both sides remained measured.[33]

The sources emphasize the crucial importance of allies in these conflicts. Romans relied especially on Bithynians, Cappadocians, Paphlagonians, and Galatians. Two recently published letters by Quintus Oppius show that they could also request and receive levies from cities in Asia Minor, including citizens, unfranchised residents, and slaves.

An unexpected dimension began to develop: Rome demanded that kings pay the costs of their own restoration, and that Mithradates pay 'damages.' These demands led to further impoverishment of Nicomedes, by no means the last monarch to fall seriously into debt to Rome. The next step was incitement of two allies, Nicomedes and Ariobarzanes, to the attack on Pontus. In the absence of evidence that the Senate had authorized such behaviour, the later charge that Aquillius had caused the ensuing war must be regarded seriously. Not only did financial demands followed by invasion constitute grounds for retaliation by Mithradates, but the demand of Aquillius that Mithradates refrain from a military response added a gratuitous insult that he could hardly afford to endure. Thus the greatest conflict that Rome ever entered in Asia Minor came about as the consequence not of considered state policy, but of misjudgment, possible intrigue (greed was charged), and unilateral action by relatively low-ranking officials. The rapid successes of Mithradates, leading to the conquest of virtually all of Asia Minor and much of Greece, did in military terms erase the rights Rome exercised there as conqueror of Antiochus III and Perseus and Corinth, and even as heir of Attalus III. Romans recognized the tenure of territory by right of conquest, as when Pompey later claimed the remnants of the Seleucid Empire as conqueror of Tigranes, himself the victor over the last effective Seleucids. However, the conqueror must *hold* his new ground, and this Mithradates proved unable to do.[34]

The record of Rome's participation in this great crisis reveals unevenness of policy. What seems a deliberate provocation of Mithradates by Aquillius – Appian clearly believed it to be so – arose from Roman party strife, with the partisans of both Marius and Sulla desiring a war for pecuniary and domestic reasons. During the war, Roman field commanders presented a bizarre display. Sulla was declared 'an enemy of Rome' by his opponents back home but led onward anyway. His nominal successor, L. Valerius Flaccus, was opposed and eventually murdered by his own legate, C. Flavius Fimbria. L. Licinius Lucullus refused to co-operate by sea with Fimbria, thus allowing Mithradates to slip away when trapped at Pitane. Still, Rome muddled through. Faced with the necessity of recovering the lands it had taken by force and diplomacy, it did just that. By 85 BC, Sulla and Mithradates had met to conclude a peace through which Mithradates retired to his own Pontic holdings. However, the treaty was not concluded in writing and was never formally ratified by the Senate; ambassadors from Mithradates were twice prevented from signing it in 80/79. Nevertheless, Sulla considered a treaty to be in force in 82 and the Senate apparently agreed, making a final anomalous touch to a strange war.[35]

What Appian calls the Second Mithradatic War began in 83, lasted three years, and should not have occurred at all. Sulla's legate, L. Licinius Murena, began it not only without sanction from Rome but also against explicit instructions not to attack Mithradates. Aulus Gabinius came to remind him of this too late, after a severe defeat inflicted by the Pontic forces. Murena was excited to his unwarranted offensive by the counsels of Archelaus, the probable son and former general of Mithradates. Archelaus had defected at the report that Mithradates viewed with disfavour his ineffectuality in negotiating terms of the recent peace with Sulla. Murena followed the hardly disinterested advice of Archelaus and opened hostilities, to which Mithradates responded, as in the case of Nicomedes's invasion six years before, by first seeking accommodation with Rome. His embassy to the Senate did bring a certain Calidius to order Murena to desist, since Mithradates had not violated the treaty. But Murena ventured on, and only the armed opposition of Gordius and Mithradates brought him up short.

Among the tangible results of this pointless escapade was the betrothal of a daughter of Mithradates to a son of Ariobarzanes I. The marriage gave Cappadocia its Queen Athenais Philostorgos II, long a figure of intrigue on behalf of later Pontic interests there. As another consequence, further portions of Cappadocia were added to the territories that Mithradates already held, probably including the rich priesthood at Comana. This loss annoyed Ariobarzanes I and in 79 he induced Rome to threaten Mithradates in the matter. The response of Mithradates was typical: disgruntled compliance with an order to withdraw, followed the next year by an invasion of Cappadocia by Tigranes, his helpful son-in-law. This attack, far more serious than any previous one, led to a virtual depopulation of Mazaca in favour of the new fortress-capital Tigranocerta. The miserable Cappadocians braced for another round in the struggle.[36]

The Third Mithradatic War was not long in coming. After the usual dynastic preparations, Mithradates opened hostilities in early 73. By this time two

Roman commanders were in place and awaiting him. M. Cotta held Bithynia, its last king having died during the previous winter (§ 2). L. Lucullus, proconsul of Cilicia, took overall command, and the conflict was on.

Again, the military details cannot occupy this examination, but aspects of the war shed light on the operation of dynastic politics during the most severe challenge to Mithradates thus far. His generals knew that Cappadocia under Ariobarzanes would afford Roman forces easy access to the Pontic frontier, and so one occupying force went there. Another army, under Eumachus, advanced into Phrygia and Pisidia, and some fighting apparently occurred in Mysia, where the grateful inhabitants recorded their gratitude to a commander serving under Lucullus 'because he saved them in the war with Mithridates.' However, the alliance of Galatians to Rome proved decisive. Under Deiotarus I, these tribes had now begun to achieve a degree of unification that rendered them formidable antagonists, especially to Mithradates after his massacre of their nobility (§ 4). A large force of Galatians assisted Lucullus against the Pontic King. The general Archelaus offered his traitorous support to Rome. It was now that people began to fail Mithradates seriously in his reliance on the fundamental devices of dynastic politics. His son Machares delivered no forces from the Crimea, and the Scythians offered only thin and unreliable contingents; his daughters had gone there fruitlessly, as did Diocles now. Even Tigranes required some urging by his wife, Cleopatra, daughter of Mithradates, before he remembered his obligations. A mission to the current Parthian monarch, Sinatruces, failed despite earlier ties between Pontus and Parthia (and, through Tigranes's daughter Aryazate-Automa, between Parthia and Armenia). Further erosion within the royal house of Pontus took Diocles and then Phoenix over to the Romans. Several important lieutenants followed.[37]

This inability of Mithradates to bolster the courage of his subordinates led to a panic in the ranks and to defeat in 71, followed by his own flight to Tigranes, who received him with unexpected coolness. This response arose not only out of apprehension that the escapades of Mithradates might draw the forces of Rome against the yet uncompleted empire of Tigranes, but also out of his ambition to succeed both Mithradates II of Parthia and Mithradates Eupator as the pre-eminent Eastern monarch. He had already adopted the title 'King of Kings,' had subjugated portions of the Parthian Empire, and had conquered the Seleucids (see § 11).

However, when Lucullus sent Appius Claudius Pulcher to demand the surrender of the fugitive, Tigranes refused. The result was his involvement too in war with Rome. Desertions from the cause of Mithradates continued, though by no means on a wholesale basis. For instance, the garrison commander in Sinope intrigued with Lucullus, but lost his life when detected; his successor resisted to the end, as too had commanders in Amisus and Heraclea. Lucullus wisely granted freedom to the cities he conquered, and an extant bronze tablet in Rome shows an attempt by Mark Antony's uncle to restore matters at Termessus Maior in Pisidia to the position they had before the First Mithradatic War. The unkindest cut of all came when Machares, ruling the Crimea for his father, requested enrolment as a 'friend and ally of the Romans' (§ 15). Tigranes, who may not have expected this combination of resolve and success for the Romans, now decided to act and joined with Mithradates in advancing to meet Lucullus, who had determined to invade Armenia itself despite the lack of a clear mandate from Rome and the obvious, understandable reluctance of his troops.[38]

The danger presented by the coalition of these two kings, both allied now to Phraates III of Parthia, who had succeeded Sinatruces in 70 BC, could hardly be regarded lightly. Even the victory of Lucullus over Tigranes in 69, followed by the capitulation of some watchful minor kings and the reinvigoration of Ariobarzanes I, still failed to prevent Mithradates from regaining by 67 much of the position he previously enjoyed. Political considerations in Rome hampered Lucullus and soon eroded his sphere of command formally; for a time he fought on illegally, in a tradition not unknown during these wars. By 66, most of the Roman work of the previous seven years had been undone, with Pontus again in the hands of Mithradates and Ariobarzanes once more ejected from Cappadocia by Tigranes (§ 17). It took until 63 for Romans finally to break Mithradates Eupator. Even then they benefited from intrigue and disloyalty at the Pontic court, this time involving the son and successor, Pharnaces II (§ 15), who recognized before Mithradates did the change now wrought in the political forces of Asia Minor.[39]

§ 4. Galatia

The territory in Asia Minor formerly known as Phrygia did not rank among its most desirable regions, for the most part being taken up by a treeless, semi-arid plateau known for its extremes of hot and cold. The generally unproductive nature of the country promoted the raids upon more prosperous neighbours for which the Galatians became notorious. They may in fact have been forced there by pressure from the surrounding long-settled tribes, after their arrival in the third century before Christ. Their Celtic ruling class organized itself into a complicated tribal system, which constituted an anomaly in Asia Minor. Over the centuries, the aristocracy largely absorbed the Greek language, but Celtic remained in use at least until the fourth century after Christ.

Possession of a few rivers, most notably the Upper Sangarius and much of the Halys with its tributaries, allowed the region a modicum of agriculture, much of it carried on by the subjugated population of Phrygians and Cappadocians. The towns of Gordium and Ancyra survived from earlier times, and both Tavium and Pessinus became noteworthy by the first century. Mithradation, the fortress of Mithradates Eupator (§§ 3, 15), stood in nominally Galatian territory.

The central location of Galatia and the relative ease of access it enjoyed to Cappadocia, Pontus, and other states, led to early accommodations with the Romans, who could partly relieve its political isolation. The resulting alliance proved of greater importance in the affairs of Asia Minor after 100 BC than the size of Galatia might seem to warrant. The warlike nature of its inhabitants and their appetite for plunder made Galatia a name to reckon with as Mithradates, on one side, and Rome, on the other, prepared for what proved to be a generation of conflict.

The Tetrarchs

The position of Galatia during these tumultuous years differed markedly from that of its neighbours. Organization under tetrarchs rather than a single king rendered it vulnerable to piecemeal conquest as well as to tribal dissension. In addition, the territorial claims exercised by the four tribes of the Galatians tended to be more flexible than those of their neighbours because of their comparatively recent arrival in Asia Minor and because of the lack of natural boundaries atop the Anatolian Plateau. Thus, for instance, after the bequest of Attalus III portions of his territories adjoining Galatia, including some over which Galatians had exercised hegemony in the past, went to their powerful neighbours Mithradates V of Pontus and Ariarathes V of Cappadocia. Adjacent kingdoms remained aloof from the Celts, who lacked both the Hellenic and the Iranian heritage that furnished so rich a source of local pride. The Galatians had achieved their homeland comparatively recently, in the third century, maintaining themselves by arms and diplomacy. By 100 BC their reputation as interlopers in contrast with the ancient monarchies around them had not faded. Only with the reign of Deiotarus I did they fully enter the 'Eastern dynastic network,' with at least a semblance of unity under a king and with intermarriage into Anatolian royal houses.

Galatians knew better than to take for granted their tenure of this amorphous homeland. It was hardly that a longing existed in Asia Minor for the Phrygians whom they had dislodged (though their local *phylai* preserved ancient Phrygian arrangements), but that no sentiment existed in favour of the conquerors: this lack of support caused their insecurity and forced reliance on a well-earned military reputation. It also promoted adherence to their long-standing alliance with Rome. Each party worked to the advantage of the other. In the dangerous years at the opening of the century, Rome could well use a steadfast ally who bordered Roman territory in the west and southwest, and shared borders in other directions with Bithynia, Paphlagonia, Pontus, and Cappadocia. All of these became theatres of war, and Galatia could not have been better placed for access to them. Though suffering repeatedly at the hands of Mithradates, Galatia survived to see his downfall. Despite some vacillation by one or another tribal group, Galatians supplied formidable contingents to precipitate that downfall.[40]

The Threat of Mithradates

At the accession of Mithradates Eupator in 120 BC, those in Rome who had opposed granting Phrygia Maior to his father now prevailed, obtaining the revocation of that decree and the annexation of Phrygia to the new Roman province of Asia. The resentment of Mithradates smouldered for nearly two decades, intensified by the recognition that Galatia, now lying adjacent to Roman territory, constituted a foothold for the distant republic. Accordingly, he combined with Nicomedes III of Bithynia to partition Paphlagonia, and in preparation for an advance on Phrygia he occupied some portion of Galatia, which separated both Paphlagonia and Pontus from the intended prey. To secure the newly acquired Galatian territory he constructed a fortress, Mithradation, at a point where eastern Galatia met the western border of Pontus.

In approaching Galatia, Mithradates, like Rome, found a multiplicity of individuals with whom he must deal. This difficulty arose from the system of tetrarchies, by which each of the four divisions of each of the three Galatian tribes possessed its own ruler, or tetrarch. Thus no fewer than twelve chieftains, at least in theory, ruled the Galatian people, and these did not always agree. Mithradates could expect to win over some of them during his first war with Rome, and Galatian troops can be discovered under his banner. But Galatians had also, along with Phrygians, joined Manius Aquillius in the recent effort to support Ariobarzanes; these retained their adherence to Rome during the war. Joined increasingly by others, they persisted as allies on into the campaigns of Lucullus.[41]

The Massacre

Mithradates brought upon himself the growing defections among the Galatians. He distrusted them from the outset and this led him to a mistake. Fearing Roman possession of Galatia, he determined to make it securely his own. In his view, that entailed removal of the tribal aristocracy, without whom he mistakenly assumed that the population of Celtic-speakers adrift in a sea of Hellenes and Iranians must follow him. At a banquet he perfidiously massacred the Galatian nobles and tetrarchs, of whom only three princes managed to escape. But he launched no general attack on the Galatian population, and hoped that this abstention settled his problem there. In the event, it guaranteed opposition to him after 86 under the remaining leaders, including the future king, Deiotarus. A governor whom Mithradates installed in Galatia could not maintain himself against a rising fomented by the three survivors, and by the close of the first war the Pontic King agreed to renounce his designs on Galatia. Nevertheless, since 'national' opinion need not compel every individual, a number of Galatians supported Mithradates in one way or another during the second war.[42]

Deiotarus I

During that war the majority of the Galatians fought against Mithradates. For the first time they appeared not in tribal contingents but under a unified command. Deiotarus was a tetrarch of the Tolistobogii, a tribe that had long since dealt in its own name with Greek states, as had the priesthood at Pessinus in the Tolistobogian territory. Deiotarus takes the prominent role henceforward in ancient accounts of Galatian affairs, though the developments that were to make him sole tetrarch of the tribe and later King of Galatia lay in the future. By the time of the second war, in 83, he must have reached mature years, for he was to be 'very old' in 42 BC, though still active.

In the third war between Rome and Mithradates, Galatians distinguished themselves. When Lucullus advanced against Pontus in 72, his route lay through Bithynia and Galatia, with thirty thousand Galatians said to have joined him as bearers and soldiers. The logistical problems from which Roman forces were to suffer in the centuries ahead during campaigns to contest Eastern Anatolia with the Parthians were mitigated by routes through allied territory in Pontus and Commagene, but these had not yet come available. Lacking alternatives, Romans relied now on Galatia. Galatian auxiliaries came near to capturing Mithradates himself and then went on to assist Lucullus against Tigranes. In these and other matters Deiotarus acquitted himself so well that by 63 he provided a 'new thing' for Galatia – kingship (§ 16), recognized by Pompey.[43]

§ 5. Cappadocia

The great treeless plateau of Cappadocia presented a formidable expanse, easily traversed by comparison with much of Asia Minor, but accessible only after passing rugged mountains or – coming from the east – the Euphrates. Further, it required lengthy supply lines for invasion. The dryness of the western reaches gave way very gradually in the eastern end of the country. On the plateau, the severe winters reduced major production to cereals and some fruits; there were also extensive pasture lands. Two major rivers traversed or bounded Cappadocia, the Halys and the Euphrates. In the south, the Taurus and Antitaurus ranges supplied timber and constituted a barrier. Considerable wealth accrued to the kingdom from its mines. In Christian times, Cappadocia's notable paucity of cities led to an anomalous form of organization, large districts containing mainly villages and towns.

Since the kings claimed descent from Darius, the long occupation by Persia lent a certain 'validity' to the Ariarathid line of kings that governed the country after Alexander. The encroachments by Pontus, which moved outward from what had once been Cappadocian territory, met steadfast resistance.

Cappadocia appeared an improbable site to precipitate the heaviest Roman involvement in Eastern dynastic politics, but a number of factors contributed to its selection. Cappadocia adjoined Rome's most steadfast dynastic allies, the Galatians and (after the death of Nicomedes III) the Kingdom of Bithynia. It also bordered the holdings of Rome's most dangerous enemy, Mithradates Eupator. To the east, it met the Euphrates and possessed the crossing at Tomisa, before seizure of it by Tigranes. Beyond lay Atropatene (§ 25), of high strategic value and, later in the century, a Roman ally. Past it there stretched the Parthian Empire, with which Romans were to open official contact early in the century during a dramatic meeting 'on the Euphrates' in Cappadocia between a Parthian envoy and Sulla, with the Cappadocian King in attendance. South of Cappadocia were Commagene, by now an established independent kingdom (§ 6), and Cilicia, a notoriously troubled region. About 100 BC, Cilicia Tracheia would require for nearly two centuries more the services of neighbouring dynasts, and Cilicia Pedias relied on at least one local dynasty, the Tarcondimotids (§ 18).[44]

The Last Ariarathids

In addition to its geographical importance, Cappadocia invited outside intervention now in another way: its ruling house, the Ariarathids, had fallen by about 110 BC into an increasingly steep decline, soon fatal. Intermarriage with Seleucids and Attalids had not so much strengthened the line as diluted it. With the Attalid kingdom in Roman hands and the Seleucids increasingly in disarray, the Ariarathids found that their major marriage alliance was with the overwhelming Mithradates, through Laodice, his sister, wife of Ariarathes VI. After the death of Ariarathes, she married Nicomedes III of Bithynia, no friend of the Ariarathids, and her daughter wed Nicomedes IV. Circumstances of time and place rapidly overtook the failing Ariarathids and proved too much for them early in the first century. Their final struggles brought both Mithradates and Rome deep into Cappadocian affairs. The effort to dislodge or maintain their successors – the dynasty of Ariobarzanes – kept the outside parties there.

First, the events surrounding the demise of the Ariarathids, some aspects of which were discussed above (§§ 2, 3). The assassination of Ariarathes VI about 111 BC through the machinations of Mithradates Eupator brought to the Cappadocian throne the son of this man by Laodice, sister of Mithradates. The expectation of the Pontic King – that he would now control Cappadocia through the agency of his sister as regent for Ariarathes VII (optimistically named *Philometor*) – fell before the intransigence of Laodice. She attempted to maintain herself without Mithradates by marrying Nicomedes III after his invasion of Cappadocia, but the couple had to flee to Bithynia. Armed conflict arose because, in Justin's account, young Ariarathes could not tolerate the return of Gordius, murderer of his father. He did not resist alone, since others in the East had come to fear the rise of Mithradates; thus he fought 'with the aid of neighbouring kings.' This phrase may cover a renewed effort by Laodice and Nicomedes, and assistance by one or more of the Galatian tetrarchs; it could refer as well to contingents sent by the neighbouring King of Commagene, Samos, who had nothing to gain from a Pontic assumption of Cappadocia.[45]

In the event, Mithradates proved too much for the coalition by despatching his young relative during a supposed truce. This action cleared the way for his own son, who assumed the Cappadocian dynastic name Ariarathes (IX) and began a reign that extended over some fifteen years, despite interruptions. He started about 100 BC, though the evidence, mainly numismatic, allows no precision despite valiant efforts by scholars. It also fails to settle the problem of the second son of Laodice, Ariarathes VIII, whether he ruled in opposition to Ariarathes IX, or in sequence, or in alternation. What does seem clear is that a struggle by some of the Cappadocian nobility – outraged at the imposition of Ariarathes IX by the Pontic house – arose in support of this second son of Ariarathes VI but failed. His position was perhaps not even strong enough to support a coinage, though notorious difficulties of interpretation surrounding the Cappadocian royal issues do not permit the exclusion of this possibility, and some coins have now been attributed to him.

In this general context occurred the visit of Marius to Cappadocia and his interview with Mithradates, whom he suspected of intending armed aggression on Cappadocia. The injunction of Marius to be stronger than Rome or obey it implied a conflict that began only after some years' delay but still endured some thirty-six years after the meeting.[46]

After Mithradates drove this last Ariarathid too from the throne, Ariarathes IX, the prince from Pontus, ruled for what remained in his initial period of perhaps five years. The final effort of Laodice and Nicomedes, supported by a portion of the Cappadocian nobility, produced yet a third candidate purporting to be a son of Ariarathes VI, though this one was widely believed to be spurious. At this juncture both parties finally had recourse to Rome, which had long been a 'friend and ally' of the Cappadocians. The Senate in Rome assumed that the situation resembled that of the Attalids more than thirty years before in that a long-standing royal line had reached the point of cessation. The majority of the senators disbelieved the claims put forward for this 'son' of Ariarathes VI, on the one hand, and considered too attenuated the claims of Ariarathes IX, on the other, even if he was descended from Ariarathes V. Other members of the family could have been brought from the Greeks of the Seleucid house, where a plethora of princes existed, but these were of even more distant connection to the Iranians of the Cappadocian royal house than Ariarathes IX, and might have proved unacceptable locally because of enduring coldness between the two houses. This coldness dated back to the days of Ariarathes V, who had renounced a marriage alliance to the family of Demetrius I in 160; he simultaneously broke off 'friendship' with the Seleucids and declared his good will towards Rome. That may account for the mild tone of a senatorial decree about 155 BC in response to his siege of Priene. Similarly, the previous marriage of the Cappadocian princess Stratonice, sister of Ariarathes V, to Eumenes II of Pergamon and then to Attalus II proved of no avail now. Even had offspring remained, the Attalids no longer had any standing locally.[47]

Finally, any children produced by Laodice and Nicomedes would be unacceptable to Mithradates and to most of the Cappadocian nobility, in the first case because of the demonstrated perfidy of the couple to him and in the second because neither was a true Ariarathid.

The New Dynasty of Ariobarzanes I

The determination of the senators in Rome that the Ariarathids had 'died out' was true on political if not familial grounds. Events such as the later marriage of Archelaus, son of the renegade general of Mithradates, to Berenice IV of Egypt (§ 23) show the lengths to which the dynastic aristocracy could go in assuring acceptable royal partners. Further, Pontic blood would flow in the veins of Cappadocian kings in future. But given the circumstances of about 95 BC, when Mithradates Eupator had arranged the murder or exile of no fewer than three Cappadocian kings and their recent replacement by his own son, many Cappadocian nobles must have despaired of their national future should the current situation long continue. Observing the failure of the deputations sent by Mithradates and by Nicomedes to Rome, they might, on the one hand, welcome a fresh beginning and, on the other, reject the Senate's suggestion of 'freedom,' for herein lay an invitation to Mithradates. They rightly preferred a king chosen locally.

The Cappadocians selected a king 'from among themselves.' What does the rather casual account of Strabo here imply? The nobles tended to stand close to the royal house by descent or marriage. At the great cult-site in Comana, as at its homonymous analogue in Pontus, the priests derived specifically from the same family as the kings and ranked second to them, with revenues and armed forces of their own. Furnished with royal recognition, nobles controlled the ten administrative divisions of the country, termed *strategiai*; one of these went to the quasi-royal priest of Comana, who acted as the *strategos* of Cataonia.[48]

Not only was the organization of Cappadocia unusual, but so was the relationship between king and nobles. When Romans concluded the first treaty of friendship and alliance with Cappadocians, Strabo regards it as unique in being framed not for a people (*ethnos*) or a king alone, but jointly for king and *ethnos*. This latter received its representation by the nobility, for Cappadocia was notoriously poor in cities, possessing only two in the days of Strabo and but three more by the time of Ptolemy. Instead, villages or towns widely dotted the countryside, and the landed nobility dwelt in 'fortresses' (*erumata, phrouria, tetrapurgia*). Any firm centralized control over the nobles proved at best difficult, and by the days of Ariobarzanes III (§ 17) virtually impossible, though they did return to the regular payment of taxes under Archelaus.[49]

Thus the circumstances of the election of Ariobarzanes to form a new dynasty appear to be as follows. Romans had long dealt directly both with the Ariarathid monarchs and with their powerful nobility. When both nobles and Rome realized that the dynastic evolution of the country had reached an impasse, with claims increasingly attenuated and the danger of intervention from Pontus and Bithynia unacceptably high, they agreed that a new dynasty, drawn from the nobles, provided the most reliable solution. Only the nobles' concurrence augured success in a country governed as Cappadocia was. As the dismal record of the coming thirty years was to prove, no precautions in their regard were too large.

Hence Ariobarzanes. To some, his election seemed less useful to the country than a strong alliance with Mithradates Eupator would have been, and this group continued its intrigues on behalf of Eupator and his son, Ariarathes IX, for decades. But others regarded the support of Rome as preferable to *de facto* absorption by Pontus, and during the century to come before Roman incorporation of Cappadocia this mutual alliance did work to the advantage of both groups, despite its financial cost to Cappadocia, *inanis* by Cicero's day (§ 17).

The implications for Rome of the accession of Ariobarzanes became clear early in his reign, requiring the armed intervention of Sulla to maintain him against Mithradates. The Roman commitment became virtually interminable so long as Mithradates lived. Ariobarzanes fled his kingdom at least five times during a reign of three decades, once journeying all the way to Rome.

Whence Ariobarzanes? Little can be deduced here, but a few clues do appear. The seat of the Ariarathid kings lay around Mazaca in east-central Cappadocia (Calder-Bean, co-ordinates Je), site of the later Caesaria (modern Kayseri). Strabo implies a mixture of royal and noble fortresses (*phrouria*) in the kingdom, apparently even in the district around Mazaca itself. Presumably the new dynasty arose in this vicinity. When a member of it, Ariarathes X, long afterward contended with the rival Sisines, his own holdings lay here and probably at Ariaratheia, whereas his opponent's were farther west, beyond Mazaca, and included a possibly alternative *basileion*. The dynasty of Ariobarzanes ruled where its predecessors had, though not without continuing local opposition.[50]

Thus it is inferred that the origin of Ariobarzanes lay in the general area later controlled by his descendants. This theory of origin cannot command certain assent, since the new dynasty would wish to control the lands of the old, both for reasons of policy and for access to the cattle and horse pastures offered by this part of Cappadocia. This region was also the one in which it was most likely that the nobility would elect the most powerful member of their own class, which was concentrated hereabouts except for the scattered holders of the ten *strategiai*.

Why 'Ariobarzanes'? Whether this constituted the given name of the new king or went to him upon his accession cannot be determined, but full warrant for its use as a throne-name in the Eastern pattern derived from its antiquity as a royal name, renowned both in Cappadocian and in Pontic history. The father of the founder of the Pontic royal line, Mithradates I, was an Ariobarzanes, as was his other son, who also ruled Pontus. The holdings of that Mithradates also included territory previously regarded as part of Cappadocia.

As a royal name, Ariobarzanes reached back even to the period when the Persian satrapy of Cappadocia existed in two divisions but when Pontus had not yet emerged separately. We know of an Ariobarzanes acting as satrap here about 365 BC.[51]

Ariobarzanes and Mithradates

Thence Ariobarzanes. Whether or not he adopted this name to conciliate the strong faction favouring Pontic control of Cappadocia, he did have to contend with this group later, and he spent his reign in conflict with Mithradates, who repeatedly ejected him or had it done by Tigranes. In 81 BC, Romans urged Ariobarzanes to marry Ariobarzanes II to the daughter of Mithradates. The text of Appian suggests that Ariobarzanes I himself married the four-year-old princess, but the situation demands his son. This marriage is reflected in an inscription from Athens naming the wife of Ariobarzanes II (and mother of Ariobarzanes III) as Athenais Philostorgos – the same name as that borne by the wife of Ariobarzanes I in another inscription. Thus we find successive, homonymous queens, the second a daughter of Mithradates but named after the first to promote dynastic continuity. The hope must have been, if this reconstruction is right, that the dreaded sovereign of Pontus might be persuaded to cease his direct attacks on Cappadocia, relying instead on the dynastic bond to accomplish his larger aims. Mithradates could be allowed to expect that the strong ties between Cappadocia and Rome might in this way weaken, and the country move towards his orbit. For his part, Ariobarzanes sought to emphasize Cappadocia's Seleucid ties through that double Greek name for his wife and daughter. The Seleucids had not yet finished as a power in the East.[52]

The gloomy details of the expulsions by Mithradates or Tigranes need not burden this discussion. Ariobarzanes I satisfied neither Mithradates nor a proportion of his subjects, who disliked his reliance on Rome. Ariobarzanes took to styling himself *Philoromaios* in formal inscriptions and on a coin otherwise modelled after traditional Ariarathid forms. This title was a new one among Eastern monarchs, adopted soon by Antiochus I of Commagene but never popular, given the increasing hostility to Rome eastward from the urbanized western portions of Asia Minor. This title and what some regarded as ignominious haste to Rome (*Romam contendit*) by Ariobarzanes during one of his five or six exiles, to say nothing of the continued presence of Roman representatives in Cappadocia as it fought with an interrelated neighbouring dynasty, convinced some nobles that their position might be eroding. Particularly unwelcome would be an ever-stronger central monarchy, supported by Roman interventions. Nobles could also foresee the treatment forthcoming from Mithradates should he prevail in Cappadocia. They received salutary example from the Galatian tetrarchs he destroyed.

Hence a steady opposition to Ariobarzanes from within as well as without, allowing Ariarathes IX, son of Mithradates, to eke out his claimed fifteen regnal years. The military record of these turbulent years shows an element of the Cappadocians fighting consistently *against* Roman forces sent to assist Ariobarzanes. He did not himself enjoy the highest martial repute, considered 'quite sluggish' (*segnis admodum*), an impression reinforced by his coin-portraits. Gordius, an agent of Mithradates long before Ariobarzanes acceded, remained for some time after that. The party that favoured Pontic control of Cappadocia endured at least into the reign of Ariobarzanes III (c. 53-42 BC).[53]

Mithradates Eupator did command respect throughout the regions adjoining Cappadocia, even in his declining years. Despite their misgivings as he neared seventy and persisted in contending with Roman armies, the Iranian populations in and around Armenia continued to favour him because of his kinship and royal position, and retained their hatred of the Romans, whom they feared as outsiders.[54]

Ariobarzanes soldiered on through his reign, optimistically issuing a coinage whenever he could, despite spending something like one-third of the time in exile. Because of the ambivalence of his own countrymen and the only sporadic effectiveness of Roman support, Ariobarzanes had to endure a chronically unsettled state of things. Ceding land when he had to, recovering it when he might, and even losing many subjects to deportation by Tigranes in the troubled period after the death of Sulla, he carried on. Despite his assistance to Lucullus in the successful campaign of 69 BC, Ariobarzanes had to withstand two years later depredations so severe that Cicero could pronounce his entire kingdom 'in the hands of the enemy.' Only in 63 could he at last breathe freely, with Mithradates finally broken. When he abdicated soon afterward in favour of his son, 'happy was he who lay down the kingdom, sad he to whom it was given.'[55]

Nevertheless, Ariobarzanes I left an important legacy. Cappadocia remained intact despite the change of dynasty and the attacks of Mithradates and Tigranes. Its holdings now included Tomisa and part of Sophene on the left bank of the Euphrates, with the addition of strategic lands in the west. The joy of Ariobarzanes upon retiring probably mingled with satisfaction. Both responses were fully warranted, but so was the apprehension of his successor (§ 17).[56]

3

The Levant

The term 'Levant' here includes Commagene, Emesa, Syria, Lebanon, Palestine, the territory of the Nabataeans, and Judaea. Egypt is treated in Chapter 4.

§ 6. Commagene

Commagene, which Strabo calls 'small, but extremely fertile,' was known for its fruit, geese, and overall prosperity, to which its position along the Euphrates contributed. Great trade routes passed through or near the country, mainly from Asia Minor or Syria across the river into Mesopotamia, but also from the Levant northward, towards Melitene. The generally rugged nature of the area, traversed by a range of the Taurus Mountains, did not deter the population from full use of the land-area, then as now. Cult-sanctuaries (*hierothesia*) in sites considered inaccessible by inhabitants of gentler lands remained in regular use for centuries, in pursuit of a remarkably syncretistic Iranian-Hellenic religious and nationalistic system. Finally, the kingdom profited from possession of iron mines so rich that it merited description as the land 'where iron grows' (*ubi ferrum nascitur*). By Roman imperial times, its king could be regarded as 'possessing immense inherited wealth, richest of the subject-kings,' and 'most prosperous of all the kings allied to Rome.' Commagene's position at the juncture of Hellenic, Semitic, and Iranian lands and its control of the important Euphrates crossings allowed the kingdom an influence disproportionate to its physical size.

By the beginning of the first century before Christ, this ancient land was in its seventh decade of independence under its own royal line, after centuries of domination by a branch of the Armenian royal family, from which its rulers claimed descent. The satrap Ptolemaios revolted from Seleucid control about 163 BC, and the national era dating from this event can be found in use more than two hundred years later. About 135 BC, under King Samos, the nation discovered for itself a niche between the Iranian world bordering it on the east and the Greek world to the west. Like Cappadocia, its Graeco-Iranian neighbour on the north, it carried forward strong elements of both societies. In the period just ahead it exhibited a high degree of syncretism between two cultures and religions. During the reign of Mithradates I, from about 95 to about 70 BC, this deliberate process received strong impetus, to be carried to its culmination by his son, Antiochus I (§ 19).[1]

Ptolemaios and Samos

After early military adventures against Cappadocian holdings under its first monarch, Ptolemaios, Commagene confined itself to internal consolidation and sound external alliances. The greatest threat to security had been presented by the Seleucids from whom he revolted in 163, but King Samos, his son, coped well with them. The attention of Samos to construction of the dynasty has left a vivid commemoration in the great rock relief of him overlooking the Euphrates at Gerger, and probably in the name of the major dynastic city, Samosata.

By the first century any problems from the Seleucids were replaced by an eastward shift in the alignments of power; first the growing empire of Parthia under Mithradates II and then that of Tigranes of Armenia were to endanger and then engulf the little kingdom. Only at the end of the period here considered (96-69 BC) could Commagenians once more look after their own affairs undisturbed, with Tigranes and Mithradates both in temporary eclipse, but their occupation of Cappadocia still to come in 67 BC (§ 5).

Mithradates I Kallinikos

Early in the century, King Samos acquired for his son and successor, Mithradates I Kallinikos, a Seleucid princess. This marriage, endlessly celebrated in the dynasty's inscriptions, brought to Commagene as queen the daughter of Antiochus VIII Grypus (§ 8), Laodice Thea Philadelphos. As her epithet ('She Who Loves Her Brothers') reminded contemporaries, the marriage also joined to this dynastic house her five brothers, all of whom reigned in the final years of Seleucid power. On her mother's side, Laodice furnished a connection with the Ptolemies as daughter of Cleopatra Tryphaena, herself among the offspring of Cleopatra III and Ptolemy VIII Euergetes II Physcon (§ 10). To advertise this distinguished marriage,

Laodice's new husband adopted Grypus's surname, *Kallinikos* ('Gloriously Victorious').

Any initial contact between Commagenians and Romans at the opening of the century has escaped documentation. In the years after Sulla's meeting with a representative of the Parthians 'on the Euphrates' north of Commagene, Romans must have realized the importance of Commagene, which possessed even better crossings into Mesopotamia than Cappadocia did. None the less, no evidence of early relations survives, though indirect contact certainly existed, for Commagene found itself caught up in the struggles surrounding it, first those of the Seleucids with the Parthians and then those of the Armenian Tigranes with the Greek states southwest of him (§ 11).

Soon after the marriage, which sent Laodice to Commagene, Antiochus VIII Grypus died, probably in 96 BC. In the struggles that ensued, all five of Laodice's brothers joined, as did their half-brother Antiochus X Eusebes (§ 8). The conflict of Eusebes with Parthia led to his defeat in 92 and may have involved an invasion by Parthian forces through Commagene, that is, by way of Zeugma. In this area, which belonged to Commagene during the early first century and probably before, was the Euphrates crossing favoured by Parthians. It had been used since the days of Alexander the Great, and probably before him by the Persians and Assyrians. Romans learned the value of Euphrates crossings during the conflict with Mithradates Eupator, when he fled beyond the Euphrates after a defeat by Lucullus, and in their battles with Tigranes, who had crossed into Syria, Cappadocia, and Commagene (§ 8). Pompey took care later to secure these Euphrates crossings in the hands of reliable allies.[2]

The greatest challenge to Commagene under Mithradates I was presented by Tigranes. As the Seleucids weakened, their outposts near the Euphrates and beyond fell either to Tigranes or to Mithradates II of Parthia. Between these two a marriage connection existed and from them Commagenians could expect little good. At the death of Mithradates II, Tigranes adopted his title, 'King of Kings' (§ 11). This title involved Commagene, for the grand design of Tigranes included succession to the Seleucids, which required possession of Syria. Hence occupation of Commagene, which lay on his way to Antioch and which it was prudent to secure behind him. One account implies his possession of the kingdom as early as 87/86; he certainly controlled it by 83, when his occupation of Antioch was complete (§ 8). Some preliminary fighting with Seleucids in the vicinity of Commagene occurred, but no tradition survives of resistance by Commagenians. They tended towards prudence.[3]

The relationship of the Commagenian monarch to Tigranes would now be that of a legitimate king subordinate to the King of Kings, on the Parthian model. The new status produced an adaptation of the distinctive Armenian tiara (*kitaris*) on the sculpture and coinage of Commagene. This practice began with Antiochus I, son and successor of Mithradates; he was already ruling by 69, with an accession date so far unknown. Whether or not he adopted this tiara before the defeat of Tigranes, he retained it for his preferred crown, as a 'successor' (*diadochos*) of the King of Kings locally. He proudly terms himself 'first to adopt the *kitaris*' in the new inscription from Sofraz Köy, and leads off with this phrase just after reciting his titles.

Commagenians greeted with relief the defeat of Tigranes in 69 BC. The standing temptation that this wealthy country constituted to its large neighbours rendered its survival precarious if it were not allied with a more powerful nation. Thus arose the paeans to its Seleucid marriage, and its care to forge similar ties to the Parthian royal house, to Atropatene, to Judaea, and to Emesa during the decades to come. Thus too its readiness to offer alliance to the Romans when they conquered Tigranes. Among the first monarchs to approach the victorious Lucullus in 69 we find Antiochus I. Save for one incident with Antony and an interruption under Tiberius, the resulting alliance remained firm for more than 140 years.[4]

§ 7. Emesa

Emesa, a kingdom based on a city (modern Homs), constituted an Arab state within Syria. Though Emesa bordered the Orontes River, its relative prosperity was apparently founded not so much on agriculture as on the pastoral life Arabs preferred. The kingdom lay north of the Anti-Lebanon Mountains. To its east the desert began almost immediately, home to the Arabs, whom Greeks called 'tent-dwellers' (*Skenitai*). Oases, such as Palmyra, and cities on the Euphrates, such as Dura-Europus, stood out in that desert, with Parthia beyond. The long and varied history of the lands east and north of Emesa, which had formed separate parts of the Assyrian and then Persian empires before the Seleucids came, had left a richly textured society difficult for the government based in Antioch to control. Emesa emerged from this background to achieve its independence at some time in the Hellenistic centuries, and participated in the overthrow of the Seleucids.

Nothing in the obscure early history of Emesa adumbrated the eventual importance of the little kingdom, which later furnished for the 'Eastern dynastic network' a number of kings active internationally and of queens intermarried with allied dynasties. Only traces of the kingdom appear before the first century BC, though it evidently arose from some antiquity. Unlike a number of cities in its vicinity, Emesa received no Greek colony during the centuries when Seleucids and Lagids pursued active settlement there. It retained its native name with no trace of any Hellenic one, also unlike its neighbours.

Emesa developed rapidly after 100 BC, assuming a disproportionate share in the dynastic activities of Syria. Its adherence to the Roman cause became especially notable by Cicero's day, when Emesenes stood in the forefront of allies providing support against threatened or real Parthian invasions. Despite difficulties at the close of the Roman civil wars, Emesene kings long continued to participate in dynastic politics. They served in the campaigns of Nero to control Armenia, and one ruled Armenia Minor. During the Jewish Wars, forces from Emesa joined those sent from Commagene or supplied by Agrippa II, and contributed to the Roman victory. A king from Emesa even saw service against his Commagenian kinsmen when Vespasian decided to terminate that kingdom's independence. After Emesa in turn lost its autonomy, it supplied notable senators active in Roman service. As the strangest development of all, aristocrats from Emesa eventually joined the imperial house in Rome – notably the Empress Julia Domna with her sons Caracalla and Geta, her great-nephew Elagabalus, and others (see stemma of Emesa).

After an efflorescence for some four centuries, Emesa then relapsed into such obscurity that Libanius, writing late in the fourth century, can speak of it as 'no longer a city' though it 'continues to send ambassadors and crowns to the emperors, knowing its poverty but ashamed to fall from the number of cities.'[5]

Azizus

Emesa owed this prominence between periods of obscurity partly to its favourable location, with connections eastward to the Arab Skenitai and to Palmyra, but it appears first in the sources for a dynastic incident, and that an ambiguous one. In 88/87 BC, the Seleucid Demetrius III Eukairos ('Well-Timed') besieged his brother Philip I Philadelphos ('Lover of His Brother' – both surnames ironic, as events proved) in Beroea (Aleppo). Philip enjoyed the support of the dynast of Beroea, of the Parthian governor of Mesopotamia, and of a certain 'Azizus, *phylarch* of the Arabs.' This name 'Azizus' suggests Emesa, where it long constituted a personal one for kings of the dynasty. But it also ranked as an important name, both sacred and personal, through much of the East; indeed, one meets it there today. Not only in Emesa but also in Edessa, Palmyra, and elsewhere did the Semitic divinity Aziz (*sc.* 'strength') appear; one delightful syncretism even yielded an Apollo Pythius Aziz, though the usual equation was with Ares. The name alone, therefore, is inconclusive during this incident.[6]

This Azizus is a *phylarch*, a term also applied to Sampsigeramus I of Emesa. An Azizus later worked with Sampsigeramus to restore Philip II Barypous, son of the Philip previously assisted by Azizus the phylarch. The references could be to the same man, judging from the relatively important position he held in both anecdotes. Philip II even received his diadem and restoration from Azizus. Further warfare was prevented only by the joint plot of Azizus and Sampsigeramus to depose both Philip and his rival, Antiochus XIII Asiaticus, and to 'divide the Kingdom of Syria' between themselves. Sampsigeramus put Antiochus to death and Azizus put Philip to flight. Then Pompey put an end to the Seleucids.

Sampsigeramus I

Whether or not this first Azizus ruled a portion of the territory controlled by Emesa cannot be ascertained, no more than can the possibility of his reigning jointly with Sampsigeramus (who later did share the rule with his son). But with the kingship of Sampsigeramus the record grows clearer. Most of his reign falls in the period after Lucullus and Pompey appeared locally (§ 20), but several indications put the inception of it well back in the first century. He therefore had to deal in some fashion with Tigranes, whose rule in Syria from 83 to 69 included difficulty with local kings, many of whom accordingly intrigued with Romans.[7]

What Sampsigeramus witnessed in these years made him a strong supporter of Rome. The chaotic final years of the Seleucids promoted neither stability nor confidence, nor were the fourteen years in Syria that Tigranes ruled much better, though in some eyes 'he controlled a most tranquil realm.' During this time his reign was 'to the Greeks not intolerable, but burdensome.' He was still spending a portion of his energies in 72-70 BC attempting to subdue cities in Phoenicia, and was so engaged when Lucullus sent Appius Claudius Pulcher, his brother-in-law, to Antioch for negotiations. Tigranes also attempted to settle the nomadic Arabs nearer to his own forces for greater control, and in various ways humiliated their leaders, who probably included Sampsigeramus.[8]

In something like a quarter-century of rule remaining to him after Tigranes left (70 or 69 BC), Sampsigeramus won praise for his competent rule at Arethusa and for his military assistance to Rome. His combination with Azizus about 66 helped fill the local vacuum. Once Pompey arrived to ratify the expulsion of the last Seleucids and to organize the allied or subject regions of the Levant, Sampsigeramus saw his task as one of stabilizing his kingdom. Under difficult conditions, he did this well (§ 20).

§ 8. Seleucid Syria

The empire of the Seleucids embraced some of the most varied and difficult territory in all of the East, and even its base, Syria, often resisted unified control during its long history. From the coastal cities to the fertile river lands of Cilicia Pedias, Syria, and the Lebanon, to the great ranges of the Taurus, the Amanus, the Lebanon, and the Anti-Lebanon, to the vast deserts eastward, Greater Syria was a land of extreme diversity.

The first third of the last century before Christ proved fatal to the Seleucids, but at the outset of the period few could have definitely foretold this. Reverses had occurred, and dangerous rivals existed in Pontus and Parthia, with Armenia to come, but the intentions of Rome remained unclear, and Seleucids may not have appreciated this danger. Turbulence in Italy early in the century helped blur for Easterners outlines of the larger situation. Not knowing the future, the last dozen Seleucids behaved as their predecessors had done for more than two centuries. Their coins depict the sometimes arrogant, often corpulent visages of the final members of the dynasty. Their policies reveal the continuing disposition to sacrifice men in internecine struggles, with some involvement by the Ptolemies. Their marriages show an unwavering resolve to maintain the dynasty by traditional methods. Their military activity concentrated on consolidation of their reduced holdings but did include attempts at expansion against neighbours such as the Judaeans or Nabataeans, and at recovering lands lost to the Parthians. The mistaken assumption of these last scions of the line was that the real threat to their empire lay in their circle of neighbouring kingdoms, not in Armenia or Rome.[9]

In this period Seleucids apparently forged no further marriage ties with Parthia or Pontus or Cappadocia, though they did with Egypt (§ 10). About 96 BC Laodice, daughter of Antiochus VIII Grypus, married the neighbouring Commagenian Mithradates I Kallinikos. Long afterward the descendants of this marriage proclaimed the connection, a matter of pride in the East for centuries after the Seleucids fell. Early in the second century after Christ the last of these, 'King' C. Iulius Epiphanes Philopappus, left proud Seleucid claims on his extant monument atop the Hill of the Muses in Athens, two hundred years after this important marriage.

Other marriages reflect continuing Seleucid ties to the Ptolemies. Antiochus X Eusebes (ruled 95-83) was the son of Cleopatra IV, daughter of Ptolemy VIII Physcon. His five royal relatives, the sons of Antiochus Grypus, also had a Ptolemaic mother, as had Grypus himself. These final Ptolemies in Syria endured almost as long as the Seleucids did. One of the last acts by Tigranes of Armenia before quitting Syria was to end the life of Cleopatra Selene, wife of Antiochus X, who had herself been 'ruling Syria.'[10]

Elsewhere the dynastic ramifications of the Seleucids had become attenuated by 100 BC. The King of Pontus, Mithradates Eupator, had a Seleucid mother, another Laodice, daughter of Antiochus IV Epiphanes. But his plans included no deepening of the bond and probably aimed at replacement of the Seleucids. In Cappadocia, the Seleucid element had been weakening since Ariarathes IV, who married a daughter of Antiochus III. By the end of the second century, the only remaining Seleucid was Laodice, the half-Seleucid, half-Pontic sister of Mithradates Eupator, who was married to Ariarathes VI and was then ejected to join her second husband, Nicomedes III, in Bithynia. Seleucids had spread their dynasty too far. Claims that they enjoyed by inheritance could now be exercised also by others.

The Sons of Antiochus VIII Grypus

The desperate history of the five sons of Antiochus Grypus and of their rival Antiochus X Eusebes cannot be treated here. Between 96 and 83 BC, all six of them had ruled and gone. The decisive factor in their 'sudden' eclipse was not Rome, nor even Parthia, but the unexpected extension of Armenia into an empire under Tigranes the Great. Parthian absorption of Seleucid possessions east of the Euphrates constituted no direct threat to their survival, but Tigranes chose to bring the conflict home to Syria. The last six Seleucids themselves provided the climate for intervention. As they weakened, others rose. To the south, the Nabataeans attained unprecedented importance. The Jews under Alexander Jannaeus, sometimes supported by factions in Egypt, involved Seleucids in dangerous skirmishes and won (§ 9). To the east, Emesa began its rise under Sampsigeramus I (§ 7), and to the northeast Laodice's marriage in Commagene entailed recognition of its autonomy (§ 6). This marriage was meant to benefit the partisans of Antiochus VIII Grypus as well, for it joined to them a cohesive dynasty, nominally Iranian and strategically located. Only the coming of Tigranes upset that calculation.

However unprofitable these final decades of struggle proved, they afford a useful glimpse of dynastic politics in full operation. In the conflict of Grypus with his half-brother Cyzicenus (they shared the same mother, Cleopatra Thea), two principles of dynastic rule appeared. One was that when two claimants arose, no grounds for secure tenure outweighed the fact of possession, at least by now. Grypus had witnessed an application of this 'rule' in the expulsion and death of his own father, Demetrius II Nicator, at the hands of Alexander Zebinas. It operated again in the murder of Seleucus V, his brother, then it came to apply to Grypus himself. After eliminating

Zebinas, he found himself dislodged in turn a dozen years later by Cyzicenus, whose formal claims rested on being the son of Antiochus VII Sidetes. For some two years (113 and 112 BC), Cyzicenus ruled alone.[11]

A second principle of dynastic rule revealed itself: when quiet possession proves impracticable, then *divide* among legitimate claimants. Grypus gradually recovered much of his position and an uneasy division resulted: 'he controlled Syria, and Cyzicenus controlled Coele.' Such an arrangement may not ordinarily constitute a 'principle,' but it does show expediency in administration of dynastic properties in times of conflict. Coele-Syria had probably been one of four new southern satrapies added by the Seleucids to their northern ones after the battle of Panium in the reign of Antiochus III, and this incident shows the disposition to regard such divisions as worth maintaining during a crisis. A dynast in difficulty instinctively assumes control of a recognizable segment of the family's traditional holdings.

Cyzicenus, assisted by his relative Ptolemy IX Lathyros, constituted a problem during the remaining reign of Grypus. We may see in the marriage of his daughter to Mithradates of Commagene an attempt by Grypus to restrict Cyzicenus from moving north by securing his own ally there. Cyzicenus maintained his opposition and only in 95, the year after Grypus died, did Cyzicenus in turn fall to Seleucus VI, the eldest son and successor of Grypus. This event did not place the rule of the Seleucids once more in the hands of a single monarch, for Antiochus X Eusebes, son of Cyzicenus, now claimed succession. Once more the matter had to be settled by war.[12]

The feebleness from which Grypus and Cyzicenus had suffered grew more acute among their survivors. As six kings struggled for supremacy during the thirteen years from Grypus to Tigranes (96-83 BC), indications of popular disaffection emerged, precipitated by conviction that the legitimacy of rule expected for an Eastern king was eroding. One example can suffice. Eusebes succeeded his father and drove into exile the successor of Grypus, Seleucus VI, who fled to Cilicia. This region lay within the traditional holdings of the dynasty but was one inferior in dignity to possession of Syria; especially in Tracheia, matters tended towards control by small dynasties (§ 18). At Mopsuhestia, Seleucus reached a Seleucid palace and began to raise funds for his campaign of reinstatement. Then occurred a noteworthy incident. The citizenry not only resisted his demands, but also set fire to his place of refuge and killed him. An inglorious end, from an unexpected source, but the days of high Seleucid pretensions were passing. Little were the Cilicians to know that diminution of Seleucid power locally was to bring them not more freedom but less: Tigranes soon rushed into the vacuum and began his mass transfers of the hapless population to Tigranocerta (§ 11).

Despite his only partial claim to the throne, Antiochus X Eusebes achieved rule of Syria. The remaining four sons of Grypus could not brook what they viewed as usurpation and tried one by one to gain all or part of Syria. Antiochus XI Epiphanes Philadelphos attempted it by war and fell. Philip I Philadelphos managed to rule over 'a certain portion of Syria.' Another of the brothers, Demetrius III, entered the fray when Ptolemy IX Lathyros intervened, bringing him from Cnidus – a convenient place for supernumerary Seleucids to await employment – to Damascus, where he installed him as king.[13]

Antiochus Eusebes, for his part, took on the Parthians. One account has him killed this way; another suggests that he ruled on until Tigranes arrived in 83. Rather than concerting their attack on Eusebes, Philip and Demetrius went to war with each other. Demetrius then allowed himself to be drawn into conflict against the Judaean Alexander Jannaeus, whom Josephus describes as at war with 'the Syrians.' Demetrius, his cognomen changing rapidly from *Eukairos* ('Timely') towards *Akairos* ('Untimely'), as found in some manuscripts, faced Arabian and even Parthian contingents, then disappeared into honourable captivity at the Parthian court of Mithradates II, where he remained until death. This dispersal of the Seleucids and scattering of their energies entailed greater dangers than they realized. Mithradates and Tigranes would have taxed the resources of even a united Seleucid monarchy. Disunited, the last kings could only await their fate.

The last son of Grypus, Antiochus XII Dionysus, gained power in Damascus after Demetrius, but repeated the pattern of fraternal strife, this time with the only other remaining son of Grypus, Philip I. After dangerous confrontations with Judaeans, Antiochus XII met an advancing Nabataean king, probably Obodas I (§ 9), and lost his life. Coele-Syria then fell under Nabataean control. These events had all occurred by 86 or 85, and left Philip as the only survivor of the five sons of Grypus, who had begun their stormy series of successions a decade before. Antiochus X Eusebes may have remained in power elsewhere in Syria still, and two young princes awaited their turn: Philip II Barypous, son of Philip I, and Antiochus XIII Asiaticus, son of Eusebes. But Tigranes ended all that.[14]

The Coming of Tigranes

For the rest, a dismal tale. The King of Kings arrived about 83, if not before, and in effect terminated the dynasty. The two princes took refuge in Cilicia, probably Tracheia, where they remained until after the defeat of Tigranes. Antiochus then crept back onto the Seleucid throne, with the approval of Lucullus, the victor, but there soon ensued the predictable conflict with his remaining relative, Philip II.

At this juncture the impatient and eager regional dynasts decided that enough was enough. Sampsigeramus I of Emesa and the Arab phylarch Azizus put an end to Seleucid rule and perhaps to the life of Antiochus XIII. That left Philip II, who fled to Antioch after eluding a similar design by the two Arabs intending to divide Syria between them.

The arrival of Pompey in the midst of this last act in Seleucid imperial history settled matters. He recognized no lingering rights of tenure for the Seleucids; simple military succession after conquest would decide the issue. Tigranes had conquered Antiochus, who had fled to 'a corner of Cilicia' and lurked there (*in angulo Ciliciae latuerit*). Romans had in turn conquered Tigranes. It was therefore 'not fitting' for Seleucids now rather than Romans to rule Syria. Antiochus or Philip could hardly expect to enjoy the rewards of another's victory (*alieni operis praemia*).[15]

Thus passed the Seleucid Empire after 250 years. Despite this ignominious end, its considerable achievements won continuing respect in the East. The value of descent from the Seleucids remained high among Greek dynasts or aristocrats, and the Seleucid era continued on in local use for centuries.

§ 9. Palestine, the Nabataeans, Judaea

The narrow fertile strip that lies along the Mediterranean coastline of Syria and Palestine widens south of the Lebanon Mountains as the coast curves southwestward towards Egypt. The Leontes River flows southward towards the sea. It rises not far from the headwaters of the Orontes, which flows northward. The Leontes reaches the Mediterranean south of the Lebanon, after flowing for some miles near and parallel to the Jordan, which in turn courses southward to feed the Sea of Galilee and the salty Dead Sea. Thus these important rivers in series follow the north-south orientation of the coastline and the mountain ranges, because they rise in these mountains and are contained by them. This geography in turn has determined population patterns in the region of comparative fertility west of the great Arabian desert. Of the three regions discussed in this section, the two occupied by the Palestinians and the Judaeans offered a more desirable environment than that occupied by the Nabataeans. Hence some of the strains recorded here between Nabataeans and the occupants of both Damascus and Judaea.

With the exception of the Ptolemies in Egypt, the dynasts of the regions south of Syria entered the 'Eastern dynastic network' relatively late, on present evidence. Not until the first century after Christ can the kings of Commagene, Emesa, Judaea, and Nabataea be discerned as fully engaged in the types of international royal involvement that had long characterized the relations of Ptolemies, Seleucids, Cappadocians, and others. Until the mid-second century BC, many regions were subject to the Seleucids. Even later, the smaller dynasties of Palestine tended to remain self-contained. Further, intermarriage was to occur during the first century BC, involving the Judaean and other royal houses, though at first on no such scale as was traditional in Anatolia. After the consolidation of these relatively new states, dynastic co-operation extended itself to an almost unprecedented degree in the first century after Christ.

This delay in the achievement of cohesive dynastic houses stemmed partly from the long hold of the Seleucids on the region. By about 100 BC, as the Seleucids slid towards oblivion, a cluster of principalities can be detected at various stages of growth in southern Syria, in Lebanon, and in Palestine. Traces in the literary and epigraphical sources provide the names of several dynasts, but sometimes little more than that. A few can be studied in sufficient detail to support historical reconstruction.

A certain Mennaeus and Ptolemy, his son, ruled the Ituraeans of the Anti-Lebanon. The principality furnished well-defined tetrarchies and some of their rulers far into the first century after Christ (§ 22). In Nabataea, the reigns of Aretas II, Obodas I, and Aretas III occurred during the period studied here. The Judaean monarchy under Alexander Jannaeus and Alexandra Salome underwent a period of foreign military conflict and domestic religious crisis. A number of small dynasts (or 'tyrants,' as at Byblos) arose as the Seleucids declined, but many fell in turn to the expanding Judaean power. More detail on these should clarify their activity.

I. Ituraeans

Ptolemy, Son of Mennaeus

First, Ituraea. Not far from Arethusa, ruled by Sampsigeramus I of Emesa and his son (§§ 7, 20), lay Chalcis and Heliopolis (Baalbek), 'which were subject to Ptolemy the son of Mennaeus.' This man also ruled the plain of Massyas, 'and the mountainous district of the Ituraeans.' Intermingled with them were 'Arabs,' the convenient ancient term for groups hard to distinguish in this region; their names show a mixture of Aramaic and Greek. Those of the mountains lived by 'robbery' (or so it seemed to their more settled neighbours); those of the Massyas lowlands, by farming. This plain separates the Lebanon range from the Anti-Lebanon and could serve as the base of an extensive territory stretching westward to the Mediterranean. The holdings of Ptolemy constituted in fact the largest political entity between Syria and Emesa to the north and Judaea to the south.[16]

In the local scramble to replace the weakening Seleucids, Ituraeans and Judaeans achieved the greatest gains. These could occur at mutual expense.

During the reign of the Judaean Aristobulus I and of Mennaeus, father of Ptolemy, the Ituraeans controlled Galilee. They shared a frontier with the Jews, and entered into conflict with them. Aristobulus spent part of his one-year reign (104-103 BC) successfully contending for a portion of their holdings, probably in Galilee.

The Ituraeans pursued an expansionist policy. If the known founder of Chalcis, 'Monikos,' is our Mennaeus, he had seen the advantage of basing his dynasty in the plain of Massyas, where Chalcis lay. He need not have been the founder of the dynasty too, but he probably initiated the extension of territory the Ituraeans enjoyed at late-Seleucid expense. No details survive of his activity, with the record confined to numerous but unhelpful mentions of him merely as the father of Ptolemy. Surely, however, he began the work his son finished: that of building up a kingdom against local rivals among the Judaeans, Nabataeans, and Seleucids, with the growing power of Emesa evident to the east. The Ituraean holdings by about 90 BC not only extended to the coast, but also virtually surrounded Damascus – where apprehension arose.[17]

A tradition hostile to Ptolemy, whom Josephus speaks of as 'a base man,' probably reflects his pressure on Damascus, to which he was a 'difficult neighbour.' The city had already suffered from the successive sons of Antiochus Grypus seeking to establish themselves there. Ptolemy operated for a time in reciprocity with the youngest of these, Antiochus XII Dionysus, who took control of Damascus about 87 BC but lost his life to an unnamed Arab king. Whoever this Arab was (see below), the Nabataean Aretas III soon gained by the death of Antiochus XII, for the inhabitants of Damascus, 'through hatred of Ptolemy, son of Mennaeus,' invited him in and pronounced him 'King of Coele-Syria'! This event was unwelcome to the Seleucid Philip I, who had failed in an attempt to replace his brother in Damascus, and probably also to Alexander Jannaeus, who had fought Antiochus XII but soon afterward suffered a defeat inflicted by Aretas III. To Ptolemy the repulse proved only a temporary discouragement, for some fifteen years later we find Alexandra of Judaea, wife and successor of Jannaeus, sending troops towards Damascus to counter the 'continual oppression' Ptolemy inflicted there.

By the time of these events, the scope for local dynastic manoeuvre had begun to diminish rapidly. Tigranes, long in control of the former Seleucid holdings in Syria, became master of Damascus too by about 72, after the Judaean expedition against the troublesome Ptolemy, who on one view first drove the Nabataeans from Damascus. Josephus links that event loosely with the siege of Ptolemais by Tigranes, who finally captured it and Cleopatra Selene just before news arrived that Lucullus was besieging Tigranocerta.

Upon the withdrawal of Tigranes, Damascus became autonomous, with both Aretas III and Ptolemy turning their attentions elsewhere.[18]

Ptolemy survived the coming of Pompey and then of Caesar. He married into the Judaean line and entered its politics. On his death, which did not occur until 40 BC, the succession passed uneventfully to his son. Members of the extended family continued to rule portions of the original kingdom for generations, and tetrarchies drawn from its territory remained under the control of relatives as late as the reign of Claudius, AD 41-54 (§ 22.I).

The diminution of Seleucid control had contributed to the efflorescence of this and other local powers. The process by which these might in turn have encapsulated the smaller principalities was partly interrupted by the Romans, from Pompey onward, but in part it continued. The dynasties that retained their coherence and continued to increase in the century to come lay in Judaea, Emesa, and the Nabataean portion of Arabia.

II. The Nabataeans

The second dynasty treated here, that of the Nabataeans, presents a number of difficulties but amply repays examination. Nabataeans controlled a recognized territory for some four hundred years and frequently entered the larger history of the Levant. The aspect of their development that impinges on affairs in the neighbouring Palestinian and Judaean states between 100 and 70 BC requires treatment here (after 70 BC: § 22.II).

Aretas I

The kingship that developed among the Nabataeans appeared to Strabo an effective one. He considers the kingdom 'very well governed' and the king a man 'of the people' (*demotikos*). The clearly articulated system he describes had been in his own lifetime brought into sharper focus by the expedition of Aelius Gallus about 26-25 BC. The scope of the institution of 'king' among Nabataeans (*mlk* in the Aramaic of their inscriptions) and whether it stood as an exact equivalent of *basileus* await full examination, but by the early second century BC, an inscription mentions 'Aretas, King [*mlk*] of the Nabataeans,' perhaps the same man as the 'tyrant of the Arabs' known from a passage in 2 Maccabees in a context of 168 BC.[19]

Relations between Nabataeans and Seleucids had been governed nominally by a pact of friendship after the raid on Petra of Demetrius I Poliorcetes about 312 BC, but this pact rested on maintaining exclusive spheres of interest. By the late second century before Christ, the expanding Nabataean power had begun to intrude where Seleucids accorded it no welcome; open conflict then ensued during the early first century. Relations with Jews from Judas Maccabaeus (c. 168-163 BC) to Alexander Jannaeus ranged from friendly to bellicose. Nabataeans sought to protect their incense trade route from Hasmonaean expansion into the eastern Transjordan. What Strabo characterizes as 'frequent' Nabataean raids on Syria before Rome held it probably fell largely within the period 110-70 BC, when constant Seleucid warfare, internally and with both Ptolemies and Parthians, drew the Nabataeans farther north, until they finally took Damascus. When many cities of Syria managed to free themselves or else fell to local 'tyrants,' the process attracted Nabataeans, as it later did Romans. Easier conquests lay here than in the Ituraean and Judaean kingdoms. Syrian and even Egyptian territory became, about 100 BC, 'prey to the previously unwarlike race of Arabs,' and this movement north and east continued. The Nabataeans could utilize a great trade route, which had lain open at least since Persian and then Ptolemaic times. It ran from Bostra through Dumata to the Persian Gulf, and also served as a military road.

Rabbel I

A possible son, 'Rabbel, King of the Nabataeans, son of 1Haretat [Aretas], King of the Nabataeans' or 'Rabbel, King of the Arabs,' may have ruled after Aretas I. However, the inscription identifying his father preserves only the final 'T' of the name, and could therefore refer to Obodat (Obodas I, below). Other considerations slightly favour the view that this monarch ruled soon after Aretas I.[20]

Aretas II

In the initial period, four Nabataean kings appear in the historical record, two named Aretas, one called Rabbel, and an Obodas. From external evidence both of the kings bearing the name Aretas can be fixed chronologically, as can Obodas. King Aretas I is mentioned in a biblical passage datable to 168 BC (see above). More than half a century later, in the conflict of the Judaean Alexander Jannaeus with Ptolemy IX Lathyros, we hear of another 'Aretas, King of the Arabs.' During the protracted struggle over control of Gaza, which had not ended until about 96 BC, the Gazaeans kept looking for assistance from this Aretas II, who failed to provide it.

Another ancient reference may belong to Aretas II, equated with the *rex Herotimus* who became contemptuous of the weakening Ptolemies and Seleucids, and who 'attacked now Egypt, now Syria.' Under him, the Nabataeans and perhaps associated Arab tribes had consolidated into a strong power, 'and he had made great the name of the Arabs among the powerless forces of the neighbouring peoples.' Also in his reign may appear the first dynastic coins.[21]

Obodas I

Whether Aretas II ruled the whole of the lands covered by the expression *nb1tw* ('Naba1tu') cannot be determined, but it is likely, and in any case we soon hear of another 'King of the Arabs' named Obodas (variants in transcription: Obedas and Obodat). An inscription at Petra mentions 'year 1 of Obodat, King of Naba1tu, son of 1Haretat, King of Naba1tu': the successor of Aretas II was his son. He had acceded by 94 or 93 BC, when Alexander Jannaeus added to his own troubles by opening a front in Gaulanitis against 'Obedas, King of the Arabs' – our Obodas I. Another passage shows Jannaeus forced to cede some territory to 'the King of the Arabs.'

These struggles were by no means inconsiderable. Archaeological evidence of a severe disruption in settlement patterns of Nabataean towns in the Negev has been ascribed to the conquest of Gaza and of 'the twelve cities [Jannaeus] took from the Arabs' when he fought them around 96. This resulted in abandonment of some sites for most of the first century before Christ. A town 'of the Nabataeans' called Oboda, the burial site of 'King Obodas, whom they consider a god,' may also appear in the list of destroyed sites.

One confrontation with neighbouring dynasts belongs to the period when Obodas I reigned, though not attributed to him by name. The Seleucid Antiochus XII proceeded 'against the Arabs' and encountered disaster, losing his life to an unnamed 'Arabian' king. Apparently this was still Obodas.[22]

Aretas III

The reign of Aretas III followed hard upon, with the invitation from Damascus for him to become 'King of Coele-Syria' and to oppose Ptolemy of Chalcis. About the long career of Aretas (c. 87-62 BC) we have better information, including coins, and we know that he was the son of Obodas I.

The coins, notably a series at Damascus from 84 to 72 BC, closely follow in type the bronze issues of Demetrius III Eukairos, who ruled there from about 96 until 88 or 87, followed briefly by his brothers Antiochus XII and Philip I. Those of Demetrius constituted a more plentiful model than those of his two ill-starred brothers could, and in his 'diadochic' issues Aretas III now stated that succession at Damascus had devolved legitimately upon him, both by right of conquest over Antiochus XII (whether he or Obodas I had achieved this) and by invitation from the inhabitants. He entered enthusiastically into the spirit of ruling a Greek city and began to call himself 'King Aretas, Lover of the Greeks.'[23]

The coins demonstrate that he maintained his position at Damascus despite conflict with Alexander Jannaeus, with whom he fought one battle in Judaea (near Adida, modern el-1Haditha). He won, and brought Nabataean power potentially deep into Judaea; possession of the town would let him control the region near Lydda and thus the main road from Joppa (Tel Aviv) to Jerusalem. Fortunately for the Judaeans, Alexander was able to conclude a treaty by which Aretas withdrew from Judaea, aware that his forces were too far from their bases for effective control. Then Jannaeus spent three years fighting east of the Jordan. He had once almost lost his life to Obodas I, but no record survives of his now coming into armed conflict with Aretas III, who must have had no territorial claims there. Jannaeus fulfilled an ambition of long standing by capturing Amathus, seat of the wealthy Theodore, son of Zeno.

Nabataeans became involved indirectly in Judaean affairs again after the death of Alexander Jannaeus in 76. His widow, Alexandra Salome, succeeded and began to favour the Pharisees, with whom Jannaeus had been in continual conflict. This change of policy drew immediate denunciation as likely to send opponents of the Pharisees flying to 'Aretas the Arab and the other princes.' These former enemies of Jannaeus would now delight in receiving their recent adversaries as suppliants.

Aretas soon withdrew from Damascus. Alexandra's expedition against it went to oppose not him but Ptolemy of Chalcis, so Aretas must have left. Then Tigranes arrived in Damascus about 72. His coins reflect control there until he left in 69 to oppose Lucullus. Aretas contented himself after the loss of Damascus with an even more active role in the internecine politics of Judaea, while unwittingly preparing for a nominal 'conquest' of his kingdom by Pompey (§ 22).[24]

III. Judaea

Contacts between the Judaean state and Rome have been seen as early as 161 BC, during the reign of Judas Maccabaeus, leading to an agreement renewed under Jonathan, with a *senatus consultum* under Simon. That a state in revolt from the Seleucids should turn to Rome during this period occasions no surprise, but the sources do not promote great confidence. With the reign of John Hyrcanus, which ended in 104, the record is a little better, but still unsatisfactory. Much of the first half-century of the new state's history remains obscure.

The early years of the first century before Christ are better attested. Judaea was dominated in this period by Alexander Jannaeus (103-76 BC) and his wife, Alexandra (76-67). In addition to opposing their neighbours in Syria, Chalcis, and Nabataea, they also contended with the Ptolemies. This meant dealing with Cleopatra III, her sons Ptolemy IX Lathyros and Ptolemy X Alexander I; indirectly with her daughter in Syria, Cleopatra Selene, wife of three Seleucids; and finally with Ptolemy XI Alexander II, Cleopatra Berenice III, and Ptolemy XII Auletes, her Egyptian grandchildren. The complications raised by the conflicts of these with the Seleucids and with one another spilled over into Judaea with considerable force, but Alexander Jannaeus was a match for them.

Alexander Jannaeus

The turbulent reign of Jannaeus involved a brief period of conflict with external princes (to 96 BC), one of internal party strife (to 88 BC), and another of external war (especially from 85 to his death in 76).

The first period embroiled him with Ptolemy Lathyros. Jannaeus attempted to annex four cities on the coast: Ptolemais (Ake; Acre) in Phoenicia; Dora (Tantura, south of Carmel); Straton's Tower (Caesarea); and Gaza (Tell el Ajjul). Josephus has him taking advantage of the struggle between Antiochus VIII Grypus and Antiochus IX Cyzicenus, his half-brother. The native ruler of Dora and Straton's Tower, Zoilus, aspired to a more secure position also, 'because of the conflict between the kings.' Zoilus rendered no effective assistance at Ptolemais and joined the people of Gaza in appealing to Ptolemy IX, who later, however, found it expedient to sacrifice him to Jannaeus.

Ptolemy Lathyros entered the struggle for dynastic reasons of his own, and because he received an invitation to do so, which accorded with his strategic aims. His mother, Cleopatra III, had expelled him from Egypt, where she ruled as regent for her younger son, Ptolemy X. Now Lathyros held Cyprus but longed for more: possession of the southern coast of Palestine. The addition of Ptolemais could serve as a bulwark against the waning Seleucids and as a reminder of his ancestors' hold on the city, renamed for Ptolemy II from the native Ake. To these dreams envoys added the prospect of joining Sidon to holdings that would reach through the territory of Zoilus down to Gaza. They easily persuaded him to the dangerous escapade.[25]

Then the citizenry in Ptolemais had second thoughts, fearing that they would come into the power of a *despotes* and that the Jewish conflict would widen for them into one with Egypt as well. Josephus recognizes the paralegal present station of Lathyros – and probably his character as locally perceived – with this term, *despotes*. Elsewhere he employs *basileus* when speaking of Ptolemies, and *tyrannos* when referring to local rulers in the cities of Syria and Palestine. But legitimacy can arise from arms, so Lathyros came ashore anyway. His presence, reinforced by the continued enthusiasm for him of Zoilus and the Gazaeans, induced Jannaeus to withdraw, requesting an attack on Lathyros by Cleopatra III, just as the people of Ptolemais had feared. However, Jannaeus also opened negotiations with Lathyros. When this duplicity came to light Lathyros, the proposed saviour of Ptolemais, had to become its besieger, with eventual success. An advance through Galilee to the Jordan brought him into battle with Jannaeus and, victorious, into possession of some Judaean territory. This advance precipitated a pre-emptive expedition by his mother into Judaea, with a flanking force sent into Phoenicia under Ptolemy X Alexander I. The wretched inhabitants of Ptolemais soon found themselves enduring another siege, also successful. Lathyros failed in a sudden attempt on Egypt and had to work his way back to Cyprus by way of Gaza. Cleopatra and Jannaeus concluded a peace, freeing the Jewish army for conquests beyond the Jordan and for a punitive siege of Gaza, which, disappointed in its hopes of assistance from Lathyros and from Aretas II, succumbed.

In due course, beginning about 94 or 93, Jannaeus engaged 'the Arabs' of Moab and Galaaditis and made them tributary; then he attempted conquest of Obodas I in Gaulanitis and nearly lost his life.

Jannaeus devoted the ensuing six years to serious domestic challenges, mainly from the Pharisees. After appalling slaughter he found himself facing an external threat again, this time from the Seleucid Demetrius III Eukairos, invited into the conflict by the opponents of Jannaeus. A state of undeclared war subsisted between Jannaeus and 'the Syrians' about 93, early in the period of unremitting conflict among the five sons left by Antiochus VIII. They fought one another and Antiochus IX Cyzicenus, then his son Antiochus X Eusebes (§ 8). Despite a victory over Jannaeus, Demetrius declined further battle. He aimed at higher things, returning to Syria for a siege of Philip, his brother, and eventually a captive's death in Parthia.[26]

Alexander Jannaeus rebuilt his fortunes, but the penchant of his opponents for summoning outside assistance did force him to restore 'to the King of the Arabs' (either Obodas I or Aretas III) the lands he had taken about 93 in Galaaditis and Moab. After an inconclusive brush with Antiochus XII, who easily breached the Judaean lines on his way to perish in Arabia, Jannaeus renewed his attacks east of the Jordan, and died so engaged some years later, in 76 BC.

His legacy demonstrated both positive and negative aspects. All but one of the major cities along the coast from Phoenicia to Egypt now belonged to the Judaeans, as did a large tract east of the Jordan, containing several cities. But he left many cities half ruined and their Greek inhabitants permanently hostile, though he sought on his coins to portray himself as a legitimate successor to the Seleucids. Only after the Romans appeared were some cities reconstructed; others, as in Nabataea, remained deserted for nearly a century and some permanently. This treatment of cities and his reputation for cruelty left a negative impression of Jannaeus in the minds of contemporaries, as well as an undying bitterness among his opponents, the Pharisees, who were now to have their day. Nevertheless, he had successfully resisted Seleucid, Ptolemaic, and Nabataean incursions and had continued his predecessor's policy of containing the Ituraeans. Even the dangerous Tigranes, in Syria since 83, remained beyond the borders of Judaea, and the skilful Alexandra was to keep him there.[27]

Alexandra Salome

Eager to rule, Alexandra, wife of Jannaeus, succeeded in 76. Although her reversal of her husband's policy regarding the Pharisees alienated her son Aristobulus, she contrived to occupy him with military duties, and Hyrcanus, his brother, with the office of high priest, despite both being of an age to rule. She built up the armed forces through domestic levies and recruitment of foreign mercenaries to the point where she became 'fearsome to external dynasts.' Then she dispatched Aristobulus to Damascus, ostensibly to rescue it from the pressures of Ptolemy of Chalcis, who tried to succeed Aretas III there. Aristobulus failed and Damascus soon lay within the orbit of Tigranes, who had been working his way southward, 'subjecting to himself some cities of Phoenicia.'

Tigranes had long impended. What saved Judaea from him now was an advance accommodation made by Alexandra. She learned that he was besieging Ptolemais as part of his campaign against Cleopatra Selene, who controlled much of Syria as wife and putative successor to the expelled Antiochus X Eusebes. Selene's Ptolemaic parentage (Ptolemy VIII Physcon and Cleopatra III) also provided her with the type of claim to the seaboard cities that Lathyros, her brother, had attempted to exercise in Ptolemais twenty years earlier. She urged the inhabitants of Ptolemais to resist Tigranes and they did, for which they paid dearly. Selene withdrew to Seleuceia (Zeugma), but her time had run its course; when Tigranes returned to Armenia he left behind the corpse of the last Ptolemaic-Seleucid queen.

However, gifts and envoys sent to Tigranes by Alexandra had bought valuable time. Doubtless Judaea lay in the long-term plans of Tigranes, but the delay in advancing on it proved permanent. His departure in 69 BC occasioned fervent sighs in Judaea.

The reign of Alexandra brought not only peace, but also prosperity, with no foreign wars of consequence and with relative harmony among domestic factions. What she proved unable to do, however, was to forestall impending trouble among the strong religious and political factions of the Jewish state. One of her sons, the future Aristobulus II, became increasingly dangerous to internal order as head of the Sadducees. Alexandra's death in 67 coincided with the inception of civil war between Aristobulus and Hyrcanus II, his brother, a war that she had authorized. The respite had ended and just beyond the receding shadow of Tigranes approached a greater threat in Pompey (§ 22).[28]

IV. Minor Dynasts

A final aspect of the political composition of the Levant in the first three decades of the last century before Christ was the proliferation of local rulers in Syria, Phoenicia, and Palestine. Not only did the larger dynasties of Ituraea, the Nabataeans, and Judaea achieve new prominence as the Seleucids declined, but a bewildering array of minor rulers, usually termed *tyrannoi*, also arose. A number of free cities appeared in the last years of the second century and early in the first; some of these had royal grants of freedom and others simply declared their own autonomy, as Damascus did when Tigranes left.

In some instances these small rulers had occupied a similar station previously, but in the main their current position was achieved in response to the internal weakening of the Seleucid and Ptolemaic structures that had dominated this part of the Near East for more than two centuries now. Present evidence permits no systematic study of these numerous rulers, who seldom gain more than passing mention in the sources and who usually left no prominent dynasties to succeed them, at least west of the Euphrates (east of it: § 12). Their diversity contributes to an understanding of dynastic processes in the Near East, where no vacuum of authority was long tolerated. The larger movements are well documented. Persians had come to power in succession to states of great antiquity; Seleucids and Ptolemies followed and were now to be replaced by Rome; it in turn gave way to Byzantine and Arab rule. The smaller entities more easily escape notice, but local traditions in the East long maintained native names and families, often impervious to the change of empires overhead.

In the northern regions, we know of a number of rulers from about 100 BC until the coming of the Romans. Byblos, the ancient residence of the mythical Cyprian Cinyras, had an unnamed 'tyrant' whom Pompey beheaded. Pompey encountered others. Ptolemy of Chalcis bought his own recognition (§ 22), but a relative of his, Dionysius of Tripolis, fared less well and also suffered beheading. The submission of a certain 'Bacchius Judaeus' appears on a coin of commemoration. A Jew named Silas ruled a Lebanese fortress called Lysias, which Pompey destroyed. In addition to these, a number of princes and kings – including Zarbienus of Gordyene (§ 12) – had been assembled by Tigranes at Antioch, but for the most part their identity cannot be determined.

Theodore, ruler of Philadelphia (Rabbath Ammon) in Transjordan, with Gadara and Amathus, tempted Alexander Jannaeus, who coveted the treasury that had descended from Theodore's father, Zeno Cotylas, ruler there in the days of Antiochus VII Sidetes. Later, Alexandra's son Aristobulus gathered an army from 'Lebanon and Trachonitis and the monarchs.' In the reign of Jannaeus, Zoilus had ruled Straton's Tower and Dora, as above. The murderer of Antiochus Grypus in 96 was a certain Heracleon, a local ruler whose son, Dionysius, ruled not only a town named for Heracleon but also Bambyce and Beroea. The latter was taken from Straton, who ruled it about 88 BC and from there initiated the overthrow of Demetrius III, aided by Azizus, the Arab phylarch (§ 7). In addition to all these are recorded numerous Arab chieftains, such as Alchaedamnus, King of the Rhambaeans along the right bank of the Euphrates and himself a late contemporary of Ptolemy of Chalcis. The roll could continue.[29]

No region on earth demonstrated greater complexity than did the Levant, where the continual mixing of immigrant groups from Sumerian, Akkadian, Babylonian, Assyrian, and Persian times produced by the days of Alexander the Great a richly textured society of Semites and Iranians now coming under Greek control, then Roman. The East's habitual easy tolerance of diversity preserved local differences among the populations of Syria and Palestine, which remained partly unaffected by the Greeks and Romans. The most far-reaching restructuring of these societies lay deep in the future, when the adherents of Islam completed the Arab territorial expansion that their Nabataean ancestors had initiated. In the interval much occurred.

4

Egypt

Egypt, aptly termed 'the gift of the Nile' by Hecataeus, consisted of three main zones: the Nile Valley from the first cataract northward to Memphis; the Delta, from Memphis to the Mediterranean; and the flanking portions of the Arabian, Western, and Libyan deserts. Out of a total land area for Egypt of nearly 400,000 square miles, the Delta occupied only 8500 and the Nile Valley about 4800. These relatively tiny portions, which were cultivable, enjoyed the nearly impassable protection of those which were not.

Of its total length of some 4000 miles, the Nile flows through Egypt for little more than 400, from about 24 to 31 degrees north latitude. However, the small percentage of its length that the river expends in Egypt constitutes the most important part, bearing rich silt to distribute along its banks (in a valley never more than 30 miles wide) and through its seven mouths into the level, rich expanse of the Delta, 'the land which is always rising.' A remarkably stable climate results from the country's position: it lies north and west of the Indian Ocean's monsoons, and – except for the Delta – south of the Mediterranean's winter storms.

As one of the earliest of the great civilizations, Egypt learned well before 3000 BC to conserve and utilize the mighty river from which its prosperity derived. After its conquest by Alexander in 332 BC, Egypt formed a valuable portion of his empire, to be ruled for three centuries by the same Macedonian family, from Ptolemy I to Cleopatra VII. The rule of the Ptolemies constituted an epoch in Graeco-Roman as much as in Egyptian history.

§ 10. The Ptolemies of Egypt

Internal problems plagued the Ptolemaic house after the death in 116 BC of Ptolemy VIII Euergetes II Physcon. Egypt played a limited role in the

Mithradatic Wars, but the ambitious widow of Physcon, Cleopatra III, had energies to spare for foreign intrigue, as Syrians and Judaeans soon learned. The struggle of Ptolemy IX Lathyros with his mother nearly engulfed the Judaean kingdom of Alexander Jannaeus in a fatal war, and the ramifications of his family's activity were felt in Syria. One sister of Lathyros was Cleopatra IV, to whom he had been married and with whom he engendered Cleopatra Berenice, born about 120. However, about 115 Cleopatra IV went as wife to the Seleucid Antiochus VII Sidetes. By that time the reigning Seleucid, Antiochus VIII Grypus, son of Cleopatra Thea and Demetrius II Nicator, was already married to Tryphaena, sister of Cleopatra IV and Lathyros. The two Ptolemaic sisters entered enthusiastically into the conflict that erupted between their Seleucid husbands, Grypus and Cyzicenus, in 113. The struggle cost the sisters their lives. About 104, Cleopatra III sent another of her daughters, Cleopatra Selene (also formerly married to Lathyros), to become the wife of Grypus. The death of Cleopatra III in 101 removed a most volatile element from the contemporary scene, but her two sons remained. Though the peace that Cleopatra had concluded with Alexander Jannaeus held, Selene and her husband, Grypus, remained at odds with Cyzicenus, and this conflict later touched Judaea. By 101 Ptolemy Apion was ruling Cyrene, and others of the dynasty soon to be heard from were alive: Ptolemy XI Alexander II, Ptolemy XII Auletes, and Cleopatra Berenice III. More detail will elucidate that summary, concentrating first on the two brothers, Ptolemy X Alexander I and Ptolemy IX Lathyros.[1]

Ptolemy X Alexander I
(c. 141-88 BC; *PP* 14555)

During the years 107-88 BC, Ptolemy X reigned in Egypt; by 101 he was furnished with Berenice III as his queen. She was the daughter of his antagonist and older brother, Lathyros. She was chosen as queen to neutralize any longing for him among those who had sought to eject Ptolemy Alexander on the charge of murdering his mother, Cleopatra III, in 101. Documents had been dated by mother and son at least until 104, and his own era began in 114/113, well back in her regency, but Alexander was attempting to put some distance between himself and his mother after her recent adventures in Palestine. Ptolemais fell to her in 102, and she briefly considered a reconquest of Judaea before settling for an alliance with Alexander Jannaeus, formulaically described as her 'kinsman.' Ptolemy Alexander had seen service in this adventure of hers and doubtless realized that it accorded ill with Egypt's real interests, since the basic purpose of the expedition was to frustrate the ambitions of Lathyros, his brother, who took advantage of her absence to attempt Egypt, though in vain.

Ptolemy Alexander, more interested in quiet tenure of his throne – usurped from his older brother – than in foreign conquest, had come to fear his volatile mother and her policies. Her demise, whether or not at his hands, permitted him a few years of relative peace in Egypt. He employed the respite by sinking into such indolence that he grew too fat to walk, and was highly unpopular with his subjects. His insouciance during the years 101-88 resulted not from any period of objective calm but from his own character. Inscriptions reveal him continuing the pious activities of a Ptolemaic ruler at home, but no record of any activity abroad survives. This despite the death of his former ally, Grypus, in 96 and the activity of his sister, Cleopatra Selene, widow of Grypus and now wife of their former enemy Cyzicenus, then of Antiochus X, son of Cyzicenus. Alexander's brother, Lathyros, remained watchful in Cyprus and was to have his day ruling Egypt (88-80).[2]

A relative, the possibly illegitimate son of Physcon, now ruled Cyrene: Ptolemy Apion crowned his tenure by willing it to the Romans! Romans were to make no organizational progress there from the time of the will in 96 BC until after 74. When Lucullus visited it in the winter of 87/86 BC, he found it disturbed 'because of a succession of tyrannies and wars' and restored order, for the moment.

That was not the first time a Ptolemaic regent of Cyrene had done such a thing, for Ptolemy Euergetes II (Physcon) purportedly drew up a will with similar import during his rule there in 163-145 BC, probably as self-protection against Ptolemy VI Philometor. his brother. An inscription found there reflects this. A potentially very important facet of the urge by Euergetes II towards consolidation of the dynasty would be a marriage between a daughter of his named Berenice and Psherenptah (Psenptais), son of the current high priest of Memphis, Petubastis (Petobastis), who may have assisted Euergetes in his dynastic conflicts about 130 BC. Berenice is described as 'the younger sister of the King Ptolemy whom men call Alexander,' implying that the marriage occurred during his reign (141-88 BC). This suggestion would indicate a dramatic initiative by the Ptolemaic house in allying itself by marriage to an important native line of priests. The reconstruction has initiated a lively scholarly debate.

Euergetes II achieved a notable 'friendship' with Romans, which Scipio Aemilianus sought to renew during his visit to Egypt about 140/39 BC. Some contact with Romans occurred in the years after that, though probably on a private basis, as when the senator Lucius Memmius visited Egypt in 112 and received gratifying treatment. The bequest in 96 of a contiguous portion of Ptolemaic territory in Cyrene and its potential transfer to foreign hands should have stirred Ptolemy Alexander from his lethargy. By the time his older brother succeeded him in 88 the situation was by no means irreversible for the Ptolemies, especially with Romans distracted by the first war with

Mithradates Eupator. However, Lathyros directed his attention towards Syria, regarding Cyrene as of little value save for its production of silphium.[3]

The dynastic marriage of Alexander I to Cleopatra Berenice III served him well in these years. Her title, *Philadelphos*, helped contemporaries forget that she was the niece, not the sister, of the King. The text of an oath from Heracleopolis dated to 99 BC shows Cleopatra Berenice clearly described as his 'sister' (*adelphē*). *Philadelphos* could be used in Ptolemaic practice for joint rule by brother and sister; in this case it blurred the descent of Berenice from Lathyros, who still languished on Cyprus. Alexander needed whatever 'legitimacy' he might obtain. He also adopted *Philometor* during the lifetime of his mother; his brother Lathyros employed it too.

Domestic discontent with Alexander forced him to flee in 89, but he raised forces in Syria, perhaps with the assistance of Cleopatra Selene, his sister, by this time serving as queen to her third Seleucid husband, Antiochus X Eusebes. The next year Alexander's final expulsion, to Lycia, was achieved by his enemies. He met his death attacking his brother's kingdom in Cyprus. He did not leave a happy memory locally, and his name may have been omitted from official lists of the Ptolemies, or at least from the one Strabo followed. Lathyros attempted a *damnatio memoriae* of his brother, retrojecting his own reign in Egypt on monuments and in official records. In this he was strictly justified, as the oldest son of Ptolemy Physcon (*OGIS* 170). His reign had been interrupted rather than terminated; the machinations of Cleopatra III and Ptolemy X Alexander I led to two preliminary interruptions, in his eighth and ninth years, before the longer one beginning in his eleventh. Egyptians clearly preferred him to his brother, and despite spending the years 107-88 BC out of Egypt, most of them in Cyprus, Lathyros dated himself as legitimate ruler of Egypt from September 117 BC. His death fell between September 81 and September 80, his thirty-seventh regnal year. These evolutions occasioned some confusion among the populace and even the scribes. One external text from 100 BC shows that foreigners regarded the Ptolemaic realm then as three separate kingdoms, that of Cyrene (Ptolemy Apion), of Egypt (Ptolemy X Alexander I), and of Cyprus (Ptolemy IX Lathyros).[4]

Ptolemy IX Philometor Soter II Lathyros (c. 142-81/80 BC; *PP* 14554)

Known even in antiquity as 'the Second Saviour' (Soter II; Soter I was Ptolemy I), or less reverently as 'Chickpea' (*Lathyros*), Ptolemy IX led a more active life than did his corpulent brother. Most known Egyptian contacts with outside dynasts derived from his policies. His initial period of rule in Egypt, from 116 to 107, fell under the dominance of his mother, Cleopatra III, whom Ptolemy Physcon had carefully named regent for whichever of their sons she chose to associate with herself on the throne. In the event, she chose both, in succession, and allowed neither much scope for exercise of power. Her preference from the outset for Alexander finally won out, and her third attempt to install him in his brother's place succeeded. None of this occurred without dissent and even bloodshed. When she forced Lathyros to abandon his wife, Cleopatra IV, and take another sister-wife, Cleopatra Selene, the disappointed former wife raised an army in Cyprus. The theatre of operations widened when Cleopatra IV took these forces to Syria for service with Antiochus IX Cyzicenus, whom she married. This embroiled her with her sister, Tryphaena, wife of Antiochus VIII Grypus. The two Seleucids continued their mutual struggle and in the process sacrificed the two Ptolemaic sisters. All these events had occurred by 112/111 BC.

Two texts shed light on the obscure first rule of Lathyros. One, a difficult passage in Josephus, might reveal that he was a 'friend and ally' of the Romans, with a preferential commercial position in the harbours of the Jewish allies of Rome. But the reference to 'Ptolemy, King of Alexandria' may mean Ptolemy X Alexander I, who also ruled at Alexandria in the period at issue (114-107 BC). Since ancient texts are helpless in resisting emendation, if the 'King Antiochus, son of Antiochus' here can become 'King Antiochus, son of Demetrius' the passage will refer not to Cyzicenus but to either Grypus (son of Demetrius II) or Sidetes (son of Demetrius I). Choose the latter of these and we alter the Ptolemy in question to Physcon, with a date back as far as 135, since the document also mentions Hyrcanus as high priest of the Jews. Rather than Physcon, it seems preferable to see either Lathyros or Alexander here, but the passage cannot be relied upon.

The other text, variously dated 109-107 BC, is an inscription from 'King Antiochus to King Ptolemy, also known as Alexander, his brother.' It notifies him that Seleucia-in-Pieria has become a free city. The Seleucid here must be either Grypus or Cyzicenus and Ptolemy is Alexander I, probably still on Cyprus awaiting his accession in 107. The letter seems an attempt to avert trouble should the Ptolemies wish to exercise residual claims to Seleucia. It goes to him because of the proximity of Cyprus and the usefulness of Seleucia to Ptolemies sailing to Syria from there. Soon after this, Lathyros was in fact to base himself in Seleucia, 'free city' or not.[5]

The fortunes of Lathyros turned in 107, when Cleopatra III probably tried to kill him and did at least drive him 'alive ... out of her hands' away from Egypt. He lodged at Seleucia-in-Pieria as the ally of Cyzicenus, formerly married to Cleopatra IV, Lathyros's sister. From his own base in Coele-Syria, Cyzicenus assisted Lathyros against Grypus. Meanwhile, Lathyros launched a successful drive against Cyprus in 105; from there he could intervene in the affairs of Judaea (§ 9). He remained there until his return to Egypt in 88 for a second period of rule, though traces of local sentiment for him in Egypt exist during this interval.

The alliance between Lathyros and Cyzicenus seasoned him militarily, as did his mother's opposition to him and her alliance with Grypus. She sent troops against him and aroused opposition to him in both Alexandria and Cyprus. After her death in 101 the opposition from Egypt dwindled as his obese brother sank farther into the ancestral throne, but his alliance to Cyzicenus kept him occupied with Syrian affairs. Even after the death of Cyzicenus in 95, Lathyros retained ties to Syria through his sister Cleopatra Selene. This forceful woman, previously queen to Lathyros, then to Grypus, and finally to Cyzicenus, now married Antiochus X Eusebes, son of Cyzicenus, who ruled or tried to from 95 until the coming of Tigranes in 83. Selene survived all this only to find her death at the hands of Tigranes on his way back to Armenia in 70/69 BC. Throughout this period Lathyros allowed no family sentiment to interfere with his own policies, and engaged effectively in the struggle among the remaining sons of Grypus. He brought Demetrius III from Cnidus and installed him as king in Damascus about 95 BC.[6]

The return of Lathyros to Egypt after his brother's fall by October 88, was not the serene affair he wished. Thebes had been in revolt under Alexander and required a struggle to subdue. Externally, matters were coming to a head both among the Seleucids and in the activity of Romans in Asia Minor, where the first war with Mithradates had begun. It was to no one's advantage to have in Egypt such a weak monarch as Alexander when Mithradates began to cast his eyes towards the Ptolemies while marshalling dynastic allies (see below). In Syria, Demetrius III Eukairos, the appointee of Lathyros at Damascus, lost his life soon after Lathyros returned to Egypt. Antiochus XII died in battle with the Nabataean Obodas I or Aretas III (§ 9). Antiochus X Eusebes, married to Cleopatra Selene now, probably died at the hands of Tigranes in 83, though one source has him alive to welcome Pompey. Selene remained ambitious even after his death (see below).

The conflict with Mithradates Eupator soon touched Egypt. In late 87 or early 86, L. Licinius Lucullus, serving as proquaestor in the East while Sulla carried on his siege of Athens, arrived in Alexandria after eluding the fleet of Mithradates. Sulla required ships and was issuing a blanket appeal to 'the kings and cities' of Libya, Egypt, and Syria in the hope that they saw Mithradates as a common enemy. Lathyros sought good relations with Rome and welcomed Lucullus lavishly. The Mithradatic War had engulfed by now an heir to the Ptolemaic throne, Ptolemy XI Alexander II, the nephew of Lathyros and son of Ptolemy X Alexander I. This youth had been sent to Cos by Cleopatra III about 102, probably along with the children of Lathyros and Selene. In 89/88 the people of Cos surrendered him to Mithradates. He later escaped and fled to Sulla, but at the time of the embassy by Lucullus he must have been still in the hands of Mithradates. This prince was too important to abandon, and Lathyros 'feared for the issue of this war.' Lest he antagonize Mithradates, he supplied no Egyptian forces to Lucullus; lest he antagonize Rome, he conveyed Lucullus to Cyprus and offered him costly gifts. Then, guessing wrongly as to the outcome of the hostilities, he abandoned his understanding with Rome. His successors could later be said to represent a strain among the Ptolemies that made them 'fearless of foreigners,' having yet suffered no evils from outside. With more experience, Lathyros learned better and lived his final years in apprehension at seeing Alexander II in the hands of Sulla, who later declared him king, without legal authority to do so but on the argument that no legitimate male heir to the throne remained.[7]

For the rest, the reign of Lathyros exhibits a range of dynastic and domestic activities. His building program achieved works of some distinction, dating for the most part from his first period of rule and stemming from the initiatives of Cleopatra III. Together they left traces of this activity as far south as Nubia. Even during his exile on Cyprus, Lathyros extended benefactions to Didyma and maintained the Ptolemies' traditional contact with Delos as well as with the people and cults of Cyprus. In Athens, Pausanias notes that statues of Lathyros and Berenice III, his daughter, stood before the Odeum.

The long life of Lathyros witnessed the last flowering of traditional Ptolemaic involvement in the affairs of Syria, and also the final period basically independent of Roman intervention. Even at that, Roman intrusions into the affairs of the kingdom had begun by his reign. Rome, the conqueror of Antiochus the Great, father-in-law of Ptolemy V Epiphanes, was unlikely to remain much longer at a distance.

The period in which Lathyros lived constituted a watershed in Egyptian affairs, as in much of the East. At the beginning of his reign in 116 he could look northward to a Syria that had invaded Egypt as recently as 168, and was now united under a sole monarch, his relative Antiochus VIII Grypus, son of his cousin Cleopatra Thea and husband of his sister Tryphaena. To the east, Parthia under Mithradates II had increased pressure on the Seleucids, but this seemed no disadvantage to the Egyptians. In Anatolia, the Ariarathids still reigned in apparent security, and beyond them the youthful Mithradates Eupator presented no apparent challenge. Bithynia prospered under Nicomedes III, and the Galatians kept to themselves. Thrace had, to be sure, engaged in obscure skirmishes with the Romans, but they in turn were busy elsewhere and appeared slow to take advantage of their new possession in Asia.

When the reign of Lathyros ended about March 80 BC, Grypus and Cyzicenus were gone, with two of his sisters who had joined them as queens. The five sons of Grypus and their cousin Eusebes had bludgeoned one another into oblivion; Tigranes now occupied Syria and was moving southward. In Parthia, the death of Mithradates about 87 had begun a period of serious internal strife. In Anatolia, the Ariarathids had disappeared and the new dynasty of Ariobarzanes fought desperately against Mithradates, now grown to an adulthood which had recently convulsed Asia and drawn Rome into a major war. Bithynia languished under the weak Nicomedes IV and in six years was to be Rome's. The Galatians, decimated by Mithradates, fought on the side of Rome; so did part of Thrace, with part opposed. Romans appeared everywhere, with the Egyptian prince Ptolemy XI Alexander II a captive in Rome and the former Egyptian possessions in Cyrene theirs ostensibly by testamentary inheritance. Of the Egyptian royal family only Cleopatra Selene, sister and former wife of Lathyros, remained active abroad, dislodged by Tigranes but determined to rule again. At home were Berenice III, ready to succeed, and the possibly illegitimate children of Lathyros, Ptolemy XII Auletes and Cleopatra V. Such were the changes by the time he took his last breath, perhaps a sigh.[8]

Cleopatra Berenice III
(c. 120-80 BC; *PP* 14522)

Pausanias viewed Berenice III as the 'only legitimate one of the children' of Ptolemy IX Lathyros, despite the possibility that both Ptolemy XII Auletes and Cleopatra V had sprung from a union of the indisputably legitimate Cleopatra Selene with Lathyros. The mother of Berenice was Cleopatra IV. The formula 'sister and wife,' applied later to Berenice's titulature after her marriage to Alexander I, refers only to the joint reign and not to a common parentage.

When Berenice was about four years old her mother left for Syria at the insistence of Cleopatra III and there married Antiochus IX Cyzicenus. Berenice remained behind. She spent some of her early years in Cyprus, where first her uncle Alexander I and then her father, Lathyros, ruled, as the designs of Cleopatra III worked themselves out. But by 101 BC she had gone as wife to Alexander I, and ruled jointly with him; the first documents reflecting their dual sovereignty date from late in that year. Though lapses in the record make it difficult to say, she probably ruled with him until his exile in 89, and appears to have been a popular queen. Her contemporary Cicero termed her 'beloved and pleasing to the populace.'[9]

Ptolemy Alexander had to flee Egypt in 89 – 'driven into exile by a gathering of the populace' – to a refuge at Myra in Lycia. Berenice and at least one of his own children were with him. Presumably the later Ptolemy XI Alexander II, 'brought up in Cos' after Cleopatra III sent him there, had not yet been surrendered to Mithradates, but no record survives of contact between him and his father at this juncture.

When Lathyros defeated his brother and regained Egypt in 88, he brought his daughter with him. As a former queen of Egypt she was too valuable to leave either in Asia Minor or in private life, so she soon appears associated with her father on the throne of Egypt. Since 91/90 she had been calling herself no longer Berenice but Cleopatra, a name by now almost as necessary to the queens of Egypt as Ptolemy was to the kings. Under this name, or in two instances as 'Cleopatra, also called Berenice,' she graced the official records as co-regent until the death of her father in 81/80.

For a moment in history, Berenice ruled alone, apparently from March to September 80 BC. However, neither her popularity nor the domestic and international situation would permit her to continue without a husband. The son of Ptolemy X Alexander I languished in Rome, but he had been named on official documents as a third co-regent back as far as 101/100 BC. The temptation to bring him home was strong among some Alexandrians, and to Sulla. Though Ptolemy Auletes had reached an age to rule, being older in fact than Alexander, his legitimacy was either questionable or said to be. The story went round that Egypt now possessed no legitimate male sovereign but Alexander, and that 'the women of the dynasty desired to have a man of the royal house ruling.' This curious statement probably resulted from a sincere, perhaps successful, attempt to obtain Berenice's assent. The return of Alexander was presumably just as welcome to most of the men, despite one scholar's serene picture of an Egypt under Berenice's governance resting from its recent dynastic quarrels. Whatever the full story, Romans duly shipped Ptolemy XI eastward and Berenice prepared to share power, gladly or not.[10]

Ptolemy XI Alexander II
(80 BC; *PP* 14557)

Once installed, Alexander II proved a less than happy choice. Sulla's expectation of monetary gain from returning the young prince, now about twenty-one, to his 'wealthy kingdom' failed to take Alexander's character into account. Ensconced in Egypt, he scorned the base degrees by which he did ascend and proceeded to offend the Alexandrians, relying on the support of Sulla. Whether imposed upon the Alexandrians, as Appian's language implies, or summoned by them, as Porphyry states, he ruled for a grand total of nineteen dismal days.

In his need for funds, Sulla hoped for much from Alexander. Now dictator in Rome, Sulla had not forgotten Egypt's failure to render assistance when Lucullus sought it. He also remembered vividly that portion of the Ptolemies' vast wealth that he had seen when the treasure sent by Cleopatra III to Cos passed from the possession of Mithradates into the trembling hands of Sulla himself. He had admired a robe purporting to descend from Alexander the Great and he wondered what else lay in the vaults at Alexandria. However, he overestimated his agent.

Alexander II took Berenice to wife. Aged about forty, she promised not numerous offspring but the seal of legitimacy. Whether she was the cousin of Alexander or his mother, and whether the marriage in fact occurred or was inferred in antiquity from joint rule, her usefulness passed as soon as Alexander was officially associated on the throne with her. So at least he concluded and found time in his nineteen days to have her killed, assuming that quiet tenure of the throne would pass to him as her successor and as son of Ptolemy X. In this he fatally misjudged the temper of the Alexandrians, who seized him in their rage and destroyed him by a public quasi-sacrifice in the gymnasium.

Thus by September 80 BC the brief reign of Alexander II had left Egypt with two serious problems. The first was that the legitimate line of the Ptolemies, with the exception of Cleopatra Selene, the recent Queen of Syria, had either died out or was alleged to have done so, for Ptolemy XII Auletes was termed by some a *nothos* ('bastard'). This version could have derived from the putative intermarriage of the native line of Memphite priests with the Ptolemies during the reign of Ptolemy VIII Euergetes II Physcon (see above). The second problem was the reputed existence now of another in the expanding series of testamentary bequests to Rome (Asia; Cyrene; soon Bithynia), for Alexander II 'left' Egypt and Cyprus to Rome. The document, if authentic, had doubtless constituted the price of Sulla's support before his accession.

To discuss the second matter first. It is clear that a contemporary, Cicero, had heard of this document, though he acknowledges that 'it is said, on the contrary, that there was no testament.' Now, an intention by a king to leave his kingdom posthumously to an outside authority presumably exceeds his powers. The success or failure of such a bequest rests on the comparative strengths of the beneficiary and of the king's dynasty. In this case, Rome had entered a period of domestic distraction and Egypt still had dynastic options.

The testament brought no immediate result, except perhaps the Roman expedition to collect treasure that the king had deposited, allegedly for Romans, in Tyre. The 'bequest' remained for possible future use: 'Who of you does not know that that kingdom is said to have been made over to the Roman people by a testament of King Alexas?' It was still necessary to press Roman demands later, and Crassus in 65 during his censorship adopted a 'dangerous and forcible' policy of attempting to impose tribute on a still independent Egypt.[11]

Ptolemy XII Theos Philopator Philadelphos Auletes (80-51 BC; *PP* 14558)

The other problem at the death of Alexander II presented an immediate and pressing challenge: with whom to replace him? *Two* sons of Lathyros came forward; one eventually proceeded to Cyprus and the other, baldly known in the sources as *Ptolemaios Nothos*, acceded in Alexandria. This son is the polyonymous Ptolemy XII (who eventually added *Neos Dionysos* to the ample repertory of titles recited above): 'Great King, the God, New Dionysos, Lover of Father, Lover of Brother' and, popularly, 'Flute-Player' (*Auletes*) or 'Bastard' (*Nothos*) – some of these more welcome than others. The remarks of Pompeius Trogus show him a son of Ptolemy IX Lathyros, but the mother is unknown although reputed in antiquity to be a concubine.

First the circumstances of his accession, then of his birth. He acceded between June and September 80; he reigned, with interruptions and indignities, until 'year 30' in 51 BC. However, his official coronation occurred only in 76/75 BC. This and other anomalies require discussion.

At Alexander's death in 80, Auletes was in Syria, according to Cicero. His brother, the subsequent King of Cyprus, might have been there as well. By now Tigranes controlled Syria. Cleopatra Selene, mother of Auletes unless the reports of his illegitimacy were true, remained in the vicinity. Her Seleucid son by Antiochus X Eusebes lived on also, probably in Cilicia; this was Antiochus XIII Asiaticus, later accused of hiding there during the occupation of Syria by Tigranes (§ 8). Her husband, Eusebes, might not have survived Tigranes in 83; the report that he did probably confuses him with Asiaticus. Only Selene left any trace of active involvement in dynastic affairs during the period 83-69, and paid for it with her life. In 75, she pressed the cause of her sons by Eusebes before the Senate in Rome, demanding not the throne of Syria but that of Egypt (see below).

Why Ptolemaic princes in Syria in 80? One thinks of the young Ptolemies captured by Mithradates Eupator at Cos and taken to Pontus. Ptolemy XI Alexander II escaped and reached Sulla, thence Rome, and finally the throne in Alexandria. However, Mithradates retained at least two princes. His aspirations included a marriage alliance with Egypt: two daughters were 'betrothed to the kings of Egypt and of Cyprus.' But the plan apparently failed, for the princesses were still in Pontus with their father in 63 BC. The possibility exists that the two betrothed Ptolemies were not the current but the future kings of Egypt and Cyprus, and that they subsequently entered Syria after it came under the control of Tigranes, the son-in-law and ally of Mithradates.[12]

Whatever his route, Auletes arrived in Egypt by late 80 and by January 79 married his sister Cleopatra V Tryphaena. The royal couple include among their titles both *Philopator* and *Philadelphos*, as well as *Theoi*, 'Gods.' Evidently they were truly brother and sister, but difficulties arise in determining their parentage. In antiquity three sources question the legitimacy of Auletes. To Pompeius Trogus he was a *nothos*; to Pausanias his sister or half-sister Berenice III was 'the only legitimate one' of the children of Lathyros; to Cicero he was royal 'neither in birth nor in spirit.' But we know that in 107 BC, Lathyros 'already had two sons from Selene' (*ex Selene iam duos filios habebat*); these were indisputably legitimate, since both parents themselves were, as children of Ptolemy VIII Physcon and Cleopatra III. Cleopatra presumably included them among the royal children she sent to Cos in 103. Porphyry alludes to Auletes simply as 'son of Ptolemy Soter [Lathyros] and brother of the aforementioned Cleopatra [Berenice III],' with no hint of illegitimacy. He also refers to Cleopatra VII as 'daughter of this man [Auletes] and last of the race of the Lagids' – unsullied by the supposed bastard birth of her father. Cicero elsewhere portrays Auletes and his brother as true Ptolemies, though in a context where his argument would otherwise suffer. Pompeius Trogus regards Auletes and his brother Ptolemy, King of Cyprus, as sons of Lathyros but Auletes as a *nothos*, and therefore son of a concubine. Inscriptions attest other children for Lathyros; that Auletes was among his children seems without doubt. Was Selene the mother of Auletes?

Difficulties arise. Selene left Egypt to marry Antiochus VIII Grypus about 104 BC, leaving her *duos filios* by Lathyros in the hands of Cleopatra III. But Lathyros had fled Egypt in 107, so Auletes, if a son of this pair, would be at least twenty-seven when he acceded in 80 BC. Should Cicero have described him as a *puer*? This objection is not decisive: Cicero had contempt for Auletes and might regard him as a 'stripling' because of his lack of other qualities. Was 'royal neither in birth nor in spirit' spoken literally?[13]

Granted that *Romans* might have put about the story that Auletes sprang from an unroyal union if he rivalled a Roman ally such as Alexander II in 80, no advantage in doing so remained after the death of that protégé of Sulla.

Rather the reverse, since Romans recognized the rule of Auletes. With an Eastern policy as yet unformed and Cyrene still not taken up, Romans in a period of severe strain at home had nothing to gain from instability among the Egyptians, especially with Mithradates at his prime and Tigranes advancing from Syria southward.

The imputation of bastardy seems more likely of Eastern origin. Its genesis *could* lie in the suggested marriage of an otherwise unattested sister of Lathyros named Berenice to Psherenptah (Psenptais) of the hereditary family of high priests at Memphis. She bore him a son, Petubastis, with whom the royal family in Alexandria would then be linked. His son in turn, another Psherenptah (Psenptais), who crowned Auletes, noted on his funeral stele that Auletes had multiple wives, each capable of producing 'royal children' – legitimate offspring. If Lathyros too was believed to engage in the type of liaison his sister did, ample warrant would exist for contemporaries to consider that deviance from long-standing Ptolemaic marital practice had appeared in the dynasty. Hence 'bastardy' for Auletes, a convenient charge by his enemies but apparently not seriously entertained by his Alexandrian subjects.

The Vienna stele recording a 'Berenice' married to Psherenptah (Psenptais) of Memphis *might* refer to a non-royal Greek woman, with an inconclusive reference to 'Ptolemy whom men call Alexander.' However, the high priests would desire only a woman of high birth, given the option. If they got one in her, it might explain not only the imputation of illegitimacy to Auletes, but also another set of anomalies: his delayed crowning and its site, in Alexandria instead of Memphis.

To return to Petubastis, son of Berenice and Psherenptah (Psenptais). In 103, the year Cleopatra III prepared for conflict with her son Lathyros, then in Cyprus, by sending her treasures and grandchildren to Cos, Psherenptah died. His son and successor, Petubastis, journeyed to Alexandria for investiture by Ptolemy X Alexander I.[14]

Petubastis still held office after the death of Lathyros in 80, when first Berenice III and then – jointly with her – Ptolemy XI Alexander II occupied the throne in Alexandria. Petubastis had received honours that put him high in the governing structure of Egypt, with a quasi-royal 'coronation' that must have greatly impressed those outside Alexandria. His son is even alleged to have claimed a form of sovereignty by birth.

Conjoined with this background is the curious sequence of events after 80 BC. Though 'year 1' for Auletes begins in the autumn of 80, and documents dated by regnal years are known almost immediately, his coronation did not take place until 76/75 BC, when he became 'New Osiris' (*Neos Dionysos*, for Greeks) and received his crown not from Petubastis but from Psherenptah

(Psenptais III, *PP* 5376), who succeeded his father in that year as high priest at Memphis. Sufficient documentation exists from the third and fifth regnal years of Auletes to demonstrate that he had duly acceded though he was not yet crowned, since no reason occurs to accomplish the ceremony a *second* time in 76/75. The documents employ regnal years for a reign officially begun in 80 BC.

The solution to this little mystery may lie in the wording of the stele on which Psherenptah (Psenptais III) records his coronation of Auletes in 76/75. After noting his own accession in the sentence immediately prior, he says: 'I set the adornment of the serpent-crown upon the head of the King on the day that he took possession of Upper Egypt and Lower Egypt, and performed all the rites ...' Does this mean that during the previous four years Auletes had controlled only Alexandria, with Petubastis claiming a type of suzerainty over the rest of the country? The troubled situation and his own postulated proximity to the royal line, if his wife was a full sister of Lathyros and Alexander I, might have inspired him to a partition of the country with the poorly regarded Auletes. Only upon the death of Petubastis was Egypt free to acknowledge but one sovereign again, duly crowned by a man who claimed royal birth but received only his priesthood, and that from the man he was to crown. 'I lived thirteen years in the presence of my father. There went forth a command from the King, the lord of the land, the Father-loving Sister-loving God, the New Osiris, son of the Sun, Lord of Diadems, Ptolemy, that the high office of high priest of Memphis should be conferred upon me, I being then fourteen years old.' The boy aspired to no control of Egyptian lands for himself; he crowned Auletes and closed the apparent rift.

Another incident may throw further light on this. About the same time, Cleopatra Selene stirred. Her desire to repair her crumbling fortunes must have been no secret at the court of Auletes, her son or nephew. By 76/75 BC, her husband, Eusebes, was either dead or deposed; Tigranes ruled at Antioch. Selene continued the struggle as she was able, being reported successively as 'ruling in Syria,' besieged by Tigranes in Ptolemais, imprisoned at Seleucia/Zeugma, and slain. On her way to this gloomy end she tried about 75 to press the claims of her sons by Eusebes, one of whom was Antiochus XIII Asiaticus. She knew better than to expect Roman assistance in recovering Syria, which would have entailed a war with Tigranes, not yet declared an enemy of Rome. She hoped rather to obtain for them, and for herself, the Ptolemaic succession in *Egypt*. 'You know that Kings of Syria, young sons of King Antiochus, were lately in Rome, not on account of the Kingdom of Syria ... but because they considered that the Kingdom of Egypt belonged to themselves and their mother, Selene.' She may have put forward against Auletes, incumbent but as yet unrecognized by Rome, the charge of illegitimacy, stressing instead the pedigree of her Seleucid-Ptolemaic sons. Some warrant for concern on her part and that of Rome might exist if Auletes was an irregular ruler before his coronation by Psherenptah. In this wider context the ceremony occurred. The possibility remains that it was a second ceremony, one of reconfirmation, arising from apprehension regarding Selene's trip to Rome.

The Roman Senate found itself not yet prepared to take sides against Auletes, though it did, insofar as Cicero represents its deliberations, oppose the claims of Tigranes by declaring that these sons of Cleopatra Selene and Antiochus Eusebes had full title to the kingdom not of Egypt but of Syria, transmitted to them 'by their father and ancestors.'[15]

For the moment, the throne of Auletes appeared secure. He was to hold it until 51 BC, with one interruption, which his daughter Berenice IV filled, briefly assisted by the Pontic noble Archelaus (§ 23). However, soon after the challenge from Selene, Auletes received notice that good relations with Rome should occupy his attention in future, for about 74 Rome at last took up the bequest of Ptolemy Apion in Cyrene and became the neighbour of the newly crowned Auletes. Whether or not these events were related, Rome had begun to show new interest in the East, where Bithynia came to it also in 74. With a Roman border now some five hundred miles west of Alexandria and the Ptolemaic possessions reduced to just Cyprus and Egypt, Auletes grew thoughtful.

5

Dynasties beyond the Euphrates, 100-69

The vast expanse of mountains, plains, steppes, and salt deserts (the Dasht-i Kavir and the Dasht-i Lut on the Iranian plateau) that lay beyond the Euphrates sustained a population of Iranians and Semites who created some of antiquity's greatest empires – the Assyrian, Babylonian, Median, Persian, Parthian, and Sassanian. Important trade routes spanned the region from south to north and from west to east; the most important, the Khurasan route, stretched from Ctesiphon (near Seleucia-on-the-Tigris and Babylon) right through to China. Over the millennia, interpenetration of peoples on the plains of Mesopotamia produced one of the most intensive racial mixtures in the entire ancient world. By contrast, the mountains of Western Iran, which loomed over this region, presented a more nearly uniform ethnic composition, as home to the hardy tribes who would rather inhabit a harsh land and rule than live among cultivated plains or orchards and be ruled, 'for soft countries breed soft men' (Hdt. 9.122, contrasting Mesopotamia with the Zagros highlands).

§ 11. Armenia

The great tableland of Armenia merges into a system of plateaus from Asia Minor to Northern Iran. Its overall altitude varies from 2400 to 6000 feet, with consequent alterations in terrain and plant cover. The east-west direction of the Pontic, Taurus, and subsidiary ranges – all well south of the Caucasus – divides Armenia into zones, which preclude easy movement from south to north. Some mountains rise to great height, especially Ararat at 17,000 feet, followed by Little Ararat, the Tendurek, the Alagöz, Bingöl Dagh, Mt Sipan, and the northern chains flowing from Nemrud Dagh. These and their subsidiaries further impede travel over much of the country.

A few large plains, most notably the one eastward of the Erzerum Plateau and northeast of Mt Ararat along the Araxes River, allowed agriculture and contained Artaxata, the largest city. The Araxes and Kyros rivers drained eastward to the Caspian Sea; the headwaters of the Euphrates arose in Armenia and drained southwestward.

The Euphrates allowed an avenue into the country, but in general the combination of rugged terrain and severe weather served as an impediment to invasions, which tended to accomplish little over the long term. Attacks by Parthians and Romans alike generally failed to penetrate far, or served only briefly to alter the course of Armenian affairs. However, one important battle occurred, against Tigranes in 69 BC, near Tigranocerta just above the Upper Tigris. After it Tigranes retired to his mountainous kingdom for another long period of rule.

Tigranes the Great

The reign of Tigranes the Great, founder of the only considerable empire the Armenians achieved in antiquity, coincided with those of the most notable of the Pontic and Parthian kings, Mithradates VI Eupator and Mithradates II. Both allied themselves with Tigranes by marriage and the three together presented to the nascent empire of Rome in the East the most serious obstacle it encountered.

About 100 BC none could have predicted the success of Tigranes. By then some forty years old, he had spent much of his life at the Parthian court, where Mithradates retained him as 'a hostage given to the Parthians a long time before.' But events began to move rapidly in the East. Cappadocia fell to Mithradates Eupator and witnessed his son briefly taking power there. Furnished with a new dynasty under Ariobarzanes I, it entered about 96 into some thirty-three years of turmoil before Mithradates was crushed. During much of that period Cappadocia was also to suffer from Tigranes, who acceded to his ancestral throne at the outset of this generation of fighting.

Several events in conjunction explain this timing. One was the expulsion of Ariobarzanes by Eupator, for the first time drawing Romans to the Euphrates region diplomatically and militarily; the initial meeting between Parthians and Romans was consequent on the expedition of Sulla. A second event was war between Mithradates of Parthia and Artavasdes I of Armenia, uncle of Tigranes. A third was domestic trouble after 96 between Mithradates II and his oldest son, Gotarzes, promoting an impulse to consolidate Parthia's frontiers (§ 13). Somewhere in this period, in response to these local evolutions, and very close to the usually accepted date (95 BC), fell the accession of Tigranes. Since the Armenians paid to Parthia for him a ransom of seventy rich valleys, they wished his return; the presumption must be that Artavasdes I had died or been killed, leaving Tigranes their choice for succession. His vigour could not have passed unremarked in Parthia and must have rendered him a reliable appointee in Arsacid eyes as, just beyond Armenia, the clouds of war built on the northwestern horizon around the rising King of Pontus.

Tigranes was a full descendant of the Artaxiad dynasty, which had by this time controlled the greater part of Armenia for nearly a century. It arose when Artaxias, the general of the Seleucid Antiochus III, proclaimed himself king in 189/188. His claim to descent from the previous Orontid dynasty assured local legitimacy. The view of Strabo that Parthia had 'not even once' ruled Armenians might not strictly apply to the period before Tigranes, when the Parthian 'King of Kings' held at least nominal higher supremacy there. However, it did apply to the period during and after his reign. If Parthians had hoped to exert through Tigranes a *de facto* hegemony over Armenia, they received a sharp disappointment.[1]

For more than a century after the accession of Tigranes, Parthia perforce tolerated his independence and that of his robust descendants. Parthians had larger problems eastward. Only when the Armenian dynasty expired early in the first century after Christ did Parthians renew their quest for dominance there, now with Rome as an indirect adversary. After half a century of struggle, Parthia won an acceptable solution from Nero: control of Armenia by a line of Arsacid kings recognized by Rome in return for 'friendship and alliance,' with investiture by the emperor. By then (AD 66), the dynasty of Tigranes was gone, although its descendants continued elsewhere in positions of prominence.

Tigranes built his power rapidly and recovered the seventy valleys. For good measure he detached from the Parthians a number of their own dependencies and eventually laid waste portions of Parthia itself. Probably this aggressive behaviour fell after the death of Mithradates II about 87; Tigranes respected the old king, to whom he sent one of his daughters, Aryazate-Automa. But in the chaotic period after 87 no Parthian force could long withstand him, and 'frequent' Parthian counter-attacks uniformly failed because 'Tigranes resisted vigorously.'[2]

The reign of Tigranes fell into phases reflecting the larger political movements of his day. In the first eight years (95-87 BC) he fought with increasing prominence in the struggle between his father-in-law, Mithradates Eupator, and the Roman protégé Ariobarzanes I of Cappadocia. Then in a second phase (86-70) following the death of the Parthian Mithradates II, 'King of Kings,' Tigranes assumed that title as he moved east and south to consolidate his nascent empire, engulfing Parthian possessions in Mesopotamia and then crossing the Euphrates into Commagene, Cilicia, and Syria. The repercussions reached into Judaea, Nabataea, even Egypt, as we have seen. Finally, a third phase (69-55) brought him into direct conflict with Rome and his last years passed mainly within his ancestral kingdom. For all three phases our sources concentrate on international events and present little information about his domestic work. (The present section treats the first two phases, section 24 the third.)

Tigranes and His Neighbours

In the initial period, soon after his accession, Tigranes moved westward towards the Euphrates. Just as Eupator began by consolidating behind him the Pontic coast and the northern reaches of his kingdom, so did Tigranes secure his northwest first, perhaps in concert with Mithradates. The intervening kingdom, Sophene, belonged to a descendant of Zariadras, one of the two generals who had taken over Armenia and its environs about 189 BC, after the defeat of Antiochus III. The other, Artaxias, was the ancestor of Tigranes, but both families were by now probably related, to judge by their proximity and nomenclature (Artaxias was himself son of a Zariadras), though the rulers of Sophene primarily sprang from the Orontid line (§ 6). Tigranes let nothing deter him and soon stood at the Euphrates, as *kurios* ('overlord') of the Sophenian dynast. The Sophenian line continued, now serving Tigranes.[3]

This move placed him across the great river from the Cappadocians, who held the western terminus of the crossing, at Melitene. Cappadocians aspired to the eastern terminus at Tomisa in Sophene; Tigranes could by holding it perform a service to himself and to Mithradates Eupator in his attempt to control Cappadocia. Accordingly, the daughter of Mithradates journeyed to the court of Tigranes and an alliance joined Armenia with Pontus, much to the apprehension of Ariobarzanes. The rising fortunes of Tigranes now gave him indirect standing in Cappadocia too, as brother-in-law of its intermittent king from Pontus, Ariarathes IX, son of Eupator. Tigranes made life miserable for Ariobarzanes; as many as five times he drove that unfortunate from the country, usually with devastation and once depopulating part of Cappadocia to furnish settlers for his new dynastic capital at Tigranocerta (see below).

Tigranes served not as a tool of his father-in-law but as a defender of Armenian interests. The Roman advance towards the Euphrates, when the first war with Mithradates broke out six years after the accession of Tigranes, combined with the Parthians' interest in subjugating a circle of kingdoms, persuaded him that defence lay in conquest – an activity he enjoyed.

Armenian forces came into conflict with Sulla during the Roman campaign to assist Ariobarzanes, and if Tigranes had not previously aspired to restoration of ancient Armenian dominion over parts of Cappadocia and probably all of Commagene, he began to now.[4]

A catalyst lay in the meeting of Sulla with a Parthian representative, held ominously on the Euphrates at the border of the nascent Armenian Empire. This meeting occurred apparently at the request of Mithradates II, for Sulla met 'Parthians requiring alliance and friendship' – hardly welcome news to Tigranes. The 'first of the Romans' to receive such overtures initiated a successful series of negotiations. Tigranes must have viewed with apprehension any alliance between Romans west of him and Parthians south. The divisions at the Parthian court during the late years of Mithradates from 96 to 87 did involve disturbances in the north (§ 13). They might have touched Armenia; hence the steady pressure by Tigranes on Cappadocia and on contiguous portions of the Parthian Empire. During the decades to come he grew increasingly isolated as his own empire grew. At one point later he allegedly refused even to receive Eupator after a severe defeat suffered by the Pontic forces, and his mistrust of the Parthians received ample justification far into the reign of Phraates III (70-57 BC).

Nevertheless, early in his reign all was well. Sometime before 88 BC, Tigranes placed a daughter among the queens of Parthia. Mithradates II lists her among his three main wives on a parchment from Avroman in Kurdistan. Tigranes could not permanently avoid hostilities this way, but the marriage does reveal that no serious breach had occurred after his recovery of the seventy valleys. Peace prevailed at the death of Mithradates II about 87, but a reciprocity existed between Armenian and Parthian strength; with the old King gone, Tigranes might aspire to more.[5]

Tigranes, King of Kings

Thus the second period of his reign. He had been called 'Great King' during the rule of Mithradates II. Only one title higher than that existed in Eastern protocol. Tigranes looked about and could descry none more deserving of it than himself. He became the 'King of Kings.' Coins proudly proclaim this and he strove to prove worthy.

The title challenged the Parthian successors of Mithradates II, but Orodes I and Sinatruces had troubles enough domestically and had to content themselves with salvaging what they could. Only after the defeat of Tigranes in 69 BC did opposition to him become feasible, and even then Phraates III approached with caution.

From the other quarter of his world, Tigranes expected no opposition either. Mithradates Eupator had his hands full with dynastic and military problems in Pontus, Cappadocia, Bithynia, Galatia, and elsewhere; Tigranes could call himself 'King of Kings' if he liked. All he required of the Armenian monarch was establishment of a secure allied power to the east. Eupator also had a standing alliance with Parthia, forged in the last years of Mithradates II, perhaps by 89 BC. This alliance held firm during the first two wars between Eupator and Rome. Parthians expected Mithradates and Tigranes to resist Roman designs on eastern Anatolia, forming a convenient buffer zone. They forced no breach with Eupator over the behaviour of his son-in-law and kept the alliance nominally in force. Only with the signal defeats of both monarchs in 69 did they hesitantly renew the Roman alliance concluded after the visit of Sulla. The revival of both kings for a final efflorescence in 67 confirmed the wisdom of watchful neutrality in Parthia.[6]

During the first two phases of his reign, from 95 to about 80 in particular, Tigranes engaged in nearly incessant warfare. Besides Sophene, he acquired all areas contiguous to his kingdom, from the Iberian (§ 25) and Albanian regions of the Caucasus to the kingdoms south and east: Atropatene (§ 25), Gordyene, Osrhoene, Adiabene, the areas 'about Ninus' and 'about Arbela' near the Tigris, and eventually 'the rest of Mesopotamia' (§ 12). He probably also penetrated Greater Media – reducing its satrap to his own service – and moved thence to Ecbatana itself. These acquisitions proved useful during future campaigns, when forces drawn from the new constituents of his empire served loyally. The small kingdoms enjoyed remarkable stability, sometimes preserving the same dynastic house for many centuries, as in Atropatene (§ 25), Characene, Elymais, Osrhoene, and Persis (§ 12). They constituted useful subdivisions of an empire, for Tigranes and for Parthia. Part of these sovereigns' loyalty to Tigranes sprang from his utilization of the ancient dynastic device of intermarriage. Besides the ties a Pontic wife and a daughter at the Parthian court provided, he linked his dynasty to that of Atropatene by sending a daughter to its king, another Mithradates. Support for him from Darius of Media may reflect such an alliance by marriage, and there must have been others (§ 24).

Tigranocerta

As an adjunct to this traditional method of consolidation, Tigranes founded a new capital, named for himself and located closer to his new possessions in Mesopotamia. The intention was certainly dynastic: he chose the spot where he had assumed the Armenian throne, probably on the way home from Parthia. The new capital's position south of the Anti-Taurus and northeast of the upper Tigris signalled his continued attention to the adjacent lands of

Media and Parthia. Possession of Sophene to the west created a buffer zone against possible Roman incursions across the Euphrates.

Tigranes sought here to represent not only the Iranian world of his ancestors, but also the Greek world of the dying Seleucids. A policy of enforced Hellenization required Greek immigrants; obtaining them proved relatively simple. He razed twelve cities and transported the stunned inhabitants across the Euphrates to take up their new quarters. Other settlers arrived, no more willingly, from his imperial possessions in Cilicia, Gordyene, Adiabene, even 'Assyria.' Most came from the core of Cappadocia, the royal district of Mazaca. This hit hard at Ariobarzanes, whose power arose there, like that of the Ariarathids before him (§ 5); Tigranes had done his homework. He also took no chances with his own nobles, whom he concentrated in Tigranocerta as a measure of control (a technique later useful at Antioch). To complete these preparations for empire, he instituted a twofold system of defence, with a primary group of Greek mercenaries backed by a native contingent under his viceroy. Not surprisingly, a high degree of mutual distrust characterized the new settlers.

Tigranocerta was no ephemeral creation. Lucullus did his best to destroy it in 69, dismissing the inhabitants to their original towns and leaving it a 'small village.' But it survived to Strabo's day and continued to be inhabited for centuries. Tigranes had chosen its site well, though its role as a fortress did not survive his as an emperor.[7]

Tigranes and the Seleucids

The real goal of Tigranes in all this lay to the west. Internal conflict in Parthia after the death of Mithradates II enabled Tigranes to consolidate his position as the most formidable king east of the Euphrates. He concluded an alliance with the successors of Mithradates. Then he turned towards Syria: 'all accepted Tigranes, King of Armenia, strengthened in addition to his domestic forces by a Parthian alliance and by relationship to Mithradates.' His conquests and alliances with the Arab chieftains or kings along the Euphrates allowed him a secure crossing there. Some of these long remained loyal to him, as is revealed for instance by the tale of 'royal guides' who attempted to delay the emissary of Lucullus to Tigranes about 71. But many, like King Zarbienus of Gordyene, defected by 69 BC.

Perhaps as early as 86, Tigranes utilized his possession of Sophene and Osrhoene to advance across the Euphrates into Commagene and northern Syria. With these secured behind him, he advanced easily to Antioch, where coins and literary testimony place him by at least 83 BC. The enormous forces he was reputed to command – 300,000 to 500,000 men – proved too large for the weak residue of Seleucid strength. Even allowing for ancient exaggeration and for subsequent increase of his followers, he must have appeared with a formidable army.[8]

Once installed, Tigranes left no doubt of his intentions. His dynasty would succeed that of the Seleucids; he was a 'successor' (*diadochos*). Accordingly, his coinage continued the era of Philip I, last of the five sons of Antiochus VIII Grypus; it carefully reflected local usage at Antioch and then Damascus. He systematically conquered the remnants of the Seleucid house, forcing Antiochus XIII and Philip II into Cilicia Tracheia for refuge. Perhaps Cleopatra Selene went too, and the rumours that Antiochus XII survived show the confusion of the time.

Tigranes exacerbated the Seleucids' situation by conquering Cilicia Pedias – probably in 78, while again invading Cappadocia – forcing them deep into Tracheia, as far as the Olba area. This occurrence gave rise to the later remark of Pompey that Antiochus XIII had 'hidden in a corner of Cilicia.' Seleucid rule effectively ceased with Tigranes, despite an abortive attempt to revive it after 69 BC (§ 8). An odd series of coins for Philip II mounting to 'year 29' (63 BC) might even show him alive as a shadow till Pompey settled Syria.

What might we think of this interlude in the long history of Syria? With the acute vision of hindsight, ancients and moderns alike have regarded it as doomed to failure. At the time, it appeared anything but that. Tigranes was now master of the former Parthian (and before them, Seleucid) satrapies between the middle Euphrates and the Tigris. His control extended even farther east, into Adiabene, Atropatene, and Media; conquered, related, or allied kings ruled out there in his interest. Beyond, and farther to the south in Mesopotamia, Parthia dominated but suffered from domestic upheaval, with Gotarzes I perhaps still holding lower Mesopotamia, and Orodes I disputing the Arsacid throne with him. To the north, Tigranes now controlled not only his ancestral realm in Armenia, but also the adjacent regions of Gordyene, Arzanene, and Sophene. His father-in-law was building an empire adjoining these on the north and west, where Cappadocia had proved vulnerable to the two kings. Not for years to come was the question of Cappadocia settled against them.[9]

In Syria, Tigranes held power so firmly that in 75 BC Cleopatra Selene petitioned Rome for assistance in gaining not Syria but Egypt. She was no fool (§ 10), and she could tell that Romans were years away from opposing Tigranes in Syria, if ever. When they finally arrived, some fourteen years after he did, they came the long way round, following campaigns against Eupator that reached Armenia and drew Tigranes home, rudely interrupting his enthusiastic conquests in Phoenicia.

As for internal opposition, Tigranes saw little to dread in 83. The nearby

Nabataeans, whether led by Obodas I or by Aretas III, struck no chill to his heart. The Judaean house of Alexander Jannaeus and his wife, Alexandra, presented no threat. It later concluded a truce; he took Damascus and turned towards Phoenicia. As for the Ptolemies, their own divisions rendered them less than formidable in 83 or after. Although Ptolemy IX Lathyros offered Tigranes a more worthy opponent than his corpulent brother would have before 88, Tigranes looked with something less than awe on a man whose mother had stripped him of two sister-wives and thrust him into seventeen years of exile.

In sum, the only misjudgment Tigranes made as he invaded Syria was underestimating the eventual Roman threat, and in 83 BC even that lay years ahead. His successful and stable tenure of Syria – *tranquillissimo regno* – did terminate the Seleucid dynasty, save for the attempts of Antiochus XIII and Philip II to restore themselves after 69 BC. Without the unexpected counterweight of Roman successes in the north, Tigranes might have ruled far longer and even have founded a successor-state. But by the logic that gave him Syria through conquest of the Seleucids, Romans after 69 claimed it through conquest of him. Pompey dismissed Antiochus XIII on these grounds as one seeking to enjoy the 'rewards of another's work.' The years of consolidation that Tigranes put into Syria cushioned the transition from the Seleucid Empire, then two and one-half centuries old, to the nascent Roman Empire. Tigranes had preserved the basic Seleucid system, especially the cities – other than those destroyed by Alexander Jannaeus and awaiting reconstruction by Pompey. In the case of Tigranes, the rewards of another's work went not to Antiochus XIII but to Rome.[10]

Despite the tradition that Syrians had originally welcomed Tigranes, replacing as he did the tumultuous last Seleucids, they shed no tears to see him go. His decade and a half had involved Syria indirectly in conflicts beyond the Taurus, for which it possessed little enthusiasm, and in warfare to the south. By 70 BC, Tigranes had become abusive and apprehensive, keeping a number of kings and princes under a form of detention at Antioch. He inflicted various humiliations, converting them into attendants who ran alongside his chariot, and daily reminding them of their subjection. The method was perhaps better understood by Iranians than by Hellenes, for his rule 'was not unbearable to the Greeks, but difficult.' When their chance came, they took it. So did the enforced inhabitants of Tigranocerta, who opened its massive new portals with alacrity. Despite the loyalty of his numerous allies and the work of garrison-commanders, such as Gouras, his brother, holding Nisibis for him, Tigranes learned that he had misjudged Lucullus and that the haughty tone he had taken in their correspondence might prove an embarrassment. He also repented his cavalier treatment of Mithradates Eupator, whom he had refused to see for some eighteen months, allowing him to wear away the time in one of his fortresses. The Roman demand that he surrender his aged father-in-law provoked a refusal and precipitated the third phase in the lively career of Tigranes (§ 24).

Tigranes turned northeast, but he worried about the activity of Cleopatra Selene until he should return. She had fled Ptolemais, which he was besieging when word came of Lucullus in Armenia; she now found herself under siege in Seleucia/Zeugma on the Euphrates, right on his way home. Pausing only to encompass her execution and thereby terminate a chapter in Syrian and Egyptian history, Tigranes moved eastward to open another in Armenian, Pontic, and Roman history (§ 24).[11]

§ 12. Trans-Euphrates Dynasties, I

An important portion of the royalty that constituted the government of the East lay between the Euphrates and Parthia. Not only Armenia, here treated separately (§§ 11 and 24), and the dynasties of Iberia and Atropatene (treated in § 25), but a number of smaller dynasties ruled parts of this crucial region. They included the dynasties of Sophene, Osrhoene, Adiabene, Gordyene, Characene, Susiana, Elymais, and Persis. Beyond lay Media, Hyrcania, the territory of the Kushans, and other distant parts of Parthia only incidentally included here (§§ 13 and 26). Much of Mesopotamia, with a rich local history, lay in a complex of governmental arrangements, from free towns to territories of local sheikhs, princes, or even kings.

Over almost all of this enormous area, Parthian authority imposed itself by the first century after Christ. Even Armenia received an Arsacid ruler, with Roman recognition after AD 66. By the well-established pattern of Parthian government, scope for semi-independent rulers of several descriptions existed under a type of hegemony by a 'King of Kings.' Hereditary kings ruled portions of this western extremity of the Parthian Empire.

Sophene

Sophene lay contiguous to Greater Armenia, between it and the Upper Euphrates. So placed, it constituted the first land a traveller (or army) from Cappadocia encountered after crossing the Euphrates at Tomisa. It stood in the same relation to the Iranian world in this regard as did Commagene on the opposite side, downriver. Its position brought it very early into the conflict between Romans and Armenians, and it retained an importance out of proportion to its size, again like Commagene. The first official meeting between representatives of Rome and Parthia took place in the vicinity of this crossing between Cappadocia and Sophene.

This kingdom has no reliable known history before the time of the Seleucid Antiochus III ('the Great'), though local traditions have been suggested. The revolt of Zariadris from Antiochus established a kingdom here in the early second century before Christ, and the sketchy record does provide some obscure names (Mithrobuzanes; Orontes) among his successors. However, proximity to Armenia led to periods of domination, perhaps already by the reign of Orontes III (c. 318-260 BC); Orontids also ruled Commagene for a time. Tigranes the Great of Armenia incorporated Sophene soon after his accession, about 95 BC. Later, his homonymous son ruled it briefly as an appointee of Pompey. (Lucan could dismiss its men as 'effeminate' because he knew only the fact of conquest and required picturesque descriptions for his portrait of Pompey.) The kingdom of Sophene later lost itself in the complexities of local history as the Romans struggled with Parthia for control of Armenia. One king of Sophene, Sohaemus, went there from Emesa as part of a major dynastic mobilization by Nero. Kings in Sophene can be traced at least until AD 298.[12]

Osrhoene

Adjacent to Sophene on the south, with a western border along the left bank of the Euphrates, lay Osrhoene, with its capital at Edessa (Antiochia ad Callirhoen; modern Urfa). After incorporation in the Persian satrapal system before Alexander, the region became a Macedonian colony under Seleucus I. For centuries, Hellenic usage prevailed in the government of Edessa; evidently some offices endured in the period of the Semitic monarchy, which otherwise employed local royal institutions. Parthians exercised an overlordship during much of the period of the kingdom, which held territory considered essential because it lay along the Euphrates. Its important position gave the kingdom a role in events of the first century before Christ, and far beyond.

Its twenty-eight known kings ruled over a total expanse of some 350 years. A troubled textual tradition leaves several dates of inception: 'year 1880 of Abraham'; Olympiad 161; 'year 180' Seleucid – in our terms, 137/136 to 132/131 BC, with probability favouring the latter. The rulers are known variously in the sources as phylarchs, toparchs, archons, dynasts, or kings. The names of the earlier monarchs were similar to those of the Nabataeans; gradually most of them settled on either Abgar (of whom there were eleven) or Ma'nû (nine of them). These monarchs include two who still bore the royal title after Caracalla made Osrhoene a province in AD 216 – as known, for instance, from a coin reading 'Emperor Gordian; King Abgar.'[13]

An early disposition to favour Rome as a counterweight to Parthia reversed itself when Crassus launched his ill-considered attack in 53 BC. Abgar II sided with the Parthians in the battle at Carrhae and rendered important service. The Roman cause locally was not strengthened by Antony's and Herod's siege of Samosata, just across the Euphrates, fifteen years later (§ 22). Osrhoene retained for many decades the wariness engendered by what it witnessed in the mid-first century.

At an early stage of Christianity, Edessa became an important centre of the new faith. Some regarded King Abgar V as the first Christian king, and the Turin Shroud reportedly spent centuries at Edessa. However, adherence to local cults continued to characterize the kingdom even after the introduction of Christianity, giving it a rich mixture of syncretistic beliefs – for which its neighbour Commagene had been famous a century earlier.[14]

Adiabene

South of Armenia, lying along the western border of Atropatene and northwest of Media, the Kingdom of Adiabene contained the headwaters of the Greater and Lesser Zab rivers as well as some 350 kilometres of the Upper Tigris. It formed a transitional zone from the Arabs on its west and south to the Iranians on its north and east. Strabo notes the position of Adiabene surrounded by Medes, Armenians, Parthians, and 'Babylonians.' It had formed an important part of ancient Assyria, as realized by writers even in classical times. In an imaginative flight of etymology, Ammianus derives its curious name from the Greek for 'to cross' with an *alpha* privative added (*a-diabainein*, 'not to cross') because it lay between large rivers and 'could not be reached by fording.' The suffix *-ene* was added by the Seleucid system, in which Adiabene formed an eparchy. As Tarn points out, an eparchy often developed – after the Seleucid demise – into a kingdom, since its governor, like that of a satrapy, had a royal structure ready to hand, usually including a palace. The Iranian name appears to have been *Natunia*, as known from epigraphical evidence.[15]

The royal history of Adiabene presents difficulties in the first century BC, though the kingdom does receive random mentions during the campaigns of Lucullus against Tigranes the Great of Armenia, who had taken many of its inhabitants to swell the population of Tigranocerta (§ 11). Tigranes used nearby Nisibis (properly in Mygdonia) for his imperial purposes, and issued a distinctive coinage there. The natives of Adiabene were clearly not Greek even after the centuries of Seleucid control; Plutarch distinguishes them from Greeks, as do their inscriptions. In the days of Tigranes, they had proceeded to royal institutions: even though the Seleucids had finally lost power at the time of his war with Lucullus, his Adiabenian ally was already a king.[16]

The kingdom grew stronger. By the first century AD, it had assumed a recognized place among the small kingdoms of the vicinity, and it had grown large enough for lively internal court intrigue, as well as for a structure including 'nobles, satraps, and commanders.' King Monobazus Bazaeus had to send his favourite son, Izates, away to King Abennerigus of Characene (see below) for protection from his jealous brothers. In Eastern fashion, the lad there received a warm welcome, a dynastic wife, and a territory to rule. On his father's death in AD 36, he succeeded to the throne of Adiabene, where he ruled until AD 55. He had not been the oldest son, but he succeeded by the decision of his father; similarly, despite leaving twenty-four sons, he chose his brother as successor. The Adiabenian kingship enjoyed this strong prerogative. Josephus takes unusual interest in it, probably because Izates and his mother, Helen, converted to Judaism. The 'three pyramids' they built as tombs near Jerusalem survived for modern rediscovery.[17]

Centuries of lying between Rome and Parthia took some toll on the kingdom. Trajan briefly incorporated it into his new province of Assyria. It allied itself with Rome and then fought against it under Severus; later, it opposed Caracalla and suffered the loss of its royal tombs. Parthia came successfully to its aid, though too late for the tombs; a large indemnity resulted, partly in compensation for their destruction.[18]

The dynasty of Hatra, when it arose, appears to have been fostered by the kings and policies of Adiabene. A statue of the Adiabenian Izates was used about a century after his death in an official cult at Hatra, where he was revered as a local ancestor. After a period of rule by 'lords' (*maria*), of whom six are known from local texts, Hatra was ruled from the mid-second century AD by kings, of whom five are known from Hatrene and Roman documents, including Sanatruq (Sanatruces) I (reigning AD 176/77).[19]

Gordyene

This kingdom lay north of Adiabene and east of the Upper Tigris; Armenia stretched to its north, Atropatene to its east. Strabo traces its origin back to the mythological son of Triptolemus, Gordys.[20]

The location of Gordyene made it vulnerable to Armenian expansion, which engulfed it early in the reign of Tigranes. When opposition to Tigranes developed strongly over twenty years later, its king, Zarbienus, agreed with Appius Claudius Pulcher in Antioch to co-operate with the Roman effort against him. Zarbienus was among a group of 'dynasts who obeyed the Armenian grudgingly.' None the less, when Lucullus began the siege of Tigranocerta, among the forces opposing him were not only Armenians but Gordyeni. Perhaps this co-operation was enforced by the continued presence inside Tigranocerta of the Gordyeni whom he is known to have carried there, or perhaps the characteristic action of Tigranes on learning of the treason in Antioch – to execute Zarbienus and his family – had its desired effect.[21]

During the period of conflict following the defeat of Tigranes in 69 BC, while Tigranes himself, Tigranes the Younger, the Arsacid King Phraates III, Mithradates Eupator, and the Roman Pompey, all manoeuvred for new alignments, Gordyene changed hands rapidly. At one point, Phraates invaded and occupied it, then a lieutenant of Pompey did, then Tigranes received it in turn from him. By this time (64-63 BC), no further mention is made of a king in Gordyene, nor is one named in Pompey's triumph among those conquered. Since Pompey's lieutenant turned the country over to Tigranes immediately, it did not apparently constitute a 'conquest.' Without a king to defend it, since Zarbienus did not have a successor, it could only pass back and forth between Armenia and Parthia, with Atropatene and Rome interested observers.[22]

Gordyene receives no regular mention in the decades to come, though the name did remain in use, as incidents reveal during the first centuries before and after Christ. A remark by Appian implies that the name had survived to his day (c. AD 115), though the region itself and Sophene were 'now governed together with Cappadocia.' The retrenchments by Hadrian after AD 118 probably ended this arrangement.[23]

Characene

The Babylonian district of Characene, also known as Mesene, dated back as a separate entity at least to the days of Alexander the Great. He ordered a city, Alexandria on the Tigris, built near the confluence of that river with the Eulaeus. Macedonian colonists joined the native population there. After subsequent destruction of the artificial town, and despite the rivalry of a nearby Arab settlement, gradually a Seleucid eparchy based on a rebuilt city, renamed Antiochia, rose to enjoy much of the Seleucid trade passing through southern Mesopotamia. Late in the second century before Christ, its eparch, Hyspaosines, spent some twenty years as a loyal officer of the declining Seleucids, but then joined the gathering movement to independence in Mesopotamia.[24]

For some three hundred years, a sequence of kings successfully ruled here, though after the late second century usually under Parthian hegemony. Since Characene (or Charax Spasinou) lay outside the normal range of classical literature, these are known mainly through the coinage. Some of the clues coins provide, such as those of Hyspaosines overstruck by a type of

Mithradates II of Parthia, require nothing further to convey their ominous message. None the less, Characene managed its affairs well and retained its identity despite Parthia and then the Armenian Empire of Tigranes.[25]

The potential rivalry of this kingdom with the Nabataeans did not for the most part involve conflict. What seems rather to have been mutually beneficial co-operation reflects itself in the mention by Pliny that those from Petra often visited a city in Characene. From the perspective of his native land, Isidore of Charax wrote early in the first century after Christ of the flourishing eastern trade routes. Recent studies have confirmed that a great commercial and military road ran from Bostra via Dumata to the Persian Gulf.[26]

The role of King Abennerigus (Abinerglos) in sheltering Izates of Adiabene has been mentioned above. Kings of Characene are met with more frequently in the early second century, when Roman military interest briefly brings the region into focus for classical authors. Attambelus and Artabazus appear suddenly in the record, the latter defeated but then restored to his position with Parthian help. In AD 150/151, the Parthian King Vologaeses IV (III) recorded his victory over King Meherdates (Mithradates), son of Pacorus, of Characene, on a bronze statue of Heracles found *in situ* in the temple of Apollo at Seleucia. A damaged limestone statue of a standing, cuirassed god attests to the level of artistic activity there. As with most of its neighbours, Characene depended on symbiosis with the great empires on either side. This relationship it maintained until the Sassanians arrived, apparently ending the dynasty about AD 225.[27]

Elymais

Lying between Babylonia and Persis, bordering Media, Sittacene, Susiana, and Characene on its east, north, and west, this kingdom enjoyed as well a considerable expanse of coastline along the upper Persian Gulf. So situated, it occupied a place of importance in the affairs of the Parthian Empire. It might seem to have lain south of the major zones of commercial activity, but this impression would be false: the kingdom in fact commanded surprising wealth, as revealed on several occasions in Seleucid and Parthian history.[28]

As ancient Elam, the region had taken a prominent part in the history of the Babylonian, Assyrian, and Persian empires. In classical times, it began a series of kings in the second century before Christ. They usually took the same throne-name, Kamnaskires. So did the kings of adjacent Susiana. It is tempting to postulate one line of kings ruling both regions, but the history of the two differed in fundamental respects and appears to preclude this. Elymais and Susiana fought each other on at least one occasion. Elymais earned the reputation of avoiding subjection to Parthia, whereas Susiana constituted a firm ally. The reputation of Elymais rests, however, mainly on the testimony of Strabo, who notes the prosperity and military might of the country, then remarks that its king 'declines to be subject to the king of the Parthians as others are' (nor had Elymais obeyed the Macedonians). This is demonstrably untrue of Elymais in the reign of the Parthian Mithradates I, when wealth stored in its temple of Artemis drew him there for enormous plunder, and he 'added this people to his kingdom.' Seleucids proved unable to resist the wealth of Elymais either, according to ancient accounts. Antiochus III, despite having received military assistance from Elymais at Magnesia, plundered its temple of Bel, but perished on this expedition. Similarly, Antiochus IV sought the riches of the temple of Artemis there and died on the way home. Demetrius II Nicator enjoyed help from Elymais in fighting Parthians. Phraates III may have governed the area for Parthia, and evidently took silver for his coinage from that tempting temple.[29]

In the first century only glimpses remain, as when the King of Elymais had contact with Pompey by letter. In AD 35, during the struggle for the Parthian throne between Abdagaeses and Artabanus, Elymais could be considered an important ally of one faction, and this alliance was compatible with Roman support, suggesting good relations between Rome and Elymais.[30]

About AD 224, Elymais joined the Sassanian Empire, not by prior consent, and prepared for lively centuries ahead.

Persis

Far down along the Persian Gulf lay Persis (Parsa; Fars), bounded on the east and north by the Parthian Empire, on the northwest by Elymais, and everywhere else by water. It included Persepolis and its treasures. During the first century after Christ, it was to undergo a rapid extension at the expense of Carmania, so that by AD 60 it bounded Hyrcania and the Kingdom of Gondophares, both previously separated from it.[31]

In the eighth century before Christ, Persians began to settle this region, which was to bear their name. They retained it through Achaemenid times; the last Achaemenid was buried near Persepolis after Alexander's conquest. Initially, Alexander recognized a Persian as satrap and after his death another, Orxines. After his execution, a member of Alexander's Bodyguards, Peucestas, acceded. He was later deposed by Antigonus. A contingent of Macedonian settlers assisted in organizing the satrapy under its new government, and Magnesia on the Maeander helped form a city in Persis. Some of the Persian nobles Alexander used as officers may have come from Persis. The land was renowned for a flourishing population, 'the most warlike of the Persians.'[32]

The Seleucids retained Persis at least until the reign of Antiochus III, finding it disposed to assist them rather than await the oncoming Mithradates I of Parthia. The Parthians regained this region and recognized its ruler as a king. Like the kings of Elymais and Characene, he issued silver coins, bearing Aramaic or Pahlavi legends. From the coinage, a record of some twenty-four kings can be formed, covering about five centuries.[33]

Persis is described as a free state in the *Periplus of the Erythraean Sea*, but Strabo considers it 'lessened in power by the Macedonians and still more by the Parthians' who take a position as its overlords. As Strabo expresses this relationship, 'the Persians have kings who are subjected to other kings ... those of the Parthians.'[34]

A salient feature of Persis was its religious syncretism, perhaps a model for that employed in Commagene. Greek equivalents existed there for such Iranian gods as Ahuramazda (Zeus Megistos), or Mithra (Apollo and Helios), or Anahita (Artemis). Nothing quite as elaborate as the Commagenian 'Apollo-Mithras-Helios-Hermes' or 'Heracles Verethragna' has appeared, but plainly the two Graeco-Iranian kingdoms used the same approach.

When the Sassanians took power, Persis became the one kingdom nearby that did not have to dread their coming, for they arose there. Their revolt broke out early in the third century and proved fatal to the Parthian Empire of the Arsacids. Ardashir (Artaxerxes), grandson of Sasan, moved to the kingship of Persis and then to the position of successor to the Arsacids.[35]

The small kingdoms of Mesopotamia need not be dismissed in our accounts of the region. Such terms as 'petty' king have the wrong connotation in English for the position these kings enjoyed; so of course do 'kinglet' or 'princeling' and the unthinking use of such equivalents. The smaller scale of holdings did not preclude these kings from exerting influence on the Seleucid, Parthian, and Roman policies involving the region. Time and again a conflict could be influenced or even decided with their help or by taking refuge among them. Most exercised virtually complete independence in their kingdoms, insulated from outside attack by deserts, distance, and force of arms. Enough intermarriage occurred among them to constitute a dynastic network of their own. That network's interconnections with the larger ones to the west (Greek) and east (Iranian) remain obscure, but might have been considerable, to judge from the case of Emesa. Our meagre knowledge artificially reduces their importance. As the oldest and once the most powerful of the regions here studied, the 'Land between the Rivers' earned more respect than we might surmise now.

§ 13. Parthia

The enormous Iranian Plateau is bounded by impressive mountain ranges:

the Zagros in the west, those of Atropatene and beyond them Armenia to the northwest, the Elburz Mountains in the north below the Caspian Sea, the heavy complex of mountains of the 'Upper Country' (homeland of the Parthians) between the Caspian and the Oxus and in Bactria, and the formidable Hindu Kush in the east. Though the country 'opens' to an extent southward, this is only to the Persian Desert – to Carmania and Gedrosia and Arachosia. This location promoted a sort of splendid isolation by nature from much of the course of classical history; the lands of the Greeks and Romans lay far to the west of Parthia proper, beyond the Euphrates. An outlet onto the Mediterranean would be useful and was soon achieved (§ 26), but was hardly essential. More to the point was Mesopotamia, for good reason one of the first sites of higher civilization, and a standing temptation to Parthians, who meant to have it and did (as 'Kings of Kings') once the Seleucids were gone, despite interruptions by Armenians and Romans.

The position of the Parthian Empire early in the last century before Christ paralleled those of Pontus and Armenia, but with direct consequences of longer duration than in either. The empire claimed unbroken succession of kings from its foundation by 'Arsaces' about 248 BC. It ruled Iran, claimed parts of Asia Minor, and from the outset it cultivated good relations with the Greeks, for instance through dedications at Delos already in 178-175 BC by Phriapatius or Phraates I, his son. Major expansion came initially through the work of the great Mithradates I (171-138 BC). His son, Phraates II (138-128 BC), and his brother, Artabanus II (128-123 BC), passed the new Empire intact to the second great conqueror of the dynasty, Artabanus's son Mithradates II (123-87 BC). The initial advantage that Mithradates enjoyed over his redoubtable contemporaries, Eupator and Tigranes, stemmed from this previous consolidation of the Parthian state and its extension to empire, both processes well advanced before his reign. Furnished with the claim to descent from Artaxerxes II of the Achaemenids, Parthians regarded themselves as the heirs of the Persian Empire and forced others to agree. A consequence was potential claim to Syria, where Seleucids had replaced Persians by right of conquest and now risked the fate they had inflicted. By the reign of Mithradates I, Seleucid decline had begun to accelerate and in the view of Strabo it contributed to the rise of Parthia. Nothing in dynastic politics precluded potential extension of Arsacid power into Asia Minor, where Persia had once ruled. Only resistance by the Greek kingdoms formed since Alexander's day and now bolstered by Romans was to decide the succession to the Seleucids. The Parthian position was clear: all former Seleucid territory east of the Euphrates belonged to the Arsacids, and perhaps some of that to the west. On one view, Parthian policy for a century, beginning with Mithradates II, sought possession of Asia Minor and much of the Levant.

Despite two centuries spent by Rome and its dynastic allies disputing this demarcation, in Hadrian's reign the *limes* had not significantly altered. Questions as to the boundary in Armenia and Northern Mesopotamia endured into Byzantine times, but centuries of diplomacy and warfare had settled one issue of continuing importance. By the late first century AD, the world was viewed as divided into two great empires (ancients blissfully ignored what lay beyond the Indus): 'the two highest empires, of the Romans and the Parthians.' In its more than 475 years of dynastic activity, the Arsacid house accomplished much and with pride could hand on the results to its Sassanian successors.[36]

Mithradates II Euergetes Epiphanes Philhellene

Mithradates II could afford no complacency in his long reign (123-87 BC). He inherited two major problems from his predecessors and witnessed the development of another. Perpetual instability in the eastern regions of the Parthian Empire plagued it at all stages of its history, and the chronic unrest of Mesopotamia worsened early in the reign of Mithradates. The third problem became equally serious: the rapid rise to empire of Pontus and Armenia, drawing Romans eastward to confront Eupator and Tigranes.

Mithradates faced challenges in the east and met them with vigour. The tradition preserved by Strabo of Parthian conquests in 'Scythia' and Bactria at two different periods reflects the work of Mithradates II and Phraates III, his nephew. The problem worsened with the eruption of the Sakai into Parthia; this began some seven years before the accession of Mithradates II and sent a dangerous group of nomads westward by at least two separate routes. A long struggle followed, with noteworthy consequences. For one, the effort left the important region south of the Caspian intact and stable; from Mithradates II to Vologaeses I in the reign of Nero the same Parthian dynasty can be traced ruling Hyrcania. Despite enormous difficulties, Mithradates left for posterity a memory of decisive though vaguely perceived success: 'With the Scythians he contended successfully at various times and became the avenger of the wrong done to his ancestors.' Another consequence of distraction in the east was reduction of Parthian activity in the west at a time of rapid political evolution there.[37]

It also may have saved Armenia for its own dynasty. Probably early in his reign, before turning eastward, Mithradates II 'waged war on the Armenians.' The cause cannot now be discerned, but the result can: Tigranes went to Parthia as a hostage, where he remained 'a long time' before his release about 95 BC. In the meantime, Artavasdes I, the victim of this invasion, ruled on in Armenia.

Mithradates II and Gotarzes I Autokrator Philopator

The second of his major problems, trouble in Mesopotamia, most plagued the reign of Mithradates and persisted among his successors. At least by 128, to judge from coinage, the native dynast of Characene (§ 12), Hyspaosines, detached Babylon. Both Phraates II and Artabanus II attempted to deal with this event by assigning the region to Himerus, the Hyrcanian viceroy of Mesopotamia. His successful deportation of Babylonians to Media encouraged in him aspiration to rival kingship. By 121, however, the hold of Mithradates on Babylon was firm enough to be signalled by overstriking the coins of Hyspaosines. A record from the same year shows 'Great Arsaces' ruling there. The Behistun inscription mentions a 'satrap of satraps' probably assigned to rule Babylon before 110 BC, or Seleucid year 202 as reckoned in Babylonia. Mithradates is still 'Great King' in this text, whereas by 110 he was using 'King of Kings' on another text from Babylon.[38]

This picture of control re-established in Mesopotamia can be deceptive. The great inscriptions cut by Persian and Parthian Kings for centuries on a cliff-face at Behistun mentions a satrap named Gotarzes, who was the son of Mithradates. Nothing to wonder at there: the oldest son receives an important command and will one day succeed his father. However, he had long to wait. The 'satrap of satraps' from before 110 remains lodged in Babylon as late as October 91, impatient to succeed. A tablet for the 'King of Kings' shows no upward mobility for Gotarzes, after twenty years. Thus a sign of trouble: 'Arsaces, King, whose name is Gotarzes' on an undated Babylonian document. The response of Mithradates came at once. A tablet dated March 90 bears an ominous message: 'Arsaces, King, who has expelled Gotarzes ...'

This challenge from his son threatened Mithradates from as early as 96/95, when the coinage mentions an *Autokrator* in Seleucia and Susa. This may reflect a temporary arrangement by which Gotarzes took control of the southwestern part of the empire in the place of his father, still the 'King of Kings.' That freed Mithradates for operations in the north and east, with one other pressing matter first: a revolt by the later Orodes I, his brother, who may have dislodged him from a portion of the empire by 91 BC.[39]

In this context occurred two important developments: the release of Tigranes to ascend the throne of Armenia, and the mission by an envoy of Mithradates to meet Sulla on the Euphrates. Alterations can also be observed in the policy of Mithradates towards the Seleucids. More on all of these presently.

To conclude the woeful tale of events in Babylonia. Mithradates alternately gained and lost control of Media, Babylon, and even of Seleucia and Susa during the late 90s. Gotarzes held on for a time, then lost not to Mithradates but to Orodes. About the time of the death of Mithradates, two Babylonian tablets speak of 'Arsaces, who has expelled Gotarzes, King, and Ashi'abatum, his wife.' They bear dates in 88/87 and 87/86 = Arsacid 160-161 and Seleucid 224-225, Babylonian era). This expulsion, with the need to repeat it a year later, constitutes the last heard of Gotarzes. Whether or not Mithradates lived to witness these events, Orodes I did. His name re-emerges in the record as late as 80/79, when Sinatruces expelled him in his turn. Small wonder that the period after Mithradates appeared later to Trogus as one with 'a changing succession of very many kings among the Parthians.' The confusion reflects itself in the coinage, with mints being forced to alter existing issues as rapid changes of monarchs or their jurisdictions occurred.[40]

Parthia and Armenia

What followed from these distractions in the last years of Mithradates? First, consider Armenia. The release of Tigranes may have come as a response to these internal problems, to the (inferred) death of Artavasdes I, to the appearance in Cappadocia of a new dynasty, to the dangerous increase in activity by Eupator, to the sudden vacuum of authority in Syria at the death of Grypus and the disruptions caused by the Judaean Jannaeus, to gathering difficulties in the east, and/or to need for those seventy rich valleys in the north as counterweight to Orodes there. All or some of these. At any rate, Mithradates II sought to tie himself firmly to Tigranes and, with him, to the rapidly rising Mithradates Eupator. Thus the treaty with Eupator and the marriage link with Tigranes, Eupator's son-in-law.

The parchment from Avroman in Kurdistan showing Aryazate-Automa among the wives of Mithradates II dates to November 88 BC. The marriage could have taken place well before that, since Tigranes, by then aged about fifty, probably had numerous progeny, some from before his accession and some after. The document is valuable not only in shedding this unexpected light on the dynastic arrangements, but also in revealing the willingness of Mithradates already to accord Tigranes a title higher than his own son dared assume: that of 'Great King.' Whether or not he expected significant assistance from the robust Armenian, Mithradates had adequately gauged his man. Tigranes would be a comforting ally on the borders of Atropatene. However, following the death of Mithradates about 87, Tigranes became a formidable antagonist to subsequent Parthians in their 'frequent' encounters. The tradition that 'Tigranes, as no other, brought low the Parthian power' must derive from this second phase of his reign. If recovery of the seventy valleys had not already occurred, it did now, and beyond these lay Parthian holdings in Northern Mesopotamia, which fell in serried array to the new 'King of Kings.' Neither Orodes I nor the aged Sinatruces I commanded the respect of Tigranes; not until the accession of Phraates III in 70 did he have cause for anything but disdain. He had to face an attack from Phraates, supported by Pompey, about 66 BC (§ 24).[41]

Parthia and the Seleucids

The relations of Mithradates II and the Seleucids oscillated in correspondence with Parthia's internal problems. The triple challenge presented by the expansionist policies of Tigranes, Mithradates Eupator, and Rome would normally have brought more response from Parthia than it did. In addition, disruptions within the Seleucid and Ptolemaic dynasties early in the century might under other circumstances have provoked Parthian opportunism, especially when the heirs of Grypus and Cyzicenus launched themselves after 96/95 into their damaging struggle for succession. But precisely now (96 to 90 BC) Mithradates suffered that internal opposition from Gotarzes and then Orodes. Parthians consequently involved themselves only sporadically in Syrian affairs during the dozen years until Tigranes removed the temptation by invading the country himself. They may have engaged with Antiochus X Eusebes, who is variously reported as having died at their hands, having fled to their court, having survived until Tigranes arrived, or even having lasted until Pompey appeared. Late in his reign, Mithradates received Demetrius III Eukairos/Akairos as either a captive or a hostage in Parthia, retaining him in honour until he died. But for the most part, Parthia failed to exploit advantages offered by the rapid decline of the Seleucids. Instead, Tigranes did, then Rome.

Mithradates would have liked closer ties to the Greek lands. His titles included *Philhellene* and he meant this, as an inscription from Babylon and another at Delos from early in his reign demonstrate. His family had married into the Seleucids not long previously: a Parthian princess named Rhodogune, daughter of Mithradates I, married Demetrius II Nicator. Phraates II, her brother, married Laodice, sister of Antiochus VIII Grypus. Further intermarriage occurred later with the Graeco-Iranian dynasties: §§ 19, 24. Parthian coinage favoured traditional Greek usages, and Parthian policy promoted diplomatic relations with the major Greek kingdoms, as well as encouragement for the Greek commercial element within the Parthian Empire. Several cities retained their local Greek governmental institutions. Susa demonstrates a *gymnasiarch* in 75 BC, and other 'Greek' offices are still evident in AD 21, mentioned in a letter from the Parthian King.[42]

Parthia and Rome

Finally, Rome. Indirect contact between the two states dating back to the mid-second century seems not unlikely, given, for instance, their mutual interest in Delos. A letter mentioned in the Old Testament purportedly from a Roman consul to the Parthian monarch 'Arsaces' (the common throne-name) cannot be dismissed out of hand, but adequate documentation of formal contacts begins only in the early first century before Christ. When the first Roman official, Sulla, appeared on the Euphrates during the internal dislocations in Cappadocia, Mithradates II of Parthia moved rapidly. To the seasoned old king, alliance with Romans could seem useful. Roman support of Ariobarzanes might indirectly protect Parthia from Eupator and Tigranes. Beyond a certain point, Mithradates would not welcome growth of the new empires in Pontus and Armenia, so he took the initiative. The accounts of this meeting agree that his agents were the ones to initiate it, seeking 'the friendship of the Roman people.' *Parthorum legati a rege Arsace missi, venerunt ad Sullam, ut amicitiam populi Romani peterent*. It is oft repeated in the sources that this constituted the first Parthian overture to Rome: *ad eum primum omnium Romanorum* and the like. The sequel demonstrates that this arose from serious intent: *amicitia* ('friendship') did result. The successors of Mithradates must have allowed it to lapse, for Pompey 'renewed it' (*renovavit amicitiam*) in the days of Phraates III. But it began with Mithradates.

Why with him? Two obvious reasons: Mithradates needed support, and Romans for the first time had appeared officially and militarily on the Euphrates. No record of prior diplomatic contact exists (aside from that vague biblical passage) to diminish the credit that belongs to Mithradates for having discerned the importance of relations between the two states. Against the background of dynastic vigour in Asia Minor, predicting the future 'division of the world' between Rome and Parthia exceeded the foresight of statesmen then, but recognizing their impending succession to Seleucids and Ptolemies lay well within the grasp of Mithradates.

Although the mission of Sulla to the East was on behalf of Ariobarzanes, nothing precluded him from meeting envoys. By the same token, he had no authority to conclude a binding alliance. He also had little idea of the immense extent of the Parthian Empire and of its potential importance to Rome. Whether the gratuitous arrogance and pomposity imputed to him at this suitably ceremonious encounter did constitute the 'diplomatic blunder' with which he has been charged, a residue of ill-feeling on the part of Mithradates ensued. Authentic or not, the story of his putting the ambassador to death for allowing Sulla to assume a position of primacy at the meeting – by seating himself in the centre – must rest on the real displeasure of the great Parthian, who considered himself humiliated not by another king but by a politician from a distant city-state. The indirect results of this meeting included the alliance with Mithradates Eupator and the marriage tie with Tigranes. The hopes of Mithradates II of finding in Rome a counterweight to these two received a rebuff in the behaviour of Sulla. 'Friendship' did ensue, but the practical Parthian hedged his bets – as he probably would have done anyway.[43]

Despite his difficulties, Mithradates II earned the title accorded him by posterity: 'the Great' (*rex Mithridates cognomine Magnus*). The appellation sprang from his accomplishments, *cui res gestae Magni cognomen dedere.* His vigorous reign not only preserved the state at a dangerous time but added 'many peoples to the Parthian realm.' In contrast to his somnolent contemporary, Ptolemy X Alexander I, Mithradates 'waged many wars with his neighbours with distinction.'

His other title, 'King of Kings,' enjoyed a curious history in the period to follow. Our admittedly incomplete evidence suggests that a certain reluctance among his rivals and immediate successors (Gotarzes I, Orodes I, Sinatruces, Phraates III) for some thirty years prevented their assumption of the title. Apparently, only Tigranes used 'King of Kings' now, substituting it for his previous 'Great King' upon the death of Mithradates. It was not until the death of Tigranes that the title reappeared in Parthia with Mithradates III and Orodes II, after whom it became an appurtenance of the Arsacid throne for centuries. Did this hiatus after Mithradates II arise from an insistence by Tigranes that he alone should hold the title? At least ostensibly, to retain credibility the title should belong to but one king at a time, though the matter may not be that simple (see note 44), and the practice in Iranian lands could differ from that previously followed by the Seleucids. In any case, Artavasdes I of Atropatene – a partial 'successor' (*diadochos*) of Tigranes – and the Pontic King Pharnaces II, son of Eupator, both used 'King of Kings.' So had Eupator, if we can credit that claim made on an inscription for Queen Dynamis, his granddaughter.[44]

Sinatruces I Theopator Euergetes Eusebes

About 79 BC, Orodes I was driven from Babylon. There may have been a brief succession by a son of Gotarzes known only as *Philopator* from his coinage. By 78 or 77, a man in his eightieth year returned from either exile or command at the fringe of the empire, restored by 'the Sacauracian Scyths.' This was Sinatruces, brother of Mithradates II and father of Phraates III. The succession may have occurred two years before his authority extended across the empire. He remained for a time in the east, with Tigranes established on the western periphery of the Parthian dominion, and now partly within it. Whether this had been foreseen by Mithradates in his careful planning some twenty years before or not, the accord did work. Tigranes regarded Sinatruces as a caretaker, and began building and populating Tigranocerta, his imposing new capital within former Parthian territory, in the first years of Sinatruces. By 78 BC Tigranes controlled, in addition to Syria and Armenia, several former Parthian dependencies, especially Gordyene, Adiabene, and Atropatene. Sophene too had once lain within the orbit of Parthian interest. On the other hand, coins of Sinatruces circulated as far north as Iberia.

Although Tigranes could mount incursions deep into Mesopotamia from Tigranocerta, his preoccupation with Syria precluded such actions. He may also have deliberately avoided provocation. The authority of Sinatruces nominally extended over lower Mesopotamia, though his coinage reflects a certain unsteadiness there. Perhaps his greatest service to Parthia was in maintaining the restless eastern part of the empire, for he did little in the west. The one time he was called upon, by Mithradates Eupator, he failed to respond. If the purported letter of Eupator to 'King Arsaces' can, as some scholars believe, be assigned to late in the reign of Sinatruces rather than to early in that of his son, who acceded in 70/69 BC, it shows the aged monarch angered over the behaviour of Tigranes – for drawing Romans towards Parthia or for preying on Parthian lands – but far from the struggle (*te remoto procul*). However, the letter probably belongs to Phraates III, his son, whose policies and attitudes towards his Iranian fellow-monarchs were to entail initiatives unwelcome to Rome as western currents of change reached Parthia at last (§ 26).[45]

Illustrations

Nicomedes II of Bithynia
British Museum

Mithradates VI Eupator of Pontus
BMC Pontus, viii.4

Anatolian Plateau in Ancient Galatia
Richard D. Sullivan

Ariobarzanes I of Cappadocia
BMC Galatia, etc. vii.5

Possibly Queen Laodice of Commagene,
daughter of Antiochus VIII Grypus
By permission of Professor F.K. Dörner

The view outward from a volcanic-cone habitation
near Göreme (in Cappadocia)
Richard D. Sullivan

Antiochus I of Commagene, with 'Armenian' tiara
British Museum

Cleopatra Thea and Antiochus VIII Grypus
BMC Seleucids, xxiii.2

Rock-cut structures at Petra, the Nabataean capital
J.A. Hammerton, *Wonders of the Past*, I (New York 1933)

Ptolemy XII Auletes
British Museum

Tigranes the Great of Armenia
Ashmolean Museum, Oxford

View eastward from Nemrud Dagh
across the Euphrates into Mesopotamia (Osrhoene)
Richard D. Sullivan

Hatra: ruins of the great palace
G. Rawlinson, *The Sixth Great Oriental Monarchy ... Parthia* (London 1870)

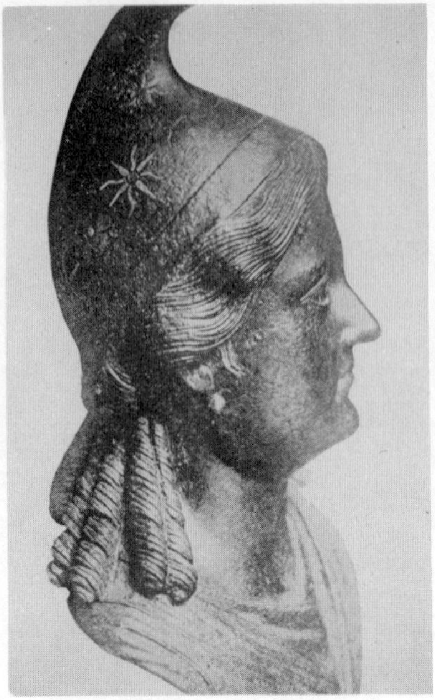

Queen Dynamis of Bosporus
G. Macurdy, *Vassal Queens* (Baltimore 1937)

Polemo I of Pontus
Ashmolean Museum, Oxford

The ruins at Susa, *circa* 1920
J.A. Hammerton, *Wonders of the Past*, III (New York 1933)

Mithradates II of Parthia
BMC Parthia, viii.4

Tarcondimotus I of Cilicia
BMC Cilicia, xxxix.8

Archelaus I of Cappadocia
BMC Galatia, vii.4

Temple at Elaeussa-Sebaste, Cilicia. Sea behind
Richard D. Sullivan

134

Emesa: unknown member of Royal Family
Damascus Museum

Commagene: colossi atop Nemrud Dagh
Richard D. Sullivan

Jerusalem: Mt Moriah's 'Dome of the Rock'
J.A. Hammerton, *Wonders of the Past*, IV (New York 1933)

Cleopatra VII; Antony on obverse
BMC Ptolemies, xxxi.7

Antony as triumvir; Cleopatra on reverse
BMC Ptolemies, xxxi.7

Cleopatra VII holding Ptolemy XV
BMC Ptolemies, xxx.6

Cleopatra as Isis; temple at Denderah
E.R. Bevan, *Ptolemaic Dynasty* (London 1927)

Artavasdes I of Atropatene
Numismatic Chronicle 1937: 250–254

OPPOSITE

top Phraates III of Parthia
BMC Parthia, xi.1

middle Orodes II of Parthia
Ashmolean Museum, Oxford

bottom Pacorus I of Parthia
BMC Parthia, xviii.12

The ruins of the Nabataean city of Humayma, founded by Aretas III
Building debris and two cisterns
Professor John Oleson

PART II

The East in the Generation of Actium, 69–30 BC

By 70 BC, Asia Minor had changed more rapidly in one generation than it had previously altered in centuries. Not since Alexander had the region witnessed such rapid political evolution, as Romans took up the position partly prepared for them by their conquest of Antiochus III at Magnesia and the subsequent peace of 188 BC. Since 100 BC, Mithradates Eupator had swept across Asia Minor and into Greece, to be driven back by Romans with their Greek allies. Tigranes the Great had assumed the title 'King of Kings' and all that went with it, forging an Armenian Empire that stretched to unheard-of limits. Tigranes had defeated the Seleucids and occupied their seat of empire, Syria. His departure and defeat were now at hand, but for the Seleucids the damage had been done. In these years, Cappadocia had become a battlefield and the major testing-ground for Roman claims to more of Asia Minor. Its monarch had called himself *Philoromaios* and had survived the local reaction against this. The Kingdom of Bithynia, adjoining Roman Asia, had now become Roman territory, by authentic or contrived testament. Galatia had materially assisted Romans, a record that persisted in the half century to come – the brief span remaining in its independent history. By 70, Commagene may have changed monarchs, or in any case soon would; another *Philoromaios* proved valuable to Romans there, though not without serious strains and some warfare. In the years just ahead, fighting and rapid change enveloped Judaea and large parts of Palestine. Emesa came for the first time to international attention during the Seleucid eclipse. Egypt stood on the threshold of a new relationship to Rome, and of civil strife. The Nabataeans moved towards an altered status regarding both Judaea and Egypt, and some fighting with Romans lay just ahead. In 70/69, when the Parthian monarch, Sinatruces, was replaced by Phraates III, his son, the rapid alteration of old balances with the west demanded re-examination of existing policies towards Armenia, Pontus, and Rome, to say nothing of Syria and Palestine. One result was to be armed Parthian incursions into Asia Minor, with unwelcome consequences for the monarchs of Commagene and Judaea.

The period of nearly forty years until the battle of Actium in 31 BC witnessed major changes in the East as the balance west of the Euphrates shifted towards Rome in ways predictable but by no means inevitable.

6

Asia Minor in the Generation before Actium

§ 14. Thrace: The Odrysian-Astaean Dynasty

By 70 BC, much of Thrace had long since moved towards one of its salient characteristics for the next century: close involvement with Rome. The accession of the Odrysian-Astaean Sadalas I can be fixed at 87 or thereabouts, but the date of his death remains obscure; conversely, the date at which his successor, Cotys IV, died is known to be about 44, but that of his accession lies beyond our records.[1] Similarly, the regnal years of the Sapaean Cotys VI cannot be determined with confidence, though his reign had probably ended about 48. This obscurity masks an important stage in Thracian history, when some tribes fought against Rome and others against Mithradates Eupator. The potential dangers of this situation later waned as the power of Eupator did, when rather than waste themselves on internecine struggles the dynasts of Thrace moved towards unification though not unanimity. The details of this process escape the historical record at first, but then come rapidly into the light.[2]

At the opening of this period, the issue of Thracian alliance had by no means been settled, since that of Mithradates Eupator had not. Some Thracians had co-operated enthusiastically with him in 88 and had served his armies as allies and mercenaries. Their repeated raids into Macedonia assisted his war effort against Rome. The difficulty of access to the inland tribes spared them from reprisals for the time, though in 72/71 Lucullus penetrated as far as Uscudama (later Hadrianopolis) and defeated the Bessi there. The coastal dynasties remained with Rome, and other Thracian allies of Mithradates began defecting to Rome during its campaigns in Asia Minor throughout 69 and 68; Thracians helped Lucullus defeat Tigranes in 69. Some later rejoined Mithradates as he achieved successes near Armenia. As did others, Thracians plainly waited upon the outcome of the Mithradatic Wars before committing themselves.[3]

Cotys IV

The threat of Mithradates no longer affected Thracian politics by 63, but this hardly removed the basic reason for dissension within the country, for a fundamental choice remained: to stand with or against Rome. Traces of internal discord over this matter remain for decades in Thracian politics. Romans tended to force the issue by invading portions of Thracian territory, from 61 BC onward, though a campaign in that year by C. Antonius Hibrida ended in his defeat. The Bessi and other Thracians lost a battle to C. Octavius in 60/59 BC. About 57 BC the Bessi came into conflict with the Odrysian-Astaean house led by Cotys IV. The occasion involved Rome and stands as an example of the bizarre circumstances increasingly surrounding political activity in the East. In 58, Cicero had been exiled, with the approval of a consul for that year, L. Calpurnius Piso, Caesar's father-in-law. In 57, Piso served as governor of Macedonia. There, according to the indignant account of Cicero two years later, he received Rabocentus, ruler of the Bessi. The Bessi had decided, for the time, to co-operate with Roman forces, and now offered military support. Cotys IV, wary of any move tending to strengthen these tribal rivals, offered a bribe of three hundred talents (in Cicero's not disinterested account), which Piso accepted. The murder of Rabocentus and his delegation followed. Small wonder that the Bessi long remained dangerous to Romans and to their Thracian allies. Piso also attacked the Dentheletae, an important tribe living along the Strymon River and potentially a bulwark for Romans on the eastern border of Macedonia. Their record had by and large been one of alliance with Rome. The consequences of Piso's aggressive policy towards them now included considerable damage and disruption as far south as Thessalonica.[4]

Cotys IV held with Rome even as its own internal troubles mounted. Before Pharsalus, in support of Pompey he sent not only an armed force but also Sadalas, his son. Most of the Thracian tribes found themselves involved in this conflict, including even the Bessi; the Sapaean Rhescuporis I fought as well (see below). A large cavalry force furnished by Cotys ranged as far afield as Thessaly. Another under the command of Sadalas did combine with a Pompeian contingent to inflict a signal defeat on Cassius in Thessaly.[5]

In these dangerous circumstances, at least some portions of Thrace enjoyed strong dynastic government, as reflected in military policy and royal coinage.[6]

Sadalas II

How long Cotys survived the period of supporting Pompey cannot be determined. Caesar tended to spare Pompey's adherents and did so in the case of Sadalas. The lack of further mention of Cotys need not show him dead yet, but a coinage showing his son with the royal title does show a smooth transition, and the coin makes a point of continuing the father's numismatic type.[7]

By this time, the mid-first century before Christ, Thracians had begun an important move towards dynastic unification. Amid the bewildering proliferation of tribes in Thrace, four stood out as especially noteworthy during this period: the Bessi, the Sapaeans, the Astae, and the ancient house of the Odrysians, formerly the most powerful in Thrace. The treachery of Cotys IV during the governorship of Piso had perhaps weakened the Bessi, but need not have entailed their submission to the Odrysians, as sometimes suggested. It did fit with an apparent policy of unification now between the Odrysian and Astaean dynasties, thus solidifying control of a block of territory sweeping northeastward from Cypsela on the lower Hebrus past the lands of the Bessi to Odessus on the Black Sea, and including the strip of coast south of there controlled by the Astae. So powerful did this alliance become that Bizye, the Astaean capital, is later described by Pliny simply as 'the citadel of the kings of Thrace' (modern Viza retains its name). Further unification added the Sapaean dynasty to this partnership. Since the foreign policy of these three dynasties, excluding the Bessi, tended to favour Rome, Thrace became a useful and strategically placed ally in the stormy decades after Pharsalus, rather than the seat of incessant warfare it potentially constituted. Even so, much internal fighting lay ahead.[8]

Sadalas probably continued his alliance to Romans and would have seen service in the projected campaign of Caesar against the Dacians in Thrace, had Caesar survived. Thrace now constituted the only major region in Europe south of the Danube with enduring opposition to Rome still evident, and Caesar presumably intended to meet this opposition.[9]

The problem had recently become unusually serious through rapid expansion of the holdings of Burebistas, King of the Getae. During a period of some fifteen years preceding the death of Caesar, this energetic man presided over an extension of Getic rule from its Transdanubian base to regions of Thrace. An inscription dated to 49/48 BC from Dionysopolis in Thrace has him in possession of 'all' the adjacent territory on both sides of the Danube. His forces threatened or captured numerous Greek cities – to some of which they had once paid tribute – along the Pontic coast, from

Apollonia, Mesembria, and Dionysopolis to as far north as Olbia. It has been suggested that his motive was less to gain wealth than to check the Roman advance, consciously carrying forward the program of Mithradates Eupator. Not only did he threaten the system of alliances Romans had built up among the southern Thracians, but he began to bear such alarming designations as 'King Burebistas, foremost and greatest of the kings of Thrace.' It may seem odd for a king of the Getae to speak of himself this way, but the Getae did speak the same language as the Thracians, according to Strabo, and may have aspired to full hegemony. It was this expansion that Caesar intended to oppose (so *Aeneid* 7.604: 'bring upon the Getae the sorrows of war'), and his grant of citizenship to a resident of the Crimea may reflect a policy of containing the Getae from the East. Burebistas perished in 45 or 44 and his quasi-empire, lacking any structure other than dependence on him, began to crumble. None the less, his successor, Dicomes, offered to assist Antony and Cleopatra against Octavian at Actium. A century later, continuing disturbances show the difficulty of controlling this entire region.[10]

During the last period of the reign of Burebistas, Sadalas II doubtless prepared to join Romans in resisting him. Later, outsiders writing of the confusing number and claims of Thracian rulers designated them as *reguli* or, in the case of Sadalas, a 'kinglet' (*basiliskos*). But coins and inscriptions reveal that Sadalas viewed his rule as a full kingship not only of the Odrysian-Astaean house but of all Thrace: 'Sadalas, King of the Thracians.' Since the coastal territories threatened by Burebistas included part of those claimed by the Astae, this title may be a reaction by Sadalas. At the death of Burebistas Sadalas moved swiftly to reoccupy these lands and even add to them some of the Getic possessions around Odessus. However pretentious the title to which he aspired, the movement towards national unity that he fostered through his son's marriage to a Sapaean princess (see below) did later produce a sole 'King of the Thracians,' though briefly, in Rhoemetalces I.[11]

A tradition that Sadalas II died 'childless' represents only a dearth of information in Dio's sources. An inscription by Cotys V records that 'King Cotys honours King Sadalas and Queen Polemocratia, his parents ...' This queen appears in a vivid story preserved by Appian in the context of 42 BC. Sadalas II had fallen in battle. Brutus took control of the kingdom and began hostilities against the restive Bessi. In collecting troops and funds for battle against Octavian and Antony, he received Polemocratia and gladly accepted her offer of the royal treasures left by her late husband, Sadalas. In return, she requested protection for her son, the later Cotys V, whom Brutus lodged in Cyzicus. Since the son is described as a young boy, his accession was deferred. According to Dio, Sadalas bequeathed his territory to the Romans, as another in the series of 'inheritances' added to Asia, Bithynia, Cyrene, and Egypt in these heady times. Nothing apparently came of it, but an interregnum among the Odrysian-Astaean rulers may have given rise to the story. How long that was cannot be determined, but a King Sadalas (III) shown ruling at the time of Actium in 31 may have been another son of Sadalas II, or a close male relative, fighting on the side of Antony. The Odrysian-Astaean kingdom passed not long after Actium to Cotys V. After his death it devolved, by way of a guardianship exercised through the then-intermarried Sapaean line, upon Rhescuporis II, his son.[12]

The Sapaeans: Rhescuporis I

The last of the three main Thracian dynasties (excluding, among others, the only marginally less active Dentheletae and Bessi) moved from obscurity early in the first century before Christ to an important position by mid-century. As seen above (§ 1), Cotys VI presents only a dim figure on present evidence, and may not even have claimed the royal title, though he did revive the Sapaean house from dormancy.

At Pharsalus in 48 BC, Pompey's allies included a force provided by the Odrysian-Astaean King Cotys IV, and one 'from Macedonia' under the command of 'Rhascypolis, a man of outstanding courage.' This must be Rhescuporis I, son of Cotys VI of the Sapaeans: the exact spelling of that name eluded Caesar. Locating 'Rhascypolis' in adjacent Macedonia presents no problem, since Sapaean territory ran along the lower Nestus River. Caesar has just mentioned Thrace in this sentence as the homeland of Cotys VI, and proceeds naturally towards Macedonia in turning to Rhescuporis.[13]

In the mobilizations after the murder of Caesar, Rhescuporis chose to support Brutus and Cassius, lending them valuable assistance through his knowledge of the mountainous terrain east of Philippi. Lieutenants of Antony and Octavian occupied the mountain passes of his territory, but he led the forces of Brutus to Philippi by a circuitous route. However, Rhascus, his brother, provided similar assistance to Antony. This arose from the brothers' shrewd assessment of the course Roman politics had taken. Rather than guess at this phase of the civil wars, they concerted a policy by which one would be on the winning side and could intercede for the other. So it proved: Rhescuporis retained his throne, after timely desertion from Brutus, and pardoned his rascal brother, Rhascus.[14]

Though Rhescuporis may have struck those outside Thrace as one of a confusing array of 'princes' or 'dynasts' or 'kinglets' – Dio refers to him vaguely as 'a certain dynast' – he acquired the title of king, whether or not his father had. One Athenian inscription honours him as 'King Rhascuporis, son of Cotys' (not *King* Cotys) and another refers to him in honouring his son: 'King Cotys, son of King Rhescuporis.' An inscription from Bizye uses the same terms in according his son honours from a group of Romans there.

Like his contemporaries in the Odrysian-Astaean line, Cotys IV and Sadalas II, Rhescuporis brought his portion of Thrace safely through two dangerous Roman conflicts between 48 and 42 BC, culminating in the battles of Pharsalus and Philippi. The appearance of hostile Roman forces in his own country must have encouraged him to promote closer ties among the dynasties of Thrace, a policy that his son carried out. Maintenance of good relations with the Athenians also ranked among his priorities. Since none could foresee the increasingly troubled evolution of political arrangements in the East, prudent rulers maintained wide cultural contacts, adjusted military policy as events dictated, and waited. The presence of Thracians as a distinct group alongside Roman colonists in distant Apollonia (on the Pisidian-Phrygian border near Apamea) affords a glimpse of what might be a minor diaspora, with recognized status in a Greek city.[15]

Cotys VII

Rhescuporis I disappears from our meagre records about 42 BC, though he could have reigned longer. The reign of his son Cotys VII had to fall in the interval between Philippi (42 BC), when Rhescuporis was still active, and Actium (31 BC), when Rhoemetalces I, his grandson, bore the title of King in Thrace.

Cotys sired two kings and one queen of Thrace. Of particular dynastic importance ranked the queen, a daughter whose name is now lost but who married Cotys V of the Odrysian-Astaean line of Thracian kings. This policy of consolidation responded to the threat posed by the Roman civil wars, which involved the East too and found their resolution through three battles in the near or distant neighbourhood of Thrace (Pharsalus; Philippi; Actium). The luxury of internecine strife had become unaffordable in Thrace; for that which did occur in the decades ahead, Thracians paid a price partly determined by Rome.

The new marriage joined all three of the major Thracian dynasties, and their large block of contiguous territories. Outside this new arrangement still lay the dangerous Bessi and, on present evidence, the Dentheletae – the latter allied to Rome. The Bessi were encircled by hostile tribes now, but gave a strong account of themselves for years to come; as late as 11 BC they were to drive Rhoemetalces I temporarily from his throne and kill Rhescuporis II, the son born to Cotys V through this Sapaean marriage.[16]

Inscriptions from Athens and Bizye honour King Cotys VII and mention his father, Rhescuporis I. Others, from Bizye and Hisarlak, mention him as grandfather of Rhoemetalces II. A possible joint coinage with Rhescuporis more likely stems from the reign of his namesake, and grandson, Cotys VIII. Otherwise, Cotys escapes mention by the sources, despite an important reign.[17]

Rhoemetalces I

The full reign of this king extends beyond the scope of the present study, but merits brief discussion by way of summary. His policies and problems mirror the experience of Thracian kings before and after him. He dealt successfully with Romans, though finding it expedient to switch allegiance from Antony to Octavian, provoking the remark by Octavian that he appreciated treachery but not traitors. He furthered his father's policy of intermarriage, reinforcing the dynasty internally by marrying his son Rhescuporis III to a daughter of his other son Cotys VIII. He also arranged the marriage of Cotys to Antonia Tryphaena of the Pontic dynasty. Among her relatives or their children reigned kings or queens of Pontus, Armenia, Armenia Minor, Cilicia, Bosporus, and Thrace itself.[18]

Rhoemetalces also served as guardian for the children of his sister's husband, Cotys V of the Odrysian-Astaean line; these included King Rhescuporis II, killed in 11 BC by the Bessi. They had suffered a reverse at the hands of Rhoemetalces, assisted by Rome, and now took revenge, dislodging Rhoemetalces too from his throne. Despite this shock he recovered to rule Thrace and to hand on the kingdom intact at his death, late in the reign of Augustus.[19]

Located where they were, as the last obstacle before Asia Minor to Romans advancing by land, most of the Thracian tribes chose co-operation. North of them lay dangerous peoples along the Danube, especially Dacians and Getae. Romans could not afford to deal with these until Thrace itself stood in their camp, and Thracians could benefit from Roman assistance.

Thracians chose as well to cultivate firm ties with other dynasties of the East. Their overall policies retained the nation's freedom until AD 46, with subsequent fighting for half a dozen years more. Personnel from the dynasty remained active much longer.[20]

In some five centuries of independence, Thrace gave a surprisingly good account of itself.

§ 15. Pontus

The final years of Mithradates Eupator did not lack drama, though his weakening position induced even Tigranes to take his part warily. Recalled from Syria to defend Armenia from Lucullus, Tigranes found that Mithradates had fled in 71 BC before the oncoming Romans and lingered now in Armenia. By late 70, all of Pontus south of the Black Sea lay in Roman hands. Tigranes granted his father-in-law a refuge but, according to a curious tale from antiquity, he refused for some eighteen months to receive Mithradates personally.[21]

The campaigns of Lucullus failed to break the two monarchs, but constituted the beginning of their end, and with them fell the empires each had constructed. Neither went quietly. Lucullus advanced through Pontus and, thanks to the Roman alliance with Ariobarzanes I of Cappadocia, crossed the Euphrates without hindrance into Sophene. Thus, Sophene passed, as claimed, from Tigranes to Lucullus, who entrusted its defence to Ariobarzanes. Advancing southeastward towards Tigranocerta, the fortress constructed by Tigranes, Lucullus defeated him, in 69 BC.[22]

This Roman victory carried important consequences for several dynasts. Antiochus I of Commagene soon sought alliance with Lucullus, since the claims of Tigranes to Osrhoene (as overlord) and to Cilicia Pedias (as its occupier) now collapsed, leaving Romans as the potential neighbours of Commagene (§ 19). Cappadocians breathed easier, since the depredations of Tigranes had been severe; unfortunately for them, they would be again. The Seleucids hoped to recover their throne, removed by Tigranes about 86 BC, but they were not to succeed for long (§ 21).

A remarkable document, composed years later by Sallust, purports to represent a letter written by Mithradates Eupator to Phraates III of Parthia after the Roman defeat of Tigranes. Its sentiments at least partly accord with those of Mithradates in 69/68. Tigranes no longer constitutes a rival to Parthian power; he will accept alliance on their terms. Romans have become the common enemy, opposing monarchs everywhere, forging a will in Asia, or frustrating legitimate succession in Bithynia. Ptolemy Auletes must purchase an uneasy peace with Rome. The Roman civil wars only postpone the coming trial of strength. Conquest of Tigranes and Mithradates will bring the theatre of war to Parthia's frontier. Timely alliance of these three kingdoms could deprive the Romans of alliances or supplies.[23]

An approach to Phraates by Mithradates and Tigranes jointly is attested elsewhere. Doubtless they used arguments such as these regarding Rome, though not Tigranes. But the careful Parthian saw no less danger to himself in them, and judged his potential antagonists of equal strength. He chose a type of neutrality, furnishing no aid and concluding a pact of 'friendship and alliance' with Lucullus to complement existing understandings with the two kings.[24]

Phraates correctly assessed the position. Contrary to the claim in Sallust's 'Letter of Mithridates' to him, the Roman force by no means lacked allies. Before the battle with Tigranes in 69, assistance came from the Galatians of Deiotarus and from Ariobarzanes I of Cappadocia. At the battle itself, Thracian allies distinguished themselves. An attempt by Lucullus to detach Zarbienus of Gordyene from Tigranes succeeded, though it later cost that king his life. After the victory, about the purported time of the letter, Lucullus received offers of alliance from others in the vicinity: 'Arabs' and Sophenians and former sub-kings under Tigranes. The Roman force did not lack friends, because the rule of Tigranes and Mithradates been locally perceived as harsh.[25]

These two carried on; in the winter of 69/68 they raised a force that did stop Lucullus short of Armenia, aided by the increasing reluctance of Roman troops to venture so far afield. Though losing Nisibis to him the following winter, Tigranes happily saw him withdraw in 67 to meet the challenge presented in Pontus by Mithradates, who had returned from Armenia late in 68. Mithradates easily raised from his subjects a force to augment that given him by Tigranes, since they preferred his rule to 'ill-treatment' by the Roman 'foreigner,' and since the claims of hereditary kingship yet carried weight in Pontus.[26]

The old king still knew how to fight. After a number of surprisingly effective engagements with Romans left behind to hold Pontus, and after some skilled sparring with Lucullus, Mithradates regained his kingdom by late in 67 and once more issued a royal coinage. Lucullus, victim of political opposition back in Rome, found himself stripped of his command and unable to inspire his army to take the field against Tigranes, who was approaching Cappadocia in the campaigning season of 67. The senatorial proposal to make Pontus a province had been premature; the conquests of Lucullus appeared to have evaporated.[27]

The situation, however, could not be so easily remedied by the two monarchs. Mithradates, now in his mid-sixties, was increasingly expected by his sons to stand aside. He required their support, on the Iranian system of using close relatives to govern portions of the wider state. Two of the sons were to fail him. For his part, Tigranes had suffered an irreversible blow to his prestige. The fearsome conqueror had lost a major battle and fled before the Romans, in 69. Defections among the kings who had comprised his empire deprived him of strategic territories like Commagene; Syria could no longer be considered his; Cilicia now lay out of reach, given the loss of these two regions. The first recourse for Tigranes became the invasion of Cappadocia.

Whatever Mithradates might have expected from this invasion by his son-in-law, he met with disappointment. Tigranes had to withdraw as three new elements came into conjunction: the replacement of Lucullus by Pompey; the assumption by the Parthian monarch, Phraates III, of an active international policy; and the entry of Tigranes's son into the conflict. An invasion of Armenia by these last two drew Tigranes homeward in 66 and left Mithradates facing Pompey, who must have helped arrange this diversion, and who concluded a separate peace with Tigranes.[28]

Mithradates found himself isolated. Pompey, possessing a degree of authority from Rome which Lucullus had lacked, moved decisively against the faltering old king. Perceiving the vanity of reliance on Tigranes, Mithradates had but two options: another attempt at alliance with Phraates III, or escape northward, whence he might return with renewed strength. He even contemplated making a circuit of the Black Sea and descending through Thrace to cut the Roman lines at the Bosporus. When Phraates III declined co-operation, having decided that Pompey offered him more than Pontus now could, and when a trial of arms proved inconclusive, the indomitable Mithradates turned north. An outlying possession of his beckoned, ruled by a faithless son, Machares.[29]

Machares had already seen his future as divorced from his father's, and had made a treaty of friendship and alliance with Lucullus. His holdings in the Crimea may have seemed sufficiently distant from Pontus that he could escape reprisal by Mithradates. He had reckoned without the will and the worsening circumstances of Mithradates, who had ascertained from Pompey that nothing short of capitulation could avert fighting, and who discovered that Tigranes now denied him both assistance and refuge. Tigranes had problems of his own with the younger Tigranes, supported by Phraates III, and rightly foresaw that Mithradates could bring only trouble. A disastrous defeat by Pompey reduced the Pontic army to a comparative handful, with which Mithradates was fortunate to reach Colchis late in 66 BC.[30]

To the end, Mithradates behaved like a traditional Eastern king, the only style he recognized. His son had disobeyed and must be removed; to effect this, Mithradates should form marriage and military alliances with other dynasts, using his large number of remaining offspring. To his credit, the effort met with surprising success. After spending the winter of 66/65 in Colchis, once ruled for him by another son, he recovered the Crimean portion of his kingdom, including Panticapaeum, and did away with Machares. Ample resources brought with him and what remained of his authority after some fifty-five years of rule let Mithradates raise an army and prepare for further battle.[31]

The ambitions of Mithradates now exceeded those of his subjects. To the earlier plan of descending through Thrace he added a bizarre scheme for attacking Italy itself. Pharnaces, his son, already designated heir, could brook no further military adventures for the kingdom. The army agreed and acclaimed him king. Mithradates at last recognized the inevitable and took his own life.[32]

Thus passed the man who had constituted the greatest threat to Roman ambitions in Asia Minor, where thrice he engaged Romans in serious wars and long delayed their advance across the vast territory between their province of Asia and the Euphrates. Their other antagonist here, Tigranes, proved by comparison an easy foe, trusting more to the remoteness of his kingdom and the ruggedness of its terrain than to his military prowess, despite his earlier success at empire-building. Watching these two, the third great power in the East, the Parthians, preferred to avert hostilities through diplomacy. Mithradates considered this method himself and did practise it on occasion, as in the case of Cappadocia when first made an issue by Romans.

Pompey twice declined peace offers and forced the outcome favourable to Rome. Though the nascent Roman Empire found rule by kings necessary for over a century more in Pontus, as it did in Commagene, parts of Cilicia, and for a lesser period in Cappadocia, from now on the relationship was usually one of mutual respect, not antagonism. The rejoicing in Rome at the death of Mithradates recognized the magnitude of the threat he had presented.[33]

Decisive action by Pompey forestalled further trouble. Having failed to overtake Mithradates as he fled northward in 65, Pompey campaigned in Pontus, Armenia, Iberia, and Colchis before turning to Syria and the troubled affairs of the Judaean monarchs (§ 22). At the news of Mithradates's death in 63, Pompey undertook a rapid march to the Black Sea, which he reached by autumn.[34]

Pharnaces II

News of this swift approach by his father's conqueror removed any tendency Pharnaces had towards indecision. Upon arriving at Amisus on the Pontic coast, Pompey discovered envoys from Pharnaces already awaiting him. They bore hostages, gifts, and the expected offer of surrender after defeat; for good measure they brought the body of Mithradates. Pharnaces requested the usual reward for such obeisance: recognition as king in succession to his father, and alliance with Rome. Pompey recognized his rule in Bosporus but not Pontus, which he continued to pacify during the remainder of 63 and early in 62. He also enrolled Pharnaces among the formal friends and allies of Rome. Five other sons of Eupator were led in Pompey's triumph.[35]

By international norms, Rome could now take title to the Pontic remainder of the kingdom of Mithradates. Holding it would be another matter, as would determination of boundaries. After due deliberation these were fixed to locate the new province of Pontus along the coast east of Bithynia and north of Paphlagonia. Still under royal rule in the vicinity were Paphlagonia, Galatia, Cappadocia, and Armenia Minor, with Commagene and Armenia beyond. A large portion of the former Kingdom of Pontus also lay outside the new province and for another 120 years was to be ruled by kings, though conflict between Pharnaces and Rome beset the initial years of this period.[36]

Pontus presented unusual problems to Roman organization, since its mixture of royal domains, sacred precincts like Comana, independent Greek cities on the coast, and an almost totally rural interior proved intractable to any but dynastic rule. Pompey recognized this by utilizing neighbouring dynasts, such as Deiotarus, to handle the inland tribes, and leaving Paphlagonia to native kings. Some cities went to dynastic control as well. Later, Antony returned to the system of royal control for virtually the entire kingdom.[37]

The reign of Pharnaces II proved predictably expansive. His recognition as king by Pompey rested on his legitimate succession to Mithradates Eupator, but those who had favoured his father's rule could hardly forget the conspiracy that marked its end. Roman support for him seemed to them 'a reward for murder,' in Dio's phrase, and his use of the title *Philoromaios* must have exacerbated internal discontent. At the same time, Roman favour brought little in the way of assistance. The ancestral kingdom lay divided among numerous occupiers or organizers of the new Roman province: Attalus and Pylaemenes of Paphlagonia; Deiotarus of Galatia; priest-rulers like Archelaus, son of Eupator's renegade general; Aristarchus in Colchis. Behind the barrier constituted by these, let Pharnaces hold the Bosporus if he could; any wider sphere of ambition seemed precluded.[38]

Pharnaces saw things otherwise. The ruler of Phanagoria, Castor, had revolted against his father and in return received from Pompey the title 'friend of the Romans.' Pharnaces decided to recover control of this city, despite the risk, and did. An expansion of his overlordship among the tribes of the Maeotic coast and the southern reaches of Scythia brought him tribute and a self-appointed position as 'Great King of Kings.' A new Pontic threat had begun.[39]

The date of the first encroachments by Pharnaces II on the territories now claimed by Rome cannot be recovered. Certainly he foresaw the consequences of the Roman civil wars and determined to take advantage of them. He apparently entered the field as early as 50 or 49, with hostilities in Colchis, on his way south, and destruction levels traceable even today. By the fall of 48, after Pharsalus, he can be described as 'in Pontus.' Desperate Pompeians sent to him there asking that he join the war effort against Caesar, an appeal that Pharnaces later claimed he declined; nor did he assist Caesar as others nearby did. He also gained, at the expense of Deiotarus and Ariobarzanes, portions of 'Armenia' (i.e., Armenia Minor: Tigranes would not be so easy a foe) and Cappadocia, as well as Pontic cities governed from Bithynia, including part of Bithynia itself. These two kings, steadfast allies of Rome, cried out for assistance. Caesar's legate in Asia, Cn. Domitius Calvinus, responded by raising what forces he could spare from those levied for the Alexandrian War and advanced with them on Pontus.[40]

The Roman force seemed hardly adequate to the task. Only one legion could be spared, and two more – trained in the Roman manner – were supplied by Deiotarus, with cavalry from him and from Ariobarzanes. The mobilizations effected on Caesar's behalf by Mithradates of Pergamon, a relative of Pharnaces II but not well disposed to him, had transferred to Egypt much of the dynastic manpower otherwise available. This force must have been on its way now, since it arrived in time for the battle, whereas one legion sent by Calvinus did not. The small force remaining in Pontus had to meet the seasoned army of Pharnaces without much hope of reinforcements.[41]

Pharnaces offered compromise, withdrawing from Cappadocia but arguing that Armenia Minor belonged to him by right, as part of his father's dominions; he awaited a decision by Caesar himself. Calvinus replied that no legal distinction existed between the two occupations; nothing remained for Caesar to decide. Calvinus rejected further representations, maintaining that Rome had a duty to recover kingdoms taken from allies (Deiotarus, in this case). The battle ensued near Nicopolis, resulting in a severe Roman defeat. Once more Pontus lay open to a king from the house of Mithradates Eupator.[42]

For some six months, Pharnaces tried ruthlessly to raise funds and use them to recover full control of Pontus, with eventual success. In the spring of 47, Caesar resolved to meet this challenge, having assured the position of Cleopatra and Ptolemy XIV, her brother. Moving northward, he achieved or reaffirmed alliance with several kings: Antiochus I of Commagene; Iamblichus I of Emesa, who had assisted him in Egypt; Tarcondimotus I of Cilicia; Ariobarzanes III of Cappadocia and his restless brother, the later King Ariarathes X; and Deiotarus I of Galatia. He removed Archelaus from the priesthood at Pontic Comana; Archelaus was the son of the late husband of Queen Berenice IV of Egypt and father of the later King of Cappadocia. Having settled relations with all these kingdoms, Caesar could securely advance against Pharnaces II, waiting watchfully in Pontus.[43]

Caesar accorded Pharnaces the respect due an antagonist who had defeated a Roman army (at Nicopolis). Safely in Italy, Cicero could indulge in feigned ignorance: 'Who would think that this Pharnaces, whoever he is, could bring terror to Asia?' At least three exchanges of envoys settled the terms on which Pharnaces might avoid battle, since as a 'foreign king' he had invaded territory of the Romans or their allies. He must make restitution; pay over the sums that Roman conquerors usually receive from their new 'friends'; withdraw from Pontus. Pharnaces ostensibly acceded, doubtless expecting Caesar to hurry on to Rome and leave him free for further advances in Pontus. For his part, Pharnaces could no longer count on support from his holdings in Bosporus: Asander, who ruled there for him, had already begun a revolt that proved fatal to Pharnaces. On both sides, therefore, existed reason to hasten a resolution. Caesar decided to accomplish it by battle.[44]

Pharnaces took his stand at Zela, where Eupator in 67 had defeated Triarius, lieutenant of Lucullus. The rapidity of attack (*Caesarina celeritas*) characteristic of Caesar brought him promptly to Zela. Pharnaces underestimated the Roman force, having defeated one, and misjudged the terrain. His advance uphill against Caesar brought predictable disaster. As Caesar soon announced, he had come, seen, and conquered.[45]

Pharnaces escaped to the sea and thence to his kingdom in Bosporus, but the treacherous Asander fought and killed him there. What had seemed to many in the East a noble dream pursued by his father and handed on to him now evaporated. For the second time a king of Pontus defeated by Romans had died after domestic betrayal. Hereditary kings ruled in Bosporus for centuries more, but Pontus stood on the verge now of a new dynasty, apparently unrelated to the old. Before this occurred, one more king of Pontus (Darius) emerged from the line of Mithradates. Bosporus made Mithradates's granddaughter its queen (Dynamis). The 'King Mithradates Philopator and Philadelphos, son of Mithradates' known from an inscription in Rome is probably not another son of Eupator, as Mommsen thought, but rather Mithradates V, son of Mithradates IV and father of Eupator.[46]

Mithradates of Pergamon

After Zela and before the rule of Darius, Caesar's friend Mithradates found further scope for his ambition. He had assisted Caesar in Egypt with a strong allied force gathered through his own prestige in Asia Minor. His benefactions to his native city won him respect there, as inscriptions attest, and the title of 'New Founder.' He had accompanied Caesar to Pontus and now received recognition fitting his 'royal birth and upbringing' – the kingship of Bosporus and rule in one of the Galatian tetrarchies previously occupied by Deiotarus. This last he took up 'by right of descent and relationship' through his father, who was connected to the Galatian tetrarchs. Bosporus came to him partly through his mother, said to have been a concubine of Eupator, by whom he was raised. He has even been thought a bastard son of Eupator, an ancient view linking him with the Pontic line.[47]

For his task in Bosporus, Mithradates of Pergamon received from Caesar recognition as king and encouragement to undertake war against Asander, who had rather expected such honour himself as reward for despatching Caesar's enemy Pharnaces. Caesar could take no chances of this usurper building up personal power among the Greek cities and Iranian tribes of the Bosporus. Better to install the tried-and-true Mithradates, with his claim to birth in the house of Eupator, even if through a concubine. The main object of the exercise lay in no doubt: 'by the interposition of a most friendly king he [Caesar] secured the provinces of the Roman people from barbarian and hostile kings.' This served as well to block the rise of any sons of Pharnaces, always a danger given the prestige in Bosporus of the house of Eupator. It also may have dealt another blow to the struggling Colchians, though the worst destruction levels there probably date to 50 or 49. Finally, securing Bosporus in reliable hands would check the eastward expansion of Thrace and, it was said, give Caesar a strategic ally for his campaign against the Getae under Burebistas, and then against Parthia. This careful planning came to nought when Asander defeated Mithradates and continued his own rule over Bosporus.[48]

Asander and Dynamis

This blow to the Romans' plans for Bosporus proved only temporary, for Asander realized the value of their support and sought it. Eventually Rome recognized him as king, after a brief period in which he used the titles *archon* and 'ethnarch.' In a reign lasting until about 27 BC and a life that endured till age ninety-three, Asander came to enjoy the title 'Great King of Kings,' as Pharnaces had, and employed the epithet *Philoromaios*, as Pharnaces had not. The good relations his successors had with Rome probably began with him. The stable kingdom ruling Bosporus for centuries to come developed from his foundations.[49]

Essential to this ranked descent from Mithradates Eupator. Asander arranged this for *his* descendants by marrying Dynamis, whose inscriptions include one honouring her as 'Queen Dynamis, daughter of Great King Pharnaces, the son of King of Kings Mithradates Eupator' – impressive credentials for Bosporus. This remarkable woman, who later married King Polemo and helped re-establish unified rule over Pontus and Bosporus, cultivated special ties with Augustus and Livia, and at one point ruled Bosporus alone. She also ruled alongside one Scribonius, whose adoption of a Roman name failed to save him from the wrath of the Bosporans. In a career lying outside the scope of this study, she completed her husband's work of establishing Bosporus on firm new foundations, linked as well to the dynasty of Thrace.[50]

Dynamis and Asander may have borne progeny who governed Bosporus, if they produced King Aspurgus, who ruled beginning late in the reign of Augustus. Aspurgus proved able to exercise and transmit authority in Bosporus. His marriage to Gepaepyris, daughter of Cotys VIII of Thrace and Antonia Tryphaena of Pontus (the daughter of King Polemo I), produced a royal line that ruled Bosporus until at least the late third century.[51]

Darius

After removal of Pharnaces and then Mithradates of Pergamon, the core of the Pontic kingdom lacked a king. Sons and daughters of Pharnaces – grandchildren of Mithradates Eupator – remained available. Caesar had shown some disposition to remove territory from Rome's formerly reliable ally Deiotarus, who might otherwise have resumed his strong position on the borders of Pontus. The portion of Galatia granted Mithradates of Pergamon came available after his defeat in the Bosporus. On several counts, some restoration of the house of Mithradates Eupator became advisable, so about 39 BC a grandson of his (Darius) acceded as King of Pontus. In addition, a son of Pharnaces soon emerged with the startling name Arsaces (the Parthian royal name).

Caesar had previously passed over claimants from the family of Eupator, hoping that Mithradates of Pergamon and Deiotarus could keep the peace. But defeat of Mithradates and the death, about 40 BC, of both Deiotarus of Galatia and Attalus of Paphlagonia left a dearth of leadership in these important regions. In Galatia and a portion of Paphlagonia, this was filled by Castor, the successor of Deiotarus. Pontus once more received a king, through Antony's recognition of Darius, son of Pharnaces. Important cities or regions previously freed by Pompey or Caesar came again under royal control, perhaps now; these included Amisus, Phazemonitis, Amaseia, and others.[52]

The return of Pontus to a king reversed the arrangements of Pompey. Only after Actium did a slow return to free status begin for some cities; the kingdom itself remained under the house of Polemo I. Despite Roman support, the reign of Darius may not have fostered pleasant memories: the later dynastic era of Pythodoris, Polemo's Queen, began in 47 BC, ignoring the action of Antony in returning Pontus to this descendant of Mithradates Eupator. In any case, the reign of Darius appears short, probably from 39 to 37 BC. Perhaps it was terminated by Polemo I.[53]

Arsaces

One final Mithradatic interlude seems to have played itself out. Suddenly another son of Pharnaces appeared, bearing the Parthian dynastic name Arsaces, attempting to rule Phazemonitis without external recognition. He was dislodged by Polemo I and by Lycomedes, presumably the man who had been Caesar's appointee as priest of Comana, termed a 'king' by Strabo. This incident fell in 37 or early 36. It constitutes the last direct attempt at rule in Pontus by the descendants of Mithradates, excepting only the joint activity of Dynamis, his granddaughter, as Queen of both Bosporus and Pontus when married to Polemo I.[54]

Polemo I

The refoundation of the Kingdom of Pontus took a strange form. Antony's attempt to order the East along traditional lines but also establish personal power there could produce startling results. When Archelaus assumed the throne of Cappadocia (§ 17), this could not strictly be justified on grounds of royal descent; nor could the accession of Herod in Judaea (§ 22). Darius in Pontus, Amyntas in Pisidia (§ 16), and others did descend indisputably from kings. Suddenly in 37 on the throne of Pontus appeared a king evidently unconnected with the family of Mithradates Eupator. He enjoyed no claim to ancient descent from the Achaemenid Darius the Great, unlike the dynasty that now passed after purportedly ruling Pontus for five hundred years. In fact, the new king bore no discernible connection with royalty anywhere. His father was a local orator and aristocrat in Laodicea on the Lycus, a certain Zeno, who distinguished himself during the Parthian attack of 40 BC (§ 26), but could pass no title to his son. Yet the son, Polemo, appears 'holding' Iconium in Lycaonia, probably held part of Isauria (transferred to Amyntas in 36 BC), is attested as ruling 'parts of Cilicia' -- probably nearby Tracheia – with the royal title, was 'considered worthy of a kingdom,' and during Antony's campaign of 36 participated as 'King of Pontus.'[55]

Barring discovery of an unsuspected link between the family of Zeno and Eastern royalty, Polemo stands out as the main exception to the dictum that kings there required birth into the 'dynastic aristocracy.' Even the suspect cases – Lycomedes of Comana, Archelaus of Cappadocia, Mithradates of Pergamon, Herod of Judaea – claimed previous connection with royalty or government before recognition as king. Deiotarus of Galatia held a quasi-royal position (tetrarch) in Galatia and could convert into a king. Asander in Bosporus fought his way to royal recognition, and married Queen Dynamis for good measure. Tarcondimotus of Cilicia had only local standing through his father and his rule remained local, though distinguished by the royal title. The kings of Emesa began as phylarchs, a locally equivalent title.

Only with Polemo does the view hold that an outside power could 'make' kings in the East from non-royal stock. Later, Rome could transfer them about, as with Zeno-Artaxias in Armenia, who succeeded thanks in part to his royal connections, or Tigranes V and VI, who failed there despite theirs. Exceptionally vigorous monarchs like Deiotarus or, under the empire, Polemo II, Antiochus IV of Commagene, Archelaus I of Cappadocia, Sohaemus of Emesa, and others might exercise rule in regions distant from their own, but their royal credentials admitted no question. Polemo remains a puzzle.[56]

Once appointed, however, he moved with vigour into his new role. Disposing of any threat by the remaining kings descended from Eupator – Darius and Arsaces – he achieved sufficient control of Pontus to let him assist Antony in the Parthian campaign. He accomplished little there and even fell captive to the forces which were fighting for Artavasdes I of Atropatene and Phraates IV of Parthia. A ransom returned him, wiser, home.[57]

Whether or not Polemo retained responsibilities in Cilicia, the rule of Pontus led him eastward and northward; he even held Colchis. He continued his services to Antony, who used Polemo as an emissary to Artavasdes, with whom Antony later attempted a marriage alliance. Antony also recognized Polemo as king in Armenia Minor, which left him facing a potential antagonist in the Armenian king, with a further problem presented by the kingdom of Bosporus. Polemo later solved that by marrying its queen, Dynamis, and occupying the kingdom.[58]

Though launched upon his career by Antony and by his own previous valour, Polemo understood the precarious position of his ally. He showed Antony honour and loyalty while these remained appropriate, securing the northeastern mountain passes of Asia Minor for the ambitious plans laid by the Roman and his Egyptian partner. Caesarion was to be 'King of Kings' and one of those sub-kings was to be Polemo. This plan extended the original motives of Antony in recognizing him king in Pontus despite no previous connections there: to offset the family of Eupator and to ensure that Polemo had no basis of authority except through Antony himself. Another motive was financial: the vigorous king paid the tribute Antony required of him, an irregularity characteristic of the triumvir's relations with his royal 'appointees.' Polemo became the only ally giving noteworthy service on the Parthian campaign, and continuing in ways large and small to acknowledge his debt to Antony, perhaps even with an unusual coinage naming the triumvir on its reverse.[59]

This loyalty did not extend to folly. As the fortunes of Antony waned, Polemo thought long and hard. His kingship had succeeded, but must have seemed tenuous locally, dependent on Polemo's ability to withstand such potential antagonists as Artaxias II in Armenia, an implacable foe of Antony after his father, Artavasdes II, was transported in 34 BC to Alexandria, whence he never returned. The presence of Queen Dynamis in Bosporus, with legitimate claims to the throne of Pontus, could not have reassured Polemo, before he married her.

When Actium came in 31, Polemo neither failed nor entirely met the highest test of adherence to Antony. Many kings attended in person, but 'from Pontus, Polemo sent an army.' A monarch unafraid before the Parthians would not hesitate to present himself at Actium unless he suspected the outcome; no known threat kept him in Pontus.[60]

Polemo remained on his throne after Actium. No other contender for control of Pontus could present the advantages for Romans that Polemo could; his vigour assured a barrier to Armenian movements westward, and a check on Parthian advances into Asia Minor. Augustus recognized his kingship and in 26 BC he formally became a 'friend and ally' of Rome. His marriage with Dynamis and then with Pythodoris, reputed a granddaughter of Antony and daughter of an aristocrat in Tralles, supplied Polemo and his family with credentials for another century of rule after Actium. Among those tracing their lineage to Polemo I were to be Queen Antonia Tryphaena of Thrace; King Rhoemetalces III of Thrace; King Zeno-Artaxias of Armenia; King Polemo II of Cilicia and Pontus; King Cotys IX of Armenia Minor; and Queen Gepaepyris of Bosporus. The new dynasty of Pontus creditably succeeded the old.[61]

§ 16. Galatia

The period of Mithradatic wars and Roman civil wars forced major changes in Galatia. Much of the conflict with Mithradates occurred in the neighbourhood of Galatia, and some of it inside. The stress of such major upheavals proved too great for the old Galatian system of tetrarchies and tribes. Before 40 BC, it had largely broken down and been replaced by kingship, the more normal pattern for Asia Minor. This came under challenge and for a time yielded not one king but two. Resolution of the impasse led by the time of Actium to a single monarch again.

Deiotarus I and Brogitarus

Deiotarus I proved a reliable Roman ally during the Mithradatic campaigns of Lucullus and Pompey, just as he had earlier (§ 4). The thirty thousand Galatians who accompanied Lucullus into Pontus late in the summer of 72 must have been gathered through the efforts of Deiotarus, and they performed well. The sources often mention both infantry and cavalry during the campaign as it moved towards Armenia.[62]

After the overthrow of Mithradates Eupator, Pompey sought to stabilize the regions previously at issue. Besides his short-lived conversion of Pontus into a province, he dealt with Armenia Minor (possibly recognizing Deiotarus there), Galatia, and Paphlagonia. He also recognized within Colchis a king ready to meet future incursions from the ruler of the Bosporus, currently Pharnaces, son of Eupator.

On dynastic grounds, all this proved straightforward. The Galatians already had an organization, though too complex to permit administration on usual Eastern lines. With the eager co-operation of Deiotarus, this system of a dozen local rulers now became a parallel system of three tribal chiefs, each replacing the original four tetrarchs of that tribe. Deiotarus ruled the Tolistobogii; Brogitarus, husband of a daughter of Deiotarus, ruled the Trocmi; Castor Tarcondarius, husband of another, ruled the Tectosages. In addition, Deiotarus received the rich Gazelonitis, Pharnacia, and Trapezusia, later with Armenia Minor, a dangerous region if not in reliable hands. Two princes, perhaps of Bithynian ancestry, with dynastic claims to Paphlagonia, divided that country with Pompey's recognition. Colchis, ruled by Aristarchus, prepared to delay the southward advance of Pharnaces, if and when it came.[63]

These arrangements by Pompey had to be ratified in Rome; in Galatia, they must be maintained by force. A segment of the population hardly welcomed foreign rearticulation of their long-standing form of government, and Rome would be of little assistance against these people as it approached its own civil war. Deiotarus maintained the new position with such severity that numerous Galatians fled him. Perhaps to strengthen his hand, the Roman Senate in 59 recognized him as king, further outraging some Galatians. To compound the problem, an irregular recognition of Brogitarus too as king followed in 58 BC.[64]

Deiotarus regarded his sons-in-law more as rivals than colleagues. Brogitarus had a sister named Adobogiona, who was the mother of Mithradates of Pergamon. This branch of the family could indeed threaten the position of Deiotarus, as when Caesar later removed part of his holdings in favour of Mithradates. With Brogitarus also termed 'king' and *Philo-*

romaios, the impediment to Deiotarus stood clear for Galatians to see. The question 'King of *what*?' did not take long to arise, since the old tetrarchal tribes required no king. Were there to be a monarch, he should be king of Galatia, and there should be only one.[65]

This rivalry lasted at least six years; the coinage of Brogitarus mounts that high. He held eastern Galatia and Armenia Minor, either removed from the control of Deiotarus or not yet under him. In addition, Brogitarus held the strategic Mithradation; at least by 56 he controlled the sanctuary at Pessinus, provoking a denunciation by Cicero, who favoured Deiotarus. Perhaps it was Brogitarus who ordered a century-old letter from the Attalid King to the priest at Pessinus recopied, and set up there now to remind others of that priesthood's esteemed position. How long after 53 he reigned or even survived cannot be determined. When Caesar arrived in 47, Deiotarus controlled 'nearly all' of Galatia, part of which he had taken by force 'a few years before.' He also 'without doubt' had been recognized by the Senate as King of Armenia Minor. If Brogitarus remained among the 'other tetrarchs' still in place by 47, his power must have been much eroded.[66]

Deiotarus and Rome

During Cicero's governorship of Cilicia, Deiotarus proved a crucial ally. Cicero found him a 'most faithful king and one most friendly to our republic' when the Parthians invaded in 51. Whether Brogitarus still lived or not, Deiotarus seems the only tetrarch to have responded with a considerable force, at one point doubling the troops available to Cicero. He used the title *Philoromaios* with full intentions of carrying out its implications.[67]

When the Roman civil war broke out in 49, Deiotarus had a dangerous choice to make. Both Pompey and Caesar could claim his allegiance. Pompey had supported him as tetrarch, and Caesar had done him services in 59 when consul: these had to do with territorial accessions and perhaps the kingship. By this time, Deiotarus had through his own efforts assumed a paramount position in Galatia – against local custom, his peers claimed – and had added to his holdings a portion of Armenia. He had much to protect. Like his fellow tetrarchs he mistakenly assumed that Pompey's would be the cause to support. Despite such advanced age that he required assistance to mount his horse, Deiotarus led his cavalry personally into battle at Pharsalus.[68]

The defeat of Pompey had serious consequences for Deiotarus. Pharnaces took advantage of the distractions to occupy Colchis. 'Since Deiotarus was away,' he also laid claim to Cappadocia and Armenia, including Armenia Minor, to which he asserted the right of succession. Caesar did not regard Deiotarus with high favour after Pharsalus, though his policy, of necessity, was to recognize the many kings who had responded loyally to the call of Pompey. Before dealing with Deiotarus, Caesar transferred to Ariobarzanes III of Cappadocia a part of Armenia Minor held until 48 by Deiotarus. After the defeat of Pharnaces in 47, a part went to Deiotarus, but Ariobarzanes retained a part too, in each case for ease of defence. About this time Cicero suspected that Caesar's motivation in any curtailments was anger at the support Deiotarus gave Pompey.[69]

Deiotarus had too firm a hold on Galatia and too well-connected a family of tetrarchs, princesses, and potential kings to be dismissed lightly, especially given his ties to Caesar's ally Mithradates of Pergamon. There was also in 48 a need to utilize his strength in the attempt to repulse Pharnaces at the battle of Nicopolis. Deiotarus served well and suffered losses so severe that two legions that he led, trained on the Roman model, retained only enough manpower for one. Deiotarus did send a body of cavalry – allegedly of inferior quality – to Caesar's aid in Alexandria. He included considerable funds, always a prime concern of Roman leaders when in the East.[70]

As Caesar approached Galatia in 47, Deiotarus went out to meet him, uneasy about previous support for Pompey and about complaints of Galatians regarding his anomalous powers. He defended his actions in the civil war by pointing out that he could not act as a judge between two contending Romans. Caesar responded that his own services to Deiotarus during his consulship in 59 should have counted for more and accused Deiotarus of making an unwise choice. However, a number of considerations disposed him to renew the alliance: benefactions to him by Deiotarus; old ties of friendship and hospitality; the high position and advanced age of Deiotarus; support for him by his wide circle of friends. An unstated but major consideration remained the power and wealth of the King.[71]

With amicable relations ostensibly re-established, Deiotarus helped fight Pharnaces II at Zela. Caesar enjoyed his hospitality, lodging in fortresses or palaces belonging to him. This did not persuade Caesar to recognize as much territory for Deiotarus as the King wished. Mithradates of Pergamon assumed, in addition to the Bosporan kingdom, a tetrarchy occupied previously by Deiotarus, doubtless that of the Trocmi, once under Brogitarus. In addition, 'part of Armenia' went to Ariobarzanes III of Cappadocia, probably Armenia Minor, despite the Roman Senate's former recognition of Deiotarus as its king.[72]

After a typical Roman sojourn in the East, seeing him hurry from Egypt through the Levant and into Asia Minor for battle, Caesar now departed in haste for Rome, leaving a long series of semi-solutions to dynastic problems, with further fighting in their train. In Egypt, Judaea, and Bosporus rivalries continued, the one in Bosporus killing Caesar's protégé Mithradates of

Pergamon. This removed a rival for Deiotarus but did not as yet expand his control of Galatia to the extent known after Caesar's death, for the tetrarchy of the Trocmi remained vacant after Mithradates died.[73]

Deiotarus had more serious problems than impediments to his territorial ambitions. Romans appreciated his power among the Galatians, but viewed with concern the continuing opposition he faced there. Before Caesar left Asia Minor, objections arose to the new arrangements in Galatia. Castor Tarcondarius, son-in-law of Deiotarus, stood to lose heavily, with his rule reduced to a portion of the tetrarchy of the Tectosages. At Nicaea in Bithynia, Marcus Brutus delivered a spirited defence of Deiotarus, but Caesar remained dubious and even hostile. A later embassy from Deiotarus regarding arrangements in Galatia, probably after the death of Mithradates of Pergamon, reached Caesar in Spain but received no decision beyond vague reassurance. Upon Caesar's return to Rome other Galatian envoys waited to protest the activities of the old king, and some came as well from him.[74]

In 45 occurred what Cicero terms an affair so bizarre that its like had never been heard of in Rome. A deputation led by Castor II, son of Castor Tarcondarius, accused Deiotarus of having plotted against Caesar's life after Zela, when the Roman victor lodged with him in Galatia. An extraordinary 'trial' of this charge occurred in Caesar's private house. Cicero, who described himself as a former guest of Deiotarus and as a friend, and who had even lodged his own son and nephew with Deiotarus while governor of Cilicia, defended the king in a speech still extant.[75]

Not surprisingly, the speech lauds Deiotarus for his many kingly virtues, known to the Roman people since his youth and proved on many campaigns undertaken as an ally. It well demonstrates the preposterousness of the charge, and of the 'accidental' collapse of the supposed plot. It points out the reasons for Deiotarus having supported Pompey in the confusion attending Roman civil strife. It glosses over the one motive Deiotarus would have had for opposition to Caesar in 47: the transfer of territories to other kings or tetrarchs.

Thanks to support from Brutus and the presence of other influential Romans who had dealt with Deiotarus, such as Cn. Domitius Calvinus, no judgment against the king occurred now. Caesar had perhaps arranged the affair as a means of curbing the aspirations of Deiotarus and assuring either his reliability or his removal when the projected Parthian campaign would come his way. Caesar did not live to use this device, but it had been readied.[76]

Once Caesar was removed, Deiotarus decided that the turmoil in Rome freed him for sole kingship in Galatia. Before this could be accomplished, other claimants had to be dislodged. Mithradates of Pergamon was no more, but there still remained Deiotarus Philopator, the son of Deiotarus; Castor

Tarcondarius, tetrarch of the Tectosages; and Castor II. Philopator had received Roman recognition as king in 51 and had been seen as the logical successor of Deiotarus. But when the battle of Philippi was fought in 42, the troops of Deiotarus were not led by his son, and no further mention of him occurs. From an inscription in his name, apparently an epitaph, it can be inferred that he died about 43. He is called 'king' as well as tetrarch of the Tolistobogii and Trocmi, titles also given to his father in the text. The inference would be that Castor Tarcondarius lived on as tetrarch of the Tectosages. Deiotarus later attended to that difficulty by murdering this son-in-law and his own daughter in their fortress. Castor Tarcondarius had known and approved the action of his son (Castor II) against Deiotarus before Caesar in 45; as affairs in Galatia moved increasingly away from the old traditions, the murder of a fellow tetrarch now became a matter of policy.[77]

Further rivalry always threatened at Pessinus, southwest of Gordion and 'the greatest emporium' of this part of Asia Minor. The priests here were virtual 'rulers' (*dynastai*), like their analogues at Comana in Cappadocia and Pontus (where one Galatian prince later served). Interestingly, an Attalid inscription of about 159 BC was recopied in the late first century BC and erected at Pessinus, perhaps to reassert the ancient prerogatives of this priesthood.

Deiotarus had lodged his hopes of a personal dynasty mainly in his son, whom he betrothed to a daughter of King Artavasdes II of Armenia in 50 BC, a match with important implications if it did occur, and a reason for Caesar's doubts about the old king. In 43, there remained only Deiotarus as the paramount ruler in Galatia. Castor II, son of the murdered Tarcondarius, survived, but his enmity and the allegation that his family had not sprung from tetrarchal origins prevented him as yet from assuming a full place in Galatia.[78]

Galatians could judge no better than others which side would prevail in the latest Roman civil war, but Deiotarus had enough experience not to wait on events. In April 44 he had through a timely bribe already secured Antony's recognition of his kingship. In 43, he can be detected on the side of L. Tillius Cimber, one of the murderers of Caesar, in a successful battle against the Caesarian Dolabella. Though first refusing assistance to Cassius, he joined the allies of Brutus in 42. He sent forces to Philippi under Amyntas, but by prior arrangement they transferred to Octavian and Antony after the first battle.[79]

No datable traces of the old Galatian remain after these notices regarding Philippi, though a coin of his commemorating a victory and honouring Antony's wife, Fulvia, appeared after the battle. Both Attalus, King of

Paphlagonia since Pompey's settlement, and Deiotarus 'had died in Galatia' by 40 BC. The succession passed to 'a certain Castor [II]' then.[80]

In one generation, the king had brought Galatia from a tribal society to a kingdom. His name could still be taken with pride by a descendant in the second century after Christ. In his long reign he dealt closely with prominent Roman generals or statesmen – Pompey, Cato, Cicero, Caesar, Brutus, Antony. He acted in concert with, or sometimes in opposition to, fellow dynasts throughout the East such as Ariobarzanes III of Cappadocia, Antiochus I of Commagene, Tarcondimotus I of Cilicia, and Iamblichus I of Emesa. He betrothed his son to the Armenian daughter of Artavasdes II, and consolidated the Galatian families of tetrarchs through intermarriage with his own relatives. His support against Mithradates Eupator and Pharnaces II helped transform the East during a critical period in its evolution, and he led the dynasts' resistance to the Parthian invasion of 51 BC. He also maintained the East's traditional link with Athens. A legacy of his strong military organization of Galatians along Roman military lines remained for some 175 years, the *Legio XXII Deiotariana*, its activity clearly traceable in papyri and inscriptions.[81]

Castor II

By 40 BC, only Castor and his sons remained of the major figures connected with Galatia in the generation now past: Deiotarus I; Deiotarus Philopator, his son; Brogitarus; Mithradates of Pergamon; Castor Tarcondarius; and Domnilaus, his brother (who fought and probably fell at Pharsalus). These men were now gone, but a son of Domnilaus, Adiatorix, lived on to rule Heraclea Pontica, and his son, Dytcutus, became the priest at Pontic Comana (see below).

Castor succeeded to the holdings of Deiotarus, and to a portion of those in Paphlagonia previously ruled by Attalus. This solved the immediate problem of a ruler here, about the time Antony recognized Darius, son of Pharnaces, in a portion of Pontus (§ 15), and soon others elsewhere. Castor may have been at hand in Rome, since his presence in any part of Galatia before Deiotarus died would have been unlikely, given that pugnacious monarch's power to take revenge for Castor's accusation of him to Caesar in 45. The murder of his father and mother by Deiotarus constituted reminder enough of the danger.[82]

Once installed in Galatia and recognized by the Roman Senate, Castor II ruled only four years. By 36 BC we find Antony recognizing Amyntas as ruler of Galatia, and a portion of Paphlagonia going to Deiotarus IV Philadelphos, son of Castor. Unless Castor died young from an unrecorded mischance, this action of Antony's constituted deposition. It could have sprung from several considerations, among them Castor's previous friendship with Caesar and his failure to offer noteworthy resistance to the Parthians under Labienus during their invasion of 41/40, if his succession had occurred by then. In the royal appointments of 39 BC, Antony had recognized, for parts of Cilicia and Lycaonia, King Polemo, son of a hero of the Parthian raids and himself active against them (§ 15). Antony had put in other hands portions of the former holdings of Deiotarus, such as parts of the Pontic coast and Gazelonitis now under Darius, son of Pharnaces. Other new dynasts arose that year under Antony's aegis: Archelaus in Cappadocia (§ 17); Herod, recognized the year before for Judaea (§ 22); Amyntas – later King of Galatia – in Pisidia. All of these paid large sums for their positions. All except Darius shared the two characteristics of proven ability and absence of direct hereditary claim to their new kingdoms. Archelaus and Herod (after his marriage in 37 BC) could boast indirect royal ties of birth or marriage; Amyntas and Polemo apparently had none. All four relied in varying degrees on Antony's support against domestic resistance, which assured him of their loyalty for the attack on Parthia. In 37/36, Antony further consolidated his allies by replacing Darius with Polemo and Castor with Amyntas, in each case removing an heir to the throne in favour of an unrelated newcomer.[83]

Deiotarus Philadelphos and Deiotarus Philopator

The removal of Castor II left in Galatia only his sons as legitimate descendants of the tetrarchs. From Strabo we know that Castor II had a son named Deiotarus who ruled Paphlagonia, including Gangra. He was to be its last ruler, with a new era from 6/5 BC presumably signalling the advent of Roman control. His coinage reveals the royal title – 'King Deiotarus Philadelphos' – and the name, presumably, of his mother, 'Queen Adobogiona'; he also may have had a royal brother, 'King Deiotarus Philopator.' The suggestion that Philopator served as co-regent with Castor II or now with Philadelphos cannot be demonstrated. If yet another 'King Deiotarus' did exist in Galatia, he probably ruled over part of Paphlagonia under the regency of his mother and was then followed by his brother.[84]

Philadelphos ruled Paphlagonia for some thirty years, with Amyntas now king in Galatia. Little trace remains of his reign beyond its success in retaining the kingdom. At Actium, he brought a contingent in person to support Antony but made a timely transfer to the side of Octavian, thus preserving his kingdom another quarter of a century. At his death or removal in 6/5 BC, he was the last reigning member of the Galatian tetrarchal and royal lines.[85]

Domnilaus, Adiatorix, Dyteutus

Another branch of the tetrarchal lines requires brief consideration here. Castor Tarcondarius, tetrarch of the Tectosages, had a brother at the battle of Pharsalus, a certain Domnilaus. He is presumably the 'tetrarch of the Galatians' mentioned by Strabo. He cannot be seen as a successor of Brogitarus, but rather as an associate in the tetrarchy of the Tectosages with Castor Tarcondarius, a partial return to the Galatian system in use before Pompey's intervention. The two fought at Pharsalus on the side of Pompey, Domnilaus in person and Castor represented by his son, Castor II. Domnilaus may have died there, for no further mention of him occurs. Presumably his territory went to Deiotarus, described a year later as holding virtually all of Galatia.[86]

Domnilaus left a son named Adiatorix. The 'other tetrarchs' who had opposed the unprecedented position of Deiotarus I in 47 BC may have included him. Given the extent of control Deiotarus enjoyed after the removal of Brogitarus and Castor Tarcondarius, these others probably had little scope for rule, despite belonging to the tetrarchal families. Adiatorix received no known territory during the distributions of Caesar after Zela in 47, for reasons unknown but very likely connected with the ambitions of Deiotarus, who had still to brook the continued rule of Castor Tarcondarius over the Tectosages and no doubt argued against proliferation of rulers. As soon as he could, he removed Castor Tarcondarius by murder, but was apparently unable to lay his hands on Adiatorix.[87]

In his policy of encouraging the extension of royal or princely control in the East, Antony settled Adiatorix as ruler over a portion of Heraclea Pontica, adjacent to a colony founded by Caesar. The temptation to win military honours with, as he asserted, the connivance of Antony proved irresistible. One night 'a little before Actium' Adiatorix fell upon the Romans there and slaughtered them. Octavian hardly received him with glad cries after his victory. Leading him and his family in triumph, he ordered Adiatorix executed with his eldest son, Dyteutus. At this point a younger brother successfully offered to die for Dyteutus, who survived to become the shaken successor of Lycomedes as priest in Pontic Comana.[88]

The story need not be thought too graphic for credibility, since Dyteutus remained priest in Strabo's day; such a tale would have currency when attached to the holder of so important a priesthood.[89]

Amyntas

The man termed both 'secretary' and 'general' during the lifetime of Deiotarus became 'king' after it. Succeeding Deiotarus, Castor II died or was deposed following a short reign, for reasons suggested above. During this same period, 40-36 BC, Amyntas had not been idle. By representing Deiotarus well at Philippi he struck Antony as a useful ally, potentially loyal because presumably not in the main line of descent. In 39, Antony recognized him as king in Pisidia and part of Lycaonia.[90]

Despite his Macedonian name, Amyntas need not have stood completely outside the families of the tetrarchs; some mixing of Hellenic nomenclature in the dynasty had occurred by his lifetime. Other Galatian uses of Amyntas are attested, though perhaps only in response to his. Neither of his previous offices (*grammateus* and *strategos*) is incompatible with tetrarchal descent, but neither proves it. That he bore some relationship to the many noble families in Galatia must be postulated, but we can go no further.[91]

Like Polemo, appointed at the same time and for a region nearby (around Iconium and parts of Cilicia Tracheia [§ 15]), Amyntas ruled with vigour. The main quality Antony sought among his allied kings was success in ruling firmly, in order to promote stability in the East and to accomplish two specific goals: raising money for the Parthian campaign, and providing military support during it. An eventual purpose, not clearly foreseen at the time of the initial appointments, was to erect an Eastern rampart of kings allied to Antony. The plan came to include the formal overlordship of Caesarion as 'King of Kings,' bolstered by the Roman triumvir and the Egyptian queen. Men like Amyntas fitted well into this bizarre scheme.[92]

By 36 BC, Amyntas stood as full King of Galatia. When Strabo wrote half a century later, the transition from Deiotarus I to Amyntas, both as sole rulers, appeared uninterrupted, ignoring the four years of Castor II. In addition to Galatia, Amyntas acquired parts of Phrygia and Pamphylia, possibly with the addition in 36 of the rest of Lycaonia and at least part of Isauria, previously held by Polemo I, now busy in the north. Later Amyntas was to hold Elaeussa in Cilicia Tracheia, after Cleopatra's defeat.[93]

The bitter campaigns Amyntas fought during his reign (39-25 BC) involved him with mountain tribes previously considered indomitable. His greatest difficulties lay with the Pisidians and Cilicians along the Taurus, and with rulers repeatedly characterized by Strabo as tyrants, such as Antipater of Derbe. What encouragement he had from his Roman allies is difficult to determine. He probably acted on a request to maintain order and regularize the administration of these difficult lands. One of his conquests came over a minor Roman appointee, but most of them involved tribes likely to resist all 'pacification' and consequent imposts. One such group, the Homanadenses, later became formidable antagonists to his Roman successors as well. His coinage attests to his widespread activity and to his attempt at conciliating the Greek cities of these vast regions. In his reign Amyntas seldom found the comforts of home in Ancyra, but in this he only followed the lead of Deiotarus.[94]

When the doleful Eastern monarchs assembled at Actium, Amyntas attended. His relations with Antony had always run smoothly, but like most of his fellow dynasts he needed no instruction in the identification of doomed military causes, and soon changed to a 'better and more useful' alliance. During the twilight of Antony's career in the months after Actium, Amyntas displayed his adherence to the new arrangement with Octavian, for instance stoutly attempting to bar passage of the gladiators from Cyzicus who sought to aid Antony.[95]

Octavian saw the value of Amyntas, who returned to his kingdom after Actium. His effort to control mountain tribes continued throughout his reign. He held some of Cilicia Tracheia, which became an important theatre of dynastic activity for another century, witnessing rule by Archelaus of Cappadocia and his son, by Polemo II of Pontus, Antiochus IV of Commagene, and King Alexander of Judaea. In 25 BC, Amyntas fell still fighting in these mountains, against the Homanadenses.[96]

Children of Amyntas remained, and Deiotarus Philadelphos ruled in Paphlagonia. Other Galatians of the tetrarchal line lived on, such as Ateporix, the Antonian appointee ruling Caranitis. But Augustus decided the time had come for Roman rule in Galatia. Estates of Amyntas – including perhaps the 'servi Amyntiani' – fell as private property to Augustus, with the remainder of the kingdom converted into a Roman province. Since the territory for which Rome had recognized the rule of Amyntas included vast tracts not under either Roman or Galatian control at the time (39 and 36 BC), he had been forced to conquer about half of his 'own' kingdom. The subsequent Homanadensian conflict demonstrates how much of this work remained. Strabo's implication that the entire kingdom of Amyntas had been incorporated by Rome at his death cannot furnish precise geographical information, especially in troubled Cilicia Tracheia, where other kings continued the struggle. What Amyntas securely held could be taken up, not always without fighting; what he merely contended for remained open to future arrangements.[97]

Galatians proved strong rulers in Asia Minor, and among the most useful Roman allies. After the disappearance of their tetrarchs and then of their kings, they passed – perhaps not peacefully – into the Roman provincial system, in 25 BC, a dubious reward for their years of loyalty. A scion of their dynasties, Deiotarus Philadelphos, remained as King of Paphlagonia until about 6 BC. The great families continued their important social role for centuries more. They included such wealthy notables as C. Iulius Severus of Ancyra – who terms himself a 'descendant of King Deiotarus' and of other kings or tetrarchs, including the Attalids of Pergamon (recalling Mithradates of that city, related to Deiotarus I); 'first of the Greeks'; 'cousin' of Easterners who served in the Roman Senate, among them King Alexander of Cilicia. Galatians continued to speak their own language until at least the days of St Jerome, who heard there in the late fourth century a tongue akin to that of the Gauls in Europe. The educated Galatians also used Greek, as we see on their inscriptions, and like their remote kin in Gaul prided themselves on their knowledge of Greek. Favorinus of Arelate in Gaul travelled to Greek lands and was pleased 'being a Galatian [Gaul], to speak Greek.' The 'growing cultural commerce between Gauls and the Greek East' in the second century continued this development.

Galatians in Asia remained faithful indefinitely to their long-standing allegiance to Rome, as for instance during the invasion of Zenobia up to Bithynia late in the third century. Galatia had been one 'key' to Asia Minor.[98]

§ 17. Cappadocia

To recapitulate, the reign of Ariobarzanes I could only be characterized as troubled, with opposition from within and without, involvement in the Roman campaigns locally, severe financial imposts, and reliance on distracted Romans as their own internal problems increased. Ariobarzanes found himself facing Mithradates Eupator of Pontus and Tigranes the Great of Armenia on several occasions; they were often assisted by a Cappadocian faction. When standing alone he suffered repeated defeats. With Roman assistance he did better, and must have watched with satisfaction the successes of Deiotarus against Eupator. He joined Lucullus in the major campaign which culminated in 69 with the defeat of Tigranes and Eupator (§ 24). Ariobarzanes proved an effective ally of the Romans, securing the Euphrates crossing at Tomisa and some of Sophene, giving him a strategic foothold beyond the river. With the fall of Tigranocerta, which Tigranes had populated by deportations from Cappadocia, Ariobarzanes must have received back home numbers of supporters forever opposed to the Armenian and his ally in Pontus.[99]

Unfortunately for Ariobarzanes, neither Mithradates nor Tigranes remained long quiescent. Lucullus had serious problems with his army. In 67, Pontus was almost entirely recovered by the king, who with Tigranes again invaded Cappadocia. In the alarmed words of Cicero, 'The entire kingdom of Ariobarzanes is in the hands of its enemies' (67/66 BC).[100]

The campaigns of Pompey changed all that. Still planning for empire, Mithradates fled to Bosporus for a confrontation with Machares, followed by his own death when Pharnaces supplanted him. Tigranes remained in the background during this stage of the conflict; his days of empire had passed. Pompey recognized the rule of Ariobarzanes, with additions. At last Cappadocia appeared peaceful, and against this background Ariobarzanes abdicated, in 64, 63, or possibly 62. The succession took place in the presence of Pompey, perhaps with a gentle push, for the old king seemed an unreliable support for Pompey's ambitions in such a critical region. No one doubted his capacity to absorb trauma and repeated expulsion, but he had reached the point where he was eager to abdicate. His son succeeded apprehensively. 'Happy was he who lay down the throne, sad he to whom it was given.'[101]

Ariobarzanes had ruled at least thirty-two years during a frightful period for Cappadocians. His innovative *Philoromaios*, 'friend of Rome,' must have seemed his only consolation during five or six exiles. Perhaps against the odds, he not only survived the unprecedented local dominance of Eupator and Tigranes, but also founded a dynasty able to maintain itself in the vacuum created by disappearance of the ancient Ariarathid line. His happiness on retiring contained both relief and satisfaction.[102]

Ariobarzanes II Philopator

The son distinguished himself from his father but honoured the paternal achievements by omitting *Philoromaios* in favour of *Philopator*. In turn, his own son was to become Ariobarzanes III *Eusebes* ('Pious') *Philoromaios*.

'He who loves his father' may seem a harmless enough sobriquet, but its meaning stood plainly for three distinct groups to see: citizens of the newly stabilized Cappadocia; Pontic adherents both within the kingdom and remaining without, now under Cappadocian, Galatian, or Roman rule; and inhabitants of the new territories over which Pompey had recently recognized Cappadocian hegemony.

The territory now under Cappadocian rule formed an extensive block. In the east it began with Sophene beyond the Euphrates and possibly Gordyene, where King Zarbienus had defected to Lucullus and later paid Tigranes with his life. Roman recognition of Cappadocian rule here followed the same lines as for Amyntas of Galatia in much of his territory: encouragement to go forth and fight for it. The traditional kingdom of Cappadocia reverted 'to Ariobarzanes' after the final expulsion of Tigranes and Mithradates from it; this is Ariobarzanes I, who then 'while still living put his entire kingdom into the hands of his son.' This included strategic portions of Lycaonia and Cilicia. At Cybistra in Lycaonia (Tyanitis) – 'the region in Cappadocia that touches Cilicia' – Cicero believed in 51 that he could best defend both Cilicia and Cappadocia from Parthians advancing by way of Syria, to which Cappadocia 'lies open' otherwise.[103]

The reign of Ariobarzanes II began against a background of external calm. Since 65, Tigranes had been quiescent in Armenia proper; by 63, Mithradates Eupator was dead. Trouble with Parthia lay unsuspected in the future. Of concern to Ariobarzanes, internal matters ranked highest, followed by restoration of 'normal' relations with external dynasts and with Athens. From clear epigraphical evidence and unclear source evidence, the name and descent of his wife have been recovered. Appian mentions a betrothal 'to Ariobarzanes' of a young daughter of Mithradates Eupator in 81 BC. On grounds of age, this probably refers to Ariobarzanes II rather than to his father. Conditions in Cappadocia which promoted the betrothal changed little over the following decade and one-half, so a marriage probably ensued. This mollified Eupator, still hoping to control Cappadocia through a relative, and it also gave satisfaction to the pro-Pontic faction in Cappadocia. It furnished Ariobarzanes II with a queen who could take on a name useful to the new dynasty: that of her mother-in-law, wife of Ariobarzanes I.[104]

The two wives are both named Queen Athenais Philostorgos. Both married a King Ariobarzanes. In an effort to win acceptance during its second decade of existence, the dynasty married its first crown prince to a well-connected princess whom it named after its first queen. This reconstruction accounts for the wording of Athenian inscriptions honouring two kings, each 'son of' an Athenais Philostorgos. A mother-regent would not fit the formula in the text for 'Ariobarzanes [III] Eusebes Philoromaios,' described as 'son of King Ariobarzanes [II] Philopator and of Queen Athenais Philostorgos [II].'[105]

If Athenais Philostorgos II indeed sprang from Mithradates Eupator, she later lived up to her inheritance. About age thirty-five in 50 BC, she ruled for her son, Ariobarzanes III, in a manner dangerous to him (see below) and damaging to Roman interests. Cicero found a situation bordering on war in the kingdom then.[106]

Meanwhile, in the calm before a storm, Ariobarzanes II developed his rule along traditional lines, including a dynastic coinage for at least eight years, cautiously featuring a Pontic symbol. This coinage preserves vivid testimony to the difficult position of the king, a Roman ally with a Pontic wife and enemies on his northern border should Pharnaces II succeed in restoring his father's kingdom in Pontus, as he later briefly did.[107]

Ariobarzanes did what he could to cultivate Athenians in particular, rebuilding the Odeum burned during Sulla's occupation of Athens, and enrolling his sons among the Ephebes there. He secured grateful mention from the Athenians as 'benefactor' of the city. One conjecture also connects him with an honorary inscription found in Rome.[108]

Indications of internal trouble began at least by 57 BC, when Ariobarzanes resorted to the proconsul Aulus Gabinius, whom he bribed to kill unspecified enemies of his. A group of royal advisers who had served his father remained loyal to him throughout his reign and into that of his son, but they did not save him from the machinations of those opposed to Rome. Ariobarzanes II was murdered by assassins at court, perhaps with the involvement of his wife.[109]

Ariobarzanes III Eusebes Philoromaios

The reign of the third member of the dynasty began in such dangerous circumstances that in Rome the Senate took what Cicero calls the unprecedented step of ordering him to assume responsibility for the king's personal safety. Much lay at issue. Some feared that the kingdom might slip into the hands of those still opposed to Rome and ally itself with Pharnaces II, or the Armenian Artavasdes II (son of Tigranes), or the Parthian Orodes II. That would threaten the progress made by Lucullus and Pompey. Deiotarus alone could have offered no effective opposition to such a coalition, nor could Antiochus I of Commagene limit the consequences.[110]

Ariobarzanes III began his reign apparently under the regency of his mother, Athenais Philostorgos II, daughter of Eupator. Whether or not she led the faction that murdered her husband, she lost little time in pursuing an anti-Roman policy. In the first year of her regency (52 BC), she managed the banishment of two pro-Roman Cappadocians, one of them a friend of Cato. When Cicero arrived at Cybistra in 51 during his governorship of Cilicia (§ 18), he effected their restoration and promoted their interests at court.[111]

The circumstances of Ariobarzanes III appeared dangerous in the extreme to Cicero, who congratulated himself on having saved the young king's life. Cicero did what he could to surround him with friends and counsellors left from the days of his grandfather. He also managed the removal from Cappadocia of a threatening priest, probably of Comana, who possessed armed adherents and seemed likely to use them in revolt against the king. So serious did the prospect of internal war appear to Ariobarzanes that he even requested troops from Cicero, who declined knowing that his own would be needed against the Parthians.[112]

An external threat aided by the faction inside Cappadocia could be foreseen. In the Bosporus, Pharnaces II, son of Eupator, had for more than a decade been consolidating power over his subjects and hegemony among neighbouring tribes. He prepared for an attack on Pontus to recover his father's kingdom there; this was accomplished during 49 and 48. Cappadocia, in the meanwhile, lay 'open to Syria' and also vulnerable to Armenia under Artavasdes II.[113]

Expecting attack from one direction by the Parthians and from another by Armenia, Cicero relied on Deiotarus of Galatia. He expressed confidence in

Tarcondimotus of Cilicia and Iamblichus I of Emesa, but both could afford only limited assistance. Antiochus I of Commagene assisted but was known to have ties to Parthia. As for Ariobarzanes III, Cicero praised his loyalty but expected nothing from one who could barely maintain himself, and whose kingdom was 'stripped bare' (*inanis*), largely by Roman creditors. For the rest, auxiliaries available to Rome were so weakened and alienated as to prove unreliable; Cicero ascribes this to the severity and inequity of Roman rule.[114]

Successful resistance to the Parthian invasion in 51 removed that threat, but internal unrest and external invasion did not constitute the kingdom's only problems. Enormous debts had built up, mainly owed to Pompey and, less pressingly, to Brutus. Appius Claudius Pulcher, governing Cilicia in 53-51, may have encouraged special taxes in Cappadocia to pay these off. Ariobarzanes had either inherited or accrued a debt to Pompey alone of something over three thousand talents; even the interest amounted to more than he could pay. The helpful Cicero arranged a repayment scheme of some thirty-three talents per month, but this staggering sum still failed to cover interest, much less principal. A kingdom so seriously weakened by its own ally needed no enemies.[115]

Cicero played to public opinion in his effort to shore up the position of Ariobarzanes III. At one point in 51 he wrote specifically 'to the consuls, praetors, tribunes of the plebs, and Senate' in Rome to report his accomplishments and to praise the qualities of Ariobarzanes. Cicero aspired to honour from the Senate and wrote early in 50 asking Cato to promote this. Cato did so in a more restrained way than Cicero hoped, but the Cappadocian affair did redound to Cicero's credit. He himself never lost sight of his main aim: to get safely back to Rome.[116]

After the invasion of 51 and the threat of one in 50, Parthians, preoccupied with matters in their own distant east, failed to take advantage of an otherwise favourable military situation in Cappadocia. As Romans flailed one another in the civil warfare of 49 and 48 BC, Parthians might have pressed westward across the Euphrates in combination with the resurgent empire of Pontus under Pharnaces II, and with the alliance of Armenia under Artavasdes II. But these three powers preferred to remain unallied, and let the opportunity pass. Eastern kings assessing the situation participated with lagging steps in 48 BC at Pharsalus, demonstrating by the paucity of the forces they contributed that they felt little confidence in the outcome. Whichever Roman faction they supported might lose, as occurred when most honoured their alliances with Pompey. Further, the weakening of Rome which the overall conflict entailed left Asia Minor and the Levant exposed to Parthian incursions, which did begin late in the decade. Watchful waiting, with the nominal support of Rome, appeared to most dynasts the only safe course now.

When the civil war broke out, Cappadocia participated. Like the other Eastern kings, Ariobarzanes III sent troops on the side of Pompey, and like them he sent a limited force (of five hundred). His brother, the future King Ariarathes X, led the contingent.[117]

In the aftermath, Caesar trusted Ariobarzanes more than he did Deiotarus of Galatia (§ 16). In the distribution of territories that Caesar made after conquering Pharnaces II in Pontus, a portion of 'Armenia,' probably Armenia Minor, went from Deiotarus to Ariobarzanes.[118]

The domestic situation remained troubled. Ariarathes had been seen by some in 51/50 as a useful figure in the contemplated revolution against his brother. This revolution had been forestalled by Cicero and the adherents of Ariobarzanes III, with no loss of credit to Ariarathes. But by 47 he had grown impatient for a share in the kingdom's governance. He must have been yet a youth, for in 51 his brother had been termed *adulescens* by Cicero, and Ariarathes was the younger of the two. The party that had worked on the younger brother then may have continued to do so now, for the remarks of Caesar regarding domestic dissension in the East in 47 probably included Cappadocia, through which he travelled on the way to Zela.[119]

Caesar knew the factional danger in Cappadocia – that Ariarathes might claim his portion of hereditary rule and interfere with his brother's. Caesar arranged for the young man to assume a measure of responsibility, though whether as regent of a portion of Armenia Minor or as priest in Cappadocian Comana remains unclear. If an emended text allows the second conclusion, this fits the policy of Caesar at the time in securing this priesthood and its analogue in Pontus, where he transferred the office from Archelaus, father of the later king, to Lycomedes, a Bithynian noble of Cappadocian royal descent. The close ties of both cult-sites, the apparent links between important residents of Comana and the royal family traceable through nomenclature, and the strong position of the priests rendered imperative tenure there by a vigorous supporter of the king.

In Cappadocian Comana, this priest, like his fellow in Pontus, was well armed and regarded as second only to the king in power and authority. The previous holder of the office had recently (in 51 BC) caused Ariobarzanes III difficulties verging on revolution and had been expelled from the kingdom with Cicero's assistance. If the priest referred to here is the Cappadocian one, the expulsion was only temporary; Caesar must have decided to settle the matter more effectively by appointing Prince Ariarathes. Assurance of the superior position of Ariobarzanes accompanied whichever appointment went to his brother, who would be 'under his command and authority' as before.[120]

After the battle of Zela in 47 removed the threat of Pharnaces II, who like his father had not stopped short of occupying Cappadocia during the brief restoration of his ancestral kingdom in Pontus, Ariobarzanes III could breathe easier. This respite did not long endure, for his restless brother grew discontented with the settlement arranged by Caesar. By May 45 he turned up in Rome, seeking, in the wry view of Cicero, 'to buy some kingdom from Caesar.' Cicero finds him unable 'as things are now' to enter 'his own' kingdom, either the one he expects to inherit or more likely the territory accorded him by Caesar in 47. In view of his previous 'great service' to the brothers, Cicero invites Ariarathes to stay with him.[121]

The incident need not show an ejection of Ariarathes by his brother, but only dissatisfaction at his distance from the throne. As it happened, he had not long to wait. Whatever action Caesar contemplated on the request, his murder ten months later disconcerted Easterners. They had to forecast the winning party, and many played safe by honouring Brutus and Cassius in the brief interval between the murder in 44 and their defeat at Philippi in 42. In Cappadocia, Ariobarzanes III answered the demand of Cassius for support by hesitating, neither opposing Brutus and Cassius nor allying his kingdom with them. To this Cassius responded by sending his cavalry into Cappadocia, where they killed Ariobarzanes and seized his treasures. Any justification needed was provided by the indebtedness of Ariobarzanes to Pompey; the vast debt owing in 51 could hardly have been discharged by 42 BC.[122]

The decade that Ariobarzanes III ruled had been one of the roughest in recent memory, with a Parthian invasion across the Euphrates, a renewed threat in Pontus (by Pharnaces II), and two Roman battles (Pharsalus, and now Philippi approaching). The epithet *Philoromaios* that Ariobarzanes bore seemed ironic in face of the financial exactions of Pompey and Brutus at the beginning of his reign and of Brutus and Cassius at its end. His benefactions to Athens as commemorated by a surviving inscription show him attempting to assume a normal place among the dynasts of the East, as too does his epithet, *Eusebes* ('Pious'). But the machinations of the Pontic faction – probably including his mother – and the increasing turmoil among Romans kept his reign unsettled. His brother's impatience hardly added to his peace of mind. Finally the Roman greed that plagued his reign proved fatal in 42 BC.[123]

Ariarathes X Eusebes Philadelphos

The younger brother of Ariobarzanes succeeded to his own throne, not one he had sought to 'buy from Caesar' three years before. With him the ancient throne-name of the Cappadocian kings revived. It had been held in the dynasty of Ariobarzanes only by the interloper from Pontus, Ariarathes IX, son of Mithradates Eupator. Whether or not his Pontic mother's influence lay behind its imposition on the new king, this was not merely assumed for the occasion: as a prince he had already been called Ariarathes when visiting Cicero in 51.[124]

The epithet *Eusebes* ('Pious') need not derive from a priesthood at Comana, since any Eastern king could profitably use it, as his brother had, but its propaganda value would be high. His other epithet, *Philadelphos* ('Lover of Brother'), reassured Cappadocians and their neighbours that the change of monarch constituted no change of dynasty, as its fourth king acceded.

The faction that in 51 attempted to use Ariarathes as the focus of its conspiracy against his brother remained in 42. Little detail survives regarding the brief reign of Ariarathes, but a general wariness of Rome was inevitable, given the murder of his brother by Cassius, the civil war among Romans, and those debts. Ariarathes had fought once before for Romans, on the side of Pompey at Pharsalus, and had good reason not to repeat the experience at Philippi. With the national treasures and military supplies removed by Cassius, Ariarathes had to remain passive during the upheavals of 42-38 BC. The Parthian invasions beginning in 40 caused disruptions among some Eastern dynasties, notably Judaea, where the Parthians effected a change of monarch. Commagene, neighbour to Cappadocia, had Parthians passing through it during the campaigns, then taking refuge at Samosata after the fall of Pacorus. Antiochus I of Commagene endured a siege by Antony and Herod, but retained his throne (§ 19).[125]

This Parthian invasion did no harm to Cappadocia, perhaps for the same reason as led to Roman displeasure with Commagene: Ariarathes may have conciliated Parthia. The faction in Cappadocia which opposed Rome hoped to take advantage of Roman distraction now, and probably wasted little sentiment on Antony or Octavian, though the murder of Ariobarzanes III by the troops of Cassius had occurred on the grounds that he was 'plotting' against Cassius and Brutus, and 'favoured their enemies.' Given strong anti-Roman sentiment in Cappadocia, this and a related prediction of 'upheaval and revolt' were well grounded.[126]

Pontus previously supported the anti-Roman party within Cappadocia, but at the beginning of the reign of Ariarathes Pontus was Roman territory. By 39 BC, the ties to Pontus of his mother, Queen Athenais Philostorgos II, if she yet lived, led to the Pontic nobility as before, but beyond them now stood a king – Polemo I, recognized by Antony and maintaining alliance with Rome. The Cappadocian royal family had no known relationship to Polemo. Hence the Pontic star which had appeared on some coins of Ariobarzanes III occurs no longer. Cappadocia assumed a stance of watchful coexistence.[127]

The sparse coinage of Ariarathes as presently known begins only in his fourth year and runs to his sixth. If this initial silence reflects difficulties in assuming his throne after 42, that occasions little surprise. He had not long to wait for further trouble.[128]

Ariarathes became the final monarch in the three generations achieved by the dynasty of Ariobarzanes. He did not rule unchallenged, even early in his reign. Appian, in a passage with a context of 41 BC, suggests a rival already in the person of one Sisines. Antony admired this man's mother, Glaphyra, and Antony is said to have recognized him as King of Cappadocia. Since a mother so named, admired by Antony, and the awarding of the kingdom to her son also characterize the situation of Archelaus in 36 BC, this passage may have confused Sisines and Archelaus. Ariarathes X appears to have ruled for six years, between 42 and 36. Tacitus suggests a date around 36 for inception of the reign of Archelaus. Only if Ariarathes began to date his regnal years about 47, when recognized by Caesar for a portion of Armenia Minor (if he did not in fact receive the priesthood in Comana then), would his six years on the coinage leave room for replacement of him in 41 by 'Sisines,' who on that view ruled till 36, when replaced by Archelaus. With a later change of name, perhaps on recognition as king by Antony, Sisines could have *been* Archelaus, given the tradition about his mother, but nothing securely attests the activity of Sisines, or his recognition in 41 as king.[129]

Though practically nothing has survived to indicate the character of Ariarathes, one tale of Strabo's connects him with an ill-conceived water-diversion project. This miscarried and caused downstream Galatians to refer the matter to Rome, obtaining from him a fine. The story remains too unclear to indicate the tenor of his reign, but does contain the judgment that his actions were 'childish pranks.'[130]

When the reign of Ariarathes X terminated, at the latest by 36 BC, it may have occurred through Antony arranging his ejection by Archelaus, the successor. Thus the dynasty of Ariobarzanes ended, obscurely and with violence. The sixty-odd years of its existence had occurred during one of the wildest periods of Cappadocian history, as of Asia Minor in general. Cappadocians congratulated themselves that the dynasty had survived the attacks of Mithradates Eupator and Tigranes the Great, with Parthians threatening on the southern and eastern borders. It had also surmounted the crises caused by Roman desire for its wealth. The international situation had eased by 36, but dangers remained. The change of dynasty now brought a capable man who ruled for half a century, through the late career of Antony and the entire reign of Augustus.

Archelaus I Philopatris Ktistes

Archelaus had been active in the field against Ariarathes even before his recognition by Antony, and his family had previous acquaintance with the triumvir. The reputed charms of his mother, Glaphyra, did not cause this appointment, though they might have intensified Antony's interest in it.[131]

The suitability of Archelaus included high descent, which had led to acquaintance with Antony. Archelaus was specifically 'not related to them' – in context, to the Cappadocians, not merely the ruling family of Ariobarzanes. His ancestry lay in Pontus with the general named Archelaus, a possible son of Mithradates Eupator who fought with distinction early in the century. The son of this man served as priest at Pontic Comana and briefly ascended the throne of Egypt as husband to Berenice IV. His death at the hands of Gabinius provided the occasion for Antony, his previous 'companion and guest-friend,' to honour him posthumously. The son of this second Archelaus succeeded him at Comana, and sired the fourth Archelaus, the King.[132]

The connections of these great priesthoods at Pontic and Cappadocian Comana with the respective royal houses had always been close. The priest ranked 'second after the king' and possessed a considerable revenue of his own, sufficient to maintain a large armed force. The priest who threatened Ariobarzanes III in 51 when Cicero was present presumably came from Cappadocian Comana, though he did rapidly vacate the kingdom when attacked, as a Pontic priest might readily do. Either priesthood could serve as a platform from which to launch a campaign for the kingship in both countries, given dynastic intermarriage.[133]

The following considerations, then, supported the advancement of Archelaus to kingship: he descended from a Pontic general; imputed descent from Mithradates Eupator enhanced his local position without compromising his alliance to Rome; his grandfather had been of sufficient eminence to achieve marriage with Queen Berenice IV of Egypt and jointly rule there; service by his father and grandfather as priests at Pontic Comana placed the family high in the nobility of Cappadocia and Pontus. Finally, recognition of Archelaus for rule in Cappadocia might disarm opposition to Polemo I in Pontus. The father of Archelaus once stood second from the Pontic throne, leaving Archelaus with higher potential claims than Polemo had. His support for Polemo gave him welcome assistance.

Archelaus could break off the dynasty of Ariobarzanes and begin a new one on grounds of appropriate descent. The faction lately active in support of Ariarathes X and his Pontic mother found itself bereft of its anti-Roman agent and unable to maintain that Archelaus lacked credentials for ruling Cappadocia. His fifty-year reign ratified the soundness of his accession.[134]

Antony now, in 36, had two strong adherents ruling side by side in Pontus and Cappadocia. Antony's admiration for the grandfather and mother of Archelaus predisposed him to confidence in the young king, which proved justified.[135]

As matters degenerated towards civil war, Archelaus maintained his alliance on a personal basis. He doubtless supported the effort of Antony against Parthia and Armenia. Even if he had an Armenian wife (see below), this fact would not weigh against policy, nor can the marriage be confidently dated so early. At Actium, Archelaus left no doubt of his position, not only supporting Antony but even attending in person.[136]

After the death of Antony and Cleopatra in 30 BC, Octavian and his victorious administration spent a decade mainly concerned with matters in the West. This began with deposition of several Eastern kings, including the son of Tarcondimotus in Cilicia (§ 18) and Alexander, the brother of Iamblichus in Emesa (§ 20); both dynasties resumed their rule at least by 20 BC. Three kings who had been recognized by Antony continued to rule: Polemo in Pontus, perhaps without recognition by Rome until 26 BC; Amyntas in Galatia (which was soon to become a province); and Archelaus in Cappadocia.[137]

The reign of Archelaus endured for some half a century and ranked as a success both for Cappadocians and for Romans. Archelaus considered the change of dynasty a clear break with the past and expressed this in his title, *Ktistes* ('Founder'). Cappadocians had endured sixty years of warfare, multiple ejections of Ariobarzanes I, occupations and deportations by Eupator or Tigranes, internal struggles of the pro-Pontic and pro-Roman factions, enormous debts, and the murder of two, perhaps three, of the four kings in the dynasty. A 'Founder' came forward almost as a saviour; at Comana, an inscription honours him as *Philopatris*, *Ktistes*, and *Soter* ('Saviour'). To signal this change Archelaus also employed that title *Philopatris* ('Lover of the Country'). He aspired to show his new subjects that his outside origin in no way diminished his determination to rule Cappadocia well; the title need not be seen as an antithesis to *Philoromaios*, as taken by two of his predecessors (Ariobarzanes I and III). Initially recognized by Antony, he had no need to remind anyone of the Roman alliance, but his aim, shown throughout his long reign, was to rule as an independent monarch, promoting the good of his subjects and their defence. He also, like his early contemporaries Artavasdes II of Armenia and his son-in-law King Juba II of Mauretania, wrote at least one work of literature, apparently of ethnographic interest.[138]

Troubles did occur at times in the years to come. At least one incident caused his subjects to oppose him so strongly that it involved an appeal to Rome. The grounds of the charge remain unknown, but its importance drew into the case no less a figure than the future emperor Tiberius, here beginning his civil career with a defence of Archelaus. An unspecified incident in which he felt wronged by his own brother, whose name has not survived, occurred sometime in the first three decades of his reign. He was also drawn, as a peacemaker, into matters affecting the Judaean house, and with Herod he met M. Titius, governor of Syria.[139]

The reign of Archelaus witnessed a strong break with the miseries of recent Cappadocian history. He administered the kingdom well and took on in addition the territories of Armenia Minor and Cilicia Tracheia, where he built a palace at Elaeussa. He maintained good relations with the royalty of the East and with the Athenians. His first wife may have derived from the Armenian dynasty, passing on lineage that prompted Augustus to describe their grandson as 'descended from the royal family of the Armenians.' Their daughter, Glaphyra, married a son of Herod the Great and took an exceptionally high place at court, considering herself in descent superior to the other princesses there. She later married Juba II of Mauretania, and finally returned to the Judaean court for yet another marriage there. Glaphyra's descendants included two kings of Armenia and one in part of Cilicia. A son of Archelaus ruled on after him in a portion of Cilicia Tracheia.[140]

The largest dynastic coup achieved by Archelaus was his second marriage, to Queen Pythodoris of Pontus, after the death of her husband Polemo I. At one stroke this marriage united the control of an extensive territory: Pontus, Armenia Minor, Cappadocia, and part of Cilicia. Once the health of Archelaus failed to the point of his requiring a 'guardian' for his realm, but he recovered; a muted power struggle may lie behind this incident. Soon after the death of Augustus he stood trial in Rome, charged perhaps with revolution. Certainly Tiberius came to dislike him. The position of Archelaus had become uncomfortably strong in the important region he ruled. By AD 18 he was dead and his kingdom became a province. His widow ruled on in Pontus for years longer, and her family controlled it until the end of the reign of Polemo II, about AD 63.[141]

Cappadocia had formed the theatre wherein occurred some of the most important events in the East early in the first century before Christ, and it seldom remained far from the centre of affairs down to Actium. Its wealth, size, and location rendered the tumult of its history in those seventy years almost inevitable, but its contributions were noteworthy.

§ 18. Cilicia. The Tarcondimotids

The rugged Taurus Mountains, termed 'the boundary of Asia' by Arrian

(*Anab.* 5.6), cut off from Asia Minor its lower coastal region, from Pamphylia to Syria. This formidable range can be passed in only a few places in the west, notably the Valley of the Calycadnus and the 'Cilician Gates' north of Tarsus. In the east, routes pass from Hierapolis Castabala to Anazarbus and beyond. The very rough region known as Cilicia Tracheia ('Rough' Cilicia) supported small, virtually uncontainable tribes, left under the control of Eastern kings even during the period of Roman activity nearby after Pompey. The more amenable regions of Cilicia Pedias ('Level'), similarly controlled by local tribal leaders, joined somewhat more readily in the larger affairs of the day. Even so, the tribes in the Amanus Range and others in the Taurus resisted external control. Only one major dynastic house arose from the two Cilicias in the first century BC, that of Tarcondimotus. Other notables, including lines of priests, existed in both Cilicias. No one felt much disposition towards terming them 'kings,' though a notable external exception arose in the first century AD in the person of King Polemo II (see below).

The two portions of Cilicia presented quite different aspects during the period 100-30 BC. About 102, M. Antonius (Antony's grandfather) hauled a fleet across the Isthmus of Corinth 'to go to Side' in Pamphylia. His object was to attack pirate bases in Cilicia Tracheia, which a contemporary law terms 'a province.' It specifies that the kings of Cyprus, Egypt, Cyrene, and Syria be notified and asked to help suppress piracy. Nothing further is heard of a 'province' for twenty years, and Cilicia Tracheia remained under nominal Seleucid control until the conquest of Syria by Tigranes the Great in 83 BC. Even after that it served as a place of refuge for two of the last Seleucid monarchs (§ 21). When Tigranes returned to Armenia about 70 BC, to face Lucullus the next year in battle, Tracheia reverted fully to Seleucid control, however intermittent and short-lived, then passed by right of conquest to Rome. Its pacification remained another matter, requiring well over a century of effort by a long series of Eastern dynasts. Notable among these stood Amyntas of Galatia; Archelaus I of Cappadocia and then his son; Polemo I and II of Pontus; Antiochus IV of Commagene; then his son-in-law, the Judaean-Cappadocian King Alexander.

Since Tracheia never formed the seat of a major dynasty during the period 63-30, that is, after the Seleucids' demise and before Octavian assumed overlordship there, it lies beyond the scope of this study, as do its line of priests at Olba and its other small dynasties or 'tyrannies.' Its importance as a region difficult to control or as a refuge for pirates before – and after – Pompey's expedition against them often brings it obliquely into the present study. Its timber does too: Cleopatra wished to control it, lacking an equivalent source of lumber for shipbuilding. The choice by Archelaus of Cappadocia to reside at Elaeussa (later Elaeussa-Sebaste) some of the time arose partly from its attractiveness, but mainly from considerations of strategy. It formed, for instance, a convenient place to deal with Herod and on another occasion with his sons. The Roman decision to delay attempts at occupying Cilicia Tracheia was prudent. As Strabo puts it, 'All things considered, it seemed best for the territories [Cilicia Tracheia] to be ruled by kings rather than to be under Roman governors.' So matters stood until the reign of Vespasian.[142]

The case differed with Cilicia Pedias, the level, fertile portion adjoining Syria. Among the number of small dynasties there, one did rise to a position of some eminence, with personnel known for more than eighty years, from before 64 BC until at least AD 17. The accessibility of Cilicia Pedias rendered it more susceptible to domination, whether by external kings, by Romans, or by an internal dynasty. It experienced all three during the first century, with control of portions by Armenia and Cappadocia, with a Roman province after Pompey, and with the dynasty of the Tarcondimotids.[143]

Tarcondimotus I

The presumed founder of the dynasty emerges into the historical record only in the time of Pompey, though his father may have held high local position before him. An inscription from Hierapolis Castabala calls him 'Tarcondimotus, toparch, son of Strato.' As Strabo puts it when discussing local 'tyrants' and dynasts, 'in our time a noteworthy man became lord of all and was proclaimed king by the Romans ... Tarcondimotus.' Whether his father had before him been one of the local rulers cannot be ascertained. That is not improbable in Cilicia, where even small districts tended to have local rulers. None the less, the dynasty's rise to importance came, as Strabo says, through the work of Tarcondimotus.[144]

The dynasty arose on the flanks of the Amanus range in the east of Cilicia, a region characterized by age-old movements of people, by lively commerce, and by the proliferation of small tribes. It extended at its fullest to encompass the territory from Hierapolis Castabala in the east to Anazarbus in the north, and also included Elaeussa, which lay west of Tarsus. This region in the west may have been obtained through the strong naval force Tarcondimotus possessed. In addition, he must have had access to the sea nearer to Hierapolis Castabala, in order to maintain his navy, though the only coastal region specifically mentioned for him in the sources is that encompassing Elaeussa.[145]

Whatever the local position of Tarcondimotus before Pompey's arrival in Cilicia, he received major impetus towards local dominance then. Pompey's triumph in 61 included Cilicia and a representation of the conquered pirates. Whether Tarcondimotus figured in the dispositions made between 67 and 63 cannot be discerned, but his rise to prominence in a region with so many local rulers accelerated with the arrangements of Pompey.[146]

Clear testimony exists of his position as a reliable ally of Rome by the time of Cicero's arrival in the East a decade later. The local population of Cilicia might have looked forward to the coming of Parthians, as Cicero says, or it might not. In either case a strong dynast in Cilicia, one of the regions most exposed to their advance, could only benefit Roman interests. Cicero refers to Tarcondimotus as 'our most faithful ally beyond the Taurus and the most friendly to the Roman people.' Tarcondimotus had decided on which side his interests lay during the Parthian invasion of Pacorus I, son of Orodes II, in 51, and had reported the oncoming Parthians to Cicero. Along with Iamblichus I of Emesa, likewise affected by the Parthian decision to advance through Syria, Tarcondimotus looked to employ Roman resistance to the Iranians now rather than suffer the uncertain consequences of an occupation. Antiochus I of Commagene assisted too, though mistrusted by Cicero, and eventually Deiotarus of Galatia supplied effective military contingents. In Cicero's eyes, apart from Tarcondimotus and Deiotarus 'the other kings and "tyrants" are reliable neither in resources nor in attitudes.'[147]

Tarcondimotus doubtless waited on events, as did his fellow kings. As Cicero put it, 'I knew that our allies were uncertainly disposed and hung on the expectation of revolutionary developments'; he hoped nevertheless to win especially Cilicia over. It had in part revolted from the control of Romans or their ally, Tarcondimotus; some 'of the Cilician people were in arms' now. Cicero advanced from the west of Cilicia (near the frontier with Lycaonia and Cappadocia) in the fall of 51 BC as the Parthians crossed the Euphrates into Syria from the east. The dominions of Tarcondimotus lay imperilled, depending on the line of march Parthians took after establishing themselves and causing an uprising in Syria.[148]

Cicero regards the district near where Tarcondimotus ruled, the Amanus, as in the hands of 'a perpetual enemy' in October 51; some of the tribesmen there had 'never obeyed even the kings' (the Seleucids) and 'were now most keenly awaiting the arrival of the Parthians.' Cicero fears for the Roman possessions in Cilicia and Syria.[149]

Cicero shows awareness of the allied kings' position and that of the populace under Roman rule in Cilicia and Syria. They waver because they 'don't dare appear overtly inimical to the Parthians'; because taxation, interest, and debts weigh on the cities; because they are alienated 'by the severity and inequity of our rule' in the provinces. These lands are threatened, and in them 'the revenues of the Roman people are contained.'[150]

Amid this turmoil, Tarcondimotus stood out in Cicero's eyes as reliable. He had probably not assumed yet the title of king, for Cicero omits it in referring to him, contrary to his usual but not invariable practice for kings. Presumably during Cicero's governorship he remained a 'toparch,' an appropriate local title, and became 'king' after his signal service during the Parthian scare of 51/50. How long after remains unclear, perhaps not until the Eastern sojourn of Caesar – after whom he named a daughter – or even of Antony.[151]

The fate of Crassus in 53, occurring not far from Cilicia, and now the invasion of the Parthians in 51, might have given Tarcondimotus pause, since part of the local population preferred Parthians to Romans, his allies. In February 50 Cicero feared a greater invasion from the Parthians, who were wintering in Roman territory. In addition to that threat, Roman losses also occurred on the Amanus at the hands of the tribesmen there. With the Amanus region bordered by territory either in Parthian hands (Syria; Cyrrhestica) or ruled by a vacillating king (Antiochus of Commagene), new emphasis came to lie on the reliability of Tarcondimotus.[152]

After the Parthian invasions, Tarcondimotus had only a short period for further organization of his holdings, now more secure but not exempt from further threats. He utilized a basically Hellenistic organization, as attested by inscriptions found during the expedition of Heberdey and Wilhelm. We find the terms *dēmos* and *polis*, both before and after his recognition as king, and *stratēgos*, *phylarch*, *dēmiourgos*, *archupēretēs* after. A group of aristocrats known as 'the first and most honoured friends of the king' assisted in extending the authority of Tarcondimotus over the vicinity. A powerful state began to rise in Cilicia.[153]

Whether or not Pompey had promoted the rise of Tarcondimotus, when the test came in 48 Tarcondimotus behaved as if he had. Not only did he support the side of Pompey, but he 'assisted him greatly with ships' in connection with the battle of Pharsalus. Caesar later exacted no vengeance for this support of his rival. After the winter spent in Alexandria, Caesar presumably dealt directly with Tarcondimotus on his way north in 47, either when receiving the 'kings, rulers, and dynasts neighbouring the province [Syria]' or else in Tarsus, to which he summoned 'all the states of this province [Cilicia].' Tarcondimotus had been a 'friend of the Roman people' by 51 BC if not before, so no further enhancement of his status in Roman eyes was necessary in 47. Caesar might have merely renewed the *amicitia*, but the possibility remains that he recognized Tarcondimotus as king. For whatever reason, naming a daughter 'Julia' must constitute an expression of gratitude to Caesar (not to Octavian, since Tarcondimotus died at Actium), and perhaps Roman citizenship came to the dynast now.[154]

Tarcondimotus would have taken part in Caesar's Parthian expedition had Caesar lived. He escaped not only this duty but perhaps also service at Philippi, though the absence of mention cannot demonstrate this. By 40 BC, when once again Parthians crossed the Euphrates in his vicinity and swept westward, Tarcondimotus had decided to follow his alliance with Rome, for no hint of trouble with Antony exists, and their relations became exceptionally warm. If not king before, Tarcondimotus became one now, during Antony's years in the East. He commemorated the close relationship to Antony by issuing an extraordinary coinage, bearing the legend 'King Tarcondimotus *Philantonius*.'[155]

Though Tarcondimotus co-operated with Antony, relations with Cleopatra might be strained. She tended to view other dynasts with suspicion, especially those controlling territory she coveted. Her assumption of a part of Cilicia Tracheia for its lumber supply may have been at the expense of Tarcondimotus, who possessed holdings there. The geographical references to this cannot furnish sufficient precision to be sure, but in any case it caused no overt trouble. Antony tended in these matters, as when Cleopatra desired territory from Herod or the Nabataeans, to arrange enough of an acquisition to placate her (e.g., Herod's balsam groves) but not to alienate his ally. So it must have been with Tarcondimotus.[156]

At Actium, Tarcondimotus assisted Antony. 'Tarcondemus, King of Upper Cilicia' in Plutarch's record is the same man; in other accounts he is known to have attended in person. 'Upper Cilicia' presumably envisions the territory around Anazarbus, where he also ruled, and at Hierapolis-Castabala.[157]

Unlike some of his fellow dynasts at Actium, Tarcondimotus did not flee when the imminent loss of Antony's cause became apparent. This confirmed Cicero's estimate of him twenty years before as a most loyal ally. He took part in the naval warfare and lost his life in an engagement with Agrippa.[158]

The rapid rise of this man to kingship in a region heretofore characterized as 'ruled by several tyrants' sprang from a conjunction of factors. It coincided with the collapse of Seleucid control of Cilicia, which had provided a framework for local rulers, until the replacement of these kings by Tigranes in Syria and parts of Cilicia. It arose contemporaneously with Pompey's action in supplanting Seleucid by Roman rule, and with the dramatic clearing of most pirates from their bases in Cilicia Tracheia. It fell in the context of Parthian success against Romans at Carrhae and during their invasions of 51-50 and 40-38. The letters of Cicero show Tarcondimotus a reliable Roman ally in 51. He then took part both at Pharsalus and Actium. The unprecedented construction of a Cilician dynasty can be explained by this set of circumstances.[159]

The Successors of Tarcondimotus

Although the subsequent history of the little dynasty lies outside the terms of this study, a brief indication of its course is necessary. Besides the daughter named Julia, Tarcondimotus left two sons, Tarcondimotus II and Philopator I. They took up responsibility in the kingdom after his death in 31, as can be discerned from the incident of the gladiators moving from Cyzicus towards Egypt to assist Antony and Cleopatra. The intervening dynasts altered their previous support of the doomed pair to join Octavian in reaping the fruits of his victory at Actium, so the gladiators had to fight their way to Syria. Among those attempting to impede their progress stood 'the sons of Tarcondimotus in Cilicia,' as well as Amyntas of Galatia and later even Herod. These had been among 'the firmest friends' of Antony – while circumstances warranted.[160]

In the aftermath of Actium, Octavian deposed some rulers, as in Emesa, and did not reinstate their dynasties until 20 BC. This occurred too in Cilicia, where 'he also deposed ... Philopator [I], the son of Tarcondimotus.' In Dio's account, the deposition precedes by some months the activity of 'the sons of Tarcondimotus' in resisting passage of the Antonian gladiators. A period in which the kingdom of Tarcondimotus lay without leadership would be dangerous, leading to such disturbances as later occurred when King Philopator II died. Other sons must have succeeded, whether with Roman recognition or not. Mentions of 'King Philopator' in the dynasty's coins and inscriptions probably refer to his later namesake.[161]

Whatever the activity of the dynasty in the decade after Actium, by 20 BC Augustus realized that a return to the former alliance with strong dynasties in the Euphrates region must govern Roman policy. Negotiations with King Phraates IV of Parthia for return of the standards lost by Crassus required on the Roman side a visible rampart of dynastic allies, precisely in the kingdoms that lay near the Euphrates frontier: Cappadocia, Commagene, Cilicia, Emesa, and Judaea. It can be no accident that three of these received new monarchs in 20 BC: Iamblichus II in Emesa, Mithradates III in Commagene, and 'Tarcondimotus, the son of Tarcondimotus, the Kingdom of Cilicia, which his father held' except for some coastal regions transferred to Archelaus I of Cappadocia. Archelaus and Herod already firmly held the other two of these 'border' kingdoms.[162]

The dynasty continued to rule its portion of Cilicia into the reign of

Tiberius. Inscriptions speak of a 'King Tarcondimotus Philopator' and his son '[C. Jul]ius Strato'; of another Julia, this one termed 'Queen Julia the Younger'; of Styrax, 'Father of Kings'; and others. In a region as difficult to govern as Cilicia Pedias, reliable rulers retained their usefulness on into the Roman Empire. In adjacent Cilicia Tracheia, allied kings maintained order until late in the first century after Christ. The descendants of Tarcondimotus joined an important group of royal supporters of the new order.[163]

7

The Levant

§ 19. Commagene

The conquest of Tigranes by Lucullus in 69 BC released Commagene from its status as a reluctant sub-kingdom, one of the many that had warranted assumption by Tigranes of the title King of Kings. The king over whom he claimed lordship in Commagene had been Mithradates I Kallinikos, with his Seleucid wife, Laodice, the daughter of Antiochus Grypus and sister of five Seleucid kings (§ 6). The last of these were attempting to rule Syria (§ 21). Commagene lay for the moment in an unquiet situation. Neighbouring Cappadocia still experienced disruption until 67, and not until 63 could Mithradates Eupator be considered no longer a threat.[1]

Antiochus I

At some time before the defeat of Tigranes, a change of monarch occurred in Commagene, for among the kings who offered alliance to Lucullus after his victory stood Antiochus I of Commagene, son of Mithradates and Laodice. A coin attributed to him bearing Seleucid rather than his later characteristic Armenian devices could mark this initial period of rule. Despite inauspicious beginnings, his reign proved one of the most exuberant in the kingdom's history, resulting in the imposing monuments still evident there, and in continuation of a stable dynasty well-connected to Eastern royalty and their aristocratic successors for another 140 years.[2]

Antiochus did not begin well, apart from promptly approaching Lucullus. The strategic position of Commagene on the Euphrates, permitting access to Parthia, did not escape the notice of either Lucullus or Pompey. A strong kingdom there allied to Rome could furnish a bulwark against Parthia and

Mesopotamia. It could also provide a base of operations against its other neighbours, Syria, Cilicia, and Cappadocia – all scenes of trouble in varying degrees during these years.[3]

Lucullus and Pompey may both have contended against the young king of Commagene; Pompey 'fought him into friendship.' Antiochus became an ally of Rome and even followed the recent usage of Ariobarzanes I of Cappadocia in terming himself *Philoromaios*. Pompey recognized his kingdom and added strategic holdings across the Euphrates, as he did also in the case of Ariobarzanes. Commagene and Cappadocia both assumed an important place in Pompey's vision of a stable block of allied territories on the western fringe of Mesopotamia.[4]

Antiochus had local, Iranian concerns as well. His position as a successor of Tigranes had caused him to assume a version of the Armenian tiara, the first in his dynasty to do so. His dedication to the Iranian gods caused his celebrated syncretistic portrayal of them with Greek gods, producing such marvels as Zeus-Oromasdes, Artagnes-Heracles-Ares, and Apollo-Mithra-Helios-Hermes. His sympathy for the Parthians led to intermarriage of the two royal houses, and later an accusation of collaboration. Antiochus did not become an unequivocal Roman ally, but rather a cautious statesman waiting upon the outcome of Rome's civil wars and of its growing conflict with Parthia.[5]

Easterners well understood that warfare among themselves only facilitated the Roman conquests that had now begun in earnest. For their part, Romans had healthy respect for Parthia, and were grateful that it had abstained from aiding Mithradates Eupator and Tigranes. Pompey took care to confirm Phraates III as 'friend and ally.'[6]

He also bolstered his new ally in Commagene. Antiochus enjoyed a period of calm and prosperity after the accommodation reached with Pompey. He may have commemorated their alliance by the era reflected on a horoscope discovered atop Nemruḍ Dagh, showing that an event of importance had taken place in 62 BC. Antiochus assumed the *toga praetexta* during Caesar's consulship in 59. The alliance with Rome might prove useful, should Tigranes stir again, or Parthia invade, as it later did. The threat from Mithradates Eupator had passed, but Antiochus required prudence in his alignments if Parthia was to remain amicable. To balance the Roman alliance Antiochus achieved one with Parthia too, cementing it by a marriage of his daughter to the Parthian monarch, Orodes II. A recently published inscription identifies her: 'Great King Mithradates [II], son of Great King Antiochus [I] and of Queen Isias, erects this representation to the imperishable memory and honour of Queen Laodice, sister of the king and wife of the King of Kings, Orodes.' The children of this marriage were later described as being of higher lineage than one son of Orodes II by a different queen. Commagene commanded high regard among its Iranian neighbours.[7]

Antiochus received a shock in 53 BC. He watched the forces of Crassus cross the Euphrates for an attack on Parthia, from which most failed to return. This disaster made him thoughtful, demonstrating as it did the effectiveness of the Parthians on their own ground, using tactics that presented unprecedented difficulties for Romans. Antiochus bore a primary responsibility to his own kingdom and now had good reason for caution regarding alliance to Rome and possible provocation of Parthia. If he still retained his holdings across the Euphrates, at the expense of King Abgar of Osrhoene (§ 12), he viewed with concern the shift away from Rome in that kingdom's foreign policy after Carrhae. Antiochus stepped even more carefully henceforward.[8]

The dual nature of the foreign policy of Antiochus did not escape Roman notice. Cicero later remarks that many considered him of dubious loyalty; though an *amicus* of Rome, he fell in a class of allies whom Cicero distrusted as 'not daring to break openly' with Parthia. Cicero contributed to the hesitation of Antiochus by ridiculing him, a dangerous habit for one who as governor came to rely on such allies as Antiochus when the Parthians did invade.[9]

That invasion fell in 51 BC and brought the Parthians right through Commagene. Antiochus sent legates to announce the invasion to Cicero in Cilicia. The mobilizations in 51 and 50 included several of his fellow kings: Ariobarzanes III of Cappadocia, Deiotarus I of Galatia, Tarcondimotus I of Cilicia, and Iamblichus I of Emesa. In his alarm, Cicero noted the vulnerability of Cappadocia, Cilicia, and Syria to the Parthians, and that 'the remainder of Asia' could fall to them as well. More than a decade later, Parthians did penetrate far into Asia Minor, but in 51 they apparently intended not conquest so much as plunder. The strong showing of the allies, one Roman victory, and some astute diplomacy removed the threat by the summer of 50 BC.[10]

Antiochus proved himself reliable on this occasion, despite some apparent wavering among the populations of the East. He informed the Roman Senate and Cicero of the threat, which some feared would also involve an attack on Cappadocia by Artavasdes II of Armenia. Fear firmed the alliance.[11]

As the Roman civil war approached, the problem for Antiochus, as for most Eastern kings, lay in forecasting the consequences. He chose the course most of them did, to support Pompey, but to do so only nominally. Two hundred Commagenian troops appeared at Pharsalus, a ridiculously low number considering the wealth and populousness of Commagene but one in line with the practice of the watchful Eastern allies.[12]

After his victory, Caesar adopted a policy of recognizing monarchs who had remained loyal to their commitments, even though these were to Pompey. Antiochus retained his kingdom, joining the 'kings, tyrants, and dynasts' who met Caesar in Syria as he advanced northward against Pharnaces II in 47 BC.[13]

The role of Antiochus had Caesar lived to carry out his campaign against Parthia must remain a matter of conjecture, but his position astride the Euphrates, with the ancestral kingdom west of the river and additional territory east of it, would have involved him. Osrhoene veered from its former loyalty after Carrhae, so Caesar knew better than to rely on it. His most convenient Eastern ally for crossing into Parthia and retaining a secure foothold upon the Euphrates would be Antiochus.[14]

Whether or not Antiochus would have proved reliable for Caesar, he was allegedly not faithful to his Roman alliance four years later when the Parthians crossed the Euphrates under Pacorus I. This fine general, who proved both successful and popular before his untimely death, married a daughter of Tigranes the Great of Armenia. His father, Orodes II, had wed a daughter of Antiochus of Commagene. Whether she was the mother of Pacorus cannot be determined, but in any case he and his Parthian force received some co-operation from Antiochus. In 40 and 39, his campaign pushed deeper into Asia Minor than anyone could have foreseen. His death in 38 prevented Parthia from following up these successes in Asia Minor and Judaea, or in any way consolidating its advantage.[15]

This left Antiochus isolated in Samosata, awaiting the Roman reaction. It came in the person of Antony, who declared that Antiochus had co-operated with Pacorus, and had received Parthian fugitives in 38. Herod of Judaea found time to join in the resulting siege, which failed because of the strength of Samosata. Antiochus realized that the main objective of his assailants had to be monetary, and secured their withdrawal with a healthy bribe. Antiochus had been an ally of Rome since before Pompey, and now bought the expensive privilege of remaining so.[16]

The events of these years must have ranked among the 'great dangers' Antiochus records that he escaped during his more than thirty years' rule. Parthians advancing from one direction with Romans and Herod approaching from another did focus his attention. Among the measures that he took to consolidate his dynasty's rule was the series of magnificent cult-complexes throughout Commagene, culminating in those at Arsameia and atop Nemrud Dagh, visible for miles. The cost of this must have been high for peasants and villagers, many with land expropriated and with conversion themselves to the status of *hierodouloi* ('temple-slaves'), but Antiochus would not have apologized. In the inscribed record of his intentions, his concern with maintaining the traditions of his ancestors stands alongside more predictable cult matters, such as piety and the protection of Commagene itself. To ensure the untroubled succession of his son, he also arranged an association on the throne, reflected in a joint coinage.[17]

Whether Antiochus survived to witness the start of Antony's Parthian campaign in 36 cannot be demonstrated. Soon after the accession of Phraates IV in 38/37 BC, the grandsons of Antiochus in Parthia fell victim to the new Arsacid monarch. So did Antiochus, according to Dio's unsupported testimony, and possibly Laodice did too. In any case, the Commagenian ruler who eventually commemorates the death of those grandsons' mother, Laodice, is 'Great King Mithradates,' her brother.[18]

Mithradates II

Mithradates II continued the policies of his father, preserving the alliance with Antony presumably made after the siege of Samosata. He retained his father's epithet *Philoromaios*, adding *Philhellenos* and for balance employing the Iranian tiara used by his grandfather. The Armenian tiara favoured by his father had by now served its purpose of proclaiming Antiochus a 'successor' of Tigranes the Great. In the dynastic tradition Mithradates added an imposing monument of his own, another *hierothesion*. Positioned on the road to Nemrud Dagh, which rears imposingly behind it in the distance, with the cult-site of Arsameia in between, the tomb held the remains of three women: the mother of Mithradates, a sister, and the sister's daughter. A touching inscription records the early death of this sister, named Antiochis after her father, and provides the reason for the monument: to accord his mother this final tribute.

'This is the hierothesion of Isias, whom Great King Mithradates ... thought worthy of this last honour, she being his own mother. But first the girl Antiochis lay here, sister of the king by the same mother. She was the most beautiful of women; her life was short, but long will be her honours in the long time [to come]. Both of these, as you see, are here, and after them the granddaughter of Isias, Aka, daughter of Antiochis. This is a memorial by the King of her life along with theirs.'

Thus the commemoration of three generations of queens. Another inscription also honours Laodice, the sister who became queen in Parthia.

This monument by Mithradates completes the extant series of major cult dedications in Commagene. His successors had too much on their minds for continuation of such large-scale dynastic and religious statements, though the cult of Antiochus and that of Zeus at Doliche endured for centuries.[19]

At Actium, Mithradates joined the kings allied to Antony, perhaps attending in person. Octavian recognized his continued rule, though with a transfer of Zeugma to the province of Syria. Mithradates may have ruled for another decade, though a possible Antiochus 'II' is known. Whether this man was a king or not, he did come into conflict with his brother, for which Octavian had him condemned in 29 BC, fearing disruptions in this crucial region. Afterwards, Commagenian kings carried on for a century to come.[20]

Commagene fared exceptionally well. Its revolt from Seleucid domination in 163 BC had succeeded and its attempt to forge an independent course did too, except for a period of domination by Tigranes and another by Rome during the reign of Tiberius. The kingdom entered enthusiastically into the system of intermarriage prevalent in the East, with eventual relatives in the dynasties of Emesa, Judaea, Cappadocia, Atropatene, Parthia, and perhaps Pontus. A remarkable king, Antiochus IV, ruling in Cilicia as well as Commagene, lived through the reigns of at least seven Roman emperors and into Vespasian's, who worried about his 'neighbourliness' with Parthia, and required the region for the planned eastern frontier. Even after the incorporation of Commagene by Rome in AD 72, some 235 years since independence began, Antiochus enjoyed a sojourn in Lacedaemonia, where the family had relatives, and then found an honorable place at Rome for his last years. His sons were at first well received in Parthia, and then joined him in Rome. His son-in-law became the last king in Cilicia (King Alexander). His granddaughter (Julia Balbilla) accompanied the Emperor Hadrian to Egypt and left extant poetry on the Colossi of Memnon there. His grandson, the grandly named C. Iulius Antiochus Epiphanes Philopappus, still termed 'king' by Easterners, served as Roman consul and Athenian archon, leaving an imposing monument that stands yet on the Museion Hill in Athens, facing the Parthenon.[21]

An Iranian-Hellenic monarchy ruled by kings who came to hold Roman citizenship, Commagene furnishes one of the most striking examples of the long historical process that substituted Roman for Seleucid or local government but left Parthia intact. Even more than most, Commagene stood 'between two empires.'

§ 20. Emesa

After the departure of Tigranes of Armenia from Syria, the Kingdom of Emesa took part enthusiastically in the struggles of the last Seleucids. King Sampsigeramus I of Emesa and Azizus, another Arab dynast (whose name also appears later among Emesene royalty), combined to block the attempted return of Antiochus XIII Asiaticus, despite the previous wishes of Lucullus. The death of Antiochus at the hands of Sampsigeramus brought forward

Philip II for a brief reign, but the day of the Seleucids had passed, and local populations bore no further allegiance to them. Sampsigeramus and Azizus even envisioned a partition of Syria between themselves, but in postulating a vacuum into which they might step they underestimated the ambitions of Rome.[22]

Sampsigeramus I

The defeat of Tigranes in Armenia during the year 69 BC provided Rome with a claim on Syria without further warfare, and Pompey explicitly exercised it. The Seleucids lost the country to Tigranes and Tigranes lost it to Rome; there need be no further discussion. Pompey required some fighting to gain firm control of Syria, including battles with such neighbours as Commagene, Judaea, the Nabataeans, and some princes in Lebanon, but no clear indication exists of armed struggle with Emesa. The later record of Sampsigeramus suggests that he made peace rapidly with Lucullus or Pompey after observing the experience of Tigranes. Having become an ally of the Romans, he remained faithful to his word. By ruling a stable state in the territory of Emesa, which stretched as far as Arẹthusa, he cushioned the lightly protected Syria.[23]

In recognizing the rule of Sampsigeramus over Emesa, Pompey acted on sound information. This dynast did not yet enjoy the title of 'king' among neighbouring Arab rulers, though Greeks presumably so regarded his position; Plutarch and Dio employ 'king' or 'dynast' for some of his contemporaries, but Strabo and Josephus prefer 'phylarch' for Azizus, Sampsigeramus, and his son Iamblichus. Whatever his title, Sampsigeramus could be relied upon. Given the weak Roman garrison in Syria, the presence of an ally bordering territory under potential threat by Judaeans, Nabataeans, and Parthians would be welcome to Pompey in 63, when he moved to Damascus on his advance against Judaea and the Nabataeans. This would have been the time for reaching an accommodation, and Sampsigeramus may have escaped the fighting that characterized the advance of Pompey through the territory of small dynasts in Lebanon. Arethusa, which he controlled, adopted a new era in 64/63, suggesting this as the time of a settlement between Sampsigeramus and Pompey.[24]

Whether their dealings led to a formal alliance, much less to payment by Emesa, is questionable, but the policy of Sampsigeramus clearly favoured co-operation with Rome. The general settlement effected by Pompey in the region included Emesa, by all indications, and when the Parthian threat became acute in 51 BC, the phylarch of Emesa duly notified Cicero as proconsul of Cilicia.[25]

Sampsigeramus may have been still alive in 51, but the ruler named by Cicero is his son Iamblichus I. Cicero could have confused Iamblichus, from whom the message came, with his father, though the only indication that Sampsigeramus lived on is an inconclusive one. To postulate shared rule between father and son on the model of Commagene later (§ 19) requires more knowledge of the political workings of Emesa than lies to hand. No firm conclusion as to the date of succession can be drawn.[26]

Iamblichus I

Iamblichus I appears known to Cicero in 51 BC more by hearsay than in person, but his repute is favourable: 'well-intentioned and a friend to our republic.' Cicero received this report in September on the same day as a similar one arrived from Tarcondimotus. A previous message from Antiochus I of Commagene had not convinced Cicero, who was far from the scene on the southwestern border of Cappadocia, but he considered these dynasts more reliable, and he also had intelligence of risings among some of the Cilicians. Accordingly, Cicero mobilized what forces he could, both Roman and allied.[27]

The strong co-operation of dynasts in Emesa, Commagene, Cilicia, Galatia, and perhaps Judaea helped Roman forces resist the Parthian incursion of 51-50 BC. Ariobarzanes III of Cappadocia had problems of his own and presumably gave no effective assistance against the Parthians, but in preparing to defend his own realm against possible Armenian attack he assisted the more general cause south of him (§ 17). Thus a rampart of allies along the Euphrates from Cappadocia through Commagene to Emesa and Judaea supported the Roman governors involved: Cicero in Cilicia, Cassius and then M. Calpurnius Bibulus in Syria. This system was the one envisioned by Pompey a dozen years earlier and it did work this time, despite internal problems in both Cappadocia and Judaea. The part played by Emesa was relatively minor, but at the time when Cicero explicitly feared any admixture of 'Arabs' with the invading Parthians, the trustworthiness of this one Arab ally cheered him.[28]

Less happy days lay ahead, as Roman civil strife broke into open warfare. Whichever side, if either, Emesa supported at Pharsalus, it did assist Caesar later, when Mithradates of Pergamon gathered a relief force for him at Alexandria in 47. Among the Syrian and Arab allies who sent forces to Egypt stood 'the dynast Iamblichus,' the young ruler of Emesa.[29]

The effort of this group of dynastic allies to relieve Caesar from an increasingly difficult position in Alexandria succeeded. Later in 47, during his reception in Syria of dynastic delegations, Caesar doubtless sought to retain the arrangement with Emesa, which would have been especially useful if his Parthian campaign had occurred.[30]

Other local consequences of the Roman civil wars affected Emesa. During the struggle of the Pompeian Q. Caecilius Bassus to seize and hold Syria from 46 to 43, he enjoyed the support of 'neighbouring phylarchs' as well as that of the Parthians. Among the cities upon which he could rely stood 'Arethusa, a city of Sampsigeramus and of his son Iamblichus, phylarchs of the state of Emesa.' Thus Emesa may have found itself consecutively both supporting Caesar and opposing his adherents. Eastern rulers could foresee no more clearly than Romans did the result of this conflict. Both Pompey and Caesar had claimed in 49/48 to speak on behalf of the Roman Senate, so that even a formal treaty, if one existed, would scarcely have provided guidance to wary Emesenes during the period down to Pharsalus.[31]

Whether or not the passage quoted above demonstrates Sampsigeramus still alive after 46, during the Syrian adventures of Caecilius Bassus, Iamblichus I ruled now too. The conflict raging nearby was described as considerable, and the Parthian relief force in 45 BC as a large one. A Jewish contingent came from Antipater as well, supporting Caesar. The position of Iamblichus became dangerous. Not only did he risk joining the losing Roman side, as he did, but now that the Parthians had sporadically joined the local fighting he could become involved in such Roman punitive expeditions as the one Caesar contemplated. Cicero expected war in the East even after Caesar's murder in March 44. After Philippi in 42, the initiative lay with Parthians; they responded by launching the invasion of 40-38 BC.[32]

During the previous Parthian invasion, in 51 BC, both Iamblichus of Emesa and Antiochus of Commagene had taken the Roman side. This time they apparently did not. Antiochus, at any rate, drew the accusation of having collaborated with Parthia. No direct mention of Iamblichus reveals his response, but it could hardly have been openly pro-Roman with a Parthian nominee now installed in neighbouring Judaea, and with the Nabataean Malichus co-operating with Parthia. Emesa had nothing to gain from Parthian hegemony in the region, but could hardly afford to become an isolated Roman ally, with Rome itself still unsettled. The appearance of Antony in the East may have caught Iamblichus in a posture of less than complete loyalty to Rome, and temporarily cost him the control of Arethusa, if this is the city Antony granted to the fugitive Parthian noble Monaeses, whom he later returned to Phraates IV as a gesture of good will.[33]

Whether or not Antony intended to utilize Emesene assistance for his unsuccessful war effort against Parthia, he must have held serious doubts about Iamblichus now. In the stark record that has survived of these fateful years, a casual mention dating from the last days before Actium reveals that

Iamblichus remained an ally of Antony and personally attended the preparations for battle. But Antony's increasing suspicion at the mounting number of defections from his camp fell upon his Emesene ally. He 'executed Iamblichus, King of certain Arabs' and others besides him. The terming of Iamblichus here as 'king' indicates that the man named is the ruler of Emesa.[34]

The Successors

At this critical juncture, then, Emesa found itself without a ruler. The succession devolved without delay upon Alexander, brother of Iamblichus, for we find him ruling already in the aftermath of Actium, when Octavian deposed some dynasts he considered unreliable. After being led in Octavian's triumph, Alexander suffered execution as his brother had. Whether left to fend for itself or not, Emesa produced no recorded king for a decade after this.[35]

The chequered story of relations between Emesa and Rome in late republican times hardly boded well for the future, yet the dynasts of Emesa were to achieve surprising success. Iamblichus II received his hereditary domain at least by 20 BC. By the time Sampsigeramus II, his son, reigned, the Emesene ruler claimed to be 'Great King' and also ranked as a Roman citizen. Intermarriage with the dynasties of Judaea, Commagene, and Atropatene further expanded the influence of Emesa. As the Roman Empire gradually incorporated Eastern dynasties during the century after Actium, the Emesene King stood among the group of royal allies paradoxically instrumental in furthering that process, especially under Nero. By the reign of Vespasian, after Emesa assisted in the absorption of Commagene, the only remaining kings west of the Euphrates were Agrippa II of the Judaean house, King Alexander of Cilicia, and two members of the dynasty of Emesa (see stemma). No proof exists that the kingdom of Emesa was separately incorporated into the network of Roman provinces made from the former kingdoms. Whether or not it was, a possible relative ruled Armenia about AD 170 and other apparent descendants of the dynasty stood ready for one final, spectacular chapter in local history late in the second century AD. At that time Julia Maesa, her sister Julia Domna (wife of Septimius Severus), Domna's son Caracalla, and Maesa's grandson Elagabalus, together furnished the Roman Empire with a ruling family derived from the Emesene branch of the Eastern dynastic aristocracy.[36]

§ 21. The Last Seleucids

As discussed in § 8, the once-mighty Seleucid Empire virtually caused its own demise during the first decades of the last century before Christ.

Following the death in 96 BC of Antiochus VIII Grypus, his five sons spent the final years of the Empire in internecine strife and in open hostilities with a number of antagonists – Judaeans, Nabataeans, Parthians, Emesenes, Ptolemy IX Lathyros in Cyprus, and finally Tigranes the Great of Armenia. Their relative Antiochus IX Cyzicenus, after murdering Grypus, joined in the fray but fell in 95 before Seleucus VI Epiphanes Nicator, son of Grypus, who himself perished in Cilicia later that year. Antiochus X Eusebes, son of Cyzicenus, continued the struggle until the coming of Tigranes sometime after 86, probably not until 83. The remaining sons of Grypus died in these domestic conflicts or in Parthian captivity or were killed by the Nabataeans. Philip I Philadelphos, the final son of Grypus, survived until 83; after him his son, Philip II Barypous ('Heavy-Foot'), belied his epithet by escaping to survive the years of Tigranes's local rule.[37]

Antiochus XIII

Antiochus XIII Asiaticus, son of Antiochus X Eusebes, also survived the coming of Tigranes, probably by concealment in Cilicia Tracheia. Since Antiochus XII, son of Grypus, had not ruled beyond about 87 or 86, these two princes, Philip II and Antiochus XIII, constituted the hopes of the Seleucid house after 83. With Roman support, they re-emerged after Tigranes removed Cleopatra Selene, formerly wife of Grypus. Following the embassy to him in Antioch by Appius Claudius Pulcher, Tigranes left for battle with Lucullus and lost in 69 BC.[38]

Lucullus recognized Antiochus XIII as King of Syria in 69, thus returning the situation nominally to what it had been some fourteen years before, at the arrival of Tigranes. To maintain the Seleucids proved more difficult than Lucullus realized: former subjects had grown too used to independence. Only Syria would have been feasible for Antiochus to control. Emesa prepared to resist incorporation by the restored Seleucid, and proved willing to assassinate him.[39]

Philip II

No union of Antiochus XIII with Philip II occurred to prevent trouble from external enemies. Instead, they followed the recent Seleucid pattern of contending with each other. Meanwhile, Syrian cities declared themselves independent.[40]

Under the circumstances, Pompey found no reason not to claim the conqueror's right to territory. Tigranes had defeated the Seleucids, who should not profit from the Roman victory. A decade before this, the Senate had declared the sons of Cleopatra Selene and Antiochus X Eusebes to be undisputed kings of Syria by right of descent from their father and their ancestors, during their visit to Rome in 76/75 BC. This recognition had not accepted Tigranes's conquest of Syria, which the Senate deliberately ignored. However, conquest of him now afforded opportunity to Rome, and for Roman commerce. A rich and important region, strategically located in the Levant, fell painlessly into Roman hands as the struggle that transferred its possession occurred far away, near Tigranocerta. No diplomatic niceties regarding Seleucid claims impeded Roman acceptance of the prize. Numerous dedications to Pompey by various Greek cities after 67 BC show their awareness of this transformation.[41]

Seleucid history ended with Philip II Barypous and the final months of rule by Antiochus XIII Asiaticus during his second reign in 65/64 BC. The action of Pompey in refusing further recognition to the fatally weakened Seleucids converted Syria into Roman territory, since Syria 'did not have neighbouring kings' to rule there. The succession of governors which began with M. Aemilius Scaurus in 65 reflected in its complexity the confusions of Roman civil war, but no opportunity for re-establishment of Seleucid rule presented itself. Only withdrawal by Rome would have permitted this, and local sentiment would not have tolerated it.[42]

Seleucid weakness and collapse contributed largely to the Roman occupation of the East, which had begun after Seleucid defeat at Magnesia and now received a significant extension. The resulting imbalances throughout former Seleucid territory contributed to the near-chaos of the thirty-five years following Pompey's action in 65. Egypt, Judaea, and Cappadocia suffered severe internal strains in those years as did Galatia, Thrace, and Pontus to a lesser degree. Commagene, Emesa, and Cilicia Pedias fared somewhat better; Cilicia Tracheia did worse. In all of these, the consequences of Seleucid departure proved profound.

Descendants

The Seleucid name did not vanish from the dynasties of the East. Its importance can be traced in Commagene, where the pride of Antiochus I in his Seleucid mother and her ancestry receives inscribed commemoration and statuary. This sentiment remained strong among descendants so distant as the Commagenian 'King' C. Iulius Epiphanes Philopappus and his sister, in the second century AD, as expressed through his monument in Athens and her poetry in Egypt. Descent from the Seleucids long mattered in the East, where use of the Seleucid era continued for centuries.[43]

Some members of the Seleucid royal house survived the Roman conquest of Syria. After the departure of Ptolemy XII Auletes from Egypt for Rome, his daughter ruled as Berenice IV. She required a dynastic husband. In 57 BC, the search turned up three Seleucid princes or former kings. One may have been Antiochus XIII Asiaticus, deposed as King of Syria about seven years before, or a brother; he died of an illness before the marriage could occur. The second was apparently Philip II Barypous, but the proconsul of Syria, Aulus Gabinius, blocked the marriage. The third, named Seleucus, son of Cleopatra Selene, succeeded but found himself rejected by Berenice after a few days. Berenice turned to Archelaus, grandfather of the later King of Cappadocia.[44]

Other royal descendants of the last Seleucid kings existed, as for instance the Cleopatra and Antiochis considered daughters of Antiochus XII. A family with 'royal honours' at Apamea in the time of Trajan had had possible ties with Eastern kings or local tetrarchs, including Dexandros, apparently first Syrian priest of the imperial cult.[45]

The inglorious departure of the Seleucids from their once-proud imperial position tends to obscure the importance of their work. Their arrival in the East with Alexander's conquest replaced a well-established Persian Empire with a Greek one. A population of Semites and Iranians stretching from the Mediterranean to India came under Seleucid dominion and part remained so for nearly three centuries. Portions of the Seleucid Empire coalesced into kingdoms, especially in the second century, and survived the collapse in Syria. Many of the kingdoms treated in this book were at one time considered Seleucid.

One legacy of the Seleucids lay in the spread of these kingdoms, largely Hellenized west of the Euphrates, or combining native and Greek elements. Pontus, Cappadocia, and Commagene blended Iranian with Greek; Judaea and the Nabataeans mixed Semitic with Greek. Even Parthians adopted Hellenic usages until the first century after Christ. Cilicia founded a combined native and Greek dynasty, that of Tarcondimotus. Rome inherited the advantages of this structure and utilized it in the slow building of its own empire.

A final legacy of the Seleucids was cities throughout the East, particularly in coastal areas. Some of these lay in ruins by 65/64, as for instance the coastal towns destroyed by the Judaeans, but a large percentage later revived.

East of the Euphrates, the Seleucids in their decline had promoted the Parthian Empire. Now, in losing their Syrian Empire, they promoted the Roman.

§ 22. Palestine, the Nabataeans, Judaea

The complex society of this region took advantage of the departure of

Tigranes to seize what it could of his Syrian and Palestinian territories. The last Seleucids crept forth from their 'corner of Cilicia' but local chiefs, especially in Emesa, resisted their return (§§ 20-21). Pompey declared Syria Roman.

This declaration did not in itself settle the question of the emergent smaller dynasts, who aspired to a modest place among the larger territories mainly controlled by the Judaeans, Emesenes, Nabataeans, or Romans. To a limited extent they found it, but replaced the uniformity of Seleucid imperial rule with greater diversity than could be maintained. The emergence of the four larger powers to replace the absent Seleucids left limited room for the smaller dynasties. Tigranes, the catalyst for this momentous alteration in the Levant, confined himself after 69 to some fourteen years' further rule in the Kingdom of Armenia, leaving to local manoeuvre and to Rome the determination of who ruled what in Palestine.[46]

I. Ituraeans

Ptolemy, Son of Mennaeus

Among the claimants remained the Ituraeans, still controlled by Ptolemy, the son of Mennaeus. His attempt to rule Damascus had brought the Nabataean Aretas III to dislodge him and issue a coinage there from about 86 to 72. One view has Ptolemy drive the Nabataeans out again about 72, but if so, he proved no more welcome to the people of Damascus than he had in 86. They summoned to their aid an abortive expedition from Judaea and then a more successful one from Tigranes, who ruled Damascus for about two years before departing, and may have left it before he left Syria. Neither the Nabataeans nor Ptolemy evidently regained Damascus, which in turn Pompey reached in 63 BC.[47]

Ptolemy met the advance of Pompey into his region with characteristic sagacity by paying a bribe of a thousand talents, though not before his territory suffered some depredations. His political position remained 'dynast,' not king; the coinage also calls him 'tetrarch' and 'high-priest.' Despite the tradition by which Josephus terms him 'base,' he enjoyed the confidence of the Judaeans and married his son into that dynasty.

At the execution of Alexander, son of the Judaean Aristobulus II (§ 22.III), Ptolemy received his children. He also received Alexandra, Alexander's sister, as his wife. The hand of this Judaean princess came as a boost to his ambitions, but Philippion, his son, had married her first. By provoking his father, the lad found an early grave, passing the wide-eyed bride on to higher station. Ptolemy used his enhanced status to befriend Antigonus, Alexandra's brother, who later moved to the throne of Judaea before succumbing to Herod's attacks.[48]

When Antony came to the East in 41, Ptolemy was still alive. An envoy sent to Antony, 'Josephus, son of Mennaeus,' might have been his brother, to judge from the unusual patronymic. The following year, 'at the same time' as the invasion of Syria by Pacorus (§ 26) and the Parthians, Ptolemy died. Josephus reports the conjunction but specifies no causal relationship. Whether or not he fell in battle, his son promptly espoused the Parthian cause. Lysanias concluded 'friendship' with Antigonus, the new Parthian protégé, apparently with the Parthian satrap Barzaphranes as intermediary.[49]

Lysanias

Though the territory Lysanias inherited is described as a 'principality' and not a 'kingdom,' he may have won recognition as a king by Antony, perhaps among the group of new kings (Archelaus, Polemo, Amyntas) on whom Antony relied. The sequence of events must have been that Lysanias first withdrew his support from Antigonus, a necessary action anyway after the victory of Herod in 37. He won Antony's confidence and became a useful regional adherent.[50]

Lysanias aspired to local succession to the last Seleucids, using coin types consistent with theirs. He was not to have scope for this, being caught up in the larger fate of his region. Antony's decision to present Cleopatra with Phoenicia, Coele-Syria, Cyprus, parts of Cilicia, or Judaea, and Nabataean Arabia involved minimal trauma to all concerned but Lysanias, whom she specifically wished removed. In those heady days, Antony regarded as his own to bestow or remove not only local territories, but local lives; Antigonus, former King of Judaea, and Lysanias both succumbed to this attitude. Even Antony required a pretext, which was that Lysanias, like many in the Levant, had co-operated with Pacorus in his invasion, not an unlikely charge since he had supported Antigonus, brother of his father's Judaean wife and the Parthian nominee for King of Judaea.[51]

Otherwise Lysanias committed no more serious an offence than to inherit territory coveted by Cleopatra. He probably lost part of it in 36, and his life in 34. His close relationship to Antigonus had excited suspicion to mingle with Cleopatra's cupidity.

Cleopatra got what she wanted, and began a coinage to say so. She also used in Ituraea the same technique she did with Herod's balsam groves and her new holdings in Arabia. She leased the territories to their former owners. This gave her revenue without the trouble and expense of occupation or administration, and it set up the relationship of overlord which she now desired for herself and her children. About a decade later, Zenodorus, the apparent son of Lysanias, is noted ruling 'the holdings of Lysanias, which he had leased' previously.[52]

After Actium, matters remained as they stood for a time, with Zenodorus presumably holding the region without tribute. Herod acquired a portion of the Kingdom of Ituraea, but kept his newly rebuilt cities of Caesarea and Sebaste outside its borders, which reached to his own. The kingdom tended later to split into as many as four portions and to be handed on within Herod's dynasty. The phrases 'tetrarchy of Lysanias' (a later ruler of Abila) and 'region called the Kingdom of Lysanias' appear until the mid-first century AD. Herod's grandson of the same name ruled Chalcis, with the title of king. Another grandson, Agrippa I, took up as an inheritance, recognized by Claudius, the entire kingdom of Herod and portions of Ituraea mentioned separately. In AD 50/51, King Agrippa II received Chalcis, still termed a separate tetrarchy; this was reflected in his eras.[53]

The Ituraeans and their rulers have received few words of appreciation from subsequent generations, ranging from the sneers of Josephus at Ptolemy to the current use of 'robber' or 'bandit chieftain' and the like. However, they ruled a most difficult region during times of unprecedented strain. They enjoyed prosperity sufficient to permit social stability (and the enormous bribe of a thousand talents for Pompey). The chaos which could have prevailed in the absence of authority did not, for which these rulers deserve credit.

II. The Nabataeans

In the nature of Near Eastern politics during the period 70-30 BC, Nabataeans would come to 'international' attention only if they physically appeared in Syria, Judaea, or in what Egypt considered its wider sphere of interest, as in fact they did. The Syrian Empire of Tigranes did not reach their territory, and after he left the last Seleucids found themselves too weakened for adventures into the desert. The Roman heirs of the Seleucids had no leisure to advance into Arabia yet.

Despite these considerations, Nabataeans do appear surprisingly often in the record of these years, partly because of their involvement in the politics of Judaea. Nabataean rule of Damascus ended only in 72; their armies appeared in the fraternal struggles of Aristobulus and Hyrcanus in Judaea; their presence was discernible as far east as Palmyra; Roman forces did advance upon them; they assisted Caesar in the Alexandrian War; they found themselves accused of co-operation with Parthia; the dynastic struggle of Herod involved them at several points; Cleopatra desired and received a portion of their territory; they assisted in the final defeat of Antony and Cleopatra, when back in Egypt after Actium.

Aretas III

The seizure of Damascus by Aretas about 86 led to some fourteen years' rule, announced by a series of coins and the epithet 'Philhellene.' By modelling his coins exactly on those of the Seleucids at Damascus, Aretas declared succession to them in that city. However, the inhabitants preferred freedom and arranged his ejection, either by Ptolemy, son of Mennaeus, or by Tigranes. This ejection left them no better off than before; a coin of Tigranes from Damascus in 'year 242' (Seleucid), or 71 BC, shows Aretas III gone by then. Life had not been easy for Damascenes in these years. Only the departure of Tigranes allowed resumption of independence and normal coinage there.[54]

Expulsion from Damascus did not end the concerns of Aretas III with affairs in Syria, Palestine, or Judaea. These all lay within the Nabataeans' sphere of interest, as to a lesser extent did some of the smaller kingdoms (§ 12) between Arabia and Parthia. To retain their independence, Arabs had to rely on their remoteness, the inhospitable desert, and sufficient military prowess to deter invasions, one of which impended.

Judaean affairs began to involve the Nabataeans, perhaps more than the Arabs wished. Antipater, governor of Idumaea and father of Herod the Great, had a wife 'of distinguished Arabian family' and through this marriage he 'brought the King of the Arabs into close relationship' with himself. The 'King of the Arabs' here and Antipater's wife must have been Nabataeans, to be spoken of in these terms. When the dynastic struggle in Judaea grew to involve Antipater, he and his protégé, Hyrcanus II, found Petra the logical place of recourse.[55]

Aretas III allowed himself to be drawn into the Judaean maelstrom. In this he acted not as unwisely as it later seemed, for manipulating neighbouring dynasties in one's own favour had long constituted an accepted device among Eastern kings. In this case, however, the consequences proved greater than he expected. Providing an army to attack Jerusalem in support of Hyrcanus should have led to no more serious consequences than similar actions did throughout Hellenistic history, and the event proved that Aretas, Antipater, and Hyrcanus had correctly gauged the unpopularity of their adversary, Aristobulus, brother of Hyrcanus. This time, however, the presence of Roman forces in the vicinity upset whatever balance Aretas relied upon. He withdrew towards Arabia when the Romans sided with Aristobulus, who took heart and pursued him, evidently winning a major victory at Papyron.[56]

When Pompey arrived in Judaea, among other projects he envisioned some sort of expedition into Nabataean Arabia, though they characteristically declared themselves 'ready to do his bidding.' This was to be more than a visit of inspection. That is evident from reference to 'the army he had ready for the Nabataeans,' and because his *legatus*, M. Aemilius Scaurus, launched a definite attack soon afterward, with no known additional provocation. The motive must have been financial, unless the blind urge for further conquest drove Pompey in all directions at once. Scaurus got nowhere in his siege of Petra, but did receive a useful bribe, and later issued an inappropriate coinage. The coin depicts Aretas III kneeling, and features a camel for those who might otherwise miss the point. Pompey included the Arabs in his triumph, but the campaign engendered no enduring results. Arabia had not been conquered, despite the Roman claims, and it pursued its affairs as before, though a trifle more warily.[57]

The ancient reputation of Nabataeans for being 'unwarlike' arose in part from their circumspection. Their methods involved mobile raiding rather than confrontations; this kept their revenues high and their losses low. Battles with more conventional forces ended quickly, with the Arabs riding off and their adversaries claiming exorbitant enemy losses. The victory of Aristobulus at Papyron supposedly involved heavy Arab casualties, but these are the claims of the winning side. The campaign of Scaurus must have engendered no losses at all, except financially. Another ambitious Roman, however, learned of these campaigns and of the monetary rewards possible, and found himself unable to resist an adventure of his own. This was the new governor of Syria, Aulus Gabinius.

Gabinius arrived in Syria during 57 BC and launched into a series of campaigns. He accomplished or projected military action in Judaea, Parthia, Egypt, and Arabia. The most lucrative of these was the restoration of Ptolemy XII Auletes in 55, for which he 'earned' ten thousand talents (§ 23). Soon after this, Gabinius advanced against the Nabataeans and won a battle. This presumably involved a skirmish and a bribe, on the Nabataean pattern.[58]

Obodas II

Numismatic evidence suggests that a new Nabataean monarch came and went sometime in the seven years between the last notice of Aretas III (the attack by Scaurus in 62) and the first mention of Malichus I, ruling by about 56. However, most of the evidence adduced for this ruler fits at least as well the reign of Obodas I in the early years of the century (§ 9). Only an unusual coinage may reveal the existence of this second Obodas in the sequence of Nabataean rulers; it attests at least three regnal years. Beyond that, the silence of the sources and the ambiguity of the inscribed mention make Obodas II a tenuous figure in present reconstructions. Nabataean history must remain at present dark for this period.[59]

Malichus I

The attack by Gabinius in 55 probably fell upon a new king, Malichus. Estimates for the inception of his reign vary from 60 to 50 BC. Attempts to work backward from the coinage of his successor, Obodas 'III,' permit some confidence in a date about the middle of this range, but no precision. Even the name of the new king (*mlk*) raises doubt; as the Nabataean word for 'king,' it leaves him with the throne-name 'King King'! None the less, there it stands in the coin inscriptions.[60]

A passage in Cicero once thought to refer to the Nabataean king in 54 BC as *Busrenum* ('man from Bostra') in conjunction with Antiochus I of Commagene has been subjected to recent scrutiny. Arguments as to the status of King Malichus among Romans should not be based on it now and should not have been previously; we have no other evidence that he either had or sought civic honours there (the passage refers to wearing of the *toga praetexta*). However, one of our few bits of evidence for his reign does indicate a disposition to assist Romans in the East. The force under Mithradates of Pergamon coming to Caesar's relief in 47 met with resistance at Pelusium, but received timely aid from 'the chiefs of Arabia,' persuaded by Antipater of Judaea. In part, this consisted of 'cavalry from Malchus, King of the Nabataeans.'[61]

Malichus had an interest in Roman activities in the East but no obligations beyond those dictated by prudence. Antipater 'persuaded the Arabs, being their guest-friend' when Caesar needed this assistance. The victory over Nabataeans by Gabinius in 56 or 55, whatever its scale, had not been an act of state. It had in fact involved illegal action on his part. The Nabataeans might have regarded themselves as allies of Rome when it suited their interests, but Caesar's war against Cleopatra's belligerent brother (§ 23) promised no benefit to Arabia, so the Nabataean involvement required persuasion. Cleopatra's future behaviour towards the Nabataeans caused them to regret this support.[62]

Good relations continued between Malichus I and Antipater, who deposited large sums of money in Petra in the years before his death in 43 BC. The purpose was to provide a safe store of capital beyond the reach of warring factions in Judaea. Though Antipater and his son Phasael did not live to claim these funds, his other son, Herod, did. The Parthian invasions of 40-38 drove him from Judaea, now ruled by the Hasmonaean Antigonus. Herod expected to find refuge with Malichus, but obtained neither that nor the funds. Malichus sided with the Parthians and saw only trouble ahead in welcoming Herod, even alleging a Parthian warning against it. The later assertion by Josephus that his main motive was retention of the funds can be discounted, given the Nabataean's wealth and the military importance of this situation.[63]

The policy he adopted in 40 cost Malichus a 'large sum' paid as a quasi-indemnity to P. Ventidius, whose Roman force reversed the momentum of the Parthians accompanying the renegade Labienus (§ 26). Ventidius moved on to govern Syria, but his own superior, Antony, had worse measures in store for Malichus, who soon saw the entreaties of Cleopatra for a portion of his territory successful. Antony grandly presented several countries or kingdoms to Cleopatra or her children; these included 'large areas of Arabia, the territories of Malchus and of the Ituraeans' (after his execution of Lysanias). Antony had no title to these and no authority to distribute them, but for a time the 'grants' satisfied her.[64]

Cleopatra had longed for control of the entire Nabataean realm, as well as Judaea, and sought the deaths of both Malichus and Herod. Antony came to his senses over this point, but did give her part of the Nabataean coastline on the Red Sea. Though not effectively occupying these, she exacted a rental for them. The tale that Herod had to stand guarantor for the payments of his wealthier fellow dynast presumably stems from the anti-Nabataean source Josephus used. It reflects the lack of harmony between Jews and Arabs at that time. The two former allies were linked by the marriage of Herod's mother but no longer by shared political sentiments. Herod's increasing inclination towards Antony was to lead, in fact, to a Judaean-Nabataean war.[65]

By 32 BC the situation had degenerated to the point where Herod, urged on by Antony and Cleopatra, decided to invade Arabia. His pretext was that Malichus had ceased his payments on the lease from Cleopatra. Her motive was to weaken the two kings whose removal she had not been able to accomplish, and a force of hers joined this pointless confrontation. Antony declined Herod's offer of support – but accepted troops from Malichus – in the campaign that terminated at Actium, asking instead that Herod continue his warfare against Malichus. Three battles produced two Jewish victories, the final one of such proportion that Herod could be deemed conqueror of the Nabataean kingdom, and 'protector [*prostates*] of the nation.'[66]

Whatever advantage arose from this contest went to Herod, as it would have even if Antony and Cleopatra had not lost at Actium. The episode remains a puzzling chapter in the long annals of Jewish-Arabian relations in antiquity. Further, the loss of Herod's support at Actium was a misjudgment by Antony. Herod made his own peace with Octavian in 30, and the Nabataeans proved helpful by burning the Egyptian ships transported into the Arabian Gulf for Cleopatra's escape.[67]

One final consequence of this upheaval in Eastern affairs lay in the fate of the former king, Hyrcanus II of Judaea, whom Herod had brought back from Parthian captivity but now feared. Hyrcanus had more claim to the throne than Herod did, and might have proved dangerous to Herod if an alliance with Octavian had not been concluded soon after Actium. Hyrcanus grew suspicious of Herod's intentions and arranged to flee to Malichus I. When the matter came to light, he was executed as a traitor.[68]

Malichus I apparently died not long after these events, though the report of Josephus that Cleopatra somehow managed his death after all cannot be credited. She would have had to do this from a distance, with negligible remaining forces, while facing her own and Antony's defeat in 31 and death in 30 BC.[69]

After the vagaries of these past decades, Nabataeans were to enjoy some 140 years of further independence. These were not altogether untroubled years. Adventures such as the Roman-Judaean-Nabataean expedition against Arabia Felix in 26 and 25 BC effected no major change in Nabataean affairs. Even after the Roman province came in AD 106, with traces of vigorous military activity at least until Septimius Severus, the royal history of the region had not ended forever. By the early fourth century the title 'King of All the Arabs' (a different dynasty with a different sphere of control) signalled an eventful future.[70]

III. Judaea

Alexander Jannaeus, son of Hyrcanus I and brother of Aristobulus I, died in 76 BC after a sometimes violent reign. His widow, who had probably been as well the widow of Aristobulus, was Alexandra Salome.[71]

The destruction wrought by Jannaeus on the coastal towns, which understandably later welcomed Pompey and then Cleopatra rather than further Jewish rule, was not reversed in the reign of Alexandra. She did avert an invasion by Tigranes, through bribery and the lucky intervention of Lucullus, who invaded Armenia and drew its king homeward.

Domestically she failed to bridge the widening chasm between Sadducees and Pharisees, who had discovered in the successors of Hyrcanus the means for their own political advancement, and who now worked through her sons, Aristobulus II and Hyrcanus II. She died as matters edged into civil war between them, probably in 67 BC, with Hyrcanus succeeding her.[72]

Aristobulus II and Hyrcanus II (67-40 BC)

Many Jews held a low opinion of the young Hyrcanus, whom they considered too weak to manage practical matters of state, and too fond of leisure. In contrast, Aristobulus appeared energetic and bold. The brothers themselves hardly regarded each other with fraternal admiration. The more active Aristobulus seemed to his sibling a man given to disturbances and the use of force. Hyrcanus seemed to Aristobulus deserving of contempt for his ineffectuality.[73]

To this personal incompatibility, the divided Jewish aristocracy added further strain. The Pharisees, during the reign of Alexandra, 'held the power whereas she held the title.'[74] Their activity 'appeared no different from that of full rulers.' Aristobulus utilized the resulting disaffection among the Sadducees to dislodge his brother, perhaps after only three months of rule.[75]

This situation could not fail to endanger the Judaeans. Instability in so crucially located an area invited territorial incursions by the waiting Nabataeans, who had lost possessions to John Hyrcanus and Alexander Jannaeus, his son. It might also tempt the Egyptians. Ptolemy Auletes received the honour of a coinage from Ascalon, which aspired to freedom from Judaean occupation; so later did Cleopatra VII, his daughter, who was to hunger for and eventually receive portions of Judaean territory. On the fringes lingered minor threats from the rulers of Chalcis, also ambitious for adjacent lands. Finally, approaching soon from Syria, the first Roman army to enter Palestine threatened the very existence of an independent Judaean state.

An important new element entered Jewish politics at this point: the Idumaeans, represented by Antipater, father of Herod the Great. Like his father before him, Antipater governed Idumaea.[76] He discerned immediately the potential value to himself of the weak and manageable Hyrcanus; he also found an excuse for disturbing the arrangement that had seen Aristobulus succeed to the throne. Antipater asserted that Hyrcanus, as the elder, should rule, a position to which he soon persuaded 'the powerful of the Jews.'[77]

This faction, led by Antipater, convinced Hyrcanus that his life of leisure might become no life at all, should Aristobulus as monarch resolve to deprive him of it. An arrangement concluded with the Nabataean King, Aretas III, offered a refuge, and a base from which the restoration of Hyrcanus might be accomplished. Antipater and Hyrcanus slipped out of Jerusalem by night and took the journey to Petra.[78]

Performance of a service to one faction of the Judaean state against another might not interest the Nabataeans, whose relations there ranged from intermarriage to warfare. But a favour to Antipater the Idumaean, his 'very good friend,' ranked among the priorities of Aretas III. The gifts and flattery of Antipater assisted his cause too, and Hyrcanus promised the return of twelve cities, which his father, Alexander Jannaeus, and his grandfather,

Hyrcanus I, had taken by force from the Nabataeans. At some point, a marriage between Antipater and Kypros, possibly the daughter of Aretas III, cemented this friendship.[79]

The advantages which might stem from installation of Hyrcanus in Judaea, with Antipater behind the throne, induced Aretas III to offer them his armed support. Aristobulus lost the ensuing conflict, deserted by the people and even by his soldiers. Timely flight to the Temple Mount preserved his life, but Aretas and the inhabitants of Jerusalem began a siege, during the Passover, in the spring of 65 BC.[80]

These incidents need not have become important. Factional quarrels in Judaea, as in the Near East or in Rome, constituted no more than interruptions in the normal flow of political and military affairs. A victory by Antipater, supporting Hyrcanus II and assisted by Aretas III, might have altered the balance of Judaean politics in favour of the Idumaeans and would have stabilized relations with the Nabataeans, to the eventual benefit of Herod, Antipater's son.

However, circumstances at the moment were unusual. Dynastic problems in Judaea interested the Romans, who had lately taken control of Syria, in 65 BC, sending an occupying force and soon a governor. Pompey arrived there late in 64. The temptation to intervene in the Judaean civil strife could not be resisted; proximity furnished the pretext and further glory or wealth the motive. In this way, Judaea invited serious compromise of its own independence, now less than three generations old since the Maccabaean revolt from Seleucid control.[81]

By drawing a Roman army into Judaea in 65 BC, Hyrcanus forfeited the assistance of Aretas, who withdrew on receiving from Aemilius Scaurus the threat of an attack involving 'Romans and Pompey.' Their military reputation after the early campaigns against Mithradates Eupator and Tigranes sufficed to deter the prudent Aretas. Nabataeans seldom borrowed trouble. Though a strong Judaea did not accord with their policy, neither did causing a Roman occupation there.[82] For his part, Scaurus aided the side of Aristobulus mainly for a large bribe, which 'came before justice.' He had also formed a low opinion of Hyrcanus. Aristobulus derived sufficient impetus from this Roman intervention that he pursued and defeated the withdrawing forces of Aretas, which were accompanied by Hyrcanus. Antipater's brother, Phallion, fell in the engagement.[83]

This situation settled nothing. Both brothers and their parties now perceived the advantage of Roman assistance. In the winter of 64/63 BC, while in Syria, and in 63 at Damascus, Pompey received envoys and gifts from local dynasts, including Ptolemy Auletes of Egypt (§ 23). Both Judaeans sent to him, but neither received support as yet.[84] The advance of

Pompey to Damascus in 63 distressed the minor dynasts lying in his path, including the Ituraean Ptolemy, son of Mennaeus. This further persuaded the Judaean antagonists of the need for winning his support. They appeared in Damascus, but a third deputation to Pompey from Judaea opposed them both in seeking a return to theocracy rather than kingship.[85]

The embassies to Damascus had no immediate result, for Pompey refused support of any faction. Deciding between Hyrcanus – backed by Antipater and some thousand of the Judaean aristocracy – on the one hand and his reputedly more competent brother on the other was premature, given the position against kingship of a possible majority (Josephus says the *ethnos* was opposed). Better to defer alliance. Pompey ostensibly looked ahead to the expedition against the Nabataeans (§ 22.II above); in fact, he probably intended what occurred, an armed march against Jerusalem.

The incident said to have provoked this is vague enough. Aristobulus accompanied Pompey some way on his campaign and then withdrew; in his 'anger' Pompey decided to pursue him instead of advancing against the Nabataeans. He had expressly feared the ability of Aristobulus to rouse Judaea and block him. Given the military danger of leaving a divided Judaea behind him, he decided to intervene there beforehand, and had been awaiting a pretext. Another factor now arose. The situation that had caused him apprehension in 65/64 had been only partly altered. Parthia still presented the danger of a combination with Armenia, despite the Roman alliance of Tigranes, who ruled on there until his death nearly a decade later. News of the death of Mithradates Eupator did not reach Pompey until he had already set out in pursuit of Aristobulus. The old King of Pontus had remained a threat until 63 BC, as his son Pharnaces II was to be after him, despite nominal alliance to Rome with the title 'friend and ally.' A campaign deep into Arabia lay out of the question since Phraates III and Tigranes had obviously realized that their interests were not Rome's, as Dio specifically notes. Pompey needed to move north from Judaea as soon as he could. Thus came the feint at the Nabataeans and the attack on Jerusalem.[86]

Dio preserves an echo of another pretext for the invasion: Aristobulus and his brother had 'mistreated' Phoenicia, doubtless a reference to Judaean possession of the cities overthrown by Hyrcanus I and Alexander Jannaeus, soon to be freed by Pompey.[87] A third pretext was the appeal for returning to priestly rule made ostensibly by a majority, and the party of Hyrcanus showed itself ready to co-operate in wresting Jerusalem from Aristobulus. This group allowed Pompey into the city, where he laid siege to the followers of Aristobulus in the Temple enclosure, defended by its precipitous sides and its fortifications.[88] After some three months, conquest and massacre ensued in the fall of 63 BC.

This victory did not in itself give Rome possession of the Judaean kingdom, unlike the victory over Tigranes, which had indirectly given it Syria. In this case, a legitimate successor existed in the person of Hyrcanus. The conquest came with his help and could be viewed as undertaken on his behalf. Pompey could not conquer and hold too much of the East: most of it must be left to its native monarchs. In Judaea, a long tradition of rule by priests offered a ready-made solution to the problem of assuring a stable ally between Syria and Arabia. Hyrcanus II could continue as high priest, satisfying the wish of some Judaeans. The country would remain under its own leaders, without the contest over kingship. To ensure this, Aristobulus went as a captive to Rome.[89] The potential strain between the power of the high priesthood and that of the king, sometimes held by the same man as was the case later with Hyrcanus II, was finally removed by Herod the Great.[90] Until then, priestly rule supported by aristocrats usually sufficed.[91]

After Pompey

The period from Pompey's conquest until the accession of Herod, 63-37 BC, witnessed bizarre happenings in Palestine. The Judaean kingdom: (i) experienced rule by high priests and even by aristocratic councils; (ii) lost some of its territory and paid tribute to Rome; (iii) fought Romans on more than one further occasion; (iv) stood in battle against Nabataeans or merely watched while Romans did; (v) saw one of the high priests carried off by Parthians into captivity; (vi) and finally had its kingship pass to a Parthian nominee and then from the class of hereditary high priests to a man 'from the common people' (as Josephus characterizes the family of Herod).[92]

i. *The High Priest* Though not now formally a king, Hyrcanus II exercised considerable powers, especially at first. Rule by a high priest only followed tradition, and constituted a return to aristocratic government, which was considered the wishes of the majority in early 63. Hyrcanus controlled the army and through the aristocracy he could look after finances; he provided the assessments Rome required, without direct intervention by Roman officials. An innovation by the governor of Syria subdivided the country into five regional aristocratic councils, but these probably endured only a short time, if in fact they ever functioned at all.[93]

The balance did apparently shift towards aristocratic rule until the time of Herod. In this quarter-century (63-37 BC), Rome itself underwent such turmoil that no consistent policy towards Judaea evolved. Pompey, Caesar, Antony, and some sixteen Roman governors of Syria all dealt with Judaea in various ways. Aware that the nation exhibited great complexity of religious, political, and class sentiment, with a diversity of attitudes concerning its relation to Rome, taxation, foreign policy, and domestic government, these Romans operated with care. Apart from some overbearing acts such as the intervention of Aulus Gabinius, or acts of outright sacrilege and thievery, including the spoliation of Temple treasures by M. Licinius Crassus, Romans employed caution in dealing with the Jews.

Pompey acceded to the wishes of perhaps the majority of the population in recognizing Hyrcanus as *archiereus* (high priest) but not *basileus* (king). In the years to follow, a bewildering assembly of titles also appeared in the country. Antipater, father of Herod, became *epimeletes* (roughly equivalent to 'governor') 'of the Jews' or 'of Judaea,' and later *epitropos* (financial agent) in Judaea, though not yet the formal equivalent of a procurator. Hyrcanus, once king – and still, like his successor, Antigonus, termed so by the Jews – became 'ethnarch of the Jews' in Caesar's terminology, as well as high priest. Eventually he and his children became 'friends and allies' of the Romans. The great local influence and, in Roman eyes, reliability of Antipater won for him unofficial recognition from Gabinius, who acted at Jerusalem 'as Antipater wished.' Caesar gave him Roman citizenship and freedom from taxation, and at one point virtual ruling power. Herod became *strategos* (governor) of Coele-Syria, or in another, improbable version, *epimeletes* 'of all Syria.' He and his brother held the office of *strategos* in Jerusalem and Galilee. Later, they became 'tetrarchs' administering all Judaea.[94]

This proliferation of offices held by so few demonstrates that Romans primarily sought a reliable ally here and were prepared to recognize local traditions as necessary. Given the complex interrelationship between politics and religion in Judaea, as well as the changing Roman personnel and policies in the East, such diversity had to result.

ii. *Territorial Losses* The territorial reductions suffered by the Judaean state after Pompey's conquest constituted a severe curtailment, especially in removing the maritime cities conquered by Hyrcanus I and Jannaeus. This coastal strip, from Dora (Tantura, north of the later Caesarea) in the north to the ancient city of Raphia in the south, covered the main Judaean outlet to the Mediterranean. The loss of nearly a dozen cities and of this sea-access could have proved serious to the state, had not Joppa (near modern Tel Aviv) and then Caesarea in the centre of this strip come back into its possession. Pompey also deprived the Judaeans of some holdings in Samaritis, Galilee, Idumaea, and the area later known as the Decapolis. Coin eras suggest that he created a separate administrative unit in the Decapolis about 63 BC, but most of the cities themselves were ancient Semitic foundations. The Jewish state shrank to Judaea itself with the remaining portions of Samaritis, Galilee,

Idumaea, and the narrow territory across the Jordan known as Peraea. Many of the cities thus freed from Jewish control, some of them termed by Josephus 'for a long time deserted,' were rebuilt, most during the Syrian governorship of Aulus Gabinius (57-55 BC). In gratitude at being freed from Jewish control, these adopted the 'Pompeian' era on their coinage, usually after some delay.[95]

Following his abbreviated account of these territorial reductions, Josephus pauses to remark that at this point the Jewish state lost its liberty and became subjected to Rome, adding that the kingship devolved no longer on those who were high priests by descent, but on men drawn from the ordinary populace. The first statement retrojects the conditions of his own day: in 63 BC much fighting lay ahead before the Jewish state could be termed 'subjected' by Rome. The second remark telescopes his narrative by anticipating the accession of Herod more than twenty-five years later. That turning-point in Judaean history reflected not only Pompey's conquest but also the efforts of his Roman successors and of those Jewish rulers who co-operated, avoiding the incessant warfare that the situation threatened.[96]

The co-operation of Antipater and his two sons, Herod and Phasael, proved especially advantageous to Romans down to the time of Antony. It was largely confidence in Antipater, and the memory of his assistance in the 'Alexandrian War,' that induced Caesar to honour the persistent request of Hyrcanus to rebuild the walls of Jerusalem and to restore vital territories to the Jews. These were the seaport of Joppa and portions of the former holdings of the Seleucids and of dynasts in Syria and Phoenicia.[97] As a reliable ally of the Romans, Judaea was to embark on a period of renewed prosperity under Herod after 37 BC.

iii. *Conflicts with Rome* In the decade after Pompey, no fewer than four armed conflicts broke out between Jews and Romans. Pompey took the unfortunate Aristobulus with him to Rome as a captive, along with his two sons. The intention appears to have been humiliation of a former ruler who had proved rebellious, for Aristobulus went fettered and two years afterward had to walk in Pompey's triumph in Rome (61 BC). One of his two sons, Alexander, had escaped on the journey to Rome and found his way back home. His presence was no more welcome to Hyrcanus than that of his father had been. However, Alexander found favour among Jews opposed to Rome, and collected an army with which he was in rebellion by 57, when Aulus Gabinius arrived in Syria. The activity of Gabinius in rebuilding cities removed by Pompey from Jewish control helped incite Alexander to warfare against Jewish and Roman forces alike. A battle near Jerusalem went against him. This became the occasion for the reconstitution by Gabinius of the

Jewish state into five districts, a move Josephus describes as a change from monarchic rule to aristocracy; but the arrangement probably soon lapsed. Caesar's later recognition of Hyrcanus as ethnarch settled things formally.[98]

In 56, Aristobulus escaped from Rome and gathered followers in Judaea. His son Antigonus escaped with him; his other son, the defeated Alexander, lived on to fight again. Aristobulus lost to a Roman force sent by Gabinius and found himself returned to Rome, but his wife, who had collaborated with Gabinius, won the release of their children.

In 55 the third conflict broke out as Alexander took advantage of the absence of Gabinius in Egypt for restoration of Ptolemy Auletes. He massacred Romans and threatened Syria. Antipater appeared at Pelusium as envoy between Gabinius and Alexander, but could not effect peace. A large force of Jews fought Gabinius near Mount Tabor and lost. Gabinius then arranged matters at Jerusalem 'as Antipater wished.' Alexander survived until 49, when Pompey ordered Scipio Nasica, governor of Syria, to execute him. By that time, Pompeians had also poisoned Aristobulus, newly arrived in Syria after his release by Caesar.[99]

The fourth conflict involved not the royal family of Aristobulus and his sons, but a former commander (*hypostrategos*) at Jerusalem: Peitholaus. This man had led Jewish troops against Alexander in the first conflict but had deserted the pro-Roman party in the second, and presumably also in the third. During the Syrian governorship of C. Cassius Longinus (53-51 BC) – the former quaestor of Crassus and later conspirator against Caesar – Peitholaus attempted to 'carry on the rebellion of Aristobulus.' However, Antipater called in Cassius. Peitholaus fell, and Cassius sent large numbers of Jews into slavery.[100]

These rebellions of the first ten or twelve years after the conquest by Pompey sprang from deeper roots than loyalty to the Hasmonaeans, since Hyrcanus could claim that lineage as well as his brother Aristobulus could. The revolts appear more factional than nationalistic, with the participants regarding Rome as another in the series of antagonists the Jewish state had faced, from the Seleucids to the Ptolemies to the Nabataeans, now to the Romans, and finally to the Parthians, soon to enter Judaean politics in force.

The ancient threat from Egypt lay dormant during the struggle of Auletes for his throne, his exile in Rome, his reinstatement, and the troubled succession of Cleopatra and her brother. But Nabataeans abode closer to Judaea; their good relations with Antipater led even to a marriage alliance. Kypros, wife of Antipater, was probably a daughter of Aretas III. The marriage specifically promoted 'friendship' between the two. However, it did not prove strong enough to provide Herod a welcome years later when he fled towards Petra.[101]

iv. *Conflicts with the Nabataeans* Nabataean coolness towards the Jews represented nothing new, and in 63 Pompey had enjoyed the assistance of Aristobulus when he set out ostensibly for Arabia. A timely diversion won him Jerusalem and the Jewish state, but Rome still needed to show the eagles in Nabataea. Whether or not Pompey envisioned a zone of Roman control encompassing portions of traditionally Nabataean holdings, he knew that the Arabs had held Damascus and a portion of Coele-Syria only a few years before. They had even invaded Judaea during the reign of Alexander Jannaeus. An incursion by Romans might help keep them at bay, with the Jewish state as an ally adjoining Nabataean territory.[102] When the invasion did occur after the departure of Pompey, under M. Aemilius Scaurus, governor of Syria, it had to be assisted by Antipater, the son-in-law of Aretas III! Antipater arranged a bribe, and Scaurus was said to be as eager as Aretas for an end to the 'war,' on which he later congratulated himself with a coin.[103]

The Nabataeans proved accommodating to Roman demands. Their military repute ranked lower than Rome's and their interests lay in maintaining the commerce on which the desert state depended. Roman motives arose more from simple need of funds than from concern over brigandage, control of caravan routes, or any threat to Syria from the Nabataeans. The wealthy kingdom cheerfully provided funds in return for peace. Lest he incur the charge of meddling in Jewish affairs, Aretas remained away when ordered to.[104]

The successors of Scaurus as governors of Syria, L. Marcius Philippus (61-60 BC) and Cn. Cornelius Lentulus Marcellinus (59-58), spent much of their terms in conflict with 'neighbouring Arabs' – not necessarily Nabataeans. The term covered local tribes: Emesenes, Ituraeans, Rhambaeans, and others.[105]

Aulus Gabinius did attack the Nabataeans after his defeat of the Jewish rebel Alexander, in 55. Relations between Gabinius and Antipater, the friend of the Nabataeans, remained smooth. Perhaps Gabinius hoped for intercession by Antipater similar to that during the campaign of Scaurus seven years before, resulting in a bribe but no fighting. In this case the ploy failed and a battle was necessary to obtain the transfer of gold.[106]

For some years, Nabataeans lived without further Judaean trouble. However, the Parthian invasion of Syria and Palestine in 40 BC brought local alignments under severe strain, since the Parthians deposed one Jewish king and installed another.[107]

King Malichus I stayed mainly out of Jewish affairs. Even when Herod sought refuge with him in 40 after the Parthian capture of Hyrcanus, Malichus refused, alleging that the Parthians forbade it. Their occupation of Judaea and Palestine that year threatened the Nabataeans from three directions, too dangerous a situation to ignore even though Herod could claim relationship through his father. Herod was forced to move on towards Rome by way of Cleopatra in Alexandria, despite tardy second thoughts by the wavering Malichus.[108]

Except for an intrigue with Hyrcanus (see below), henceforth Nabataeans tried to remain far enough from the tumult in Judaea to avoid trouble.[109]

v. *Conflict with Parthia* Judaean dealings with Parthia in the quarter-century after Pompey and before Herod (63-37 BC) at first presented no particular difficulty. Roman governors of Syria tramped off repeatedly on Parthian 'campaigns'; Caesar wished to as well, and later Antony had his adventures. But Judaea largely escaped the consequences of these stirrings until they suddenly hit home in 40 BC. Parthians decided, after their defeat of Crassus in 53, to take advantage of the increasing disarray among Romans in the East. Among other consequences of the Roman civil wars, the governorship of Syria became a prize for which candidates might even fight to the death, sometimes with Parthian involvement. The Pompeian Q. Caecilius Bassus contended, in the years 46-43 BC, with a series of Caesarians; the rivalry then continued between Cassius and an appointee of Antony. By the summer of 40, Parthians in force occupied Syria, much of southern Asia Minor, most of Phoenicia, and Palestine, including Judaea. Their alleged accomplices included Antiochus I of Commagene, the Nabataean Malichus I, and Antigonus the Hasmonaean, son of Aristobulus. The Parthians took Hyrcanus into captivity.[110]

vi. *Kings Antigonus and Herod* The Parthians rewarded Antigonus by supporting him as 'king and high priest.' The Romans responded in 40 BC by recognizing Herod as king. He had made his way to Rome and sought Antony's support, relying on their favourable relations since 41. A portion of the Jewish state, especially the aristocracy, had opposed the rapid rise of Herod and would resist him now; on the other hand, Herod seemed the strongest candidate available. Though other Romans, for instance Asinius Pollio, have also been seen as keenly interested in Judaean affairs, by and large Rome temporized now, appointing Herod but giving *de facto* recognition to Antigonus. Herod would have to win his own throne.[111]

By 40 BC, most of the dynasts who had seen the turning-point in Jewish affairs after Pompey's invasion of 63 were no longer a factor. Aristobulus II and one son, Alexander, were both dead. Hyrcanus II, brother of Aristobulus, was a Parthian captive, destined never to rule again and to meet his death at Herod's hands in 30 BC. Antipater, father of Herod and perhaps the most influential Jew during the generation of confusion after Pompey, died by poison about 43 at the hands of an ambitious Jew named Malchus (not the

Nabataean King). Phasael, Herod's brother, committed suicide in 40 after falling into Parthian hands. Antigonus, the other son of Aristobulus II, ruled the Jewish state and awaited the onslaught of Herod; there could not be two kings of the Jews.[112]

King Antigonus versus King Herod, 40-37 BC

Herod's rise to kingship had rested on secure foundations. His father, Antipater, enjoyed wide respect from Jews as well as Romans, and Herod succeeded to a good portion of this. After initial difficulties with Hyrcanus, which nearly terminated his career at its outset, he managed to win a betrothal to Mariamme, granddaughter of Hyrcanus by his daughter, Alexandra, and his nephew, Alexander, son of Aristobulus. The prospect of this marriage bode well for harmony between the factions that had supported either Hyrcanus or Aristobulus, and it promised for Herod the Hasmonaean connection that his own Idumaean and Arab parentage had failed to provide. The marriage did not take place until 37 BC, but Herod had previously announced it, to his advantage. In 40, his ostensible purpose in journeying to Rome was to obtain the kingship not for himself but for his prospective brother-in-law, another Hasmonaean named Aristobulus. He expected that Romans would recognize only a member of the existing line, as was their practice.[113]

By 40 BC, Herod had served as governor of Galilee, guardian of the armory, governor of Coele-Syria, and tetrarch of Judaea. He had enthusiastically raised funds for Cassius and had favourably impressed Antony; his promise of more money augmented his appeal now. His recognition by Antony and Octavian as King of Judaea in 40 constituted the Roman response to the Parthians' support of Antigonus. It was a time of Roman political insecurity. The aftermath of Philippi and the recent strains between Antony and Octavian precluded extensive military commitments against Parthia. However, Antony noted that if Herod were king, Romans would benefit in contending with Parthia, especially since Antigonus had received that same title from Parthians, thus 'slighting the Romans.'[114]

Herod lost little time before contending with Antigonus for the real kingship. A supporting Roman force struggled with the Parthian occupiers in Syria during 39 BC, and marched without result into Judaea. That same year, Herod began his conquests, winning Joppa and Masada, with a portion of Galilee. At one point, his support from Rome faded when Ventidius accepted a bribe from Antigonus. Josephus in fact notes that this diversion of a Roman force into Judaea 'was a device to obtain money' from the king, not unlikely given the chronic need for funds to support these Roman expeditionary forces.[115] With some renewed Roman assistance, Herod managed to reach the area of Jerusalem to attack Antigonus, who denounced him to the Romans as 'a commoner, Idumaean, and half-Jew' unworthy of the kingship. The royal power should remain within its present line, Antigonus declared, which also accorded with Roman practice in dealing with allies. If the appointment of Antigonus by Parthians caused insuperable obstacles to peace, he would abdicate in favour of another Hasmonaean of the priestly class.[116]

These arguments, backed by money, probably carried some weight with the Roman commander, Pompaedius Silo, lieutenant of P. Ventidius, governor of Syria. Silo proved to have more appetite for plundering Jericho than for besieging Jerusalem. Antigonus remained active in bribery, so the Romans lived at ease for the time being.[117]

For his part, Herod or his forces campaigned on in Idumaea, Samaria, and Galilee. In the spring of 38, Ventidius instructed Silo to assist Herod and then bring him to help resist the Parthian Pacorus I.[118] Herod delayed for a spectacular campaign against resisters in the caves of Galilee, with ineffectual assistance from a Roman force sent by Ventidius on Antony's orders. After the Roman success over the Parthians in Syria early in the summer of 38 BC, Ventidius and then Antony moved against Antiochus I of Commagene on the grounds that he had aided the Parthians. Their withdrawal left Antiochus facing a siege in Samosata. He gazed out not only at Antony, but also at Herod.[119]

Finding himself assailed by his fellow king occasioned Antiochus no surprise. As son of a Seleucid princess, Antiochus partly represented the royal house that had once dominated Judaea. As alleged collaborator with the Parthians, he had assisted the power behind the throne of Herod's rival, Antigonus. As 'enemy' of the Romans, he incurred as well the enmity of Rome's ally, Herod. The siege now provided Herod with an opportunity to repay Antony for support in his bid for kingship. Herod determined for all these reasons to appear in person before Samosata and did, despite a perilous journey.[120]

Herod's arrival is said to have determined the outcome of the siege. Antiochus saw the advantage of co-operation and became an ally of Antony.

Herod's return found a new crisis in the death of Joseph, his brother, who had been assisting the Herodian effort in Idumaea and Judaea with the help of a Roman force. The populace in parts of Galilee and Judaea revolted against the partisans of Herod. With his recruits and two Roman legions supplied by Antony, Herod defeated the army of Antigonus at Jericho and by the spring of 37 he was besieging Jerusalem itself.[121]

The siege constituted a paradigm of international politics in this region and period: a Jewish army representing the established Hasmonaean royal line and supported by the Parthians fought another Jewish army led by a 'commoner' recognized as king by Rome and supported by a Roman commander 'sent as an ally' by Antony. The combination of chronic internal discord in Judaea with its critical geographical and political position had drawn the two great powers of the day into conflict there. To underline his dynastic intention, and still apprehensive regarding his non-royal descent, Herod married his fiancée during the siege itself. Mariamme brought him a much-needed connection to the royal line: her father was Alexander, son of Aristobulus II, and her mother was Alexandra, daughter of Hyrcanus II. At one stroke Herod planned to harmonize the parties that had polarized around Mariamme's two royal grandfathers, and to ignore the 'Parthian' interval established by Antigonus after them. With his own military vigour and his new royal wife, he might now complete the siege and claim sole kingship.[122]

Thanks to the recent restoration of Jerusalem's fortifications, the siege endured until July or later, but the combination of Herod's force with a Roman one left the outcome in little doubt. The Parthians rendered no assistance to their nominee. Antigonus surrendered not to Herod but to Sosius, who sent him to Antony for execution. Herod averted desecration of the Temple by his Roman allies and prepared for unopposed kingship.

King Herod the Great

His recognition as king in Rome in 40 BC had not been accepted in Judaea, where Antigonus was regarded by the nobility as the legitimate king. Herod took steps to claim a kingship dating from 40 – among them the issuance in 37 of four coinages bearing an unprecedented feature in Jewish coins, a date ('year 3'). This feature he thought likely to enhance his new position, but some months later he abandoned this 'false' era and dated from his conquest of Antigonus, thus facilitating an amnesty and conciliating Jewish opinion. A coin of his suggests that he cultivated Greek opinion too by ascribing this victory to the Dioscuri.[123]

The task of winning over his subjects to this termination of Hasmonaean rule lay before Herod even after his military victory. As an Idumaean, a 'half-Jew,' and a Roman protégé, he could be considered – in Cleopatra's words – not among the 'true kings' of the country, with no real claim to its rule.[124] In addition, he faced the hostility of his wife's mother, Alexandra, whose father, Hyrcanus II, complicated matters after accepting Herod's invitation to return from Parthian captivity. Ineligible to serve as high priest through loss of his ears, a mutilation designed at the time of his capture to ensure this ineligibility, Hyrcanus II could nevertheless help 'legitimize' Herod's rule. He might, however, become a living reminder of the change that Herod had wrought. Among preparations for kingship after victory in

37, Herod executed a number of prominent and wealthy Jews, confiscating their resources, thus deepening the nobility's dislike of him. He also had to worry about Cleopatra, who regarded invidiously his accession and his friendship with Antony, and who maintained a strong friendship with Alexandra.[125]

Herod precipated trouble with Alexandra by ignoring her son when choosing a new high priest and instead appointing a Jew from Babylon. The intent was to remove this valuable office from Hasmonaean hands.[126] Alexandra requested that Cleopatra persuade Antony to influence Herod on behalf of her son. Herod regarded this as the first step in an attempt to supplant him in the kingship itself. Alexandra denied it, and on her undertaking not to interfere with his own rule, Herod transferred the high priesthood to her son, Aristobulus. This was the (then future) brother-in-law for whom Herod had undertaken to obtain kingship at Rome in 40, but he wished him well removed from such aspirations now. Herod also believed that the office of high priest should be divorced from that of king.[127]

Antony had no intention of intervening in matters like this, with his respect for the prerogatives of kings and for Herod personally. But the lad's personal charm came to Antony's attention and this worried Herod. He put an insupportably tight watch on the boy and Alexandra. They tried having themselves smuggled out of Jerusalem in coffins for attempted flight to Cleopatra. This sort of thing finally provoked Herod to arrange that young Aristobulus be submerged in a pool at Jericho until the bubbles stopped. Antony summoned him to an accounting. Herod went, furnished with the usual bribes.[128]

Cleopatra's attempt to get Herod removed failed. Antony, lubricated by the lavish gifts of Herod, declared that a king would not be a king if he had to explain his rule to another. Cleopatra seriously hoped to control part of Herod's territory, just as she aspired to Arabia, Syria, and even Cilicia, in restored Ptolemaic glory. She did obtain Herod's groves around Jericho, which she leased back to him.[129]

The charming story of Cleopatra's attempt to seduce Herod when they met in Judaea after seeing Antony off to Armenia shows nothing about the two rulers but their reputations, in her case for lasciviousness and in his for political calculation. That he came near to killing her seems unlikely, in view of the potential consequences; that he wished to need not be doubted.[130]

The threat from Cleopatra remained active as long as she did. Complications arising from Herod's having guaranteed payment to her not only for himself, but also for the Nabataean Malichus I – an odd action, reported without explanation by Josephus – led to a remarkable scene. Three armies (Judaeans, Nabataeans, and a force sent by Cleopatra) contended over issues rapidly becoming unclear even to the participants. Unlike previous confrontations in Hellenistic times, this one entailed Roman intervention, for Antony at Cleopatra's urging instigated the attack by Herod on the Nabataeans, while Cleopatra prepared a force for service in Nabataea, presumably with Antony's knowledge. They saw little to lose in letting Herod and Malichus distract each other. Antony declined a force offered by Herod for service against Octavian, and sent him off to Arabia.[131]

On the eve of Actium, these three kingdoms remained autonomous. Herod mentioned this in regard to Malichus and believed it of himself and Cleopatra: a monarch was a monarch.[132] The anomalous position was Antony's, influencing actions in the East more by his relation to Cleopatra than through any 'authority' from Rome, which disclaimed him as the party of Octavian prevailed. Herod acknowledged that Antony, as his patron and ally, had presented a small portion of his territory to Cleopatra. He hardly welcomed this, but accepted it in the interests of avoiding trouble with her and retaining good relations with him. Herod's main efforts now went into the difficult series of battles with the Arabs, with one catastrophic loss but ultimate victory.[133]

Herod returned from his campaign against the Arabs to find himself in an extremely dangerous situation. The battle of Actium had broken the power of Antony; the *philia* that had contributed to Herod's success now might lead to his downfall. On the other hand, Octavian himself was said to be apprehensive about Herod, for if he were to combine with the remaining forces of Antony and Cleopatra, and summon assistance from the Arabs, whom he had just defeated and over whom he had achieved the status of 'protector' (*prostates*), considerable difficulty would arise for Octavian, whose recent naval victory was scant preparation for desert campaigning. It lay in the interest of both parties to reach an accommodation.[134]

Herod also faced problems at home. The aged Hyrcanus remained alive, now the last Hasmonaean, regarded by many as more worthy of the kingship than Herod was. Alexandra, daughter of Hyrcanus and mother-in-law of Herod, remained hostile and ambitious. The Nabataean King, Malichus I, recently defeated by Herod, appreciated the prospects of greater freedom if Herod were supplanted by Hyrcanus. Whether these three combined in fact or only in the mind of Herod, he determined to have Hyrcanus executed on a charge of treason, and did. He also feared domestic problems that might arise involving his wife, Mariamme, his mother, and Salome, his sister, now married to his former enemy, Costobar. Accordingly, he left the women and his own children in custody during his trip to meet Octavian. In the next three years, Herod was to execute Mariamme, Alexandra, and Costobar; he had already executed Salome's first husband, Joseph.[135]

Herod journeyed to meet Octavian on the island of Rhodes, probably in the spring of 30 BC. He had been perhaps the most useful of the kings allied to Antony, with the exception of Polemo I, but Antony's defeat released Herod from further obligations. He had not taken part at Actium, but had sent supplies; rather than deny his services to Antony, he emphasized them to establish his credit as a loyal ally. The strategy succeeded; Octavian knew the record of Herod and his family in supporting Roman interests in the East, and he rightly foresaw usefulness to himself. Herod had already performed a service in helping the governor of Syria intercept the gladiators moving to assist Antony. His ample purse and his proven military prowess assured his value as an ally. The conqueror recognized his kingship and accepted the *philia* Herod offered.[136]

Herod knew what he must do. On the campaign against Antony and Cleopatra, he assisted Octavian without reserve; for once the family of Herod had chosen the winning side. After Antony and the hated Cleopatra were gone, Herod began the most successful and prosperous period of his life, with restoration of territories taken from the Jews by Cleopatra and before her by Pompey. So great did Herod's prestige become that distant Greek states invoked his aid, as when Ilium successfully sought his intervention after Agrippa levied a heavy fine against it. His vast building programs, begun early in his reign – interrupted at Jerusalem by the earthquake of 31 BC but later redoubled – brought new construction even into areas previously unsettled. Increasing domestic problems were to return late in his reign before his grisly death, but for the time being the relationship with Octavian during the formative years of the principate worked to their mutual benefit. In the century to come, Herod's descendants and relatives by marriage formed the core of the 'Eastern dynastic network' that governed much of the Near East. Until late in the first century AD, 'Great King Marcus Iulius Agrippa, son of Great King Agrippa,' Herod's great-grandson, carried on the work of this remarkable dynasty.[137]

8

Egypt

§ 23. The Last Ptolemies

Ptolemy XII Neos Dionysos Philopator Philadelphos Auletes (*PP* 14558)

By 70 BC, with Roman armies in the East pursuing Mithradates Eupator and Tigranes, a strong Egyptian ruler might have resisted the gathering eclipse of his kingdom and tried to reassert Egyptian claims in the Levant. Instead, Ptolemy Auletes lay slack, if we are to credit ancient perceptions, and earned his epithet *Auletes* ('Flute-Player'). This tradition of his idleness and his prowess with the flute, vying with others in contests on the instrument, could have easily been developed by a party hostile to him at court. The picture of him accompanying on the flute the subsidence of the Ptolemaic Empire appears too vivid not to elicit some scepticism now. Such pictures formed easily in antiquity (Sardanapalus on his cushions; Nero fiddling).[1] Doubtless the prospect of venturing forth into an almost certain losing effort at restoration of Egyptian glory held little appeal. Better to let others deal with Tigranes and Mithradates, in the hope of retaining Egypt. The revenues of Egypt flowed undiminished, despite charges of misadministration levelled at Auletes and his court; the sources emphasize his great wealth. An inscription from 62 BC shows the Egyptians still maintaining an official standing in the Arabian Gulf, source of luxuries from beyond. Ptolemy XII had the means to live as he chose; his sobriquets *Auletes* and *Neos Dionysos* ('New Dionysos' or Bacchus) indicate the directions he sometimes took.[2]

The tradition imputing bastard birth to Auletes might have impeded his rule, if this view gained currency, but the Ptolemaic court viewed such matters with less severity than Romans would. His father was Ptolemy IX

Soter II, but the identity and credentials of his mother remain in doubt. The postulated intermarriage of the Ptolemaic family with the line of high priests at Memphis could provide ample scepticism at court, should Auletes's mother have derived from this connection (see stemma).[3] The status of *nothos* ('bastard') could have hampered Auletes in relations with his people, by whom he was deeply disliked. An amusing bust of him as a bacchant captures the indolence, weakness, and unmanliness popularly ascribed to him, whether as king or god.[4]

The widespread ancient impression of repeated revolts against Auletes by his subjects in 65, 63, and 58 may have arisen out of the one clear interruption of his reign, from summer 58 to April 55 BC.[5] Conversely, it may stem from actual incidents that have escaped documentation, as well as from the repeated instances of unrest in the country for economic reasons. The presence of restless elements in Alexandria can be detected throughout his reign. They opposed him for a number of reasons: nationalistic convictions; apprehension at continued loss of traditional Egyptian possessions in Cyrene (claimed since the reign of Ptolemy I), Cyprus, Palestine, and Syria; despair at extinction of the Seleucid branch of the Ptolemaic line; disgust at the weakness of this current representative of the once-robust dynasty; contempt for his reputed illegitimacy; and in due course, resentment of Roman interference.[6]

We must recall that in Egypt, an alien dynasty ruled by force over a society inured to foreign domination and long indifferent to it. The transition from Persian to Macedonian hegemony had little affected the mass of the population. Art forms remained largely as they had for millennia; foreign wars passed unnoticed unless requisitions intruded on the ancient pace of life in the land upstream from Alexandria. The lavishness at court caused no pride among those whose labour provided it and who had little stake in the wider fortunes of the dynasty. Occasionally native resentment erupted in notable rioting, but for the most part the countryside remained quiet, which, together with the pacific foreign policy of Auletes, gave a misleading impression of Egyptians as 'unwarlike.' They were not so, in and around Alexandria, and a papyrus from soon after Cleopatra's death calls 'the Egyptians around Thebes ... more warlike than the others.'[7]

Underlying the increasing domestic troubles of Auletes lurked a social phenomenon dangerous to continued Ptolemaic rule. As the dynasty weakened, along with the Seleucids, the masses of Egypt grew ever more assertive. Especially among the lower classes, upon whom the burden of this increasingly expensive state fell most heavily, the combination of limited resources and restricted upward mobility heightened frustration whenever unusual exactions befell them, such as those Auletes required to pay his huge bribes to Pompey and Caesar. On the other hand, a group of 159 papyri from Heracleopolis mainly covering the period from 'Year 18' of Auletes (64/63 BC) to 'year 8' of Cleopatra (45/44) clearly demonstrates continuity and personal loyalty among the officials appointed by Auletes. Some may have joined him in exile, and others can be detected proceeding from his service into Cleopatra's.

The few did rise through the grades of society. The army had become virtually professional, with a strong mixture of Egyptians, Greeks, and foreigners, including adventurers from Syria, Cilicia, and farther north. A strong camaraderie prompted such dedications as one from the second century BC in which 'the main body of cavalry in Alexandria' honour their *strategos* as 'fellow campaigner' and 'kinsman' (an honourific, not meant literally). However, discipline broke down after the return of Auletes from exile. Fugitive slaves, as Caesar later complains, and even Romans from the force used to reinstall Auletes in 55, settled into the slack and enjoyable life of Alexandria. In addition, criminals and exiles flocked to the city. The army contained a loyal element, long in Ptolemaic service, which proved useful to Auletes more than once; city garrisons helped assure stability.[8] This mixed army, with its own social and religious traditions and an increasing percentage of soldiers married to native women, provided one of the few avenues of advancement for members of the lower and middle classes. The Alexandrians too were already 'mixed' when Polybius visited in the late second century. The process intensified under Auletes, especially after his restoration in 55, when Romans from the army of Gabinius married native women and sired children.[9]

The population resident in and near Alexandria became a fusion of ethnic strains, with no intrinsic reason for loyalty to the Ptolemies. Its lower and middle classes found few opportunities available in the other areas open to them – the administration itself or agriculture. The ablest and most fortunate might rise in either sphere, but unfortunately for them, when popular revolts did occur, the targets were the wealthy classes, the landowners, and the government itself.

The upper classes progressed towards a certain admixture with their Greek rulers. Higher posts in the government, the diplomatic service, the army, and the valuable priesthoods lay open to well-born or well-connected native Egyptians, especially those with a knowledge of Greek. The native clergy sometimes bore part-Greek nomenclature, and at the highest court levels successful natives spoke fluent Greek, a virtual prerequisite. The Ptolemies gained a certain notoriety for their inability to speak Egyptian and this disdain caused ill will. Cleopatra won special praise for her facility with this and several other languages of her subjects or dynastic neighbours.[10]

In the reign of Auletes, a danger greater than disaffection by some of his subjects arose from the claims of Rome. These took the form of accepting 'bequests' regarding Cyrene and Egypt itself, or of naked intervention, as in Cyprus. A worse danger lay in Roman ambitions to extract some of Egypt's fabled wealth, or even to transform that nation into a Roman province.

As to the bequests (§ 10), that of Cyrene nominally made in 96 had now been taken up, in 74, though conversion into a province took a decade longer. Income from royal estates and the import of silphium constituted the extent of Roman interest in the region for some time, and the *de facto* interregnum for a generation after 96 caused the anarchy observed by Lucullus during his visit there in 86 BC.[11] The alleged bequest of Egypt itself by Ptolemy XI Alexander II after his nineteen days' reign in 80 had not yet been acted upon, and doubts as to its authenticity persisted among Romans. If the bequest was genuine, failure of Romans to take it up appears odd, for Egypt's wealth beckoned and the difficulties of ruling it – though undeniable – should not have deterred a state willing to exercise rule by now in Cyrene, Bithynia, and Asia. In fact, no Roman assumption of Egypt occurred until the reign of Augustus, who can boast, 'I added Egypt to the domain of the Roman people.'[12]

Auletes himself was to ask Pompey's assistance, and Caesar considered converting Egypt into a province, during his months in Alexandria. However, he rejected it lest it prove one day a seat of Roman revolution. Augustus may have had this in mind when accounting for his decision 'on the example of our ancestors' not to convert Armenia into a province.[13]

Auletes was not to know in advance of his success and that of Cleopatra, his daughter, in retaining Egyptian independence for some forty years more. He knew that Romans had become increasingly interested in Egypt, and even before he fell into the clutches of Roman money-lenders he must have dealt with Italian merchants. The famous visit of Scipio Aemilianus in 140/139 BC had produced a glowing account of Egypt's wealth, populousness, and impressive cities. It had been followed by a group of Roman traders settled in Alexandria probably by 127, and a spectacular visit by a Roman senator in 112 BC.[14] Within the lifetime of Auletes, Lucullus had visited Egypt (87/86 BC), with important consequences for Egyptian autonomy (§ 10). A rare glimpse of Egyptian attitudes to Rome occurs in an anecdote of Diodorus derived from his visit there. About 60 BC, a Roman embassy arrived in Egypt and Diodorus affirms that care was taken not to offend its members. But an incident involving a Roman either resident in Alexandria or visiting there provides a vivid insight into the ambivalence of local attitudes. The Roman had been observed killing a cat, an animal still sacred in Egypt, and the enraged populace decided to punish him, despite the 'general fear of Rome' locally. Auletes heard of the incident and rushed officers to defend the Roman, but the mob succeeded in hanging him.[15]

Against this background, Auletes must have watched apprehensively any Roman debates on the future of Egypt. Some have thought that Pompey entered the country in 67; in 65, a debate over conversion of Egypt into a province allegedly occurred; in 63, Auletes entered the shifting alignments of politicians by seeking to bring Pompey to his court; and in 59, he offered bribes to Caesar to effect his recognition as 'friend and ally' of Rome. Now to examine these important stages more closely.

A passage in Lucan recites the extent of Pompey's campaigns and mentions that 'the middle zone in torrid Egypt is known to me, and Syene, where the shadows nowhere diverge [from the perpendicular].'[16] Pompey's career leaves room for such a visit only between his campaign against the Cilician pirates and his movement northward in the new command against Mithradates, that is, either late in 67 or early in 66 BC.[17] Since this winter was spent either in Cilicia or nearby in Asia Minor, a journey to Egypt and as far south as Syene could have been worked into the time available, though Pompey had no mandate to go there.[18] A remark of Appian, appropriate to the context of 63 BC, that Pompey did not enter Egypt need refer only to that year, not to his entire span of work in the East from 67 to 62 BC. No record survives of contact in 67/66 between Pompey and the Nabataean King, Aretas, but that need not preclude a trip to Egypt then.[19] Pompey's activity in the East affected Egypt in many ways, as Appian probably stressed in his lost *Egyptian History*, which he says will deal with this question. This reference cannot prove a trip there in 67, though for many reasons such a journey was advisable for one intending to control the East.[20] The detail mentioned by Lucan, that Pompey's experience also included Syene, suggests a trip undertaken in company with Auletes, for the temple at nearby Philae had an especial appeal to the young king, as attested by his numerous inscriptions there.[21]

Whether or not Pompey visited the king in 67, Egypt lay on the minds of some Romans. Covetous eyes were cast in its direction during 65, when M. Licinius Crassus introduced a bill to send Caesar there. The aim, 'to make Egypt tributary to Rome,' appeared dangerous to others and his colleague Catulus opposed the idea successfully. In a speech two years later, Cicero notes the openness of designs on Egypt by this group in 65 BC.[22] The details of their scheme lie now obscure, but some heady scent wafted across the Mediterranean that year, possibly stirred by a brief expulsion of Auletes.[23]

By 63, the temptation had become irresistible.[24] The combination of local unrest, of contempt for a king regarded as weak, and of his own predilection to look for Roman assistance made further contact inevitable, especially with

Pompey in the East.[25] The danger to Eastern monarchs of Pompey's presence after passage of the *lex Manilia* was tempered by his removal of the threat posed by Tigranes and Mithradates Eupator. To Auletes, plagued by problems at home, Pompey appeared an important ally. Cleopatra Selene was now six or seven years dead at the hands of Tigranes, and the remaining Seleucid princes had lost their power if not their lives. Far from daring to reassert lingering Ptolemaic claims in Syria, Auletes showered on Pompey gifts and offers of armed assistance, hoping to induce him to enter Egypt in a show of support for the monarch.[26] But Pompey declined, despite – as events were to show – an abiding interest in obtaining an Egyptian command.

Other Romans aspired to the same assignment. Cicero fulminated in the Senate against a group now planning to take up the 'bequest' of Ptolemy XI Alexander II, despite doubts that it ever existed. Cicero implies that the men involved in 63 were largely the same ones who had failed two years before. Now, instead of proceeding openly to make Egypt tributary, they hoped to take up the putative inheritance through a commission of *decemviri*. He accuses P. Rullus and his colleagues of intending to achieve by subterfuge that which they had failed to attain openly. In his rhetoric, Rullus 'will sell Alexandria, will sell Egypt' and will come into control 'of a most wealthy city, a most beautiful countryside ... a most opulent kingdom.'[27]

Added to the attractions of the kingdom lay the deficiencies of the king, 'whom nearly all agree to be royal neither in birth nor in spirit.'[28] What better set of circumstances to warrant intervention? A rich land with a weak king of bastard birth provided every incentive. Pompey declined the visit but accepted the rich gifts and auxiliaries. He knew that Egypt hung ripe for plucking, but the visit would not secure it for him. Better to return to Rome and secure a command for Egypt, in the meantime using his supporters to block similar attempts by others, which were not long in coming.

In the meantime, Ptolemy Auletes ruled on. A *prostagma* from 11 December 63 shows him forbidding unauthorized entrance to sacred treasuries, probably a routine measure but one useful in demonstrating continued smooth functioning of his bureaucracy. For the moment his throne stood secure.[29] It shook within five years for two reasons connected with Rome – the enormous sums Auletes raised to bribe Caesar, and the Roman seizure of his brother's kingdom in Cyprus.

Auletes precipitated some of his own troubles with Rome, for he sought the two-edged sword of Roman military assistance against his own subjects. He also schemed for recognition as 'friend and ally,' since ambitious foreign generals would lay hands less often on the territory of friends than of enemies. After averting a threat from Crassus and Caesar in 65, and failing to obtain Pompey's assistance in 63, Auletes achieved his first major success through Caesar and Pompey in 59, probably in February or March.[30] As before, rumour had Caesar pondering the annexation of Egypt to Rome. The prospect ranked low on Auletes's list of desiderata, but he determined to turn it to his advantage. Caesar aspired to wealth, which Auletes possessed. Might not a mutually beneficial redistribution occur?

Caesar secured for Auletes recognition as *socius* and *amicus*. Certain little costs attached to such an effort, it was understood; expenditure by Auletes of the enormous sum of six thousand talents recompensed Caesar. None openly employed the term *bribe*, but such the transaction seemed later.[31] Auletes borrowed from Roman financiers and relied on his own purse or domestic exactions to pay it. Perhaps this occasioned his initial indebtedness to Rabirius Postumus.[32]

The sums appeared worth it at the time, and the ties were duly completed 'both by law and by decree of the Senate.'[33] The new relationship of Egypt to Rome does not escape several ancient authors; it was a matter of moment even among recent changes in the East after Pompey. Many 'friends and allies' of Rome ruled there, with the ancient Kingdom of Egypt now added to their number.[34]

Auletes proclaimed decrees to let the populace share his joy, to judge from a papyrus.[35] Of more immediate concern to them loomed the six thousand talents, part of which he had to collect 'by force from the Egyptians.'[36] Taxes had already been too heavy, and the Alexandrines showed their wrath repeatedly.[37] The sum required bulked large even for an Egyptian king, especially when confiscatory rates of interest weighted the scale. The debt was to grow so enormous that despite a decade of payments nearly half of it remained at the death of Auletes for his successors to discharge.[38]

To compel obedience, he might rely on a reasonably well-disciplined domestic force, though it was falsely alleged that he 'lacked mercenaries' and required but could not obtain 'foreign forces.'[39] Auletes needed to pacify his subjects by attending to religious duties expected of the monarch, and proved more diligent than the image of his indolent life at court suggests. One text details a journey of inspection he undertook throughout Egypt, complete with religious festivities.[40] Another, mentioned above, shows him regulating access to temple treasuries. His name and titles stand proudly on a granite effigy of a crocodile ('great god Petesuchos') from Crocodilopolis-Arsinoe, dated 16 April 58 BC.[41] Especially numerous dedications at Philae to Isis – appropriate for 'New Dionysos' (Horus) and 'New Osiris' – appear from his reign.[42] He completed some two centuries' work by the Ptolemies on the temple at Edfu (see below).[43] At a number of other sites he completed or signed his name to the work of others. The purpose lay in his need for 'legitimacy' in the popular view – hence carvings of him as a traditional Pharaoh.[44]

Ptolemy of Cyprus
(*PP* 14559)

Another problem proved more dangerous to Auletes than any yet faced in Alexandria during his reign: the loss of Cyprus. Though later temporarily reversed under Cleopatra, this proved in 58 a severe blow to the stability of Egypt and to the reign of Auletes, leading perhaps to his deposition.[45]

Ptolemy of Cyprus had assumed his throne in 80, after the death of his father, Ptolemy IX Soter II Lathyros.[46] He appears to have been of sterner stuff than Auletes, his brother, and in this case it worked against him, to the extent that he provoked the illegal act that cost him his kingdom.

Some years before, perhaps in 67, P. Clodius Pulcher had fallen captive to Cilician pirates.[47] The story became somewhat garbled in transmission, but presents clear outlines. The pirates demanded a ransom he could not pay. Whether on their suggestion – seeking to provoke a distracting enmity between Rome and Cyprus – or on his own initiative, Clodius requested payment from Ptolemy of Cyprus. Ptolemy did pay, but the sum, perhaps two talents, was deemed insufficient and was returned. None the less, the pirates released Clodius.

Did Ptolemy of Cyprus have any obligation in this affair? Neither he nor his brother had yet been named 'friend and ally' of Rome by the mid-sixties. In fact, Ptolemy of Cyprus probably never became one, despite a later tradition that he had.[48] The testimony of Cicero is clear, in a context which would have induced him to claim allied status if he could: 'King Ptolemy ... had not yet been termed "ally" by the Senate ... [but] ... was a king who, if not yet an "ally", was still not an enemy.'[49] A vague understanding that he came under Roman protection (*fretus imperio populi Romani*) conferred no obligation on him, and in the event did nothing to protect him from Roman interference.

Acting partly from motives of revenge, Clodius moved against Cyprus as tribune of the people for 58, and appointed Cato to the task without ships or troops.[50] The inevitable inducement of financial reward also bulked large in his thinking. Some seven thousand silver talents eventually reached Rome, delivered by Cato, who discerned no moral problem in thus acquiring by force, on the authority of a tribune, a portion of the Ptolemies' domains.[51] The charge probably ran that Ptolemy had assisted the pirates; the countervailing plea that he had remained a friendly king guilty of no wrongdoing was not made in time. An all-purpose accusation, that of bad character, also served.[52]

Ptolemy of Cyprus faced this aggression with dignity, choosing suicide rather than futile resistance in the absence of aid from Auletes. The suggested position as priest in the temple of Aphrodite at Paphos hardly appealed to a king.[53]

No reasonable grounds had been put forward for this seizure. The pique of Clodius hardly justified annexation, since Cyprus offered no threat to Rome, though pirates might use it.[54] Nor had Ptolemy threatened Rome when betrothed to a daughter of Mithradates Eupator years before.[55] It was immaterial that Eupator had formerly encouraged the Cilician pirates.[56] Basically, the annexation had to rest on the grounds that Rome could accomplish the act, and chose to, while the East slowly recovered from the wars of the previous thirty years.[57]

As expected, the Alexandrians reacted to the news with rage, for the most part directing it at Auletes. Despite his recent alliance, he found no way to resist this action – a result doubtless foreseen by Clodius in appointing Cato to take control of Cyprus. Auletes did nothing, and probably paid for it with ejection from his throne.[58]

Exile of Auletes, 58-55 BC

Since antiquity the questions raised by this departure have resisted solution. One strand of testimony ascribes it to revolt in Alexandria.[59] Dio has him slip away so quietly that his absence took some time to discover. The papyri may show that his finance minister (*dioiketes*), Hephaistion, shared his exile and return.[60] A second strand has him merely interested in a trip to Rome, perhaps as a precaution, with a leisurely course through Rhodes and Athens. Plutarch states that he left under no compulsion and without apparent reason, though elsewhere he says 'in some anger and disagreement with the citizens.' The catalyst was provided by the ambitions of Pompey for a command, using his agent Theophanes to work on Auletes.[61] The latest date for Auletes to be discerned reigning and in Egypt is 11 August 58, or 'year 23, Mesore 10.'[62] But his 'year 24' (7 September 58 to 5 September 57) is equated with Berenice's 'year 1,' so that he must have remained until at least its beginning.[63] Papyri which might attest a 'year 25' for him (i.e., 6 September 57 to 5 September 56) do not certainly bear this date; inscriptions from Philae to him in that year, and the date in December 57 for him on the pylon at Edfu (see below), do not prove him still resident.[64] It seems most likely that his absence began in the autumn of 58; it was to endure until the spring of 55, a long period abroad with important consequences.[65]

From the beginning, it was fraught with conspiracy, bribery, and indignities. On the way to Rome he visited Rhodes and met his late brother's enemy, Cato, who advised his return to Alexandria and offered assistance.[66] This assistance ought to have been welcome to Auletes, who had left his family behind and expected further unrest in Alexandria, but he knew Roman politics and regarded Pompey as a more reliable source of support than Cato was. Either he declined, or the offer had not been made seriously, for he continued towards Rome, apparently by way of Athens, where Cleopatra, his daughter, may have stayed, and where monuments to his ancestors included recent ones for Lathyros and Berenice III.[67]

On arrival in Rome, Auletes met with a good reception, taken in hand by no less an advocate than Pompey and brought before the Senate.[68] Many in Rome regarded Pompey as instigator of the trip by Auletes, with future military gains in mind.[69] But it was to prove a political struggle of the first magnitude, an issue so intractable because of party interests that it dragged on for years and influenced not only Egyptian affairs, but also careers in Rome.

Meanwhile, the Alexandrian harboured no illusions as to the dangers of the situation. They sent an embassy of one hundred members to counteract the activities of Auletes in Rome. Their dislike of him, combined with a satisfactory appointment of two queens in his stead (see below), led them to oppose with vigour any plan to restore him by force of Roman arms. Auletes learned of the ambassadors' approach and forestalled it, using borrowed money to hire assassins, who intercepted and cut up the embassy on its way to Rome from Puteoli. The game had turned serious.[70]

By the autumn of 57, a topic of interest in Rome concerned the restoration of Auletes. The Senate decreed this, calling upon the consul P. Lentulus Spinther, designated for the next year to govern Cilicia, with the addition of Cyprus.[71] Auletes preferred restoration by Pompey, which met the desires of Pompey too: what better stepping-stone to further advancement than troops, a navy, and a segment of Egypt's wealth from a grateful Auletes?[72] Cicero knows this to be Pompey's intention, and that Auletes will co-operate.[73]

The matter became too important to ignore, and the opportunity too great to lose. A bizarre device blocked the proposed restoration. Timely discovery by Cato of a Sibylline oracle appeared to forbid the restoration should that require a band of men (*cum multitudine hominum*), as of course it would. Even Cicero, who regarded this as a sham, dared not suggest a course contradicting the oracle.[74]

Voices rose in the Senate this autumn against Auletes, citing both his murders of Alexandrian envoys and his bribing of Romans. He rapidly became quite unpopular, but retained a few powerful supporters. It appeared politic for him to withdraw and operate through an agent (Ammonius), hoping still to effect restoration by Pompey. He left Rome and took refuge at the temple of Artemis in Ephesus, a safer location for him now than Rome.[75]

All through the early months of 56 the struggle continued, with a variety of proposals, each unsuitable to one faction or another. Pompey did not approve of the one that would employ Lentulus for the restoration, but the Sibylline prohibition, however transparent, could not be ignored. Pompey had to wait, opposed by Clodius, C. Cato, and others, and sometimes feigning indifference (*Syriam spernens*). In August, Cicero was still attempting to find a way around the oracle by having Lentulus Spinther recover the king's throne for him while Auletes waited in Ptolemais, thus somehow obviating the need for employing the 'band of men' it forbade. This desperate counsel would allow Spinther to 'hold' (*tenere possis*) Alexandria and Egypt. And so in Rome, at Cicero's favourite time for writing such letters, burned the pre-dawn lamp.[76]

Romans continued for months to salivate over the potential command in Egypt, while Cicero fed Spinther frequent portions of encouragement ('... for you, with Egypt almost in sight ...'). The attractions of this command had been lost on no one in Rome. The religious issue came forward basically 'lest anyone wish to visit Alexandria through desire of a military command.' For that reason, what had become something of a scramble for the post did not find a ready resolution, as the year 56 wore on.[77]

The severe unrest in Rome during 57 and 56 retarded progress towards restoration of Auletes. Egyptians watched with apprehension, aware that their country lay exposed to a new combination of dangerous adversaries. To the west, Cyrene had become a Roman province, with a governor now attestably present; to the north, Cyprus had fallen after centuries of Ptolemaic rule. Syria, long an object of Ptolemaic aspirations, had become a Roman province too; its governors in these years came into armed conflict with two neighbours of Egypt, the Nabataeans and the Jews. By 57, Aulus Gabinius had arrived in Syria and in two years was to undertake the armed restoration of Auletes.[78] Apprehension mounted in Egypt.

The antipathy Egyptians felt for Auletes affected Romans too. Many desired to be rid of the question. Egyptians had another reason for viewing his proposed restoration with distaste: they had found a better ruler, his daughter.

Berenice IV (*PP* 14504)

On realizing that Auletes had fled to Rome in 58, the Alexandrians examined their royal family and discerned a candidate for rule. Strabo described the children of Auletes as two infant sons not yet to be considered for rule and 'three daughters, of whom one, the eldest, was legitimate.'[79] Whether or not Auletes himself could be regarded as legitimate, no unpleasant questions were asked about Berenice, who began to rule probably in the autumn of 58, her 'year 1' equated with his 'year 24' (7 September 58 to 5 September 57).[80]

On some ancient testimony, a certain Cleopatra Tryphaena ruled with Berenice for the first year.[81] Can this be the wife of Auletes, attested in the papyri and inscriptions for a decade after their marriage in or before 79 BC?[82] She seemingly disappears from the papyri after February 68, and scholars have thought her either dead or disgraced by then.[83]

However, a papyrus confirms the ancient tradition of two queens, and a more dramatic piece of evidence that she still lived can be found on a temple.[84] For nearly two centuries, at least since the reign of Euergetes I, the Ptolemies had been constructing and embellishing the temple at Edfu. Even as the departure of Auletes for Rome occurred in 58, his workmen were putting the final touches to massive cedar-and-bronze doors at its entrance, and carvings were appearing on the pylons. Among the representations stands the following inscription, published in 1870: 'Ptolemy the New Dionysos with his sister and wife, Queen Cleopatra also called Tryphaena.'[85] However, Porphyry, who reports this year of dual reign, regards Berenice's associate as not the wife but the daughter of Auletes, that is, Cleopatra VI.[86] Can this inscription outweigh the testimony of Porphyry and the previous silence of our extant documents?

It can. Rule by two sisters does not make sense, but rule of the eldest daughter supported by association with her mother, queen for over twenty years by now, does. The temple is dedicated in 'year 25, 1 Choiak,' or December 57 BC. Auletes had long since left for Rome, but Berenice and Cleopatra Tryphaena were probably regarded as vice-regents rather than regents in their own right, in the absence of formal deposition of Auletes. It would be in their interest to maintain the façade of continuity by honouring Queen Cleopatra alongside Auletes at Edfu. The inscription does, after all, describe her as both queen and *sister*, and can only mean the wife of Auletes. Had she died by this time, the logical dedication would have been to Auletes and Berenice, as eldest daughter, not to Auletes and the younger Cleopatra VI.

The objection that Cleopatra V Tryphaena 'disappears' from the documents after early 68 begs the question here, where the mention fits only her. If the dedication is posthumous, then we must ask why such honours arise for a queen dead now some ten years. The strained conjectures have less to recommend them than does the simple postulate that she lived still; her absence from the few documents we have of the preceding decade must be otherwise explained.[87] Her participation in government, as the former and present queen, probably did much to render the interregnum acceptable to the Alexandrians, who wished a full succession to Auletes. The death of

Cleopatra V after a year of joint rule left Berenice unchallenged on the throne of the Ptolemies.

But here lay the rub. For a period, documents refer only to her ('Queen Berenice, the Goddess Manifest'). With no tradition of rule by a queen alone, the Alexandrines sought a dynastic husband for her.[88] Perhaps a regime solid enough to supplant that of Auletes and forestall his impending restoration by Romans could be established. Interestingly, thoughts turned first to the Seleucids, who could still supply princes for potential rule in Egypt, and whose new-found leisure after the conquests of Tigranes and Pompey provided opportunity for acceptance of such assignments. One prince suggested was probably Antiochus XIII Asiaticus, the son of Cleopatra Selene (*PP* 14520), who with his brother had journeyed to Rome in 75 BC hoping to gain the throne of Egypt. But Antiochus may later have been killed by Sampsigeramus I of Emesa, as Diodorus asserts. In that case, the man named Antiochus found now for Berenice would be his relative, but his death from an 'illness' terminated the arrangement. Attention turned to the former king, Philip II Barypous, who had ruled briefly in Syria around 66 BC.[89] However, Aulus Gabinius, proconsul of Syria from 57 to 55 BC, blocked the move, concerned at this obvious strengthening of Ptolemaic connections and weakening of Pompey's prospects for restoration of an even more unwelcome Auletes.[90]

Finally a candidate succeeded, another son of Cleopatra Selene named Seleucus. Marriage ensued and all seemed right with the Ptolemaic world. Then, unfortunately, his lineage came into question at court, prompted perhaps by his rather rough personal qualities, which earned him the sobriquet *Kubiosaktes*, 'seller of cubed tunny-fish.' Berenice allowed her delicacy of sentiment to prevail and after a few days of marriage had him strangled.[91] His nickname, if not his person, so caught the imagination of the irrepressible Alexandrians that they still remembered it over a century later and applied it to Vespasian.[92]

The long traditions of the Pharaohs, and now of the Ptolemies' three centuries, deserved better than this, so a new search began. In Syria, Gabinius had received by early in 56 BC a member of the royal family of Pontus, Archelaus. The man proclaimed this connection and was understood to be asserting that he was the son of Mithradates Eupator, of whom he does seem to have been a grandson. His father had served Mithradates and he himself had been recognized by Pompey as priest of Pontic Comana, a traditional place for princes to serve, as Cappadocian dynasts did in their own Comana. He left for further adventures, with his son succeeding him in the priesthood. He was now living in Syria, with some intention of joining a Parthian expedition planned by his 'friend' Gabinius.[93]

Because of his high descent, Archelaus was viewed with suspicion by Gabinius, who detained him. An invitation from Egypt arrived, inducing Archelaus to buy his freedom. Whether brought secretly away by agents of the Ptolemaic court or on his own initiative, he appeared in Alexandria and won acceptance as the second groom for Berenice.[94] As a descendant of the Pontic royal house, Archelaus already enjoyed distant relationship to the Ptolemies, partly by way of Seleucid connections with both lines. Among these Seleucids in Pontus had been the mother of Mithradates and great-grandmother of Archelaus, Laodice, daughter of Antiochus IV Epiphanes. Berenice's great-aunt, Cleopatra Thea, numbered among her sons Antiochus VIII Grypus, grandfather of the King Philip II whom she had just tried to marry. Berenice's grandmother, Cleopatra Selene, had married no fewer than three Seleucid kings. The earlier betrothal of Berenice's father, Auletes, and Ptolemy of Cyprus, her uncle, to daughters of Eupator would have furthered ties between Egypt and Pontus. The present marriage of Archelaus and Berenice represented one more effort in Alexandria at pursuing traditional intermarriage. The measures Cleopatra VII took in this regard for herself and her children in the decades to come demonstrates the continuing instinct for marriage alliances.[95]

The marriage occurred by April 56 BC and gave every evidence of success. Livy refers to Archelaus simply as the man 'whom the Egyptians had recognized as their king,' which seems to have been the prevailing attitude. A smooth transition to joint rule reflected itself in the official titulature adopted for court documents, and in a dual regnal era. So stood the royal governance of Egypt for something like a year, and it would have endured longer had Egyptians got their way.[96]

However, Aulus Gabinius, proconsul of Syria, determined with Pompey to ignore the Sibylline prohibition – for which Cicero later rebuked him – and to restore Auletes 'against the wishes of the state' of Rome. Romans had voted against the restoration, despite their weariness of the 'Alexandrian question' and the rampant bribery by Auletes. The ambitions of Gabinius and Pompey impelled them to an illegal act for which Gabinius would later stand trial, though rescued by Pompey's influence.[97]

Berenice had foreseen the danger; 'she feared the Romans, but was unable to accomplish anything suitable.' After at most a year of rule with her, Archelaus had no means of mounting vigorous resistance. The unreliable army at Alexandria disliked Auletes and feared his return, but saw little future in supporting Archelaus; some made timely defections to Auletes.[98]

Gabinius experienced little difficulty with the military side. The excuse that the navy of Archelaus might harass Syrian waters with piracy furnished a pretext for invasion. Gabinius wavered before the dangers presented by the march to Pelusium but was steadied by his cavalry commander, Mark Antony. At Pelusium Auletes gave further reason for the reluctance of Egyptians to receive him again by nearly effecting a massacre, prevented only by the intercession of Antony.[99] The resistance put up by Archelaus and his troops, though ineffective, did suffice to characterize what followed as a 'war' (*bellum*).[100]

Archelaus fell in battle, allegedly slain by Gabinius himself. This constituted a serious breach of international practice, since Egyptians regarded his rule with Berenice as legitimate and had recognized both. Antony, who knew Archelaus previously, perhaps in Syria, treated the body well and won praise for this from the family, the later rulers of Cappadocia.[101] Antony then moved for the first time into the perfumed vicinity of the young princess Cleopatra. He was at once enkindled.[102]

Auletes Restored

So Auletes returned to his court. The apprehensions of the Alexandrians proved well founded. Acting from motives of vengeance and desire for funds, Auletes executed a number of wealthy subjects. The slaughter that he initiated did not stop even at his daughter. He regarded her as a usurper rather than a caretaker, since at his hasty departure he had not appointed her in his stead. Her dual era with Archelaus showed that Egyptians were preparing to continue indefinitely without Auletes, an attitude of which he certainly knew. However, his 'year 27' on documents as far afield as Thebes shows him ruling as if no break had occurred.[103]

The spoliation of the wealthy renewed their hatred for Auletes, shared by much of the population of Alexandria.[104] The peasants upriver toiled as ever and delighted in their crops, gifts of Nile silt, abundant sunshine, and favourable temperatures. The name of Auletes rang only distantly there.

The situation in Alexandria remained tense. Gabinius left for Syria, where the Judaean Alexander had begun killing Romans.[105] Part of his forces returned with him to Syria, eventually finding their way into the army of Pompey in the civil wars.[106] It is notable that when Crassus succeeded Gabinius in Syria his proposed sphere of control included not only Syria but also Egypt. The stability of the restored regime remained a concern. Crassus had larger things on his mind and in 53 disappeared eastward into Parthia, where he and his head remained separately. In Rome, relations worsened between Caesar and Pompey. As the Roman civil wars approached, Auletes was left on his own.[107]

Auletes took care of his forces. These included a Roman contingent left by Gabinius as a garrison, protecting the hated king from his own people.[108] He won the Roman troops' loyalty by rewarding them with a life of luxury. Seven years later, Caesar observed that the Ptolemaic army, a collection which included Greeks, native Egyptians, Gauls, Germans, fugitives, brigands, and some Gabinian troops, still constituted a formidable force. However, these Romans had taken native wives and no longer retained 'the name and discipline of the Roman people.'[109]

Auletes now faced enormous debts to the Romans. His financial condition before departure to Rome might not have been so secure as Strabo, for instance, believed. His call for assistance from Caesar in 59 cost him heavily and led to borrowings from Roman financiers, who had developed to an art the practice of lending money at high rates of interest. In one case, Ariobarzanes III in Cappadocia, king of a once-wealthy realm, could not even pay the interest on his debt to Pompey.[110] Auletes fell into the toils of Roman financiers before his trip to Rome. In his oration for Rabirius Postumus, Cicero implies that he had lent Auletes money before his exile, and Postumus certainly was in Egypt after the restoration, claiming later that he had been forced to remain as a virtual *dioiketes* (treasurer) for Auletes. Financial expertise was hardly lacking in Egypt, where the oldest continuous political office in the world (that of Pharaoh) still functioned under the Ptolemies. The real motive was to ensure that the king repaid his abundant debts.[111]

These arose from three sources: bribes to Caesar, interest on the original sum, and the new amounts necessary to effect restoration. On the original six thousand talents, Auletes paid such interest that even after his death four years later, he still owed more than half. The figure given is 17.5 million drachmas remaining.[112] In Roman terms, Auletes had borrowed 384 million sesterces, an almost incomprehensible sum, which at the prevailing rate of 1 per cent per month would have him paying some 160 talents per month in interest alone! The exact amount owing to Caesar in 55 cannot be determined, but must have been substantial. When he arrived in Alexandria in 48, seven years after the restoration, he remitted part of the debt but still demanded 10 million drachmas for support of his army there, and carried off much gold and silver, ostensibly to pay the debt.[113]

This deplorable tale does not complete the financial woes of Auletes. In addition to the sums incurred in 59 and 55, he had promised Gabinius a handsome remuneration, estimated as high as 10,000 talents, for illegal diversion of his forces from Syria. Cicero denounces this as the selling of a Roman army to a foreign king, but the legal niceties bothered Auletes less than did the cost and its payment.[114] The allegation that Rabirius Postumus had instigated the attack on Alexandria by Gabinius seems a not improbable one, in context. A great deal of money lay at stake, owed or promised.[115] What progress Auletes made on the second borrowing cannot be ascertained, but the steady efforts of Rabirius Postumus to drain the kingdom must have credited Auletes with at least some of the principal.

The Alexandrians came to regard Rabirius as a virtual overlord, according to the official deposition against him as paraphrased by Cicero.[116] Rabirius entered Egypt soon after the restoration, to work against such expenditures by the king as a large gift of ivory to Apollo at Didyma.[117] In Cicero's courtroom speech, this action by Rabirius becomes one not of rapacity or even financial prudence, but rather one of incaution, which results in Rabirius's finding himself dragooned into service as the king's treasurer. The terms are clear: lest the royal purse disgorge handsome sums for indulgence of whims, Rabirius undertakes to manage the kingdom's wealth. He must be 'appointed' *dioiketes*. If he assumes the Greek cloak, that constitutes – so runs the argument of Cicero – the price paid for later retaining his toga and recovering his and others' loans. All this he does reluctantly under virtual coercion by the King.[118]

Those who could believe a tale like this did so. Rabirius accomplished his work efficiently during a term in 'office' that ran to 54 BC.[119] He represented himself and friends who had lent money to Auletes through him, perhaps also Pompey and Caesar and apparently Gabinius, for whom he undertook to raise the promised ten thousand talents. Fearing eventual outrage (which came) from the Alexandrians when they discovered his systematic draining of the state, Postumus kept for himself and his friends a portion of the funds raised for Gabinius. Better paid now than later. To avert little surprises at the last moment, Rabirius exported vast wealth concealed under mundane cargoes in the holds of ships dispatched to Puteoli.[120] Gabinius did get his money, though only for the military expenses, it was claimed.[121]

Perhaps in December 54, this massive transfer of wealth provoked the Alexandrians to imprison Postumus and then deport him to catch up if he could with the fortune sent on ahead.[122] Auletes watched him over the horizon with relief. However, he could not forget the remaining debts, since his Roman creditors did not; in their eyes, the obligations even devolved upon his successors – Ptolemy XIII, Ptolemy XIV, Cleopatra VII, and Arsinoe IV. The debt served later as one pretext for the usurpation of Ganymedes (see below). Roman intervention restored Auletes but not tranquillity; the financial consequences only exacerbated divisions at court, as the period after his death was to demonstrate. The special 'guardianship' Romans later claimed over Egypt supposedly at the behest of Auletes stemmed largely from anxiety over the remaining debt.[123]

What Auletes achieved by recourse to Rome appeared to many not worth the consequences: recognition as 'friend and ally' with a few oaths and treaties in exchange for crushing financial obligations that conferred on later arrivals like Pompey and Caesar a pretext to intervene as 'guardians' in Egyptian financial and political matters.[124] For the time being the restored monarch did enjoy a certain prosperity despite the depredations of Rabirius. The coinage of Auletes, previous to his exile woefully debased, began after it to recover towards the level of silver content expected of Ptolemaic coins.[125]

Auletes passed the remainder of his life without major incident. Alert Romans tabulated his accounts and took further steps to ensure payment. Ptolemy would compose a testament. Unlike those of his predecessors in Egypt and Cyrene or of his early contemporary Nicomedes IV of Bithynia, this one provided not for inheritance by Rome but for succession by his children, under conditions protecting the 'investment' of Romans. The primary heirs were to be the elder of the two sons and the elder of the two daughters, that is Ptolemy XIII (*PP* 14560) and Cleopatra VII (*PP* 14525), elder daughter now that Berenice IV had been murdered.[126] The two young monarchs were 'to cohabit in accordance with Egyptian custom and to rule jointly.'[127]

The terms of the testament as we have it, at second or even third hand, provided for guaranteed succession.[128] So deep had mistrust run that Auletes felt impelled to call upon Rome, if the document is genuine, for external assistance in establishing his children upon his own throne. There would be factions and in this the future demonstrated the foresight of Auletes. The arrangement included provision for Romans to ensure that succession take place as he arranged it. 'In the same testament Ptolemy solemnly enjoins the Roman people through all the gods, and through the treaties that he had concluded at Rome, that these things be done.'[129] This concern to shift onto Rome some responsibility constitutes a realistic assessment of the abiding situation.

As a further safeguard, Auletes ordered that the testament be drawn in duplicate. Besides the deposit copy in Alexandria another would lie in the treasury (*in aerario*) at Rome. However, Pompey received it instead; allegedly, the political situation in Rome (*per publicas occupationes*) prevented deposit as Auletes wished. No evidence exists that the copy, far too valuable a document for exposure to the possible designs of one's rivals, *ever* left Pompey's hands. He laid it by to help exchange a rainy day in Rome for a sunny one in Alexandria, though when that contingency did arise the result hardly matched his expectations.

This arrangement, in Roman eyes a type of 'guardianship,' whatever it may have meant to Auletes, cannot be dated precisely.[130] Its general form must have been worked out before the restoration, but the document itself clearly followed that happy event ('treaties that he had concluded at Rome'). It probably lay closer to 55 than to 51, the year of his death.

The strategy of depositing a second copy in Rome contributed to an uneventful transition, as Cleopatra VII and Ptolemy XIII came forward.

Whether Auletes also associated his heirs with him in government remains questionable. He certainly called attention to them, if inscriptions from Philae and elsewhere reflect the royal wishes. A papyrus from 55, the year of his restoration, terms him 'the elder Ptolemy': is this to call attention to his son? It cannot refer to Ptolemy of Cyprus, a younger brother of Ptolemy Auletes and now three years dead. The reference can only be to Auletes considered together with his young son Ptolemy XIII. In an inscription of 52, the year before his death, the children become 'the gods, the new *Philadelphoi.*' This last is a useful title, with the force of 'loving brothers and sisters' – a consideration when two princes and two princesses succeed, especially from so contentious a family. Papyri with indication of two regnal eras seem to reflect joint rule but in likelihood do not; 'year 30, which is also year 1' need not show association so much as close succession, well planned and smoothly attained.[131]

How should history judge Auletes? His depravities and frivolities have been well reflected in literature and in such unexpected sources as the 'shameless inscription' by one of his catamites.[132] The disparaging remarks of Strabo and others, the undeniable hatred of many Alexandrians, the contempt of Romans, such as Cicero, all combine to leave a negative impression of him now.

However, some weight must lie on the other pan of the scale. To survive under conditions of the mid-first century required resourcefulness for an Egyptian monarch. When Auletes began his reign, Tigranes and Mithradates Eupator still dominated Asia Minor, controlling territory once claimed by the Ptolemies. Egypt itself lay beyond their reach but not their aspirations. Seleucids, related to the Ptolemies, threatened Auletes when Selene, his aunt, presented her two sons in Rome, claiming not Syria but Egypt. Auletes helplessly watched annexation of Cyrene and of his brother's kingdom in Cyprus. He gained recognition as friend and ally of Rome, and arranged to regain his own throne and depose his daughter. Furnished with Roman treaties, sworn guarantees, contingents such as the army left by Gabinius, and the support of Pompey or Caesar, he brought his kingdom through a period of extreme threat to its very existence. He picked his way with sufficient care to hand it down intact despite disturbances in local and international politics during the last decade of his life. The financial exactions by Roman usurers did not fatally weaken his realm, nor did he neglect the traditional Pharaonic and Ptolemaic methods of consolidation. Statues and temples and inscriptions to the gods continued to be produced at his orders and sometimes under his personal supervision. His officials demonstrated stability and loyalty. A certain vigour marks this reign of some thirty years. It did manage to meet the most severe external challenges that Egypt had faced since the days of Seleucid occupation a century before. Even the internal disruptions did not prevent the reign from ending well. Though one hesitates to affirm that Auletes had reasons to sound his own flute, he ended life better than most expected: he died from disease, not intrigue.[133]

Cleopatra VII Philopator Philadelphos (*PP* 14525)
Ptolemy XIII Theos Philadelphos (*PP* 14560)

The death of Auletes occurred before 22 March 51 BC and he cannot be proved alive after 22 February that year.[134] The inscription indicating him dead by March, from the Bucheum at Hermonthis near Thebes, provides no certain evidence, since *he* might have sent Cleopatra (see below). Estimates of the time necessary for her to journey from Alexandria to Thebes have little bearing, since the last dated document for Auletes comes from Philae, so far upriver that the production of an inscription to him might fall weeks after the order to have it cut. We are reminded of a similar lag after his exile in 58, when at Edfu and Philae inscriptions long suggest him still in the country. Cicero does not hear of his death until 30 June 51 BC, and again nothing can be deduced precisely, since news to Rome travelled slowly. A text for Cleopatra in 'year 1, Mecheir' could show her ruling already by February 51, but the reading is not definite. She has even been detected already ruling in the autumn of 52 BC, but again through a doubtful reading; this would have been in association with Auletes.[135]

The texts dated 'year 30 = year 1' have been explained as reflecting the succession. Auletes completed twenty-nine years of rule, as stated in the Ptolemaic 'Canon,' and was in his thirtieth when he died; Cleopatra's 'year 1' absorbs the fraction he completed of his thirtieth year, usually in silence except for a few texts with the equation above.[136] However, another solution has been put forward: Cleopatra concealed the death of her father for a time, meanwhile maintaining that they ruled together![137] This solves one problem, the double-dated papyri, by creating a greater one. The picture of Cleopatra launching herself with glistening eyes into a fictitious double-reign while her father mouldered in a palace chamber awaiting an official death and burial can only repel. The fractious Alexandrian court, especially the portion of it disposed to favour her brother over herself, would never have let such a scheme succeed. The evidence points clearly to a normal succession, carefully managed.[138]

The remarkable inscription from the Bucheum that initiates the reign of Cleopatra and Ptolemy XIII reflects the care that these last Ptolemies took to fulfil the religious duties expected of them, but its real significance lies deeper. Its date is 'year 1, Phamenoth 19' or 22 March 51, squarely at the beginning of their joint reign. Since a scribe in the Heracleopolite nome could still on 15 February 51 write 'year 30, Mecheir 14' for Auletes, he might be considered yet alive, though ill, when Cleopatra set out for Hermonthis. But his death and their coronation preceded the trip. Cleopatra is 'Queen' and Ptolemy XIII 'King' by the time of the installation on 22 March, so even if Auletes had lived on into February, he was not alive by this time in March, unless the brother and sister were *associated* in rule with him now, a postulate untenable in the absence of better evidence.[139]

What seems a remarkably fortuitous circumstance of the bull's death at the opening of the new joint reign is deceptive: an interval of years could occur between the death of the bull and the formal installation of a new one by the monarch. In this case the bull was born two years before! The apparent coincidence was in fact long in the planning, as Auletes neared the end of his life, with installation deliberately set to follow his death. He and the astute Cleopatra realized the value in distant Thebes of her presence at the installation; her popularity in the Thebaid later reflects this act at the opening of her reign.[140] After about thirty years of rule by Auletes, the transition would be a momentous occasion. The careful planning that marked it by installation of a new Buchis, representing no less a deity than Amon-Re and occurring in a district both crucial to the Ptolemies and distant from the court in Alexandria, was done wisely.

This need not have required the presence of Ptolemy XIII, which remains an open question. The King usually did attend in person, but in this case Cleopatra's presence might have sufficed.[141] The inscription records Ptolemy's participation in a formulaic manner that fails to guarantee the fact, though the attendance of both at the ceremony would have been politic.

The case is clearer with Cleopatra. The wording attesting her presence is quite unparalleled and almost certainly commemorates her taking part in person at the ceremonies in Thebes.[142] The new bull 'reached Thebes, his place of installation .... He was installed by the King himself in year 1, Phamenoth 19 [22 March 51 BC]. The Queen, the Lady of the Two Lands ... the goddess who loves her father, rowed him in the barque of Amun, together with the boats of the King, all the inhabitants of Thebes and Hermonthis and priests being with him ...'[143]

Cleopatra doubtless enjoyed all this. Even at nineteen (with Ptolemy now about eleven), the new queen understood how to conduct herself. She had known for years that the title was to be hers, and her eight years' seniority to Ptolemy XIII rendered her queenship a full one despite the requirement of Auletes's will that the pair rule jointly.[144] Her relative prominence in the

Bucheum text need not indicate that she had eclipsed her brother; neither should a papyrus from later this year dating by her name alone.[145] Her participation at Thebes came as a joint act with her brother, whether he journeyed there or not, and she performed the rites with conviction.

Her other titles presumably struck her as in no way inappropriate. Ancient Egyptian titulature such as 'Lady of the Two Lands' (Upper and Lower Egypt, a distinction now over three millennia old, at least since Narmer's day) and the action of helping to row the Buchis bespeak a solemn ceremony, seriously performed before a large assemblage of her subjects. She also took seriously the title 'goddess,' already provided for in her father's nomenclature for his children. She later identified herself with the goddess Isis, and her brother as Osiris; in years to come a succession of males (Caesar, Caesarion, Antony, two more sons) and a daughter would be drawn into her divine orbit as incarnations of ancient gods. The vague line between highly fortunate mortals and gods in Greek eyes, and between the ruler and the gods in Egyptian eyes, constituted not impediment but opportunity for Cleopatra.[146]

The epithet *Philopator*, 'loving one's father,' served for the public, but we have little indication of Cleopatra's true attitudes towards her father. She might have accompanied him into exile in 58, if the trace of her in Athens is authentic, though she could have been sent there earlier as other Ptolemaic children had. She was back in Alexandria when he returned, and no record exists of her being with him during the exile. At the time of his restoration in 55, Auletes killed her elder sister, Queen Berenice IV, either before her eyes or at least within her ken. Cleopatra was then about fifteen.[147] However, in many respects she was truly her father's daughter: the opportunism that marked his reign marked hers, and even the political ruthlessness leading to murder of a close family member was common to both (in her case, the victims were perhaps Ptolemy XIV and certainly her sister Arsinoe). Both shared the qualities of ambition limited by no scruple; of hard-eyed realism recognizing both the threat and the utility of Rome; of determination to turn the rapid dynastic and imperial developments of the late first century to personal and national advantage; of energy; of intelligence. Auletes had used *Philopator* for the same reasons Cleopatra did: succession and legitimacy remained prime requisites for rule in Egypt.

The inscription from the Bucheum demonstrates at the outset of Cleopatra's reign the multifaceted character it consistently displayed. She was noted for being 'at ease' with her subjects and for mastery of the many languages of Egypt and its neighbours. These included not only Egyptian but also Ethiopian, Somalian ('Troglodyte'), Arabic, Hebrew, and Aramaic ('Syrian') in addition to a presumed later admixture of Latin. Greek, her native tongue, brought her total to eight, a not inconsiderable achievement among the Ptolemies, traditionally disdainful of others' languages.[148] In her remarkable career, unaware that she would be the last member of her line to rule, she was to attempt not only a refoundation of the Ptolemaic dynasty on a firmer basis, through traditional Egyptian supports, but also an extension of the state to its former imperial bounds and then – through Antony and their children – far beyond, even into Media. This woman, so beautiful that 'many men would have purchased by death a night with her' (an impression borne out by some statues but not by most of her coin portraits), aimed at more than the captivation of such as Caesar and Antony. She attempted and might have achieved her share of an 'Empire of the East' had fate deflected on timely occasions (Caesar's murder; Octavian's career; Actium). But the future lay not with Cleopatra.[149]

Auletes had accurately gauged his daughter's queenly spirit and would have approved the way she swung into her new role, but he had underestimated the impediments to joint rule. Cleopatra did not balk at the title *Philadelphos* ('loving one's sibling') that Auletes had bestowed on his children. Removing it from her titulature might cause domestic difficulties, and neither she nor Ptolemy XIII need abide by it, as events demonstrated. If her sister Berenice had been forced by public opinion to take a consort, so must she. Rather than seek one externally as Berenice had done, she could assume as consort her brother, still a minor and easier to eclipse than a less manipulable adult. This had been the wish of Auletes in directing the pair to cohabit and rule jointly. So began the initial phase of her remarkable reign.[150]

The Joint Reign

Cleopatra had no intention of ruling figuratively, with the real power vested in a regent, though many at home and abroad expected the joint reign to take that form. To Romans, the initial question at news of Auletes's death concerned not the succession but the regency of Potheinos. Caelius remarks to Cicero: 'It has been reported to us and is held to be the case that the King of Alexandria has died. Write me in detail what you advise, how that kingdom is conducting itself, and who is acting as vice-regent (*quis procuret*).'[151] This neatly sums up the problems Cleopatra had to meet: her brother's share in power, the expectations at court that she would submit to the regency of Potheinos, and the keen interest which Romans took in this transition. Romans were moving towards their own civil war now, by 51. In addition to financial gains made by some from restoration of Auletes four years before, more might be available, a tempting source of funds for the approaching conflict. The debt of Auletes to Caesar passed to the children with only a portion remitted.[152] Pompey too had claims to make.

A polarization developed at the Ptolemaic court over the problem posed by Rome. Ptolemy XIII and his advisers recoiled from the close co-operation previously favoured by Auletes and now by Cleopatra, but for some four years the pair nominally ruled together.[153]

Rome presented only one of several problems. We hear of drought and a disastrously low rising of the Nile in these years (some eight feet instead of the normal twenty-seven in 48 BC), with crop failures, desertion of villages, famine, even rioting.[154] An inability to pay taxes impaired state revenues. At the beginning of 'year 3' (5 September 50 to 3 September 49) may stand an ominous royal decree, a *prostagma* issued in the name of the king and the queen, in that order. This wording may or may not show Ptolemy now in the ascendant; a nodding or literal-minded scribe could do the deed, relying on such formulations as the will of Auletes, which did mention the son first. But the ominous facet of the document lies in its content, not its reflection of intrigues at court. Merchants of wheat or pulse in 'the nomes above Memphis' may not convey these products to 'the low country' (the Delta) or the Thebaid, on pain of death, though they may do so freely to Alexandria. Rewards for informants are high. The decree is duly posted and will be enforced by the *strategos.*[155] It derives from a dangerous situation in Egypt and, among measures taken generally to promote agricultural stability, demonstrates the cynical concentration at court on assuring the food supply for Alexandria by preventing merchants from seeking higher profits elsewhere. The decree reflects the Ptolemaic taste for monopoly and control, here exacerbated by agricultural scarcity.

The determination of Cleopatra to assume personal direction of the kingdom in its dealings with Rome appears during an instructive incident this year, 50 BC. The forces of Parthia, flushed with triumph after their annihilation of Crassus in 53, occupied portions of Asia Minor and Syria in 51. The Parthian monarch, Orodes II, at some time in his kingship numbered among his wives a daughter of the Commagenian king, Antiochus I. Conjunction of these two could be dangerous. The prospect of more trouble than he could handle reminded the governor of Syria, M. Calpurnius Bibulus, of the force previously left by Gabinius in Alexandria to assist Auletes. Early in 50 he sent two of his sons to summon these troops to Syria, but instead the Gabinians murdered the pair. Cleopatra promptly arrested the culprits, sending them under guard to Bibulus.[156]

The incident has its interesting aspects: Roman recourse to these remaining 'Gabinians'; their own reluctance to forsake Alexandria and families for duties on behalf of Rome against Parthia, where one could get hurt; Cleopatra's ability to control the Gabinians sufficiently to apprehend the killers; her wish not to offend the Roman governor of Syria. This, perhaps Cleopatra's first substantial decision as queen, demonstrates mature judgment. She not only smoothly averted provocation of the Roman governor, but also retained the Gabinians in Egypt. No record remains of Bibulus pressing for their services after this incident.

What of the Ptolemaic court in the years after Auletes died? With Parthians in the territories formerly claimed by Ptolemies and now by Romans, the polarity at court increased between those willing to placate Rome and those wishing either to ignore it or to forge alliances in the East that would bolster Egyptian independence. An intense struggle created disruptions by the fourth year, though initially the joint monarchy may have proceeded smoothly.

Installation of the Buchis in March 51 took place in the name of both monarchs. It can hardly be used to prove ascendancy of one over the other. Omissions of one of the two names in official documents, or alteration of their relative order, have been taken to reflect fluctuations in their standing at court, but this too can be overestimated. For instance, Cleopatra appears alone in a document from 29 August 51, early in the reign.[157] However, her brother remained in the kingship, with an active faction at court supporting him.

A council to serve both monarchs existed, probably headed in 51 BC by Hephaistion (*PP* 31), *dioiketes* after the return of Auletes in 55, but interrupted by the irregular term of Rabirius Postumus in 55 and 54.[158] Hephaistion's successors, Protarchus and then Ptolemaios, remain shadows. Presumably the council initially treated Cleopatra with greater deference than her brother because of her age, but an eclipse of the more even-handed ministers occurred, with the stronger position won by those favouring the more manipulable Ptolemy, who as a male could carry their anti-Roman convictions farther. So they believed, not the last ones to underestimate Cleopatra.

Potheinos, tutor of Ptolemy XIII, led this group, rising through his personal influence over the boy to a position of supreme executive power. The youthfulness of Ptolemy, often commented on by the sources, promoted the activity of Potheinos and of what came to constitute a powerful but irregular council.[159] The terms for it vary so widely that its anomalous nature stands out: 'council of the most powerful'; of 'chamberlains and tutors'; of 'advisers'; of 'relations and friends'; of 'friends of the king' (not necessarily including Cleopatra); even of 'eunuchs.' The traditional inner groupings of the Ptolemaic court, the *syngeneis* and *protoi philoi* and appointed officials, had begun to evolve into a collection of partisans, though largely formed from men of proven ability and political experience.[160] Plutarch notes that local power lay now so readily available that any who wished could achieve it. The permanent 'cabinet' included a rhetorician,

Theodotus of Chios, and Achillas 'the Egyptian,' described by Caesar as *praefectus regius*.[161] Cleopatra had her own *philoi*, probably in part a different group, including Apollodorus of Sicily.[162]

Potheinos began as tutor, but his power grew apace during the first four years of the joint monarchy, and came to exceed that of the *dioiketes*, especially of Ptolemaios in year 4. His control extended not only over finance but also over the general administration of the kingdom, as the man who 'conducted all matters' in the words of Plutarch.[163] Ultimately, his position grew so anomalous that the sources accord him an unprecedented range of titles and approximations: tutor, friend of the king, chief adviser, overseer, financial administrator, vice-regent, the inevitable 'eunuch.'[164]

So ran the government of Egypt. Several documents from 'year 2' show the dual monarchy in place and all apparently well in Egypt, at least politically, from 5 September 51 to 4 September 50.[165] This year of gathering storm in Italy leaves no visible reflection in the papyri of Egypt.

'Year 3' (5 September 50 to 3 September 49) proved more lively. Caesar cast his die, Pompey fled Rome, and the long-smouldering Roman civil war broke forth. Egypt's insulation from disruptions abroad neared an end.

In this year a puzzling formula creeps into some but not all of the papyri. Variously, it reads 'in the first year, but also termed the third' or simply 'of the first and third year.' Alongside texts of this type we find others dated merely 'year 3.'[166] The known texts do not yield an intelligible pattern for the third year, since papyri with 'year 3' occur both before and after those with 'year 1 = 3.'[167] Finally, several texts from this year present anomalous citations of the rulers. The papyrus discussed above, from October 50, that prohibits diversion of crops from Alexandria shows both ruling but names the king first. Another from this year lets Cleopatra stand first, and perhaps alone, as she had in a papyrus of the previous year.[168]

What may we make of these puzzling texts? A great deal, some think: a 'revolution' at court with a 'final expulsion of Ptolemy XIII from the kingship.'[169] This appears too strong for the evidence, especially since Ptolemy remained in power during 48. In the Ptolemaic court of the day anything might occur, and could be reflected in the papyri, but these irregularities cannot alone justify such major postulations. Too many possibilities then arise. Cleopatra might have aspired to rule with Ptolemy XIV (now ten or eleven) in violation of her father's will. Or, she might have taken into her bosom Arsinoe IV, now about twenty; her later hatred of this younger sister need not have begun yet and Arsinoe did share her exile in 49/48. Any interruption was brief, judging from the reflection in the regnal eras on papyri. Whatever transpired occurred only during June and July 49, with restoration of joint rule thereafter, if it had been broken at all.[170]

Something must explain the adoption of two regnal eras ('year 3 = 1'), but without better evidence we cannot surmise a promotion of Ptolemy XIV in his brother's or sister's stead, or of Cleopatra in his.[171] Other than playing musical kings, we must postulate an event in this period that seemed at the time to justify an additional era, but was soon dropped. Was it connected with Cleopatra's exile, which was caused by her brother's resentful adherents?[172] Cleopatra's ejection stemmed from motives internal to the court, not from disaffection or uprising by the populace. She had already tried to remove her brother from their joint throne, and now instead he and his friends expelled her.[173]

Cleopatra's Exile

In late spring or early summer of 49 both monarchs were ruling together in Alexandria. We know this because Pompey's son had left Rome for Egypt in early March, and found Cleopatra enough in evidence on his arrival that he fell captive to her charms.[174] However, late in 49 a meeting of Pompeians in Thessalonica behaved as if only Ptolemy XIII ruled in Egypt. Other notices demonstrate that Cleopatra had been expelled from Alexandria.[175] The vagueness of testimony that this expulsion had occurred 'lately' or 'a few months before' the autumn of 48 suggests that it could have been late in 49; precise inquiries were not made after Pharsalus. The flight of Pompey from Italy in 49 and the appearance of his son that summer in Egypt requesting assistance brought home to the anti-Roman party around Ptolemy XIII the dangers that involvement could pose. In sending off 50 or 60 ships to help, Egypt became a participant, though the ships never engaged.[176]

During her exile, Cleopatra remained busy; she journeyed to the Thebaid, managed to have a coinage dedicated to her in Ascalon during 49 BC, and raised an army in Syria with which to fight her brother, all by September 48. The early part of her exile, probably beginning in her 'year 3,' which terminated on 3 September 49, might account for the formula 'year 1 = 3.' However, this appears too early, since one text uses that formula before June 49 BC.[177] Had she left this early, her exile would have taken some fifteen months by September 48. That formula must at present go unexplained.

Cleopatra's choice of the Thebaid as her first refuge sprang from reasonable considerations. The area was reputed to be 'warlike' still, as it had been in the 25th and 26th dynasties. Its remoteness could later make it seem to have been 'not subject to the kings' and promoted revolts from Alexandrian control, as would occur again after Cleopatra's reign. She was remembered fondly by the aristocracy and officials of Thebes for her dedication of the Buchis in 51, but more important was the recent service there of Callimachus. This man, an honorary 'kinsman' of her father, had served as *epistrategos* or *Thebarch* from as early as 78 and probably down to the death of Auletes. After an impressive career there he moved to Alexandria as *epistolographos*.[178]

Whether or not her ties with those around Thebes helped her, Cleopatra moved on to Palestine and Syria during her 'year 4' – 4 September 49 to 3 September 48. The assistance she might expect from coastal cities such as Ascalon arose from their distaste for Jewish rule and their perception of Egyptian sovereigns as potential allies against it. Ascalon had honoured her father, Auletes, and her grandfather, Lathyros, with coinages, and now placed her portrait on an issue too, beginning in 49 and continuing for years.[179] In addition, Cleopatra might expect assistance from the Nabataeans, uneasy about the expanding Judaean kingdom and alert to the opportunities she might present. Further aid might come from states in the Lebanon and from the Kingdom of Emesa, since she thought that these viewed with apprehension the local disruptions caused by Roman activity in Syria.

Appian's vague remark that she 'was raising an army around Syria' did not mean within that country itself. Its governor, Q. Metellus Scipio, had no leisure for the exiled queen; he was engaged in raising 'large forces' for the civil war. For this he required corresponding exactions 'from the cities and local rulers' and two years' requisitions from his province's *publicani*, hardly measures to promote local tranquillity. He nearly stripped the great temple at Ephesus. He later conveyed two legions to Pompey and led them personally at Pharsalus.[180]

Cleopatra could expect no aid from Scipio against her brother, who was now under the 'tutelage' of Pompey, Scipio's son-in-law. From principalities and kingdoms drawn into the war, she received contingents, gradually furnishing an army. All realized that realignments approached, however hard they were to foretell. Prudent eastern kings sent contingents to Pompey, though in measure.[181]

Meanwhile, a strange event occurred. An increasingly desperate Pompey had fled to Greece with most of the senators from Rome. At Thessalonica, probably late in 49, they took an odd decision by which Ptolemy XIII, now ruling alone, became in their eyes a ward of Pompey. The relationship, termed a *tutela*, had no validity in Egypt, but Roman guardianships had been claimed there as early as 200 BC. (M. Aemilius Lepidus for Ptolemy V Epiphanes), and these Romans hoped that such a tie would assure Egyptian support.[182] In conjunction with the will of Auletes, which Pompey had, this claim gave him a personal standing in the East. His son had succeeded in obtaining ships and men in Egypt. The decision to arrange a special relationship with Egypt and to recognize Ptolemy XIII as a 'friend and ally' of Rome, which his father had been, was a shrewd one.[183]

Pompey soon had need of this unusual relationship. Fleeing after Pharsalus in August 48, he considered refuge with Orodes II of Parthia.[184] This was not the aberration it seems, for the conquest by Pompey and Lucullus of Tigranes and Mithradates Eupator had done a service to Parthia. Pompey had achieved *philia* with Phraates III, and had sent to Parthia before the battle of Pharsalus to seek aid if possible or neutrality if not.[185] His instincts were sound; the tolerant Parthians held him blameless for the indiscretions of Crassus and would not have dishonoured their suppliant or his wife, as some feared. But advisers prevailed and he veered to thoughts of Juba, King of Mauretania. However, Juba appeared on reflection to be of insufficient stature for the occasion.[186]

That left Egypt, where ruled his nominal protégé. Pompey had opposed Caesar's projected annexation of Egypt and now hoped for his reward. In 48, Egypt retained its attractiveness, especially financially, as 'a great realm, still both prosperous and strong in ships, crops, and money.'[187] The proximity of Egypt, its friendliness to Pompey, and the will of Auletes, all encouraged him. Thus Pompey turned from the civil war he had lost to the kingdom he had not gained.

Pompey's fate did not lack drama. Approaching by sea towards the warring forces of Cleopatra and her brother in September 48, he sought out Ptolemy's camp near Pelusium. Before landing he prudently announced himself to Ptolemy. In the advisers' debate that ensued, the prevailing view clearly demarcated the shrinking range of choices open to these last Ptolemies. If they rejected Pompey, they reasoned, he and perhaps Caesar would conceive an enmity that one day would be dangerous; if they received Pompey, he would attempt to control Egypt and Caesar would become its enemy. The services that Pompey had rendered Auletes hardly carried weight with the counsellors of Ptolemy XIII, some of whom had probably agreed with the ejection of Auletes ten years before for his dealings with Rome. Seeing no alternative, the group decoyed Pompey into a boat and there inflicted on him an ignominious end in a corner of the Egypt he had once schemed to use as a political springboard.[188]

Ptolemy XIII did not prevent his death and suffered considerable opprobrium from ancient writers, for instance as 'that most vile king, acting on the advice of eunuchs.' However, the *tutela* Pompey purportedly received from the displaced senators at Thessalonica the year before had not sought the consent of the Egyptians. Ptolemy's advisers saw little for their interests in the arrangement. Hoping to remain outside Rome's civil war and to defeat Cleopatra in the skirmishing near Pelusium, they tried to chart an independent course for Egypt.[189]

The action did not please Caesar as it had been expected to, but it did refocus events. The civil war between Ptolemy XIII and Cleopatra simmered on, but Ptolemy withdrew towards Alexandria, where Caesar landed in October 48 BC.[190]

Caesar and Cleopatra

Caesar had his hands full there. The Alexandrians found his consular regalia and lictors unimpressive, and resented a foreign official parading thus to the palace. They began a street war against wandering legionaries. Caesar imperiously summoned both Ptolemy and Cleopatra back to Alexandria, regarding the will of Auletes as his warrant.[191] Potheinos left the force at Pelusium confronting Cleopatra and brought Ptolemy back. Marvellous stories result. Potheinos agreed to supply Caesar's soldiers with grain, but measured out the oldest and worst. At state dinners he used dishes of wood or pottery, explaining that Caesar had spirited away the golden and silver ones to satisfy Auletes's debt. Cleopatra evaded the force at Pelusium and arrived in Alexandria clandestinely by boat, thence into the palace rolled in a carpet, stepping forth like a girl from the birthday cake at a fraternal organization's annual party. Caesar, appreciative of a well-shaped ankle anyway, was awed by this apparition shimmering on the scented air of Alexandria.[192]

At this point began one of the great romances, the creation not of dramatist or poet but of two notable figures at a turning-point in history. Ancients frequently levelled at Caesar the charge of allowing his heart to rule his head, and certainly he did take risks during this sojourn in Alexandria. But the political situation had evolved to the point where he would have come here anyway. With Rome now in new possession of Cyrene, Cyprus, and Syria, with the Ptolemaic state threatening disintegration, and with Caesar fresh from the conquest of Gaul and then Pompey, someone would have to ascertain the condition of Egypt. Given its wealth and an honourable opportunity to settle its affairs, Caesar could not have resisted, especially with his debts there still uncollected.

The remarkable aspect of his visit is his renunciation of conquest. Divided Gauls bore no likeness to quarrelling Ptolemies; a tribal society differed from a national one, rich in tradition. Surprisingly, Caesar may even have arranged that Cyprus return to the Ptolemaic fold, initially as a means of employing the supernumerary Ptolemy XIV and Arsinoe. During the ensuing 'Alexandrian War' Ptolemy XIII fell – not by Caesar's hand – and Arsinoe proved an implacable foe whose exile Caesar finally encompassed.[193] He arranged for Ptolemy XIV a philadelphic marriage and joint rule with Cleopatra.[194] None of this bespeaks an aim at territorial aggrandizement. On the eve of Roman absorption of the most impressive kingdom in classical history, Caesar attempted to restore the prestige of the Ptolemaic house and left a garrison to ensure its stability. As *socii et amici*, the rulers of Egypt would stand with a flank of other independent monarchs at the southern and eastern extremities of the Mediterranean world, all enjoying their ancient freedoms while forming a bulwark against Parthia.

First Caesar must conquer, and it proved no foregone conclusion. As so often, a Roman force contending with an Eastern one found itself rescued from a difficult situation by timely assistance from other Easterners. Roman successes lay as much in the diplomatic as they did in the military field, and so it was with Caesar in 47. His small contingent of Roman legionaries received naval and ground support furnished by allies from Rhodes, Pontus, Lycia, Asia, Syria, and Cilicia. He had archers from Crete and cavalry from the Nabataeans.[195] The arrival of the Thirty-Seventh Legion, a fragment of Pompey's forces, with supplies and munitions was an occasion of joy to him.[196] But the saving force was that which arrived under Mithradates of Pergamon, related to King Deiotarus of Galatia and closely connected to Mithradates Eupator. Among his associates would have been Archelaus, the father of that Archelaus, friend of Antony, who had a decade before married Berenice IV of Egypt.[197] Mithradates led a large army of recruits, raised through his own efforts in Syria and Cilicia and through his personal prestige in Asia (*magnae nobilitatis domi*). He had become a loyal friend of Caesar, who sent him on this recruiting drive at the beginning of the war.[198]

The forces brought by Mithradates show the 'Eastern dynastic network' operating at the full. The Judaean Antipater, married to the Arabian princess Kypros, mother of Herod the Great, took part in the battle at Pelusium himself. He had gained the friendship of 'the King of Arabia through this alliance by marriage' and by his agency the Nabataeans assisted too.[199] So did Iamblichus of Emesa, living on Mount Lebanon, ranked among 'the rulers of Syria.'[200] Through such a dynastic mobilization Caesar saved himself.

During the war in Alexandria, most of the notable or notorious officials of Ptolemy XIII perished. Caesar ended the life of Potheinos, possibly the most effective opponent of Roman aggression in Egypt.[201] Arsinoe IV, acclaimed sovereign by the Egyptians as a member of the royal family so far untainted by association with the Romans, used Ganymedes to put Achillas to death.[202] Others fell here and there.[203] By the time of Caesar's victory (27 March 47), it may have seemed possible to start afresh, with Ptolemy XIII now gone too, and Arsinoe powerless. Had Caesar lived, the history of Ptolemaic Egypt might have ended here, not with a clang but a simper.[204]

What of the dangerous Arsinoe, lately termed queen by a faction, and former enemy of Caesar?[205] Now a prisoner, she was to march in Caesar's triumph at Rome.[206] Later, like her father, Arsinoe proceeded from Rome to the safety of Ephesus. Unfortunately for her, this did not lie beyond

Cleopatra's reach, and the day came, probably in 41, when gentle Antony on her orders dragged Arsinoe forth for execution.[207]

The exact arrangements made beyond reinstallation of Cleopatra are difficult to determine. Cleopatra's regnal era continued as if never interrupted, now in 'year 5' (4 September 48 to 3 September 47). To it was joined 'year 1' of Ptolemy XIV, so that again a double era prevailed ('year 5 which is also year 1').[208] Conjectural restorations have attributed a distinct era to him, and these would have the reigns just one year apart, necessitating the postulate that he joined Cleopatra on the throne briefly in 50 BC. After predictable eclipse, on this view he re-emerges alongside Cleopatra with a dual era in her seventh year but only a single era in her eighth. So far the evidence forces such grasping at straws.[209]

The sources reflect the ancient perception of this reign – that it essentially omitted Ptolemy XIV. After recording the death of Ptolemy XIII in battle with Caesar, most sources merely remark that Cleopatra succeeded him, and she 'alone proceeded to have all the power.'[210] Since the documents so far discovered carry only Cleopatra's era, can it be that she abrogated an arrangement of which Porphyry's source knew? If so, her experience with Ptolemy XIII and his powerful friends may have determined her on this course: Caesar had gone on to Syria, and what he didn't know about the implementation of his arrangements would not hurt him.

The interval between Caesar's victory in Egypt, on 27 March 47, and his departure for Syria and then Pontus has been variously calculated at from two to ten weeks.[211] This may leave time for the celebrated and romantic cruise with Cleopatra up the Nile, though it goes unmentioned in contemporary accounts of the campaign. Caesar himself, Cicero, the *de Bello Alexandrino*, Livy, Strabo, Nicholas of Damascus, Velleius, Josephus, even Plutarch all remain silent about the story. Lucan, writing about 110 years later (he died in AD 65, still working on the poem), appears to lay the groundwork for it by having Caesar express an interest in seeking the unknown source (*ignotum caput*) of the Nile.[212] Whether the finished version would have taken the couple on a Nile cruise cannot be told, but the interesting juxtaposition of that prospect with abandonment of military duty echoed a persistent theme. Suetonius, writing some 165 years later (his *Lives of the Caesars* appeared in 120), reduces it again to the level of aspiration: Caesar would have taken the voyage with her but his soldiers refused to follow.[213] Appian, writing about AD 140, by now has four hundred ships in procession up the Nile and Caesar 'taking pleasure in her.'[214] Finally, by Dio's time the story has waned: Caesar is drawn away 'against his will' by the threat of Pharnaces, though Cleopatra had sought to detain him longer.[215]

Whether or not he cruised the Nile, the traditional Egyptian welcome for foreign dignitaries (one recalls Scipio Aemilianus in 139), Caesar had much on his mind besides the charms of Cleopatra: Pompeians in Africa, Pharnaces in Pontus, problems in Italy during the aftermath of civil war. If he left by early April 47, then in the unreformed, seasonal calendar this was late January, a bad time for travel by sea or land from Egypt to Syria. However, for Caesar the time had come to exchange romantic for military conquest. The predictable statues commemorating his victory at Pharsalus had begun to appear, especially in the western cities of Asia Minor, but he must now face Pharnaces in the forbidding interior.[216]

Egypt had been spared, since the defeated faction had yielded now to a more 'legitimate' group, Cleopatra being older at twenty-three than her vanquished brother at fifteen. As victor, Caesar could have followed the precedent of Cyprus and the earlier rumoured bequest to justify annexation, but decades of trouble might have resulted.[217] To make Egypt a province courted risk, as Caesar well knew.[218] Enforced conversion into a province of a kingdom whose ruler had been recognized as *amicus* and *socius* would not have accorded with Roman traditions to date. Augustus later wrote: 'I added Egypt to the domain of the Roman people' and at the same point he recorded, 'I might have made Armenia Maior a province ... but preferred to hand it over to Tigranes [III] *on the example of our ancestors* [emphasis added].'[219] He could have had Caesar's action of 47 BC in mind. For political reasons, Cyprus had been seized; as the conqueror who ended Seleucid history, Pompey had annexed Syria; on the rationale of bequests the Attalid kingdom, Bithynia, and Cyrene had joined this list. However, other annexations lay still in the future, as Roman policy evolved and its power to force its will on Eastern monarchs increased.

Caesar left a garrison of three legions, later increased to four. The commander of the initial three, a freedman named Rufio, seems an inappropriate selection. But the remark of Suetonius that Caesar feared the potential of Egypt for rebellion explains the choice: a man of humble birth would have difficulty persuading Romans and Egyptians to follow him.[220] In conflict with the army of Ptolemy XIII, Caesar had developed respect for it. The legions left behind sufficed to neutralize this broken force, but not to constitute a military occupation of Egypt.[221] What made this feasible in Caesar's eyes was his judgment of Cleopatra, who had been rescued from great difficulty by him and whose loyalty could be counted on. Her revenues remained more than adequate for the support of these troops and for the smooth running of her monarchy.[222]

A concise passage in *de Bello Alexandrino* 33 clearly sets forth the major considerations now. The legions are left so that the rule of these two monarchs might be more firmly established. This is necessary for two reasons: they have no claim to the favour of their people since they had been loyal to the hated Romans, and they have been on the throne only a few days, so that they lack the authority of an established reign. (Cleopatra had been restored after exile and much bloodshed; Ptolemy XIV ruled only because of his brother's death.) The troops would protect the royal pair 'if they remained in faithfulness' to Rome, and that would be conducive to 'the dignity of our empire and to the public weal.' If they became 'ungrateful' (*ingrati*), the troops could nudge them towards a sounder view of the new realities. Caesar took few chances, off the battlefield.

The queenship of Cleopatra seemed once again secure. With Ptolemy XIII and his anti-Roman advisers dead and a Roman garrison at her disposal, she could rule on a basis more firm than ever. Ptolemy XIV could be dominated in a way that Ptolemy XIII in 51-49 BC could not, for he lacked such advisers as Potheinos.

She did not miss the chance afforded by Caesar's restoration of Ptolemaic rule over Cyprus when he had recognized Ptolemy XIV and Arsinoe there. Ptolemy's rule endured long enough for coinages, apparently, with special honours for Isis on two of the issues – an oblique reference to Cleopatra, the 'new Isis'?[223] The evidence suggests that Cleopatra now ruled this old possession of her dynasty and had no intention of letting it drift away again. Two *strategoi*, a *gymnasiarch* of Salamis, and a prefect attest her administration of the island in the decade after Caesar left.[224]

Caesarion

Cleopatra had a son, Ptolemy XV Caesar Theos Philopator Philometor ('Caesarion'; *PP* 14562). In antiquity, the child's paternity was questioned, and so is it still, along with the date of his birth.[225] Caesar is said to have allowed his name for the boy, and Antony is quoted as declaring to the Senate that Caesar had acknowledged paternity.[226] At least one tract was written against the idea, probably after Caesar's death, by his former friend C. Oppius.[227] The date of Caesarion's birth is given on a demotic stele as 'year 5, Payni 23, the day of the birth of the Pharaoh Caesar.' This would be early September 47 BC in the unreformed calendar, or 23 June 47 in the Julian calendar. Since that was not in force until January 45, this demotic text was composed after then, if it is Julian – perhaps on the return of Cleopatra from Rome in 44 BC.[228] If written before 45, the text seems unlikely to speak of the young child as 'the Pharaoh Caesar' while Ptolemy XIV still ruled. Probability favours 44 BC as the year this was composed.

As to the liaison, no point in adding to the tide of speculation except to note that Caesar's fondness for women made one likely during the winter of 48/47, when he and Cleopatra both used the palace in Alexandria as headquarters. That he was already married made little difference. Cleopatra's marriages with her brothers lent 'legitimate' birth to this child, conceived perhaps while her first husband, Ptolemy XIII, still lived (though at war with her), or more likely after her marriage to Ptolemy XIV. She need not have feared public criticism of bearing the child out of wedlock, given the frequency of bastardy, real or imputed, among the late Ptolemies, with her father a recent example, and herself one as well, in one ancient view. Presumably such behaviour for a queen raised more eyebrows than for a king, but having begun to wade through slaughter back to her throne, Cleopatra cared little for eyebrows.[229]

If the child was his, Caesar might have dreamed of 'a new thing in Egypt': a Ptolemaic queen married to a Roman statesman, or at least joining him in altering the dynasty's blood-lines. Caesar envisioned for himself a kind of amalgam of Hellenistic and Roman ruling styles, and he was to die for it. An intaglio probably dating from the close of the Alexandrian war depicts him in both Roman and Ptolemaic styles.[230] He was soon to transfer the issue of his Eastern policies to Rome itself.

In summoning Cleopatra and Ptolemy XIV (with Caesarion?) to Rome, Caesar underlined his intention of developing a strong Roman presence in the East, with his own personal ties to the Ptolemies. His lavish honours for Cleopatra, which aroused predictable clucking from Cicero and others, included a statue of her in the new Temple of Venus Genetrix, thus associating her with the alleged founder of the Julian *gens*. This dangerous precedent constituted one of the highest honours a Roman could bestow on a foreign ruler.[231] It accorded with Cleopatra's self-portrayal in Egypt as a living incarnation of Isis (Aphrodite to her Greek subjects, and Venus to the scowling Romans). A coin effigy later depicts her in this form with Caesarion as Horus (Eros; Cupid). To strict Romans the statue in the Temple of Venus amounted to an Eastern form of blasphemy; Caesar's association with it did him no credit; nor did his statue in the Temple of Quirinus, associated with the site since before the founding of Rome.[232] At the same time, a building reportedly rising in Caesar's honour near the Great Harbour in Alexandria (the 'Caesareum,' mentioned by one wide-eyed author in a pamphlet on the Seven Wonders) seemed to many in Rome inconsistent with the deeds of a Roman magistrate and general, as did anything like a cult for him.[233]

If Caesarion was in fact alive, acknowledged by Caesar, and visible to concerned or dyspeptic Romans, unhappy reflections accompanied the installation of Cleopatra 'across the Tiber in her gardens.' Her real or imagined haughtiness (*superbia*) hardly increased her welcome. On her side, she condescended to the Romans in Caesar's circle as mere politicians; on theirs, she as a queen once exiled by her own people and rescued ostensibly by Roman arms (omitting consideration of the decisive Eastern forces which relieved Caesar) ranked probably as a client, even a suppliant. The situation could not be conducive to good relations, especially if their son would inherit Egypt one day and rule as the first half-Roman Ptolemy.[234]

Despite the odium that she aroused, notably in Cicero (*Reginam odi*), Cleopatra accomplished her designs in Rome. With Roman legions and her palace bureaucracy holding Egypt, she could administer the realm with Ptolemy at her side for safekeeping.[235] Except for one possible trip back, she abode in Rome and impressed important politicians there. Now recognized as *socius* and *amicus*, as her father had been, she needed fear little for her position while Caesar lived. After his murder no one hindered her return to Egypt as its undisputed queen.[236]

Caesar may have gone so far as to encourage C. Helvius Cinna, tribune for 44, to draft legislation by which Caesar might marry 'as many wives as he wished,' for the purpose of begetting children.[237] This could include Cleopatra and legitimize their son. The report that he also aspired to a form of kingship, with a base or even a residence in Alexandria, arose from this and from his extraordinary honour to Cleopatra in the new temple.[238]

After the Ides of March

A timely discovery in the *Sibylline Books* once again proved politically useful, though not in the way expected. A passage was interpreted to read that the Parthians could be conquered only by a king; Caesar should receive this title.[239] If the *quindecimviri sacris faciundis* really did emerge with this 'finding,' whether at Caesar's instigation or through their own inspiration, it constituted a fatal miscalculation, and spurred the conspirators to their deed.[240]

Did Caesar aspire so high? Some royal usages were congenial to the *imperator*. His allowing a statue of himself in the Temple of Quirinus rose above precedent, though not necessarily above mortal station. The record of his deportment in Alexandria hardly soothed troubled brows, especially when he later introduced rites of Dionysos into Rome, despite previous prohibitions.[241]

After Caesar's murder Cleopatra returned in the spring of 44 to Egypt. Cicero implies that she had left Rome by 15 April. A document in Egypt names her with Ptolemy XIV in July, though neither monarch had to be physically present for this.[242] By September, if not before, Ptolemy XIV was dead. The event fell in Cleopatra's 'year 8,' corresponding to his reported 'year 4' (that is, between 3 September 45 and 2 September 44).[243] The sources have him killed by her.[244] In view of her ambitions, especially with Caesarion available for joint rule, Ptolemy XIV was expendable. His death let Cleopatra rule as she wished.[245]

Cleopatra's association with Caesarion became a co-regency. By 'year 11' (3 September 42 to 1 September 41), both are named on the documents; one restored text would show this practice in effect a year earlier.[246] Her son in no way hindered Cleopatra. The party which had once coalesced around her brother, Ptolemy XIII, had long since broken. The murders of Ptolemy XIV in 44 and Arsinoe in 41 forestalled any reformation of it.

Cleopatra's apprehensions regarding Arsinoe were well-founded. This energetic younger sister had acted decisively during the Alexandrian War and had been hailed by a faction as queen. She grew to like the title and could have been dangerous while at Ephesus, where she had been received as a queen. The proximity of the ancient Ptolemaic possession of Cyprus, now under the control of a prefect disloyal to Cleopatra (who later fled to Tyre and was delivered up to her), might have given Arsinoe the base and forces she needed for rebellion, as in the days of Lathyros. Her hatred for Cleopatra and opportunities for mischief during the Roman civil war should have tempted her, whether or not they did. Antony permanently removed the threat, at Cleopatra's behest.[247]

In the meantime, the astute Queen had worked out a plan for Roman recognition of Caesarion's kingship. She had seen the usefulness of Roman alliance in her father's lifetime and then at first hand in her own. She must have contemplated generations of rule for the Ptolemies descended from her, beginning with the fruit of her liaison with Caesar. By now it would have made no difference had the boy not been Caesar's: she could claim he was, with none to deny. Monuments in Egypt were soon to proclaim this version of Caesarion's paternity for all to see: 'On behalf of Queen Cleopatra the Goddess who loves her father and of King Ptolemy also called Caesar, the God who loves his father and mother, and of their ancestors ...'[248]

In preparation, she approached the appointee of Antony for governor of Syria, P. Cornelius Dolabella. He had to contest the appointment, ultimately unsuccessfully, with the candidate of the murdered Caesar, C. Cassius Longinus. But in the interval, Cleopatra dealt with him. She had begun to present herself not only as Isis to her awed subjects, but as Hathor, with Caesarion associated. He must be king too, with external acknowledgment of the title. The stele 'announcing' his birth used 'king' for him and must have been composed now, for it apparently used the Julian, not the uncorrected calendar. She determined to obtain recognition for him by at least a faction of the disturbed Roman state, against further invasion of

Egypt. Joint rule of a queen with a king who was also Caesar's son might prove sufficient bulwark.

She sent Dolabella ships and money during his attempt to secure Asia Minor for Antony, and he declared that Caesarion could be considered king. This lay entirely beyond his powers, since Egypt remained a sovereign, allied country, but it met her wishes. Subsequently, it achieved a measure of legality through ratification by the triumvirs.[249] This course entailed some risk, for Cassius was also in the East, raising forces in Syria; he twice called upon Cleopatra to assist, but she excused herself on the grounds of famine and pestilence in Egypt. She was in fact aiding Dolabella at the time. Fortunately for her, Cassius was to die the year after Dolabella did in 43 BC.[250] He was recalled by Brutus when at the point of leaving for Egypt, 'to punish the queen' and to prevent her from assisting Octavian and Antony with a large fleet.[251] She later told Antony that she had sailed, and that the fleet was destroyed by a storm.[252]

An interesting facet of this manoeuvring is that Cleopatra may have already regained some of the Ptolemaic possessions in the vicinity of Syria and Lebanon. The Tyrians and the Aradii are mentioned for their failure to consult her before aiding Cassius![253] Her later designs on portions of Palestine and Arabia were no break with her past.

Antony and Cleopatra

After Philippi, a victory some considered 'entirely due to him,' Antony's repute 'was at its apogee' in Appian's view. His father (M. Antonius Creticus), uncle, and grandfather had all earned reputations in the East, from which he benefited. In the spring of 41, Antony came to Asia, first Bithynia and then Ephesus. In both places he received deputations from the Jews, whose internal difficulties had reached new heights. His mission in Asia was clear: to punish some allies of Brutus and Cassius, but mainly to collect money.[254] In settling financial matters with the allies, he also put their minds at rest regarding territorial ambitions by Romans: all were to keep what they possessed before.[255] The funds, in turn, would pay soldiers the wages and bounties promised before Philippi, and would supply the expedition against the Parthians that Caesar had contemplated and that Antony now undertook to lead. It did not take long before he mused upon the riches of Egypt.[256]

Antony summoned Cleopatra to meet him in Cilicia, and after some regal delay she did. A previous incident at Ephesus, whether Antony had fully understood it or not, explains what next occurred. He had been hailed upon arrival there as another epiphany of Dionysos; Easterners welcomed opportunities to elevate a king or commander and enjoy a revel. A full procession had been accorded him, and Cleopatra heard of it. As the daughter of one 'New Dionysos,' and as mother of a son by a second one, she saw opportunity for a spectacle at Tarsus with a third one which would edify the masses for years to come. To his Dionysos (Horus) she would play Aphrodite (Isis/Hathor).[257]

Thus occurred the most fondly remembered event of her career, and perhaps his too. She floated up the Cydnus River to Tarsus. Antony came to gaze on Cleopatra too, and he fell captive.[258] Her strategy worked marvellously, for word went out that Aphrodite was disporting herself with Dionysos 'for the good of Asia'![259]

Thus began Cleopatra's second great romance, with Antony thrashing in her toils or lap and soon carried off to Alexandria for the winter of 41/40. Romans were not to approve, but Caesar had become a god recently, though not while living, and Antony knew that in the East apotheosis even ere demise remained both possible and politic.

The portrait of Antony lost in love and unmindful of his larger purposes vividly distorts the situation. The winter passed pleasantly enough, to be sure, since Antony was fond of revelry, flattery, and women.[260] To be plucked from the ranks of rough soldiers and hailed as a god might turn even more mature heads than his. However, behind it all lay design. Egypt made a fine base from which to arrange a campaign against Parthia. For her part, Cleopatra had required a number of little services, including the murder of Arsinoe at Ephesus; the execution of her disloyal governor of Cyprus; the despatch of a pretender who had arisen at Aradus claiming to be Ptolemy XIII, not drowned after all. There were others, too.[261]

A final memento of her year with Antony appeared in the fall of 40, some months after his departure: twins. These were Alexander Helios and Cleopatra Selene, both destined to enter the dynastic plans of their parents. Alexander went for betrothal but not marriage to Iotape I, daughter of Artavasdes of Atropatene; Selene married Juba II of Mauretania.[262]

Antony's absence lasted over three years. Rather than vest all her plans in his fortunes, Cleopatra busied herself with the traditional concerns of Ptolemaic monarchs. A building program always ranked high among these, and hers would be second to none. Featured on monuments in her incarnation as Isis/Hathor, she promoted the official portrait of Caesarion as Horus. If cut adrift by the Romans, she could rely on the attributes of her position as queen and goddess.

Numerous buildings bear her name and that of Caesarion, reflecting a spate of activity after the association in 'year 11' (42/41). These included new buildings – mainly religious – and rebuilt existing ones. Coptos, Armant, Athribis, Hermonthis all reveal her hand.[263] She and Caesarion stood proudly depicted on great monuments like the temple of Hathor at Dendera, in traditional Egyptian style. At the same time, her two newer children, named after the Sun-God (Alexander Helios) and the Moon-Goddess (Cleopatra Selene), could prepare for their own period of divine rule.

Cleopatra, the living goddess with a divine child by one Roman and two more by another, prepared for participation in the expected Golden Age. Lest anyone in the East forget the heights attempted, Antony and Cleopatra together in the decade left to them were to demonstrate untiringly their position as the New Dionysos and the New Aphrodite.[264] They learned too late that the coming Golden Age contained no place for them.[265] Such happy Vergilian predictions as that 'a great new order of the centuries is born' portended the eclipse, not the apogee, of Egypt. An intermingled Macedonian-Roman dynasty in Egypt might have fit the cry, 'now a new progeny is sent down from high heaven,' but this was not to be either.[266]

Another ambition of Cleopatra was to restore whatever she could of the ancient Ptolemaic and even Pharaonic hegemony in the Levant. Tuthmose and Ramses had turned back before reaching Asia Minor, but she might go on. Her aspirations encompassed portions of Cilicia as well as Arabia, Judaea, Lebanon, and Syria, with planned rule elsewhere in Asia Minor, Mesopotamia, and Iran by way of Antony or her children.

Cleopatra proceeded along lines practised by Eastern dynasts for centuries. She entertained Herod in 40 BC during his flight from the Parthians.[267] For unstated reasons Cleopatra attempted to enrol Herod, driven from his tetrarchy, in her own service, as commander of a rather vague expedition she claimed to be preparing.[268] The ulterior motive was to divert him from Rome, where she foresaw his success in winning recognition for his bid to rule. This weakened her own position in the Levant, where among her lists of desiderata lay some of Herod's territory in the maritime regions of Palestine.[269] Cleopatra relented and helped Herod proceed to Rome. As in the days of Caesar and Auletes, Roman recognition for any needful but not needy monarch came at a price. Herod had no funds with him but promised money once king.[270] Antony recognized him as King of Judaea in 40, and he proved a strong monarch.[271]

Dynastic Mobilizations

After Octavian, Antony, and Sextus Pompeius came to terms at Misenum in 39, Antony began in earnest his dynastic mobilizations of the East.[272] Besides Cleopatra's Egypt, these included kings from established houses, rulers drawn from collateral lines, or non-royal aristocratic families. Among existing royalty stood Darius, son of Pharnaces II of Pontus;[273] Herod;

Artavasdes I of Atropatene (who required armed persuasion but then became a valuable ally);[274] Artavasdes II of Armenia (son of Tigranes the Great); Amyntas (son of Deiotarus) in Pisidia and Galatia;[275] and after a conflict, Antiochus I of Commagene. By establishing good relations with these, Antony secured support from regions to the north, west, and south – to be left progressively behind him on the march east against Parthia, the known objective of this undeclared war.[276]

In the category of kings drawn from collateral royal lines stood Archelaus of Cappadocia, connected to the ruling families of Pontus and Cappadocia but not himself in the main lines of descent in the dynasty of Ariobarzanes.[277]

Those of not attestably royal origins included Amyntas of Galatia, former secretary to Deiotarus.[278] Polemo I, who assumed part of Cilicia and then took Pontus and Bosporus, came only from an aristocratic family in Laodicea. His second queen, Pythodoris, had similar origins in Tralles, but his first queen had been a Pontic princess. The other major ruler in Cilicia was Tarcondimotus ('Philantonius'), whom Antony may have found in an existing line of dynasts there.[279] At Actium, 'Philadelphos, King of Paphlagonia' was to attend.[280] In all, these crowned heads formed a powerful group of allies, controlling a block of territories from Egypt to the Black Sea.[281]

Cleopatra became fully involved in this dynastic mobilization. When Antony sent Octavia back to Rome in 37 and then journeyed to Syria, summoning Cleopatra, rumours flew, as once before in Rome. But great matters were afoot.[282]

Cleopatra brought to Syria with her in 37 her two children by Antony, and by 36 she presented him a third, Ptolemy Philadelphos.[283] She sought to formalize their union, as the phrase used to go. Some form of oriental marriage occurred now, in 37/36 BC. It alienated Romans but allowed Antony quasi-royal status among Easterners. The sentiments Plutarch quotes for him, that aristocracies proceed by the issue of many kings and that his own ancestor, Heracles, did not limit his progeny to one womb, bothered no one in the East. He did not divorce Octavia yet, and now 'had two wives at once, a thing no Roman had ever dared.' But the question 'Wife or concubine?' has been warm since antiquity.[284]

In this year, 37/36 BC, Antony began distributions of territory to Cleopatra and their children, behaving like a monarch. Some assumed him ready for the step upward from Roman consul to Eastern king, reportedly like Caesar before him. A magistracy was temporary but kingship was for life. The associated prestige was equivalent within both systems, but personal gain decidedly accrued more to the king. A tradition arose that Antony 'forgot the name of his fatherland, and the toga, and the fasces' and lost himself in the trappings of kingship, 'lacking only a crown' to be king. The Hellenistic King and the coming Roman Emperor curiously converge in the fading figure of Antony.[285]

Distributions and First Campaign

Discussion of dynastic arrangements by Antony appears under each dynasty, but the 'distributions' to Cleopatra from 37/36 to 34 can be mentioned here, treating the series of them together. Antony tried to follow local usage. From Cilicia southward, regions once Ptolemaic returned for a final period to Egypt. In Cilicia Tracheia, potentially useful for timber, Cleopatra laid claim to Elaeussa, Hamaxia, and part of the interior; this and adjacent portions were subsequently controlled by Amyntas of Galatia, Archelaus I of Cappadocia, and by Polemo I of Pontus.[286] Later still this rugged region, left for kings to rule, came under the sway of Polemo II, Archelaus II, and the Commagenian Antiochus IV.[287]

Distributions from 37 to 34 BC included other areas desired by Cleopatra. If Cyprus had again been lost, it was once more recovered for Ptolemaic rule. Ptolemais in Lebanon issued a joint coinage, but it was on the authority of Antony, whose head adorns the obverse, rather than that of Cleopatra, whose bust appears on the reverse, though the dating (38/37 BC) is by her era. Lysanias, son of Ptolemy of Chalcis, met his death because of Cleopatra's insatiable desires for land here; Porphyry associates her new double era (beginning 37/36) with this desire for land. The balsam-producing tracts around Jericho fell to her, and Herod had to bribe her to leave it at that.[288]

As discussed in §§ 24-26, in 36 BC Antony ventured 'tardily' eastward against Parthia, but soon returned, overeager to curtail the campaign, some thought.[289] He met Cleopatra in a village between Berytus and Sidon; she brought money and clothing for the soldiers.[290] By 36, Antony was issuing a coin with an Armenian tiara to commemorate a reverse inflicted on Artavasdes II of Armenia by his lieutenant, P. Canidius Crassus. It may depict Antony in a pose characteristic of the coins of Alexander, after whom Antony's son was named and whom he could now emulate with Armenians, Atropatenians, and Parthians as the foe rather than Achaemenids.[291]

In this year, 36 BC, Cleopatra's fortunes appear at their apogee. Revenues flowed in from her new as well as her old domains. The Ptolemaic Empire seemed on the way to restoration and even augmentation should Antony succeed in Iran. A number of cities in Syria and Lebanon began to honour her, some with new eras. Coins reflect her 'presence' in Damascus, Berytus, Arados, Balanea, Tripolis. She and Antony continued to share a coinage from Ptolemais Ake, with her portrait relegated to the reverse but dating by a new era of hers.[292]

A new era conjoined with the existing ones on the Ptolemaic documents comes as no surprise. Papyri and inscriptions bearing regnal dates as from 'year 16 = year 1' (1 September 37 to 31 August 36) carry on to the end of her reign. There seems no need to postulate joint rule with Caesarion to explain these, and his position as 'King of Kings' did not begin until 34. This new era of Cleopatra instead reflects reacquisition of Ptolemaic lands in the Levant beginning in 37/36 BC. Since Caesarion had already been named on her documents, 'year 16 = 1' did not refer to him; any era for him should have begun by 42 BC, which was only her 'year 11,' not 'year 16.' The formula signalled rather that Cleopatra now began her own 'new order of the centuries' by starting afresh.[293]

The distributions caused predictable resentment in Rome.[294] Antony and Cleopatra forged on anyway. In early 35 both were back in Alexandria with their little family. The unsuccessful expedition of 36 left dynastic arrangements in the East as before, but Antony realized that so poor a showing could endanger his entire position. Through the able Polemo I, on missions to and from Artavasdes of Atropatene in early 35 BC, he achieved a treaty of 'friendship and alliance' that looked towards conquest of Parthia, and his other allies (in Commagene, Galatia, Cappadocia) prepared to co-operate.[295] However, their adherence to Roman causes varied in proportion to Roman success. Alliance with *anyone* against Parthia was a dangerous game, and Antony – increasingly unsupported by the rest of the Roman state – had shown himself in 36 a slender reed (§ 26). Extremely heavy losses, inconclusive results, and misjudgments such as the gruelling late-fall march back to the coast eroded confidence, and he knew it.[296] So for 35 he projected a campaign not against Parthia, but first against *Armenia*, whose king had left at a most inopportune time in 36 BC.[297] After that he would effect a junction with Artavasdes of Atropatene and march on Parthia.[298] However, the expedition barely got under way before he had to postpone it.[299]

He and Cleopatra had proceeded to Syria when word arrived that Octavia was coming with supplies, funds, and two thousand soldiers (a token amount: he had lost many times that number in 36). Cleopatra perceived the threat of reunion and exerted her full womanly panoply in preventing it and drawing him back to Alexandria. This incident reveals a real need for manpower, and reluctance among the royal allies.[300]

A problem seemingly remote to Antony had recently neared: that of Sextus Pompeius. He arrived in the East during Antony's campaign of 36. Hearing of its failure, he aspired to supplant Antony and began secret embassies to Polemo in Pontus, Cotys VII in Thrace, and Artavasdes II in Armenia. With hopes high he also sent to Phraates IV in Parthia, but Antony intercepted these messengers. Amyntas of Galatia joined a force of native troops raised in Asia by Antony's governor there, Furnius; Pompeius gathered Roman colonists in Lampsacus. After several successes he had to flee before Antony's reinforcements from Syria. King Amyntas, Furnius, and Titius caught up with him in Bithynia (his object was Armenia). His execution, at Miletus, was ordered lest he reach Cleopatra – favourable to him long before – and disrupt Antony's plans, in which he did not figure.[301] This diversion of troops and of 120 ships (plus the 70 coming 'from Sicily' or from Octavia) delayed Antony so far into the campaigning season of 35 that it, not Cleopatra's designs, prevented his campaign.

He was free for dynastic problems instead. The matter of Aristobulus, son of Herod's mother-in-law, Alexandra, had come to a head when Herod had the youth drowned.[302] This fell late in 35, and led Antony – at Cleopatra's urging – to summon Herod for an accounting at Laodicea before his own departure eastward in 34. Herod's kingship had been supported by Antony both in 40 at Rome and when won in 37 BC.[303]

Antony had too much at stake to interfere with this strong monarch, whose kingdom had to be secure before the coming expedition would dare leave it in the rear. In Herod's words, Antony said an accounting from a king meant that he was none, and treated him with honour, telling Cleopatra not to meddle in dynastic affairs. His wish did prevail – perhaps at the cost of further gifts to Cleopatra of territory in 'Coele-Syria.' A coin probably from 34 issued in Syria calls her the 'younger Goddess' in possible reference to her great-aunt Cleopatra Thea, vividly remembered in Syria as the wife of three Seleucid kings and mother of Antiochus VIII Grypus (§ 8). Antony graces the coin's obverse.[304]

The Second Campaign

During the enforced lull of 35/34 BC, Antony attempted a dynastic arrangement of his own. His object still lay in Parthia, but his disastrous experience in 36 convinced him that Artavasdes of Armenia must be neutralized first, through diplomacy or arms. He offered his son Alexander Helios for marriage to a daughter of Artavasdes.[305] Dio considers this a ploy, but it may have been sincere. Antony's thoughts ran towards a dynasty. A successful arrangement might have freed him for an attack on Parthia. But the offer lapsed and he had to confront the Armenian.[306] In due course the same offer was accepted by the Median Artavasdes.[307]

Antony set off eastwards again in 34, accompanied by Cleopatra as far as the Euphrates. She returned via Apamea and Damascus, then Judaea, where she once again met Herod.[308] In the generally censorious view of Jews, Cleopatra presented no model of chastity. It may be true that Caesar, Antony, and perhaps (back in 49) the son of Pompey constituted the only men in her life, but rumour had other partners for her. On this occasion in 34, Josephus has her, fresh from the embrace of Antony, attempt that of Herod. But the Judaean had already suffered when she intervened in the selection of a high priest.[309] He had no illusion as to her ultimate designs on his kingdom: he had to lease from her for two hundred talents some of his own lands detached by Antony. He denied himself with ease the pleasure of her body, but with difficulty that of her murder. His advisers dissuaded him from thus offending Antony (and changing history), so instead he conducted her respectfully to Pelusium – the one probable element in the entire tale – laden with gifts, and waved her home.[310] Through all this she concentrated on her own advantage. Even the Nabataeans had to be rescued by Herod from becoming 'slaves of Cleopatra,' and at that they lost maritime portions of their lands to her.[311]

Antony's campaign never reached Parthia, but it allowed him to claim a specious conquest of Armenia by capture of the monarch, Artavasdes II, son of Tigranes. Nothing in fact changed: Artaxias II, his son, succeeded and no interregnum ensued. The incident did permit Antony a royal captive for Cleopatra. He also issued a splendid coinage by 32, with his head and Cleopatra's and the legend ARMENIA DEVICTA. He was not even averse to sporting an Armenian tiara on his coins.[312]

Since this 'victory' had resulted from a surprise seizure of the king, with the *chrysophylakes* of Armenia declining to turn over its gold and the populace refusing battle, Antony's hold on Armenia would not have been acknowledged by its inhabitants. The king and his retinue refused obeisance (*proskynesis*) to Cleopatra, too. But Antony and she chose to make this occasion the grand ceremony in Alexandria with which to begin their dynasty. She became 'Queen of Kings,' Caesarion 'King of Kings,' and new territorial arrangements were set.[313]

The Kings of Kings

A second 'King of Kings' also appeared in the East. Alexander Helios was to rule in succession to Artavasdes II, who like his father Tigranes had assumed this title.[314] Antony and Cleopatra were serious, as subsequent use of the title demonstrates.[315]

Alexander was to take over Armenia – ignoring Artaxias and the still living Artavasdes II. He also 'received' Media Atropatene, presently in the hands of the allied Artavasdes I, to whose daughter he was betrothed. This would take effect on the death of the present king, one must suppose. He was also to rule Parthia and 'as far as India,' but the matter of conquest should be arranged first.[316]

A third 'King of Kings,' in Plutarch's view, was to be Ptolemy Philadelphos, who received Syria, Phoenicia, and Asia Minor. The distribution seems feasible, but further multiplication of the East's most exclusive title verged on absurdity. Still, removing Syria from Cleopatra's direct control made good sense and could save future strife: she had already encompassed several executions there, including King Lysanias of Chalcis. The arrangement would also keep her at greater distance from Herod.[317]

Cleopatra herself, now 'Queen of Kings' and soon also 'of Sons who are Kings' (CLEOPATRAE REGINAE REGVM FILIORVM REGVM) – the most awesome titles yet in the East – took Egypt and Cyprus. Caesarion, 'King of Kings,' was to rule jointly.[318] Finally, Cleopatra Selene took Cyrene, now ostensibly returned to Ptolemaic control.[319]

Appropriate costume and ritual attended all this, with the religious element prominent. Cleopatra is the 'New Isis' and soon 'Wife of Amon.'[320] Antony associates with her as the 'New Liber' (Dionysos), a god himself. An inscription from 'year 19, which is 4, Choiak 29' (28 December 34 BC) calls him 'Great Antony, inimitable among lovers' – echoing both Dionysos and Antony's society of 'Inimitable Livers.'[321] Coins continue this divine titulature for Cleopatra as the 'New Goddess.'[322]

All this met with predictably little enthusiasm in Rome, as did Antony's attempt to have his actions ratified. The alleged will of Antony even contained reference to it, and drew further support away from Antony.[323]

This last great ceremony of the Ptolemaic court, however ironic its pretension to validity, exposes the dichotomy of practice between East and West. Antony had no right to distribute the lands of kings among his children or to reverse the Roman conquest of such countries as Syria. Likewise for those regions now to be under the suzerainty of Caesarion and of Antony's sons through the rubric 'King of Kings'; this rare title had elsewhere been assumed by right of conquest (or of succession, among Parthians). The kings of Emesa, Commagene, Cilicia, Cappadocia, Galatia, Pontus and elsewhere were now suddenly to be under a Ptolemaic-Roman higher sovereignty.

The system would not have worked. Granted that some of these kings had been recognized originally by Antony himself, they all ruled areas traditionally under kings and unprepared for change. To compel them would not have been possible, since they themselves furnished most of the manpower for Eastern campaigns. The Roman method of winning them over or absorbing them piecemeal during a period of two centuries succeeded. Antony's method would not have for long, even without Octavian, who when his turn came had the good sense and sound advice to leave the kings alone. An expedition against one or two of them was always feasible, bolstered by Eastern allies. Wholesale warfare against them all was unthinkable in Antony's day, and his policy risked extensive alienations if he tried to carry it out against so many monarchs. Small wonder that antiquity regarded these distributions as the work of a pair increasingly out of touch with reality in the luxury and debauch of that idyllic world in Alexandria.[324]

Inscriptional evidence vividly demonstrates Octavian moving to supersede Antony, though their rivalry was not yet settled. Octavian had addressed the city in his own name alone as early as 39/38 BC, and we find joint triumviral decrees, but side by side with them now appears unilateral action by Octavian in portions of Antony's sphere of authority in Asia Minor.

Actium

Antony had by 33 become, at various places and times since 42, a 'New Dionysos' (like Auletes) , Osiris, the 'betrothed of Athena,' a 'God,' and the honorand of a temple by Cleopatra, the 'New Goddess.'[325] He had also become a general whose major prize, Parthia, eluded him, and who drew from Octavian an accusation of slothfulness before the Senate, in contrast with his own busy but inconclusive Illyrian campaigns.[326] His attempts to win land allotments for his veterans brought from Octavian the riposte that they should seek them in Media and Parthia since they had gained these for Rome. This unsubtle jibe reached Antony in Armenia, late in 33 BC.[327] He had gone there for another try at Parthia but instead negotiated with Artavasdes of Atropatene, acquired Iotape I, his daughter, as promised bride for Alexander Helios, and gave away some of Armenia to Artavasdes in his favourite prerogative of command: territorial distribution. Then he withdrew to Ephesus to meet Cleopatra and mobilize dynasts for war with Octavian, should it come. His troops followed, leaving to Artaxias his father's kingdom in Armenia. Antony and Cleopatra spent the winter of 33/32 in Ephesus; even gods require shelter.[328]

Open criticism of him by Octavian in 33 drew a letter from Antony.[329] It opens plaintively: 'What has changed you?' (*Quid te mutavit?*) It rushes on to say that if Octavian's coolness has arisen because of Cleopatra there should be no breach over this, since the affair has lasted nine years (dating from their meeting in Cilicia in 41) and since Octavian has had affairs of his own. The naïveté of the letter shows it a late paraphrase, selective and salacious, not a direct quotation. The situation called for discussion at the military and political level, though both knew that the dynastic ambitions of Cleopatra and of Antony through her lay at the base of the coming conflict.[330]

Antony contributed to the discord by divorcing Octavia in 32, causing further defections. The dynastic marriage of a daughter of his, Antonia, to

Pythodorus of Tralles would have further ruffled feelings if it occurred.[331] Matters proceeded to disguised, then open preparations for war.[332]

A solemn declaration of war followed not against Antony, though he had been stripped of his consulship and all other authority, but against Cleopatra.[333] Thus no *civil* war, and Octavian could later characterize this as a war undertaken 'on behalf of the Republic.' Cleopatra constituted an enemy far easier to justify than was Antony: a woman, an oriental, a corrupter of Antony, a harlot, a power-mad schemer who aspired 'to rule even in the city [of Rome].'[334] Antony had contributed to this charge by allowing sculptures of himself all about the Roman and Greek world. The colossal head that survives yet in Alexandria, the 'orientalizing' busts, the statues and paintings were reported to Romans and helped convince them that he had become 'not Roman but Egyptian, not Antony but Serapion.'[335] The representations of him as Osiris or Dionysos, with Cleopatra as Selene or Isis, 'more than anything else made him appear bewitched by her.'[336] Octavian announced that the war was to be with her eunuch, chambermaid, and others, since they now managed the kingdom, and she Antony.[337] The *Sibylline Oracles* could, as on occasions in the reign of Auletes, provide suitably frightening passages regarding an oncoming Eastern *despoina*, the feminine gender of the word from which we derive 'despot.'[338]

In the East, Cleopatra contributed to Antony's problems by insisting on a place in the deliberations, as well she might on grounds of her long experience as queen and as purveyor by Antony's own admission of most ships in their force.[339] Attempts to get her away from the army and even back to Egypt failed. Antony wished it himself early in 32, but after their move to Athens that summer he abandoned the notion.[340] Herod claimed later to have advised Antony to kill her.[341] The pilfering of art objects on her behalf[342] continued even during preparations at Ephesus, and sacred groves fell for ship-timbers at Cos.[343] These events and rumours such as his bestowing on Cleopatra the great libraries at Pergamon, worked against Antony in both East and West.[344]

Despite these problems the Eastern allies, the backbone of his force, began to assemble. They included, besides Egyptians, forces from Kings Iamblichus of Emesa, Tarcondimotus in Cilicia, Archelaus of Cappadocia, Mithradates II of Commagene, Sadalas III of Thrace, Polemo I of Pontus, Amyntas of Galatia (and Lycaonia), Artavasdes I of Atropatene, Malichus of the Nabataeans, Herod of Judaea, and others.[345] Some kings attended in person. Herod intended to, but was sent off to a pointless war with the Nabataeans.[346]

In October 32, the royal pair moved from Athens westward to Patrai, which issued a coin with Cleopatra as Isis.[347] A line of battle formed from an anchor-point in Cyrene, where Antony had four legions, to Corcyra, with reserves in Syria and Egypt. A series of island or port stations linked the extremes of the line, as for instance the outpost of King Bocchus of Libya at Methone.[348]

Easterners remained loyal when it made sense to. If not, not. One Roman might be preferable to another but none might be better still. After centuries of independence they could envision a future without Rome, and in these battles they put in an appearance but tried not to get carried away.

So at Actium, where wavering had begun even among Antony's Romans.[349] Antony's command came into question among his adherents, who nearly replaced him.[350] Friction between Antony and Cleopatra hardly reassured their followers; the story of his fear that she might poison him owes more to Roman imagination and Medea than to reality, but the core lay there in disagreements over tactics.[351] Hence allied defections. The cavalry of Amyntas wheeled towards home – in the overheated imagination of Horace – at the sight of Cleopatra's retinue and pavilion. Amyntas himself and Deiotarus opted for Octavian.[352] King Philadelphos of Paphlagonia proved no firmer.[353]

The vanquished reveal mistakes to the critical eye, and on 2 September 31, Antony and Cleopatra did so at Actium, mainly by losing. Not aware that the Roman Empire had begun, they preserved themselves through flight.[354] On reaching the coast of Libya, they returned to Egypt separately.[355] Cleopatra prepared a spectacular transfer of her remaining fleet from the Mediterranean to the Arabian Gulf, intending to move through the Red Sea to a new home, 'fleeing slavery and war' alike.[356] But the Nabataeans burned her ships as they appeared.

Unfortunately, King Artavasdes of Armenia remained yet in Alexandria and Cleopatra arrived before Antony. She reasoned that sending his head to Artavasdes I of Atropatene would further his alliance with Antony and herself, so she did.[357] This alliance constituted part of a projected mobilization of Eastern kings for a final defence of the royal pair's dream.[358] Should this fail they would sail to Spain and detach it through their great resources remaining in Alexandria.[359] Such counsels of desperation, authentic or invented by the malicious, came to naught as Eastern kings prepared for another transition. Their relations with Pompey, then Caesar, and now Antony had all foundered. Antony retained no basis other than Cleopatra on which to build dynastic alliances, and she no longer sufficed; of the large number of adherents once established throughout the East, no states or dynasts now heeded the call.[360] Only a group of their gladiators training in Cyzicus for expected celebratory games remained loyal, and set out for Egypt. After conflict with King Amyntas in Galatia and the sons of Tarcondimotus in Cilicia they failed to pass Q. Didius, governor of Syria.

With no response from Antony to their messages, they came to terms with Didius and settled for the time being in Daphnae.[361] They were later deceived, dispersed, and destroyed.

Herod had seen enough and lost no time changing allegiances, even assisting Didius against the gladiators.[362] In the spring of 30 BC he hastened to Rhodes, where Octavian was preparing to advance on Egypt. Later that summer he rejoined Octavian at Ptolemais and assisted him on the journey to Egypt.[363]

The final manoeuvres of Antony and Cleopatra included use of their two sons by previous mates: Caesarion, reputed son of Caesar, and Antyllus, Antony's son by Fulvia. These were to serve as a focus of resurgent Egyptian zeal for the war, believing that 'a man now served as their king' – a curious sentiment under the circumstances, with candidates for rule being a queen, two boys, and a Roman ex-triumvir. Should Antony and Cleopatra fall, these youths were to lead on. This prospect later furnished Octavian a pretext for despatching them both.[364]

Antony and Cleopatra also wrote to Octavian. Cleopatra sought to retain Egypt for her children, if not herself. In addition to their joint proposals for peace, she sent without Antony's knowledge rich gifts in the hope of detaching herself from Antony if it came to that.[365] Octavian returned placatory answers to Cleopatra and none at all to Antony, who even sent him Antyllus and a quantity of gold. (Octavian retained the money but not the boy.) He had learned of Cleopatra's plan to immolate herself and her enormous wealth in a tomb under construction for the purpose.[366] Octavian urged her to sacrifice Antony but keep her treasures safe. From Herod he knew what wealth the East could provide, and meant to have all of it he could.[367]

With Antony's former legions in Libya advancing against him from the west and Octavian from the northeast in the summer of 30, the military situation in Egypt became untenable. Some troops in Egypt remained loyal and fought well; Cleopatra's bodyguard of Galatians persisted and were later transferred with honour to the service of Herod. Enough ships remained that a papyrus a few years later can mention refurbishing 'the fleet of Cleopatra'; however, she proved unable to utilize it during her final crisis.[368]

She may have given orders to yield Pelusium and abate resistance, foreseeing Octavian's victory and hoping to win favour. One excited account has her relying on her ability to captivate yet a third powerful Roman, retain her realm, and rule in Rome after all.[369]

Bizarre final scenes ensued, novelistic as much as historical. Cleopatra retreated to her tomb and surrounding treasures. Antony arrived, a Romeo to her Juliet, and thinking her dead stabbed himself. She, alive (some said the sequence was her design), could not re-emerge since cunning Egyptian doors, once closed, will not reopen. She peeped out the top. Antony, not yet dead, demanded entrance; ropes raised him in time for expiry on her bosom.[370] She 'took heart' regarding Octavian and awaited him, passing the time by embalming Antony.

Cleopatra's remaining efforts went towards securing a position for herself and her children. She came to realize that detention in Rome loomed inevitably. She could have come to terms with that had not the prospect of being led in a Roman triumph, like her sister Arsinoe years before, brought home the approaching humiliations. Hence the decision to rasp her last gasp in the clasp of an asp.[371] She requested burial beside Antony, after a death unanimously described as dignified and royal, on 17 Mesore of 'year 22' (10 August 30 BC), at age thirty-nine. Her kingdom, wealthiest in existence 'except for [that of] Arsaces' in Parthia, now formed the prize that financed many of the remaining accomplishments of Octavian and helped secure the position of his successors.[372]

Somewhat more cynically, one must wonder how Octavian would dare leave her alive as a vivid reminder of the 'maddened' Antony and the internecine war. The crafty politician who now assumed the rewards of his victory did not need Cleopatra in his triumph, or in Rome. Better to arrange a quiet murder out of her subjects' sight, and to satisfy curiosity by the vivid tale of the asp?

Caesarion, sent for safety to Ethiopia and aiming for India, was persuaded or forced to return, purportedly to succeed his mother. Like Antyllus, he had to die.[373] However, the children of Antony and Cleopatra survived. They all, formerly well tutored by Nicolaus of Damascus, went now to Octavia to be raised among her own children.[374] About 20 BC, Cleopatra Selene married Juba II of Mauretania and ruled with him there. Two children of theirs, Drusilla and King Ptolemy, took up dynastic marriages in the Roman Empire. The fates of Alexander Helios and of his brother, the last Ptolemy, remain obscure.[375]

Besides the indelible image of Cleopatra in literature from that time forward, cults for her left traces from as early as AD 4 on into the third century.[376]

Thus passed the independence of Egypt, the Ptolemaic dynasty, and history's most famous woman. More than any other single event, her dramatic downfall, with the ruin of Antony's hopes, appears to mark the transition in 30 BC from royal rule in the East to Roman hegemony up to the Euphrates. However, the impression is deceptive, and that process was not to be completed for a century yet. At the time of her death, most of the East remained royal.

9

Dynasties beyond the Euphrates

§ 24. Armenia

When Tigranes left Syria – after first ending the lively career of Cleopatra Selene – and returned to face Lucullus in Armenia, he proceeded unwittingly to change the political distributions of much of the Near East. Before the battle near Tigranocerta in 69, Tigranes ranked as 'King of Kings' in name and substance. After it, he retained only his own kingdom and found enemies on all sides, including his own son, though he later recovered some territory and the grand title. Probably no single battle in the East so advanced Roman fortunes as this one, since it removed the major threat of Tigranes and Eupator (though both did live to fight again) and broke their empires. At the same time, it provided Rome a title to Syria, as victor over Tigranes, the conqueror of the Seleucids.[1]

The Last Years of Tigranes

Both Tigranes and Lucullus relied on their respective dynastic allies. Therefore the defection of Machares (brother-in-law of Tigranes), then holding the Bosporus for his father, Mithradates, seemed to Lucullus a crucial development. Cavalry from allies in Thrace and Galatia, with the disaffection of the Greeks inside Tigranocerta, contributed to his success. So did desertion by elements in the army of Tigranes – especially contingents from Sophene, Gordyene, and 'Arabia' – allowing Roman victory in a situation otherwise inconclusive.[2]

Panics and mutinies among Roman forces show the misgivings of the soldiery when facing such remote and alien populations. Problems with logistics attended the expedition, forcing dependence on allies. In 69 BC, the line of march had to be through Galatia, with supplies furnished and transported for the Roman forces by the Galatians themselves.[3]

Not least among resources available to the two Eastern monarchs for use against Rome was their wealth, usually stored in well-dispersed fortresses under heavy guard. The main treasury of Tigranes was of great size but Pompey, despite his need of money, could not force the guardians to open their vaults. He had to settle for payments – 'more than agreed upon' – relayed to him through the defeated king. Other rich treasuries of Tigranes lay near Artaxata itself, and account for the ease with which Tigranes met Pompey's terms of payment.[4]

Territorially, the Roman success out here was transitory; areas 'conquered' by Rome could rapidly return to native control. This applied most strongly to the Iranian borderlands, including Armenia. For one example, Gordyene was never really occupied by Rome, and soon reverted to the Parthians. In accounting for the inconclusive results of Roman efforts in Armenia, Dio sees popular loyalty to the Eastern monarchs as a key factor, ascribing it to 'legitimacy' of the monarchy. Thracian mercenaries disliked the Roman foreigner and joined the attack on their Roman employers, aided by slaves whom Mithradates had slyly declared that he intended to free. Both sides relied upon allied or hired manpower, both sometimes using the same men. These Thracians had formerly served Mithradates, going over to Rome for higher pay. Likewise, Commagene was now detached by Rome from Tigranes. Its king Antiochus – and one of the 'Arab' dynasts, Alchaudonius – aided Lucullus in 69, and transmitted to him the information that Tigranes and Mithradates were attempting to bring over the Parthian monarch.[5]

Despite his defeat by Lucullus, Tigranes entered the field again, occupying Cappadocia in 67. He took advantage of Lucullus's difficulties with his Roman political opponents and his own army. Tigranes required a military success to retrieve the international prestige he had lost in 69, especially since his allies began defecting immediately. For a time, he refused to acknowledge that his days of empire were ending, but the invasion of Armenia by Phraates III of Parthia and the son of Tigranes forced the former 'King of Kings' to concentrate on his own kingdom. The replacement of Lucullus by Pompey with extraordinary powers brought into the field a more formidable antagonist. Tigranes recognized that even his own kingdom's security could not be taken for granted any longer, and made peace with Pompey. This removed from Mithradates Eupator his last support, and proved indirectly fatal to him.[6]

Throughout the conflict between Tigranes and Lucullus, Phraates III of Parthia tried to maintain good relations with both Tigranes and Mithradates while avoiding provocation for war with Rome. A projected Roman alliance broke down upon evidence that he was also cultivating Tigranes, but Lucullus achieved 'friendship and alliance' with Phraates, who saw in Tigranes a greater threat than he saw in Rome. After all, Tigranes and his father-in-law together had been paramount in Asia, and Tigranes 'the most powerful king of the time.'[7]

Parthian reaction to this opportunity of neutralizing Tigranes took a dynastic form. The younger Tigranes, supported by Phraates III, moved against his father at Artaxata in 66 BC. Pompey intervened and a settlement along territorial lines distinguished between Armenian dynastic lands and later conquests. The elder Tigranes recovered 'his entire paternal realm' but lost the lands he had conquered. Besides parts of Cappadocia, Cilicia, Syria, and Phoenicia, these conquests were regarded as including Sophene. Pompey recognized the family's claim to Sophene, but insisted that Tigranes turn over its rule to his son, thus keeping an area so dangerously near Cappadocia out of the Armenian king's hands. After the later defection of Tigranes the Younger (see below), Sophene was added to the Cappadocian holdings of the restored Ariobarzanes. Portions of Upper Mesopotamia reverted to more local control, for instance by Abgar of Osrhoene and 'the Arab' Alchaudonius, King of the Rhambaeans, both of whom forgot their Roman alliance by the time Crassus arrived. Gordyene, conquered long before by Tigranes, and ruled for him by the faithless Zarbienus, came under his control again for a time after 69 and then went to his son when Sophene did.[8]

Tigranes ruled on for some fourteen years after the defeat of 69, though restricted after 65 BC mainly to his own kingdom. Payment of a large sum ensured his enrolment as 'friend and ally of Rome.' A version of events current in Rome about nine years later has Tigranes removing his diadem and Pompey replacing it in a field ceremony. The formal alliance of Tigranes to Rome provided at least nominal support for that dawning empire's ambitions beyond the Euphrates. Positioned below Iberia and above Atropatene and Parthia, this strong monarchy controlled a strategic territory. At least by 66/65, his coins call him 'Philhellene' in Mesopotamia, and returning confidence allowed Tigranes to resume the use of 'Great King' (66-55 BC) and then even 'King of Kings' (62-57 BC) during his final years of rule, however inappropriate the titles by that time.[9]

Intermarriage

The dynastic practice of Tigranes throughout his reign led to extensive intermarriage with other dynasties, and the effects were discernible for centuries. The marriage of Tigranes to Cleopatra, daughter of Mithradates Eupator of Pontus, had provided him with access to one of the most extensive royal families in the East. His offspring, by her and other wives, extended his own influence into other lines of kings. He could ill afford to ignore the Parthians, and arranged a match between his daughter and the Parthian King Mithradates II, as well as the marriage of a daughter to Pacorus I, the son of Orodes II. A third Parthian marriage in the Armenian house was that of his rebellious son Tigranes the Younger to a daughter of Phraates III, though this took place under circumstances adverse to Tigranes the Great.

Tigranes could control an empire, but not his sons. He met Tigranes the Younger in battle. Another son, Zariadres, had a similar falling out with his father. He was supported in this – like his brother – by the Armenian nobility, whose role in the nation's affairs was an active one in the two centuries ahead. Zariadres lost his life to Tigranes, and another son was killed by his father for prematurely seizing the diadem from the recumbent Tigranes after a hunting accident, as the story went.[10]

As partial successor of Mithradates II of Parthia after 86 BC, Tigranes had entered a dynastic network and advanced it through his numerous progeny. As discussed in § 11, a parchment from Avroman in Kurdistan shows that Mithradates II had married a daughter of Tigranes named Aryazate-Automa (the names may show respectively her Iranian and her claimed Greek descent). His daughter enjoyed full standing among the Parthian queens of Mithradates in the Avroman text, where she is named *before* the second sister-wife. As father-in-law of the 'Great King' of Parthia, Tigranes later advanced military claims to succeed to parts of his empire.[11]

A daughter of Tigranes married the ruler of Media Atropatene. In recounting the manoeuvres by Mithradates Eupator against Lucullus in 67 BC, Dio mentions a diversion by 'the other Mithridates, from Media, son-in-law of Tigranes.' Whether this means that his origins lay in Atropatene or merely that he ruled there as appointee of Tigranes must remain undecided. However, Dio's wording implies familiarity with a figure who would not have been obscure in the records of Rome's early encounters with dynasts of East Anatolia, given the vigorous participation of Tigranes and his many relatives or descendants in these.[12]

Appian mentions another dynast of Atropatene allied (and perhaps related) to Tigranes. In 64 BC, Pompey 'fought Darius the Mede,' perhaps 'formerly allied to Tigranes.' His triumph in Rome listed this man among the 'conquered kings.'[13]

By way of summary and forecast, it is well to note that the marital tie of Tigranes the Great to Mithradates Eupator long affected the Armenian house and was clearly traceable in imperial times. The Zeno (renamed Artaxias: *PIR*^{2} A 1168) who was to be put forward as Armenian king from 18 to 34 AD descended from King Polemo I of Pontus, who had married Dynamis (*PIR*^{2} D

211), granddaughter of Mithradates Eupator. As niece of Cleopatra – the wife of Tigranes the Great – she was also a cousin of King Artavasdes of Armenia. The sister of Zeno-Artaxias, Antonia Tryphaena (*PIR*^{2} A 900; J 397), was to link him as well to the house of Cotys in Thrace. As the stemmata show, this closely linked dynasty ruling in Thrace, Pontus, and Bosporus continued its ties with the Armenian house and with the lines related to it – including Judaea – well into the first century AD. The King Cotys (*PIR*^{2} C 1555) who was to rule in Armenia Minor sprang also from this house: his mother was Antonia Tryphaena. Polemo II, his brother (*PIR*^{2} J 472), ruled Cilicia, and briefly married Berenice, Herod the Great's great-granddaughter (J 651).[14]

The Work of Tigranes

Despite his reputation for cruelty and the terror his name inspired, Tigranes the Great performed a distinguished service to the Armenian nation during his long reign of some forty years (95-55 BC). He secured the country and expanded its territory at a time when kingdoms in the East had begun to be threatened by the Seleucid collapse, the growth of Parthia, the campaigns of Mithradates Eupator, and the advance of Rome. Tigranes gave Armenia its greatest period of empire, and a legacy of stability. His dynasty ruled on after him and his country escaped domination from without. These were not inconsiderable achievements, though for Easterners the role Tigranes took in the rise and fall of Eupator, his harassment of Ariobarzanes I in Cappadocia, the deportations from Cilicia to settle Tigranocerta, and the critical occupation of Syria, which resulted in its absorption by Rome, all loomed large in memory. To balance the often hostile narratives of classical historians, later accounts such as that by Moses of Chorene demonstrate the longevity of positive memory as well.

Tigranes survived until at least 56 BC, and perhaps 55, as known from mentions and coinage. He left a robust successor, Artavasdes II, fully worthy of his heritage. Another son, the Younger Tigranes, gave his father less comfort.[15]

Tigranes the Younger

The man known by this name never quite ruled Armenia, and is not enumerated among the Artaxiad monarchs. None the less, he came closer to it than some wished, including his father. After his defeat at the hands of Lucullus, Tigranes the Great, 'handing over to his son the diadem and the insignia of rule, fled to one of his fortresses,' according to Memnon, with a similar version in Plutarch. At some point late in the reign of Tigranes and early in that of the Parthian Phraates III (70-57 BC), Tigranes the Younger is said by Appian to have been 'crowned' by his father. The occasion and the son may be the same in all three accounts; Tigranes presumably intended an association of his son on the throne rather than retirement for himself.[16]

Whatever the hopes of Tigranes, they met with disappointment. The Prince-King 'soon deserted and fought him; defeated, he fled to Phraates, King of the Parthians, who had recently received the government from his father, Sinatruces.' This event must have occurred in 69 or 68, cemented by marriage to a daughter of Phraates. Romans took advantage of it, for Pompey in his negotiations with Phraates provided the ambitious young Tigranes an opportunity. So did the discontent of a faction among the Armenian aristocracy. In 66 the younger Tigranes approached Pompey, who received him even 'though he was a maternal grandson of Mithridates [Eupator].' Phraates had by now arranged 'friendship' with Pompey, and decided to resolve his problems with Tigranes the Great by invading Armenia in company with the younger Tigranes. They penetrated as far as Artaxata, but the withdrawal of Phraates left son facing father, and the older man won. Since Mithradates Eupator could no longer be of service to either side, the son returned to Pompey, who decided on an advance of his own against Armenia. This brought the capitulation of Tigranes the Great, followed by 'friendship' and – a major incentive for Pompey – an indemnity.[17]

Pompey wished the younger Tigranes to rule Sophene and perhaps Gordyene, both of which the elder had conquered. But a falling-out left the younger Tigranes in disfavour with Pompey, and then a captive. Under a series of custodial arrangements, including a trip to Rome for humiliation in Pompey's triumph, he languished until 58 BC. In that year, P. Clodius accepted a bribe and released him, after which he is heard of no more.[18]

Tigranes the Great saw to it that his rebel son had no scope for further adventures against him. In his declining years, he had available another son, Artavasdes II, who proved a vigorous and worthy successor. He contrasts sharply with the opportunistic Tigranes the Younger, whose dealings with Parthians, Romans, and Armenians brought lasting benefit to none, including himself.

Artavasdes II (55-34 BC)

Artavasdes apparently derived from a different mother than had the younger Tigranes and his two brothers, both killed by their father. He succeeded to the throne by 55 BC, possibly a year earlier. Tigranes the Great lived at least until 56.[19]

From his father, Artavasdes received the advice not to provoke either Parthians or Romans to conflict, but to attempt an independent policy. He began as a 'friend to the Romans' but later threw in his lot with Parthia in the face of a Roman invasion, and ultimately paid for it by proceeding as a captive to Alexandria, where he may have died at Cleopatra's hands about the time of Actium.[20]

At his accession, he fully intended to carry on the dynastic work of his father, not in warfare but in royal intermarriage and alliance. Early in his reign, about 50 BC, Artavasdes betrothed one of his daughters to a son of Deiotarus I of the Galatian tetrarchal and royal line. Through this match – if the marriage did take place – the Armenian line gained relatives among the ruling class in Pontus, Pergamon, Paphlagonia (Deiotarus Philadelphos), and Galatia. Deiotarus held the title of king in neighbouring Armenia Minor, c. 51-41 BC.[21]

During the reign of Artavasdes, even closer ties with the Arsacids are visible. A sister of Orodes II of Parthia (58-39 BC) had married Tigranes the Younger about 68 BC. Another sister of Orodes went to Artavasdes about 53 BC, and Pacorus I, son of Orodes, reinforced the link by his marriage to the sister of Artavasdes II. Pacorus was important to the plans of Orodes, and this marriage reflects the policy of both houses. Besides gaining recognition for his ability as a leader, Pacorus later ruled jointly with Orodes and issued coins of his own (§ 26). The death of Pacorus in Cyrrhestica (38 BC) led to a severe curtailment of Parthian efforts there. No record of his Armenian wife's subsequent activity remains.[22]

The period of Artavasdes II is also noteworthy for the increasing adoption of Hellenic cultural elements by the royalty of Armenia and Parthia. Plutarch reflects on Greek penetration into both of these houses; Ionian Greek *hetairai* are ancestresses of some Arsacids. We learn that Artavasdes actually wrote Greek works, 'some of which survive.' In this he perhaps inspired his late contemporary, King Archelaus I of Cappadocia (§ 17).[23]

In perhaps the first year of his reign, Artavasdes faced a difficult situation. When M. Licinius Crassus left Rome late in 55 BC to assume his command in Syria, the new King of Armenia was unaware that Crassus might interpret his tenure of Syria as a mandate to attack Parthia. Looseness of interpretation in this post had recently allowed A. Gabinius to attempt installation of the Parthian prince Mithradates, but he got no farther than the Euphrates, though he did restore Ptolemy XII Auletes to Egypt in 55. Whether or not he possessed some sort of *imperium infinitum* in Roman eyes, this would have no application in Parthia or Armenia; 'friendship and alliance' could not be stretched to indicate subjection. Any advance into Parthia by the new Syrian governor would be an act of war.[24]

Nevertheless, Artavasdes began his reign in line with his father's policy of adherence to the Roman alliance. He offered a strong force to assist Crassus in the spring of 54, despite his knowledge that Parthia, like Armenia, enjoyed 'friendship and alliance' with Rome. In effect, he was willing, in order to fulfil his undertaking in one pact, to help Crassus break another. For his part, the Parthian King Orodes II had no intention of passively allowing either a Roman advance into his territory or a significant Armenian measure of assistance. He demanded an explanation from Crassus of his crossing into Mesopotamia, and he prepared to block any force that Artavasdes might send from Armenia. This last proved unnecessary, for in 53 BC Crassus declined the Armenian offer to guide him and lost crucial military assistance. He apparently regarded Armenia as an inconsequential ally, an easy conquest itself if matters came to that.[25]

Crassus proceeded to meet his destiny at Carrhae in 53 BC. The disaster influenced local policies for years to come, and lured Artavasdes from fidelity to the Roman alliance. An ancient tradition has the marriage of his sister to Pacorus I occur just as the campaign of Crassus ended in disaster, with the wedding celebration enlivened by a performance of the *Bacchae* featuring the severed head of Crassus in the role of Pentheus. The conjunction is too neat, but the marriage occurred in the period of Carrhae, perhaps as a consequence. Artavasdes could no longer be relied upon as a Roman ally.[26]

Two years later, when Cicero went to Cilicia as governor, he felt some apprehension regarding Artavasdes. In the fall of 51 he made camp near Cybistra 'so that Artavasdes, the Armenian King, whatever his policy might be, would know that an army of the Roman people was not far from his territory.' Cicero had heard that 'the Armenian King was about to make an attack on Cappadocia'; in the context of the Parthian invasion of Syria that year, this could be a dangerous situation. The alliance of the two monarchies, reinforced by a double royal marriage, threatened Roman interests late in 51 BC.[27]

The blundering of Crassus had contributed to converting a Roman ally into a Parthian one, despite the territorial disputes then current between the two monarchies. Cicero faced the consequences in 51 and 50, with Parthians invading and Armenians thought likely to. Cicero did what he could to prop up Cappadocia by strengthening the resolve of Ariobarzanes III, but refused troops to him and confined his initial military efforts to occupying the westernmost passes at Cybistra. This protected Lycaonia, but potentially sacrificed Cappadocia. Cicero attempted to disguise this in his letter to Cato in August 51. Dependent on the wavering 'fidelity of our allies,' especially in Galatia and Commagene, Cicero endured a precarious situation not of his own making.[28]

Secure in his alliance with Parthia and the apparent lack of a further threat from Rome, Artavasdes aspired to resume the imperial work of his father. At least by 51/50 BC, his coinage takes up the title 'King of Kings' once borne by Tigranes and still used in Parthia. By 38/37 BC he also adopted an echo of the title Tigranes used, *Theos* ('the God'); in his case, it became *Theios* ('Divine'). He utilized the same tiara his father had, currently also favoured by Antiochus I of Commagene and by Artavasdes I of Atropatene (§ 25). Artavasdes issued a coinage readily recognizable as harmonious with his father's, even including one of the Mesopotamian types; presumably he desired to rule there and at one time in his long reign did. Especially welcome to him would have been obtaining a portion of Media Atropatene, where King Artavasdes I lived in enmity with the Armenians.[29]

Artavasdes ruled with competence as the situation worsened in Rome. Caesar's intended expedition against the Parthians in 44 BC might have aimed at him too, since his attitude as early as 51 had been suspect. The murder of Caesar removed this threat, but in due course Antony's appearance in the East presented another. The political situation in Parthia altered in 38 BC when Pacorus I, son of the Arsacid King Orodes II, fell after leading the successful Parthian invasions of Asia Minor, Syria, and Judaea. This was followed about 38/37 BC by the death of Orodes and the succession of Phraates IV. Phraates decided to take no chances of further rivalry and murdered his half-brothers, the sons of Orodes by a daughter of Antiochus I of Commagene. This dangerous situation soon involved both Rome and Armenia, as noble Parthians, especially a certain Monaeses, fled westward seeking help.[30]

Monaeses fired the imagination of Antony with the prospects of glory to be achieved by invading Parthia. Attacking a 'friend and ally' could appear impolite, but it was given out that Phraates IV had murdered his father, and here lay the necessary pretext, since Orodes had been a Roman ally. At the same time, a campaign by P. Canidius Crassus against the Iberians and Albanians north of Armenia succeeded, and made Artavasdes of Armenia apprehensive. Finally to be weighed now in 36 BC were two considerations: that Artavasdes I of Atropatene, the enemy south of Armenia, might profitably be weakened by a Roman invasion, and that he had allied himself with the new Parthian monarch. Antony had the further incentive that Parthia had not returned the standards and captives remaining there since the battle of Carrhae seventeen years earlier.[31]

The situation led to a bizarre culmination, in 36 BC. When Antony proceeded against Parthia and met his assembled allied kings, he found them numerous, and 'the greatest of all Artavasdes of Armenia,' bringing a force of thirteen thousand. Relying on the advice of Artavasdes, Antony found himself led not directly against Parthia but through 'mountainous and roadless regions, and circuitous ways' to Atropatene, part of which he devastated. This settled a score for Artavasdes of Armenia, but did little to advance the fortunes of Antony. Ultimately, after what appeared to contemporaries as treachery against his Roman ally, Artavasdes withdrew to Armenia and left the Romans to fend for themselves while winter and Phraates IV approached. The Roman withdrawal was disastrous (§ 26), but Antony chose to pronounce this botched campaign a victory. The 'Armenian' tiara which now appeared on his coinage copied the version of the King of Atropatene, Artavasdes I, his nominal foe, not that of Artavasdes II of Armenia, his erstwhile ally. Antony had determined to snatch a propaganda victory from this misadventure. Similarly, when he seized the Armenian king in 34, his coinage blossomed with ANTONI(US) ARMENIA DEVICTA, despite the perfidious nature of the 'conquest.'[32]

Leaving Polemo I of Pontus behind as a captive, Antony obtained supplies from Artavasdes and withdrew to Egypt, meditating vengeance on the Armenian and a renewed attack on the Parthians.[33]

The blunders by Crassus early in Artavasdes's reign were echoed by Antony's at the end of it: in each instance the result was increased Armenian alienation and espousal of Parthia. In 34, Artavasdes renewed dealings with Antony. The marriage alliance now artfully proposed by Antony to offset Armenian misgivings struck neither party as anomalous – Antony had soon learned the role of dynastic intermarriage in the East – but the only outcome was Antony's treacherous seizure of Artavasdes, and attempts on his treasuries.[34]

Captivity in Alexandria for the monarch and his retinue had unfortunate results, from the Roman point of view. A son of Artavasdes, Artaxias (also called Artaxes), soon succeeded him, distrustful of Romans and disposed towards alliance with the Parthians. In his account of events in AD 16, Tacitus remarks that the ill-feeling in Armenia had still not disappeared by that time – thirty-six years after the death of Artaxias, and fifty since the seizure of Artavasdes II. About 31 BC, another consequence of the ensuing local upheavals – complicated by hatred for Rome – may have been alliance through marriage of the Atropatenian and Hyrcanian dynasties. The fusion yielded powerful Arsacid rulers in Vonones II and Artabanus III, both of whom were to leave numerous progeny to rule Parthia, Atropatene, and Hyrcania.[35]

Antony's arrangements on behalf of his own children bore little fruit, but his methods were anchored in the Eastern dynastic tradition. He gave Caesarion the title 'King of Kings'; he used one dynasty against another (Artavasdes the Armenian against Artavasdes the Mede); he planned dynastic intermarriage of his own (his son Alexander to Iotape, daughter of

Artavasdes the Mede: Alexander had previously been suggested for a daughter of Artavasdes of Armenia); and he distributed territories to dynasts he himself recognized (Armenia Minor to Polemo, Galatia to Amyntas, Cappadocia to Archelaus). It is likely that in retaining Antony's distributions for much of the East, Augustus or his advisers recognized that these dynasties would be most able to control their respective populations, though the choice among available and mutually acceptable individuals could be flexible.[36]

Artaxias II (34-20 BC)

At the seizure of Artavasdes by Antony in 34 BC, his son Artaxias II evaded detention. There was no interregnum, and he appeared almost immediately as King of Armenia. The detailed account of Dio reveals a strong reaction among the Armenian citizenry to Antony's seizure of Artavasdes: they refused him access to the king's treasuries, and 'those bearing arms' chose Artaxias king. Artaxias withdrew to the Parthian king before Antony's advance into Armenia.[37]

Some Armenians submitted voluntarily to Antony, whereas Artaxias was supported by most of the nobility and by the pro-Parthian faction evident at least since Tigranes the Younger appeared. The aunt of Artaxias, sister-in-law of the reigning Phraates IV, could still have been at the Parthian court with the children she had borne to Pacorus I, who had died four years before. Artaxias reappeared with Parthian assistance, recapturing both Armenia and the kingdom in Media Atropatene of Antony's ally Artavasdes. Even though his brothers were in Roman hands after being discovered among the royal hostages at Alexandria, Artaxias massacred the remaining Romans in Armenia and sent Artavasdes of Atropatene flying for refuge to Rome. The long reign (33-20 BC) of Artaxias back in Armenia proved unfortunate for Roman designs on Eastern Anatolia.[38]

Artavasdes of Armenia left at his death (apparently in 30 BC, perhaps at Cleopatra's hands) two other sons besides Artaxias and the daughter betrothed into the Galatian house. All three sons bore traditional Armenian royal names, and became the first Armenian rulers after Actium. Through these legitimate heirs to the throne, Rome made major efforts at gaining influence in Armenia. Strabo optimistically but erroneously recapitulates Armenian history between Actium and his own day by saying that all successors of Artavasdes 'ruled under Caesar and the Romans.' Rome's first Armenian 'appointees' left much to be desired in the eyes of Augustus, and elements of the eventual failure of his policy for the region were already evident. The Parthian-supported, anti-Roman Artaxias II occupied the throne of Armenia during the first decade of the Augustan principate. Perhaps the later renaming – to Artaxias – of the Armenian King Zeno was an appeal to Armenian loyalties after the forty years of turmoil that were to follow the death of Artaxias II in 20 BC.[39]

The claim of Augustus that he might have made Armenia a province in 20 BC would have been true only were he prepared for an extensive military effort on behalf of the faction discontented with Artaxias II. Even then, the reaction of the Arsacids and most Armenians would have been sharp; the conciliatory Phraates IV could not be pressed too hard. Allied kings were unready for mobilization then also. Armenia remained a prize for Romans to contest with the Arsacids of Parthia until the compromise reached in the reign of Nero, which in effect ceded control to Parthia but saved face for Rome. After Artaxias II, Tigranes III, Tigranes IV, Erato, and Artavasdes III, the disappearance of the line which had descended from Tigranes and his forebears left Augustus with the virtually insuperable problem of locating kings from the Eastern dynasties who could also win acceptance in Armenia. He and his successors attempted to use several kings from Atropatene; they sent in Tigranes V and Tigranes VI, descended from Archelaus of Cappadocia and Herod the Great; they supported two Iberians (§ 25); they recognized the successful Pontic prince Zeno-Artaxias. The policy ultimately failed, with a long series of Arsacids assuming control of Armenia, beginning intermittently early in the first century. The Parthians 'definitively planted an Arsacid ruler on the Armenian throne in AD 66, as they had earlier on that of Media Atropatene.' Armenia remained an issue for centuries, with Rome tending to claim small but tightly organized portions and the Parthians enjoying alliances with the major parts. A formal division along such lines between Rome and Persia appeared by the late fourth century AD.[40]

§ 25. Trans-Euphrates Dynasties, II

A number of small Mesopotamian dynasties in the vicinity of Armenia – beginning with Sophene in Upper Mesopotamia – continued their regional rule right through the period 69-30 BC, and are discussed in § 12. Iberia and Atropatene, two other regions with a strong dynastic tradition and an important role in events, receive study here.[41]

Iberia

These two dynasties shared in Roman eyes one overwhelming advantage: strategic proximity to Armenia. A line of allied kings in either or both would confer advantage on such an enemy as Rome became of the Artaxiads in

Armenia. Despite occasional professions of amity, the permanent relationship between Rome and Armenia remained one of watchful hostility. Obtaining allies on the Armenian frontiers became Roman policy for at least a century, beginning with Pompey.[42]

Whether or not the Iberians were distinct as early as the fifth century, when they have been identified with the 'Sospires' of Herodotus, they did enjoy a stable line of monarchs from the early third century before Christ to the late sixth century after. They employed their own national era, they co-operated with the Seleucids in a policy of containing Armenia, and they intermarried with the Armenians – all characteristics of the flexible East.[43]

Iberia had avoided subjugation by the Macedonians during Alexander's campaigns, though he later sent an expedition to the vicinity, and this entered local tradition as a 'conquest.' Iberians 'were not subject to Medes or Persians, and escaped Macedonian rule,' according to Plutarch. Their independence did not unduly isolate them from contact with neighbouring peoples to the north, with whom they intermarried and traded. Caravans, rich cities, prosperous estates are mentioned. Their dress showed contact with Armenians and Medes, as did their language. They preferred farming and peace to warfare, but could give a formidable account of themselves when necessary. Their lancers fought for Tigranes the Great, and appear among the allies of Mithradates Eupator. None the less, during the reign of the Parthian Sinatruces (78/77 – 70/69 BC), his coins circulated in Iberia. Their religious and social organization resembled that in Pontus and Cappadocia, with a priestly caste second to the kings, and the military, farming, and common classes ranked below. Of course, ancients noticed the homonymy between Asiatic Iberia and Hispanic Iberia; Appian remarks that they have no similarity 'in custom or language,' though some had postulated a connection between them.[44]

Iberia remained by choice aloof from the surrounding struggle when it could, but fought for Tigranes in 69 at Tigranocerta. Its inhabitants in 66 demonstrated, under King Artoces, their reluctance to permit Mithradates Eupator access to the region of Chotene in Armenia, though they failed to stop him. By the same logic, they resisted Pompey when he arrived in the vicinity during his pursuit of Mithradates, but they were forced to capitulate. An arrangement for a time made Iberians into allies of Rome. The 'three leaders of the Iberians' who were led in Pompey's triumph had doubtless been demanded of Artoces as a pledge, and so were some of his children.[45]

King Artoces died about 63 BC, to be succeeded by Pharnabazus II, his son. This king married an Artaxiad princess and ruled some thirty-three years, to 30 BC. His adherence to the Roman alliance wavered, and in 36 BC, P. Canidius Crassus advanced against him in battle. A Roman victory led to another alliance. Pharnabazus took seriously the consequent obligation of campaigning against his own neighbour, King Zober of Albania.[46]

Actium and its consequences made no immediate impact on Iberia, but the gradual approach of Rome did. By the beginning of the first century after Christ, the Artaxiad dynasty, which Tigranes the Great had so strengthened, grew enfeebled, necessitating a dolorous series of outside kings for Armenia, supported by Rome. These drew on Atropatene, Judaea, and Pontus. Eventually they included two Iberians. Despite strong Roman efforts to support these kings, only Zeno-Artaxias of Pontus enjoyed any success.[47]

Though Iberians co-operated with Romans in a mutual attempt to impede Armenia, they retained an independent outlook that occasionally led to conflict. Strabo, writing early in the first century, regarded Iberians as easily dominated, but quick to revolt if not watched closely or if vigorous leaders arose. Rome relied on a natural community of interest with the Iberians, who feared and disliked the Parthians, from whose domination they could boast themselves to have remained free. For their part, Parthians in AD 35 could describe King Pharasmanes I as 'the contemptible Iberian with a mercenary army' while they prepared for battle. This did not prevent the Iberian force from prevailing over the Arsacid King Artabanus.[48]

During the stormy period from AD 35 to 54, the two Iberians were to rule Armenia with Roman support. Mithradates, brother of the Iberian King Pharasmanes, and Radamistus, son of the same king, both held the country with his co-operation, but after them the Roman effort there began to slide precipitously.[49]

Following a century of involvement in the politics of the Roman effort to advance beyond the Euphrates, Iberia returned to its independent ways, with centuries of its own monarchs to come.[50]

Atropatene

The region known in antiquity as Atropatene, 'Atropatian' Media, Media Atropatene, or Media Minor (modern Azerbaijan) bordered Armenia on its north and Media proper on its southeast. To its west lay Adiabene; to its northwest, Gordyene. Its southern boundary ran contiguous to the northern limits of the Parthian kingdom. Both Strabo and Pliny clearly distinguish Atropatene from Media and from Armenia.[51]

Its location guaranteed that Atropatene would constitute an important object of interest to Armenians and Parthians, who disputed its control or alliance for centuries. When Rome advanced to the area, Atropatene also entered the plans of Antony and then Augustus as they sought a foothold beyond Mesopotamia from which operations might be conducted against either Parthia or Armenia. Antony betrothed a son to an Atropatenian princess, who went after his death to Commagene with results long important in the East. The last princes of Atropatene served as kings of Armenia in the attempt of Augustus to detach it from Arsacid control after the line of Tigranes perished.

The eponymous founder of the dynasty began as a satrap of Media, in which Atropatene previously lay incorporated, though distinct, as shown on the Persepolis reliefs. At the battle of Gaugamela in 331, Atropates led the Medes, with three other contingents attached (Cadusians, Albanians, Sacesinians), part of a vast army in support of the Persian Darius III. After his victory, Alexander transferred Media to the Persian Oxodates on the supposition that his recent imprisonment under Darius would render him now more trustworthy. Subsequent dissatisfaction with him led Alexander instead to return Atropates to his former satrapy. During the remainder of Alexander's life, Atropates performed various services, such as delivering a Median pretender to him at Pasargadae or sending to him at the nearby plain of Nesaea one hundred women equipped for cavalry duty. Alexander reconfirmed his governorship late in his life and in 324 married a daughter of his to Perdiccas. After the death of Alexander, division of Media left Atropates with the northwest territory which came to bear his name.[52]

Atropates 'prevented his country from falling under Macedonian subjection.' He achieved the title of king, on Strabo's testimony, and managed to organize a distinct state. From the time of his reign, 'the succession from him has been preserved until the present' (early first century after Christ); Strabo either wrote this by about AD 9 or else had in mind descendants no longer ruling (see below). The succession constituted a strong dynastic tradition, achieved in the usual twofold manner: by vigorous defence of the country and by royal intermarriage. His descendants lie for the most part in obscurity during the first three centuries after him, though one glimpse reveals a King Artabazanes about a century after him. Antiochus III, after suppressing the rebellion of Molon, decided to follow up his success by advancing against 'the dynasts of the barbarians' bordering his domain on the east. The 'most powerful and vigorous of those dynasts' was Artabazanes, whose domain 'remains yet under the Persians, after being overlooked in Alexander's time.' Since 'a very old man' now (220 BC), he chose not to resist the attack of Antiochus, and concluded peace with him. From the description by Polybius of the territory Artabazanes ruled, he was dynast of Atropatene; the source followed by Polybius apparently did not accord him the title of king. In remarking that Atropatene remained 'under the Persians,' Polybius presumably distinguishes it from territories dominated by the Seleucids when he wrote Book V, midway in the second century before Christ. Some sort of overlordship by the Parthians at that time remains possible, even though Atropatene had its own ruler. Strabo's tradition cannot prove full independence at all periods.[53]

Glimpses of the kingdom must suffice, for the period before the first century, and these usually permit no conclusions. When Zariadras and Artaxias became kings, recognized by Rome, after the defeat of Antiochus III and the subsequent treaty of Apamea in 188 BC, Artaxias I enlarged his portion of Armenia by moving south of Artaxata into Caspiane, Phaunene (Phauene), and Basoropeda, taking them 'from the Medes' of Atropatene. This need not mean conquest of Atropatene, and the succession probably continued. The military alliance between Artaxias and Timarchus, 'Satrap of Media' about 162 BC, might reveal one of the rulers of Atropatene, but might also refer to Media Maior. Atropatene could seem more likely, as being nearer and also potentially within the sphere of Roman interests, since the same man had recently appealed to Rome for recognition and received a *senatus consultum* terming him 'king.' However, Timarchus held Babylon also. While this cannot determine which Media lay under his control, Media Maior had somewhat better access to Babylon.[54]

Marriage alliances helped to consolidate the kingdom. The successors of Atropates 'arranged marriages with the kings of the Armenians and of the Syrians, and after that with those of the Parthians.' This important statement can be substantiated by scraps of evidence. When Strabo wrote this, Atropatenian marriages with all three of these royal houses had left traces discernible still.[55]

First, Armenia. How far back Strabo intends his remark to apply cannot be determined. Certainly, intermarriage between Armenian satraps and the 'Hyrcanian' rulers can be postulated from so remote a period as the fifth century, when Hydarnes III ruled both areas. Orontes I, his grandson, founded the Orontid line in Armenia and thus passed on this dual heritage. This was long before Atropates.[56]

The attested connections between the Orontids and the ruling houses in Parthia or in Commagene, with the intermarriage in turn between those two houses and Atropatene (see below), could also have been in Strabo's mind. More precise, however, was the evidence that Tigranes the Great had married a daughter of his to the King of Atropatene. During the Roman campaign of 67 BC against Mithradates Eupator, they were attacked by 'the other Mithridates, the one from Media, son-in-law of Tigranes.' That 'Media' here meant Media Atropatene can be presumed by its much greater proximity to the theatre of war; it also lay within the sphere of overlordship formerly claimed by Tigranes as 'King of Kings' when the marriage may have taken place. He had subdued 'all other nations' in his vicinity, which included Atropatene but not Media, far more defensible by the Arsacids; he specifically held Atropatene among his 'subjects.'[57]

The marriage-alliance with Tigranes presumably dated to the period after the death of the Arsacid Mithradates II, when Tigranes rose to the status of 'King of Kings.' In addition to the assistance of his son-in-law, he also apparently derived military support from one 'Darius the Mede,' with whom Pompey fought 'either because he had been an ally of Antiochus [of Commagene] or of Tigranes.' This vague report by Appian permits no certain dating, though Darius must have ruled about 65 BC, considering the chronology of Pompey's campaigns. Since an advance by Pompey to Media Maior is impossible, this conflict with Darius must have involved the other Media, Atropatene, probably during the dispute with Phraates III over control of Gordyene in 65/64 BC. Pompey's lieutenant, L. Afranius, invaded Gordyene and could have come into conflict with the ruler of adjacent Atropatene then; the battle could also have occurred when A. Gabinius advanced to the Tigris in 65.[58]

The existence of two monarchs at virtually the same time in Atropatene can of course be explained by succession. When 'the kings of the Medes and Adiabeni' aided Tigranes in 69 BC, the monarch would have been Mithradates, on this view; he lived still in 67. When Pompey's lieutenant won a victory against Darius the Mede in 65/64, that king would have recently acceded. The second postulate available, that one or the other ruled Media Maior, appears most unlikely considering the distances involved. The conjunction of 'Medes and Adiabeni' in the report for 69 is appropriate if referring to Atropatene, which lay adjacent to Adiabene, but less so for the more distant Media Major. Appian seems uncertain as to the course of events in his report of Darius, but presumably got the name right. The king of 'the Medes' from whom Pompey received an embassy in 65 could be either Darius or Mithradates on the present reconstruction, since the succession apparently fell about then.[59]

Pompey received 'favourably' the overtures of the 'King of Media' in 65. This could be either monarch. 'Medes' had been among the allies of Eupator, whose fortunes were now in decline. The impulse to seek accommodation with Pompey also reflected the advance of the Parthian Phraates III into Gordyene. A king of Atropatene would respond with alacrity to this invasion of neighbouring territory, probably assuming that he had more to fear from Parthia than from distant Rome.[60]

An attempt to see in Darius of Media the 'Unknown Parthian King' of Warwick Wroth's classification of the Arsacid coinage would explain anomalies in the monograms of some drachms and tetradrachms. His usurpation of the Parthian throne, or rather contention for it with Phraates

III, would fall about 65 BC. Though this solves a problem in classification of the Arsacid royal coinage, it rests on evidence too slight to inspire confidence.[61]

Returning to Strabo's summary of Atropatenian intermarriage, we find, besides Armenians, 'kings of the Syrians, and after that of the Parthians' as partners. 'Syrians' should mean Seleucids, and that would not occasion surprise, but no evidence survives. It could, however, loosely include the Commagenians, with whom the Seleucids were intermarried, and even the royal house of Emesa, which did receive a princess of Atropatenian lineage.[62]

Artavasdes I

Whether they wished it or not, the people of Atropatene and Media were to be drawn into the battles of the late first century. Thus, 'Medes' appeared at Philippi. When Antony attempted an invasion of Parthia in 36, he found himself instead attacking Atropatene, then 'allied to Parthia'; he devastated a portion of it and claimed victory. The failure of his military efforts beyond the Euphrates in 34 did not deter him from attempting a marriage alliance with the very king he had previously attacked, Artavasdes I of Atropatene. This ambitious monarch styled himself 'King of Kings' and affected on his coinage a tiara proclaiming him a local successor of Tigranes. He agreed to betroth his daughter, Iotape, though 'still small,' to Alexander Helios, son of Antony and Cleopatra.[63]

The betrothal collapsed when Antony's fortunes did, though by then the little princess had been taken to Alexandria for marriage. Octavian discovered her there after his conquest of Egypt in 30, and sent her back to Atropatene. In due course, she turned up as Queen of Commagene, married to King Mithradates III. The consequences of this union can be traced for a century among the dynasties of the East, specifically Commagene, Emesa, and Judaea. Seven queens or princesses named Iotape appear in the dynastic records. Her daughter, Iotape II, married her son, Antiochus III; another philadelphic marriage united her grandchildren by this couple, Iotape VI Philadelphos and Antiochus IV Epiphanes, the last full King of Commagene, ruling till AD 72 or 73. His daughter, Iotape VII, married King Alexander of the Judaean house, a distant descendant of Archelaus I of Cappadocia who proceeded to the rule of Cilicia and then to the Roman Senate.[64]

In the dynasty of Emesa, Iotape III, daughter of the Atropatenian princess, married Sampsigeramus II and became by him mother of two kings of Emesa, Sohaemus and Azizus, as well as of Iotape IV, who married the Judaean Aristobulus, grandson of Herod the Great; their daughter was Iotape V.[65]

Such the 'Syrian' marriages of the Atropatenian house. Strabo also mentions '... after that the Kings of the Parthians' as marriage partners. This claim can best be examined after returning to discuss the reign of Artavasdes I and its consequences.

Through the agency of Polemo I of Pontus, by 35/34 BC Artavasdes I of Atropatene forgot his anger at the depredations of Antony in 36 and abrogated his Parthian alliance. One consequence was the betrothal of the princess Iotape to Alexander Helios. Another was the annexation by Artavasdes of some land then in Armenia, in the territory called Symbace. This fertile and strategic region could not have been better placed for Atropatenian interests, and its possession appeared at first assured by the captivity of Artavasdes II of Armenia. Antony's exultant coinage in 32 BC reflected his view of the situation by proclaiming this a 'conquest': ANTONI(US) ARMENIA DEVICTA.[66]

To watching Parthians, these events appeared dangerous. When in 34 BC Antony took his 'counsellor' Artavasdes II of Armenia away for captivity in Alexandria, charging that the king had 'betrayed' him, the reaction locally came without delay. Artaxias II, son of the Armenian king, achieved the throne and immediately fled to Parthia for assistance. The 'crime of Antony' in seizing Artavasdes 'under pretense of friendship' made Artaxias II a foe of the Romans and he 'defended himself and his kingdom by the power of the Arsacids.' Artaxias executed Romans left in Armenia by Antony. The bitterness had remained in Armenia for half a century when Tacitus wrote that account.[67]

Artavasdes I of Atropatene did not long benefit from his association with Antony. His coinage as 'King of Kings' could belong to this period of augmented holdings and seeks to designate Artavasdes a successor locally. A female figure, sometimes kneeling, also appears on his coinage; this has been taken to symbolize the territory in Armenia which now submitted to him.[68]

The moment of glory soon passed. Strengthened 'by the power of the Arsacids,' Artaxias II attacked Atropatene and defeated Artavasdes in 33 BC. Dio says, 'Armenia was lost [to Rome], along with Media,' and remained in Arsacid or Armenian hands until 20 BC or later. Romans had regarded Armenia as an ally for most of the time since the conquest of Tigranes by Lucullus in 69, and the defeat of the Armenian Artavasdes II by Antony appeared to reinforce this claim; hence the legend ARMENIA RECEPTA on coins. Whether or not captured as Dio says, the Atropatenian Artavasdes reached Augustus, joining the small list of 'kings [who] fled to me as suppliants.' In 30 BC he received Iotape back. He may have made his way to Atropatene, though it more likely remained in Arsacid hands for a decade or more after 33 BC. Artavasdes received Armenia Minor to rule, presumably from Augustus since Antony's candidate had been Polemo I of Pontus. By 20 BC he had died, perhaps in Rome.[69]

The progeny of Artavasdes ruled on after him, though insecurely, beginning in 20 BC. Augustus wished to use them as rulers of Armenia too, after Artaxias II died, but determined resistance from Armenians restricted Ariobarzanes II, his son, and Artavasdes II, his grandson, to reigns there of about two years each, between AD 2 and 6. Other descendants appear in the record of the East, one perhaps ruling Atropatene about AD 9. The branch of the family founded by Iotape I, who married King Mithradates III of Commagene, flourished, but the succession in Atropatene slipped into Arsacid hands by the reign of Artabanus III (II) and his brother, Vonones II, who between them controlled it for most of the period from AD 12 to 51. Both in policy and in coinage Artabanus demonstrated that an era of lesser accommodation between Parthia and Rome had begun.[70]

This returns the study finally to Strabo, who in his enumeration of the dynasties allied by marriage with Atropatene concludes: 'after [the kings of the Armenians and the Syrians] they intermarried with those of the Parthians.' About AD 10, late in Strabo's lifetime and a decade or so before his death, a new Parthian monarch appeared. This was the formidable Artabanus III.[71]

This king began to rule both Parthia (AD 10) and Atropatene (AD 12) at a time when Strabo was still writing. The Arsacid Vonones I also ruled Atropatene briefly (AD 12/13). Strabo knows that the Atropatenians have 'come into friendship with Caesar' but 'at the same time are cultivating the Parthians' – apparently during his own day. He must be thinking of the rapid alternation of kings in Atropatene from AD 2 to 18, if the passage was written that late. No fewer than six kings occupied the Atropatenian throne in those years, three Roman nominees and three from the Arsacid house. Yet Strabo mentions in a nearby passage that the line of succession from Atropates 'is preserved until now.' Unless he has slipped, or strains his statement by thinking only of descendants who no longer rule but still live on (as some did: see below), Strabo must consider the Arsacid occupation of the Atropatenian throne consonant with the claim of unbroken descent, as could occur if Artabanus, for instance, derived in part from the Atropatenian royal family.[72]

This latter possibility has exercised scholars for decades. Josephus implies that when Artabanus was summoned to the Parthian throne, being a member of the Arsacid royal family, he was already 'King of Media.' Tacitus agrees on his Arsacid lineage 'on his mother's side, but otherwise degenerate'; he has him reared 'among the Dahae' beyond the Caspian, north of Hyrcania. Artabanus had connections with the Hyrcanians (and, to the south, the Carmanians) later, but that cannot demonstrate his origins. Nor can the flight of Artabanus 'to the borders of Media' after a defeat by Vonones prove origins from Atropatene. Vonones subsequently fled to Armenia in similar circumstances, but no one argues from this that he originated there. In sum, this most important point must remain without proof, but with the balance inclining towards the testimony of Strabo that Atropatenian-Arsacid intermarriage had occurred by his day. Herzfeld's postulate of a marriage between an Arsacid princess and an Atropatenian prince about 31 BC would explain the acceptability of Artabanus (or for that matter of Vonones II, his brother, who also ruled both kingdoms) for the throne of either Media Atropatene or Parthia.[73]

So far and not much farther can the record take us in explicating the important testimony of Strabo regarding Atropatenian intermarriage. The record has almost entirely vanished, 'a piece of history that is, and may well remain, for the most part irretrievably lost.' Complicating that is the ancient habit of referring loosely to Atropatene as 'Media' in the first centuries before and after Christ. Nevertheless, final glimpses of the Atropatenians at work can be afforded us. As Mommsen once noted, another dynastic marriage must have occurred, one which took an Atropatenian or Armenian to the Cappadocian court for marriage to Archelaus I (36 BC–AD 17). Otherwise, it is difficult to see where Glaphyra, his daughter, derived her boast of descent from the Achaemenids, or Tigranes V, his grandson, his claim to lineage 'from the royal family of the Armenians,' as Augustus describes him.[74]

The royal Atropatenian house by no means vanished when Roman claims to Atropatene lapsed, perhaps by AD 9, certainly by AD 18. Relatives ruled on in Commagene, Emesa, and Judaea. For generations members of the dynasty survived in Italy, and can be traced by inscriptions. A branch of the Atropatenian aristocracy from Albak has been discovered living at the Armenian court around AD 100.[75]

Thus passed the valiant little dynasty begun by Atropates. Its independent survival for 340 years despite the encroachments of Alexander, the Seleucids, Armenians, Parthians, and Romans defied all odds. Its important contributions to the dynastic life around it on all sides evoke real admiration.

§ 26. Parthia

An important stage in relations between Parthia and Rome, as well as with surrounding states, was marked by the strong reign of Phraates III Theos, son of Sinatruces and his sister-wife Isbubarza. King Sinatruces, by now aged about 87, died in Olympiad 177.3, or 70/69 BC in our calendar. One reconstruction would bring this down to 68/67; another one has Phraates III associated on the throne with him as early as 74; yet another sees Phraates as governor of Elymais, raised to equal status with Sinatruces just before the old king's death. Coins begin 'year 242' Seleucid, or 70 BC. This reign witnessed the Roman invasion under Lucullus and the withdrawal of Tigranes from Syria to meet it. The defeat of Tigranes and its termination of Seleucid history curtailed the Armenian Empire and initiated new negotiations by Parthia with Roman generals in the East.[76]

Phraates III (70-57 BC)

Phraates III found it necessary to decide what foreign policy to adopt in the western portion of his huge empire. The alliance previously concluded between Parthia and Mithradates Eupator did not tempt Phraates at this point into the conflict, and he waited on events. Phraates felt no obligation to assist either Tigranes or Mithradates Eupator. Tigranes had 'humbled Parthian power as no man before him' had done. In refusing him direct assistance, Phraates only followed the policy of his father, Sinatruces, who had watched with apprehension the late career of the 'King of Kings.' Despite assurances in the purported letter of Mithradates to 'King Arsaces' that Tigranes no longer threatened Parthia and that the real enemy lay in Rome, Phraates favoured a policy of watchful waiting.[77]

The defeat of Tigranes confirmed the caution of the Parthian monarch, though neither the Pontic nor the Armenian king regarded the battle as final. Lucullus correctly surmised that Phraates might follow standard Parthian policy and remain on the sidelines. He sought to forestall a combination with Tigranes, who offered powerful inducements: return of the rich territory he had taken from Parthia, with cession of Adiabene and parts of Mesopotamia. Lucullus sent an embassy to Parthia, and received one as well. Learning that Phraates was negotiating simultaneous alliances with both Armenia and Rome (as Memnon, Appian, and Dio, all report), Lucullus ostensibly determined to invade Parthia. His own troops prevented this ill-advised resolve, if it was genuine, and he concluded 'friendship and alliance' instead, renewing the understanding between Sulla and Mithradates II, as Pompey soon renewed this one.[78]

Pompey began dangerous manoeuvres in 66 BC, involving Phraates in attacks on Armenia, while Tigranes the Younger, his father, and Mithradates Eupator, all took the field at one point or another. Pompey encouraged the invasion by Phraates as well as his support for the younger Tigranes, but Phraates had little enthusiasm for needless adventures in the northwestern extremities of his domain and withdrew, leaving the prince to his father's counter-attacks. Lacking confidence in Mithradates Eupator and now also in his father-in-law (Phraates), the young man could only flee to Pompey. When Tigranes the Elder decided against open confrontation with Pompey, the prince could be established in Sophene and perhaps Gordyene. Only the youth's own actions cost him his opportunity, with imprisonment by Pompey as the outcome.[79]

In 65, Phraates III opened negotiations with Pompey aimed at an accord, in view of the recent military successes of Pompey, which some thought inspired 'fear' among the Parthians. For his part Pompey also 'feared Parthian might' – and the Parthian Empire's vast distances. This state of mutual respect accorded with the situation; neither would benefit from a conflict with the other. Now that the threat of Mithradates Eupator was abating, Pompey may have attempted to overawe the Parthian by affecting a certain haughtiness, for instance declining to employ the full title 'King of Kings,' and addressing him as 'King' merely. For one whose coinage proudly proclaimed him 'Great King Arsaces, Just, A God Manifest, Noble, Philhellene' and who also enjoyed 'King of Kings' – 'a title on which he prided himself before all the world and before the Romans themselves' – this constituted a calculated insult. However, 'King,' 'Great King,' and 'King of Kings' could all be employed by the same monarch. Parthians cared little what formulae Romans used as long as peace and not war prevailed.[80]

Phraates failed to secure the release of Tigranes the Younger from captivity, and to conquer part of the holdings of Tigranes the Elder. Whether he seriously intended either lies open to question. The brief invasion of Armenia in support of the prince ended abruptly for the Parthian forces, and a reported second invasion had a different objective (see below). Phraates and Tigranes shared greater community of interest than either could with Rome; 'both well knew that whichever overcame the other would merely assist the affairs of the Romans and himself fall the more easily before them.' Phraates wished Tigranes to rule on, whatever diplomatic and military feints might prove necessary from time to time. The career of Mithradates Eupator had still not ended in 64 BC, but neither of these other two monarchs would miss him, as both had demonstrated.[81]

Two issues dominated the situation now, in 65 and 64. Parthians found it necessary to remind Romans that they regarded the Euphrates as their western frontier. Associated with this were nearby territorial disputes with Armenia.

When Pompey sent Gabinius across the Euphrates and up to the Tigris, this constituted a provocation. That increased when Afranius advanced into Gordyene 'in violation of the agreement with the Parthian [King]' and transferred its control from Phraates, who had occupied it, to Tigranes, who had previously ruled it. Phraates regarded Gordyene as of marginal importance, but he could not permit erosion of Parthian claims out here; hence the second invasion of Armenia.[82]

Phraates made it clear that Romans would be unwelcome across the Euphrates, the Parthian frontier since Mithradates I, back about 140 BC Pompey's flippant reply, that he would 'use the just boundary,' was given no more attention than it deserved, and Phraates continued his policy of moderate insistence on Parthian claims. Ultimately, Pompey arranged for a trio of Roman commissioners to assist in settling the boundary dispute between Parthia and Armenia. In 63, now a 'friend and ally' of the Romans, 'Phraates remained quiet.'[83]

Phraates accomplished several goals of long standing in Parthia. He saw the removal of Mithradates Eupator, a threat for over a generation by now; the Parthian and Armenian refusals to aid Eupator enabled Pompey to chase him from Asia Minor, and his treacherous sons did the rest. Second, Phraates also delighted in the neutralization of Tigranes the Great, confined now to his kingdom after a generation of self-aggrandizement partly at Parthian expense. Third, Phraates avoided any full-scale war with Rome, a consistent Parthian policy. A bit of chest-thumping had kept the potential antagonists alert, but harmed no one. Phraates reiterated the view that the Euphrates formed his western boundary, and by concluding a new pact of friendship and alliance he received tacit confirmation of this, despite the earlier reluctance of Pompey and the dangerous behaviour still to come of Gabinius and Crassus. The incorporation of Syria by Rome did not serve Parthian interests, but that only replaced Seleucid or Armenian control there; future invasions might be expected to alter this situation favourably, as they later briefly did, in 51 and 40-39. Finally, the captivity of Tigranes the Younger, his son-in-law, did not basically constitute a disservice to Phraates; the prince had proved useless militarily and regally. Marching in Pompey's triumph kept him from such mischief as 'making trouble for Pompey with the Parthians,' as he had been accused of doing. The last had not been heard from him, although Phraates hardly foresaw this. All in all, he had stepped carefully. 'Phraates and Tigranes falling into war' was a notion useful for him to project, since Pompey's self-congratulation on this event and the boundaries left Romans no excuse for further intervention.[84]

Phraates desired this friendship with Rome, a consistent Parthian aim from the time of Mithradates II until that of Orodes II, from about 100 BC to 53. As Strabo points out, the 'eagerness' of Parthians for this relationship began to abate with the invasion by Crassus, and then altered to an aggressive policy against Rome.[85]

The reign of Phraates began peacefully and continued that way once

Pompey had gone home. The Hellenization in Parthia so visible during the reign of Orodes II, his son, characterized that of Phraates too. His title, 'Philhellene,' was seriously meant, and his coinage followed the Greek model. One indication of prosperity may be the sudden change at the mint of Susa to silver coins, after half a century of bronze issues only. No matter if the silver for this came from the rich temple of Artemis in Elymais where he once governed; if Phraates did obtain it here he but followed a tradition, since Mithradates I of Parthia had plundered the same temple about 140 BC. A definite indication of prosperity and redirection came with the foundation of Ctesiphon as a winter residence for the King of Kings, if indeed this occurred under Phraates.[86]

Like his contemporary Tigranes the Great, Phraates called himself a 'God' (*Theos*), but he proved all too mortal. He fell by a 'treacherous murder' perpetrated by his two sons, who soon came into conflict with each other, with the Armenians, and with Rome. Phraates and Pompey had set a peaceful example which unfortunately their mutual successors ignored.[87]

Mithradates III (57-55 BC)

Despite some confusion in Dio's account, the coins show that Mithradates succeeded his father. The new king had, on some reconstructions, been governing Media for Phraates during the preceding dozen or so years, just as Phraates may have governed Elymais for Sinatruces prior to his own succession. This practice allowed a smooth transfer of power. The governorship and the succession support the inference that Mithradates was the eldest son. Orodes, his brother, remained for the moment outside events, perhaps in a minor post.[88]

Mithradates, the first Parthian monarch to employ his own name on his coinage, also on one issue named his father, Phraates. The motive for both uses must have been secure succession, an issue soon brought into focus by rivalry with his brother. Ironically, the parricide Mithradates also used *Eupator* ('having a good father'); *Theopator* ('having a divine father,' recalling *Theos*, the epithet of Phraates); and *Philopator* ('loving his father'). He was also *Dikaios* ('just'). Orodes II later used *Philopator* and *Theopator* too. Obviously the murder had involved powerful elements in the state and reflected internal problems that persisted during the fraternal strife of c. 57-55 BC.[89]

Mithradates demonstrated his intention of building a strong foreign policy by pursuing a full-scale war (*bellum*) with Armenia, late in the reign of Tigranes the Great. This may not have occurred in 57, since Cicero twice refers to Parthians ('Persians') that year as 'most pacific people,' though he may mean only with regard to Rome. One object of Mithradates was recovery of Gordyene, which his father had lost to Tigranes by way of Pompey. He succeeded and by 55 Parthia controlled the entire territory up to the Euphrates. However, too much warfare in the northwest still did not accord with Parthian interests, and we find Mithradates expelled 'after the Armenian war by the Parthian Senate because of his severity.'[90]

Mithradates fled into Syria in 56 BC. There he sought to persuade the governor, Aulus Gabinius, to assist in his restoration. The vague mandate under which Gabinius had proceeded to Syria included attention to 'Syrians, Arabs, and Persians' as well as Babylon. Some in Rome believed that he had a virtual *imperium infinitum*. Gabinius saw booty ahead and advanced to the Euphrates, contrary to the wishes of the Roman Senate. Before penetrating far into Parthia, he was recalled to the other major task at hand, restoring Ptolemy XII Auletes (§ 23). Thus Mithradates was left alone to cope with his brother, after appealing unsuccessfully to Gabinius on his return. He did occupy Babylon and Seleucia, issuing coins as 'King of Kings,' some showing him victorious. Orodes II besieged him in Babylon. Mithradates surrendered, hoping for mercy, but Orodes considered him 'more an enemy than a brother' and had him executed before his eyes. A coinage with kneeling Tyche and flying Nike overstruck on uncirculated issues of Mithradates proclaimed the victory of Orodes, now free to rule alone.[91]

The short and unhappy reign of Mithradates III brought in its train important consequences. Gabinius had been replaced before enjoying what seemed easy plunder in Parthia. His successor was to be the ill-advised M. Licinius Crassus.

Orodes 'II' (55-38 BC)

The monarch who achieved sole control of Parthia in 55 BC may be the first of that name in the dynasty. Attributions of a coinage in Babylon to an Orodes 'I' in 80/79 BC relied on the authenticity of an inscription referring to 'Orodes, King' dated to this year by the Seleucid and Arsacid systems. Questioning of the entire coinage may have removed this 'king' from history, but the matter will continue to be controversial.[92]

Orodes achieved unchallenged supremacy, but at first found it necessary to overstrike his brother's coins, as mentioned. He did allow another issue of his brother to circulate since it did not name him and could be taken as his own. Its epithet, *Ktistes* ('Founder'), could apply as well to Orodes, and its claim to be issued by the 'King of Kings' would fit the ambition of the new king too. An imposing and numerous coinage then emerged for nearly two decades from his reign.[93]

The power of Orodes originated in the Parthian east; his brother's was centred in Iran. Orodes had been returned from quasi-exile by the very general on whom he relied for defence of the western frontier against Romans in 55 and after. This man was the Parthian official known as 'the Surena,' both a title and a family name denoting the powerful figure who represented the great princely house of Sūrēn, enjoying the right of crowning the Arsacid King and leading his armies as commander-in-chief. During the raid of Gabinius and the abortive invasion of Crassus, this man stood in charge of the defence, which he accomplished well. His personal name has not survived.[94]

The appointment of M. Licinius Crassus, a member with Caesar and Pompey of the first 'triumvirate,' as governor of Syria fell during his own consulship, in 55. In November he left for Syria and by the summer of 54 he marched across the Euphrates. The usual motives, glory and treasure, hardly excused the attack on a 'friend and ally' of Rome; a strong segment of public opinion in Rome both foresaw his intention and opposed it.[95]

Carrhae

Crassus made a crucial error at the outset of his adventure. By advancing into Mesopotamia and leaving behind garrisons of some eight thousand men as far afield as Nicephorion and Zenodotion, he condemned himself to return there in 53. This return involved a long trip southeastward to retrieve the men, through country not so much inhospitable as highly advantageous to Parthian cavalry, since the low rolling hills constituted no impediment, and sufficient grass for the horses could be found in early summer. It also caused him to ignore the advice of Artavasdes II of Armenia, who stood ready with a force to guide him northward in an arc through the more rugged country near Armenia. When Crassus rejected this plan, Artavasdes had to withdraw this force to meet the advance of Orodes II upon Armenia, leaving Crassus the worse not so much for the loss of manpower, since he had some forty thousand men, as for that of a secure route and a native guide.

Other allies either failed to appear or proved unreliable. No mention occurs of faithful adherents like Antiochus I of Commagene, Sampsigeramus or Iamblichus of Emesa, Tarcondimotus I of Cilicia, and Ariobarzanes II or III of Cappadocia (the succession occurred this year). Hyrcanus II of Judaea might have attended but did not; this occasions no surprise when we remember that Crassus derived much of his war-chest from plundering allies, including Judaeans. The Temple in Jerusalem even yielded treasures to Crassus, which Pompey had spared. Neighbouring cities and dynasts perforce contributed as well. To obtain easy plunder in Parthia, Crassus began with it in and around Syria. Few of Rome's allies thought their interests lay in accompanying him.[96]

Two other dynasts who might have helped did not. Alchaudonius, King of the Rhambaeans, had nominally ranked as a Roman ally since the aftermath of Tigranocerta in 69. His perception of the schemes of Crassus in 53 led him to forsake that alliance and join Orodes II. His policy was simple, and suited to a small state amidst larger powers: 'he always joined the stronger.' Somewhat less openly, King Abgar II of Osrhoene also favoured Parthia but feigned adherence to Crassus. During the fighting he attacked the Roman forces, with effect.[97]

Osrhoene under Abgar II stands as a paradigm of the social and political organization Romans would face in attempting to penetrate Parthia. A ring of territories held either directly by the Arsacid monarch through viceroys or else by allied kings interposed itself between the Parthian heartland and the territories west of the Euphrates allied to Rome. The dynasty ruling Osrhoene traced its descent for more than five centuries, from just before 300 BC until just after AD 200. Despite two interregnal periods, the incorporation of a Macedonian colony at Edessa, and natural disasters such as a flood about AD 200, the kingdom held control of its lands across the Euphrates from Commagene. Its receptiveness to a Roman alliance during the campaigns of Pompey vanished before the folly of Crassus and, except for four years under Trajan and a short period after AD 165, the kingdom remained effectively outside the Roman orbit until the reign of Septimius Severus. Such were the local constituents of the forces Crassus so blithely attacked; the kings of Persis, Elymais, Adiabene, and Atropatene might be added to these, and thanks to his actions King Artavasdes II of Armenia not only withdrew from the Roman campaign but also concluded a marriage alliance with Orodes II.[98]

The unhappy details of Carrhae need not detain us. Ancients delighted in the tale that Orodes had warned Crassus of warfare to the death should he come as an act of war by the Roman state, but with leniency should he advance unofficially, an old man deranged by ambition. Crassus boasted that he would detail in Seleucia the causes of war. For answer, a Parthian indicated his own palm and declared that hair would grow there before Crassus reached the city. The disaster then seemed a punishment for arrogance as well as one sent by 'the gods who punish those who break treaties,' as Orodes had reminded him would be the case.[99]

By a serious miscalculation, Crassus assumed that Roman arms able to prevail over Armenians and Cappadocians would have no difficulty with Parthians. Instead, he learned that the recent successes of Pompey by no means assured further Roman advance. 'Pompey's one error was in underestimating the potential power, the resilience and indigestibility of the Parthian Empire. His overall scheme was conceived in an aggressive spirit at a moment of Parthian weakness.' Crassus now learned at first hand how formidable a foe Parthia and its cavalry could become, and the lesson cost him his life.[100]

Ancients well understood the importance of this battle. They invented a tale neatly encapsulating two main consequences by bringing the severed head of Crassus to the ceremony marrying the sister of Artavasdes II to Pacorus, son of Orodes II, just in time to electrify a performance of the *Bacchae*. The arrogant Crassus and the obtuse Pentheus shared the same stage for a moment. This underlined the Hellenism of the two monarchs (Artavasdes wrote Greek works, 'of which some survive' in Plutarch's day). It also symbolized the extent of Roman loss now, for until the raid of Crassus both monarchs had ranked among the allies of Rome. They had fought each other or come near to it during the campaign when Orodes advanced against Armenia to hold Crassus in check, but now their differences stood resolved. The Parthian 'desire for friendship with the Romans' temporarily ended with Crassus.[101]

After Carrhae

Parthians took advantage of their new opportunity and firmly established their border at the Euphrates, where they remained. The planned expedition of Caesar against Parthia might or might not have achieved some of its grandiose aims, but it did not occur. Parthian successes tilted eastward the balance previously established by Rome, with effects observable in Judaea, Commagene, Osrhoene, and to some extent in Cappadocia. Except for the projects of Caesar and Antony, and the Parthian invasions of 51 and 40-38 BC, only Armenia presented a serious area of contention after Carrhae.

For decades after Carrhae, wounded Roman pride recalled the humiliation and imagined the fate of those soldiers, who had 'grown old in arms under the Median King' with 'barbarian wives.' More than thirty years later Augustus considered recovery of the standards lost by Crassus (and some later by Decidius Saxa and by Antony) a major achievement, 'as if he had conquered the Parthian in some war,' in the wry phrase of Dio. 'Standards torn from the haughty columns of the Parthians' gave much to boast of, but the triumph was to be diplomatic, not military, despite the vaunting tone of Augustus and his poets.[102]

In Parthia, the loss of Syria and the victory over Crassus led to two complementary policies: Hellenization would remain strong, and Syria must be recovered. The cultivation of Hellenic usage in Parthia arose partly from the conviction that with the Seleucids gone, Parthia had inherited their legitimacy of rule in the East. Lest popular opinion discern in this an unwelcome Iranian threat, evoking memories of the long centuries during which Achaemenid Persia dominated Asia Minor and the Levant, the Arsacids muted for domestic consumption their claim to have succeeded the Persians, and instead emphasized Hellenic elements in the former Seleucid Greek territories. Thus the story that Ionian Greek *hetairai* had been ancestresses of some Arsacids, and that Orodes II, like Artavasdes II of Armenia, appreciated Greek works. The legends on the coinage of Orodes continued in Greek, as those of his successors were to do for another half-century, and he was a '*Philhellene*' there, with a series of other Greek titles. Interestingly, his attempt to render the title *Eupator* was weakened by the increasing illiteracy in Greek observable now on Parthian coinage, and became illegible as such.[103]

It was in the former Greek cities that Hellenic usage continued most visibly. Ctesiphon was enlarged by Pacorus, son of Orodes II, who 'gave it a Greek name' and made it 'the highest adornment' of Parthia ('Persia'). Seleucia (Susa) retained a large Greek element at least until the third century after Christ, with a *gerousia* in Plutarch's day. Strabo knows still of 'Greek cities in Media, foundations of the Macedonians.' Distant Hyrcania, linked to the outstanding Arsacid of the first century AD, Artabanus III, produced impressive Greek inscriptions.[104]

The second immediate consequence of Carrhae was a Parthian resolve to recover Syria, absorbed a decade before by Rome. The actions of Crassus could be seen by a later perspective as 'the inception for Romans of warfare against [Parthians].' His massive defeat conversely furnished encouragement to extend the borders of Parthia westward. In the next few years these were to reach their farthest western limits ever.[105]

Orodes II began this westward movement in 52 BC. His execution of the Surena curtailed plans for a full-scale invasion of Syria. Instead he launched raids, possibly encouraging revolt among disaffected Jews. A vigorous response by the Roman governor of Syria, C. Cassius Longinus, prevented any serious consequences for Rome this year, but worse was to follow and in 51 he faced a full-scale Parthian invasion.[106]

Pacorus I

Orodes II prepared for his advance by associating with himself on the throne Pacorus I, his able son. On one joint coinage, the legend 'King of Kings Arsaces Philhellene and Arsaces Pacorus' declares the new arrangement. A special coinage struck at Ecbatana in 51 announced the new policy and put

Parthians and Romans alike on notice as to the importance Orodes placed on the campaign. Pacorus nominally led the Parthians, but because of his youth yielded effective command to a certain Osaces, who fell at the hands of Cassius late in 51 BC.[107]

Cicero, proceeding to Cilicia as governor, thought as late as July 51 in Athens that the Parthians remained quiet, but learned on his way eastward that they had crossed the Euphrates, and found himself relying on an unsteady coalition of dynasts. Of these, Tarcondimotus of Cilicia and Deiotarus of Galatia seemed in Roman eyes the most trustworthy, with varying degrees of reliance to be placed as well on Antiochus I of Commagene, Iamblichus I of Emesa, and Ariobarzanes III of Cappadocia (though he required rather than offered assistance). Thanks in part to allied effectiveness, especially on the part of Deiotarus, Romans managed by 50 BC to withstand the Parthian drive into Syria, which had taken more the form of a swift cavalry raid for plunder than a campaign of conquest. This constituted the usual Parthian strategy.[108]

Despite heavy Parthian pressure, M. Calpurnius Bibulus, governor of Syria in 51-50, won the reputation, however dubious, of having outmanoeuvred the Parthians by fomenting internecine discord among them, especially through inducing Pacorus to aim at kingship. This must be a propaganda distortion of the truth that Orodes associated his son in the rule, probably to secure Parthia against intrigues and to present a united military front. Nevertheless, some strains may have occurred within Parthia, accounting for the absence of a campaign after preparatory skirmishes in early summer of 50. One tradition has Pacorus recalled by a suspicious father while already in Syria.[109]

For a decade the Parthians, engaged with their eastern empire, undertook no further campaigns west of the Euphrates. A hiatus in the striking of tetradrachms covers this same period. Despite Roman apprehensions in 49 BC and after, this distraction allowed the Roman civil wars to proceed without serious advantage taken by the Parthians, who supported Pompey and with whom, after his defeat, he considered taking refuge in 48. Unluckily for him, he chose Egypt instead and met his death there.[110]

The aftermath of the Roman civil war drew Parthians into Syria under Pacorus to assist the Pompeian Q. Caecilius Bassus, whose rebellion against Caesar in 46 and 45 BC touched the East. He was supported by such Eastern dynasts as Sampsigeramus I and Iamblichus I of Emesa. This did not constitute a full-scale Parthian campaign, but it proved effective, and Cicero foresaw war. It made Caesar thoughtful too. His projected war against Parthia sprang in part from this event. His careful and painstaking preparations, well advanced when cut short by his death, demonstrated how seriously he took the Parthian threat. He had learned from the mistakes of Crassus, but had little appreciation of the vast territory that would dwarf his familiar Gaul, or Spain, or Pontus.[111]

With the death of Caesar, Parthia was to remain secure from serious Roman invasion, except for the abortive attempt of Antony, until the reign of Trajan a century and one-half later. Parthians took part in the battle of Philippi in 42 BC on the side of Brutus and Cassius, but no direct consequence came of this beyond a raid on Palmyra by some cavalry Antony sent and a vague notice that Antony was 'preparing for the Parthian war' while collecting funds in the East in 41. His actions later appeared a cause of the war, which came in 40 BC.[112]

In the spring of 40, Parthians crossed the Euphrates in force. Whatever the problems Pacorus may have had with Orodes a decade before, they had been resolved by 45 when Pacorus led a force to assist Bassus, and no doubt exists of his joint kingship in 40. He commanded the army as 'King of the Parthians' and his coinage, oddly enough for a joint king, termed him 'King of Kings,' sometimes bearing his personal name, Pacorus, in addition to the usual Arsaces.[113]

Whether or not Orodes had become 'too indolent' for military campaigning in person, he had not only his robust son to call upon, but also an able Roman commander, Q. Labienus, son of Titus Labienus, Caesar's legate. Quintus had been sent into Parthia by Cassius before Philippi, asking for reinforcements. The battle caught him still there; fearing to return as a partisan of the losing side, he remained, helping to persuade Orodes and Pacorus to invade. In 41, he was in charge of the Parthian forces 'around Mesopotamia,' and when the invasion came in 40 he commanded jointly with Pacorus. A number of 'tyrants' and dynasts who had fled Antony in 41 to take refuge with the Parthians joined the expedition, expecting reinstatement. As well, Pacorus could rely on allies in Commagene, Nabataea, Ituraea, and Judaea.[114]

In Syria, Pacorus and Labienus divided forces. Antony's governor of Syria, L. Decidius Saxa, met Labienus in the field and fell. Labienus began a spectacular campaign across Asia Minor to its coast, perhaps reaching as far as Lydia and Ionia. The devastation at Mylasa in Caria later mentioned in a letter of Augustus probably dates from this incursion. The father of the future King Polemo I of Pontus won high reputation for resisting this invasion, but by the campaigning season of 39 the Parthian force held most of southern Asia Minor. In that summer, Labienus himself fell and the campaign began to collapse. A turning-point in Arsacid history approached.[115]

While Labienus drove westward, Pacorus turned south. The Hasmonaean house in Judaea remained hopeful that Hyrcanus II could yet be displaced.

Parthian assistance, made the readier by an enormous bribe, placed Antigonus, son of Aristobulus II, on the throne of Judaea from 40 BC until Herod the Great defeated him in 37. Pacorus also rapidly conquered the coast, except for Tyre, and reached Gaza by May 40, with a triumphant coinage marking this point in his progress. For the first time since the Achaemenid era, the Persian/Parthian Empire had an outlet on the Mediterranean. Reclining nearby on Cleopatra's couch, Antony sat up. Suddenly much of the East lay in Parthian hands or under the control of Parthian allies. Direct conquests included Syria and much of Palestine, with southern Asia Minor. Parthian allies included Malichus the Nabataean, Lysanias the Ituraean, Antigonus in Judaea, and – some said – Antiochus I of Commagene.[116]

The death of Labienus in 39 BC was followed by that of Pacorus in June 38, both at the hands of P. Ventidius, sent by Antony. The fall of Pacorus constituted the end of Parthian efforts, and a major psychological blow; 'the Parthians never received a greater wound in any war' than this. The Parthians withdrew beyond the Euphrates, Orodes fell into an extreme excess of grief, and it seemed that Ventidius had achieved a victory 'balancing' the defeat of Crassus. In 38 he became the first man, and the only man till Plutarch's day, to have a triumph over Parthia. He also began the siege of Antiochus I of Commagene which Antony and Herod finished.[117]

Cicero had remarked regarding the invasion of Crassus that Rome possessed no pretext for such a war. The unprecedented Parthian invasions of 51-50 and 40-38 BC showed that they agreed. Mutual mistrust lingered even during the stalemate following the death of Pacorus. Orodes II pursued the issue no farther, but the initiative was now taken by Antony, after assuring no further trouble from Commagene and helping Herod win his throne in Judaea.

The Parthian Empire administered 'half the world' in the eyes of contemporaries and might have contested more of it, but now lost the will to. Its temporary replacement of Roman power in the Levant had led to no permanent acquisitions, much like the Roman invasion of Parthia under Trajan over a century and one-half later. In both cases, a military sweep proved more feasible than enduring possession, though the effects of the Roman incursions lasted longer than did these of Pacorus, acceptable though he was. Pacorus seemed to *Syrians* among the best rulers they ever had, and his death dealt a great blow to Parthia. He commanded allied loyalty, as shown by the record of cities like Arad. By contrast, Romans were disliked for 'misgovernment' or greed and had lost control of some territory even before 51, as for instance in parts of Cilicia. Cicero tried to retrieve the situation in 51, and Antony did likewise in 38, though some damage was irremediable, such as the destruction of Mylasa. The sieges of Samosata in Commagene and of Jerusalem left the territories immediately adjoining Syria in allied hands once more. Herod recovered Hyrcanus II from Parthian captivity in 37. Antony decided the time had come to press the advantage gained by the death of Pacorus.[118]

As the siege of Samosata had shown, Antony's lieutenants fared better militarily than he did. The invasion of Parthia was to constitute his greatest failure before Actium itself. Once again the Euphrates had become the boundary between Parthia and Rome, with Parthia holding a strip west of the middle Euphrates too (*TAVO* B V 7). Antony required secure flanks before attempting an invasion across the river. In addition to the allies west of it, he needed allies east, especially in Armenia. He received a Parthian renegade who might prove useful, and Parthia underwent a change of ruler at the end of 38 or beginning of 37. Antony considered a Parthian conquest useful in maintaining his own position as Octavian's power increased, and grew eager to add the stimulation of battle to that of Cleopatra.[119]

Circumstances built towards a successful Roman invasion. Collapse of the Parthians' efforts in Syria and Judaea need cause no harm to their empire. However, the appearance of Monaeses might, for he was 'illustrious and powerful' and he came to Antony in flight from the new King of Parthia, occasioning consternation in his homeland. The best course seemed to be returning him to Parthia, asking for peace and restoration of the standards lost by Crassus. Thus Antony was given a propaganda advantage and he hoped by it to lull the Parthians before the campaign he still intended. He was even thought to have concluded a treaty with Parthia before his campaign. A remaining deficiency in the preparations was remedied when P. Canidius Crassus advanced northward against Iberia and induced Artavasdes II of Armenia to renew the Roman alliance disrupted by the invasion of Parthia which M. Licinius Crassus conducted in 53. Thus equipped, Antony advanced to challenge the untried new King of Parthia.[120]

Phraates IV (38-2 BC)

The death of Pacorus broke Orodes II and pushed him into senility. With no further interest in ruling, he looked among his thirty sons for a successor. Probably by the end of 38 BC he had chosen the eldest, Phraates IV, who proved disastrous to those around him at the time but who worked out a long and successful reign. He began by destroying potential rivals for the throne, including grandsons of Antiochus I of Commagene 'because they were better than he in excellence and, on their mother's side, in descent.' His remaining brothers succumbed, as did numbers of the aristocracy – a policy that occasioned the flight of others like Monaeses. Phraates IV did not even shrink from murdering his father, though he tried it unobtrusively at first. Removal of the distinguished old king, a second 'Founder' (*Ktistes*) of Parthia, as his coins proclaim, left Phraates and his pared administration to face the oncoming Romans. He proved more than equal to the task.[121]

Antony's campaign suffered from poor judgment and bad fortune. His route sensibly avoided the direct approach chosen by Crassus and bent northward through Armenia Minor. The support of Antiochus I of Commagene and Artavasdes II of Armenia helped assure him of a safe journey until reaching the border of Media Atropatene, but from here on matters became increasingly precarious. Artavasdes persuaded Antony that an attack on Atropatene would be an easy success since the King of Atropatene, Artavasdes I, had left his realm to assist Phraates IV. Artavasdes did not emphasize the strong fortifications of Praaspa (Phraata), capital of Atropatene, nor did he allude to the level ground for miles around it, favouring the Parthian cavalry. Antony knew of these factors, and had furnished himself with siege-engines, slingers, and cavalry. But the cumbersome engines fell behind on the way. Parthians seized and destroyed them, along with the baggage trains and some ten thousand men conducting them. Only one notable survivor of this group remained, King Polemo I of Pontus, captured and later ransomed. As to the slingers, they proved unable to protect legionaries on foot, and Antony's cavalry, much of it belonging to Artavasdes of Armenia, withdrew when he did, after one good look at the enemy.[122]

Antony found himself surrounded by a sea of celebrating Parthians and confronting a city he had no means to capture. It dawned on him that he had better make a plan. His men shared the Armenian view of the enterprise by now and reportedly Antony resorted to classic decimation, executing one in ten to encourage their resolve. Departing in defeat about the end of September, he spent three weeks and lost eight thousand more men in returning to Armenia, suffering from thirst, inadequate provisions, and Parthians. In all, he lost perhaps a third of the sixty thousand Romans (excluding forty thousand Iberian, Celtic, Armenian, and other allies) who accompanied him on this woeful journey. Antony had rushed into the campaign a year late ('at last,' sighs Livy). He hurried out of it not towards a camp in Armenia but towards the soothing air of Cleopatra's court. Bucking snowdrifts did not, for Antony, rival lolling on cushions ingesting wine, and the whole disastrous expedition took on the aspect of an interlude.

Thus far the view hostile to Antony. Writers favourable to him evidently blamed Artavasdes of Armenia for the defeat, maintaining that his cavalry, trained to fight Parthians, would have made the difference. However, this only underlines his optimism in relying on untried allies so far from Roman territory, with *two* enemy kings to face when he attacked Atropatene on the way to Parthia.[123]

One campaign leads to another. The community of interest between Artavasdes of Atropatene and Phraates IV endured while the threat from Antony did, but eroded as Phraates consolidated his position in Parthia. A break soon occurred between them. Though the repulse of Antony can be credited in part to the fortifications of Praaspa and its spirited local defenders, Phraates of Parthia also engaged the Romans personally, and his forces receive the most frequent mention during the campaign. The breach with Artavasdes arose through fear that Phraates might incorporate Atropatene, whether on grounds of its need for defence by Parthia or through the momentum engendered by the victory. Phraates had decisively overcome the challenge both from Rome and from his own dissident aristocrats. A period of expansion might ensue, despite some threat posed in the eastern part of the Parthian Empire where Phraates struggled for control.[124]

The disruption of the united front presented by Artavasdes of Atropatene and Phraates worked to the advantage of Antony. On the way back from Atropatene he conciliated Artavasdes of Armenia because he desperately required supplies for his faltering army, but his intention remained to take vengeance for the desertion of Artavasdes. The falling-out between Artavasdes of Atropatene and Phraates provided an opportunity. Artavasdes also sought revenge on the King of Armenia for having led Romans against him. Artavasdes had encountered Polemo I of Pontus during Polemo's captivity on the recent campaign; Polemo was ransomed, though the chronology is unclear and he may have remained a captive until 35. Artavasdes utilized Polemo's good relations with Antony to send him as a royal-level emissary to Antony in Alexandria, suggesting an alliance with Atropatene. Antony, seeing the very arrangement he required, accepted with alacrity and prepared for the campaign by recognizing an extension of Polemo's rule to Armenia Minor, more a strategic arrangement than a 'reward' for ambassadorial service.[125]

About this time, another Roman caught up in the civil wars, Sextus Pompeius, attempted to open relations with Parthia. However, Antony blocked this and through the assistance of King Amyntas of Galatia and of his own lieutenant, Titius, encompassed the destruction of this potentially dangerous man. A false start in 35 BC led nowhere, but Antony built up his forces for a 'Parthian' campaign, meanwhile attempting to lure Artavasdes of Armenia into his hands by suggesting intermarriage. Artavasdes wisely remained out of reach in his kingdom. The Atropatenian Artavasdes readily offered Antony the cavalry he required for an advance on Parthia. He also furnished Iotape, his daughter, for betrothal to Alexander Helios, son of Antony and Cleopatra; this furthered their plan to create an empire of royal allies under a 'King of Kings' in Egypt.[126]

Phraates IV did not achieve through his victory over Antony a permanent rapprochement with the disaffected nobles in his empire. The Parthian aristocracy had been gaining in importance at the expense of the central authority all through the first century, since the reign of Mithradates II. After the fraternal strife between Orodes II and Mithradates III, followed by the wholesale executions of Phraates IV, they had turned to Antony. His failure did not terminate their aspirations, and the prospect of his return contributed to the dissension from which Parthia was rumoured to be suffering in 35/34 BC.[127]

In the spring of 34, Antony set off ostensibly for Parthia, accompanied to the Euphrates by Cleopatra, who had her own fish to fry and reportedly tried to seduce Herod on the way home during negotiations over his balsam groves (§ 22). Antony proceeded into Armenia and laid hands on Artavasdes II at last by perfidiously detaining him after a meeting, binding him in silver chains later changed for gold. The Armenian went unhappily to Alexandria, where he perished; the legacy of this remained for decades in hatred of Rome by his son and successor, King Artaxias II. Two other sons, evidently captured now, served as Armenian kings later (Tigranes III and Artavasdes III; see stemma).[128]

Antony considered the seizure of Artavasdes a triumph and attempted to announce it in Rome as well as Alexandria, but Octavian intercepted the dispatches. He had himself been attempting secretly to enlist the aid of Artavasdes against Antony and the Atropatenian Artavasdes. The bizarre situation set two distant Iranian kings against each other as partisans of two contending Roman politicians.[129]

Antony's campaign against Parthia contented itself with this diversion and 'conquest' of Armenia. He stationed Romans there to assume control; they were later killed by Artaxias on his restoration. At first, Artavasdes of Atropatene profited by alliance with Antony, who returned in 33 to assist him successfully against the forces of Phraates and Artaxias. However, Antony's troop-withdrawal by 32 to pursue the Roman civil war left Artavasdes facing defeat. He fled Atropatene and sought asylum with Octavian, who later recovered little Iotape among the debris of Antony's and Cleopatra's dreams in Alexandria and returned her to her father.[130]

Antony, ever the optimist, had issued coins announcing the conquest of Armenia two years before he captured its king. Similarly, at the 'Donations' in Alexandria during the autumn of 34, he presented Parthia to Alexander Helios, his son, despite his failure to conquer it.

Phraates could afford amusement at this presentation of Parthia, which had withstood over twenty years of actual or threatened Roman invasions, from Gabinius and Crassus in 55-53 to Caesar in 44 to Antony in 36, 34, and 33. None of these accomplished anything. The vision of tens of thousands of Romans captured at Carrhae or left behind as casualties after Antony's invasion of 36 long haunted the Roman mind and delighted the Parthian. The 'jubilant chorus' in Rome that greeted the return of those standards over a decade later shows what a blow it had received. The series of defeats coupled with Rome's own civil war could well cause Horace to wonder, during the reign of Phraates IV, if 'this city might perish by its own right hand in accordance with the prayers of the Parthians.'[131]

The smile soon vanished from Phraates's face. His aristocrats could look no more for aid from Rome, but they could look to themselves. Phraates barely had time to issue coins with Nike crowning him, or Nike and Star, or Zeus Nikephoros commemorating his victory over Rome and its ally Artavasdes of Atropatene, before a serious threat beset his throne. A rebel appeared, Tiridates II, possibly from a part of the royal family or perhaps a renegade general of Phraates; the uncertainty began in antiquity. By 31 BC Phraates had fled his throne, 'driven into exile by his people.' When Tiridates replaced him, it was already 'in his absence.' Tiridates, with Roman encouragement, advanced so rapidly that Phraates purportedly decided to destroy his harem rather than let such a valuable source of royal blood fall into unwelcome hands.

Tiridates managed to rule, or at least claimed to, for he issued coins assuming the title 'King of Kings' and he is termed a king later by Augustus. The coins bore in abbreviated form a wondrous addition to the Parthian nomenclature: 'Emperor, Lover of the Romans' (AUTOKRATO PHILOROMAIO). Dated coins of Phraates resume at least with Seleucid 'Year 283' (29/28 BC), as he achieved reinstatement with the assistance of 'Scythians' (Dahae?) to whom he had fled.[132]

Actium had two results for Parthia. One was to remove Antony from his nibbling at Parthia's western flanks, bothersome even though he had 'preferred leisure to war.' The other was to provide a refuge for Tiridates. Octavian had become undisputed ruler of the Roman state, and remained in the East from 31 to 29 BC, after the defeat of Antony and Cleopatra. As Phraates bore down upon him, Tiridates fled to Octavian in Syria; he found time to scoop up a son of Phraates to take with him.[133]

Phraates, restored but 'unhappy' (for a time), demanded the return of Tiridates and of his son. In due course the son was returned, supposedly in exchange for the standards of Crassus. Phraates, however, well understood their significance and retained them longer. He did send four sons as hostages to Rome, whom Strabo reports still there; a sepultural inscription shows that two of them died in Italy years afterward. Despite the confidence of the likes of Horace that Phraates could be considered 'suppliant on his knees,' his supply of sons made Roman retention of those he sent, or even of the one Tiridates abducted (described as the 'youngest' son at the time and thus of no importance for the succession), a comparatively minor matter. This young man, also named Phraates, had ruled for a time, probably jointly with Tiridates, but this made him neither indispensable to Parthians nor a valuable spearhead for incursions from without.[134]

Any apprehensions Phraates felt lay more among his family and Parthia's aristocrats than in Rome. After thirty more years of rule following Actium, with the standards at last returned, with Phraates 'not overcome in war, but seeking our friendship,' and with the two powers ostensibly amicable, he died, probably in 2 BC, at the hands of a son as impatient as he had been. Phraates V (Phraataces) inherited a stable empire.[135]

The Parthians progressed a long way, as did Rome, from the time of Mithradates II at the opening of the first century before Christ until the years just following Actium. After ambivalent early dealings with Sulla, they weathered the Armenian Empire of Tigranes, with unintended Roman help. They reached 'friendship' with Pompey and repelled Crassus. King Pacorus delivered a telling counterblow to which Antony attempted a response and failed. Parthians consolidated their hold on the area beyond the Euphrates. Increasing stability in the Parthian East allowed Phraates IV, during a reign of some thirty-five years, to reach a balance with Rome, which prevailed long after him. The future held no more direct Roman invasions of Parthia until Trajan's short-lived conquests. In the meantime, the only serious bone of contention would be Armenia. Rome poured a series of kings into it from Media Atropatene, the Cappadocian-Judaean dynasty, Iberia, and even Pontus. For the rest, the future belonged locally to Parthia, from the reign of Artabanus III onward.[136]

As Moses of Chorene saw, Parthians and Romans, whether as belligerents or not, remained in contact. Parthia not only survived intact, but had in the first century come to a position of equality with Rome, dividing the known world, one of 'the two mightiest empires' and destined to remain that way, if its Sassanid successors can be considered its heirs. Not even Rome disputed its control of the lands clear to India (though Cleopatra fancied that her son could rule out there). Skirmishes confined themselves to border regions of the Parthian west. The relations of the two powers tended towards mutual recognition of sovereignty, with a border on the Euphrates, where Sulla and the ambassador of Mithradates II had begun the dialogue.[137]

PART III

The Royal East

10

The Eastern Dynastic Network

The great historical process studied herein by no means terminated at Actium in 31 BC. Kings occupied the East, including 'the greater part' (*ex parte magna*) of the provinces there claimed by Rome. As in Rome itself, probably few in the East realized the true import of that battle at the time, and many kings ruled on with no apparent reference to it. Other battles in the Roman civil wars (Pharsalus; Philippi) had come and gone, each with a different influence on arrangements in the East, including changes among the Roman generals sent there. After Lucullus, Pompey gave way to Caesar, he to Antony, and he to Octavian. Most Greek, Semitic, and Iranian rulers at first failed to realize that Actium had settled Rome's internal troubles and potentially freed her for a more active political stance in the East. Indeed, this itself, beyond a few *ad hoc* adjustments in 30, waited some ten years, until Augustus had completed necessary attentions to the Roman West and felt it incumbent upon him to turn more seriously eastward in 20 BC. Most kings, for instance Polemo I of Pontus, ruled part of that decade without the formality of renewed Roman recognition.[1]

Brief examination of the individual dynasties will demonstrate in operation a twofold historical process extending from before Actium to the century or more after. The first aspect of this process is continued rule by the previously established dynasties, with increasing reference to Rome but with maintenance of full royal government. This rule continues in each case up to the time of incorporation, which varied from Egypt – absorbed upon the death of Cleopatra – to Commagene (AD 72 or 73) and parts of the former Kingdom of Judaea (mid-nineties AD, upon the death of Agrippa II). The Kingdom of Bosporus participated in the process but avoided incorporation altogether.

The second aspect of this process after Actium lies in the increased range of use by Easterners and Romans alike of the former kings. Augustus realized the importance in the East of intermarriage among the dynasts and promoted it as he 'joined the allied kings (*reges socios*) by mutual bonds and was most ready to advise and foster intermarriage and friendship; he held them all as members and parts of the empire (*membra partesque imperii*).' This intermarriage was facilitated by the well-established practice of raising royal children in Rome, an advantage to themselves and to the building of the empire. Judaeans had long done this, and continued to, with Agrippa I present in Rome at important junctures in imperial evolution. The interrelated dynasty of Pontus-Thrace sent its princes there, and recorded them as 'raised together' with Caligula. Cappadocians had visited Rome and stayed there during the republic; presumably this continued, in spite of the difficulties of Archelaus with Tiberius. Glaphyra, his daughter, must have been well known at the court after her Judaean marriage and when preparing to marry Juba of Mauretania, whose first wife had been Cleopatra Selene, daughter of Antony and Cleopatra.[2]

Study of the kings reveals, not surprisingly, that in portions of the East dependent on the Roman alliance to maintain themselves against either internal (as in Thrace) or external (as in Bosporus) threats, cultivation of ties with Rome continued strongly. Areas with a powerful neighbour to watch warily, as in Commagene and Cappadocia, both too near Parthia for comfort, took a more circumspect approach to Rome. This range from enthusiasm to reserve reflects itself in the coinages, with celebration of Roman alliance reserved for those who most needed it, and silence for the rest.[3]

A recapitulation of dynastic history following Actium will reveal the depth and strength of royal control remaining now and for decades. A full, documented study is required for an accurate apprehension of the remaining cohesion in Eastern society under royal rule, but even a brief discussion will reinforce the arguments of this study.

In *Thrace*, the deep split between those who would support Rome and those resisting it remained. The Odrysians retained the favour of Rome during the wars following Actium, and the Dentheletae remained under treaty with Rome. Campaigns against the Bessi, and beyond them, the Dacians and Bastarnae, involved the country for many years. Intermarriage between the Odrysian-Astaean houses and the Sapaeans assured stability in the Thracian aristocracy. The Odrysian-Astaean King Cotys V, who lived until about 18 BC, married a daughter of Cotys VII of the Sapaeans. One of his children by her, King Rhescuporis II, ruled until about 11 BC. Cotys V arranged for Rhoemetalces I, brother of his wife, to serve as guardian for the children. Despite ejection at one point by the Bessi, Rhoemetalces ruled from the time of Actium until AD 13, virtually the entire reign of Augustus;

predictably, his coins honour Augustus. For a time he may have ruled Thrace alone, but later Augustus divided Thrace between Rhescuporis III, his brother, and Cotys VIII, his son. The famous contrast between these two, the former portrayed as a sullen lout and Cotys as a man of cultivation, friend of Ovid and admired by Tacitus, may be consequent on their respective fates, for Rhescuporis killed Cotys. Queen Antonia Tryphaena, daughter of Polemo I of Pontus and widow of Cotys, accused the murderer before the Roman Senate and obtained his exile to Alexandria, where he died, half a century after Cleopatra expired there.[4]

The loss of Cotys and Rhoemetalces, which occurred by AD 19, could have deprived the Thracians of royal control. However, one more scion of the unified Thracian houses, Rhoemetalces II, acceded in that year and married Pythodoris II, daughter of Antonia Tryphaena and Cotys VIII. Since Rhoemetalces II was the son of Rhescuporis III and his mother a sister of Cotys VIII, he and his new wife – named for Pythodoris I, wife of Polemo I and Queen of Pontus – joined the major blood-lines of Thrace to the vigorous dynasty of Pontus.

Another son of Cotys VIII and Antonia Tryphaena ruled as final King of Thrace. Rhoemetalces III ruled at least from 38, when confirmed by Caligula, until 46. One of his brothers, Cotys IX, ruled Armenia Minor. Another was King Polemo II of Pontus, and a sister, Queen Gepaepyris, stood at the head of a long succession of kings of Bosporus.

Antonia Tryphaena served as priestess of Livia and then of Drusilla; her sons were 'raised with' Caligula. This celebration of the Roman alliance also characterized her daughter in Bosporus and her relatives in Pontus. When Claudius decided to incorporate Thrace as a province, it required some fighting, but the groundwork had been laid long before.

Thrace, nearest to Rome of all the 'Eastern dynasties' and the only one of them now lying in Europe, constituted an abiding area of interest as the focus of Roman attention shifted to its northeast. Its pattern of steadfast support for Rome by some dynastic houses and equally unwavering opposition by others made Thrace an exceptionally difficult area to control, a task best left to local kings (as also in Cilicia Tracheia). Once reasonable pacification had occurred, Rome was free to assume provincial control of the region, as it also had in Galatia after the death of Amyntas. Thrace became a critical staging-point for the wars to come against the Dacians.[5]

The dynasty of *Pontus*, closely tied to the Thracian royal house by the marriage of Antonia Tryphaena to Cotys VIII, enjoyed considerable prominence in the East after Actium. Polemo I, recognized as king by Antony, ruled on also in the Bosporus, where he married Dynamis, granddaughter of Mithradates Eupator. Augustus recognized his holdings and the Roman Senate enrolled him among the 'friends and allies' of Rome. Polemo ruled with vigour and died in the field, fighting the Aspurgiani. His two former wives had important careers. Dynamis had previously married King Asander of Bosporus; the long line of Bosporan kings descended from her and Asander, by way of their presumed offspring, King Aspurgus, who married Gepaepyris, the granddaughter of Polemo I. Pythodoris, reputedly a granddaughter of Mark Antony, married Polemo I too and after his death ruled Pontus for many years, eventually marrying King Archelaus of Cappadocia. Their joint realms constituted a rich and extensive block of territory.[6]

Besides the marriage of his daughter, Antonia Tryphaena, into the Thracian dynasty, Polemo I also provided a son, Zeno-Artaxias, the only successful Roman nominee in Armenia. The children of Antonia ruled in Thrace (Pythodoris II, wife of Rhoemetalces II; Rhoemetalces III), or Bosporus (Gepaepyris), or Armenia Minor (Cotys IX), or Pontus (Polemo II). In addition to his duties there until his retirement about AD 64, Polemo II also ruled a portion of Cilicia, probably near that of his fellow dynast, Antiochus IV of Commagene. He evidently returned to Cilicia for his last years, as attested by a coin from the reign of Galba. A long line of aristocrats descended from this powerful dynasty, some of them later Roman senators and consuls.[7]

Pontus constituted an important territory for Rome as its interest in Armenia increased, since supplies could best be brought in from the Black Sea over the Paryadres range, or from the south with the co-operation of Commagene. The dynasty founded by Polemo I remained pro-Roman for the century of its existence. Antony's recognition of Polemo had effectively converted Pontus from the seat of Rome's greatest foe, Mithradates Eupator (and his son, Pharnaces), into that of a most reliable dynasty.

Galatia, where Deiotarus had pursued a course favourable to Rome despite some strains with Caesar, did not long survive Actium as a kingdom. It became a province in 25 BC, after the warlike and effective King Amyntas lost his life still fighting to pacify part of Cilicia Tracheia. A member of the dynasty, King Deiotarus Philadelphos, ruled on in Paphlagonia until his death, in 6/5 BC. Members of the large royal family lived on for centuries, taking a high place in Galatian society and Roman service. Among the most notable stood C. Iulius Severus of Ancyra in the second century, 'descendant of kings' (including Deiotarus) and 'first of the Greeks,' as well as a relative of notable consuls, senators, and royalty: King Alexander of Cilicia, Iulius Quadratus, Ti. Iulius Celsus Polemaeanus and his son, and C. Claudius Severus, first long-term governor of Arabia and ancestor of a son-in-law of Marcus Aurelius, just as Julius Severus was of a wife of Elagabalus.

Similarly, the extensive senatorial family of the Ti. Iulii Frugi, widely active in Western Asia Minor, may have had Galatian origins.[8]

The Galatians entered Asia Minor as strangers but won a central territory which they maintained with vigour, growing into strong Roman allies and later into an important aristocratic society within the Empire.

In *Cappadocia*, the half-century reign of Archelaus gave an excellent degree of cohesion to the troubled kingdom, especially when his marriage to Pythodoris I united under one royal pair the rule of both Cappadocia and Pontus. Despite later problems in the reign of Tiberius that led to the condemnation and death of Archelaus, his family took an important place in the dynastic network. Glaphyra, his daughter, married to two Judaean princes and to Juba II of Mauretania, became the ancestress of two Roman nominees for the kingship of Armenia (Tigranes V and VI) and of the last king of Cilicia, the same King Alexander whom C. Iulius Severus of Galatia names as relative. Alexander later stepped down to a Roman consulship. By his wife, the Commagenian princess Iotape VII, daughter of its last king, Antiochus IV, he produced other aristocrats active in the Roman system. The brother of Glaphyra, Archelaus II, participated in the wide-based effort of the remaining kings to control Cilicia Tracheia. This now constituted the only region remaining for a Cappadocian king, since the kingdom itself had been made into a Roman province after the death of Archelaus in AD 17.[9]

Cappadocia, where the Roman push into Asia Minor had begun during the first century before Christ, experienced a tumultuous time until the recognition of Archelaus by Antony allowed the kingdom its final period of stability. As the stemma shows, members of the royal family endured long afterward, both as kings in the Judaean house and as aristocrats with mixed Greek and Roman names.

In *Cilicia Pedias*, the dynasty of Tarcondimotus ruled on after he fell at Actium. Tarcondimotus II and Philopator I, his brother, demonstrated their correct reading of the new distributions of power in 30 BC when they took the field against gladiators seeking to make their way from Cyzicus to Antony's assistance in Egypt. The rule of this family was recognized by Augustus, perhaps not until 20 BC during his other arrangements of the East in the context of his dealings with Phraates IV of Parthia for the return of the standards. Julia, sister of these two, produced a royal son named Philopator (II), who was still ruling in Cilicia at the time of his death in AD 17.[10]

Cilicia Tracheia, where 'it seemed better to the Romans for kings to rule rather than Roman prefects,' constituted so severe a challenge that the work of many kings over many decades went into its pacification. Kings Amyntas of Galatia and Archelaus of Cappadocia both spent extensive parts of their reigns there, followed by the son of Archelaus, by Polemo II of Pontus, and by

Antiochus IV of Commagene. Antiochus's daughter married King Alexander of the Judaean house, a descendant of Archelaus, and he enjoyed the last reign there. Vespasian took over the region, probably as part of a plan that also involved incorporation of Commagene late in AD 72 or early in 73.[11]

Commagene continued after Actium, where Mithradates II, son of Antiochus I, fought in person for Antony. He apparently retained his throne during the decade that followed, though Octavian secured the condemnation of Antiochus 'II,' his brother, before the Senate in Rome. Octavian intervened in order to side with the incumbent monarch and prevent internal discord, especially dangerous given Commagene's location and the coming negotiations with Parthia, an empire that could not be allowed an ally here.[12]

The reign of Mithradates III included a marital tie with Atropatene. He married Iotape I, the princess previously intended by Antony for Alexander Helios. By her, he sired Queen Iotape (III) of Emesa, wife of Sampsigeramus II, and the philadelphic pair of Commagenian rulers, Antiochus III and Iotape II, whose children were the similarly philadelphic couple, Antiochus IV and Iotape VI 'Philadelphos.' Upon the death of Antiochus III in AD 17, Commagene became for some twenty years a Roman province, with its considerable revenues flowing to Rome. This premature removal of a strategic dynasty was reversed by Caligula, who restored its line by recognizing Antiochus IV as king. During the next thirty-five bellicose years, Antiochus ruled both Commagene and a portion of Cilicia Tracheia, in person serving Claudius and Nero militarily or sending his sons to other conflicts, including the war in Judaea. At its conclusion, Vespasian began to worry about the 'proximity of the kings' of Commagene and Parthia, especially in light of Parthian control of Armenia now; by combining they 'might involve the entire Roman realm in war.' Accordingly, he launched an action considered a 'Commagenian war' (*bellum Commagenicum*) at the time. Antiochus ended up honourably detained and subsidized in Rome, where his sons joined him. Among his relatives or descendants ranked King Alexander of Cilicia and the notable 'King' C. Iulius Antiochus Epiphanes Philopappus, Roman consul and first citizen of Athens, honoured by the extant monument there on the Museion Hill. Julia Balbilla, his sister, accompanied Hadrian to Egypt and left extant poetry on the Colossi of Memnon. Other descendants entered the Roman system as well.[13]

In *Emesa*, Actium brought disruption. Iamblichus I fell victim to the suspicions of Antony, who rightly foresaw defections among his wavering Eastern royal allies. Alexander, his brother, succeeded him, but met with the disfavour of Octavian, who deprived him of his sovereignty, led him in his triumph, and then executed him. The grounds remain obscure, but in any case an interruption evidently ensued. Only when Augustus began his extensive arrangements in the East in 20 BC did a new sovereign, Iamblichus II, appear in Emesa.[14]

Whether in the reign of Iamblichus or not, the expected Roman citizenship came to the rulers of Emesa, for his son and successor, Sampsigeramus II, used 'C. Iulius' on some of his inscriptions. He also used the title 'Great King' and participated in the assemblage of kings at Tiberias in AD 42, waiting upon Agrippa I of Judaea. Fellow dynasts there included Antiochus IV of Commagene; Cotys IX of the dynasty of Pontus and Thrace, then ruling Armenia Minor; Polemo II of Pontus; and Herod of Chalcis. The assemblage alarmed the governor of Syria, C. Vibius Marsus, who assumed that 'so much friendship among these dynasts did not accord with Roman interests.'[15]

King Sampsigeramus furthered the dynastic intermarriage of his day, himself taking to wife Iotape III from Commagene and Atropatene, and in turn marrying two of his children into the Judaean dynasty. His son, C. Iulius Sohaemus, ruled as King of Emesa during the two important decades following AD 54, and found himself in the thick of the Jewish War, as well as in the fighting that led to a new dynasty in Rome and to incorporation of Commagene. A woman perhaps from the dynasty, Julia Maesa, became queen by marriage to Polemo II of Pontus. Numerous aristocrats appear in the record after him, and no firm date can be given to the end of royal rule in Emesa. By ties now difficult to discern, it seems probable that the later Roman imperial family from Emesa (Julia Domna, Julia Mamaea, Elagabalus) derived from royal stock there.[16]

In *Judaea*, the family of Herod the Great came to a position of high importance in the dynastic East. His great number of offspring and descendants assured the dynasty of representation in such diverse areas as Pontus, Emesa, Nabataean Arabia, and Cappadocia. Descendants ruled not only in Judaea and its possessions but also in Armenia Minor, Cilicia, and Armenia. Of importance in the evolution of arrangements between Rome and the Eastern dynasts were Herod himself, Agrippa I, his grandson, and Agrippa II, his great-grandson. Not until the end of the first century did dynastic rule disappear entirely from among the members of Herod's house.[17]

The remaining dynasties treated in this study do not enter the present chapter because for the most part they had no role in the 'dynastic network' as it applied to relations between Rome and the East. Dynasts in Atropatene did involve themselves heavily in the Roman effort to obtain Armenia, but they and the Armenians did not actively enter the post-royal aristocracy that served Rome. Like Parthia, Atropatene retained rule by kings for centuries. The vast pool of post-royal aristocrats who poured into the Roman Senate after about AD 70 and materially influenced the government of the East did not include any significant number from beyond the Euphrates, nor from Arabia, at least before the second century. In those Semitic and Iranian lands, the royal system continued on through Byzantine times.[18]

After thousands of years, royal government in the lands west of the Euphrates gave way to the Roman Empire, but the kings' legacy of firm government and social stability went far towards making that empire possible, in the East.

11

Epilogue

I

Some outstanding individuals brought about this great transformation of the East. This study can conclude by recapitulating their contributions.

Most of the kings languish now in obscurity, as for instance do Cotys III and Sadalas I of Thrace, who probably initiated the slow unification of royal houses there and prepared the country for a most difficult century. This study has dealt with many like them, but the record also includes remarkable kings about whose work a relatively large amount is known.

Outstanding among *those* kings ranks Mithradates VI Eupator. Not only did he bring Pontus to its greatest territorial extent by his empire, but for a time he reversed many political developments of the second century before Christ. A moment in history saw Asia Minor reunited under a distant descendant of the kings of Persia, claiming to act for 'the Greeks'; he added the north coast of the Black Sea to his dominion, and invaded Greece. The failure of Darius and Xerxes four hundred years earlier seemed reversible, for a few months, but Sulla ended that dream. None the less, the long reign of Mithradates (120-63 BC) imperilled Roman ambitions in the East during almost its entire duration. The massacre of many thousand Romans demonstrated the feelings he was able to focus.

This confrontation brought in its train a number of consequences. The relations of Bithynia and Cappadocia were affected by the manoeuvres of Mithradates when he saw Laodice, his sister, previously lodged in Cappadocia, choose Nicomedes III of Bithynia after the death of her husband, Ariarathes VI. Among partial consequences of the interventions by Mithradates were the disappearance of the Ariarathid line in Cappadocia and eventually of the Bithynian dynasty, when Nicomedes IV died without an heir firmly placed on his throne. The initial kingdom to become Roman territory in the first century (Cyrene was not taken up until a generation after its nominal acquisition), Bithynia appeared well-placed as a base for the control of Pontus after Mithradates fell, but the reconquest by Pharnaces II briefly undid that arrangement, and Antony returned to the previous distributions of power when he recognized Polemo I as King of Pontus.

A second notable figure must be Ariobarzanes I of Cappadocia, not so much for his accomplishments as for his pertinacity. Despite repeated expulsions at the hands of Mithradates or Tigranes, he clung to the throne he had refounded, and after more than thirty years happily passed it to his son, who received it with justified apprehension. Cappadocia constituted the catalyst and the key for Roman operations in Asia Minor during the first half of the century; its position lent it unusual importance when dealing with Pontus, Armenia, or Parthia.

In the adjoining Kingdom of Commagene, the reign of Mithradates I Kallinikos promoted strength and unification. His marriage to a daughter of the Seleucid Antiochus VIII Grypus provided Commagene a coterie of royal relatives and, after the Seleucids fell, perhaps the mantle of successor, clearly a sentiment behind the grand *hierothesia* of Antiochus I and his son. The dynasty survived conquest by Tigranes and prospered far into the next century.

Judaea moved from the successful reign of John Hyrcanus to the violent one of Alexander Jannaeus. The succession by Alexandra Salome opened the faltering country to growing religious factions, which weakened it. Fraternal strife and Roman intervention (Pompey) lay just ahead.

In Egypt, the reign of Ptolemy Lathyros, with the vigilant presence of Cleopatra III, brought the country through a period of internal difficulty partly consequent on the Seleucid disintegration. Cleopatra Selene, another of the vigorous Ptolemaic queens during these years, promoted her cause and that of her sons in Rome, seeking not Syria but Egypt itself. She died fighting Tigranes.

The Armenian Empire of Tigranes rose and fell roughly within the first three decades of the century, but its effects reached far beyond this. Not only did he curtail the expansion of the Parthian Empire at a crucial time, but at an equally crucial time he ended the Seleucid Empire. His conquest of Syria itself drove the last Seleucids into exile, from which they emerged only to find Rome claiming to inherit the fruits of Tigranes's conquest.

Under Mithradates II, 'King of Kings,' Parthia rose to the status of great power, initially limited in the west only by Tigranes, father of one of Mithradates's wives. His immediate successors never reached the military and political levels of success he had, and the aristocracy began to gain at the expense of the central authority, but Mithradates did hand on a nation more than strong enough for the challenges to come, and among his successors Sinatruces proved able to maintain this strength. The relations of Parthia with Armenia, Pontus, and Rome soon underwent severe tests of national resolve and diplomacy, to say nothing of military threats. The pattern of insult-then-alliance begun by Marius and Sulla was to continue and intensify.

II

The second half of the period this study treats shifted from the concerns of the first (Eupator; Tigranes; Seleucids) to a crescendo of new problems. After the removal of Mithradates and Tigranes as major threats, the Seleucid Empire faltered onward only briefly and then fell before the view of Pompey that it had been defeated by Tigranes and he by Rome, so that title to Syria passed to Rome. This claim might be pressed for other Seleucid possessions as well, but that required further conquest.

Thracians continued their mixed response to Rome. Inevitably, their proximity to the battlefields of Pharsalus and Philippi involved them closely in the Roman civil wars. Their dilemma is illustrated by the tactic of Rhescuporis I and his brother, who supported opposing Romans so that one would be on the side of the victors and might preserve the other. At Actium, Rhoemetalces I defected to Octavian, who 'loved treachery but hated a traitor.' The stability of Thrace henceforward rested on the intermarriage of its Odrysian-Astaean and Sapaean royal houses, begun by Cotys V and reinforced by others. As indicated in the previous chapter, Thrace continued its odd symbiosis with Rome on one side and the Eastern dynastic network beyond.

Bithynia and Nicomedes IV had gone by 70 BC, but Galatia under Deiotarus I forged strongly onward, now to enjoy its greatest period of influence as he achieved kingship and led its formidable horsemen against Eupator and Tigranes in furtherance of the Roman alliance. Little misunderstandings with Caesar, Brogitarus, his daughter, and Castor II did not materially dampen his spirits. The kingdom he handed on to Amyntas more than maintained itself in the ceaseless fighting of the thirties, as too in the effort to pacify Cilicia Tracheia and environs. Provincial status lay just ahead, scant reward for decades of important service, but probably not unwelcome to Galatians unused to kings.

In Pontus, the aftermath of Eupator and his son left a royal vacuum in a time and place still requiring royal rule. Hence Antony's recognition of Polemo I as king there, with a century of unremitting struggle ahead.

Polemo's marriages to Dynamis and to Pythodoris assisted in consolidation of this kingdom, its adjunct territory in Bosporus, its allied dynasty in Thrace (through Antonia Tryphaena), and even a brief success in Armenia (Zeno-Artaxias). Polemo II carried Pontus into the reign of Nero and shared in the effort to conquer and pacify Cilicia Tracheia.

The unlucky successors of Ariobarzanes I retained their kingdom but watched it gradually empty of its wealth (becoming *inanis*: Cicero), mainly to meet the exactions of Pompey. Ariobarzanes III lost his life to partisans of Brutus and Cassius. But a notable king, descended from Pontic nobles and a former brief king of Egypt, ascended as Antony's appointee. Archelaus ruled half a century, leaving his land and family both strong, though Tiberius saw fit to incorporate Cappadocia as a province.

Commagene achieved a period of prosperity under Antiochus I and a reaffirmation of national prestige. Despite problems after his death and that of his son, Commagene survived for an even greater period to come.

Tarcondimotus gave his region in Cilicia a king and an active policy during the conflict with Parthia. Surprisingly, his little dynasty endured until at least the reign of Tiberius.

Emesa arose from nowhere under Sampsigeramus I to assume a role in the demise of the Seleucids and then step into the vacuum. He and Iamblichus, his son, involved themselves in the defence of Syria and environs against Parthians in 51, and appeared again when fighting from the Roman civil wars spilled into the area. The Emesenes became kings, with important work to perform in the century ahead.

In Judaea, the consequences of fraternal rivalry between Aristobulus II and Hyrcanus II led to the rise of a new family, that of Antipater, and to intervention by Pompey. The consequences let Antipater's son, Herod the Great, open a place for his new dynasty, supported by Rome. Expulsion of the Parthian nominee and last Hasmonaean, Antigonus, left Herod free for his long, stabilizing reign.

The period of Nabataean involvement in these evolutions began with support for Antipater, with major tests to come in the reign of Augustus. Aretas IV married a daughter to Herodes Antipas, son of Herod the Great, but by and large Nabataeans remained just out of reach, comfortable thus.

Egypt began its rapid slide towards Roman domination through the involvement of Ptolemy XII Auletes with Roman financiers and politicians. His subjects drove him to Rome, whence he returned in force, but the price was predictably high, financially and politically. His forceful daughter, Cleopatra VII, eclipsed her two brothers and captivated both Caesar and Antony. Her ambitions extended to arrangements that were not destined for fruition, but would have profoundly altered dynastic history.

Across the Euphrates, Tigranes ruled confined to his kingdom and passed it intact to Artavasdes II. Antony's capturing him for exile and death in Alexandria removed the last vestiges of Armenian 'friendship and alliance' with Rome.

Atropatene rose to international prominence for the first time, under Artavasdes I, and shared in Roman efforts to control Armenia. The children of Artavasdes, especially Iotape I, furthered the progress of intermarriage, especially among the dynasties bordering or near the Euphrates.

Parthia under Phraates III, Orodes II, Pacorus, and Phraates IV, the most prominent of its kings now, remained outside the action as Eupator and Tigranes were broken, then it moved to benefit from that. Despite formal friendship and alliance with Rome, it found itself facing Roman military designs by Gabinius, Crassus, Caesar, and Antony. None of these came to anything, and the period ended with mutual recognition between the two greatest powers then existing outside the Far East. Parthia regarded the Euphrates as the proper boundary with Rome, and this view prevailed by the time of Augustus.

III

One of the great transformations of history saw Asia Minor, the Levant, and Egypt altered from a royal society to a constituent of the Roman Empire. This long process reached its most important stage between roughly 100 and 30 BC. Roman statesmen began appearing in the East and the Roman state increasingly decided to intervene there, bolstered by the inheritance of Pergamon and Cyrene, then Bithynia, as well as responding to the threat of pirates and of Mithradates Eupator with Tigranes. What Romans encountered was a society already organized along royal lines and firmly controlled by its aristocracies, a type of government that Romans understood. The hundreds of persons who composed this social and political structure are imperfectly known now, but their role in mediating the gradual Roman absorption of the East can plainly be discerned.

Roman policy veered from the extremes of ignoring developments in the East to intervening militarily. The scope given a Roman commander in the East, and the distant pressures of domestic politics on him when there, combined to produce an inconsistent pattern, but its direction bore always towards financial profit and concomitant political control. A royal society can be relatively well replaced by an aristocratic one, as Rome was. Many of the kings co-operated in this process, but others resisted; either way, they led the East during this critical period.

Contingency operated as an important factor. Frequent examples remind us of this – the slackening of Parthian effort after Pacorus died, the pro-Roman leanings of Antipater's family, the choices Deiotarus made, the aspirations of Cleopatra. Each raises historical problems of its own, but the aggregate suggests that evolutions in the East occurred on a far less predetermined basis than sometimes assumed.

How stood the East, then, in 31 BC? At Actium, most of the East remained under kings, but the establishment of the Roman Empire and the consolidation of the Parthian Empire rested on a firm basis. Their replacement of the empires of the Persians, Ptolemies, and Seleucids had become irreversible, partly as the result of processes set in motion by the Empires of Eupator and Tigranes. But much remained for Eastern royalty to do.

NOTES

Chapter 1

1 BEROSSUS: See S.M. Burstein, *The 'Babyloniaca' of Berossus* (Malibu 1978; Sources from the Ancient Near East, 1, fascicle 5). That 'cultural isolation' need not have characterized the mutual relations of Seleucids and the inhabitants of Mesopotamia has been emphasized by S.M. Sherwin-White. See her article with J.A. Black, 'A Clay Tablet with Greek Letters in the Ashmolean Museum, and the "Graeco-Babyloniaca" Texts': *Iraq* 46 (1985) 131-140. See too her 'Babylonian Chronicle Fragments as a Source for Seleucid History': *JNES* 42 (1983) 265-270. ALEXANDER: The vast topic of his relations with the Greeks and Iranians of the East requires study. Some of the many relevant studies appear in the Selected Bibliography (Tarn, Herzfeld, Rostovtzeff, Bengtson, and others). See also A.J. Heisserer, *Alexander the Great and the Greeks: The Epigraphic Evidence* (Norman, Oklahoma 1980). EPARCHIES: Discussed by Tarn and Griffith (see Selected Bibliography) Ch. 4, 130-132. KINGS: The quotation regarding kings is by Cyril Toumanoff, 'Origin or Function: The Two Fundamental Concepts of the Princely Rank': *The Coat of Arms*, n.s. 7, no. 138 (1986) 4-14. For the mix of kings referred to by B. Levick, *Roman Colonies in Southern Asia Minor* (Oxford 1967) 219 f., see treatment under their respective dynasties. See too A. Lintott, 'What Was the Imperium Romanum?': *G&R* (ser. 2) 28 (1981) 53-67, esp. section IV 'Allied Kingdoms.' He says (61): 'The patron-client relationship is occasionally used in ancient sources as a metaphor for that which existed between Rome and her allies: the term "client-king" as such is a creation of post-Renaissance scholarship ... It has a drawback ... in that it may suggest that the Romans viewed these kings as clients of the Roman

people ...' See also Antony: Jos. *AJ* 15.74. Marionette: So writes R. Bernhardt, *Historia* 26 (1977) 66, note 32, of the appointees of Nicomedes III and Mithradates VI in Cappadocia (§ 5). Romans encouraged the notion of kings 'given' for vacant thrones, on which see the examination by R. Göbl, 'REX ... DATUS': *RhM* 104 (1961) 70-80.

2 LEGITIMATE LINE: References collected by Hoben 176 note 161. COINS: D. Braund, *Rome and the Friendly King* (Beckenham, Kent 1984) 123 ff. KINGS' POWERS: See below, *passim*; Schürer (Vermes and Millar) 316 f. Studies discussing the kings extensively include those (see Selected Bibliography) by Cimma; Braund; McEwan; Sands; Pani; Reinach, *Trois royaumes*; Eddy; Hoben; Bohn; Gagé, '*Basiléia*'; Olshausen. Later: J. Gagé, 'L'empereur romain et les rois': *RH* 221 (1959) 221-260. See P. Garnsey and R. Saller, *The Early Principate, Augustus to Trajan* (Oxford 1982; *G&R*, 'New Surveys in the Classics, no. 15') 8 ff. on 'clientage' (basically the older view). This term and its analogues should, as applied to Near Eastern kings, disappear from scholarly writing. As D. Braund notes (*Friendly King* 23), 'It is now generally agreed that the term "client king" is not to be understood literally: *clientela* is a metaphor ...' The most useful term is 'allied king,' reflecting *socius* and *rex*, if 'king' alone is regarded for some reason as inadequate. Levick, *Roman Colonies* 215 ff., Appendix VI, examines the question of Rome's relation to 'Client Kings, Royal Domains, and Imperial Estates' after Actium. E. Rawson, 'Caesar's Heritage: Hellenistic Kings and Their Roman Equals': *JRS* 65 (1975) 148-159; p. 156 misstates Sall. *Jug.* 65.2 (*more regum*).

3 M.I. Finley, *The Ancient Economy* (Berkeley 1973); G.E.M. de Ste Croix, *The Class Struggle in the Ancient Greek World* (London 1981).

4 MAGNESIA: The Roman victory relied heavily on allies: Tarn and Griffith 28. Even Achaeans crossed into Asia Minor to assist: *SIG*[3] 606. APAMEA: S.M. Burstein, 'The Aftermath of the Peace of Apamea': *AJAH* 5 (1980) 1 ff.; A.N. Sherwin-White, 'Roman Involvement in Anatolia, 167-88 B.C.': *JRS* 67 (1977) 62-75; A.H. McDonald, 'The Treaty of Apamea (188 B.C.)': *JRS* 57 (1967) 1-8; A.H. McDonald with F.W. Walbank, 'The Treaty of Apamea (188 B.C.): The Naval Clauses': *JRS* 59 (1969) 30-39; J. Briscoe, 'Eastern Policy and Senatorial Politics, 168-146 B.C.': *Historia* 18 (1969) 49-70; M.J. Moscovich, 'Dio Cassius and the Political Undertones of the Treaty of Apamea': *Ancient History Bulletin* 1.5 (1987) 122-126. See Selected Bibliography, books by Sherwin-White, Gruen (1984: II, 620 ff.), Liebmann-Frankfort, Harris.

5 *BAlex.* 78: *iure gentis et cognationis*. Legitimate succession: Hoben 176 note 161.

6 Detailed discussion of the historical geography of Asia Minor occurs through-

out Magie's first volume, especially Ch. 2 and 11, and pp. 369-376. See also Levick, *Roman Colonies* Ch. 2 and 8; Cary, *Geographic Background* Ch. 6; Ramsay, *Historical Geography of Asia Minor* (*passim*, but to be used with caution); Jones, *Cities*². Regional studies appear under the appropriate dynasties.

7 On Asia Minor and its wealth, see Magie, *passim*, and Broughton in *ESAR* IV. See Selected Bibliography.

8 Sullivan, *Armenian Question* 298-316, on the settlement; further bibliography below, Ch. 9, § 24.

9 PUBLICANS: E.g., Sherk, *Greek East* nos. 59 and 70; cf. 45, 65, and 68. See too *OGIS* 440; *SIG*³ 747; *IGRR* IV 262; T. Drew-Bear, *BCH* 96 (1972) 443-471; Memnon, *FGrH* 434 F 27.6 (38). EMPIRE: A useful starting-point is M.I. Finley, 'Empire in the Greco-Roman World': *G&R* 25 (1978) 1-15. See also G.W. Bowersock, *Roman Arabia* (Cambridge, Mass. 1983) 30; G. Gagé, 'L'empereur romain et les rois': *RH* 221 (1951) 221-260. The idea of 'world empire': T.S. Brown, *Phoenix* 18 (1964) 124-136.

Chapter 2

1 BEQUESTS: For Bithynia, see this chapter, § 2, notes 18-19. For Egypt and Cyrene, see Ch. 4, § 10, notes 1, 3, 11. For Asia, see *OGIS* 338, 435; *SIG*³ 694; *IGRR* IV 262; Sherk, *Greek East* nos. 39-40, 44-45. *OGIS* 338 remarks that the will of Attalus 'needs to be confirmed by the Romans' and some consider this a demonstration of its authenticity. However, a party capable of manipulating a kingdom should be able to arrange appropriate propaganda to support its action, and the bequest possibly represented not so much the intentions of Attalus himself as of a group within the nobility. Suspicions arose in antiquity. Sallust, *Hist.* 4.69.8 rhetorically terms the will 'forged' and 'unpatriotic' (*simulatoque impio testamento*). Rostovtzeff notes (*CAH* IX 226) of all these that 'the testaments of client kings were for a while a device in the foreign policy of the ruling party in the Roman Senate.' THRACE: Hdt. 5.3. On the Odrysians and the 'inner unity and strategic centre' provided by the central plain of Thrace, see N.G.L. Hammond, 'The Extent of Persian Occupation in Thrace': *Chiron* 10 (1980) 53-61. An ancient comment: Amm. Marc. 27.4.2-8. See *SEG* 33 (1983) no. 560 on 'political' inscriptions.

2 Recent studies on Thrace include: J. Wiesner, *Die Thraker* (Stuttgart 1963), esp. 155-162; Jones, *Cities*² Ch. 1; Chr. M. Danov, 'Die Thraker in dem Ostbalkan …' in *ANRW* II 7.1 (Berlin 1979) 21-185; R. Sullivan, *ANRW* II 7.1, 186-211. See too Y. Youroukova, *Coins of the Ancient Thracians* (Oxford 1976; Brit. Arch. Reports, Suppl. Ser. 4); review: W. Stancomb in *NC* (ser. 7) 18 (1978) 200; B. Isaac, *The Greek Settlements in Thrace until*

the Macedonian Conquest (Leiden 1986; Studies of the Dutch Archaeological and Historical Society, 10). For the studies of Mommsen, Dessau, and Bowersock, which concentrate on the later period, see Ch. 6, § 14. Cf. below, notes 7 and 9.

3 Arrian provides one example of this 'warlike and expansionist nature': *FGrH* 156, F 72 = A. Roos, *Flavius Arrianus, II: Scripta Minora et Fragmenta* (Leipzig 1968) 'Bithynika' Frag. 54. As late as the third century AD, Thrace drew special attention because of its 'position stratégique et les qualités militaires de ses habitants': M. Le Glay in *ZPE* 43 (1981) 175-184, esp. 184; A.G. Poulter, *Ancient Bulgaria*, I-II (Nottingham 1981). Many ancient writers remark on Thracian fierceness; e.g., Amm. Marc. 27.4. 'ASIA': The range of meaning given this term in ancient sources after Alexander's day is discussed by S.I. Oost in H.J. Dell, ed., *Ancient Macedonian Studies in Honor of Charles F. Edson* (Thessaloniki 1981; Institute for Balkan Studies, 181) 265-282. See too D.J. Georgacas, *The Names for the Asia Minor Peninsula* (Heidelberg 1971). Roman usage for the territory previously possessed by the Attalids was precise, but some ancients meant Asia Minor in general by the term, and others had Persia/Parthia in mind. The term requires careful examination in each context. Rome's proconsuls in its province of Asia around 100 BC are studied by F. Coarelli, *Epigrafia e ordine senatorio* (Rome 1982) 435-451. DELPHI: See, for instance, *SIG*^{3} 611-612; 643. DELOS: Romans are mentioned there in inscriptions from at least 193 BC: F. Durrbach, *Choix d'inscriptions de Délos* (Paris 1921-1922: hereafter, Durrbach, *Choix*) 64 (to Scipio Africanus) and 65 (renewal of 'good relations and friendship'). See also Sherk, *Greek East* nos. 9-10; 28; 47 A-D. See M.-F. Baslez and C. Vial on the slow growth of Roman and Delian recognition of mutual interest: *BCH* 111 (1987) 281-312. CULTS: The Greek East began surprisingly early to take up Roman gods or cults, though more for political than religious reasons. See Sherk, *Greek East* no. 41; cf. no. 18 for an early (c. 180 BC) trace of the cult; J. Reynolds and others, *JRS* 76 (1986) 138; R. Mellor, *Thea Rōmē. The Worship of the Goddess Roma in the Greek World* (Göttingen 1975). The sites of the cult are indicated on *TAVO* B V 6. CITIES: V. Velkov, 'Siedlungsleben im antiken Thrakien': *Eirene* 17 (1980) 45-63; Velkov, 'Das antiken Siedlungsleben in Thrakien': *Klio* 62 (1980) 5-11.

4 EARLY CONTACTS: G. Chiranky, 'Rome and Cotys, Two Problems, I: The Diplomacy of 167 B.C.; II: The Date of *SIG*^{3} 656': *Athenaeum* 60 (1982) 461-481. Whether the Scordisci can be regarded as Thracian or not, the *Periochae* of Livy use such phrases as *in Thracia cum Scordiscis ... pugnavit*: 56, 63; cf. 54 and 65. Livy, *Ab urbe condita* 40.57.7 and 41.19.7-8, distinguishes them from Thracians. Cf. Jul. Obsequens 16: *Dalmatae Scordisci*; Orosius 5.23.19: *cruentissimi atque immanissimi Scordisci erant*; Amm. Marc.

27.4.4: *saevi quondam et truces*; Florus 1.39.4: *Saevissimi omnium Thracum Scordisci fuere*. They were probably Celts of Pannonia, moving at times into Illyria and Macedonia; they demonstrate the looseness with which 'Thracian' could be used. Their victory over Cato: Dio 26.88; Florus 1.39.3; Amm. Marc. 27.4.4; Livy *Per.* 63; Eutr. 4.24. Cf. App., *Ill.* 5.12-15 for a variant account. Map: T. Reinach, *Mithridate Eupator* (Paris 1890). See also *RE* 2A (1923) 831-835. For other Roman-'Thracian' conflicts of the late second century, see B. Lenk in *RE* 6A (1937) 437-439 ('Thrake'); W.V. Harris, *War and Imperialism in Republican Rome, 327-70 B.C.* (Oxford 1979) 245 and 272. *SIG*[3] 710A mentions a victory of M. Minucius over not only the Scordisci but also over 'the Bessi and the remaining Thracians' about 107; cf. Livy *Per.* 65. APHRODISIAS: See J. Reynolds, *Aphrodisias and Rome* (London 1982). DECREE OF 129: *SIG*[3] 694. See L. Robert in *BCH* 108 (1984) 489-496; Sherk, *Greek East* no. 44; cf. 39-40 and 45. ASTYPALAEA: *IGRR* IV 1028; Sherk, *Greek East* no. 53.

DIDIUS: Amm. Marc. 27.4.10-11. See M. Hassall, M. Crawford, J. Reynolds, 'Rome and the Eastern Provinces at the End of the Second Century B.C.': *JRS* 64 (1974) 195-220, esp. 203, lines 27 ff., and 204, lines 6 ff. They locate the Caenic Chersonese as 'presumably the peninsula running down to the Bosporus' (213); Jones, *Cities*[2] 15 ff. and Map I places it above the Hellespont. On this question see also *SEG* 33 (1983) no. 868. On the document, see Sherk, *Greek East* no. 55. See too *SEG* 3 (1929) no. 378. It goes too far to say with Jones, *Cities*[2] 8, that Rome now exercised 'a vague suzerainty' over the rest of Thrace; many decades of diplomacy and warfare lay ahead. The remark also presupposes territorial ambitions in Thrace and the East that Rome did not exhibit before the Mithradatic Wars: A.N. Sherwin-White in *JRS* 67 (1977) 62-75. Cf. Ch. 6, § 18, note 142. On the date of the *SC de agro Pergameno*, see H.B. Mattingly in *AJP* 93 (1972) 412-423 (for 122 BC) and E. Badian in *JRS* 70 (1980) 202 (for 129 BC). See too Sherk, *Greek East* no. 45; *IGRR* IV 262.

5 COINS OF MOSTIS: Youroukova (above, note 2) 33-39 with Pl. xvii-xviii. The date in Head *HN*[2] 285 ('circ. B.C. 200, or later') should be brought down to a range that includes the decades after 146 BC, to judge from an overstruck coin. Mostis might have ruled long enough to be included among the Thracians mentioned by Appian and others as willing allies of Mithradates Eupator, though the stylistic arguments of Youroukova are inconclusive. See App. *Mith.* 15.54; cf. 13.44; 41.158; 57.234. See too Dio 31, Frag. 101.2; 36.9.3; Livy *Per.* 92 and 95; Sall. *Hist.* 2.80; Eutrop. 5.7 and 6.2; Orosius 5.23.20. BESSI: Reinach (above, note 4) places the Bessi southwest of the Scordisci and the Dentheletae; Jones, *Cities*[2] omits the area west of the Dentheletae on the map for Ch. 1, and indeed the Dardanians belong only

peripherally to Thracian history. LUCULLUS AGAINST THE BESSI: *qui cum durissima gente Bessorum conflixit omnium primus*, Amm. Marc. 27.4.11; Eutrop. 6.8; 6.10; Livy *Per.* 97; Oros. 6.3. Lucullus was in fact probably *not* the first Roman to fight the Bessi, who must have been involved in the second-century conflicts; in any case, he was certainly not the last. C. Octavius against them: Suet. *Aug.* 3.2. Cicero accused L. Calpurnius Piso of beheading a Bessic chieftain at the behest of the Odrysian-Astaean King Cotys IV: *Pis.* 34.84. The Bessi long continued to appear under their own name: e.g., Caes. *BCiv.* 3.4; Dio 51.25.5; 54.34.5-6.

6 DENTHELETAE: Allied to Philip V, though harshly treated by him: Livy 40.22.9-11. See Gran. Lic. (ed. Flemisch) p. 28; Cic. *Pis.* 34.84. Most of the Thracian raids recorded by Livy were into Macedonia, but Romans also raided the territory of Thrace during the Mithradatic Wars. See Livy *Per.* 70, 74, 76, 81-82, 91-92, 95, 97; 83 records Sulla's fighting against Thracians. Plut. *Sulla* 23.5 brings him into the country of the Maedi, bordering Macedonia along the Strymon. See Eutrop. 5.7. In the First Mithradatic War, Romans used the area about Byzantium as a staging-point for naval operations, and Mithradates in turn relied on his Thracian allies to assist Arcathias, his son, in invading Macedonia by way of Thrace. See App. *Mith.* 17.61-63; 18.64; 35.137; 41.156. Arcathias is not Ariarathes (App. *Mith.* 10.33; 15.50), *pace* E. Badian, *Studies in Greek and Roman History* (Oxford 1964) 177 note 56 vs. Magie, *Roman Rule* 1100 note 24 and 1105 note 41. Cf. A.N. Sherwin-White in *CQ* 71 = n.s. 27 (1977) 181 note 43, where he has Arcathias ruling Armenia, perhaps thinking of App. *Mithr* 17.63 – vs. 15.54, etc.: Arcathias commanded some cavalry from Armenia Minor, but Tigranes ruled Armenia. Bibliography on these campaigns: B. Lenk in *RE* 6A (1937) 439-441. On the historical geography of Thrace and its tribes, see further Jones, *Cities*^{2} Ch. 1.

7 THE SAPAEAN COTYS VI: H. Dessau, 'Miscellanea Epigraphica I-II': *Ephem. Epigr.* 9 (1913) 700 = *IG* III 552 = II/III^2 3442. Discussion: Kahrstedt in *RE* 1 A, 1 (1914) 256, s.v. 'Rhaskouporis nr. 2'; B. Lenk in *RE* 6 A (1937) 445 ff., 'Thrake'; G. Mihailov in *I.G.Bulg.* 399; Sullivan (above, note 2), section III. SAPAEAN ECLIPSE: Kahrstedt; Youroukova (above, note 2) 32 ff.; W.-D. von Barloewen, *Abriss der Geschichte antiker Randkulturen* (Munich 1961) p. 239, Table I; cf. note 9. RHESCUPORIS I AS DYNAST: Dio 47.25.2, though his wording – 'a certain dynast' – is vague. KING ABRUPOLIS: *SIG*^{3} 643. See also Polyb. 22.18.2; Livy 42.13.5; Sherk, *Greek East* no. 19. THASOS: Sherk, *Greek East* no. 64.

8 COTYS II AND PERSEUS: *SIG*^{3} 656. See also Livy 42.29.12, 51.10, 57.6, 67.4-5; 45.42.6; Polyb. 30.17.1 (18.12). Praise for Cotys: Polyb. 27.12 (10) and Diod. 30.3. See too Livy 44.42.2. GAIUS SENTIUS AND COTYS III:

Livy *Per.* 70; Oros. 5.18.30; Cic. *Verr.* 2.3.217; *Pis.* 34.84 (where he may ascribe to the Dentheletae a service performed rather by the Odrysian-Astaean Cotys III: Diod. 37.5a). Sentius: Broughton, *Magistrates* II, 12, 15, 18, 42, 49. COTYS III: Diod. 37.5a. See also *RE* 11 (1922) 1552 f., 'Kotys, nr. 3.' The strange coin bearing the legend ΚΟΤΥΟϹ ΧΑΡΑΚΤΗΡ, which Head *HN*^{2} 285 prudently declines to assign Cotys III, could in fact belong to him, as some have thought, but see Youroukova (above, note 2) 40 ff. SADALAS I: M. Holleaux, *Études d'épigraphie et d'histoire grecques,* I (Paris 1938) 143-159 = Holleaux, 'Décret de Chéronée relatif à la première guerre de Mithradates': *REG* 32 (1919) 320-337; Cic. *Verr.* II, 1.24.63. But see Sullivan, 'Thrace': *ANRW* II 7.2, notes 8 and 18. For an earlier Sadalas see *I.G.Bulg.* no. 307 with I. Venedikov, 'L'inscription de Sadala': *Epigraphica* 42 (1980) 7-12, concluding that this Sadalas was not an Astaean. His reign is placed late in the fourth century BC by Y. Youroukova, 'Les monnaies dans l'inscription de Sadalas': *ibid.*, 13 ff.

9 ABDERA'S APPEAL: *IGRR* IV 1558; Sherk, *Greek East* no. 26; *SIG*^{3} 656. The Roman Senate had at first favoured Cotys II (lines 25 f. with note 7). BYZANTIUM: Tac. *Ann.* 12.62; Jones, *Cities*^{2} 7, with 376 note 8. MESEMBRIA: *I.G.Bulg.* I^2 314 a; Sherk, *Greek East* no. 73. ODRYSIAN-ASTAEAN UNITY: This question provokes disagreement. The Astaeans took an independent line in 172 BC by approaching Rome (Livy 42.19.6), whereas Cotys II, specifically named an Odrysian, supported Perseus (above, note 8). But by the time of Cotys IV, the two royal houses had probably joined, and the old capital of the Astaeans at Bizye became first the capital of the two tribes jointly and then, after union with the Sapaeans, it developed into '*Bizye arx regum Thraciae*' (Plin. *N.H.* 4.11.47). On this lively controversy, pursued at least since Dessau's day, see especially G. Mihailov, *I.G.Bulg.* I^2 (Sophia 1970) 97-98 (comm. to no. 43), vs. Jones, *Cities*^{2} 377 note 11; bibliography in Sullivan (above, note 2) 190 note 9; R. Werner, 'Thraker': *Abriss der Geschichte antiker Randkulturen* (above, note 7) 117; 239; Wiesner (above, note 2) 156 ff; B. Lenk in *RE* 17 (1937) 1900-1903 ('Odrysai').

10 PRUSIAS II: Discussion and bibliography in E. Gruen, *The Hellenistic World and the Coming of Rome* (Berkeley and Los Angeles 1984) I, 117 ff. Cf. A.C. Scafuro, 'Prusias II of Bithynia and Third-Party Arbitration': *Historia* 36 (1987) 28-37. BITHYNIA: See *TAVO* B V 3 and 6; Calder-Bean, coordinates D-E, b-c. Cf. Arrian, *Bithynika,* Fragment 20 (Roos): 'the Sangarius is traversed by ships [*nausiporos*] and is the largest of the rivers in Bithynia.' See Strabo 12.3.7.543; Hdt. 1.28; 7.75; Livy 38.18. See too G. Vitucci, *Il Regno di Bitinia* (Rome 1953); B.F. Harris, *ANRW* II 7.2 (Berlin 1980) 857-901. See as well studies by F.K. Dörner: *Inschriften und Denkmäler aus Bithynien* (Berlin 1941); *Bericht über eine Reise in Bithynien* (Vienna

1952); *Tituli Asiae Minoris*, IV.1 (Vienna 1978). See too S. 2Sahin, *Bithynische Studien* (Bonn 1978) and his *Katalog der antiken Inschriften des Museums von Iznik (Nikaia)*, 1-3 (Bonn 1979-1987, with R. Merkelbach); T. Corsten, *Inschriften von Apameia (Bithynien) und Pylai* (Bonn 1987); F. Becker-Bertau, *Inschriften von Klaudiopolis*, with an Anhang by W. Weiser, *Zur Münzprägung von Bithynion* (Bonn 1986); Jones, *Cities*[2] Ch. 6; Magie Ch. 13. For the incorporation of Phrygia Maior, traditionally in 116 but possibly in 119: *OGIS* 436 = *IGRR* IV 752 = Sherk, *Greek East* no. 49. See too Magie 168 ff. and 1058 ff. notes 34 ff., with T. Drew-Bear in *Historia* 21 (1972) 44-87, esp. 83 ff. But his objection that Rome should have taken up Phrygia before 116, since its ally Mithradates V had died in 120, bears little force (see his note 29). Mithradates VI might have been considered for a time to be his father's replacement in this regard, and in any case Romans could be slow to take up the administration of newly acquired territories in this period (Cyrene – 'Roman' for some twenty years before being effectively organized; possibly Bithynia, below note 19). For Asia, see Sherk, *Greek East* nos. 39-40; 42-45; 57-58. See also *SEG* 26 (1976-1977) no. 1885. See too A.N. Sherwin-White, *Roman Foreign Policy in the East* (London 1984) Ch. IV; E.W. Gray, 'M'. Aquillius and the Organisation of the Roman Province of Asia': *Proc. Xth Internat. Cong. Class. Arch.* (Ankara 1978) 969 note 25. The view that Nicomedes III and Mithradates V had attempted to outbid each other and thus gain Phrygia is reviewed by Magie 1043 note 27 (cf. pp. 154 f. and 318). On the supposed bribe of Aquillius: Magie 1043 note 27 and 1049 note 41.

11 REFUSAL OF NICOMEDES: Diod. 36.3.1, with Magie 1093 note 57. PARTITION OF PAPHLAGONIA: Magie, *ibid.*, with p. 197; date discussed by A.N. Sherwin-White (above, note 4) 71 note 61. See too Justin 37.4.3-9 and 38.5.4 ff.; Magie 1098 note 14; Th. Liebmann-Frankfort, *La frontière orientale dans la politique extérieure de la République romaine* (Brussels 1969) 178 ff.; Justin 38.2.6.

12 CAPPADOCIAN INVASION: Justin 38.1.1 ff. This was about 102 BC: Magie 203 note m. The appeal to Rome occurred in 97/96 or later: Sherwin-White (above, note 4) 71. See too Magie 205 with 1098 note 14. 'FREEDOM': Justin 38.2.7; cf. Strabo 12.2.11.540; below, Ch. 3, § 5.

13 FINANCIAL PROBLEMS: Diod. 36.3.1, with the interpretation of Magie 1093 note 57. The mission of Verres to Thrace and to 'King Nicomedes' might have been connected with these financial dealings between the Bithynians and Rome: Cic. *Verr.* II, 1.24.63. BENEFACTIONS: Magie 318 and 1199 note 46; *OGIS* 345. Laodice is mentioned with him in lines 7, 8, and (conjecturally) 32; she bears the title of queen and is clearly identified as the daughter of King Mithradates (V).

14 DATE: Scholars usually follow Reinach, *Mithridate Eupator* (Paris 1890) 112 note 2, in dating the inception of this reign to 94. Reinach assumes that the Nicomedes of Justin 38.2.6 is still Nicomedes III ('II,' in his numeration) and that the proximity of this passage to that recording the accession of Ariobarzanes I shows him still reigning about 95. Despite disputes over the date of accession of Ariobarzanes, the assumption and the approximate date appear worth retaining. Reinach's other argument, that enough time must be allowed for Nicomedes to marry twice and sire two children *before* his temporary expulsion, need not detain us. The coins, though quite similar, do apparently portray a younger man beginning with 'Year 204' Bith. (= 94 BC): *Recueil* I Plate XXXIII, 10 with p. 232. Newer coins: Bennett (below, note 17) 470-472. POISON: Gran. Licin. 35, p. 29, ed. M. Flemisch (Leipzig 1904). DEPRAVITY: Suet. *Div. Iul.* 2 and 49; cf. *De Vir. Illustr.* 78.1; Dio 43.20.2; Plut. *Caes.* 1.3. Visit of Caesar, alluded to in a speech of his (... *pro hospitio regis Nicomedis*): Aul. Gell. 5.13.6. DELOS: *OGIS* 343, with the restoration given in Magie 1200 note 47. SOCRATES: Gran. Licin. 35, p. 29. As 'Chrestos': Justin 38.5.8; Magie 207 with 1099 note 19; Vitucci (above, note 10) 107 ff. NICOMEDES IV: The Senate in Rome recognized Nicomedes IV as king: App. *Mith.* 10.32; Memnon, *FGrH* 434, F 22.5 (30.3). MARRIAGES: Gran. Licin. 35, p. 29 f.: ... *sororem patris ducit uxorem, quae cara huic vivo fuerat. (Cum) die nono post mortua esset morbo an dolo, Nisam Ariarathis Cappadocum regis filiam accepit.*

15 SOCRATES CHRESTOS: See previous note. INVASION OF MITHRADATES: Justin 38.3.4; App. *Mith.* 13.42 and 57.232. In 10.31-33, Appian places this event *after* the first ejection of Ariobarzanes and the order from Rome that he be reinstated, and *before* the second ejection, by Mithraas and Bagoas, which occurred about 91. See too A.N. Sherwin-White in *CQ* 71 = n.s. 27 (1977) 176 ff. Despite the view of Reinach, *Mithridate Eupator* 114 note 2 and Magie 1099 note 19, the word *nuper* in Cic. *Orat.* 3.229 cannot be pressed to show Nicomedes being defended in Rome 'shortly before September 91.' But the passage does reflect the difficulty Nicomedes had in re-establishing himself, despite the original decision of the Senate for him. See also Memnon 22.5 (30).

16 RESTORATION: App. *Mith.* 11.33; Livy *Per.* 74; Justin 38.3.4 and 38.5.8: *regem Bithyniae Chreston, in quem Senatus arma decreverat.* FINANCIAL WOES: App. *Mith.* 11.36. INVASION: App. *Mith.* 11.35-12.38; Dio frag. 99.1 Boiss. AQUILLIUS: E.W. Gray (above, note 10); Broughton, *Magistrates* II, 38, 6. CASSIUS: Florus 1.40.

17 ATTEMPTED ASSASSINATION: App. *Mith.* 57.232. MURDER OF SOCRATES: Justin 38.5.8. EXPULSION OF NICOMEDES: App. *Mith.* 12.38-16.58; 57.233; Memnon 22.6-8 (31); Livy *Per.* 76, with Magie 1100 note 20.

NICOMEDES AT WAR: Magie 209-223 and 243 ff.; Vitucci (above, note 10) Ch. 5. RULE IN PAPHLAGONIA: This from a notice, out of chronological sequence, in Gran. Licin. 35, p. 28 Flem.: *Nicomedi regnum Bithyniae restituit Curio eique adiecit Paphlagoniam*. Flemisch restores the passage thus on the basis of App. *Mith.* 60.249. There were *regii agri* of his or his father's there, later acquired by Pompey: Cic. *Leg. Agr.* 1.2.6; 2.19.51. LETTER TO APHRODISIAS: Nicomedes has been seen as the author by J. Reynolds, *Aphrodisias and Rome* (London 1982; Society for the Promotion of Roman Studies, *JRS* Monograph 1) no. 4, with suggestions by K.J. Rigsby in *Phoenix* 38 (1984) 103. This has, however, been questioned by G.W. Bowersock in *Gnomon* 56 (1984) 48-53, esp. 51. In *EMC* n.s. 4 (1985) 309-317, C.P. Jones, after examination of the stone, regards only two letters of 'Nicomedes' as legible, rather than the four that Reynolds did. Though name plus title of King Nicomedes 'fits the traces in line 1' (page 316), the two letters could also fit a Roman official. From its position on the 'Archive Wall' the letter is obviously important, but unfortunately we still do not know its author. THIRD MITHRADATIC WAR: B.C. McGing, 'The Date of the Outbreak of the Third Mithridatic War': *Phoenix* 38 (1984) 12-18. DATE OF HIS DEATH: G. Perl, *Zur Chronologie* 306 f. and 330; W. Bennett in *Historia* 10 (1961) 459-472, esp. 463. Contra: Magie 1200 f. note 49 and 1204 note 5. Coins of Nicomedes to 'year 224' of the Bithynian era show him still alive in October 74, if that era began in 297, as the Pontic and Bosporan eras did. Eutropius 6.6.1 puts his death in the consulships of Lucullus and Cotta (74 BC).

18 Sall. *Hist.* 4.69.9 (Maurenbr.): *Bithyniam Nicomede mortuo diripuere, cum filius Nysa, quam reginam appellaverat, genitus haud dubie esset.* An apparent descendant of the Bithynian royal house through the marriage of Nicomedes III and the Cappadocian Nysa still existed in Caesar's day, which further supports the contention that scions of the house were available in 74: *BAlex.* 66.5, *Id [Comana] homini nobilissimo Lycomedi Bithyno adiudicavit, qui regio Cappadocum genere ortus iure minime dubio, vetustate tamen propter adversam fortunam maiorum suorum mutationemque generis intermisso sacerdotium id repetebat.* The interruption of dynastic descent here would be the eclipse of the Ariarathids by the dynasty of Ariobarzanes (§ 17). Testimony of Appian (*Mith.* 7.23) that it was not Nicomedes Philopator but his *grandson* who left the kingdom to Rome does at least reflect conviction at the time that a claimant existed. Another passage, from Sallust (*Hist.* 2.71), demonstrates the existence of a son, whom the pro-Roman faction had to denounce as illegitimate and the royalists (the *quos* here) resolved to support, presumably in Rome: *Quos adversum multi ex Bithynia volentes accurrere falsum filium arguituri.* The possible interregnum, with Ariobar-

zanes I as custodian, presumably reflects the delay in sorting out claims and counter-claims (see next note). Magie's dismay (1201 note 50) at the possibility of a Roman manoeuvre of some sort underlying this 'bequest' rests on fundamental convictions regarding ancient methods that bear examination elsewhere, though in any case ones our sources will hardly support. A suggestion sometimes made is that such clauses in royal wills would, *if known in advance*, help prevent assassination: e.g., *JRS* 67 (1977) 67. See too Braund, *Friendly King* 129-164. Outright invention remains to be considered as well. CAESAR DEFENDS NYSA: Suet. *Div. Iul.* 49.5. MITHRADATES TO BITHYNIA: App. *Mith.* 71.300. Magie, 1201 note 50, argues unconvincingly against the view that this was to install the claimant.

19 SENATE ACCEPTS: Magie 320 with 1201 f. note 51. ARIOBARZANES AS CARETAKER: Scholiasta Gronovianus to Cicero, ed. Stangl (Hildesheim 1964) p. 316: *Bithynia antea a Nicomede rege tenebatur. Iste mortuus est intestatus: pervenit ergo eius regnum ad populum Romanum. Misit ergo populus Romanus ad regnum illud tenendum Ariobarzanen.* See also Cic. *De Leg. Agr.* 2.15.40: *regnum Bithyniae, quod certe publicum est populi Romani factum*; Magie 1201 note 49. Some delay in full Roman assumption of Bithynia might also be inferred from the many coins issued in towns there during the proconsulate of C. Papirius Carbo (61-59 BC) but apparently not by his predecessors; published in *Recueil* I and I² and listed by Magie 1254 note 68. See too Broughton, *Magistrates* II, 181 and 191.

20 BLACK SEA: Polyb. 31.25.5. The treaty is *IOSPE* I² 402. See too Sherk, *Greek East* no. 30. SITE OF THE KINGDOM: *TAVO* B V 6; Magie 177 ff.; Jones, *Cities*² Ch. 6. MITHRADATES: Still fundamental is T. Reinach, *Mithridate Eupator, Roi de Pont* (Paris 1890), with a valuable appendix on sources, 417-455. See also Magie, *Roman Rule* as cited below; T. Liebmann-Frankfort (above, note 11) Part II, and especially the studies of Eckart Olshausen: 'Mithradates VI. und Rom': *ANRW* I (1972) 806-815; 'Pontos': *RE Suppl.* 15 (1978) 396-442; and on the later period, 'Pontos und Rom (63 v. Chr. - 64 n. Chr.)': *ANRW* II 7.2 (1980) 903-912. Still useful is A. von Gutschmid, *Untersuchungen über die Geschichte des pontischen Reichs* (Leipzig 1892). Mithradates in Athens: M. Thompson, *The New Style Silver Coinage of Athens* (*American Numismatic Society, Numismatic Studies* 10, 1961); Chr. Habicht, 'Zur Geschichte Athens in der Zeit Mithradates VI': *Chiron* 6 (1976) 127-142; E. Badian, 'Rome, Athens, and Mithridates': *Trav. VI*ᵉ *Congr. internat. d'études class.* (Paris 1976) 501-521 and in *AJAH* 1 (1976) 105-128; H.B. Mattingly, 'Some Third Magistrates in the Athenian New Style Silver Coinage': *JHS* 91 (1971) 85-93; D.M. Lewis, 'The Chronology of the Athenian New Style Coinage': *NC* (ser. 7) 2 (1962) 275-300. Cf. the Giresun hoard published by F. Kleiner in *ANSMusN* 19

(1974). On the dynasty see also R. Sullivan, 'Dynasts in Pontus': *ANRW* II 7.2 (1980). CHRONOLOGY: G. Perl, *Zur Chronologie der Königreiche Bithynia, Pontos, und Bosporus* (Amsterdam 1968) 299 ff. COINAGE: *Recueil* I² (1925) 12-20; Head *HN*² 501 f.; *BMC Pontus* 43-45; T. Reinach, *L'histoire par les monnaies* (Paris 1902); individual studies as cited below. CAUCASUS: Memnon, *FGrH* 434, F 22.3(30). DYNASTIC INTERMARRIAGE: J. Seibert, *Historische Beiträge zu den dynastischen Verbindungen in hellenistischer Zeit* (*Historia Einzelschriften* nr. 10; 1967) 120-134. THE DYNASTY: Polyb. 5.43.2; Strabo 10.4.10.477; Justin 37.1.5; App. *Mith.* 112.549; Memnon, *FGrH* 434, F 22.2(30); *OGIS* 368 with notes. Further: Reinach, *Mithridate Eupator* 55; Magie 1091 note 50. PARTHIAN ALLIANCE: Memnon 22.4(30); App. *Mith.* 15.54.

21 PHRYGIA MAIOR: See above, note 10. See also *OGIS* 436 = *IGRR* IV 752 = Sherk, *Roman Documents* no. 13. Phrygia free: App. *Mith.* 57.231. Resentment of Mithradates: Justin 38.5.3.; App. *Mith.* 12.39 and 15.50-51. See, in general, Liebmann-Frankfort 154-160 and Magie 169 ff. with 1058 notes 36-37. INCREASINGLY HELLENIZED: E. Olshausen, 'Zum Hellenisierungsprozess am pontischen Königshof': *Ancient Society* 5 (1974) 153-170. ARMENIA MINOR: Strabo 12.3.28.555; cf. 12.3.1.541 and 12.3.13.547, with Magie 1237 note 41; Eutropius 5.5.1; Justin 38.7.2. COLCHIS: See below, note 30. TIGRANES: App. *Mith.* 15.54; Justin 38.3.2; Plut. *Luc.* 14; Memnon, *FGrH* 434, F 29.6(43); cf. 22.4(30). Magie, 1099 note 16, dates the marriage to 93 BC, but the precise date is difficult to recover since the accession date of Tigranes is too. See also comments by E. Badian, *Studies* (above, note 6) 176 note 49. See too below, Ch. 5, § 11.

22 PAPHLAGONIA: See above, note 11. See too Magie 196 f. with 1093 note 56; *RE Suppl.* 15 (1978) col. 423.

23 CAPPADOCIA: See this chapter, § 5. Bibliography: *RE Suppl.* 15 (1978) cols. 422 ff. STANDING TREATY: This was by now over half a century old. See J. Briscoe, 'Eastern Policy and Senatorial Politics, 168-146 B.C.': *Historia* 18 (1969) 49 ff. See too Polyb. 3.5.2; 21.2(12).13; 22.1(5).1 f.; Diod. 31.28. GORDIUS: *RE* 7 (1912) 1592; Livy *Per.* 70; Plut. *Sulla* 5.6 f.; Justin 38.2.3-5. The suggestion sometimes made that Gordius himself may have aspired to kingship rests on his position as a Cappadocian noble and regent during a time of uncertain transition. But Mithradates clearly preferred to install his own son, and the Cappadocians preferred first the Ariarathids and then the house of Ariobarzanes.

24 PONTIC FACTION: R. Sullivan, 'The Dynasty of Cappadocia': *ANRW* II 7.2 (1980) sections II-IV. END OF THE ARIARATHIDS: See this chapter, § 5. COINAGE: See this chapter, § 5. Narrative for the period in Magie 202 ff. The ejection of Ariarathes VIII by Mithradates might have been an especial

affront to Rome, for he had been receiving his education in the Roman province of Asia, probably being groomed there for power; the nobles *ipsum Ariarathen nomine, ab Asia, ubi educabatur, revocant* (Justin 38.2.1).

25 EMBASSY TO ROME: Justin 38.2.1-5. Mithradates argued that his son sprang from the true Ariarathid line and even claimed to have inherited Cappadocia himself. See Florus 1.40; App. *Mith.* 12.39. App. *Mith.* 9.27-29 has the two dynasties originally joined. In *SIG*³, no. 742, Mithradates is termed 'King of Cappadocia.' For the rest, see § 5 and W.V. Harris, *War and Imperialism in Republican Rome, 327-70 B.C.* (Oxford 1979) 252 and 273.

26 THE VISIT OF MARIUS: Plut. *Mar.* 31.5. See A.N. Sherwin-White in *JRS* 67 (1977) 74 and note 87; *Roman Foreign Policy* 108-109; T.J. Luce, 'Marius and the Mithradatic Command': *Historia* 19 (1970) 161-194, but also M. Hassall et al. in *JRS* 64 (1974) 218 note 29. Sherk, *Greek East* no. 47 C with note 4 summarizes the controversy over the statue. Cf. *ILLRP* 343; *CIL* I² 845. SULLA: E. Badian, 'Sulla's Cilician Command': *Athenaeum* 37 (1959) 299-303 = his *Studies* (1964) 157-178; A.N. Sherwin-White, 'Ariobarzanes, Mithradates, and Sulla': *CQ* 71 = n.s. 27 (1977) 173-183; R. Sullivan, 'The Dynasty of Cappadocia': *ANRW* II 7.2 (1980) notes 19 and 27.

27 WITHDRAWAL: Justin 38.2.3-7; cf. 38.5.6. See also this chapter, §§ 2 and 5. Mithradates and most Easterners probably assumed they had relatively little to fear from Rome so far: Sherwin-White in *JRS* 67 (1977) 72 ff.

28 COINAGE OF ARIARATHES IX: See this chapter, § 5. Portraits widely ascribed to him may rather belong to Eupator: O. Neverov, *TE* 13 (1972) 110-118. INCEPTION OF FIRST MITHRADATIC WAR: This revision of the chronology that had been accepted since Reinach (*Mithridate Eupator* 121-123) transfers the destruction by Mithradates of forces levied by L. Cassius Longinus and Q. Oppius from the spring of 88 BC back to the campaigning season of 89, and the mobilizations back to 90 instead of the spring of 89 (Reinach 116 ff.). The suggestion is by A.N. Sherwin-White in *JRS* 67 (1977) 74 with note 86. Cf. App. *Mith.* 58.235. See too D. Glew, 'The Selling of the King: A Note on Mithridates Eupator's Propaganda in 88 B.C.': *Hermes* 105 (1977) 253-256; P. Desideri, 'Posidonio e la guerra Mitridatica': *Athenaeum* n.s. 61 (1973) 3-29; 237-269.

29 RELATIVES: Only a portion of this vast circle can be dealt with here. For a stemma of the major offspring of Mithradates, see *RE Suppl.* 15 (1978) 399-400 (Olshausen, 'Pontos'). Stemmata showing the interrelationships of the Pontic and other dynastic houses appear with the articles by R. Sullivan in *ANRW* II 8 (1977) at pp. 200, 300, 742, 912, 938, and in *ANRW* II 7.1 and 7.2. A prosopography of the major officers of Mithradates occupies pp. 166-170 of Olshausen's article cited in note 21 above. See also Seibert, *Zu den dynastischen Verbindungen* (above, note 20) 120 ff. BETROTHALS TO

PTOLEMIES: See Ch. 4, § 10, note 12. DAUGHTERS IN 'SCYTHIA': Seibert, *ibid.*; App. *Mith.* 111.536; 102.474; 108.516.

30 SATRAPAL CONTROL: E.g., App. *BCiv.* 12.4.22; 12.9.62. See too *SIG*[3] 741 = C.B. Welles, *Royal Correspondence* nos. 73 f. = Sherk, *Greek East* no. 60. ARIARATHES IX: 'Year 15' is 87 BC in the classification of B. Simonetta in *NC* (Ser. 7) 1 (1961) 40, nos. 10-11, but he begins the reign of Ariarathes in 101. See this chapter, § 5. MACHARES AND THE SCYTHIANS: App. *Mith.* 15.53; 67.281; 69.292 f.; Justin 38.3.6 f.; Magie 322, 333-335, 342, 356, 363; *RE* 14 (1928) 153. ARCATHIAS: *RE* 2 (1895) 1161; Magie 1104-1105 note 41. ARCHELAUS: *RE* 2 (1895) 450 nr. 13; Sall. *Hist.* 4.69.12; Livy *Per.* 82; App. *Mith.* 41.156-50.199 frequently; so in Plut. *Sulla.* On the descendants of this man, see Sullivan, 'Cappadocia' in *ANRW* II 7.2, notes 139 f. with *P. Grenf* II, 38. See also Ch. 4, § 10; A. Samuel, *Ptol. Chron.* 156; M. Pani, *Roma e i re d'oriente* (1972) 93 ff.; Strabo 12.3.34.558 and 17.1.11.796. OTHER OFFSPRING: *RE Suppl.* 15 (1978) 400. Possible: A. Degrassi in *BCAR* 74 (1951-1952; appeared 1954) 27 no. 8; Magie 1090 note 48. PHILOPOEMEN: App. *Mith.* 48.187. DORYLAUS: Strabo 10.4.10.477-478 and 12.3.33.557. COLCHIS: App. *Mith.* 64.266; G.F. Dunda and G.A. Lordkipanidze, 'Hellenistic Coins from the Site of Vani, in Colchis (Western Georgia)': *NC* (ser. 7) 19 (1979) 1-5; D.B. Selov, 'Colchis and the Pontic Empire of Mithridates VI': *VDI* 153 (1980) 28-43 (in Russian, with summary in English).

31 CONTINGENTS: App. *Mith.* 13.44; 15.53 f.; 17.59; Justin 38.3.6-7. DEFECTORS: See note 30. CHAEREMON: *SIG*[3] 741.

32 COMMON ENEMY: App. *Mith.* 24.91; Welles, *Royal Correspondence* no. 73; *SIG*[3] 741. ARCHON: C. Habicht, *Chiron* 6 (1976) 127 ff. APHRODISIAS, NYSA, EPHESUS: Sherk, *Greek East* nos. 59a-61; 63; J. Reynolds, *Aphrodisias and Rome* (London 1982) Documents 2-3; App. *Mith.* 61.250-62.260; *SIG*[3] 742 with *AJP* 60 (1939) 468 f. Sulla at Ephesus rewarded loyal states: App. *BCiv.* 12.9.61 f. He praises Stratoniceia in *OGIS* 441. Initial support for Mithradates came from a number of cities; App. *BCiv.* 12.4.22-23. 'KING OF KINGS': See Ch. 5, § 13, note 44. PHARNACES II: See Ch. 6, § 15. DYNAMIS: See Ch. 6, § 15, note 50.

33 AWE: Cic. *Pro Flacco* 25.60; O. Neverov, 'Mithridates as Dionysus': *SGE* 37 (1973) 41-45 and 85 (Russian and English). The gem showing him as Dionysus is perhaps from Pergamon, 80 BC. SENATORIAL PRONOUNCEMENTS: Justin 38.2.3-7; Strabo 12.2.11.540. By 'freedom' in Cappadocia Romans may have meant *autonomia* for the cities, which were not numerous there. COMMISSION UNDER AQUILLIUS: Justin 38.3.4; cf. 38.5.8. See also Livy *Per.* 74; App. *Mith.* 11.33-36; Magie 1100 note 22; E.W. Gray (above, note 10). INCOGNITO: Justin 37.3.4-5.

34 ALLIES: App. *Mith.* 11.35; 13.44; 15.53-54; 17.59; 19.74; 20.78-79. See too J. Reynolds, *Aphrodisias and Rome* (London 1982) nos. 2-3, pp. 16-20; Sherk, *Greek East* no. 59 a-b. DAMAGES: App. *Mith.* 11.33-36; Magie 208. AQUILLIUS: App. *Mith.* 12.38; 21.80. Not only party strife, but eagerness for booty and reputation lay behind Roman interest in Asia at this time. See Luce (above, note 26) 187. App. *BCiv.* 1.7.54-57: Sulla's troops eagerly foresaw loot. Vell. Pat. 2.18.6 also stresses the element of party strife behind commands for the East now.

35 FIELD-COMMANDERS: Narrative in Magie 222 ff. TREATY: App. *Mith.* 64.269; 67.282-283; 66.279; 65.272. See too D. Glew, 'Between the Wars: Mithridates Eupator and Rome, 85-73 B.C.': *Chiron* 11 (1981) 109-130; A. Keaveney, 'Studies in the *Dominatio Sullae*': *Klio* 65 (1983) 185-208; L. Raditsa, *Helikon* 9/10 (1969/1970) 632-635; A.W. Lintott, 'Mithridatica': *Historia* 25 (1976) 489-491.

36 SECOND WAR: App. *Mith.* 66.281; cf. 64.265-66.279. See too Plut. *Sulla* 16 f.; Livy *Per.* 86; Memnon, *FGrH* 434, F 36 (54). L. LICINIUS MURENA: *SIG*³ 745 = *ILS* 8772; *IG* 5.1.1454; *L'ann. ép.* 1974, no. 631.

37 THIRD WAR: Magie 292 ff.; B.C. McGing, *Phoenix* 38 (1984) 12-18; J. van Ooteghem, *L. Licinius Lucullus* (Brussels 1959) 55 ff.; Memnon 27(37)-29(43), with Magie 1206 note 9; Plut. *Luc.* 14.1; App. *Mith.* 78.342-343; 79.353-355. MYSIA: *OGIS* 445. Roman naval engagements: Sherk, *Greek East* no. 71. TIGRANES: Memnon 29.6 (43); App. *Mith.* 78.343 f. SINATRUCES: Memnon, *ibid.* PHOENIX: App. *Mith.* 79.349-350. OTHERS: Strabo 10.4.10.477-478 and 12.3.33.557; Reinach, *Mithridate Eupator* Book V, Ch. 2, pp. 318 ff.

38 PULCHER: E. Rawson in *Historia* 22 (1973) 219-239. FLIGHT TO TIGRANES AND HIS INVOLVEMENT: Livy *Per.* 97-98; Plut. *Luc.* 19-24; App. *Mith.* 82.368-83.375; Memnon 36.6 (54); Magie 1213 f. notes 34 and 38; Reinach, *Mithridate Eupator*, Ch. 3. TERMESSUS: *ILS* 38, proposed by Gaius Antonius, brother of Creticus, Antony's father. See too Magie 295 with 1176 f. note 34, and 1102 note 30; Sherk, *Greek East* no. 72.

39 THE LAST YEARS: See Ch. 6, § 15. Narrative in Magie 343-50. Some material on the letter of Mithradates: E. Bikerman in *REL* 24 (1946) 131-151 and L.F. Raditsa in *Helicon* 9/10 (1969/1970) 632 f. and 689 ff. See too E. Olshausen in *ANRW* II 7.2, p. 904, note 3. See as well Ch. 5, § 13, note 45; Ch. 6, § 15, note 23; Ch. 9, § 26, note 77. By 67 BC Cicero says of Cappadocia: *regnum Ariobarzanis ... totum est in hostium potestate* (*De Imp. Cn. Pomp.* = *Pro Lege Manilia* 2.5). Only by 63 was Mithradates no longer a threat: Dio 37.10.4. See É. Will, *Histoire politique* 411-423.

40 GALATIA: *TAVO* B V 6; *RE* 7 (1910) 520-559 (Brandis); Hoben Ch. III; Jones, *Cities*² Ch. 4; Th. Reinach in *RN* (sér. 3) 9 (1891) 20-41; Strabo

12.566 f. Others as below. GALATIAN INSCRIPTIONS AND HISTORY: E. Bosch, *Quellen zur Geschichte der Stadt Ankara im Alterum* (Ankara 1967). PHRYGIANS: E. Bosch, 'Ankara I: Die Phylen' in *Jahrbuch für kleinasiatische Forschung* 3 (1955) 57-74, esp. 62. TETRARCHS AND TRIBES: Magie 373 and 1235 ff. notes 40-42. A leisurely but useful discussion of the system by A. Zwintscher, *De Galatarum Tetrarchis et Amynta Rege Quaestiones* (Leipzig 1892) devotes pp. 5-11 to the period down to Pompey. For the period of the Mithradatic Wars, see especially F. Stähelin, *Geschichte der kleinasiatischen Galater*, 2nd ed. (Leipzig 1907) Ch. VII. TERRITORIES AFTER ATTALUS: Stähelin 85 f.; Justin 37.1.2. LONG-STANDING ALLIANCE: Romans saw early on that Galatians could be useful against the Attalids, and attempted as early as 166 to guarantee their independence: Polyb. 30.19(20).12; 31.2(28); 31.6(30).6.

41 PHRYGIA MAIOR: See above, notes 10 and 21. See too Magie 194 f.; Stähelin 86; Justin 38.5.3; App. *Mith.* 11.35; 12.39; 56.228; 57.231-232. PAPHLAGONIA: See this chapter, above, § 3. See too Magie 1093 note 57. The country had been ruled until now by two princes, both expelled by Mithradates, restored by the Romans, and then succeeded by the Galatian Castor: Magie 1234 f. note 37. The region had had its own dynasts since c. 180 BC: Polyb. 25.2.9. GALATIA INVADED: Justin 37.4.6 and Strabo 12.5.2.567. MITHRADATION: Justin 37.4.6 and Strabo 12.5.2.567. It later passed to Brogitarus, son of Deiotarus II of Galatia. See Ch. 6, § 16. On the fortress and its location see Calder-Bean, co-ordinates Jd, and W.M. Ramsay, *Social Basis* 93. GALATIAN TROOPS: App. *Mith.* 41.158; Justin 38.4.9. ASSISTING ROME: App. *Mith.* 11.35 and 17.59. The latter passage speaks of them as 'the Galatians in Asia,' perhaps to distinguish them from those nearer Pontus who co-operated with Mithradates. Later: Plut. *Luc.* 28.2; Memnon 30.1 (44).

42 MASSACRE: App. *Mith.* 46.178-179; 54.218; 58.236; Plut. *De mul. vir.* 23 (259 A-D). FAILURE OF MITHRADATES: App. *Mith.* 46.179; 55.223 with 58.240. GALATIAN ALLIES: Memnon 30.1 (44) and Plut. *Luc.* 28.2 show organized followers of Mithradates. See too App. *Mith.* 41.158. Occurrence of Celtic names among his followers – e.g., Connacorix in Memnon 29.4 (42) and 34.4 (49) – cannot support deductions as to the sentiments of the populace.

43 TOLISTOBOGII: See, for instance, *SIG*[3] 591, in which a letter 'useful' to the people of Lampsacus goes to the 'people of the Galatian Tolistoagioi' about 195 BC. On the three tribes: See Ch. 6, § 16, note 63. Pessinus dealt separately with the Attalid king about 159 BC: *OGIS* 315. See too Sherk, *Greek East* no. 29. Strabo 12.5.3.567 notes that the Attalids constructed the precinct here. See also below, Ch. 6, § 16, note 78. DEIOTARUS: Cic. *Phil.* 11.33; *Pro*

Rege Deiot. 26 f. and 37; Dio 47.24.3; Strabo 12.3.13.547; Livy *Per.* 94; App. *Mith.* 75.326; Orosius 6.2.18. GALATIAN AUXILIARIES: Plut. *Luc.* 14.1 and 28.2; Memnon *FGrH* 434, F 30 (44); Magie 1176 note 33. For an 'appreciation' of his role in the affairs of Galatia see G. Rohde, *Studien und Interpretationen* (Berlin 1963) 236 f.

44 THE SITE: Jones, *Cities*² Ch. 7; Magie 491 ff.; *ESAR* IV, 620 ff.; Gwatkin, *passim*; Ramsay, *Historical Geography* Part II, Ch. M, N, O. THE CAPPADOCIAN DYNASTY: R. Sullivan, 'The Dynasty of Cappadocia': *ANRW* II 7.2 (Berlin 1980) 1125-1168; W. Hoben, *Untersuchungen zur Stellung kleinasiatischer Dynasten in den Machtkämpfen der ausgehenden römischen Republik* (Mainz 1969) Ch. IV; M. Pani, *Roma e i re d'oriente da Augusto a Tiberio* (Bari 1972) Ch. III-V. GEOGRAPHY AND RESOURCES: T. Frank et al., *An Economic Survey of Ancient Rome* (Baltimore 1933-1940) Vol. IV; Jones, *Cities*² Ch. 7; W. Gwatkin, *Cappadocia as a Roman Procuratorial Province* (Princeton 1930 = *Univ. of Missouri Studies* no. 4) Ch. 2. ROYAL COINAGE: B. Simonetta, *The Coins of the Cappadocian Kings* (Fribourg 1977); T. Reinach, *Essai sur la numismatique des rois de Cappadoce* (Paris 1887) = *RN* (sér. 3) 4 (1886) 301-355 and 452-483 = *Trois royaumes de l'Asie Mineure: Cappadocia, Bithynia, Pontus* (Paris 1888) 1-87; B. Simonetta in *NC* (Ser. 7) 1 (1961) 9-50; 4 (1964) 83-92; 7 (1967) 7-12. See too O. Mørkholm, *NC* (ser. 7) 2 (1962) 407-411; 4 (1964) 21-25; 9 (1969) 21-31; C.M. Kraay and G.K. Jenkins, *Essays ... Robinson* (Oxford 1968) 241-258; Head *HN*² 751; *BMC Galatia, etc.*, 39 ff. MEETING ON THE EUPHRATES: Strabo 12.2.1.535.

45 MACHINATIONS OF MITHRADATES: Magie 203-204; Sullivan (above, note 44) § 1. See also above, notes 12, 15, 23-25. See too Reinach, *L'histoire par les monnaies* 172 and *BCH* 7 (1883) 347, no. 7; *OGIS* 353; G. Daux in *BCH* 57 (1933) 81-82; A.N. Sherwin-White in *CQ* 71 (1977) 180 and *Roman Foreign Policy* 105-107. *REGIBUS*: Justin 38.1.5-8; F. Durrbach, *Inscriptions de Delos* (Paris 1937) 1576 with 1902.

46 LAST ARIARATHIDS: Justin 38.2.1-4. ARIARATHES VI: He also dealt with cities and individuals far to the west. For example, he receives honours in connection with a sanctuary at Rhodes: *SEG* 33 (1983) no. 642. ARIARATHES IX: Justin 38.2.5. His claim rested also on the victory of Mithradates in Cappadocia, *quam iure gentium victor occupaverat*: Justin 38.5.6. FIFTEEN YEARS' REIGN: Simonetta (above, note 44, 1961) 41 nos. 10-11. ARIARATHES VIII: Justin 38.2.1-2; Simonetta, (above, note 44, 1961) 18. But see Mørkholm (above, note 44, 1968) 252 f. See too Plut. *Marius* 31-32; Cic. *ad Brut.* 1.5.3; App. *Mith.* 57.233; Plut. *Sulla* 5.3; T. Luce, *Historia* 19 (1970) 161-194, with *JRS* 64 (1974) 218 note 29; A.N. Sherwin-White in *JRS* 67 (1977) 62-75.

47 THIRD SON: Justin 38.2.3. RECOURSE TO ROME: Justin 38.2.4 ff. 'FREEDOM': Justin 38.2.7; Strabo 12.2.11.540. SELEUCID PRINCES: See Ch. 7, § 21. ROME AND CAPPADOCIA PREVIOUS ALLIES: Diod. 31.28; Polyb. 21.41 (43).4 f. and 45 (47); Livy 38.37.5 f. and 39.6; 42.29; Briscoe (above, note 23) 56-57. PRIENE SIEGE: *OGIS* 351; Sherk, *Greek East* no. 32.

48 PREVIOUS MARRIAGES: Seibert, *Zu den dynastischen Verbindungen* (above, note 20) Ch. IX, 112 ff. ARCHELAUS AND BERENICE IV: See above, note 30. SELECTION OF ARIOBARZANES: Justin 38.2.6-8; Strabo 12.2.11.540. NOBLES AND COMANA: Strabo 12.2.3.535 and 12.2.5-6.537; App. *Mith.* 114.560 (Pontus); *Bell. Alex.* 66; Sullivan (above, note 44) sections V-VI. *STRATEGIAI*: Strabo 12.1.2-4.534; cf. 12.1.2.533; Ptol. *Geog.* 5.6; *OGIS* 364. In Appian's day (*Mith.* 105.495) *strategeitai* can still be used to describe the administration of Gordyene and Sophene as parts of Cappadocia (§ 12). For an eleventh *strategia* see Jones, *Cities*² 177.

49 ETHNOS: Strabo 12.2.11.540. Polyb. 31.3 (cf. 8) mentions the earlier arrangements of Ariarathes V and Rome. On early treaties between Rome and the Greek East, see A.N. Sherwin-White, *Roman Foreign Policy in the East* (London 1984) Ch. 3. CITIES: Strabo 12.2.7.537-538: only two *strategiai* have cities, which are Tyana and Mazaca. He does use the term *polis* for Comana as well (12.2.3.535), but regards its Cataonian inhabitants as devoted to the cult and not as constituents of a *polis* in the usual sense. *Polismata*: Strabo 12.2.7.537. Cf. the village in Ptol. *Geog.* 5.6.13. FORTRESSES: Strabo 12.2.9.539; Jones, *Cities*² 177 ff.; Gwatkin (above, note 44) 18 ff.; Magie 1352 ff. NOBLES: Diod. 31.21; Cic. *Fam.* 15.2.4-7 and 15.4.6; *Att.* 6.1.3; Tac. *Ann.* 2.56.4.

50 DATE OF SULLA'S INTERVENTION: Proposals now range from 97/96 to 92/91 BC for this. See E. Badian, *Athenaeum* 37 (1959) 279-303 = *Studies in Greek and Roman History* (Oxford 1964) 157-178; T. Luce, *Historia* 19 (1970) 161-194; Liebmann-Frankfort 166-171; A.N. Sherwin-White, *CQ* n.s. 27 (1977) 173-183; R. Sullivan, 'Cappadocia' 1129 ff., with note 27; A. Keaveney, *LEC* 48 (1980) 149-157 and *AJP* 102 (1981) 195 f. note 3; G.V. Sumner, *Athenaeum* 56 (1978) 395 f. MIXTURE: Strabo 12.2.9.539. ARIARATHEIA: It lay east of Mazaca-Caesareia: Calder-Bean, co-ordinates Ke; Jones, *Cities*² 180 ff. and Map II. Sisines may or may not have been the later Archelaus: Sullivan (above, note 44) section V, end, with note 124. He held Nora (Calder-Bean, co-ordinates Ie) and Cadena: Strabo 12.2.6.537. Archelaus preferred possessions even farther west, and spent most of his time in Elaeussa (Strabo 12.2.7.537). The 'Ariarathes the king' of Strabo 12.2.8.538-539, who held Mazaca, is in context Ariarathes X, since his dispute locally is decided by the Romans – a far more probable circumstance for about 40 BC than for 97 BC, when the last Ariarathid except the son of Mithradates

(Ariarathes IX) had ruled. So the successors of Ariobarzanes I, including Ariarathes X, held the former Ariarathid seats, and the family may have arisen there. See further Gwatkin (above, note 44) 20-21 on Archelaus. Gwatkin does not realize here the comparative antiquity of Ariaratheia, on which see Jones, *Cities*[2] 180 with 430 f. note 1 and 431 note 12.

51 MITHRADATES KTISTES AND ARIOBARZANES: Plut. *Demetr.* 4.1-4; *RE* 2 (1896) 2860 and *Suppl.* 1 (1903) 129 f. no. 4a; Magie 189 and 1087 note 37; Strabo 12.1.4.534; *RE Suppl.* 15 (1978) 399; *RE* 15 (1932) 2157 no. 1.

52 PONTIC FACTION: For example, Plut. *Sulla* 5.3, with Sullivan (above, note 44) section II and note 28. MARRIAGE: App. *Mith.* 66.279 f. If Ariobarzanes married the young daughter of Mithradates in 81, then it was after the death of Athenais Philostorgos I, the known mother of Ariobarzanes II, who was himself old enough for the succession about 63. Athenais might have derived from the Pontic house and caused the version of Appian. INSCRIPTIONS: *OGIS* 354-356 = *IG* II/III[2] 3426-3428; Sherk, *Greek East* no. 47 H. See below, Ch. 6, § 16, note 46 and Ch. 6, § 17, note 108.

53 *PHILOROMAIOS*: Bibliography in Hoben (above, note 44) 146 f. with note 40. On the title in the East, see Sullivan (above, note 44) section II, note 22. See too *OGIS* 354-355; cf. 356, Ariobarzanes III. See also Simonetta (above, note 44, 1961) 41-44 with Plate IV, nos. 31-32. HOSTILITY: For example, Dio 36. 9.2. FLIGHT TO ROME: Justin 38.3.3; App. *Mith.* 10.31. EXPULSIONS: Hoben 148 note 46. See Ch. 5, § 11. The dating of these is hard to reconstruct; some even see a sixth exile (e.g., Simonetta, [above, note 44, 1961] 18). Presumably everyone but Ariobarzanes lost count. One 'restoration' is noted in an apparent context of 85 BC: *CIG* 6855 d, III, with the comments of T. Reinach, *Mithridate Eupator* (Paris 1890) 471. OPPOSITION TO ARIOBARZANES: Plut. *Sulla* 5.3; *Luc.* 14.6. The agent Gordius was a Cappadocian noble whom Mithradates wished *restituere in patriam*: Justin 38.1.6. So perhaps were Mithroas and Bagoas of App. *Mith.* 10.33. *SEGNIS*: Justin 38.3.2. ARIOBARZANES III: See Ch. 6, § 17.

54 HATRED: Dio 36.9.2-5.

55 COINAGE: Simonetta (above, note 44, 1961) 19 and 41-44; Reinach, *Trois Royaumes* 59 f. TROUBLE AFTER SULLA: App. *Mith.* 66.279 f. with 67.283 f.; 91.414; Plut. *Luc.* 35.5; Strabo 12.2.9.539; Dio 36.17.1. Ariobarzanes's possible tenure of Bithynia: See note 19. DEPREDATIONS: Cic. *De Imp. Cn. Pomp.* (*Pro Lege Manilia*) 2.5. BREATHE FREELY IN 63: Dio 37.10.4. But earlier that year Cicero could still stress Mithradates's determination: *Leg. Agr.* 2.19.52. HAPPY: Val. Max. 5.7, Ext. 2, *laetus erat qui regnum deponebat, tristis cui dabatur.*

56 TOMISA: Strabo 12.2.1.535. SOPHENE: App. *Mith*, 105.495 with Sullivan (above, note 44) section II and note 46. A.N. Sherwin-White, *Roman Foreign*

Policy 226 with notes 102 and 105, doubts the testimony of Appian on the grounds that Cicero implies in 51 that the eastern boundary of Cappadocia now lay on the Euphrates. Two objections: this does not disprove Appian's account of conditions over a decade earlier, and the presence of a large Parthian force on the Euphrates demonstrates nothing about previous Cappadocian claims in Sophene, which it would not under the weakened Ariobarzanes III be able to hold against Parthian incursions. LANDS IN THE WEST: App. *Mith.* 105.496; Val. Max. (above, note 55).

Chapter 3

1 COMMAGENE: Strabo 16.2.3.749; Tac. *Hist.* 2.81; Jos. *BJ* 5.461; K. Roesch, 'Kommagene – das Land "ubi ferrum nascitur"': *Antike Welt* 6 (1975) 15-17; 86. On its earlier history, see the bibliography in R. Sullivan, 'The Dynasty of Commagene': *ANRW* II 8 (Berlin 1977) 732-798, esp. sections I-III. ITS ERA: H. Seyrig, 'Sur quelques ères Syriennes, 1. L'ère des rois de Commagène': *RN* (sér. 6) 6 (1964) 51-56. ORONTID DYNASTY: C. Toumanoff, *Manuel* 403 ff. Also, his *Studies in Christian Caucasian History* (Washington 1963) 277 ff.; Jones, *Cities*[2] 242 and 451 note 22. SYNCRETISM: This went back at least to Mithradates, for Antiochus says that his father founded the *Hierothesion* at Arsameia: F.K. Dörner and T. Goell, *Arsameia am Nymphaios: die Ausgrabungen im Hierothesion des Mithradates Kallinikos von 1953 bis 1956* (Berlin 1963; Istanbuler Forschungen 23) esp. p. 41. On the excavations of 1962 to 1967, see W. Hoepfner, *Arsameia am Nymphaios II* (Berlin 1983; Ist. Forsch. 33). Dörner points out the early emphasis on Mithra by his namesake Mithradates in *AI* 17 (1978) 125-133. See Ch. 7, § 19, note 5. On the cults, see H. Waldmann, *Die kommagenischen Kultreformen unter König Mithradates I. Kallinikos und seinem Sohne Antiochus I.* (Leiden 1973). But the greater impetus for this work came from Antiochus. See esp. J. Wagner and G. Petzl, 'Eine neue Temenos-Stele des Königs Antiochus I. von Kommagene': *ZPE* 20 (1976) 201-223. See too *SEG* 26 (1976/1977) no. 1490. As the stele discovered by Dr Wagner at Sofraz Köy makes clear, Antiochus could also honour Greek gods without reference to their Iranian equivalents (though without further evidence this cannot merely be assumed to constitute a preliminary stage in his own religious thinking): *AW* 6 (1975) 51-59.

2 LAODICE: Her full titulature includes Thea and Philadelphos. Antiochus I mentions her frequently in his inscriptions; *IGLSyr* nos. 1, 3, 5, 8, 14-18, 22, 26-28, 31-35, 46-47, 52. SULLA'S MEETING: Plut. *Sulla* 5.3.5; Livy *Per.* 70; Vell. Pat. 2.24.3. See Ch. 2, § 5 and Ch. 5, § 13. TOMISA: Strabo 12.2.1.535. ZEUGMA: A. Bouché-Leclercq, *Histoire des Séleucides* (Paris

1913-1914) 420 ff. See also Dio 49.19.3; cf. 40.17.3; Jos. *AJ* 13.371. On the notion derived from this passage of Josephus that Laodice herself became involved in the fighting, see Sullivan, 'Commagene' 758-759 with notes 104-106. Zeugma's position: See J. Wagner, *Seleukeia am Euphrat/Zeugma* (Wiesbaden 1976). Later Parthian incursions through Commagene: Cic. *Fam.* 8.10.1. See also Strabo 16.1.22.746 and Frontinus 1.1.16. Commagenian possession of Seleuceia (Zeugma) and bits of Mesopotamia: App. *Mith.* 114.559. This taken with 105.495 shows the policy of Pompey later with regard to these crossings of the Euphrates.

3 SELEUCID OUTPOSTS: Strabo 14.5.2.668-669; J. Wolski in *Berytus* 12 (1956/1957) 35-52. TIGRANES IN SYRIA: Justin 40.1.4 has him ruling there *per X et VIII annos* by 69 BC and probably includes the prior conquest of North Syria (Commagene). See too App. *Syr.* 48.248. See also Schürer (Vermes and Millar) I, 134-135; Liebmann-Frankfort, *La frontière orientale* 193 f. SELEUCIDS IN COMMAGENE: Strabo 16.2.3.749 records the execution of Cleopatra Selene, former queen to three Seleucid monarchs (§§ 8 and 10), at Seleuceia (Zeugma). Cf. App. *Syr.* 48.247.

4 TIARA: R. Sullivan, 'Diadochic Coinage in Commagene': *NC* (ser. 7) 13 (1973) 18-37, with the inscription published by Wagner and Petzl (above, note 1) 213, lines 5-6. See too H. Toros, 'Tigran's Crown in Commagene': *San* 7 (1976) 65-66. See in general H.W. Ritter in *Historia* 36 (1987) 290-301 and his *Diadem und Königsherrschaft* (Munich 1965). ANTIOCHUS IN 69: Dio 36.2.5. The group mentioned in Plut. *Luc.* 29.5 might include Antiochus under the generic phrase 'Kings of the Arabs.' The reign of Antiochus: See Ch. 7, § 19. DURATION OF THE ALLIANCE: See Ch. 10.

5 THE DYNASTY OF EMESA: C. Chad, SJ, *Les dynastes d'Émèse* (Beyrouth 1972) esp. 33-62; R. Sullivan, 'The Dynasty of Emesa': *ANRW* II 8 (Berlin 1977) 198-219 with stemma; H. Seyrig in *Syria* 36 (1959) 184-192 = his *Antiquités syriennes* VI (1966) 64-72. On aspects of Emesa: F. Altheim and R. Stiehl, *Die Araber in der alten Welt*, I (Berlin 1964) 138 ff. and 355 ff.; Jones, *Cities*[2] 256 ff.; F. Altheim, 'Royal Necropolis': *Syria* 29 (1952) 204 ff. NO LONGER A CITY: Liban. *Orat.* 227, p. 42 Foerster; *Epist.* 846. For a neighbouring dynasty at Arados, 70 kilometres west of Emesa, see *IGLSyr* VII (1970) 87-90 nos. 42-45.

6 GEOGRAPHICAL ADVANTAGES: Seyrig, *Antiquités syriennes* 67 provides a sketch-map showing the road connections. See also Jones, *Cities*[2] 226, Map V; Altheim and Stiehl 138 ff. PHILIP AT BEROEA: See this chapter, § 8. This was the previous Harabu or Halman, the present Halab: Jones, *Cities*[2] 231. On its development into medieval Aleppo: J. Sauvaget, *Alep* (Paris 1941); the Hellenistic and Roman phases are covered in pp. 33-53. AZIZUS: Jos. *AJ* 13.384. The name in general: A. Alföldi in *RN* (sér. 4) 31 (1928) 256 ff.;

BMC Arabia xcv with Julian *Or.* IV 150c-d and 154a (Edessa); G. Cook, *Textbook of North-Semitic Inscriptions* (Oxford 1903) 295 f. note 1 (Palmyra); Cumont in *RE* 2.2 (1896) 2644; W. Hiempel, 'A Catalog of Near Eastern Venus Deities': *Syro-Mesopotamian Studies* 4 (1982) 51-72, esp. 18-20.

7 SAMPSIGERAMUS: Diod. 40.1a-1b. Altheim and Stiehl review the reasons for putting his reign early in the century: 162-163. See too Stähelin in *RE* 1A.2 (1920) 2226 f. See Ch. 7, § 20. TIGRANES AND THE LOCALS: Plut. *Luc.* 21.2 and 29.7.

8 TRANQUIL KINGDOM: Justin 40.1.4. Plut. *Luc.* 21.1-3 brings Appius Claudius into the microcosm Tigranes had established at Antioch. HUMILIATIONS: Plut. *Luc.* 21.4-5.

9 THE LAST SELEUCIDS: Jones, *Cities*² Ch. 10; A. Bouché-Leclercq, *Histoire des Séleucides*, I-II (Paris 1913-1914) 399-485 and 602-616; Schürer (Vermes and Millar) 125-136; G. Downey, *A History of Antioch in Syria* (Princeton N.J. 1961) 129-141; A.-J. Festugière, *Antioche payenne et chrétienne* (Paris 1959); É. Will, *Histoire politique du monde hellénistique*, II (Nancy 1967) 373-385 and 411-415; E. Bevan, *The House of Seleucus* (London 1902) 255-266. COINS: Bouché-Leclercq 661-663 with Plate IV; *BMC Seleucids* 91-105; Head *HN*² 769-773; A.R. Bellinger, 'The End of the Seleucids': *Trans. Connecticut Acad. of Arts & Sciences* 38 (1949) 51-102; E.T. Newell, *Late Seleucid Mints in Ake-Ptolemais and Damascus* (New York 1939; *Numism. Notes and Monographs*, No. 84) 59-107 with Plates I-XVII; Newell, 'The Seleucid Mint of Antioch': *Am. Journ. Numism.* 51 (1917) 98-128; *SNG ... Seleucid Kings* (Copenhagen 1959). Full recent bibliography in Schürer (Vermes and Millar) 9-10. See too G.M. Cohen, *The Seleucid Colonies* (Wiesbaden 1978); R. Bar-Kochva, *The Seleucid Army* (Cambridge, Eng. 1979); S.M. Sherwin-White, 'Babylonian Chronicle Fragments as a Source for Seleucid History': *JNES* 42 (1983) 265 ff.

10 PHILOPAPPUS: See Ch. 10. SELENE: Jos. *AJ* 13.419; *BJ* 1.116. Tigranes executed her at Seleuceia (Zeugma): Strabo 16.2.3.749. See further App. *Syr.* 48.247.

11 MITHRADATES AND LAODICE: See Ch. 2, §§ 2 and 3. GRYPUS vs. CYZICENUS: Jos. *AJ* 13.270 f.; Schürer (Vermes and Millar) 133-134.

12 DIVIDE: Euseb. *Chron.* I, col. 260 Schoene; Jones, *Cities*² 246. CYZICENUS: Jos. *AJ* 13.272 and 278; 13.366; Justin (Pomp. Trog.) *Prol.* 40.

13 FEEBLENESS: Jos. *AJ* 13.327. TRADITIONAL BOUNDARIES: App. *Mith.* 62.253; Liebmann-Frankfort 52 note 1. CILICIAN REFUGE: Jos. *AJ* 13.112, 116, 368; App. *Syr.* 69.365. SMALL DYNASTIES: A.-M. Vérilhac and G. Dagron in *REA* 76 (1974) 237-242 publish a text for a local priest-dynast formulaically termed 'the brother of the kings.' They suggest Philip I and II. Perhaps Philip II and Antiochus XIII are the kings designated, in

context. On other priests-dynasts-kings here see R. Sullivan in *NC* (ser. 7) 19 (1979) 5-20 with Plate 2. EUSEBES RULES: Jos. *AJ* 13.369. The edition of Josephus by R. Marcus (1943) misplaces note 'c' in the rendering of this passage; it should stand after the second mention of an Antiochus; the first is Antiochus X. PHILIP I: Jos. *AJ* 13.369. DEMETRIUS III: Jos. *AJ* 13.370.

14 DEATH OF EUSEBES: Schürer (Vermes and Millar) review the conflicting evidence (p. 135). On the unlikely view that he fell fighting in Commagene, see R. Sullivan, 'Commagene': *ANRW* II 8 (Berlin 1977) 758-759. DEMETRIUS *AKAIROS*: Jos. *AJ* 13.374, 376, 384-386. ANTIOCHUS XII: Jos. *AJ* 13.387-392. M. Sartre, *REA* 81 (1979) 40 with note 30, puts his death in 87 BC. E.T. Newell, *NNM* 84 (1939) 78-100: his coins continue to 86/85 BC. Meshorer 12 sees 84 BC. OBODAS I: Bowersock, *Roman Arabia* 24.

15 TIGRANES: Plut. *Luc.* 21; Dio 37.7a; Justin 40.1.3-4: *omnes ... consensere* seems an unlikely view of his rule, but by contrast with the last Seleucids he may have looked welcome to some. ANTIOCHUS AGAIN: *rex Syriae ... ab ... Lucullo appellatur*: Justin 40.2.2. TWO ARABS: Diod. 40.1a-1b. LURKING IN CILICIA: Justin 40.2.3. Philip had been there too: Diod. 40.1a. ANOTHER'S VICTORY: App. *Syr.* 49.250; Justin 40.2.3.

16 PALESTINE, NABATAEA, JUDAEA: Jones, *Cities*^{2} Ch. 10; Schürer (Vermes and Millar); Smallwood, *Jews*; Bowersock, *Roman Arabia*; *TAVO* B V 6. CHALCIS AND THE ITURAEANS: Strabo 16.2.10.753; 16.2.18-20.755-756; Polyb. 5.45.9. Geographical and ethnographic detail: Ancient toponyms appear on the map by E. Honigmann in his *Historische Topographie von Nordsyrien im Altertum* (Leipzig 1923) = *ZPalV* 46 (1923) 149-193 and 47 (1924) 1-64, with Tafel VII. See too Jones, *Cities*^{2} Ch. 10; Schürer (Vermes and Millar) 561-573, Appendix I; R. Dussaud, *Topographie historique de la Syrie antique et médiévale* (Paris 1929); A.H.M. Jones, 'The Urbanization of the Ituraean Principality': *JRS* 21 (1931) 265-275. 'ARABS': Examples in Schürer (Vermes and Millar) 562 note 4.

17 GALILEE: Jones, *JRS* 21 (1931) 265-266; Schürer (Vermes and Millar) 217 f. and note 10; Jos. *AJ* 13.318-319, in two almost parallel passages, the second taken from Strabo, who in turn followed Timagenes (*FGrH* 88 F 5). Since it is known from *BJ* 1.76 that Aristobulus had military success in Galilee, combining the passages and the information that his reign lasted only a year permits the inference that his conquest of a portion of the Ituraeans' territory occurred in Galilee. E.M. Smallwood, *The Jews under Roman Rule* (Leiden 1976) 14, wishes to shift the conquest back into the reign of John Hyrcanus on the grounds that the one-year reign of his son 'would hardly allow time for such an operation' as their conquest and 'Judaization.' But a successful campaign followed by the stipulation that those who chose to remain must convert to Judaism – which is all that Josephus says (*AJ* 13.318 f.) – need

not occupy more than a part of this year. MENNAEUS: Stephen of Byzantium, under 'Chalkis' (4). He need not be the founder of the dynasty, *pace* Jones, *Cities*² 254. However, one indication exists that the dynasty computed its era from the period when he lived. This is a coin using an era beginning c. 114 BC: Wroth in *BMC Galatia, etc.*, 281, first note. H. Seyrig is sceptical, though unconvincingly: *Syria* 27 (1950) 46-49. EXTENSION OF TERRITORY: Schürer (Vermes and Millar) 562-564; Jones, *Cities*² 254 with 454 note 37. FATHER OF PTOLEMY: Strabo 16.2.10.753. See too Jos. *BJ* 1.103, 185, 248; *AJ* 13.392 and 418; 14.39, 126, 297, 330; H. Seyrig, *RN* (sér. 5) 17 (1955) 105-107, nos. 8-12. TETRARCHS: Members of the dynasty sometimes held the title 'tetrarch and high priest' (§ 22.I). See I. Lévy in *Hommages à Joseph Bidez et à Franz Cumont*, II (Brussels 1949) 183-184; E. Renan, 'La dynastie des Lysanias d'Abilène': *MAI* 26 (1870) 49-84.

18 DIFFICULT NEIGHBOUR: Jos. *AJ* 14.39; 13.418; M. Sartre, 'Rome et les Nabatéens à la fin de la République (65-30 av. J.C.)': *REA* 81 (1979) 40 ff. DAMASCUS: Jos. *AJ* 13.387-391; *BJ* 1.99-102. The date for the campaign of Antiochus XII may be as early as 87 BC: Sartre note 30; Bowersock, *Roman Arabia* 24 f. note 47; Schürer (Vermes and Millar) 577 f. In any case, the death of Antiochus and the appeal to Aretas III should probably not be placed before 86/85; Meshorer (12) has 84. See too Newell, *Late Seleucid Mints* (1939) 86-89. JANNAEUS AND ARETAS: Jos. *BJ* 1.99-105 and *AJ* 13.387-392. OPPRESSION: Jos. *BJ* 1.115; *AJ* 13.418. TIGRANES AT PTOLEMAIS AND DAMASCUS: Jos. *AJ* 13.419-421; *BJ* 1.116; Plut. *Luc.* 21.1; Newell 95-100.

19 NABATAEANS: The basic study is G.W. Bowersock, *Roman Arabia* (Cambridge, Mass. 1983) esp. Ch. 1-3 and Bibliography, 193-211. See too Schürer (Vermes and Millar) Vol. I, Appendix II, 574-586, with bibliography. A monograph by A. Negev appears in *ANRW* II 8 (Berlin 1977) 520-686. ARETAS I: The text that A. Cowley ascribed to Aretas III in *Pal. Expl. Fund Annual* 3 (1914-1915) 145 ff. has been reattributed to Aretas I on palaeographical grounds by F. Cross in *JBL* 74 (1955) 160, n. 25. In II Macc. 5.8, we find him called 'the tyrant of the Arabs' – a loose equivalent by an outside writer. See also Bowersock, *Roman Arabia* 18, note 22; Strabo 16.4.21.779-26.784. INSCRIPTIONS: J. Euting, *Nabatäische Inschriften aus Arabien* (Berlin 1885); M. Sartre, *IGLS* XIII, 1: *Bostra (Nos. 9001 à 9472)* (Paris 1982). Some redating of inscriptions at Petra has been suggested by J. McKenzie and A. Phippen: see below, Ch. 7, § 22, note 76.

20 DEMETRIUS I: Plut. *Demet.* 7.1; Diod. 2.48.5 f.; 19.94-100. RAIDS: Strabo 16.4.21.779; Justin 39.5.5. The proximity of the Nabataean capital, Petra, to both Egypt and Judaea could be convenient or dangerous. Its road to Gaza probably facilitated the conquests of Jannaeus in the Nabataean lands after

96. On the trade conflict see Y. Shiloh in *PEQ* 119 (1987) 9. A detailed map of the Nabataean heartland appears after p. 312 in H. von Wissmann's article on the Sabaeans in *ANRW* II.9.1 (Berlin 1976). Relations between Jews and Nabataeans: J. Starcky, 'Pétra et la Nabatène,' *Dictionnaire de la Bible, Suppl. VII* (Paris 1966) 904-905 (hereafter: *SDB* 7). Nabataeans had penetrated the Hauran by the second century BC and moved steadily northward in the early first century. On their movements see R. Dussaud, *La pénétration des Arabes en Syrie avant l'Islam* (Paris 1955) Ch. II-III. See too J. Starcky in *Bibl. Arch.* 18 (1955) 84-106; F. Altheim and R. Stiehl, *Die Araber in der Alten Welt*, I (Berlin 1964) Ch. 2, 31 ff.; J. Teixidor, 'The Nabataean Presence at Palmyra': *JANES* 5 (1973) 405-409. The Nabataean capital, Petra, is now attested epigraphically under its Semitic name, *Reqem*; it was founded in biblical times (Jos. *AJ* 4.161). See J. Starcky, *RBi* 73 (1965) 95-97; *Ann. Dept. Ant. Jordan* 10 (1965) 43-49. DUMATA ROAD: Discussion and bibliography by M. Speidel in *Historia* 36 (1987) 212-221. RABBEL I: The evidence is *CIS* II 349, probably from the eighteenth year of Aretas III. See I. Lévy in J. Cantineau, *Le Nabatéen*, Vol. II (1932) 8 ff.; R. Dussaud, *La pénétration* 52-54; Starcky, *SDB* 7, 905; Negev, *ANRW* II 8, 530 (but see 535). His remark that 'The earliest Nabataean king, known by the name of Rabilos-Rabel, belongs to the end of the second century B.C. ...' is misleading unless the first comma is removed. Schürer (Vermes and Millar) 578 places Rabbel after Aretas II. Another piece of evidence, Steph. Byz. 466.5-7 = *FGrH* 675, F 25, has been much emended since Gutschmid's day: Dussaud, *La pénétration* 52-54; Starcky, *SDB* 7, 905 and *Bibl. Arch.* 18 (1955) 91; Schürer (Vermes and Millar) 578 note 12; Negev, *ANRW* II 8, 529-530. The 'Rabeibelos, King of the Nabataeans,' known from an inscription in Rome, appears to be much later: A. Degrassi, *BCAR* 74 (1951-1952; appeared 1954) 34-37 no. 20. On Rabbel II, see Bowersock, *Roman Arabia* 72 ff.

21 ARETAS II: Jos. *AJ* 13.360 and 365, where the events loosely synchronize with the death of Antiochus VIII Grypus in 96. They were, however, precipitated by the departure of Cleopatra III from Palestine; she died in 101. The campaign against Gaza thus occupied some portion of a period about five years long. For Aretas I in 168, see above. REX HEROTIMUS: Justin 39.5.6. The passage does not justify the statement that 'This Erotimus is thus to be regarded as the founder of the royal Nabataean dynasty': Schürer (Vermes and Millar) 577. See too F. Täubler, 'Der Nabatäerkönig Erotimus': *Klio* 10 (1910) 251 ff. DYNASTIC COINAGE: A coinage once attributed by De Saulcy to a Malichus I about 145 was dismissed by R. Dussaud in his 'Numismatique des rois de Nabatène': *JA* (sér. 10) 3 (1904) 189-238, esp. 192-197. In turn, his view that the dynasty's coins began only with Aretas III was questioned by E.S.G. Robinson in *NC* (ser. 5) 16 (1936) 288-291, who reattrib-

uted some issues to Aretas II: see his Pl. XVII. Study of all the coinage: Y. Meshorer, *Nabataean Coins* (Jerusalem 1975; Qedem 3: Monographs of the Institute of Archaeology, The Hebrew University of Jerusalem) 9 ff.; *BMC Arabia* xi-xxii and 1-13 with Pl. I-II; Head *HN*[2] 810 f.; H. Seyrig in *RN* (sér. 5) 17 (1955) 94 f.; Newell 95.

22 OBODAS I: G. Dalman, *Palästinische Forschungen zur Archäologie und Topographie*, II: *Neue Petra-Forschungen der Heilige Felsen von Jerusalem* (Leipzig 1912) 99-101, Nr. 90, with Abb. 68. *CIS* II 354. See also J. Starcky, *SDB* 7 (above, note 20) 906; Bowersock, *Roman Arabia* 23 f.; Jos. *AJ* 13.375; *BJ* 1.90. See too Schürer (Vermes and Millar) 220-223 on this situation. Jos. *AJ* 13.382 shows the territory ceded; Starcky (*SDB* 7, 906) notes that only in this way could Jannaeus avoid fighting on two fronts, since Demetrius III was then (about 90 BC) moving southward from Damascus into Samaria. THE TWELVE CITIES: Jos. *AJ* 14.18, with A. Negev in *PEQ* 101 (1969) 5 and 10, suggesting that Alusa and Orybda in this list correspond to Elusa and Oboda. The campaigns of Jannaeus against Gaza and these Nabataean cities (Jos. *AJ* 13.356-364) caused in his view the depopulation reflected in the archaeological record. Starcky, 906-907, notes that the divine title for Obodas in this passage from Steph. Byz. 482.15-16 corresponds to the *Theos* of Demetrius III and to *Dionysos Epiphanes* for Antiochus XII, both contemporaries of Obodas I. Another reason for considering the town of Oboda his rather than that of Obodas II in the reign of Augustus used to be the view of some scholars that the *Arabica* of Uranius, upon which the account of Stephen is based, was written by the middle of the first century BC, too early for Obodas II. A much later date, however, is argued by J.M.I. West, 'Uranius': *HSCP* 78 (1974) 282-284 (dissertation summary). See also D. Graf in *BASOR* 229 (1978) 1-26; D. Graf and M. O'Connor, *Byzantine Studies/Études Byz.* 4, Part I (1977) 52-66. Starcky's view that a series of inscriptions for Mas'ûdu, King of Liḥyân reflects 'un changement de dynastie' is unnecessarily pessimistic; nor need we speak of 'les nouveaux maîtres,' especially in view of the unfailing series of Nabataean rulers. Any disruption suffered was, as he acknowledges, brief. Other kings of Liḥyân have been identified: e.g., M. Rizack, 'A Coin with the Aramaic legend *SHRW*, a King-Governor of Liḥyân' in *ANSMusN* 29 (1984) 25-28. ANTIOCHUS XII vs. ARABS: Jos. *AJ* 13.387-391; *BJ* 1.99-102. This campaign is what has tempted scholars to emend the passage above from Stephanus of Byzantium, substituting 'Antiochus Dionysus' for the clear reading 'Antigonus the Macedonian.' OBODAS vs. ANTIOCHUS XII: G.W. Bowersock, *JRS* 65 (1975) 181; *Roman Arabia* 24 f.

23 ARETAS TO OPPOSE PTOLEMY: Jos. *BJ* 1.103 f. and *AJ* 13.392. Coins from his reign in Damascus are plentiful. See E.T. Newell, *Late Seleucid Mints*

(New York 1939) 92-94; Starcky, *SDB* 7 (above, note 20) 907 nos. 1-2. See too Dussaud, *JA* 3 (1904) 205-208 for the various issues, Damascus and elsewhere. See also *BMC Arabia* l f. with Pl. I.1-4; Meshorer 9 ff. That he was the son of Obodas I is attested by Steph. Byz. 144.19-26, s.v. 'Auara.' DIADOCHIC COINS: On this practice see R. Sullivan in *NC* (ser. 7) 13 (1973) 18-39 and Pl. 14. Tigranes himself did this in Syria, continuing the era of Philip I. ARETAS PHILHELLENE: 'of King Aretas the Philhellene.' This use of a familiar formula on a local coinage assures its acceptance. It does not constitute 'evidence of the penetration of Hellenism in the Nabataean realm at that time,' but rather reflects his possession of Damascus. Later Nabataean coins, after the loss of Damascus, avoid Greek. See Schürer (Vermes and Millar) 579; Meshorer 12-15.

24 BATTLE IN JUDAEA: Jos. *AJ* 13.392; *BJ* 1.103. Josephus provides no explicit warrant for the statement that Alexander 'was able to persuade the Nabataean King to withdraw only by making concessions' (Schürer [Vermes and Millar] 226), and it is difficult to determine what these would have been, unless monetary and not territorial. An alternative assumption is that Aretas had been warning Alexander away from his own new holdings in Damascus. EAST OF THE JORDAN: Jos. *AJ* 13.393-395 and *BJ* 1.104-105. AMATHUS: Jos. *BJ* 1.86-87 records an earlier attempt; *BJ* 1.104-105 and *AJ* 13.393-395. NABATAEANS vs. JUDAEANS: Jos. *AJ* 13.408-415; *BJ* 1.110-114. Further interventions: *AJ* 14.14 ff. and below, Ch. 7, § 22. DAMASCUS: Jos. *BJ* 1.115 and *AJ* 13.418. GIFTS TO TIGRANES: Jos. *AJ* 13.419 ff.; *BJ* 1.115 f. NOMINAL CONQUEST: Jos. *BJ* 1.159 and *AJ* 14.80-81. Difficult terrain and near-starvation induced Scaurus to suggest a bribe, which Aretas III paid; both were 'equally glad' to break off hostilities. See Ch. 7, § 22. On the expansion of Nabataeans under Aretas III, see the following as well: A.R. Bellinger, 'The Early Coinage of Roman Syria': *Studies in Roman Economy and Social History in Honor of Allan Chester Johnson* (Princeton, N. J. 1951) 58 ff.; Starcky, *SDB* 7 (note 20, above) 909 f.; A. Negev, 'The Chronology of the Middle Nabataean Period': *PEQ* 101 (1969) 5-14; F. Winnett and W. Reed, *Ancient Records from North Arabia* (Toronto 1970) III, 1: 'Inscriptions nabatéenes' 141-160 (section by J.T. Milik and J. Starcky); A. Negev, *ANRW* II 8 537 ff. In the context of developing relations with Rome, see G.W. Bowersock, 'A Report on Arabia Provincia': *JRS* 61 (1971) 221 f. (Antiochus 'XIII' is a misprint for XII.) Cf. his *Roman Arabia* Ch. 3-4. See also J. Starcky, 'The Nabataeans: A Historical Sketch': *Bibl. Arch.* 18 (1955) 84-106.

25 JUDAEAN HOUSE: For an introduction to this enormous subject see E. Schürer, *The History of the Jewish People in the Age of Jesus Christ* (Edinburgh 1973; rev. G. Vermes and F. Millar) Vol. I, abbreviated herein as Schürer

(Vermes and Millar). Also for the period after Pompey's arrival see E.M. Smallwood, *The Jews under Roman Rule* (Leiden 1976: herein as Smallwood, *Jews*), and U. Baumann, *Rom und die Juden. Die römisch-jüdaischen Beziehungen von Pompeius bis zum Tode des Herodes (63 v. Chr. - 4 v. Chr.)* (Frankfurt am Main 1983). For the early contacts of the Judaean state with Rome, see also A.N. Sherwin-White, *Roman Foreign Policy in the East* (London 1984) 70-79. Some notes on the dynasty as it developed appear in R. Sullivan, 'The Dynasty of Judaea in the First Century': *ANRW* II 8 (Berlin 1977) 296-354, with stemma. See too J. Efron, *Studies on the Hasmonean Period* (Leiden 1987; Studies in Judaism in Late Antiquity, 39). JANNAEUS vs. THE CITIES: Jos. *AJ* 13.324-325. He calls Cyzicenus the brother of Grypus; but though they shared the same mother, Cleopatra Thea, they had different fathers: Antiochus VII Sidetes and Demetrius II Nicator, respectively. ZOILUS: Jos. *AJ* 13.324-335.

26 PTOLEMY vs. JANNAEUS: Jos. *AJ* 13.324-364 with summary in *BJ* 1.86-87 gives this story in unusual detail, partly following Strabo and Nicholaus of Damascus (*AJ* 13.347). On the conquests: Jones, *Cities*[2] 455 note 39. OBODAS: Jos. *AJ* 13.374-375. Troubles between Judaeans and Nabataeans went back at least to the days of Judas Maccabaeus: Starcky, *SDB* 7 (1966) 905. But the close call with Obodas probably precipitated the violence characteristic of the campaigns of Jannaeus against Nabataeans now. JANNAEUS vs. SYRIANS: Jos. *AJ* 13.374-378. Earlier Judaean-Syrian relations: e.g., *ZPalV* 91 (1975) 191-196. DEMETRIUS: Jos. *BJ* 13.377-386; *BJ* 1.92-95. On the supporters of Philip in this conflict, 'Azizus, phylarch of the Arabs' and the Parthian governor of Mesopotamia, see this chapter, § 7.

27 LANDS TO THE ARABS: Jos. *AJ* 13.382; cf. 374. On this passage see above, note 22. FINAL CAMPAIGNS: The period of these last invasions is about 83-76, with some respite about 79. Schürer (Vermes and Millar) 225-227 with notes 23-26. See Jos. *AJ* 13.390 on the defensive line, and 13.387-391 on the death of Antiochus in his conflict with Philip and with 'the Arab king.' LEGACY: The exception along the coast was Ascalon, independent since the reign of Aristobulus and still so under the Romans. On these see the bibliography in Schürer (Vermes and Millar) 228 notes 30-32. HIS COINS: These use the Seleucid anchor, as frequent throughout the East, from Commagene to Parthia. Herod the Great may have based his own depiction of the anchor on that of Jannaeus: D. Jacobsen in *ANSMN* 31 (1986) 145-165, esp. 163. See too Meshorer 26. CRUELTY: Schürer (Vermes and Millar) esp. 224-225 note 22.

28 ALEXANDRA AND SONS: Jos. *AJ* 13.408-417; *BJ* 1.107-114. DAMASCUS: Jos. *BJ* 1.112 and 115; *AJ* 13.418; Plut. *Luc.* 21.2. PTOLEMAIS AND SELENE: Jos. *AJ* 13.419-421; *BJ* 1.116-117; Strabo 16.2.3.749; App. *Syr.*

69.367. DEATH OF ALEXANDRA: Schürer (Vermes and Millar) 231 f.; Smallwood, *Jews* 16 ff. On the dynasty now: J. Klausner in *The World History of the Jewish People*, Vol. VI, *The Hellenistic Age*, ed. A. Schalit (New Brunswick, N.J. 1972) 201-254.

29 FREE CITIES: Jones, *Cities*² 253 f. with 454 notes 35-36. Damascus free: E.T. Newell, *Late Seleucid Mints* (New York 1939) 100. BYBLOS: Strabo 16.2.18.755. Jones, *Cities*² 455 note 40, misunderstands Strabo's reference to Cinyras. PTOLEMY, DIONYSIUS, SILAS: Jos. *AJ* 14.39-40. BACCHIUS: *BMC Roman Republic* I, 490-491. He is tentatively equated, on unstated grounds, with Dionysius of Tripolis in Schürer (Vermes and Millar) 237 note 14. THEODORE AND ZENO: Jos. *AJ* 13.235 and 356 and 375; *BJ* 1.60, 86, 104. ARMY OF ARISTOBULUS: Jos. *AJ* 13.427. ZOILUS: Especially Jos. *AJ* 13.324-326. The note on this passage by R. Marcus in his edition of Josephus (1943) misunderstands *AJ* 13.334, which mentions that Zoilus joined the petition of the people of Gaza, not that he ruled there; 13.329 shows them as distinct. HERACLEON AND DIONYSIUS: Jos. *AJ* 13.365; Athen. *Deipn.* 4.153b; Strabo 16.2.7.751; Jones, *Cities*² 455 note 41. STRATON: Jos. *AJ* 13.384. ALCHAEDAMNUS: Strabo 16.2.10-11.753; App. *BCiv.* 5.1.7. On these and others back into the second century BC: Jones, *Cities*² 455 note 41. Local situation: See Ch. 7, § 22 with R. Sullivan, 'Emesa': *ANRW* II 8 (Berlin 1977) 207-209.

Chapter 4

1 EGYPT: 'Gift of the Nile' in Hdt. 2.5; 2.10; Arr. *Anab.* 5.6.5. 'Land ... always rising': Hdt. 2.14. EUERGETES II: Conditions late in the reign are reflected in *P. Tebt.* 5. *FGrH* 234 quotes Euergetes himself. See Diod. 31, Frags. 15 a and 17 c, with T.C. Skeat and E.G. Turner, *JEA* 54 (1968) 199 ff., esp. 207, on earlier disturbances. An inscription from Delos shows Roman ship owners and merchants engaged 'in the capture of Alexandria' under Euergetes: Durrbach, *Choix* 105; Sherk, *Greek East* no. 47 A. Cf. J.D. Ray, *The Archive of 1Hor* (London 1976) 12 ff. and 164 ff. See especially Otto and Bengtson (this note, below) 110-145. As an example of the mixture of nationalities already evident in Egypt now (cf. Ch. 8, § 23, notes 7-9), note the dedication offered by the Jews of Wadi Natrun: *SEG* 8 (1937) no. 366 = *SB* 7454. PTOLEMIES: The stemma employs the numbers assigned each individual by W. Peremans and E. Van 't Dack in *Prosopographia Ptolemaica*, VI (Louvain 1968 = *Studia Hellenistica* 17) 3-21 ('La Cour,' 1. 'La famille royale'). This is abbreviated hereafter as: *Pros. Ptol.* or *PP*. Sequential numbers given to homonymous members of the family (Ptolemy 'VIII,' etc.) are as given there and in *RE* 23.2 (1959) 1602-1762, 'Ptolemaios' (H. Volkmann). These differ

from earlier reconstructions by inserting the brief reign (145/144 BC) of Ptolemy Neos Philopator (see Pestman, *Chronologie* 55), son of Ptolemy VI Philometor. He becomes Ptolemy VII and each remaining member of the line thus receives a designation one higher: Ptolemy VIII (not VII) Euergetes II Physcon, and so on. Irreverent Alexandrian nicknames permit convenient identifications. The primary work on the dynasty remains that of A. Bouché-Leclercq, *Histoire des Lagides*, I-IV (Paris 1903-1907), supplemented by E. Bevan, *A History of Egypt under the Ptolemaic Dynasty* (London 1927) and other studies cited below, with H. Maehler, 'Egypt under the Last Ptolemies': *BICS* 30 (1983) 1-16. CHRONOLOGY: P.W. Pestman, *Chronologie égyptienne d'après les textes démotiques (322 av. J.-C.-453 ap. J.-C.)* (Leiden 1967: Papyrologica Lugduno-Batava, XV); A.E. Samuel, *Ptolemaic Chronology* (Munich 1962; Münchener Beiträge zur Papyrusforschung und antiken Rechtsgeschichte, 43). GENERAL: P. Meyer, *Das Heerwesen der Ptolemäer und Römer in Ägypten* (Leipzig 1900); É. Will, *Histoire politique du monde hellénistique (323-30 av. J.-C.)*, II (Nancy 1967) 356-372 and 435 f.; W. Otto and H. Bengtson, *Zur Geschichte des Niedergangs des Ptolemäerreiches* (Munich 1938 = *Abh. Bayer. Akad.*, N.F. 17); E. Olshausen, *Rom und Ägypten von 116 bis 51 v. Chr.* (Diss. Erlangen-Nürnberg 1963); T. Skeat, *The Reigns of the Ptolemies* (Munich 1954 = Münchener Beiträge zur Papyrusforschung und antiken Rechtsgeschichte, 39); P.M. Fraser, *Ptolemaic Alexandria*, 1-3 (Oxford 1970); Cimma Ch. 3, section 6. TRYPHAENA: Justin 39.2.3; Seibert, *Zu den dynastischen Verbindungen* 90 f. GRYPUS vs. CYZICENUS: Justin 39.3.12. Narrative in Bouché-Leclercq, *Lagides* 90-93. Chronology in Bevan, *History of Egypt* 328. See also Schürer (Vermes and Millar) 131 f.

2 JOINT DOCUMENTS UNTIL 104: Bernand, *Fayoum* I, 29 ff. no. 6. Cf. no. 5. See too *OGIS* 175; *SEG* 33 (1983) no. 1359. CLEOPATRA III: Bevan, *History of Egypt* 331, seeks to discount this version – attested by three sources – on the grounds that Alexander ruled on. But he had become a legitimate ruler, and the Alexandrians held no brief for Cleopatra. See also Bouché-Leclercq, *Lagides* II, 103-106 with 106 note 1; Justin 39.4.5; Athen. *Deipn.* 12.550 a; Pausanias 1.9.3. KINSMAN: Jos. *AJ* 13.352-355. ATTEMPT EGYPT: Jos. *AJ* 13.350-351. UNPOPULAR: Justin 39.4.3-6; Athen. *Deipn.* 12.550 a-b. ACTIVITIES: *SEG* 8 (1937) no. 498 is a pious dedication in his tenth year, still using the title *Philometor* a decade after the death of Cleopatra III, as he did even on joint documents with Berenice III: e.g., Bernand, *Fayoum* I, 31 f. no. 7. This combination of titles had been used by Ptolemy VI and Cleopatra II in the mid-second century: *SEG* 20 (1964) no. 498; Pestman, *Chronologie* 140 f.; J.D. Ray, *The Archive of Ḥor* (London 1976) 20 ff. no. 3. He and his sister are *Philometores* in *SEG* 8 (1937) no. 466. See too *OGIS*

176-180; 181 must belong to the period of his rule on Cyprus. See T.B. Mitford, 'Helenos, Governor of Cyprus': *JHS* 79 (1959) 97 ff., esp. 120 ff. BORROWINGS: E. Badian, *Roman Imperialism*, 2nd ed. (Ithaca, N. Y. 1968) 73.

3 CYRENE BEQUEATHED: Livy *Per.* 70; Tac. *Ann.* 14.18.2; Justin 39.5.2.; Sall. *Hist.* 2.43; Plut. *Luc.* 2.3-4. App. *BCiv.* 1.111 synchronizes the inheritance with that of Bithynia in 74, probably because Rome took no direct control of Cyrene until then. See too App. *Mith.* 121.600. Jul. Obsequens 49 supplies the date, in the consulships of Cn. Domitius and C. Cassius. See the inscription published by L. Gasperini, *QAL* 5 (1967) 53. The honorand is C. Claudius Pulcher, cos. 92. E. Rawson suggests in *Historia* 22 (1973) 230 that his relations with Cyrene might go back to the years before the death of Ptolemy Apion in 96 BC. The decision to annex probably came in 75/74: G. Perl in *Klio* 52 (1970) 320-325; W. Harris, *War and Imperialism in Republican Rome, 327-70 B.C.* (Oxford 1979) 154-155 and 267; S. Applebaum, *Jews and Greeks in Ancient Cyrene* (Leiden 1979) 63-65; D. Braund, *Liverpool Class. Monthly* 8.6 (1983) 88. See also Bouché-Leclercq, *Lagides* II, 108-109 note 1; S.I. Oost, 'Cyrene, 96-74 B.C.': *CP* 58 (1963) 11-25; J. Reynolds, *JRS* 52 (1962) 97-103; E. Badian, *JRS* 55 (1965) 110-121, esp. 119-121. Ptolemy Apion is *Pros. Ptol.* 14553; *RE* 23.2 (1959) 1737-1738, no. 29. PHYSCON: *Pros. Ptol.* 14551; Athen., *Deipn.* 12.549d-550b; *SEG* 9 (1938) 7. On this interpretation of such wills: E. Badian, *RhM* 110 (1967) 187; A.N. Sherwin-White in *JRS* 67 (1977) 66-67 and *Roman Foreign Policy* 81. See too D. Braund, *Friendly King* 129 ff. WILL OF EUERGETES II: *SEG* 9 (1938) no. 7; Sherk, *Greek East* no. 31; É. Will, *Histoire politique*, II (Nancy 1967) 300 ff. See also above, Ch. 2, § 1, note 1. PETUBASTIS: This suggestion, by E.A.E. Reymond based on her work with the late John Barns at Oxford, appeared in 'Alexandria and Memphis: Some Historical Observations': *Orientalia* 46 (1977) 1-33. I am grateful to her for discussing this with me before publication and for suggestions since on related problems. The evidence is Vienna Stele 82 = J. Quaegebeur, 'Inventaire des stèles funéraires memphites d'époque ptolémaïque': *CE* 49 (1974) 59-61, no. 32. J. Quaegebeur has expressed reservations in 'The Genealogy of the Memphite High Priest Family in the Hellenistic Period': *Studies on Ptolemaic Memphis*, ed. D.J. Crawford, J. Quaegebeur, W. Clarysse (Louvain 1980; Studia Hellenistica 24) 43 ff., esp. 77; cf. 69 no. 24, with stemma on 52. The paper of Crawford in this volume merely notes (42 note 1) Reymond's work, *pace* R. Bagnall, *CW* 76 (1982) 17. AEMILIANUS: J. Dobiáš in *Archiv orientální* 3 (1931) 245; Diodorus 33.28a; Strabo 14.5.2.669; Athen. *Deipn.* 12.549d-e, from Poseidonius. MEMMIUS: *P. Tebt.* 33; L. Mitteis and U. Wilcken, *Grundzüge und Chrestomathie der Papyruskunde* (Leipzig-Berlin 1912) no. 3. On Jos. *AJ* 14.249 see below.

4 TITLES: Pestman, *Chronologie* 72-76, 156, 161-162. *OGIS* 175, 177-179, and 740 show Ptolemy X Alexander I using *Philometor*. During the joint reign of Lathyros with Cleopatra, he used it too: Pestman 66-68 and 150-151. On the activity of Cleopatra in this regard see Bouché-Leclercq, *Lagides* II, 105 note 2. Borrowing of titles: *OGIS* 181 note 1 (end) with *JHS* 79 (1959) 120. CLEOPATRA BERENICE: She is *adelphē* and *Philadelphos* in *BGU* VIII 1735. FLIGHT OF ALEXANDER: See below, note 7. See too Justin 39.5.1; Pausan. 1.9.3. His army in Egypt had rejected him, it appears from the notice of Porphyry, *ap*. Euseb. *Chron*. I, col. 164 Schoene = *FGrH* 260, F 2.8-9. E. Badian in *RhM* 110 (1967) 178-192 ascribes the will giving Egypt to Rome to Alexander I rather than to Alexander II. He sees the death of Alexander I not occurring until the spring of 87 on the grounds that raising the fleet took time; that the termination of the reign among the scribes in Alexandria in September 88 did not follow the news of his death but only of his flight; that he thus probably lived until late 88; that he might have endured till spring, for 'common sense and ancient practice would suggest that the second naval battle was not fought before the spring of 87' (p. 184). Certainly some scholars accept this view; see Braund's review of Cimma, *Reges* in *JRS* 70 (1980) 203; *Friendly King* 134-135. A.E. Samuel, 'Year 27 = 30 and 88 BC': *CE* 40 (1965) 376-398, sees Alexander alive at least until November 88 BC. On the documents: Pestman, *Chronologie* 72 note b and 75. Egypt did not, of course, come into Roman hands until after Actium, as Augustus notes: *Aegyptum imperio populi Romani adieci, Res Gest*. 27.1. See too Ehrenberg-Jones, nos. 14 and 37; App. *Mith*. 114.557: Pompey did not enter Egypt (but see below). *DAMNATIO MEMORIAE*: Narrative in Bouché-Leclercq, *Lagides* II, 110. The passage in Strabo 17.1.11.795 f. moves from Ptolemy VIII Euergetes II directly to Ptolemy IX Soter II Lathyros, then to Ptolemy XII Auletes. Bibliography in *RE* 23.2 (1959) 1746. See Pestman 64-77 on the records; Samuel, *Ptolemaic Chronology* 147-153. EXTERNAL TEXT: This is *SEG* 3 (1929) 378 B 1.

5 LATHYROS AS SOTER II: *OGIS* 173. WIVES OF LATHYROS. Cleopatra IV: *Pros. Ptol*. 14519. The marriage was ended by her mother soon after the death of Physcon in 116. Cleopatra Selene: *Pros. Ptol*. 14520. This marriage endured from 115 until 107, when Lathyros terminated it by fleeing from his mother. Selene began her three Seleucid marriages (Grypus; Cyzicenus; Eusebes) about 104. FRIEND AND ALLY OF THE ROMANS: Jos. *AJ* 14.247-255 with esp. Schürer (Vermes and Millar) 204-206 and note 7. Pestman, *Chronologie* 66-69. Josephus may have inserted a *senatus consultum* into a passage recording a decree of Pergamon. If the 'Hyrcanus the high priest' mentioned here is Hyrcanus I during his reign, the period covered is 135-104. 'King Antiochus, son of Antiochus' should be Antiochus IX Cyzicenus,

son of Antiochus VII Sidetes; he ruled 114-95. Bouché-Leclercq, *Lagides* II, 95 note 2, plucks 'l'an 107?' out of the air – a year when both Ptolemies ruled; its convenience to scholars is its main recommendation. Emendation to *Demetrius* puts the text farther back in time, but tends to rest on circular arguments such as those in Schürer (Vermes and Millar) *ad loc.* : such activity 'contradicts all that is known of Antiochus IX' – unless this passage too 'is known of Antiochus.' This and other statements such as 'none of the later Seleucids [after Antiochus VII] ... confronted the Jews with such a display of force' do not adequately represent the military record of Cyzicenus as otherwise known. The campaign reflected in the account of Josephus could rest on possession by Cyzicenus of an adequate force, and allies from Egypt sufficient to alarm the Jews into calling for Roman help. SELEUCIA-IN-PIERIA: This is *OGIS* 257. On the controversy see Bouché-Leclercq, *Lagides* II, 602-604 and Bevan, *Egypt* 329. See too Jones, *Cities*² 253. ALLIANCE OF CYZICENUS AND LATHYROS: Jos. *AJ* 13.276-278; Justin 39.4.4.; Diod. 34-35.39a; Euseb. *Chron.* I, 260 Schoene. Jos. *BJ* 1.65 names 'Antiochus ... Aspendius' (Grypus), in mistaken contrast to the parallel passage, *AJ* 13.276.

6 LATHYROS TO CYPRUS: Justin 39.4.2: *vivum eum e manibus*. Cf. *Prol.* 39. See T.B. Mitford in *JHS* 79 (1959) 96 ff. and 103 f. OPPOSITION OF CLEOPATRA III: Mitford 125-129. Bibliography in *RE* 23.2 (1959) 1741. SELENE: App. *Syr.* 69.366; Strabo 16.2.3.749; Jos. *AJ* 13.420; *BJ* 1.116; Schürer (Vermes and Millar) 135. DEMETRIUS III: Jos. *AJ* 13.370; E.T. Newell, *Late Seleucid Mints* (New York 1939) 78-86. INTERVAL: *SEG* 8 (1937) nos. 536-537 (96 BC) = *SB* 8127-8128.

7 RETURN OF LATHYROS: *P.Strassb.* 8 and 12 (October 88); Pestman, *Chronologie* 72-76; Bevan, *Egypt* 335-337; Bouché-Leclercq, *Lagides* II, 112. See above, note 4. EXTERNAL MATTERS: App. *Syr.* 48.248; 69.366. The statement of Justin 40.2.2 (cf. Porphyry in Euseb. *Chron.* I, col. 262 Schoene) that 'Antiochus, son of Cyzicenus' (i.e., Antiochus X Eusebes) survived should probably refer rather to the son of Eusebes, Antiochus XIII Asiaticus. LUCULLUS: Plut. *Luc.* 2.2-3.3; App. *Mith.* 33.131-132. Plutarch here terms Lathyros a *meirakion*, hardly the appropriate term for a man over fifty-five. Plutarch cannot be thinking instead of Ptolemy XI Alexander II, who had been sent to Cos in 103 and was now probably still in the hands of Mithradates planning his escape to Sulla. Possibly Lathyros sent out his son, the future Ptolemy XII Auletes, to escort Lucullus into the presence. CHILDREN AT COS: Jos. *AJ* 13.349; App. *Mith.* 23.93 and *BCiv.* 1.102; Justin 39.4.1: *ex Selene iam duos filios habebat* (Lathyros). The possession by Mithradates of the future Ptolemy XI Alexander II and others restricted the freedom of manoeuvre now for Lathyros and may explain his refusal to

render Lucullus any real assistance. He subsequently 'ceased observing his alliance' with Rome: Plut. *Luc.* 3.1. On the fearlessness (partly from inexperience) of Ptolemies at this time, and the actions of Sulla, see App. *BCiv.* 1.102.

8 TRADITIONAL ACTIVITIES: *OGIS* 167-174; Pausan. 1.9.3; A.D. Nock, '*Synnaos Theos*': *HSCP* 41 (1930) 1-62, esp. 6-7; Bevan, *Egypt* 337 f. with notes 1-3 and Figs. 57-58; *RE* 23.2 (1959) 1742; *JHS* 79 (1959) 97 ff. PTOLEMY V EPIPHANES: Livy 36.4.3. SELEUCID INVASION: J.D. Ray, *The Archive of Ḥor* (London 1976) 7-29, Texts 1-3; 164-165. DEATH OF LATHYROS: Pestman, *Chronologie* 74; Skeat 37.

9 BERENICE III: Pausan. 1.9.3. Titles in Pestman, *Chronologie* 2 note 4, and 72. See too Bouché-Leclercq, *Lagides* III, 30 note 1; *OGIS* 174, from Cyprus. Attempts to fix the date of her marriage to Alexander I have been inconclusive. See the note by Bouché-Leclercq, *Lagides* II, 105 note 1. See too *RE* 11 (1922) 781-782, no. 21. *Pros. Ptol.* 14522 opts for 101. The marriage had occurred by then, since documents date by both sovereigns in 'year 14': e.g., Bernand, *Fayoum* I, 31-34, no. 7; Samuel, *Ptolemaic Chronology* 152. On her popularity: Cic. *De reg. Alex.* Frag. 9, p. 462 Schöll.

10 EXILE: Justin 39.5.1; Porphyry, *FGrH* 260, F 2.8-11 = Euseb. *Chron.* I, cols. 164 ff. Schoene. See too App. *BCiv.* 1.102. Berenice was associated with her father on the throne as 'Cleopatra' (Pestman 72); Bouché-Leclercq (II, 116 note 1) suggests the necessity now for this as a throne-name. It is true that the most powerful of the Ptolemaic women during Berenice's lifetime had all borne this name: Cleopatra II-IV. Selene: probably Tryphaena, wife of Grypus: *Pros. Ptol.* 14521; cf. *RE* 11 (1922) 787 f. and Otto and Bengtson, *Ptolemäerreiches* 50 and note 5. In addition, her father's cousin had been Cleopatra Thea, wife of three Seleucids, as her cousin Selene was to be. PTOLEMY XI ALEXANDER II: *P. Turin* 6085 names him together with Alexander I and Berenice III. Pestman maintains (72 note e and 76 note b) that this text proves Berenice the mother of Alexander II. By the time Lathyros died in 80, Alexander II was in Rome: Euseb. *Chron.* I, 166 Schoene. See also App. *BCiv.* 1.102. BERENICE RULES ALONE: Porphyry F 2.9; Euseb. *Chron.* I, 166 Schoene, for six months. Samuel, *Ptolemaic Chronology* 153; Pestman 76. Bouché-Leclercq II, 117, sees this as a respite from quarrels. Eusebius (emended) has her consent to Alexander's coming. JOINTLY: *P. Grenf.* II 38 continues its odyssey: *BASP* 16 (1979) 215.

11 REIGN OF PTOLEMY XI: App. *BCiv.* 1.102 says Sulla 'proclaimed him ruler of the Alexandrians.' However, he was 'recalled' to Alexandria, for Porphyry *ap.* Euseb. *Chron.* I, 166 Schoene. See too Plut. *Luc.* 3.1; App. *Mith.* 23.93 and 117.577; Jos. *AJ* 13.349 and 14.112. If the man Strabo means in 17.1.8.794 by 'Kokkes' and 'Pareisaktos' is Alexander I, then the boy had

precedent in distributing inherited Ptolemaic treasures. Strabo describes here the spoliation of the gold sarcophagus of Alexander the Great, probably being coined for distribution to mercenaries. See *RE* 23.2 (1959) 1744. On the relation of Ptolemy XII to Berenice, see Pestman 72-76. Cicero calls her *reginam sororem suam* (*De reg. Alex.* Frag. 9). The passage in Euseb. *Chron.* I, 166 Schoene, first mentions Cleopatra (= Berenice III), then calls Alexander II an 'ancestor of Cleopatra [VII],' then has him marry 'the aforementioned Cleopatra,' who is Berenice III again. The passage makes sense only if he is thinking of the famous Cleopatra in calling Alexander II her *progonos.* END OF THE REIGN: See the references to Porphyry; Eusebius; Cicero; Appian above in this note; *P. Oxy.* 2222. Pestman 76-77: September 80 BC. Justin *Prol.* 39 has him expelled, not killed; the scholiast to Cic. *Verr.* II, 4.27 takes him for refuge to Tyre. On the money there and the testament: Cic. *Leg. Agr.* 1.1.1 and 2.16.41-17.44; *De reg. Alex.* Frag. 9 = *Scholia Bobiensia*, 1907, p. 32 (Hildebrand) = p. 465 Schöll. See above, Ch. 2, § 1, note 1. See too Olshausen, *Rom und Ägypten* 14 note 17; 22 ff. Bibliography: *RE* 23.2 (1959) 1748, with Badian, *RhM* 110 (1967) 178-192; Braund, *Friendly King* 134. CRASSUS: Plut. *Crass.* 13.1.551.

12 DATE: Pestman, *Chronologie* 76 ff.; Samuel, *Ptolemaic Chronology* 153-156. See too *RE* 23.2 (1959) cols. 1748-1755, no. 33; *OGIS* 182-192; Will, *Histoire Politique* 437 ff. CORONATION: Reymond and Barnes, *Orientalia* 46 (1977) 13; British Museum Stela No. 886 = J. Quaegebeur, *CE* 49 (1974) 59 ff. no. 25. SYRIA: Cic. *De reg. Alex.* Frag. 9: *quum ille rex* [Ptolemy XI Alexander II] *sit interfectus, hunc puerum in Syria fuisse.* See Justin 40.2.3; App. *Syr.* 49.250 and *Mith.* 106.500; Schürer (Vermes and Millar) 135-136; Euseb. *Chron.* I, 262 Schoene. BETROTHAL: The brother, also named Ptolemy, is *Pros. Ptol.* 14559. He ruled Cyprus from 80 to 58 but did not return when his brother did from Rome: Ch. 8, § 23. On the betrothal, Seibert, *Zu den dynastischen Verbindungen* 120-121; Otto and Bengtson, *Ptolemäerreiches* 177. See also E. Bloedow, *Beiträge zur Geschichte des Ptolemaios XII.* (Diss. Würzburg 1963) 18 ff.; Heinen 169; *RE* 15 (1932) 2200; *RE Suppl.* 15 (1978) 400; above, Ch. 2, § 3, note 29. The betrothal is mentioned only in App. *Mith.* 111.536. Though ambiguous in context, the participle *syntrephomenai* probably governs *tois basileusin* also and thus shows the four royal progeny once being raised together at court. AULETES IN EGYPT: Pestman 76-83; Samuel 154-155; *BGU* 1292; F. Preisigke and W. Spiegelberg, *Die Prinz-Joachim Ostraka* (Strassburg 1914) n. 1 and pp. 20 f. TITLES: *SEG* 8 (1937) no. 468.

13 THE ROYAL COUPLE: *OGIS* 182-183; cf. 185; Bernand, *Fayoum* I, 34-37, nos. 9-10. PARENTAGE: Justin *Prol.* 39; the *Prologue* to Book 40 recognizes his paternity from Lathyros. See Pausan. 1.9.3; Cic. *Leg. Agr.* 2.16.42;

Justin 39.4.1; Jos. *AJ* 13.349. App. *BCiv.* 1.102 and *Mith.* 23.93 mention Ptolemy Alexander II specifically (as son of Alexander I), but not the other grandsons of Cleopatra III by Lathyros. Inscriptional evidence attests a son: *SEG* 9 (1938) 5. See Porphyry *FGrH* 260, F 2.12 = Euseb. *Chron.* I, 168 Schoene; Cic. *Sest.* 26.57: *eodem genere eisdemque maioribus.* Bibliography: *RE* 23.2 (1959) 1748 f. See too E. Olshausen, *Rom und Ägypten* 30 f. note 39. SELENE: Justin 39.4.4 and 39.4.1. DESCRIPTION OF AULETES: Cic. *De reg. Alex.*: *hunc puerum in Syria fuisse; Leg. Agr.* 2.16.42.

14 This is based on a restudy of the family's funerary stelae, especially British Museum Stela No. 886 and Vienna Stela No. 82. See Reymond and Barns, *Orientalia* 46 (1977) 1-33. The connection with the Ptolemies proceeds from the Vienna stela's possible mention of Berenice, wife of Psherenptah, as sister of Ptolemy X Alexander I, and assumes her a daughter of Cleopatra III and Ptolemy VIII Euergetes II. On the investiture of Petubastis II see their pp. 11 f. See too J. Quaegebeur, 'Genealogy' (above, note 3) 52 with 65-71 nos. 21-27; *PP* 5371 and 5376.

15 HONOURS FOR PETUBASTIS: Reymond and Barns, *Orientalia* 46 (1977) 1-33. PSHERENPTAH III SOVEREIGN: Reymond and Barns 12 f. with Vienna Stela No. 82. The term used is *ity*, 'king.' REGNAL YEARS OF AULETES: Pestman 77-83. STELA OF PSHERENPTAH: Reymond and Barnes 13. Bevan, *Egypt* 347 f. provides the translation quoted here. SELENE AND SONS: Jos. *AJ* 13.419-420; *BJ* 1.116; Strabo 16.2.3.749; Cic. *Verr.* II, 4.27.60-30.68. TESTAMENTARY BEQUESTS: Sall. *Hist.* 2.43; Justin 39.5.2; Livy *Per.* 70; Jul. Obsequens 49; Amm. Marc. 22.16.24; Plut. *Luc.* 2.7; App. *Mith.* 121.600. Bibliography: *RE* 23.2 (1959) 1738. PRINCES IN ROME, THEN SICILY: Cic. *Verr.* II, 4.27.60 to 4.32.71. A papyrus which might date to 'year 3' of Auletes (*BGU* 1730) reflects agricultural scarcity. Wilhelm Schubart in his introduction to *BGU* VIII (1933) 1-2, dated it rather to year 3 of Cleopatra VII by the 'discovery' (underneath the present writing) of an earlier edict to 'Heliodorus,' but this on more recent re-examination has proved unverifiable. See Bloedow 23, note 1; Fraser, *Ptol. Alex.* II, 231, n. 298. See also Ch. 8, § 23, notes 155 and 167.

Chapter 5

1 ARMENIA: Maps in Cary, *Geographic Background* Ch. VI (3); *TAVO* B V 6; Jones, *Cities*[2] Ch. 9. Bibliography by M.-L. Chaumont, 'L'Arménie entre Rome et l'Iran, I. De l'avènement d'Auguste à l'avènement de Dioclétien': *ANRW* II 9.1 (Berlin 1976) 71-194, esp. 190-193. See also: J. Wolski, 'Iran und Rom. Versuch einer historischen Wertung der gegenseitigen Beziehungen': *ANRW* II 9.1 (Berlin 1976) 195-214, and G. Widen-

gren, 'Iran, der grosse Gegner Roms: Königsgewalt, Feudalismus, Militärwesen': *ANRW* II 9.1 (Berlin 1976) 219-306 (only a portion of these last two cited are relevant to Armenia proper). For the earlier period, see the bibliography in my dissertation, *Some Dynastic Answers to the Armenian Question* (California 1970; publ. University Microfilms 1971) Ch. I-II and pp. 317 ff. Other studies as in Ch. 9, § 24 and below. TIGRANES: Justin 38.3.1 shows his detention; cf. Strabo 11.14.15.532. His date of birth as early as 140 BC can be loosely deduced from the remark of Lucian, *Macrob.* 15, that he lived eighty-five years, coupled with the evidence in Cic. *Sest.* 27.59 that he was still alive and reigning in 56 BC (*regnat hodie*), with Artavasdes I, his son, on the throne by 54 BC: Dio 40.16.2 and Plut. *Crass.* 19.1. His accession date depends on synchronization of his activity with that of Mithradates Eupator and Ariobarzanes I, who seems to have been driven from his throne soon after receiving it, with Tigranes the specific agent: Justin 38.3.1-3. See Ch. 2, § 5 for the controversy about dating this. The version of A.N. Sherwin-White in *CQ* 71 = n.s. 27 (1977) 173-183 would have Tigranes ruling by 95. Other bibliography by Hoben 148, but with a later date for the first ejection, following E. Badian in *Athenaeum* n.s. 37 (1959) 279 ff. = *Studies in Greek and Roman History* (Oxford 1964) 157-178. See too Sullivan, 'Cappadocia' 1127-1136. Plut. *Luc.* 21.6 gives twenty-five years of rule to Tigranes by 71/70 BC – which may be but need not be 'a mere approximation' (Badian 176 note 49). The marriage to Cleopatra, daughter of Mithradates, probably occurred about 93, though no certainty is possible. See too Magie 1099 notes 15-16. MITHRADATES II vs. GOTARZES: See this chapter, § 13. HIS WAR WITH ARTAVASDES I: Justin 42.4.1, resuming the narrative concerning Mithradates II broken off at 42.2.7. ARTAXIADS: See stemma. See too Strabo 11.14.15.532; Polyb. 25.2.12. The father of Artaxias was a Zariadres, as known from Aramaic marker stones: Frye, *Persia* Ch. 5, note 35. He claims Orontid descent on an Aramaic inscription: S. Der Nersessian, *The Armenians* (London 1969) 24-25. 'Not even once': Strabo 16.1.19.745; H.F. Tournebise, *Histoire politique et religieux de l'Arménie*, I (Paris 1910) 19-23 and Appendice, 761 f. no. 3. ORONTIDS: The family ruled Armenia from about 331 BC to about 188, and was replaced by the Artaxiads. See C. Toumanoff, *Studies in Christian Caucasian History* (Washington 1963) 277-305, tracing the survival of this family among princely houses of Armenia for centuries, as well as in Commagene (§ 6). See too M.J. Osborne, 'Orontes': *Historia* 22 (1973) 515-551; R.D. Wilkinson, 'Orontes, Son of Artasyras': *REArm* n.s. 7 (1970) 445-450.

2 PARTHIANS vs. TIGRANES: Strabo 11.14.15.532 and 16.1.19.745. ARME-

NIAN PROBLEM: See Ch. 9, § 24, with Ch. 10. The climax: Dio 63.1.1-8.5; A. von Gutschmid, *Geschichte Irans und seiner Nachbarländer von Alexander dem Grossen bis zum Untergang der Arsaciden* (Tübingen 1888) 79 ff.

3 ARMENIA: For maps of the eventual holdings of Tigranes, see those in *ANRW* II 9.2 at pp. 8 and 200, with C. Burney and D.M. Lang, *The Peoples of the Hills: Ancient Ararat and Caucasus* (London 1971) 190. See too E. Olshausen and J. Wagner, *TAVO* B V 6. Calder-Bean shows a portion of the area. Most of it appears in standard classical maps. For the Iranian portion: N. Debevoise, *A Political History of Parthia* (Chicago 1938) endpaper; U. Kahrstedt, *Artabanos III. und seine Erben* (Bern 1950) Maps I-II; *CAH* X 47; Jones, *Cities*[2] Maps IV-V; S. Der Nersessian, *The Armenians* (London 1969) 13; Cary, *Geographic Background* 175. SOPHENE: See this chapter, § 12 and Ch. 9, § 24. See also Th. Frankfort, 'La Sophène et Rom': *Latomus* 22 (1963) 181-190; Strabo 11.14.5-6.528-529 and 11.14.15.532. See especially C. Toumanoff, *Studies* 277-303, nos. 11-14; G. Le Rider, *RN* (sér. 6) 2 (1959/1960) 21 f. no. 22.

4 TOMISA: Strabo 12.2.1.535. MARRIAGE WITH CLEOPATRA: App. *Mith.* 15.54; Justin 38.3.2; Plut. *Luc.* 14.6; 22.5; Memnon, *FGrH* 434 F 29.6 (43.2); Magie 1099 note 16. CONFLICT WITH SULLA: Plut. *Sulla* 5.3.

5 PARTHIAN DEALINGS: See this chapter, § 13. Dates and discussion: A.N. Sherwin-White in *CQ* n.s. 27 (1977) 173-183. Other sources in R. Sullivan, 'The Dynasty of Cappadocia': *ANRW* II.7.2 (Berlin 1979) notes 19-26. See also Plut. *Sulla* 5.3.5; Livy *Per.* 70 and 100; Vell. Pat. 2.24.3; App. *Mith.* 10.31 and 57.231; Dio 36.45.3 and 36.51.1. On his spurning of Eupator: Plut. *Luc.* 22.1. PHRAATES III: Livy *Per.* 100; Dio *ibid.*; Plut. *Pomp.* 36.3; Memnon, *FGrH* 434, F 38.8 (58). See below, Ch. 9, § 26. ARYAZATE-AUTOMA TO PARTHIA: The parchment showing this daughter of Tigranes there was published by Ellis Minns in *JHS* 35 (1915) 22-65. Discussion by R. Sullivan, 'Papyri Reflecting the Eastern Dynastic Network': *ANRW* II.8 (Berlin 1977) 911-914. Remarks by K. Dobbins in *NC* (ser. 7) 15 (1975) 21 note 10.

6 COINS: P. Bedoukian in *ANSMusN* 14 (1968) 41-66; R. Sullivan in *NC* (ser. 7) 13 (1973) 18-37; Mionnet, *Suppl.* VII (Paris 1835) 725 no. 6: associated with his son; see Ch. 9, § 24, note 21. THE FEAR OF PHRAATES III: Plut. *Luc.* 30.1-2. PONTUS ALLIED WITH PARTHIA: App. *Mith.* 15.54 records a report by Pelopidas in 89 that 'Tigranes the Armenian is his son-in-law and Arsaces the Parthian his ally.'

7 CONQUESTS: Strabo 11.14.15.532 and 16.1.24.747. The satrap of Media was later pursued by Pompey 'because he had been an ally either of Antiochus [I of Commagene] or of Tigranes before that': App. *Mith.* 106.497 and 117.576. Cf. Diod. 40.4. Penetration to Ecbatana: Isidore of Charax, c. 6 (*Geog. Min.*

Didot, I, 250); Reinach, *Mithridate Eupator* 311. See also Justin, *Prol.* 41: *Tigranes ... a quo subacta est Media et Mesopotamia*; Plut. *Luc.* 27.6. INTERMARRIAGE: Dio 36.14.2: 'the other Mithridates, from Media, son-in-law of Tigranes.' This may be Atropatene, for the satrap of Media mentioned above was Darius, and both appear close contemporaries. See also Magie 338 ff. TIGRANOCERTA: *TAVO* B V 6; Strabo 16.1.23.747; 11.12.4.522; 11.14.15.532; 12.2.9.539. See too App. *Mith.* 67.285 and 84.379-381; Tac. *Ann.* 15.5; Plut. *Luc.* 14.5; 21.4; 26.1. Nobles there: App. *Mith.* 84.379 and probably 86.392. Discussion by R. Sullivan, *Armenian Question* 54-59. See also *RE* 6A (1936) 967-982; Magie 1214 note 36; Sir R. Syme, 'Tigranocerta. A Problem Misconceived': *Armies and Frontiers in Roman and Byzantine Anatolia*, ed. S. Mitchell (Oxford 1983; BAR International Series 156; British Institute of Archaeology at Ankara Monograph No. 5) 61-70. SITE: R. Hewsen, *Revue des études arméniennes* [*REArm*] n.s. 16 (1982) 111-150, esp. 140-142. See the *Tübinger Atlas des Vorderen Orients (TAVO)* B V 6 (Wiesbaden 1981). See too Th. Reinach, *Mithridate Eupator, roi de Pont* (Paris 1890) 345 ff. (hereafter: Reinach, *Mithridate* to distinguish it from the German edition, 1895); M.-L. Chaumont, 'Tigranocerte': *REArm* n.s. 16 (1982).

8 TURNED WEST: Justin 40.1.3. Perhaps as early as 86: Justin 40.1.4 says *accitus in regnum Syriae per X et VIII annos tranquillissimo regno potitus est* by 69 BC. ARAB ALLIES: Plut. *Luc.* 21.1-2; Justin, *Prol.* 41; Plin. 6.28.142; Strabo 16.1.26.747-28.748. See R. Sullivan, 'The Dynasty of Emesa': *ANRW* II.8 (Berlin 1977) 198 ff. on Arabs here. TIGRANES TO ANTIOCH: Jos. *AJ* 13.419. Strabo 11.9.2.515 ascribes his success principally to Seleucid weakness. App. *Syr.* 48.248 has him ruling Syria '14 years' by 69. On the coins see Head HN^2 772 f. Damascus: Newell, *Late Seleucid Mints* (1939) 95 ff. Tigranes in Nisibis preparatory to invasion of Syria: H. Seyrig in *RN* (sér. 5) 17 (1955) 85-128, esp. section IV.

9 TIGRANES A *DIADOCHUS*: R. Sullivan in *NC* (ser. 7) 13 (1973) 18 ff.; Schürer (Vermes and Millar) 135. CILICIA: See Ch. 3, § 8. TIGRANES'S YEARS IN SYRIA: App. *Syr.* 48.247-49.250; Memnon, *FGrH* 434 F 22; Strabo 12.2.9.539; Justin 40.2.3. THE CAPPADOCIAN QUESTION: Ariarathes IX, son of Eupator, claimed the throne at least until 88. As late as 67, Tigranes and Mithradates could hold the country: Cic. *Leg. Man.* 2.5. Dio 37.10.4: Eupator in 63. For the worst of Tigranes's invasions there, see App. *Mith.* 67.284-285; Strabo 12.2.9.539.

10 SYRIAN TENURE OF TIGRANES: App. *Syr.* 48.247-248; Cic. *Verr.* II, 4.27.61. App. *Syr.* 49.250 and *Mith.* 106.500 specify the logic of title by conquest. See too Justin 40.2.3. CITIES: Schürer (Vermes and Millar) 228 and note 32.

11 TIGRANES AND THE GREEKS: Plut. *Luc.* 21.3-5; 26.1; 29.2; Dio 36.2.1 ff.

GOURAS: Dio 36.7.4; Plut. *Luc.* 32.4. The position of Tigranes now beyond the Euphrates is covered in Plut. *Luc.* 24 ff. TIGRANES AND MITHRADATES: Dio 36.3.1-2; Plut. *Luc.* 26.3 ff.; 22.1; Magie 1213 f. note 34. SELENE: Strabo 16.2.3.749; Jos. *AJ* 13.419-421 and *BJ* 1.116.

12 SOPHENE: C. Toumanoff, *Studies in Christian Caucasian History* (Washington 1963) 277-305, and his *Manuel de généalogie et de Chronologie pour l'histoire de la Caucasie chrétienne (Arménie - Géorgie - Albanie)* (Rome 1976) 410. See too Th. Frankfort, 'La Sophene et Rome': *Latomus* 22 (1963) 181-190; *RE* 3A (1929) 1015-1019 (Weissbach). On the dynasty: J. Markwart, *Erānčahr nach der Geographie des Ps. Movsēs Xorenac'i* (Berlin 1901) 176. SOHAEMUS: Tac. *Ann.* 13.7.1, with R. Sullivan, 'Emesa': *ANRW* II 8 (Berlin 1977) 198-219, esp. 216-218. See also A.A. Barrett, 'Sohaemus, King of Emesa and Sophene': *AJP* 98 (1977) 153-159; Tac. *Ann.* 13.7; Luc. 2.587-596.

13 OSRHOENE: A. von Gutschmid, 'Untersuchungen über die Geschichte des Königreichs Osroëne': *Mémoires de l'Académie impériale des sciences de St. Pétersbourg* (sér. 7) 35 (1887) 1-49; M. Rubens-Duval, 'Histoire politique, religieuse et littéraire d'Édesse jusqu'à la Première Croisade': *JA* (sér. 8) 18 (1891) 87-133; 201-278; 381-439; 19 (1892) 5-102. A misprint at the beginning of Chapter III gives '312' BC for '132' BC as date of inception for the kingdom. See too A.R. Bellinger and C.B. Welles, 'A Third-Century Contract of Sale from Edessa in Osrhoene': *YCS* 5 (1935) 95-155, esp. 121 ff.; Jones, *Cities*^{2} Ch. 9, with 442-444, notes 4-10; H.J.W. Drijvers, 'Hatra, Palmyra, und Edessa. Die Städte der syrisch-mesopotamischen Wüste in politischer, kulturgeschichtlicher und religionsgeschichtlicher Beleuchtung': *ANRW* II 8 (Berlin 1977) 799-906; A. Bertinelli in *ANRW* 9.1 (1976) 3-45; J. Wagner, 'Provincia Osrhoenae. New Archaeological Finds Illustrating the Military Organisation under the Severan Dynasty': *Armies and Frontiers in Roman and Byzantine Anatolia*, ed. S. Mitchell (Oxford 1983; BAR International Series 156; British Institute of Archaeology at Ankara Monograph No. 5) 103-129, with Pl. 8.1-5; E. Babelon, 'Numismatique d'Édesse': *Mélanges Numismatiques* (sér. 2), 1893, 209-296; G.F. Hill, *BMC Arabia* xciv ff. and 100 ff.; U. Kahrstedt, *Artabanos III. und seine Erben* (Bern 1950) Ch. 6. See also *RE* 5 (1905) 1933-1938; 18 (1942) 1589-1590 (O. Krückmann); Head *HN*^{2} 814-815; *PIR*^{2} A 5-11; P. Naster, 'Les monnaies d'Édesse': *RBN* 114 (1968) 5-13.

14 ABGAR II: H.I. MacAdam and N.J. Munday, 'Cicero's Reference to Bostra (*Ad Q. frat.* 2.11.3)': *CP* 78 (1983) 131-136. It should be noted that Antiochus I of Commagene was not 'an Arab king.' They think Cicero refers here to Abgar (cf. Ch. 9, § 26, note 97). Useful on Zeugma: J. Wagner, *Seleukeia am Euphrat/Zeugma* (Wiesbaden 1976). See also below, Ch. 7, § 22, note 61.

RELIGION: Rubens-Duval (above, note 13) Ch. 5; H.J.W. Drijvers, *Cults and Beliefs at Edessa* (Leiden 1972); J.B. Segal, *Edessa, the 'Blessed City'* (Oxford 1970) esp. 5-22, 261-264 (maps), and 265-289 (bibliography).

15 ADIABENE: Kahrstedt (above, note 13) Ch. 6; Fraenkel in *RE* 1 (1894) 360; J. Teixidor, 'The Kingdom of Adiabene and Hatra': *Berytus* 17 (1967-68) 1-11; Strabo 16.1.19.745. ASSYRIA: Amm. Marc. 23.6.20: *Adiabena ... Assyria priscis temporibus vocitata*; Plin. *HN* 5.66. On *-ene*, see W.W. Tarn, *The Greeks in Bactria and India*, 2nd ed. (Cambridge, Eng. 1951) 2-4 and 442-445 (Appendix 2). NATUNIA: J.T. Milik, 'A propos d'un atelier monetaire d'Adiabene: Natounia': *RN* (sér. 6) 3 (1961) 51-58; cf. 2 (1959/1960) 291 and *Iraq* 29 (1967) 16-33.

16 ADIABENI: Plut. *Luc.* 26-27. NISIBIS: J. Sturm, *RE* 17 (1937) 714-757. The coin, of which an example is in the British Museum, is published by R. Sullivan in *NC* (ser. 7) 13 (1973) 18 ff. See too H. Seyrig, 'Trésor monétaire de Nisibe': *RN* (sér. 5) 17 (1955) 85-128.

17 Jos. *AJ* 20.17-96; *BJ* 1.6; 2.388 and 520; 4.567; 5.147, 262, 474; 6.356. See also N. Clarke, 'Helena's Pyramids': *PEQ* 70 (1938) 88 ff. See too *PIR*^{2} H 47; J 891; *PIR* M 490 ff.

18 TRAJAN AND LATER: Magie 608, 672-673, 686, 1554 notes 44-45.

19 HATRA: J. Teixidor (above, note 15) discusses the link with Adiabene. See too A. Maricq, 'Hatra de Sanatrouq': *Syria* 32 (1956) 273-288; Maricq, *Syria* 34 (1957) 288-296. Texts discussed by A. Caquot: *Syria* 29 (1952) 89-118; 30 (1953) 234-246; 32 (1955) 49-69 and 261-272; 40 (1963); 41 (1964). See also *RE* 7 (1912) 2516-2523; B. Aggoula, *Berytus* 18 (1969) 85-104; S. Downey, 'Cult Banks from Hatra?': *Berytus* 16 (1966) 97-109; Kahrstedt 66-68; J.M.C. Toynbee, 'Some Problems of Romano-Parthian Sculpture at Hatra': *JRS* 62 (1972) 106-110; F. Safar and M.A. Mustafa, *Hatra: the City of the Sun God* (Baghdad 1974; in Arabic); M.A.R. Colledge, 'Some Observations on Sculptors' Stone-Carving Techniques at Hatra': *Sumer* 32 (1977) 135-40; Colledge, *Parthian Art* (London 1978), *passim*; J.K. Ibrahim, *Pre-Islamic Settlements in Jazirah* (Baghdad 1986) esp. 99-115, with Pl. 67. See the series of 'Remarques sur les inscriptions Hatréens' by B. Aggoula; no. XI, in *Syria* 64 (1987) 91-106, has bibliography on the first ten of these.

20 GORDYENE: *TAVO* B V 6. Debevoise, endpaper; E. Herzfeld, *The Persian Empire* (Wiesbaden 1968) 200-201; Th. Liebmann-Frankfort 229 ff.; Kahrstedt 58-69; *RE* 7 (1912) 1594 ff.; Strabo 16.1.25.747.

21 TIGRANES: Strabo 11.14.15.532; cf. 11.14.8.529 and 16.1.1.736. ZARBIENUS: Plut. *Luc.* 21.2; 26; 29; Sall. *Hist.* 4.56 Maurenb.; E. Rawson, *Historia* 22 (1973) 231.

22 POMPEY: Strabo 16.1.24.747; Dio 37.5-7; App. *Mith.* 106.501; Plut. *Pomp.* 36; Debevoise 73 ff. POMPEY'S TRIUMPH: App. *Mith.* 114.556-118.583.

23 App. *Mith.* 105.495; Gwatkin 18 note 10; T.B. Mitford, 'Cappadocia and Armenia Minor: Historical Setting of the *Limes*': *ANRW* II 7.2 (Berlin 1980) 1169-1228.

24 CHARACENE: A. Nodelman, 'A Preliminary History of Characene': *Berytus* 13 (1960) 83-121, with Pl. 27-28; J. Hansman, 'Charax and the Karkeh': *IA* 7 (1967) 21-58 (= *Mélanges Ghirshman*, 2); E. Newell, 'Mithradates of Parthia and Hyspaosines of Charax': *NNM* 26 (New York 1925) 1-18; Weissbach in *RE* 3 (1899) 2115-2119 and 15 (1932) 1083-1084; Baumstark in *RE* 2 (1896) 2700-2718 ('Babylonia'); Kahrstedt 52-57; Debevoise 39-42. See too *OGIS* 231; Juba, *FGrH* 275, F 29-33; Plin. *NH* 6.124 and 6.139; Tarn, *CAH* IX, 584 f.

25 THE COINAGE: Much of the cumulative bibliography is available through the work of G. Le Rider, 'Monnaies de Characene': *Syria* 36 (1959) 229-253 with Pl. 19-22; his *Suse* (below, note 36); cf. his note in *RN* (sér. 6) 2 (1959/1960) 35 on coins of Tiraios II from 78/77 to 48/47 BC (Sel. 234-264). See too A. Bellinger, 'Hyspaosines of Charax': *YCS* 8 (1942) 54-67; G.F. Hill, *BMC Arabia* 200 ff.; M.R. Zamir-Dahncke, 'Phraates: ein bisher unbekanntenen Herrscher in der Charakene': *Arch. Mitt. Iran* N.F. 10 (1977) 209 ff.; Head *HN*[2] 820 ff.; Kahrstedt 52 ff.; *RN* (sér. 6) 11 (1969) 7-27 and *NC* (ser. 7) 6 (1966) 348; cf. *RN* (sér. 4) 38 (1935) 158 ff.

26 PETRA: Plin. *HN* 6.141. On the Dumata Road, see M. Speidel in *Historia* 36 (1987) 213-221. ISIDORE: W. Schoff, *The Parthian Stations of Isidore of Charax* (Philadelphia 1914). On his date, B. Mukherjee, *An Agrippan Source* (Calcutta 1969) 211-215. See too *FGrH* 781 = Müller, *Geog. Gr. Min.* I, 244 ff.

27 *PIR*[2] A 1160 and 1329; Ps.-Lucian, *Macrob.* 16; Eutrop. 8.3.1. On Artabazus: M. Rostovtzeff, *CAH* XI 118; Dio 68.28.4. THE INSCRIPTION OF VOLOGAESES: E. Quarantelli (ed.), *La Terra tra i due Fiumi* (Turin 1985. Centro Ricerche Archeologice e Scavi di Torino per il Medio Oriente e l'Asia; Il Quadrante Edizioni) pp. 420-22, no. 231, with Pls. on pp. 340-41; 421. SCULPTURE: F. Basmachi, 'Miscellanea in the Iraq Museum': *Sumer* 18, pp. 48-50. My thanks to Professor Malcolm Colledge for some details on these last two items.

28 ELYMAIS: Kahrstedt Ch. 4, 37-47; Debevoise 21-27; Weissbach in *RE* 5 (1905) 2458-2467; Tarn, *CAH* IX, Ch. XIV.

29 KINGS: *BMC Arabia*, clxxxvi ff. and 245 ff.; A. von Petrowicz, *Sammlung Petrowicz, Arsakiden Münzen* (Wien 1904) 195 f. with Tafel 25. KAMNASKIRES. T. Fischer, '*Basileos Kamnisk(e)irou*': *Chiron* 1 (1971) 169-175. DIFFERENCE WITH SUSIANA: Kahrstedt 41-47; Strabo 11.13.6.524. Strabo 16.1.1.736 distinguishes them. See too *RE* 4 A (1932) 988 (Honigmann). RELATIONS WITH PARTHIA: Strabo 16.1.18.744; Justin 41.6.8;

Debevoise 23-26; K.W. Dobbins, *NC* (ser. 7) 15 (1975) 37-39; Head *HN*[2] 822-823; *RN* (sér. 6) 11 (1969) 18-22. The rain-god of Elymais appears on the coins of Phraates III: D. Sellwood in R.A.G. Carson, *Mints, Dies, and Currency* (London 1971) 34. SELEUCID RAIDS: Bibliography in *RE* 5 (1905) 2464-2465 (Weissbach). See too Debevoise 18 note 75 and 21 note 92; Strabo 16.1.18.744; Polyb. 31.9(11); Justin 36.1.4; App. *Syr.* 66.352; D. Mendels, 'A Note on the Tradition of Antiochus IV's Death': *IEJ* 31 (1981) 53-56, with further bibliography.

30 POMPEY: Plut. *Pomp.* 36.2; Allotte de la Fuye in *RN* (sér. 4) 6 (1902) 92 ff. AD 35: Tac. *Ann.* 6.44.4.

31 PERSIS: Kahrstedt 37-47, and both maps following p. 89, showing its rapid growth between AD 38 and 60. See too *RE Suppl.* 12 (1970) 1022-1038 (W. Hinz), with map.

32 Arrian, *Anab.* 3.18; 6.28-30; 7.30; Diod. 19.14.4-5; Curtius 5.5.5-21; 10.1.22 ff.; *OGIS* 233. WARLIKE: Diod. 19.21.3.

33 *BMC Arabia* clx-clxxxii and 235-245; *CRAI* 1920, 133 ff.; Debevoise 13; 25-27.

34 Strabo 13.3.3.728; cf. 15.3.24.736. See Tarn, *CAH* IX, Ch. XIV.

35 Debevoise 268-269; Rawlinson, *Sixth Monarchy* 365-370; *PIR*[2] A 1166; Frye, *Persia* Ch. 6.

36 PARTHIA: See the maps in Debevoise, endpaper; Rawlinson, *Sixth Monarchy* Ch. 1; Kahrstedt, endpapers; Frye, *Persia* 286 ff. THE ARSACIDS: Fundamental remain the studies by N. Debevoise, *A Political History of Parthia* (Chicago 1938), W.W. Tarn in *CAH IX*, and G. Rawlinson, *The Sixth Great Oriental Monarchy ... Parthia* (London 1873). Stemma of the dynasty: R. Sullivan, 'Papyri Reflecting the Eastern Dynastic Network': *ANRW* II 8 (1977), second foldout after p. 938. See too K. Schippmann, *Grundzüge der parthischen Geschichte* (Darmstadt 1980). Highly important but difficult to use are Parthian coins, usually designating the king simply as 'Arsaces.' See D. Sellwood, *An Introduction to the Coinage of Parthia* (London 1971); Head *HN*[2] 817 ff.; W. Wroth, *BMC Parthia* (London 1903); R.H. McDowell, *Coins from Seleucia on the Tigris* (New York 1935); E. Newell, *Some Unpublished Coins of Eastern Dynasts* (New York 1926); *Sammlung Petrowicz, Arsakiden Münzen* (Vienna 1904); P. Gardner, *The Coinage of Parthia* (London 1877; repr. 1968); R.A. Olsen, 'Studies in the Coinage of the Arsacid Rulers of Parthia' (Diss. Minnesota 1968; *DA* 30, 1969, 234A); G. Le Rider, *Suse sous les Séleucides et les Parthes* (Paris 1965).

Specific studies are legion. The ones of especial use here include the following: A. Simonetta, 'Some Remarks on the Arsacid Coinage of the Period 90-57 B.C.': *NC* (ser. 7) 6 (1966) 15-40 with Pl. I-II, and his 'le contromarche della monetazione arsacide': *GNS* 30 (1980) 62-67; H. Seyrig, 'Trésor monétaire de Nisibe': *RN* (sér. 5) 17 (1955) 85-128; G. Le Rider, 'Un Trésor ... à Ninive': *IA* 7 (1967) 4-20; K.W. Dobbins, 'The Successors of Mithradates II of Parthia': *NC* (ser. 7) 15 (1975) 19-45 and Pl. 2-3; D.G. Sellwood, 'Wroth's Unknown Parthian King': *NC* (ser. 7) 5 (1965) 113-135 and Pl. X-XI; O. Mørkholm, 'The Parthian Coinage of Seleucia on the Tigris, *c.* 90-55 B.C.': *NC* (ser. 7) 20 (1980) 33-47. Useful for problems of continuity by the time of Mithradates II: D.G. Sellwood, 'Deux notes sur les drachmes arsacides': *RN* (sér. 6) 13 (1971) 154-157; M. Abgarians and D. Sellwood, 'A Hoard of Early Parthian Drachms': *NC* (ser. 7) 11 (1971) 103-119 and Pl. 20-23. Useful for dating: M.-L. Chaumont, 'Les ostraca de Nisa': *JA* 1968, 11-35, and 'Études d'histoire parthe, 1: documents royaux à Nisa': *Syria* 48 (1971) 143-164. See also E. Bickerman in *BO* 23 (1966) 15-17; a misprint dates Ostracon no. 1760 to AD 91 rather than 91 BC. Other studies: T. Fischer, *Untersuchungen zum Partherkrieg Antiochos' VII im Rahmen der Seleukidengeschichte* (Diss. München; publ. Tübingen 1970); R.N. Frye, *The Heritage of Persia* (Cleveland 1962; Mentor 1963); *The History of Ancient Iran* (Munich 1984). See too studies by G. Widengren and J. Wolski cited elsewhere. See as well M. Colledge, *Parthian Art* (London 1978); Colledge, 'Parthian Art and the Roman East': *ANRW* II 12.4; Colledge, 'Greek and Non-Greek Interaction in the Art and Architecture of the Hellenistic East' in A. Kuhrt and S. Sherwin-White (eds.), *Hellenism in the East* (London 1987) 134-162 with Figs. 4-12 and Pls. I-XIV; W. Schur in *RE* 18 (1949) 1968-2029 ('Parthia'); Tarn, *CAH* IX, Ch. XIV; A. von Gutschmid, *Geschichte Irans und seiner Nachbarländer* (Tübingen 1888) 79 ff. Also on the environs of Parthia: U. Kahrstedt, *Artabanos III. und seine Erben* (Berne 1950), with review by E.W. Gray in *JRS* 43 (1953) 164 f. Still useful: J. Vaillant, *Arsacidarum imperium, sive regum Parthorum historia*, I-II (Paris 1725 and 1728).

DESCENT OF ARSACIDS: On their putative derivation from Artaxerxes II of the Achaemenid house, see I.M. Dyadov and V.A. Livšits, *Dokumenty iz Nisy* (Moscow 1960) 20, where the site at Nisa bears the name *artaxšarakan*. See too Arrian, *Parthica*, Frag. 1, ed. Roos (Teubner 1967 = Syncell. p. 539, 14 Bonn). Athen. *Deipn.* 12.513-515 appears to take the Parthians at their own word. See also Tac. *Ann.* 6.31.1. Strabo 11.9.3.515 derives Arsaces I from 'the Scythians' or from Bactria. E. Bickerman, in *Berytus* 8 (1944) 73 ff., defends the account of Arrian, but see *BO* 23 (1966) 15 ff. and *Historia* 11 (1962) 138. See further J. Wolski, 'De Arsacidis Achaemenidarum heredibus': *Eos* 55 (1965) 152-157. H. Bengtson, *The Greeks and the Persians* (London 1969), summarizes the claim to Syria. DELOS: M.-F. Baslez and C. Vial in *BCH* 111 (1987) 281-312, esp. 282 nos. 19 and 22.

SELEUCIDS: Parthian material appears in E. Bickerman, 'The Seleucids and the Achaemenids': *La Persia e il mondo greco romano, Acad. nazionale dei*

Lincei 76 (1966) 87-117. See E. Herzfeld, *The Persian Empire: Studies in the Geography, History and Ethnography of the Ancient Near East* (Wiesbaden 1968). W. Tarn, 'Seleucid-Parthian Studies': *PBA* 16 (1930) esp. 127 ff., studies the Parthian tendency to preserve Seleucid administrative divisions, especially the *eparchia*, intermediate between the satrapy and the hyparchy and usually designated by the termination -*HNH* in its nomenclature. Cf. his *Greeks in Bactria and India*, 2nd ed. (Cambridge, Eng. 1951) 2 ff. and 442 ff., Appendix 2. Another source of Seleucid-Parthian contact had long been through the use of Parthian mercenaries there: see M. Launey, *Recherches sur les armées hellénistiques* (Paris 1949) 546 ff.; J. Wolski, 'Le rôle et l'importance des mercenaires dans l'état parthe': *IA* 5 (1965) 103-115. See too E. Badian in *JHS* 85 (1965) 160-161; Fischer, *Untersuchungen* Ch. I. Schippmann (above, this note) sees from Mithradates II to Vologaeses I a steady policy of annexing Syria and Asia Minor. TWO EMPIRES: *Duo imperia summa*: Pliny *H.N.* 5.88. Cf. Justin 41.2.4: *Parthi, penes quos velut divisione orbis cum Romanis facta, nunc Orientis imperium est.* See also Dio 40.14.3; Strabo 11.9.2.515; Herodian 4.10.2.

37 MITHRADATES AND THE EAST: *RE* I A (1920) 1770-1806 ('Sakai'), Hermann; cf. 1807-1812; E. Herzfeld, 'Sakastan, Geschichtliche Untersuchungen zu den Ausgrabungen am Kūh i Khwādja': *Arch. Mitt. aus Iran* 4 (1931) 1-116; maps at 24 and 116; *RE Suppl.* 9, 1021. See also H. Bailey, *Corpus Inscriptionum Iranicarum*, II: *Inscriptions of the Seleucid and Parthian Period from Eastern Iran and Central Asia*, Vol. 5: *Saka Documents* (London 1968); Bailey, *Khotanese Texts* Vol. 4: *Saka Texts from Khotan in the Hedin Collection* (Cambridge, Eng. 1961); Debevoise 35-38. HYRCANIA: Herzfeld 58-86; Kahrstedt 22-25; Justin 42.2.4; cf. 41.4.7 ff.; Strabo 15.2.14.727; L. Robert, *Hellenica* XI-XII (1960) 84-91. CONQUESTS: The tradition preserved by Strabo 11.9.2.515 of Parthian conquests in 'Scythia' and Bactria at two different periods probably reflects the work of Mithradates II and his uncle, Mithradates I. The Eucratides mentioned here as being 'earlier' locates the first period in the time of Mithradates I, his contemporary. Cf. Strabo 15.1.3.686; Debevoise 19-21; *RE* 15 (1932) 2208 ff.

38 ARMENIA: Justin *Prol.* 42; 42.4.2-4, continuing the account in 42.2.6. HYSPAOSINES OF CHARACENE, SON OF SAGDODONACUS: E.T. Newell, 'Mithradates of Parthia and Hyspaosines of Characene: A Numismatic Palimpsest': *Num. Notes & Monogr.* 26 (1925) 1-18; Fischer, *Partherkrieg* Ch. 3. HIMERUS: Diod. 34.21; *BMC Parthia* xxi and 23; Posidonius, *Hist.* 16, frag. 13 = *FGrH* II A, 228 = Athen. *Deipn.* 11.466b = *FHG* III 259; Debevoise 39 notes 45-47. See too Tarn, *CAH* IX 584. On the new state in Characene, see this chapter, § 12. Military adventures of Himerus: Justin, *Prol.* 42. MITHRADATES IN BABYLON: Dobbins, *NC* (ser. 7) 15 (1975) 19-45.

39 GOTARZES I AND ORODES I: Debevoise 50-52; Dobbins, *NC* (ser. 7) 15 (1975) 19-45; D.G. Sellwood, 'The Parthian Coinage of Gotarzes I, Orodes I, and Sinatruces': *NC* (ser. 7) 2 (1962) 73-89. Behistun: *OGIS* 431, with E. Herzfeld, *Am Tor von Asien* (Berlin 1920) 35 ff., from a copy made before damage to the inscription. The text preserves only the final -*THC* of the name of Mithradates; the rest is restored. Gotarzes as 'satrap of satraps' is clear. Justin 42.4.4 probably refers to Mithradates III (§ 26).

40 BABYLON: Dobbins, *NC* (ser. 7) 15 (1975) 19-45. The view that Gotarzes disappears about 86 is disputed by M.-L. Chaumont in *JA* 1968, 17 with 27 note 29; cf. her article in *Syria* 48 (1971) 157 f. She regards him as ruling until 81/80, though styled simply *Arsaces*. Since his proper name disappears but that of Orodes does re-emerge in the record of 80/79, when he was probably expelled by Sinatruces, this must remain hypothesis. The last certain notice of Gotarzes appears in Tablet xiv (Dobbins 20 f. and 43), recording his expulsion in 87/86 (Ars. 161; Sel. 225 Babyl.). CONFUSION: Justin *Prol.* 42; D. Sellwood, 'Some Politic Alterations in the Parthian Series': *Mints, Dies, and Currency*, ed. R. Carson (London 1971) 33 ff.

41 AVROMAN PARCHMENT: Published by Ellis Minns, 'Parchments of the Parthian Period from Avroman in Kurdistan': *JHS* 35 (1915) 22-65. On the controversy over its dating, see R. Sullivan, 'Papyri': *ANRW* II 8, 909-938, notes 1, 8, 14. See too R. McDowell, *Stamped and Inscribed Objects from Seleucia on the Tigris* (Ann Arbor 1935) 3, 12, 187. The remark of C.B. Welles, *Royal Correspondence* (1934) 302, no. 75, that the letter of Artabanus III (II) to Susa justifies the arguments of Rostovtzeff (*YCS* 2, 1931, 41 ff.; Sullivan, 'Papyri' note 8) in using the Parthian era alone cannot be regarded as decisive. This letter from AD 21 is a late exception to the practice of supplying the Seleucid date if only one was to be used, and it cannot be retrojected to solve the problem. By the days of Artabanus the 'Iranian reaction' against Hellenic usages beginning with Vonones I (AD 7-12) more readily allowed an Arsacid era alone. MITHRADATES IN KURDISTAN: Judging not from this parchment, which could have migrated, but from fixed monuments, the authority of Mithradates in Kurdistan and Luristan was firm. See L. Vanden Berghe, *Archéologie de l'Iran ancien* (Leiden 1966) 224-227. TIGRANES AND PARTHIA: Strabo 16.1.19.745; 11.14.15.532; Dio 36.45.3 with 36.51.1-3; Livy *Per.* 100; App. *Mith.* 87.392-393; Memnon, *FGrH* 434, F 38.8 (58); Plut. *Luc.* 21.4.

42 MITHRADATES AND THE SELEUCIDS: Jos. *AJ* 13.371, a troubled passage; see J. Dobiáš (next note) 221-224. See too Euseb. *Chron.* I, 261 Schoene; App. *Syr.* 48.246-247 and 68.359-360; Schürer (Vermes and Millar) 135; Jos. *AJ* 13.384-386. Cf. Athen. *Deipn.* 4.153 a. MARRIAGE TIE: App. *Syr.* 67.356-68.361; Justin 38.9.3-8 and 38.10.10. *PHILHELLENE*: S. Reinach in

BCH 7 (1883) 348 and A. von Sallet in *Zeitschr. für Numism.* 12 (1885) 372-375, commenting on the later *OGIS* 430. Babylon: *SEG* 7 (1934) no. 40; cf. no. 39. The rise of Parthia and then of Tigranes is clearly ascribed by Strabo to growing Seleucid weakness about 140 BC (14.5.2.669), but Parthians stayed in reasonably amicable contact. Greeks and Jews seem to have moved freely in the Parthian Empire: Justin 41.4.3-7 and 38.10.10; App. *Syr.* 67.356 and 68.360. See S. Ahmed in *AArchSyr* 17 (1967) 85-90; G. Walser in *Festgabe H. von Greyerz* (Bern 1967) 189-202. See too J. Neusner, *A History of the Jews in Babylonia, I: The Parthian Period* (Leiden 1969), with his 'The Jews East of the Euphrates and the Roman Empire, I: 1st-3rd Centuries A.D.': *ANRW* II 9.2 (Berlin 1976) 46-49; Strabo 11.9.2.515; Leibmann-Frankfort 118-133; J. Wolski in *Historia* 8 (1959) 222-38 and 11 (1962) 139-44; *Berytus* 12 (1957) 35-52; É. Will in *RPh* 40 (1966) 285. Acts 2.8-11: everybody, including Parthians, could be found in Jerusalem. Parthians favoured Greeks within the empire: Plut. *Crass.* 32.3; Strabo 11.13.6.524; F. Cumont, *CRAI* 1933, 264 ff., no. 2. A *gymnasiarch* served at Susa in Arsacid year 248 (75 BC), under Sinatruces. In *CRAI* 1932, 238-260, Cumont published the letter of AD 21 in 'Un lettre du roi Artaban III.' M. Rostovtzeff commented in 'L'Hellenisme en Mésopotamie': *Scientia* 53 (1933) 120-121. C.B. Welles republished the text in *Royal Correspondence* 299-306. The letter refers throughout to Greek institutions. Greeks in turn admired the Parthians: Dio 40.14-15. Seleucia had a large Greek population still in Dio's day (AD 229): 40.16.3. Commagenians adopted some Parthian usages: Babelon, *Rois* ccviii ff.; R. Sullivan in *NC* (ser. 7) 13 (1973) 18-39 and Pl. 14. There was some Iranian erosion of Greek usages eventually, the culmination of a cultural force descending from Persian times. See also J. Wolski, *Sprawozd. Komis. PAN Oddzial w. Krakowie* 4 (1960) 270-72 (in Polish) and his 'L'aristocratie parthe et les commencements du féodalisme en Iran': *IA* 7 (1967) 134-144; A. Ghirshman, *Iran: Parthians and Sassanians* (London 1962). Parthian envoys in Judaea: Schürer (Vermes and Millar) 221-222; J. Neusner, 'Parthian Political Ideology': *IA* 3 (1963) 40-59.

43 FIRST MENTION: I Macc. 15.22: King Arsaces. SULLA: Livy *Per.* 70; Vell. Pat. 2.24.3; Plut. *Sulla* 5.3-5. Velleius echoes Plutarch and probably used the same source, but misdated the meeting to the time of the First Mithradatic War, some five years later, assuming the actual meeting was about 94, and the outbreak of the war somewhat earlier than Reinach thought: Sherwin-White, *CQ* 171 = n.s. 27 (1977) 173-183. See too A. Keaveney, 'Roman Treaties with Parthia, circa 95 - circa 64 B.C.': *AJP* 102 (1981) 195-212. Some see no 'treaty' here at all, but rather an informal understanding. E.g., A.N. Sherwin-White, *Roman Foreign Policy* (London 1984) 219-220. Later negotiations with Phraates III: see Ch. 9, § 26, note 78; Dio 36.45.3 and 36.51.1.

Blunder: Debevoise 47; Rawlinson instead takes the view that Tigranes began his attacks on Parthia in response to this meeting, considering it more successful than perhaps it was. See also Strabo 11.14.15.532; Plut. *Luc.* 14 and 21; Fest. *Brev.* 15.2: *Primum a L. Sulla proconsule Arsaces rex Parthorum, missa legatione, amicitiam populis Romanis rogavit ac meruit.* Florus 1.46.4-6 alludes to ruptures in the arrangements concluded by Sulla and later by Pompey. Parthians and Romans remained in contact, regarding their frontier as near the Euphrates. See Jos. *AJ* 18.101 and *BJ* 7.105; Suet. *Cal.* 14.5; Dio 59.27.3 and 72.22.2; Vell. Pat. 2.101; K. Zeigler, *Die Beziehungen zwischen Rom und dem Partherreich* (Wiesbaden 1964); Moses of Khorene, *Hist. Arm.* 2.69 = *FGrH* 782 (Anhang, nr. 1); J. Dobiáš, 'Les premiers rapports des romains avec les parthes et l'occupation de la Syrie': *Archiv orientální* 3 (1931) 215-256, an excellent survey. See as well V. Gardthausen, 'Die Parther in griechisch-römischen Inschriften': *Theodor Nöldeke zum siebzigsten Geburtstag* (Giessen 1906 = *Orientalische Studien* I-II) II, 839-859; R. Ghirshman in *Syria* 49 (1972) 161-165; H. Petersen in *Berytus* 16 (1966) 61-69 (I A.D.); Liebmann-Frankfort 171 ff.; 237 ff.; 263 ff.; A. Guenther, *Beiträge zur Geschichte der Kriege zwischen Römern und Parthern* (Berlin 1922); A.G. Bokshchanin, *Parfii i Rim* (Moscow 1960-1966).

44 MITHRADATES AS 'GREAT': Justin *Prol.* 42; 42.2.4. *Multa bella*: Justin 42.2.4. KING OF KINGS: Head HN^2 819; *BMC Parthia* 30-66. The Parthians' use of 'King of Kings' may have originated with Mithradates I, though firm evidence is lacking: Gutschmid 79 ff.; Rawlinson 88; *RE* 18 (1949) 1977. On the overtones it had, see F. Taeger, *Charisma, Studien zur Geschichte des antiken Herrscherkultes* (Stuttgart 1957) 334 ff. See also R. Frye, 'The Charisma of Kingship in Ancient Iran': *IA* 4 (1964) 36-54; J.G. Griffiths, '*Basileus Basileôn*: Remarks on the History of a Title': *CP* 48 (1953) 145-154. C. Toumanoff suggests (private letter) that these distinctions among titles could be relatively fluid, and that 'King of Kings' can mean not *necessarily* 'King over other Kings' but perhaps 'King excelling other Kings.' See his *Studies in Christian Caucasian History* (Washington 1963) esp. p. 47 with note 36; pp. 50-51 with note 44; p. 77; pp. 101-106 with notes 152, 154, and 160. See also his discussion, 'Origin or Function: The Two Fundamental Concepts of Princely Rank': *The Coat of Arms*, n.s. 7, no. 138 (1986) 4-14. DYNAMIS: See Ch. 6, note 50.

45 ACCESSION OF SINATRUCES: K.W. Dobbins, *NC* (ser. 7) 15 (1975) 19-45; O. Mørkholm, *NC* (ser. 7) 19 (1980) 33-47 sees his accession in 86/85. Cf. Lucian *Macrob.* 15. No response to Mithradates Eupator: Memnon, *FGrH* 434, F 29.7 (43.2). Cf. App. *Mith.* 78.342, an incomplete version. COINS IN IBERIA: G.F. Dundua and G.A. Lordkipanidze, *NC* (ser. 7) 19

(1979) 1-5; cf. above, Ch. 2, § 3, note 30. LETTER OF EUPATOR: Sall. *Hist.* 2.69. Compare the picture of desolation after the defeat of Tigranes given by Plutarch, *Luc.* 29.1-2. On the sources of Sallust for this letter, see H. Fuchs, *Der geistige Widerstand gegen Rom in der antiken Welt* (Berlin 1938) 16 ff. Dobiáš 227 regards this as written under Sinatruces. See also R. Syme, *Sallust* (Berkeley and Los Angeles 1964) 196 and 250-251; E. Bikerman, 'La lettre de Mithridate dans les "Histoire" de Salluste': *REL* 24 (1946) 131-151. See as well Ch. 2, § 3, note 39; Ch. 6, § 15, note 23; Ch. 9, § 26, note 77.

Chapter 6

1 Y. Youroukova, *Coins of the Ancient Thracians* (Oxford 1976; BAR Supplementary Series 4) 40, provides 75 BC for the termination of the reign of Sadalas and 57 for the inception of that of Cotys, but the evidence adduced supports no certainty.

2 See Ch. 2, § 1.

3 SADALAS I AIDED SULLA: See above, Ch. 2, § 1, note 8; Sullivan, 'Thrace' 189 note 8; Dio 31, Frag. 101; App. *Mithr.* 13.44; 15.53; 41.158; 57.234. See too Livy *Per.* 74, 76, 81-83, 91-92, 95, 97; Dio 36.9.3-4. LUCULLUS: Eutrop. 6.10; Amm. Marc. 27.4.11; cf. 14.11.15; Jones, *Cities*² 14 and Map 1; Memnon, *FGrH* 434, F 1.38.3 (56).

4 CAMPAIGNS: Dio 38.10.1-2; Livy *Per.* 103; Jul. Obsequens 61a; *SIG*³ 762, line 17. See too Chr. Danov, *ANRW* 7.1, 113-118; Suet. *Aug.* 3.2 and 94.5; Cic. *Pis.* 34.84; Diod. 37.5a. Bessi as enemies: see, e.g., Dio 54.34.5 (11 BC), with Sullivan, 'Thrace' 198-199.

5 Caes. *BCiv.* 3.4 and 3.36; Dio 41.51.2; App. *BCiv.* 2.49; Flor. 2.13.5

6 Head *HN*² 286.

7 Head *HN*² 286; Sullivan, 'Thrace' 190 note 10; Youroukova 40-45; Dio 41.62.3-63.1.

8 Jones, *Cities*² 9: Cotys 'added the Bessi to his kingdom by bribing Piso to execute their prince.' The Bessi, on the contrary, took an independent line, in opposition to the Odrysians, for decades to come, though in 29 BC some of their territory fell into Odrysian hands: Dio 51.25.4-5. On Odessus, see Chr. Danov, *ANRW* II 7.1, 281-300. See also Pliny *N.H.* 4.11.57: *Bizye arx regum Thraciae.* Jones, 377 note 11, is sceptical about the union of the Astae and Odrysians. But see G. Mihailov, *I.G.Bulg.* I² (Sophia 1970) 95-98, no. 43, and Sullivan, 'Thrace' 190 note 9.

9 Suet. *Caes.* 44.3; Strabo 7.7.5.298; V. Velkov, *Klio* 63 (1981) 474.

10 GETAE: Discussion by Chr. Danov, *ANRW* II 7.1, 118-120. Their situation before the unification by Burebistas: A. Vulpe, 'Aspects significatifs dans

l'histoire et la culture des Géto-Daces': *RESE* 16 (1978) 619-631. See this chapter, § 15, on King Asander, for implications in the Bosporus. DIONYSOPOLIS: *SIG*³ 762 = Sherk, *Greek East* no. 78 = *IGRR* I 662 = *I.G.Bulg.* I² 13. BUREBISTAS: His policy may have continued that of Eupator: E. Condurachi, 'Burebista, successeur du programme politique du Mithridate VI Eupator': *AAntHung* 26 (1978) 7-14. Further on him: Z. Petre, 'L'esercito di Burebista': *QC* 2 (1980) 501-517. See too D.M. Pippidi, 'Les rois gètes et les colonies grecques de Scythie Mineure' in *Mélanges d'archéologie, d'épigraphie et d'histoire offerts à J. Carcopino* (Paris 1966) 763-770; Strabo 7.3.9-13.297. Tribute: D. Pippidi, 'Épigraphie et historiographie: à propos des relations gréco-indigènes dans le bassin de la Mer Noire': *Acta Classica Univ. Scient. Debrecen.* 3 (1967) 35-41. 'Foremost and greatest': *SIG*³ 762; App. *BCiv.* 2.110.459; *Ill.* 13; Suet. *Iul.* 44. A grant of citizenship is reflected by *IOSPE* I² 691 = Sherk, *Greek East* no. 82. For a glimpse of Roman policy in the century after the dissolution of the empire of Burebistas, the career of Ti. Plautius Silvanus (*ILS* 986) under Nero shows continued turmoil among Bastarnae, Dacians, and others. See esp. F. Conole and R.D. Milns in *Historia* 32 (1983) 183-200. See also C. Daicoviciu, 'Dakien und Rom in der Principatszeit': *ANRW* (forthcoming). DICOMES: Plut. *Ant.* 63.3-4. OLBIA: J. Vinogradov, *Olbia. Geschichte einer altgriechischen Stadt am Schwarzen Meer* (Constance 1981).

11 App. *BCiv.* 4.10.75; Head *HN*² 286; Mihailov, *I.G.Bulg.* I² (Sofia 1970) 95-98 no. 43 (Odessus). On the later dynasty, Sullivan, 'Thrace' 194.

12 Dio 47.25.1-2; App. *BCiv.* 4.10.75; Plut. *Ant.* 61; Sullivan, 'Thrace' 189-194. The apparent alternation of dynastic nomenclature between Sadalas and Cotys rests on too few examples to preclude another Sadalas as the elder son of Sadalas II. Sadalas III could be a relative who bore or assumed that name and served as regent while Cotys V remained safely in Cyzicus. GUARDIANSHIP BY RHOEMETALCES I: Dio 54.20.3; Chr. Danov in *ANRW* II 7.1, 120-122. COTYS V AFTER ACTIUM: H. Dessau in *Ephem. Epigr.* 9 (1913) 698 f.

13 Caes. *BCiv.* 3.4; Lucan 5.55; Sullivan, 'Thrace' 194-196.

14 Dio 47.25.2 and 47.48.2; App. *BCiv.* 4.11.87; 4.13.103-104; 4.17.136; Livy *Per.* 122.

15 Dio 47.25.2; *I.G.* II/III² 3442 and 3443; W. Hasluck in *ABSA* 12 (1905/1906) 178 = H. Dessau, *Ephem. Epigr.* 9 (1913) 700 and 702 note 2; *I.G.Bulg.* I² p. 98; Sullivan, 'Thrace' 194-196. APOLLONIA: S. Mitchell, 'Roman Residents and Roman Property in Southern Asia Minor': *Proc. Xth Internat. Congr. Class. Arch.* (Ankara 1978) 311-318, has removed the improbable reading 'Thracian colonists' from our understanding of *IGRR* III 314, 317-318; *MAMA* VIII 350.

16 THE MARRIAGE: Evidence reviewed in Sullivan, 'Thrace' 193-194. See too Dio 54.20.3. Cotys VII: *PIR*² C 1552. THE BESSI: Dio 51.25.4-5; 54.20.3; 54.34.5. The 'Lucius Piso' whom Dio mentions here was the son of the Piso who governed Macedonia in 57 BC. See T.C. Sarikakis, 'L. Calpurnius Piso Pontifex: A Disputed Governor of Macedonia' in H.J. Dell, ed., *Ancient Macedonian Studies in Honor of Charles F. Edson* (Thessaloniki 1981; Institute for Balkan Studies, 158) 307-314.

17 The first two inscriptions are mentioned above. See Dessau, *Ephem. Epigr.* 9 (1913) 696; *I.G.Bulg.* I² no. 43. Discussion: Sullivan, 'Thrace' 196-198 and 205-206; T. Iwanow in *StudClas* 3 (1961) 93-98.

18 Plut. *Mor.* 207 A; *Rom.* 17 (28 A). Sullivan, 'Thrace' 197-211. For an earlier Rhoemetalces, see Ch. 2, § 1, note 7.

19 Sullivan, 'Thrace' 198-200; Chr. Danov, *ANRW* II 7.1, 122-150. In *StudClas* 9 (1967) 116-119, L. Robert has put to rest a chimerical numismatic commemoration of amity between two Thracian kings in the reign of Caligula.

20 Tac. *Ann.* 12.63.3; *ILS* 849; Sullivan, 'Thrace' 207-211, and 'Pontus' *ANRW* II 7.2, 913-930. Further on Thrace: G. Bowersock, *Augustus and the Greek World* (Oxford 1965) 152-156; R.F. Hoddinott, *The Thracians* (London 1981); B. Gerov in *ANRW* II 7.1, 212-240; Chr. Danov in *ANRW* II 7.1, 21-185 and 241-300; T. Mommsen in *Ephem. Epigr.* 2 (1875) 250-263 = *Ges. Schr.* VIII (1913) 297-311; H. Dessau, *Ephem. Epigr.* 9 (1913) 691-705; J. Wiesner, *Die Thraker* (Stuttgart 1963); B. Gerov, *Landowning in Roman Thrace and Moesia* (1987). Still useful: M. Cary, *Histoire des rois de Thrace* (Paris 1752). Others as cited by R. Sullivan in *ANRW* II 7.1, 186-211. See too V. Velkov, *Eirene* 17 (1980) 45-63. On later administration here by Romans: M. Le Glay in *ZPE* 43 (1981) 175-184.

21 See Ch. 2, § 3; Magie 340-343 with 1214-1215, notes 38-44; Plut. *Luc.* 21-22; 28; E. Olshausen, *ANRW* I 1 (Berlin 1972) 806-815, and *AncSoc* 5 (1974) 153-170.

22 The campaigns are depicted in *Tübinger Atlas des Vorderen Orients (TAVO)*, B V 6 (Wiesbaden 1981), 'Kleinasien und Schwarzmeergebiet: Das Zeitalter Mithradates' d. Gr. (121-63 v. Chr.).' On Tigranocerta, see Ch. 5, § 11 and Ch. 9, § 24; Magie 343 ff.

23 Sallust *Hist.* 4.69, already regarded as a composition of the historian by Fronto in *ep. ad L. Verum* 2.142 Haines (2.126 Naber). See too E. Bickerman in *REL* 24 (1946) 131-151; L. Raditsa in *Helicon* 9/10 (1969/1970) 632-635 and 689-694; E. Pasoli, *Le Historiae e le opere minori di Sallustio* (Bologna 1965) 135-148. Its date: Debevoise 70-71 note 3. Further bibliography: E. Olshausen in *ANRW* II 7.2 (Berlin 1980) 904. See Ch. 2, § 3, note 39; Ch. 5, § 13, note 45; Ch. 9, § 26, note 77.

24 Dio 36.1 and 3; Plut. *Luc.* 30.1; Memnon, *FGrH* 434, F 1.38.8(58).

25 Memnon, *FGrH* 434, F 1.38.3 (56); Plut. *Luc.* 21 and 29; Sall. *Hist* 4.56 Maurenbr.; Dio 36.2.5.

26 Dio 36.8-9; Plut. *Luc.* 34. Lucullus had not been popular with his troops: *Luc.* 33.3-4. See too Magie 344-345. NISIBIS: *RE* 17 (1937) 714-757 (J. Sturm) esp. 730-731.

27 Magie 346-350; 1219 note 59. See also W. Waddington, E. Babelon, Th. Reinach, *Recueil général des monnaies grecques d'Asie Mineure*, I, 2nd ed. (Paris 1925; hereafter *Recueil* I^2) p. 20, with misprint '(66/7 av. J.-C)' for '67/66.'

28 Dio 36.51.1-2; Plut. *Pomp.* 36.2; App. *Mith.* 104.484-106.493; Frontinus 2.5.33.

29 App. *Mith.* 97.446-101.462; Dio 36.45.3-51.2; Livy *Per.* 100; H. Stier in *Festschr. Fritz Altheim*, I (Berlin 1969) 441-451. POMPEY'S POWERS: App. *Mith.* 97.446-447; Cic. *de Imp. Cn. Pomp. (Leg. Man.)* 52-53; Velleius 2.31. On his office now, see R.T. Ridley, 'The Extraordinary Commands of the Late Republic': *Historia* 30 (1981) 280-297. Mithradates had received the voluntary submission of places like Panticapaeum, seeming less a threat to the Greeks than did the surrounding Iranian 'barbarians'; he counted on solid support now. See too Strabo 7.4.4.

30 MACHARES: App. *Mith.* 83.365; Plut. *Luc.* 24.1; Dio 36.50.2; Livy *Per.* 98; Memnon, *FGrH* 434, F 1.37.6 (54). CAPITULATION: Dio 36.45.3-4; App. *Mith.* 98.451-452; Luc. *Phars.* 2.580-582. TIGRANES: See Ch. 9, § 24; Magie 353-358 and 1221-1226, notes 6-13. A later inscription preserves the Roman tradition of these battles, noting that Lucullus triumphed over both kings *magnis utriusque regis copiis compluribus proeliis terra marique superatis*. See also Reinach, *Mithridate Eupator* (Paris 1890) 471 no. 20; D.B. Shelov, *VDI* 1978, 55-72.

31 Strabo 11.2.13.496; Magie 359-363. Offspring were ample: Dio 36.11.4 and 36.13.1; 37.7.5; 37.10.4. See E. Olshausen in *RE Suppl.* 15 (1978) 399-400; Plut. *Luc.* 18. Coins of Eupator in Panticapaeum: K.V. Golenko, *VDI* 126 (1973) 65-87 [in Russian].

32 Dio 37.12.2 notes the increasing distance between the king and his subjects. See also Magie 364-365 with 1229-1230 note 25. Later propaganda might have Pharnaces the murderer, doubtless to discredit him after his renewed enmity with Rome. See too Magie 364 vs. 4. COLCHIS: App. *Mith.* 64.266; K.V. Golenko in *VDI* 130 (1974) 95-110 [in Russian]. LAST MONTHS OF MITHRADATES: Cic. *Leg. Agr.* 2.19.52; Dio 37.10.4.

33 REJOICING: Magie 365-367 and 1230-1231 notes 29-31. WARS: L. Robert, *Hellenica* XI-XII (Paris 1960) 82-83 note 4. Pompey's triumph featured gold and silver statues of Mithradates and paintings of scenes from his life and death. The career of Mithradates was widely reflected epigraphically. See, e.g., Reinach, *Mithridate Eupator* (Paris 1890) 456-472, App. II; *OGIS* 366-374.

34 Magie 356-365 and 1230 note 26.

35 Dio 37.14.1-3; App. *Mith.* 113.551-555; 117.572.

36 C. Papirius Carbo governed 'Bithynia and Pontus' beginning in 61 BC: Broughton, *MRR* II, 181; 191. On the troubled question of the borders of the new province, see Jones, *Cities*² 157-167; Magie 369-372; E. Olshausen, *ANRW* II 7.2 (Berlin 1980) 906-907. See too A.J. Marshall, 'Pompey's Organization of Bithynia-Pontus: Two Neglected Texts': *JRS* 58 (1968) 103-109.

37 Magie 372-374 with notes *ad loc.*

38 Plut. *Pomp.* 41; Strabo 4.310; Dio 37.14.2. THE PAPHLAGONIANS: Magie 1234-1235 note 37. A king still ruled there in 31 BC: Dio 50.13.5; Zonar. 10.29. DEIOTARUS: See this chapter, § 16; Magie 1235-1236 notes 40-41. ARCHELAUS: See this chapter, § 17, with Sullivan, 'Cappadocia' *ANRW* II 7.2 (Berlin 1980) 1149 f. ARISTARCHUS: App. *Mith.* 114.560; K. Golenko in *VDI* 130 (1974) 95-110; Head *HN*² 496.

39 App. *Mith.* 113.555; 114.560; Strabo 11.5.8.506; Hoben 12-16. See *Corpus Inscriptionum Regni Bosporani* [*CIRB*] (Moscow-Leningrad 1965) 28 = B. Lifshitz, *Epigraphica* 32 (1970) 7, no. 1; K. Golenko and P. Karyszkowski, 'The Gold Coinage of King Pharnaces of the Bosporus': *NC* (ser. 7) 12 (1972) 25-38 with Pl. 2-3.

40 App. *BCiv.* 2.87-88; Strabo 11.2.17.498; 12.3.14.547; Dio 41.63.3-4; 42.45; 42.46.3; *BAlex.* 34; Hoben 18-19. COLCHIS: Traced by G.F. Dunda and G. Lordkipanidze in *NC* (ser. 7) 19 (1979) 1-5. See above, Ch. 2, § 3, note 30.

41 Hoben 20-21 with note 59; Magie 407-409 with 1262-1263 notes 14-16. On Mithradates of Pergamon, see Ch. 8, § 23, with notes 197-198, and below, notes 47-48. Caesar had cultivated support in Pergamon and now reaped the rewards. Mithradates became a reliable ally, later ruling the Bosporus (see below): see Rostovtzeff, *SEHHW* 821 ff. Cf. *JRS* 42 (1952) 123-125; *Athenaeum* n.s. 16 (1938) 119 ff.

42 *BAlex.* 34-40.

43 *BAlex.* 41; 65-68; App. *Mith.* 121.596-597. Discussion in Ch. 6-8, §§ 16-20 and 23. Further detail in the *ANRW* studies by Sullivan cited there. On the important priesthood at Comana, now transferred by Caesar to a Bithynian of royal Cappadocian birth named Lycomedes, see below, note 54. See Sullivan, 'Cappadocia' 1149-1151. Strabo 12.3.38.560 even terms him a king. See *OGIS* 346, with notes.

44 Cic. *Fam.* 15.15.2; *BAlex.* 69-70; cf. 34 (*ab externo rege*, a view attributed to Cn. Domitius Calvinus). Asander's revolt from Pharnaces had apparently already occurred: App. *Mith.* 120.591-592; Dio 42.46-47; App. *BCiv.* 2.91.381-383. *BAlex.* 77 describes the conflict as a *maximum bellum*.

45 *BAlex.* 71-77: *tanta celeritate*; Cic. *Att.* 16.10: *Caesarina ... celeritate*. See

too Dio 42.47-48. Useful remarks by L.E. Lord in *JRS* 28 (1938) esp. 37. App. *BCiv.* 2.91 gives a Greek version of Caesar's famous *veni, vidi, vici.*

46 PHARNACES KILLED: Dio 42.47.5; App. *Mith.* 120.590-595; Strabo 13.4.3.625. *BAlex.* 76-78 records the cessation of his rule but not the manner of his death. MITHRADATES, SON OF MITHRADATES: Best summary is by Magie 1090 note 48. The text is republished by A. Degrassi, *BCAR* 74 (1951-1952; appeared 1954) 27-28 no. 10 = his *Scritti Vari* (Rome 1962) I, 415 ff. See too A.W. Lintott, *ZPE* 30 (1978) 137-144.

47 MITHRADATES: *BAlex.* 78; Strabo 13.4.3.625 and 11.2.17.498. See also Magie 1259 note 4; H. Hepding, *MDAI(A)* 34 (1909) 329-340, cf. 35 (1910) 471; 37 (1912); Chr. Habicht, *GGA* 213 (1959/1960) 152; *IGRR* IV 1682; G. Hirschfeld, *Hermes* 14 (1879) 474-475; *RE* 15 (1932) 2205 no. 15; Sherk, *Greek East* nos. 80-81. See too below, Ch. 8, § 23, notes 197-198; above, note 41. See Stähelin 92 notes 6-8 and 93 note 1: Adobogiana, wife of Deiotarus Philadelphos. However, see Hoben 118-119. B. Levick, *Roman Colonies* 124, sees in the marriage of 'Adiobogiana' [*sic*] a device for keeping then-declining Pergamon 'in the political picture.'

48 Strabo 13.4.3.625; *BAlex.* 78; Dio 42.46-48; App. *Mith.* 120.594-121.596; Magie 1267 note 32; Hoben 26-29. COLCHIS: See above, note 40. ON BUREBISTAS: See this chapter, § 14. Hoben suggests that the defeat of Mithradates might have been at sea, possibly before landing; support for this view might come from the text in Latyschev, *IOSPE* 2.25, erected at Panticapaeum by his admiral. See next note.

49 *PIR*² A 1197; Luc. *Macr.* 17. See too B. Latyschev, *Inscriptiones antiquae orae septentrionalis Ponti Euxini Graecae et Latinae* (*IOSPE*), 2nd. ed. (Petersburg 1916) 2.25 = *IGRR* I 874; Hoben 26-34.

50 Latyschev, *IOSPE* 2.356 = *IGRR* I 905; *CIRB* 31 = B. Lifshitz in *Epigraphica* 32 (1970) 7-9 no. 2; App. *BCiv.* 2.91.382; Sullivan, 'Thrace' and 'Pontus': *ANRW* II 7.1 and 7.2; M. Rostovtzeff in *JHS* 39 (1919) 88-109 and Pl. 3-4; G. Macurdy, *Vassal Queens* (Baltimore 1937) 29 ff. The later marriage of Pythodoris and Polemo (see below) need not show a break with Dynamis; Polemo might have followed the tradition of Mithradates Eupator in taking more than one wife, on the local Iranian model, *pace* Rostovtzeff. See also *PIR*² D 211; V.F. Gajdukevič, *Das Bosporanische Reich* (Amsterdam 1971) Ch. 9. The later period of reign postulated for Dynamis, c. 8 BC to AD 8, has been disputed by N. Frolova in *SA* 2 (1978) 49-61.

51 Sullivan, 'Thrace': *ANRW* II 7.1, 200-204, with stemma; *PIR*² A 1265 and G 168; Rostovtzeff, *JHS* 39 (1919) 107 ff. On the later dynasty: N. Frolova, *The Coinage of the Kingdom of the Bosporus, A.D. 69-238* (Oxford 1979; BAR Suppl. 56). See too V. Anokhin, *The Coinage of Chersonesus: IV Century B.C.–XII Century A.D.* (Oxford 1980; BAR Suppl. 69); N. Frolova, *VDI* 1977,

156-176. *IGRR* I 879 shows King Aspurgus of Bosporus to be the son of 'King Asandrochos' (Asander).

52 Dio 48.32.5; App. *BCiv.* 5.75; Strabo 12.3.13-14.547; 12.3.38-39.561; Magie 1282 note 16; Hoben 34-39; Jones, *Cities*^{2} 166-168.

53 Jones, *ibid.* The era of Pythodoris began not with Zela but later in 47: Th. Reinach in *NC* (ser. 4) 2 (1902) 1-4; Hoben 38 with note 139.

54 Strabo 12.3.38.560; Dio 51.2.2: 'Lycomedes, serving as king in part of Cappadocian Pontus.' Another warrant exists for regarding Lycomedes as locally termed a king, an inscription recording one 'Meniskos ... being a descendant of King Lycomedes': see T. Wiegand, *Didyma* II, *Die Inschriften* (A. Rehm; R. Harder; Berlin 1958) no. 107, lines 3 and 18-20, with pp. 119-121 (time of Caligula). Cf. H. Hommel in *Chiron* 6 (1976) 319-327, esp. 322 note 10. See too *PIR*^{2} L 456. On the high station of this priesthood see Sullivan, 'Cappadocia' 1149-1151. See Hoben 37 and 44-45 for the date. Comana's wealth: App. *Mith.* 64.269. See above, note 43. H. Volkmann, 'Der Zweite nach dem König': *Philologus* 92 (1937) 285-316, notes the quasi-royal status of this priest, who could on two occasions each year wear the diadem. See H.W. Ritter in *Historia* 36 (1987) 290-301 and his *Diadem und Königsherrschaft* (Munich 1965).

55 ACHAEMENID DESCENT: App. *Mith.* 112.540. LAODICEA AND ICONIUM: Jones, *Cities*^{2} Map II; S. Mitchell in *Historia* 28 (1979) 409-438. See too Strabo 14.2.24.660; 12.8.16.578; 12.6.1.568; App. *BCiv.* 5.75.319; Dio 49.25.4; Sullivan, 'Pontus': *ANRW* II 7.2 (Berlin 1980) 915-920; Hoben 39-53; Buccheim 49-53. ISAURIA: S. Mitchell in *Proc. Xth Internat. Cong. Class. Archaeol.* (Ankara 1978) 311-318, with Strabo 12.6.1-3.568-569 and App. *BCiv.* 5.75.319

56 On these other monarchs see R. Sullivan in *ANRW* II 7.1, 7.2, 8; also R. Sullivan in *Festschrift ... Dörner* (Leiden 1978) 914-939; A.A. Barrett in *AJPh* 98 (1977) 153-159.

57 Dio 49.25.4; Plut. *Ant.* 38; Hoben 39-53.

58 Dio 49.33.1-2; 54.24.4-6; Strabo 11.2.3.493 and 11.2.18.499 (Colchis).

59 Strabo 12.8.16.578. CAESARION: See Ch. 8, § 23. THE COINAGE: *Recueil* I^2 21 note. See also Sullivan, 'Pontus' 917-918 with note 14.

60 Plut. *Ant.* 61.2.

61 Strabo 12.8.16.578; Dio 53.25.1; Sullivan, 'Pontus' 918-920. POLEMO II: R. Sullivan in *NC* (ser. 7) 19 (1979) 6-20 with Pl. 2; A. Barrett, *Historia* 27 (1978) 437-448. PYTHODORIS: R. Sullivan in *ANRW* II 8 (Berlin 1977) 920 note 48 and 'Pontus' 920-922. See too *OGIS* 377 = *IGRR* IV 1407.

62 GALATIA: The effectiveness of Deiotarus against Mithradates and his generals: App. *Mith.* 17.59 and 75.326; Oros. 6.2.18. See also Memnon, *FGrH* 434, F 1.30 (44); Plut. *Luc.* 14.1; 28.2; Livy *Per.* 94 (74/73 BC); Hoben 64-66;

bibliography, note 59. Maps of Galatia at this time: R. Sherk, *ANRW* II 7.2 (Berlin 1980) 960; Jones, *Cities*[2] Map II; *TAVO* B V 6 (Tübingen 1981); Bürchner in *RE* 7 (1910) 529, 'Galatia'; Hoben Ch. III; Magie 333.

63 Th. Reinach in *RN* (sér. 3) 9 (1891) 20-41. See also Strabo 12.3.1.541; 12.3.13.547; 12.5.1-4.566-568. See further Magie 373-375 and 1235-1237 notes 40-41; 402; 426; B. Niese, 'Straboniana, IV. Galatien und seine Tetrarchen': *RhM* N.F. 38 (1883) 583-600. ARISTARCHUS: App. *Mith.* 114.560 with K. Golenko in *VDI* 130 (1974) 95-110: 'The coins confirm the testimony of Appian.' See Eutrop. *Brev.* 6.14: Pompey *Aristarchum Colchis regem imposuit,* and *Armeniam minorem Deiotaro, Galatiae regi, donavit.* See too Hoben 68-71 on the problem of Armenia Minor. See as well *BAlex.* 67; F. Adcock, *JRS* 27 (1937) 12-17.

64 FLIGHT OF GALATIANS: W.M. Ramsay, *The Social Basis of Roman Power in Asia Minor* (Aberdeen 1941) 44-45. THE KINGSHIPS: Magie 1235-1238 notes 40-41; that of Brogitarus arose through a decree of the people, engineered by Clodius. Caesar may have assisted in recognizing him as king: *BAlex.* 68. See Cic. *Har. resp.* 29 and *Att.* 14.12, with D. Braund in *LCM* 7 (1982) 39. See too E. Rawson, 'The Eastern Clientelae of Clodius and the Claudii': *Historia* 22 (1973) 219-239, esp. 236-237.

65 ADOBOGIONA: Her benefactions are recorded by an inscription found on Lesbos, *OGIS* 348; her father is a different Deiotarus. Her marriage is attested by an inscription from Pergamon calling her 'Adobogiona, daughter of Deiotarus, wife of Brogitarus, son of Deiotarus, tetrarch of the Galatian Trocmi ...': A. Ippel in *MDAI(A)* 37 (1912) 294-296. See, however, Chr. Habicht in *GGA* 213 (1959/1960) 152. See also F. Stähelin, *Geschichte der kleinasiatischen Galater,* 2nd ed. (Leipzig 1907) 88 ff. and 108. Coins of Brogitarus use *Philoromaios*: Th. Reinach, *L'histoire par les monnaies* (Paris 1902) 155 and Stähelin, *ibid.*, 90 note 2.

66 Stähelin 90 note 6; Magie 1235-1238 notes 40-41; Cic. *Sest.* 26.56; *Dom.* 50.129; *Har. Resp.* 13.28-29; *QFr* 2.7.2. (Clodius sought an embassy *aut Byzantium aut ad Brogitarum aut utrumque.*) Pessinus: See below, note 78. *BAlex.* 67: *tetrarches Gallograeciae tum quidem paene totius*; 78: *tetrarchian occupatam et possessam paucis ante annis a Deiotaro.* This 'tetrarchy' is presumably that of the Trocmi, previously held by Brogitarus; the third tetrarchy, of the Tectosages, was held by Castor Tarcondarius. See A. Zwintscher, *De Galatarum tetrarchis et Amynta Rege Quaestiones* (Leipzig 1892) 13-14 on the coins and titles of Brogitarus; A. von Sallet in *NZ* 14 (1887) 379.

67 Cic. *Fam.* 15.1.6; 15.2.2.; 15.4.5; *Att.* 5.18.2; 5.21. *Philoromaios*: Ehrenburg-Jones no. 174 = R. Arik and J. Coupry in *RA* (sér. 6) 2 (1935) 130-155, esp. 140. Castor Tarcondarius sent his son, Castor II, to join Cicero: Cic. *Deiot.* 10.28.

68 CAESAR IN 59: *BAlex.* 68; *ibid.*, 67-68 for opposition to Deiotarus internally. DEIOTARUS IN ARMENIA: Dio 41.63.3; 42.45.3. PHARSALUS: Cic. *Deiot.* 5.13; 10.28 (Castor II); Caes. *BCiv.* 3.4; App. *BCiv.* 2.8.49; Flor. 2.13.5; *BAlex.* 67-68; Dio 41.63.1. AGE: Cic. *Deiot.* 10.28.

69 Dio 41.63.3 and 42.45.3; *BAlex.* 35; Dio 41.62.3-4; 41.63.3-4; Cic. *Deiot.* 3.8. See H.-W. Ritter, 'Caesars Verfügung über Kleinarmenien im Jahre 47': *Historia* 19 (1970) 124-127; F.E. Adcock, 'Lesser Armenia and Galatia after Pompey's Settlement of the East': *JRS* 27 (1937) 12-17. Useful: Th. Reinach, *REA* 16 (1914) 3-29, esp. 8-11. See also Stähelin 93 and note 1.

70 Dio 42.46; *BAlex.* 34-40; 68; Cic. *Deiot.* 5.14; 8.22-9.24; Cic. *Att.* 6.1.14; Magie 413.

71 *BAlex.* 67-68; Cic. *Deiot.* 3.8-5.13; H.-W. Ritter, 'Caesars erstes Zusammentreffen mit Deiotarus': *Historia* 18 (1969) 255-256 (78 or 74 BC).

72 Cic. *Deiot.* 3.8; 9.24; *BAlex.* 68-69; 77; H.M.D. Parker, *The Roman Legions*, 2nd ed. (Cambridge, Eng. 1958) 64. See too Cic. *Deiot.* 3.8; 5.15; 6.17; 7.21; Strabo 12.5.2.567; Magie 1266 note 29; *BAlex.* 67 and 78; Dio 41.63.3; 42.48.3; Cic. *Phil.* 2.37.94-95; *Div.* 2.79. Discussion: Hoben 69-72 and 92-98; Magie 413 with 1267 note 31, 1259 note 4; Buccheim 110-112 notes 121 and 133.

73 Magie 414 with 1267 note 32. Hoben 101-102 puts the death of Mithradates in 46. On the tetrarchy: Hoben 108 note 260.

74 CASTOR: Discussion by Stähelin 93-94. BRUTUS: Cic. *Att.* 14.1.2 and *Brut.* 21; Tac. *Dial.* 21.6. HOSTILE: Cic. *Phil.* 2.37.94: '*Quis enim cuiquam inimicior quam Deiotaro Caesar?*' See too Cic. *Div.* 2.79; *Deiot.* 3.8. SPAIN: Cic. *Deiot.* 14.38: *bene sperare et bono esse animo*; cf. 15.41. See also Cic. *Deiot.* 15.41; Stähelin 94.

75 Cic. *Pro Rege Deiotaro ad C. Caesarem Oratio*. Cf. *Fam.* 9.12, to P. Cornelius Dolabella; *Att.* 5.17.

76 Cic. *Fam.* 6.13; *Deiot.* 11.32. Castor may have been temporarily resident in Rome, providing an opportunity for collusion with Caesar: *Deiot.* 7.21.

77 SOLE KINGSHIP: Strabo 12.5.1.567; Cic. *Phil.* 2.37.95. Antony recognized him immediately: Cic. *Att.* 14.12. See also R. Arik and J. Coupry in *RA* (sér. 6) 6 (1935) 130-155 = *Ann. ép.* 1936, 110; Magie 1236 note 40; 1266 note 29; R. Uguz, *Türk Tarih, Ark. Etn. Derg.* 2 (1934) 102 ff. and 308. See too Hoben 107; 111-112; Cic. *Att.* 5.17.2-3; *Deiot.* 13.36. Philopator was still alive in March 43. See as well Cic. *Phil.* 11.12.31-11.13.33. CASTOR'S MURDER: Strabo 12.5.3.568; Hoben 107 with note 256; Magie 1276 notes 59-60.

78 PESSINUS: Strabo 12.5.3.567. See *OGIS* 315, with bibliography on the Magna Mater cult here. Cf. Ch. 2, § 4, note 43; this chapter, § 16, note 88; this chapter, § 17, notes 120, 133 f. See too Sherk, *Greek East* no. 29. FAMILY: Cic. *Att.* 5.21; Dio 47.48.2; Zwintscher, *De Galatarum Tetrarchis* 27 ff., Cap. VI. See too Cic. *Deiot.* 11.30, perhaps invented.

79 Cic. *Att.* 14.12; 16.3; *Phil.* 2.37.94-95; Magie 426 and 1275 note 58; *Brut.* 1.6; Dio 47.24.3. See also Cic. *Phil.* 11.12.31; Dio 47.48.2; App. *BCiv.* 4.88, showing that Castor II probably also took part: 'tetrarchs of the Galatians.'

80 Dio 48.33.5; Magie 1234-1235 note 37; Hoben 110-111; Stähelin 96 ff. THE COIN: Zwintscher, 29-30; Head *HN*² 629; M. Crawford, *Roman Republican Coin Hoards* (London 1965; Royal Numismatic Society, Special Publications No. 4). See too A. von Sallet, *ZfN* 12 (1885) 371-372; M. Blanchet, *RBN* 85 (1933) 11 ff.; E. Newell, *RBN* 86 (1934) 5 ff.

81 *OGIS* 544-545; E. Bosch, *Quellen zur Geschichte der Stadt Ankara im Altertum* (Ankara 1967; T.T.K.Y. VII Ser., No. 46) 122-130 nos. 105-106; Hoben 112-116. This legion may in its early years have contained a high proportion of Galatians. It spent most of its years in Egypt, and may have been lost early in Hadrian's Jewish war of 132-135. See Magie 1321 note 34; E. Ritterling, 'Legio': *RE* 12 (1925) 1791-1797; 1224; Lesquier, *L'armée Romaine d'Égypte d'Auguste à Diocletien* (Cairo 1918) Appendix VI. Glimpses of it occur throughout this period: for instance *ILS* 1434 and 2483, with others probable; *CIG* III 4716-4719; Smallwood, *Documents ... Hadrian* no. 333. See too Pflaum, *Carrières* I and II (indices); R.K. Sherk, *GRBS* 5 (1964) 295-304 and *Greek East* no. 106 (2 BC). The wide spread of the name of Deiotarus began in the first century: e.g., P. Lambrechts in *AC* 38 (1969) 140-144. ATHENS: *OGIS* 347; *IG* II/III² 3429.

82 Magie 433; Dio 48.33.5; Hoben 116 with note 307; Strabo 12.5.3.568. Some of the imprisonments of which Deiotarus was accused had begun at least by 45: Cic. *Deiot.* 7.22, the brothers of Phidippus (6.17).

83 Hoben, *ibid.*; Dio 49.32.3; App. *BCiv.* 5.75.319; Dio 49.32.5 (Amyntas only the secretary of Deiotarus). Discussion: Hoben 36-42; Plut. *Ant.* 38; Dio 49.25.2 and 32.3.

84 Strabo 12.3.41.562; *PIR*² D 36; *PIR* P 257; Magie 1283-1284 notes 20 and 23. COINS: Magie, *ibid.*; Dressel in *ZfNum* 21, 226; H. Dessau 25, 335-343; Th. Reinach, *L'histoire par les monnaies* (Paris 1902) 151 and 162-163; Reinach, *RN* (sér. 3) 12 (1894) 414 ff.; Hoben 118-120; U. Kahrstedt, 'Frauen auf antiken Münzen': *Klio* 10 (1910) 284, dating to 36 BC.

85 Plut. *Ant.* 61.1 and 63.3; Zonar. 10.29; Dio 50.13.5. See too Jones, *Cities*² 167-168 and 426-427 notes 39-40; Strabo 12.3.41.562; Head *HN*² 506-507; *IGRR* III 137; Th. Reinach, 'Monnaie inédite de Déjotarus Philadelphe, dernier roi de Paphlagonie': *RN* (sér. 3) 9 (1891) 17-19; *Receuil* I² 166 ff.; Magie 1283 note 20.

86 Strabo 12.3.6.543. On the activity of Deiotarus Philadelphos: Hoben 78-83 and note 120; Zwintscher, 14-15 and 19; Stähelin 89-92 and 114. See also Caes. *BCiv.* 3.4, employing chiasmus, on this view; *BAlex.* 67.

87 Strabo 12.3.6.543. See too *BAlex.* 67: *ceteri tetrarchae.* These are the tetrarchs 'by birth' of Pompey's day: Strabo 12.3.1.541. See also Strabo 12.5.3.568. Adiatorix has been thought mentioned in Cic. *Fam.* 2.12.2, which dates to 50 BC, but this would have been during his father's tetrarchship and the identification is very uncertain. See too Stähelin 109; Hoben 95 note 198; Reinach, *L'histoire par les monnaies* 157-158; Magie 1287 note 27. For this name: *OGIS* 534.

88 Strabo 12.3.6.543 and 12.3.35.558-559. Antony's policy: Buccheim 50 and 56-59. See too Jones, *Cities*² 426 note 39.

89 Dyteutus has been seen as the subject of a poem by Crinagoras in the *Palatine Anthology* (7.638): G.W. Bowersock, *Hermes* 92 (1964) 255 ff. OTHER DYNASTIC PERSONNEL: C. Bosch, *Jahrb. kleinasiat. Forsch.* 2 (1952/1953) 283-293.

90 Dio 47.48.2; 48.33.5; App. *BCiv.* 5.75.319; Magie 433-434 and 1282-1283 notes 16-19.

91 *PIR*² A 573. *OGIS* 533 shows Pylaemenes, his son. See too *OGIS* 544; Zwintscher 26-27; Bosch, *Quellen* 122-130 nos. 105-106; cf. 197-198 no. 156. See further Stähelin 98 note 2, and 110; Hoben 121. Macedonian name: See remarks by L. Robert in *AC* 35 (1966) 384-385.

92 See Ch. 8, § 23, with notes 273-284, on the developing intentions of Antony and Cleopatra.

93 Dio 49.32.3; Strabo 12.5.4.568; 14.5.6.671. PHRYGIA: G.W. Bowersock in *AJPh* 91 (1970) 226-227; Chr. Habicht, *JRS* 65 (1975) 69. ISAURIA: Strabo 12.6.3.569 with S. Mitchell in *Proc. Xth Internat. Cong. Class. Arch.* (Ankara 1978) 311-318.

94 Strabo 12.6.3.569; Magie 1282-1283 note 17; 433-434. See esp. Zwintscher 31-42. ANTIPATER: M. Ballance, *AS* 7 (1957) 147 ff. and 14 (1964) 139 ff. HOMANADENSES: B. Levick, *Roman Colonies in Southern Asia Minor* (Oxford 1967) 203-214, App. V. HIS KINGDOM: Levick, 24-28; 219-220. Coins from as far afield as Side: *BMC Galatia* xvii; *Lycaonia* xviii-xix; Head *HN*² 509 and 747. See too R. Syme in *Anatolian Studies Presented to W.H. Buckler*, ed. W.M. Calder and J. Keil (Manchester 1939) 299-332; T.E. Mionnet, *Suppl.* VII (Paris 1835) 656.

95 Vell. Pat. 2.84.2; Plut. *Ant.* 61 and 63; Hor. *Ep.* 9.17-18: 'Gauls, chanting "Caesar", turned away ...' See also Dio 51.7.4.

96 Strabo 12.6.4-5.569 and 14.5.6.671. Cleopatra prized the region too: Ch. 8, § 23. On the successive dynasts, see R. Sullivan, 'King Marcus Antonius Polemo' in *NC* (ser. 7) 19 (1979) 6-20 with Plate 2.

97 CHILDREN: Dio 53.26.3; *OGIS* 533.15 and 42; *Anth. Pal.* 6.241; Zwintscher 43. ATEPORIX: Strabo 12.3.37.560; Magie 435. Except for the possible Galatian Strabo mentions here, Dyteutus, Ateporix would be the last ruler

from the Galatian tetrarchal lines. PROVINCE: Strabo 12.6.5.569; Dio 53.26.3; Levick 25-28 and 219-222. See too R.K. Sherk, *The Legates of Galatia from Augustus to Diocletian* (Baltimore 1951) 11-19; Sherk, *ANRW* II 7.2 (Berlin 1980) 954-1052. Another 'testament' has been postulated: see discussion by Levick 219. AMYNTIANI: Gwatkin 20-21; S. Mitchell, 'Iconium and Ninica': *Historia* 28 (1979) 409-438; Mitchell, *CQ* n.s. 26 (1976) 298-308; F. Robiou, *Des Gaulois d'Orient* (Paris 1866) Ch. 14, 258 ff. See also Strabo 12.5.1.567; 12.6.5.569; Dio 53.26.3; Sherk, *ANRW* II 7.2, 958-959. See as well R. Syme in *Klio* 27 (1934) 122 ff. and 30 (1937) 227 note 1 with Levick 30-32 and Sherk, *ANRW* II 7.2, 959 note 17; cf. R. Syme in *Anat. St. Buckler* 329. CILICIA TRACHEIA: T.B. Mitford, 'Roman Rough Cilicia': *ANRW* II 7.2, 1230-1261, with maps.

98 *OGIS* 544; Bosch, *Quellen* nos. 105-106 and 156. The impression among some ancients that Galatia required armed suppression, with Deiotarus I falling anachronistically to Octavian, preserves a taste of the suddenness of conversion to a province: Malalas 9, p. 221 Dindorff = Bosch no. 47; Tzetzes 1.139 = Bosch no. 48. DEIOTARUS PHILADELPHOS: See above, note 85. On these later aristocrats descended from kings, see Ch. 10 below. See also S. Mitchell in *ANRW* II 7.2 (Berlin 1980) 1053-1081, esp. 1076-1077; Mitchell, *AS* 27 (1977) 63-103; 28 (1978) 93-96; 29 (1979) 13-22. See too R. Sherk, *AJPh* (1979) 166-175; Sherk, *ANRW* II 7.2, 954-1052; P.R. Franke, *Chiron* 9 (1979) 377-382. Priesthoods Severus and others held: R. Sullivan, *Festschr. Dörner* 914-939. FAVORINUS: Philostr. *VS* 489; C.P. Jones, *HSCP* 72 (1967) 287. ZENOBIA: H.M.D. Parker, *History of the Roman World, A.D. 138-327*, 2nd ed., rev. B. Warmington (London 1958) 198-199.

99 BIBLIOGRAPHY: See Ch. 2, § 5; L. Franck, *Sources classiques concernant la Cappadoce* (Paris 1966; = *RHA* 24, 5-122) map on 10-11. The campaigns appear on *TAVO* B V 6. See also Sullivan, 'Cappadocia' 1130-1135; Cimma Ch. 3, sections 7-8; Ch. 4, sections 1-6. See too Hoben Ch. 4.4-5; Pani Ch. 3. See further Strabo 12.2.1.535. Cf. Plut. *Sulla* 5; *Luc.* 14.6: Romans often fought *Cappadocians.* SOPHENE: Coins of Ariobarzanes I appear there: *IGCH* 1741. TIGRANOCERTA: App. *Mith.* 67.284; Strabo 12.2.9.539; Ch. 5, § 11 and Ch. 9, § 24.

100 See this chapter, § 15; App. *Mith.* 91.414; Plut. *Luc.* 35.5; Dio 36.17.1; Cic. *Leg. Man.* 2.5.

101 EUPATOR STILL PLANNING: Cic. *Leg. Agr.* 2.19.52. CAPPADOCIAN RULE: App. *Mith.* 105.495-496; 114.558; see below. SUCCESSION: Val. Max. 5.7, Ext. 2; App. *Mith.* 105.496. DATE: H.B. Mattingly, *Chiron* 9 (1979) 166-167 suggests spring, 64, 'when Pompey passed through Cappadocia on his way from Amisos to Syria,' assuming with Badian that the reign began in 96 and lasted thirty-two years: *Athenaeum* n.s. 37 (1959) 279-

303. Mattingly, *AJAH* 1 (1976) 118: 'By the spring of 96 ... Ariobarzanes had been recognized as king.' A.N. Sherwin-White, *CQ* 71 = n.s. 27 (1977) 173-83, esp. 180, thinks 64-62 BC are all possible. See next note.

102 REGNAL YEARS: B. Simonetta, *NC* (ser. 7) 1 (1961) 9-50 with Pl. 2-4, esp. p. 19; Simonetta, *The Coins of the Cappadocian Kings* (*Typos* II) (Fribourg 1977). See esp. the review by O. Mørkholm, *NC* (ser. 7) 19 (1979) 242-246. T. Reinach, *Trois Royaumes* 59-60, reports thirty-third and thirty-fourth years; Simonetta cannot confirm these, but the possibility remains. See too G. Taylor, *Berytus* 20 (1971) 43-45.

103 PHILOPATOR: *OGIS* 354-356 = *IG* II/III^2 3426-3428; cf. 1039. See too *BMC Galatia* 41; Reinach, *Trois Royaumes* 61. SOPHENE AND GORDYENE: App. *Mith.* 105.491 and 495; Plut. *Luc.* 21.2 and 29.6; T. Reinach, *Mithridate Eupator* (Paris 1890) 393, note 1. THE KINGDOM: App. *Mith.* 105.495-496; 114.558; Cic. *Fam.* 15.2.2. and 15.4.4-6; Magie 375 with 1238 notes 44-45; 1249 notes 40-41. See also Strabo 12.1.1.533-4.535; 12.2.7.537; this became the 'eleventh *strategia*' of the kingdom. MAP: Calder-Bean, co-ordinates Hf; *TAVO* B V 6: southwest corner of Cappadocia; T.B. Mitford in *ANRW* II 7.2, 1215, Fig. 4.

104 TIGRANES: App. *Mith.* 105.491. Eupator: App. *Mith.* 111.540. BETROTHAL: App. *Mith.* 66.279-280; Sullivan, 'Cappadocia' 1133. See too *OGIS* 354-356; *IG* II/III^2 3426-3428; R. Sherk, *Greek East* no. 47H; *RE* 2 (1896) 2037 no. 6.

105 See *OGIS* 354-356; Th. Reinach, *RN* (sér. 3) 4 (1886) 432 ff.

106 Cic. *Fam.* 15.4.6.

107 COINAGE: Simonetta, *NC* (ser. 7) 1 (1961) 19, suggests evidence for coins of the ninth and eleventh years, but on p. 45 shows them only to the eighth. See too *BMC Galatia, etc.*, xxxii-xxxiii and 41.

108 Vitruv. 5.9.1: *odeum ... idem autem etiam incensum Mithridatico bello rex Ariobarzanes restituit*. See also App. *Mith.* 38.149; *IG* II/III^2 3426-3427 = *OGIS* 354-355. SONS: *IG* II/III^2 1039, b'+c'+p; *SEG* 22 (1967) 110 II 99; H.B. Mattingly, *Chiron* 9 (1979) 166-167: 65-63 BC. See too *SEG* 14 (1957) no. 77. E. Badian's restoration would name him with his two sons and his queen: *JRS* 58 (1968) 247-249 = *AE* 1968, 19 = Degrassi, *ILLRP* 181-181a-181b = *Scritti Vari*, I, 426 = *Imagines* added to *CIL* (Berlin 1966) 90 = *BCAR* 74 (1951-1952) 31-32 nos. 14-16. Cf. Degrassi in *BCAR* 75 (1953-1955) 69 ff. on *REG* 68 (1955) 287-288 (*Bull. ép.* no. 288). See too A.W. Lintott, *ZPE* 30 (1978) 137-144.

109 Cic. *Prov. Cons.* 4. These royal advisers were elderly by the time of Cicero's governorship in 51, when Ariobarzanes III visited him *cum paternis amicis, maioribus natu*. They had served since the days of Ariobarzanes I: *patris eius atque avi iudicio probatos*. See also Cic. *Fam.* 15.2.5-6. Cicero twice here

speaks of the death of Ariobarzanes as a *casus*, at one point adding *acerbissimus*.

110 Cic. *Fam.* 15.2.4. On Cicero's role in promoting recognition by Rome of kingship for Ariobarzanes III, see D. Braund in *LCM* 7 (1982) 39. The potential weakness of Cappadocia in Roman eyes: Plut. *Crass.* 18.4.

111 Cic. *Fam.* 15.4.6.

112 Cic. *Fam.* 15.2.4-8 and 15.4.6-7.

113 Cic. *Fam.* 15.3-4.

114 Cic. *Fam.* 15.1-4; 15.1.5: *propter acerbitatem atque iniurias imperi nostri.*

115 Magie 390; 396; 1249-1250 note 41; 1256 note 78. See too Cic. *Att.* 5.18; 6.1.3-4; 6.2.7; 6.3.5. Appius Claudius: See E. Rawson, *Historia* 22 (1973) 219-239, esp. 233. See also D.R. Shackleton Bailey, *Cicero's Letters to Atticus*, III (Cambridge, Eng. 1968) 83.

116 Cic. *Fam.* 15.2, 15.4-6. RETURN TO ROME: E.g., *Fam.* 15.12.2.

117 App. *BCiv.* 2.49 and 2.71, mistakenly calling Ariarathes king already. See too Caes. *BCiv.* 3.4; Florus 2.13.5.

118 Dio 41.63.3; 42.45-46; Cic. *Phil.* 2.94 and *Deiot.* 3.8; *BAlex.* 34-35; 67.

119 Cic. *Fam.* 15.2.6, 15.2.5; *BAlex.* 65.

120 COMANA: *BAlex.* 66 has Caesar visit the Cappadocian Comana, but the detour would have been considerable; App. *Mith.* 121.597 and Strabo 12.3.34.558 show that the appointment of Lycomedes in place of Archelaus was in Pontic Comana, leaving room at Cappadocian Comana for Ariarathes. Lycomedes can even be regarded as a 'king' in Strabo 12.3.38.560 and Dio 51.2.2. See also *Didyma II*, no. 107. See above, this chapter, § 15, note 34. Emendations: R. Harper, 'Tituli Comanorum Cappadociae': *AS* 18 (1968) 99-101. Discussion: Magie 371 and 410-411 with 1264 note 21; Ramsay, *Social Basis* 103-105; Sullivan, 'Cappadocia' 1149-1151. LINKS: Harper 102-113 shows the Gerousia at Comana honouring 'Mithratochmes, also called Ariobarzanes' in the first century BC. Other texts also reveal *Ariobarzanes* and *Athenais* used in such *agnomen* formulae. An Athenais dedicates 'on account of *philostorgia*.' CICERO IN 51: *Fam.* 15.4.6. AUTHORITY: *BAlex.* 66: *sub eius imperio ac dicione.*

121 Pharnaces did withdraw from Cappadocia when threatened by Cn. Domitius Calvinus, but menaced it again after defeating the Roman and allied force (Deiotarus and Ariobarzanes). See *BAlex.* 34-41. KINGDOM: Cic. *Att.* 13.2a: *Vult, opinor, regnum aliquod emere a Caesare.*

122 BRUTUS: Sherk, *Greek East* no. 80. CAPPADOCIA: Dio 47.33.1-4; App. *BCiv.* 4.63.272.

123 On the epithet: *OGIS* 356, and his coinage, which reaches 'year 11.' See also Simonetta in *NC* (ser. 7) 1 (1961) 46; Simonetta, *The Coins of the Cappadocian Kings* (Fribourg 1977). ATHENS: *OGIS* 356.

124 Cic. *Fam.* 15.2.6.

125 ARIARATHES AT PHARSALUS: App. *BCiv.* 2.71. CASSIUS: App. *BCiv.* 4.63.272.

126 PARTHIA: Hoben 164; 175-177. PLOTTING: App. *BCiv.* 4.63.272; Dio 47.33.2. REVOLT: Dio, *ibid.*

127 Hoben 173-176; Buccheim 55.

128 B. Simonetta in *NC* (ser. 7) 1 (1961) 19-20 and 47; Simonetta, *The Coins of the Cappadocian Kings* (Fribourg 1977); *BMC Galatia* 43.

129 THREE GENERATIONS: Strabo 12.2.11.540. Discussion: Sullivan, 'Cappadocia' 1147-1149; Hoben 177-179 and 181 note 177; Magie 1286 note 26. See too J. Raillard, *Die Anordnung des M. Antonius im Orient* (Zürich 1894) 27; App. *BCiv.* 5.7; Strabo 12.2.6.537; Tac. *Ann.* 2.42.2.

130 Dio 49.32.3; Val. Max. 9.15, Ext. 2; Pani 106-107; Strabo 12.2.8.538 f.

131 FIELD: If Archelaus can be identified with Sisinnes, he did 'attack the realm of the Cappadocians': Strabo 12.2.6.537. Antony himself is credited with 'driving out Ariarathes' in Dio 49.32.3, though presumably through the agency of Archelaus. GLAPHYRA: App. *BCiv.* 5.7; Martial, *Epig.* 11.20: *futuit Glaphyran Antonius.* Dio 49.32.3 regards her as an hetaira. An inscription from Magnesia honours her as 'Queen Glaphyra, mother of King Archelaus Philopatris': *OGIS* 361. See also Hoben 180 note 172. ARCHELAUS: Pani Ch. III, 91-145; Hoben 179-194; Gwatkin 7 ff.; Wilcken, *RE* 2 (1895) 451. See too *FGrH* II B, 123; *PIR*^{2} A 1023; Jones, *Cities*^{2} 180-181.

132 NOT RELATED: Strabo 12.2.11.540. Discussion: Sullivan, 'Cappadocia' 1151-1154; M. Pani Ch. III, 91-97. See also Plut. *Ant.* 3; Strabo 12.3.34-35.558; 17.1.11.796; Plut. *Sulla* 11.3; App. *Mith.* 114.560. See further Frontinus 1.5.18; 1.11.20; 2.3.17; 2.8.12; Memnon 40.1. Others in the family: App. *Mith.* 17.62; 49.197; Plut. *Sulla* 21.3. On the marriage to Berenice see Ch. 8, § 23. Gabinius a friend: Strabo 12.3.34.558 (in Syria, 57 or 56 BC).

133 POSITION OF THE PRIESTS: Strabo 12.2.3.535; 12.2.6.537; 12.3.32.557-36.559. See too App. *Mith.* 114.560; *BAlex.* 66; Cic. *Fam.* 15.2.5-7.

134 Lycomedes had some connection with the *Cappadocian* royal family at the time Caesar put him forward for Pontic Comana; such were the interchanges between these adjacent priesthoods and kings. See also *BAlex.* 66; Dio 51.2.2; Sullivan, 'Cappadocia' 1150. Sullivan, *ibid.*, 1153 mistakenly locates the ancestors of Archelaus in *Cappadocian* Comana. See further E. Babelon, 'Le nom de Comana': *RN* (sér. 3) 4 (1886) 439-450; Magie 1285 note 25; cf. 1234 note 36.

135 ARCHELAUS IN EGYPT: Strabo 17.1.11.797; Dio 39.58.3; Plut. *Ant.* 3; Sullivan, 'Cappadocia' 1152-1153. See also below, Ch. 8, § 23.

136 Plut. *Ant.* 61.1.

137 Dio 51.2.1-2; Strabo 12.8.16.578; Dio 53.25.1.

138 *SOTER*: V. Yorke, *JHS* 18 (1898) 317 no. 24 = *OGIS* 358, copied in 1891 by D.G. Hogarth. See also R. Harper, *AS* 18 (1968) 99-101 no. 2; Ramsay, *Social Basis* 103 no. 85. *KTISTES*: It has been suggested that Archelaus adopted this title to signal the foundation of Elaeussa-Sebaste in Rough Cilicia, but founding a new dynasty in Cappadocia was certainly more deserving of commemoration. DURATION OF REIGN: Tac. *Ann.* 2.42.2. The coins mount to 'year 49': B. Simonetta in *NC* (ser. 7) 1 (1961) 20; *BMC Cappadocia* xxxiii; Head *HN*² 752. See too Th. Reinach, 'Essai sur la numismatique des rois de Cappadoce': *RN* (sér. 3) 4 (1886) 452-482. On the titles: *OGIS* 357-361, and the coins. Pani, 104-105 (summarizing others), on his titles as 'testimoniando la polemica di Archelao contro il servilismo filoromano dei suoi predecessori' overstates the case in both directions. LITERARY WORK: Archelaus: *FGrH* II B, no. 123. Artavasdes: *FGrH* III C, no. 678. Juba: *FGrH* III A, no. 275; *PIR*² J 65.

139 HIS SUBJECTS: Suet. *Tib.* 8; Dio 57.17.3-4. THE BROTHER: Jos. *BJ* 1.507. HEROD: Jos. *AJ* 16.131 and 324-326; *BJ* 1.499-501. TITIUS: *AJ* 16.270, with the summary by T. Corbishley in *JRS* 24 (1934) 43-49; see further Ch. 9, § 26, note 135.

140 ELAEUSSA: Agnes Baldwin published coins of his struck there in *Arethusa* 17 (1927) 168-169; they were found in Caesarea (Cappadocia), bearing dates corresponding to AD 4-6. See E.A. Sydenham, *Coinage of Caesarea in Cappadocia* (London 1933) 12 ff.; E.L. Hicks, *JHS* 12 (1891) 226-228; Jos. *BJ* 1.499-512; Gwatkin 18 ff.; A. Machatschek, *Die Nekropolen und Grabmäler im Gebiet von Elaiussa Sebaste und Korykos im Rauhen Kilikien* (Wien 1967; Ergänzungsbände zu den *Tituli Asiae Minoris* 2) on the site. RELATIONS WITH OTHER DYNASTIES: In Sparta, *RE Suppl.* 12 (1970) 505-506 on C. Jul. Eurycles. See too Jos. *AJ* 16.301-310, with note by R. Marcus (Loeb 1963) *ad loc.*; Plut. *Ant.* 67; A. Spawforth, *ABSA* 73 (1978) 249-262 and Plates 34-35; Spawforth, *ABSA* 75 (1980) 203-220; G.W. Bowersock, *JRS* 51 (1961) 112 ff. Cf. I Macc. 12.5-24. Judaea: Jos. *AJ* 16.11, 74, 131, 193, 206-207, 261-270, 325-334, 356, 360, 394; 17.11, 16. Archelaus may have been the source of the name given Archelaus Herodes of Judaea (*PIR*² A 1025), his daughter's husband. See below, Ch. 7, § 22, note 137; Ch. 10, note 17. GRANDSON: *Res Gestae* 27; Tac. *Ann.* 6.40.2; this was Tigranes V, son of Glaphyra. See Sullivan, 'Cappadocia' 1164 f. GLAPHYRA: Sullivan, 'Cappadocia' 1161-1168, with article 'Glaphyra' in *The Anchor Bible Dictionary* (New York, forthcoming). Glaphyra's royal offspring were Tigranes V and VI and King Alexander. See Sullivan, 'Judaea' stemma. The connections of L. Iulius Agrippa of Apamaea (shown there) with King Alexander and therefore with Herod have been questioned: J.P. Rey-Coquais in *AAAS* 23 (1973) 55; D. Braund in *CQ* 33 (1983) 242. See too *AE* 1976 nos. 677-686; Ch. 10, note 17;

OGIS 363; *IG* II/III² 3437/8. ARCHELAUS II: Sullivan, 'Cappadocia' 1167 f.; E. Bammel, 'Die Schatzung des Archelaos': *Historia* 7 (1958) 497-500; M. Pani, 'Archelao II e la fine della dinastia dei Teucridi di Olba': *Athenaeum* n.s. 48 (1970) 327-334. On the spheres of kings there: Sullivan, *NC* (ser. 7) 19 (1979) 6-20; Tac. *Ann.* 6.41.1; A. Wilhelm in *Arch.-Epigr. Mitt.* 17 (1894) 1-6.

141 Sullivan, 'Cappadocia' 1155-1161 and 'Pontus' 920-922; Dio 57.17.3; Tac. *Ann.* 2.42. See too R.S. Rogers, *Criminal Trials and Criminal Legislation under Tiberius* (Middletown, Conn. 1935) 25 ff.; Hoben 193 notes 228-229; G.W. Bowersock, *Augustus and the Greek World* (Oxford 1965) 157-161, Appendix III; B. Levick, *CQ* n.s. 21 (1971) 478-486. On the province: W.E. Gwatkin, *Cappadocia as a Roman Procuratorial Province* (Princeton, N. J. 1930; University of Missouri Studies, V); R. Teja, 'Die römische Provinz Kappadokien in der Prinzipatszeit': *ANRW* II 7.2 (Berlin 1980) 1083-1124; T.B. Mitford, 'Cappadocia and Armenia Minor: Historical Setting of the *Limes*': *ibid.*, 1169-1228; cf. *JRS* 64 (1974) 160-175. See also Th. Liebmann-Frankfort, 'Les étapes de l'intégration de la Cappadoce dans l'empire romain': *Le Mond Grec ... Hommages à Claire Préaux*, ed. J. Bingen et al. (Bruxelles 1975) 416-425. Possible descendants of Archelaus at Comana: *AS* 18 (1968) 109-129, nos. 2, 18 and 6, 15.

142 CILICIAN GEOGRAPHY: Levick, *Colonies* Ch. 2 and 8; Jones, *Cities*² Ch. 8; T.B. Mitford, 'Roman Rough Cilicia': *ANRW* II 7.2 (1980) 1230-1261; H. Hellenkemper, *ANRW* II 7.2 (1980) 1262-1283. TRACHEIA: On M. Antonius and the pirate law see Sherk, *Greek East* nos. 54-55; M. Hassall, M. Crawford, J. Reynolds in *JRS* 64 (1974) 195-220, esp. 201-207. See too above, Ch. 2, § 1, note 4; below, this chapter, note 143 and Ch. 8, § 23, note 254. DYNASTS IN TRACHEIA: See this chapter, § 15 (Polemo I); this chapter, § 16 (Amyntas); this chapter, § 17 (Archelaus); Ch. 7, § 21 (Seleucids); Ch. 8, § 23 (Cleopatra). See also Strabo 14.5.3.669; 14.5.6.671; 12.1.4.535; 12.2.7.538; 12.2.11.540; 14.5.10.672. App. *Mith.* 92.416-96.445 centres the pirates in Tracheia. See as well Florus 1.41; *SEG* 3 (1929) no. 378; M. Hassall, M. Crawford, and J. Reynolds, 'Rome and the Eastern Provinces at the End of the Second Century B.C.': *JRS* 64 (1974) 195-220; Sullivan, 'Papyri ... Network' 927-932 (Antiochus IV) and 935-938 (King Alexander, on whom see also *Festschrift ... Dörner* 935-937); R. Sullivan, *NC* (ser. 7) 19 (1979) 6-20 (Polemo II and others at Olba). HEROD AT ELAEUSSA: Jos. *AJ* 16.131; 326; 332; *BJ* 1.456; Jones, *Cities*² Ch. 8. PIRATES: Strabo 14.5.2.668-669; 14.5.6-8.671. See too R. Seager, *Pompey, a Political Biography* (Oxford 1979) Ch. IV; J. Dobiáš in *Archiv orientální* 3 (1931) 245-256; G.E. Bean and T.B. Mitford, *Journeys in Rough Cilicia in 1962 and 1963* (Wien 1965; Denk. Oest. Akad. Wissen., Phil.-Hist. Klasse, 85). See also their *Journeys in Rough Cilicia 1964-1968* (Wien 1970). Others: see below.

143 DOMINATION BY ARMENIA AND CAPPADOCIA: See this chapter, § 17 and Ch. 9, § 24. PROVINCE: Cic. *Verr.* 2.1.95 loosely defines it as covering Lycia, Pamphylia, Pisidia, and Phrygia! Discussion: R. Syme, 'Observations on the Province of Cilicia': *Anatolian Studies Presented to W.H. Buckler* (Manchester 1939) 299-332; T.B. Mitford, *ANRW* II 7.2, 1234-1240; L.P. Doria Breglia, 'La provincia di Cilicia e gli ordinamenti di Pompeo': *RAAN* 47 (1972) 327-387. See too Magie 284-286; 1161-1163 note 12; 1165-1166 notes 15-16; Jones, *Cities*[2] 201-206 and 437; A. Sherwin-White, *JRS* 66 (1976) 1-14 and *Roman Foreign Policy* 97-101. See also Sherk, *Greek East* no. 67 on P. Servilius Vatia; Eutrop. 6.3.

144 *OGIS* 752; Strabo 14.5.18.676. THE DYNASTY: W.M. Calder, 'Colonia Caesareia Antiocheia': *JRS* 2 (1912) 79-109, esp. 105-109 ('The Tarcondimotids of Cilicia'); E. Babelon, 'Tarcondimotus, Dynaste de Cilicie': *RN* (sér. 3) 5 (1887) 378-381 with Pl. 10.9; *RE* 4A (1932) 2297-2298, 'Tarcondimotus' (Stein). The most detailed treatment is Hoben's Ch. V, 'Tarcondimotus, Dynast in Kilikien' 195-211. See also Head *HN*[2] 735; *BMC Cilicia* cxxix; T.E. Mionnet, *Supplément* VII (Paris 1835) 296-297; J. Marquardt, *Römische Staatsverwaltung*, 2nd ed. (Leipzig 1881-1885) I, 384-387; Buchheim 22-23 and 80. ITS CAPITAL: A. Dupont-Sommer and L. Robert, *La déesse de Hierapolis Castabala (Cilicie)* (Paris 1964; Bibl. arch. et hist. de l'inst. franç. d'arch. d'Istanbul, 16) esp. 38-46. THE NAME TARCONDIMOTUS: L. Zgusta, *Kleinasiatische Personennamen* (Prague 1964) 486-493, name and variants; Zgusta, *Anatolische Personennamensippen* (Prague 1964) 179 and 103-113.

145 Dio 54.9.2 mentions 'certain places beside the sea' which Tarcondimotus had controlled, but notes that these went to Archelaus of Cappadocia, along with Armenia Minor (previously ruled by Artavasdes I of Atropatene), in 20 BC. Since Archelaus is known from Strabo to have controlled Elaeussa, where he built a palace (§ 17), this must be the region to which Dio refers. The reference to Tarcondimotus as a former pirate in Lucan 9.219-225 does not constitute evidence for his early naval strength, but Dio 50.14.1 shows him at Actium participating in a sea engagement against Agrippa. Dio 41.63.1 notes that he assisted Pompey considerably with ships in 48 BC. ANAZARBUS: M. Gough, 'Anazarbus': *AS* 2 (1952) 85-150.

146 POMPEY: Magie 1240-1241 note 53; Hoben 196 note 9. Strabo's 'in our time' cannot serve as useful dating: 14.5.18.676. See too Plut. *Pomp.* 39; W.M. Calder, *JRS* 2 (1912) 105, thinks his recognition came only after the death of Ariobarzanes II about 52, since App. *Mith.* 105.496 has 'Castabala, a city of Cilicia' given by Pompey to Ariobarzanes I. Cf. M. Gough in *AS* 2 (1952) 93. B. Niese, 'Straboniana' in *RhM* 38 (1883) 567-575, goes somewhat beyond the evidence for Pompey's role regarding Tarcondimotus. See also Unger in

Philologus 55 (1896) 245-256, esp. 248; cf. 72-122, esp. 84-85; Plut. *Pomp.* 39; Hoben 196-198.

147 Cic. *Fam.* 15.1-6; 15.1.6: *reliqui reges tyrannique neque opibus satis firmi, nec voluntate sunt.*

148 Cic. *Fam.* 15.1.2-3.

149 Cic. *Fam.* 15.4.7-10.

150 Cic. *Fam.* 15.4.4: *aperte Parthis inimici esse non audent*; 15.4.2: *multas civitates acerbissimis tributis et gravissimis usuris et falso aere alieno liberavi*; 15.1.5: *propter acerbitatem atque iniurias imperi nostri aut ... imbecilla sunt ... aut ... alienata a nobis*; 15.1.5: *ne amittendae sint omnes hae provinciae, quibus vectigalia populi Romani continentur.*

151 KING: Cic. *Fam.* 15.1 refers to him merely as 'Tarcondimotus' and to Iamblichus of Emesa as phylarch, but uses 'king' for Antiochus of Commagene and Deiotarus of Galatia, just as in 15.2.4 he uses 'King Ariobarzanes.' Cf. 15.2.8, 4.3-6, 4.15, 5.1. But this practice is not invariable (e.g., *Fam.* 15.3.1: 'Antiochus of Commagene'; *QFr.* 2.12.2: 'the Commagenian'). It should not be used as evidence, though the probability remains that Tarcondimotus adopted 'king' only later. Dio 41.63.1 uses 'dynast' for him in 48 BC. TOPARCH: *OGIS* 752. See Hoben 199. Julia, his daughter (*PIR*² J 637): *OGIS* 753 = *IGRR* III 901. See also R. Heberdey and A. Wilhelm, 'Reisen in Kilikien – ausgeführt 1891 und 1892 im Auftrage der Kaiserlichen Akademie der Wissenschaften' (Wien 1896; Denkschriften der Kais. Akad. der Wiss. in Wien, Phil.-Hist. Klasse, 44) 28-31 nos. 63-66.

152 Hoben 201 with note 26. See esp. Cic. *Fam.* 15.4.10; Cic. *Att.* 5.18 and 5.21. See too Cic. *Fam.* 8.6: *sine Parthis Bibulus in Amano nescio quid cohorticularum amisit.* Cf. Cic. *Att.* 5.20.4 and 5.21.2.

153 *OGIS* 752, where Tarcondimotus is *toparch*; 754 does not refer specifically to Tarcondimotus, but he is apparently the king it names. See Heberdey and Wilhelm (above, note 151) 28-29; Strabo 14.5.18.676; Hoben 200-201; Magie 1240-1241. On this remarkable inscription, see the discussion by M. Rostovtzeff and C.B. Welles in *YCS* 2 (1931) 54; F. Cumont, *Fouilles de Dura-Europos* (Paris 1926) no. 34; *OGIS* 430. See also *IGRR* III 901; Dupont-Sommer and Robert (above, note 144) 39; F. Durrbach, *Choix d'inscriptions de Délos* (Paris 1921) no. 100.

154 PHARSALUS: Dio 41.63.1; Florus 2.13.5. VENGEANCE: Dio 41.62.3-4 and Florus 2.13.5; *BAlex.* 65-66; Magie 410 with 1264 note 19. Presumably Tarcondimotus lost Aegae now, if he had held it, for its coins show an era beginning 47. See Jones, *Cities*² 203; Calder-Bean, co-ordinates Jg. This did not constitute the only seaport of Tarcondimotus, since he retained a navy until Actium. FRIEND: Cic. *Fam.* 15.1.2. JULIA: *OGIS* 753.

155 E. Babelon, *RN* (sér. 3) 5 (1887) 378-381 with Pl. 10.9. Coins of the dynasty:

F. Imhoof-Blumer, *Kleinasiatischen Münzen* II (Wien 1902) 446-447; J. Eckhel, *Doctrina Nummorum Veterum*, III, 2nd ed. (Vienna 1828) 82-83 with M. Babelon in *Mélanges numismatique* I, 82-83; E. Babelon, *Inventaire de la collection Waddington* (Paris 1898) 469 nos. 4714-4715. See too *BMC Cilicia* cxxix-cxxx and 237-238 with Pl. 39.8; T.E. Mionnet, *Description des médailles antiques, grecques et romaines*, III (Paris 1808) 661; Mionnet, *Supplément*, VII (Paris 1835) 296; F. Grose, *Catalogue of the McClean Collection of Greek Coins, Fitzwilliam Museum* (Cambridge, Eng. 1923-1929) 304; L. Forrer, *Descriptive Catalogue of the Collection [of] Sir Herman Weber* (London 1924-1929) III, 670. See further *Müzayde Kataloğu Egger* (Prowe 1904) 84; F. Imhoof-Blumer in *ZfN* 10 (1883) 267-298, with Pl. 10; J. Bent and E. Hicks, *JHS* 11 (1890) 242 no. 11; J. Raillard, *Die Anordnungen des M. Antonius im Orient* (Zürich 1894) 29-30.

156 Strabo 14.5.6.671; 12.1.4.535 (Archelaus); Dio 54.9.2 (coastal possessions of Tarcondimotus transferred to Archelaus). See also H. Instinsky in *Studies Presented to D.M. Robinson* (St Louis 1951-1953) II, 975-979; A. Zwaenepoel, 'La politique orientale d'Antoine': *Études classiques* 18 (1950) 3-15; R. Rossi, *Marco Antonio nella lotta politica della tarda Repubblica Romana* (Trieste 1959) 118-125.

157 Plut. *Ant.* 61.1.

158 Dio 50.13.5-14.2.

159 RISE OF TARCONDIMOTUS: Strabo 14.5.18.676. See the remarks of A. Dupont-Sommer and L. Robert, *La déesse de Hierapolis Castabala* (Paris 1964) 45 ff.: 'un phénomène original et mal connu, une dynastie indigène' in the region.

160 Dio 51.7.1-7. For Herod now: Ch. 7, § 22.

161 The suggestion of G.W. Bowersock, *Augustus and the Greek World* (Oxford 1965) 44, that Strato, deposed after Actium from his tyranny at Amisus, may have belonged to the Tarcondimotid dynasty rests basically on the name, which was one of those it used. See Strabo 12.3.14.547. The father of Tarcondimotus was a Strato (above), and a '[C. Iul]ius Strato, son of King Tarcondimotus Philopator' is also known: W.M. Calder, *JRS* 2 (1912) 108 no. 43 = *AE* 1914 no. 134. See also Magie 1321 note 33; B. Levick, *Roman Colonies* 126. PHILOPATOR: Dio 51.2.2; cf. 51.7.4. The deposition of Philopator ostensibly occurred late in 31 BC; the gladiators moved south from Cyzicus on hearing the news of Actium, and would have taken some time to reach Cilicia, since King Amyntas tried to bar their way first. KING PHILOPATOR II: *IGRR* III 895 = J. Bent and E. Hicks, *JHS* 11 (1890) 242 no. 11 = Ehrenberg-Jones no. 177. See Tac. *Ann.* 2.42.5: *Antiocho Commagenorum, Philopatore Cilicum regibus defunctis turbabantur nationes* (AD 17). See too Head HN^2 735: 'Of King Philopator'; M. Gough in *AnatSt* 2 (1952) 93 no. 34.

162 KINGS IN 20 BC: Dio 54.9.2. See Sullivan, 'Emesa' 211-212; 'Cappadocia' 1155-1156; 'Commagene' 780–782; Ch. 6-7, §§ 17, 19, 20.

163 Magie 1337-1338 note 22; Heberdey and Wilhelm (above, note 151) nos. 63 ff., 87, 94. See also *OGIS* 752-754; *IGRR* III 895-901. See too Keil and Wilhelm, *JOEAI* 18 (1915) *Beiblatt* 54-60; W.M. Calder, *JRS* 2 (1912) 105-109; J. Bent and E. Hicks, *JHS* 11 (1890) 242 no. 11 = *IGRR* III 895; *SEG* 12 (1955) 519 and 535 = M. Gough, *AS* 2 (1952) 127-149; *REG* 67 (1954) 173-174 no. 238. See also *PIR* P 282; T 12; *PIR*^{2} J 637; Plin. *NH* 5.93; Ptol. *Geog.* 5.7.7, p. 900.6; Q. Curt. 3.7.5; Hierocles, *Synecd.* 706.2; *MAMA* III: J. Keil and A. Wilhelm, *Denkmaler aus dem Rauhen Kilikien* (Manchester 1931). See further A. von Domaszewski in *Philologus* 70 (1911) 448; B. Levick, *Roman Colonies in Southern Asia Minor* (Oxford 1967) 126. Perhaps the *reguli Cilicum* of Tac. *Ann.* 2.78.2 and 2.80.1 included members of the family. On Cilicia in the first century AD: Sullivan, 'King Marcus Antonius Polemo': *NC* (ser. 7) 19 (1979) 6-20, esp. 19. Its cities: H. Hellenkemper, 'Zur Entwicklung des Stadtbildes in Kilikien': *ANRW* II 7.2 (Berlin 1980) 1262-1283.

Chapter 7

1 COMMAGENE: See also Ch. 3, § 6. Eupator: Cic. *Leg. Man* 2.5; Dio 37.10.4.

2 Dio 36.2.5. The coin is discussed by J. Wagner, *MDAI(I)* 33 (1983) 222-224. He is aware that it resembles a coin of the sons of Antiochus IV. See his Pl. 53, nos. 4 and 9. THE LATER KINGDOM: Sullivan, *ANRW* II 8, 778-798.

3 J. Wagner, *Seleukeia am Euphrat/Zeugma* (Wiesbaden 1976) esp. I.2a, pp. 56-64.

4 Pliny *NH* 2.235; App. *Mith.* 106.497. *PHILOROMAIOS:* Examples are scattered throughout *OGIS* 383-405; *IGLSyr* 1-50. KINGDOMS: App. *Mith.* 114.559; 105.495; 106.499; Plut. *Pomp.* 38.2; Dio 40.4.1.

5 TIARA: R. Sullivan, *NC* (ser. 7) 13 (1973) 18-37; J. Wagner and G. Petzl, 'Eine neue Temenos-Stele des Königs Antiochos I von Kommagene': *ZPE* 20 (1976) 201-224 with Taf. VIII-X. The tiara carried wide priestly overtones as well: R.A. Stucky, 'Prètres syriens, II': *Syria* 53 (1976) 127-140, esp. 134-135. SYNCRETISM: On the cult statues, see works cited in Sullivan, *ANRW* II 8, 732-798, with F.K. Dörner's studies listed there, and his *Kommagene, Götterthrone und Königsgräber am Euphrat* (Regensburg 1981); his study of Nemrud Dagh is forthcoming. See also his 'Mithras in Kommagene': *Acta Iranica* 17 (1978) 123-133 with Pl. III-VI (*Actes du 2 Congrès international Téhéran*, IV, Études Mithraiques), and Eleanor Dörner, 'Deus Pileatus': *ibid.*, 115-122. See further J. Duchesne-Guillemin, 'Iran and Greece

in Commagene': *ibid.*, 187-199; F.K. Dörner, 'Das Problem der *propylaiai hodoi* zu den Hierothesia in Arsameia am Nymphaios und auf dem Nemrud Dagh': *Hommages à Maarten J. Vermaseren* (Leiden 1978) 322-330. See also 'Cult Inscriptions' below, note 17. IRANIAN TIES: Dio 49.23.4; J. Wagner, *MDAI(I)* 33 (1983) 208-212; C. Toumanoff, *Studies in Christian Caucasian History* (Washington 1963) 277-283 and his *Manuel de généalogie et de chronologie pour l'histoire de la Caucasie chrétienne* (Rome 1976) 403-409.

6 Dio 37.7.3-4; 36.52.4; 36.53.6; App. *Mith.* 106.501. PARTHIA: Justin 41.1.1; Dio 37.7.2; App. *ibid.*; Dio 36.51.1; Plut. *Luc.* 30. COMMAGENE: Caes. *BCiv.* 3.4.6: *magna Pompeius praemia tribuit.*

7 HOROSCOPE: O. Neugebauer and K. Van Hoesen, *Greek Horoscopes* (Philadelphia 1959) 14-16; J. Wagner in *MDAI(I)* 33 (1983) 207-208 with note 105. TOGA: Cic. *QFr.* 2.12.2. THE MARRIAGE: Dio 49.23.4, a reference merely to 'Antiochus,' without secure identification of him – though who else it could be is difficult to say, since the man is apparently a king of some note. This postulate has been confirmed by the text published by J. Wagner, 'Dynastie und Herrscherkult in Kommagene: Forschungsgeschichte und neuere Funde' in *MDAI(I)* 33 (1983) 177-224, esp. 208, with Taf. 45-53. See below, note 18.

8 On the Kingdom of Osrhoene, see Ch. 5, § 12. Abgar contended against Rome at Carrhae: bibliography by J. Wagner in *Armies and Frontiers in Roman and Byzantine Anatolia*, ed. S. Mitchell (Oxford 1983; BAR International Series 156) 103-104. and 119, note 9.

9 Cic. *Fam.* 15.1.2; 15.1.6; 15.4.4.; *QFr* 2.11(10).2. D. Braund has examined Cicero's jocose approach to Antiochus in *LCM* 7.3 (March 1982) 37-39. Cf. R. Sullivan in *ANRW* II 8, 766-768, where Cicero is shown as a 'supporter' of Antiochus but hardly his 'friend' except in the formal political and military sense, *pace* Dr Braund. Neither man trusted the other as far as he could bounce an anvil in a swamp. On the supposed reference to Bostra, see H.I. MacAdam and N.J. Munday, *CP* 78 (1983) 131-136. See below, this chapter, § 22, note 61.

10 Cic. *Fam.* 8.10.1 (... *copias Parthorum ... profectas per Commagenem*); 15.1-4; Dio 40.28-29. Debevoise 97-104 provides a full account.

11 Cic. *Fam.* 15.3.1-2; 15.4.10; Dio 40.28.4.

12 App. *BCiv.* 2.49.202; Caesar, *BCiv.* 3.4.6; Flor. 2.13.5.

13 *BAlex.* 65.

14 On the change of policy in Osrhoene see J. Wagner (above, note 8) 104 and 119, notes.

15 See Ch. 9, § 26, with Sullivan, 'Commagene' 766-768 and notes 141, 150-152. See too Dio 48.41; 49.20-22; 49.32; 49.41.

16 Plut. *Ant.* 34; Jos. *BJ* 1.321-322; Strabo 16.2.3.749; Dio 48.41.5; 49.20-22; Schürer (Vermes and Millar) 251.

17 PEASANTS: Eric Gray has emphasized the social cost of the dynastic and cult activities of Antiochus, which conferred benefits mainly on the nobility. So did much of the activity of Antiochus IV in the next century. When a portion of the populace had a chance to express itself for or against the monarchy in the reign of Tiberius, some sentiment against it probably existed, though our evidence is contradictory (Tac. *Ann.* 2.42.5 vs. Jos. *AJ* 18.53). Sullivan, 'Commagene' 784-785, wavering too. THE CULT INSCRIPTIONS: *IGLSyr* 1 = *OGIS* 383 = H. Waldmann, *Die kommagenischen Kultreformen unter König Mithradates I. Kallinikos und seinem Sohne Antiochos I.* (Leiden 1973) 62 ff. See too J. Wagner and G. Petzl, *ZPE* 20 (1976) 201-223; *SEG* 26 (1976-77) 1623; W. Clarysse, *ZPE* 23 (1976) 264; F. Dörner and T. Goell, *Arsameia am Nymphaios* (Berlin 1963); J. Wagner, 'Neue Denkmäler aus Doliche': *BJ* 182 (1982) 135-137 and 161-162, no. 4. F. Holt, 'The So-Called "Pedigree Coins" of the Bactrian Greeks': W. Heckel and R. Sullivan, *Ancient Coins of the Graeco-Roman World* (Waterloo 1984) 71-72, with note 22, demonstrates the failure of W.W. Tarn's attempt (*Greeks in Bactria and India*, 2nd ed. [Cambridge, Eng. 1951] Appendix 3) to argue Bactrian issues by analogy with the practices of Antiochus in Commagene. JOINT COINAGE: Sullivan, 'Commagene': *ANRW* II 8, 776 with notes 182-183; O. Taşyürek, *AW* 6 (1975) 42.

18 The evidence is Dio 49.23.3-4, which mentions an apparently royal Antiochus, taken with J. Wagner, *MDAI(I)* 33 (1983) 208-212. See also *SEG* 33 (1983) no. 1215. In context, Dio is thinking of Antiochus when he reports a murder by Phraates IV in this passage, despite the view of Wagner (212, note 114) that the reference is to Orodes II. The Greek text could refer to either, grammatically, but the passage has already accounted for the death of Orodes II 'through age and sorrow [at the death of Pacorus]'; it must intend to mention Antiochus. We have other evidence that Phraates murdered his father (Justin 42.5.1: *patrem interfecit*; see Ch. 9, § 26), and Dio probably should have referred to Orodes as the victim here, but as the text stands, clearly he did not. See above, note 7.

19 Details in Sullivan, 'Commagene' 776-777. See also *PIR* M 451; *IGLSyr* 50 = *OGIS* 403 = Waldmann (above, note 17) 56-57 no. K; Humann and Puchstein, 225 ff. We need not press the Greek text (as Dittenberger does, *OGIS* 403) into suggesting different fathers for Mithradates and Antiochus. Commagenian usage might not have required *homopatria* as a balance to *homometria*, especially in a text honouring the mother. Inscription for Laodice: Wagner (above, note 18). RELIGIOUS VITALITY: The vigorous centuries of this still to come have left clear traces. See Sullivan, 'Commagene': *ANRW* 798 with note 270. For the local cult of Jupiter Dolichenus see M. Hörig and E. Schwertheim, *Corpus Cultus Iovis Dolicheni (CCID)* (Leiden 1986; *EPRO*

106). See too J. Wagner, *BJ* 182 (1982) 133-166; *L'ann. épig.* 1975, no. 712; M. Maaskant-Kleibrink, 'Cachets de terre de Doliche?': *Bull. Antieke Beschaving (BABesch)* 46 (1971) 23-63, e.g., no. 5, *dexiosis* of Jupiter Dolichenus and Vespasian.

20 ACTIUM: Plut. *Ant.* 61.1-2. ZEUGMA TO SYRIA: See J. Wagner, *Seleukeia am Euphrat/Zeugma* (Wiesbaden 1976) 64. This hypothesis rests mainly on use of the Actian era on Zeugma's coinage, which hints at a change of status locally. See also J. Wagner in *BJ* 182 (1982) 136-137. ANTIOCHUS 'II': Plut. *Ant.* 61.1; Dio 52.43.1; Sullivan, 'Commagene' 775-780; *PIR* M 451-452; *PIR*^{2} A 740. Though Antiochus is usually enumerated 'II' and has thus determined the numeration of his successors in scholarly treatments, no proof exists that he ruled. The account of Dio omits the royal title and suggests that his brother Mithradates ruled on, 'in conflict' with Antiochus. The reconstruction of Bowersock, *Augustus* 57-58, assumes kingship for Antiochus and puzzling behaviour for Octavian ('With remarkable swiftness Octavian struck down the man he must have elevated two years earlier'). To condemn a king for friction with a non-royal brother, who on this view cannot have been Mithradates II, would have been unprecedented. Braund, however, finds this 'entirely plausible' (*Friendly King* 174 note 17).

21 Details in Sullivan, 'Commagene': *ANRW* II 8, 732-798. Note 4 there mistakenly substitutes *Annals* for Tac. *Hist.* 2.81.1. Rule in Cilicia: Mionnet, *Suppl.* VII (Paris 1835) 153-154; 169; 184; R. Sullivan, *NC* (ser. 7) 19 (1979) 6-20; Imhoof-Blumer, *Kl. Münz.* II, 442 ff. LACEDAEMON AND BALBILLA: Antiochus had a granddaughter, Balbilla, connected with the nobility here: A. Spawforth: below, this chapter, § 21, note 43. Connection with Ti. Claudius Balbillus has been postulated (Sullivan, 'Commagene' 796-797). On him see D. Hennig, 'Zu neuveröffentlichten Bruchstücken der "Acta Alexandrinorum"': *Chiron* 5 (1975) 317-335. See also R. Merkelbach in *ZPE* 31 (1978) 186-187; *ILS* 845; D. Kleiner, *The Monument of Philopappus in Athens* (Rome 1983). WAR AND INCORPORATION: *IGLSyr* 2796 and 2798; *ILS* 9198 and 9200; D. Kennedy, 'C. Velius Rufus': *Britannia* 14 (1983) 183-196; Suet. *Vesp.* 8.

22 See above, Ch. 3, § 7; Diod. 40.1a-1b; Justin 40.2.2; Sullivan, 'Emesa': *ANRW* II 8, 198-219; C. Chad, *Les dynastes d'Émèse* (Beyrouth 1972) 33-38. See especially the review by W. Röllig in *Wiener Zeits. für die Kunde des Morgenlandes* 65/66 (1973/1974) 283-285.

23 App. *Syr.* 49.250; Justin 40.2.3; Strabo 16.2.10-11.753.

24 Dio 36.2.5 ('a certain Arab dynast, Alchaudonius'); Plut. *Luc.* 29.7 ('Kings of the Arabs'); *ibid.*, 21.2; Plut. *Pomp.* 38.2; Dio 37.7a. PHYLARCHS: Jos. *AJ* 13.384; Strabo 16.2.10.753, cf. 16.1.28.748; Cic. *Fam.* 15.1.2. Pompey avoided fighting in Coele Syria and some other regions near Emesa: App.

Mithr. 106.499. IN LEBANON: Jos. *AJ* 14.39-40. ERA OF ARETHUSA: Sullivan, 'Emesa' 201-202 with note 13; C. Chad, *Les dynastes d'Émèse* 39. STRATEGIC LOCATION OF EMESA: Jones, *Cities*² Map V; H. Seyrig, *Syria* 36 (1959) 187.

25 TREATY: See Chad, *Les dynastes d'Émèse 41. Cic. Att.* 2.16.2 mentions a *vectigal*, but not necessarily in connection with Sampsigeramus, whose name occurs here jocosely for Pompey's. See too Cic. *Fam.* 15.1.2. POMPEY'S SETTLEMENT: Dio 37.7a; Plut. *Pomp.* 38.2; App. *Mithr.* 106.499.

26 Cic. *Fam.* 15.1.2; Strabo 16.2.10.753.

27 Cic. *Att.* 15.1-3.

28 Cic. *Fam.* 15.2; 15.4.7; 8.10.2.

29 Jos. *AJ* 14.128-129; *BJ* 1.187-188; *BAlex.* 1 and 26.

30 *BAlex.* 65.

31 Strabo 16.2.10.753; Schürer (Vermes and Millar) 248-250. Arethusa is presumably not the city freed from Jewish control by Pompey: Jos. *AJ* 14.75; *BJ* 1.156. An earlier view: Sullivan, 'Emesa' 210 with notes 75-76.

32 BASSUS IN SYRIA: Jos. *AJ* 14.268-272; Cic. *Att.* 14.9.3; Dio 47.27 and 43.51.1; App. *BCiv.* 58.

33 Dio 48.41.5; Plut. *Ant.* 37.1.

34 Dio 50.13.7.

35 *PIR*² A 497; Dio 51.2.2.

36 Sullivan, 'Emesa,' sections V-IX; Chad, 'Les dynastes d'Émèse' 45-128; *IGLSyr* V, nos. 1998-2710, esp. 2212-2217. Ruling Armenia, AD 163-175: Sohaemus, *PIR* S 546. See D. Knibbe, *JÖAI* 49 (1968-1971), *Beibl.* 24-29, no. 5 = *AE* 1972, 576. See Parthian stemma.

37 See above, Ch. 3, § 8. Summary in E. Bevan, *The House of Seleucus*, II (London 1902) 257-268. See also Schürer (Vermes and Millar) 134-136; Head *HN*² 768 ff.; Bouché-Leclercq, *Histoire des Séleucides (323-64 avant J.C.)*, II (Paris 1914) 640 ff.; E. Babelon, *Les Rois de Syrie* (Paris 1890) ccxxii-ccxxiii; *MDAI(I)* 1967, 208. PHILIP BARYPOUS: J. Dobiáš in *Listy filologické* 51 (1924) 216 ff.

38 Schürer (Vermes and Millar) 135 f. ANTIOCHUS XII: Jos. *AJ* 13.387-392. See also M. Sartre, *REA* 81 (1979) 40 with note 30: 87 BC; E.T. Newell, *NNM* 84 (1939) 78-100: coins as late as 86/85 BC; Meshorer 12: 84 BC. SELENE: Justin 39.4.4 and 40.2.3; Jos. *AJ* 13.419; *BJ* 1.116; Strabo 16.2.3.749; App. *Syr.* 48.247; 49.250; Diod. 40.1a. ROMANS: Plut. *Luc.* 21; E. Rawson, *Historia* 22 (1973) 231 and 234.

39 ANTIOCHUS XIII: Justin 40.2.2; Diod. 40.1a-1b.

40 Magie 1178 notes 37-38 and 1180 note 43; Bouché-Leclercq, I 436; G. Downey, *A History of Antioch in Syria* (Princeton, N. J. 1961) 139-142; Sullivan, 'Emesa' 199-205.

41 Justin 40.2.3; App. *Mith.* 106.500; App. *Syr.* 49.250. See Ch. 3, § 8 and Ch. 4, § 10. See too Cic. *Verr.* II, 4.27.60-4.32.71. Commerce: J. Dobiáš, *Archiv orientální* 3 (1931) 253. Pompey: Sherk, *Greek East* no. 75.

42 App. *Syr.* 70.367. No neighbouring kings (ostensibly): Plut. *Pomp.* 39.3. See also J. Dobiáš, *Archiv orientální* 3 (1931) 241. SYRIAN GOVERNORS: Schürer (Vermes and Millar) 243-253; no fewer than nineteen of these served in the period from 65 to Actium, if one counts repeated and disputed tenure of the post.

43 ANTIOCHUS AND PHILOPAPPUS: See above, this chapter, § 19, note 21, with Sullivan, 'Commagene' 755-757; 768-770; 796-797. SELEUCID DESCENT: *CIG* 4471; M. West in *ZPE* 25 (1977) 120; A. Spawforth, 'Balbilla, the Euryclids and Memorials for a Greek Magnate': *ABSA* 73 (1978) 249-261 with Pl. 34-35. SELEUCID ERA: E.g., *IGLSyr* 2212-2217; 2917. See too *OGIS* 604.

44 Philip was grandson, not son, of Antiochus VIII Grypus. See Dio 39.57.1-2; Strabo 17.1.11.796; Porphyry, *FGrH* 260, F 32 (28). See also Ch. 6, § 17 and Ch. 8, § 23. Antiochus XIII may have died at the hands of Sampsigeramus of Emesa: Diod. 40.1a-b. See this chapter, § 20.

45 Babelon, *Rois* ccxxii-ccxxiii. L. Iulius Agrippa of Apamea: Ch. 10, note 17.

46 TIGRANES: See Ch. 9, § 24. Bowersock, *Roman Arabia* 28 and 30, in a context of 65-64 BC, leaves the impression that Tigranes remained a local factor then: 'Petty princes and bandit chieftains were struggling with Tigranes of Armenia for possession of the heartland of the Seleucid empire.' Tigranes left some five years before this (cf. p. 26), prior to the last Seleucids' rule (§ 21). The view (p. 28) that 'the armies of Tigranes' fought on 'elsewhere in Syria as late as 65' cannot be supported by Jos. *BJ* 1.127 or *AJ* 14.29. The final campaigns of Tigranes occurred in Cappadocia and Armenia (§ 24), not in Syria.

47 DAMASCUS: Jos. *AJ* 13.392 and 418. The reconstruction is by M. Sartre, 'Rome et les Nabateens, à la fin de la République (65-30 av. J.C.)': *REA* 81 (1979) 37-53, esp. 40-41. See Ch. 3, § 9 and below, note 54.

48 POMPEY: Jos. *AJ* 14.38-40; Schürer (Vermes and Millar) 564. PTOLEMY'S POSITION AND MARRIAGE: Jos. *AJ* 14.126 and 297; *BJ* 1.248 and 185-186; *BMC Syria* 279-280; Buccheim, 15-18 and 25-28; H. Seyrig in *RN* (sér. 5) 17 (1955) 101-106. PHILIPPION: Jos. *AJ* 14.126; *BJ* 1.185.

49 JOSEPHUS: Jos. *AJ* 14.307. BARZAPHRANES: Jos. *BJ* 1.248-256; 433; *AJ* 14.330-346; 15.12; 20.245. Lysanias, Malichus I the Nabataean, Antiochus I of Commagene, and others 'favoured Pacorus': Dio 48.41; 49.20; 49.22; 49.32.

50 POSITION OF LYSANIAS: Jos. *AJ* 14.330; *BJ* 1.248; Dio 49.32.5; Buccheim 18-19 and 69-74; Porphyry, *FGrH* 260 F 2 (17). He may have remained a

tetrarch only, despite these later notices, but later writers do not lightly employ the royal title. The coinage calling him 'tetrarch and high priest' does not preclude later assumption of 'king,' *pace* Schürer (Vermes and Millar) 565. More to the point would be omission of the title in a reference to his son: 'to Zenodorus, son of the tetrarch Lysanias': *IGLSyr* 2851. However, identification of this Zenodorus and Lysanias as those from Chalcis in Antony's day was convincingly questioned by H. Seyrig, 'L'inscription du tétrarque Lysanias à Baalbek': A. Kuschke and E. Kutsch, ed., *Archäologie und Altes Testament: Festschrift für Karl Galling* (Tübingen 1970) 251-254. See also Schürer (Vermes and Millar) 561-573, Appendix I. See Ch. 8, § 23.

51 COINS: Babelon, *Rois* ccxi; *BMC Syria* 280; D. Sestini, *Lettere e dissertazioni numismatiche*, 6 (Firenza 1819) 101: perhaps Lysanias of Abila. See also H. Seyrig, 'Antiquités Syriennes, 42': *Syria* 27 (1950) 46-49 ('Chalcis du Liban') = *Antiquités Syriennes*, Vol. IV (1958) 108-111. On the title see I. Lévy, 'Tétrarques et Grands Prêtres Ituréens': *Hommages à Joseph Bidez et à Franz Cumont*, 2 (Brussels 1949; Collection Latomus) 183-184: 'C'est en dehors des cultes sémitiques qu'il faut chercher l'origine de la titulature de Ptolémée, fils de Mennaios et de ses deux successeurs.' FATE OF LYSANIAS: Jos. *AJ* 14.330 ff.; 15.79 and 92; *BJ* 1.248; 440; Plut. *Ant.* 36; Dio 49.32.5. Antigonus may have been killed not by Antony but by Herod: Jos. *AJ* 17.191 vs. 14.488-490, 15.6-10, 20.245.

52 ZENODORUS: Jos. *AJ* 15.344; *BJ* 1.398. The names Lysanias and Zenodorus probably alternated locally, as known from *IGLSyr* 2851 (Baalbek). The Zenodorus here is not called 'tetrarch,' as the successor of our Lysanias presumably was; H. Seyrig (see above) attributes the text rather to the later rulers of Abila. See also *PIR* Z 8; *BMC Galatia, etc.*, 281. See above, Ch. 3, § 9, note 17. CLEOPATRA'S COINAGE: H. Seyrig, *Syria* 27 (1950) 43-49 – his *Antiquités Syriennes*, Vol. IV (1958) 110 ff. See Ch. 8, § 23.

53 LATER TETRARCHY OF LYSANIAS: Jos. *AJ* 18.237 (AD 37); 20.138 (AD 53); *OGIS* 606; Luke 3.1 (AD 28). 'KINGDOM' OF LYSANIAS: Jos. *BJ* 2.215 (AD 41); 247 (AD 53). ITURAEANS: Schürer (Vermes and Millar) Appendix I, 561-573; A.H.M. Jones, 'The Urbanization of the Ituraean Principality': *JRS* 21 (1931) 265-275, with Pl. 31; Jones, *Cities*[2] 253-260; 281-282; 287-289. AGRIPPA II: H. Seyrig, *RN* (sér. 6) 6 (1964) 55-68; Th. Reinach, *REA* 16 (1914) 3-27.

54 NABATAEANS: See Ch. 3, § 9. A summary: P.C. Hammond, *The Nabataeans – Their History, Culture, and Archaeology* (Gothenburg 1973) Ch. 2. In Palmyra: J. Teixidor, *JANES* 5 (1973) 405-409. COINS: See Ch. 3, § 9 with notes 23-24. See too Meshorer, *Nabataean Coins* 9-15; G.F. Hill, *BMC Arabia, Mesopotamia, and Persia* (London 1922) xi-xxii and 1-13. EJECTION BY PTOLEMY: See this chapter, § 22.I above, note 47 on M. Sartre

in *REA* 81 (1979) 41. See too E.T. Newell, *Late Seleucid Mints in Ake-Ptolemais and Damascus, NNM* 84 (New York 1939) 92-100; R. Dessaud, 'Numismatique des rois de Nabatène': *JA* (sér. 10) 3 (1904) 205 ff.; M. Crawford, *Roman Republican Coinage*, I (Cambridge, Eng. 1974) 446 no. 422; Meshorer, 16.

55 ANTIPATER: Jos. *BJ* 1.181. See below, this chapter, § 22.III.

56 See below, this chapter, § 22.III; Bowersock, *Roman Arabia* 28 ff. See also Jos. *AJ* 14.10-21 and 29-33; *BJ* 1.123-130; Flor. 1.40: *Arabes, si quid imperaret, praesto fuere.*

57 Jos. *AJ* 14.46 and 48. PETRA: *AJ* 14.80-81; *BJ* 1.159. Bowersock, *Roman Arabia* 31-32, sees no hostile intent despite the phrasing of Josephus, and the subsequent attack by Scaurus. MOTIVE: M. Sartre, *REA* 81 (1979) 42 ff. COIN: E.A. Sydenham et al., *The Coinage of the Roman Republic* (London 1952) 151-152, nos. 912 ff. with Pl. 913; E. Babelon, *Monnaies de la république romaine*, 1 (Paris 1885) 120-121; H. Greuber, *Coins of the Roman Republic in the British Museum*, 1 (London 1910) 483-484 and Pl. 48.14.

58 GABINIUS: Jos. *AJ* 14.82-104; *BJ* 1.160-178; Schürer (Vermes and Millar) 245-246.

59 OBODAS II: Meshorer 16-20 and 87. The older studies omit this king: M. de Vogüé, *RN* (sér. 2) 13 (1868) 153-168; F. de Saulcy, *AN* 4 (1873) 1-35. R. Dussaud, *La pénétration des Arabes en Syrie avant l'Islam* (Paris 1955; Institut Français d'Archéologie de Beyrouth, Bibl. Archéol. et Historique, 59) 51-54, admits him, on insufficient evidence, to a reign from 62 to 50 BC; in *JA* (sér. 10) 3 (1904) 189 ff. and 209-210 he had it as 'vers 62-47.' A. Negev, *ANRW* II 8 (1977) 558 ff., admits no Obodas II in this period; nor does Starcky (Ch. 3, § 9, note 20) *SDB* 7 (1966) 909. In his 'Numismatics and Nabataean Chronology': *PEQ* 114 (1982) 119-127, Negev does recognize an Obodas ruling in 60 BC, but regards him as the first of that name. See also G. and A. Horsfield, 'Sela-Petra, The Rock of Edom and Nabatene': *Quarterly of the Dept. of Antiquities of Palestine* 7 (1938) 41 ff. and 8 (1939) 87 ff. Bowersock, *Roman Arabia* 34-35, believes such a monarch possible now. The inscriptions and coins may, of course, all refer to Obodas I, who is also attested by Jos. *AJ* 13.375 and *BJ* 1.90, but the coinage discussed by Meshorer does appear to warrant postulating a reign in the period 62-56 for this Obodas 'II' since the reign of Obodas I appears too early for Nabataean coins of this type. There remains the risk of a circular argument here, and the dogmatism of Dussaud (*JA* [ser. 10] 3 [1904] 197) will no longer do: 'nous ne possédons aucune monnaie antérieure à Aretas III.'

60 MALICHUS I: '60 B.C.E.' (Meshorer 20-28); 'en 56 au plus tard' (Starcky 909); 'about 58 or 57 B.C.' (Schürer [Vermes and Millar] 580); 'vers 50' (Dussaud, *La pénétration* 54). INSCRIPTIONS: Meshorer 26.

61 Cic. *QFr.* 2.11(10).3 as emended. See H.I. MacAdam and N.J. Munday, 'Cicero's Reference to Bostra (*Ad Q. Frat.* 2.11.3)': *CP* 78 (1983) 131-136. They speak of 'the impossibility of a reference to Bostra' but they admit 'a fleeting reference to Bostra in *I. Macc.* 5.27' – a passage that groups it among 'cities [which] were strong and large.' Professor Bowersock has, however, pointed out to me that the reference here may be to the southern Jordanian city of Buseirah. Apparent mentions of Bostra in Isaiah 63.1 and Jeremiah 48.24 may also refer to Buseirah. If Cicero had alluded to Bostra, it would reflect his obscure humour (e.g., plays on the name of Sampsigeramus) rather than the city's importance. M. Sartre, *IGLSyr* XIII, 1, *Bostra (Nos. 9001 à 9472)*, Paris 1982, publishes no inscriptions earlier than AD 117-120. Also on this passage: D. Braund in *LCM* 7 (1982) 37-39. See too above, this chapter, § 19, note 9. RELIEF FORCE: Jos. *AJ* 14.128-129; *BJ* 1.187; *BAlex.* 1 (cf. 26-32): *equites ab rege Nabataeorum Malcho.*

62 PERSUASION: Jos. *AJ* 14.128-129; *BJ* 1.187.

63 Jos. *AJ* 14.370-373; *BJ* 1.274-277; Dio 48.41.5; 49.32.5; Deveboise 113. The 'territories that had been conceded to the Arabs by Antipater' in Bowersock, *Roman Arabia* 39, were not lands but funds.

64 LARGE SUM: Dio 48.41.5, mentioning King Antigonus of Judaea and Antiochus I of Commagene in the same terms. TERRITORIES: Dio 49.32.5.

65 DISTRIBUTIONS: Jos. *AJ* 15.92-96 and 107; *BJ* 1.361-363. See also Plut. *Ant.* 36.2: 'as much of Arabia of the Nabataeans as inclines towards the outer sea.' Josephus provides two accounts. In one, Herod himself leases some of Arabia from Cleopatra; in the other, he pays her but is reimbursed by Malichus. The two are compatible, and reflect a short-lived arrangement in an anomalous set of circumstances. See too Bowersock, *Roman Arabia* 40-41.

66 DATE: Meshorer 23 places this in 'year 26,' but he begins in 60 BC for Malichus. JEWISH-ARAB WAR: Jos. *AJ* 16.108-161; *BJ* 1.364-385. Troops from Malichus: Plut. *Ant.* 61.2.

67 Jos. *AJ* 15.161-201; *BJ* 1.386-396; Plut. *Ant.* 69; Dio 51.7.

68 Jos. *AJ* 15.165-178; *BJ* 1.433-434.

69 DEATH OF MALICHUS: Jos. *BJ* 1.440; cf. 360.

70 Bowersock, *Roman Arabia*, Ch. 4-6; 10; an excellent bibliography occupies pp. 193-211. See too G.W. Bowersock, 'The Annexation and Initial Garrison of Arabia': *ZPE* 5 (1970) 37 ff.; D.L. Kennedy, '*Legio VI Ferrata*. The Annexation and Early Garrison of Arabia': *HSPh* 84 (1980) 283-308. Boundaries: M. Sartre, *Trois études sur l'Arabie romaine et byzantine* (Brussels 1982; Coll. Latomus 178) Ch. 1, 17-76. On the dynasty under Obodas 'III' and Aretas IV, whose daughter married into the house of Herod, see the inscription – which evidently accompanied a statue of Malichus I – published by N.I. Khairy (with J.T. Milik), 'A New Dedicatory Nabataean Inscription from Wadi

Musa': *PEQ* 113 (1981) 19-26, with Plate. See the arguments of J. Starcky and J. Strugnell, *RBi* 73 (1966) 236 ff., Text no. I. See also J. Starcky in *Hommages à André Dupont-Sommer* (Paris 1971) 151-159; Meshorer 28 ff.; Starcky, *SDB* 7 (1966) 911 ff. An inscription at Petra for 'King Malichus' was ascribed to Malichus I by J.T. Milik in J. Starcky, ed., *Le Mond de la Bible* 14 (1980) 12-15. On stylistic grounds, it is referred to Malichus II (c. AD 40-70) by J. McKenzie and A. Phippen, 'The Chronology of the Principal Monuments at Petra': *Levant* 19 (1987) 145-165. Cf. *PIR*² A 746 and 1033. See as well G.W. Bowersock, 'The Greek-Nabataean Bilingual Inscription at Ruwwäfa, Saudi Arabia': *Hommages Préaux*, sect. 5. On the expedition against Arabia Felix: S. Jameson, *JRS* 58 (1968) 71-84. Late military activity is evident, as shown by D.L. Kennedy in *Roman Frontier Studies XII 1979*, ed. W. Hanson and L. Keppie (Oxford 1980) 879-888.

71 On her status see Jos. *AJ* 13.320 with the note *ad loc.* of Marcus in the Loeb edition. See also Schürer (Vermes and Millar) 219 note 2. For bibliography on § 22.III, see Ch. 3, § 9, note 25.

72 Schürer (Vermes and Millar) 229-232; Smallwood, *Jews* 18-19. The date appears in Jos. *AJ* 14.4 as Olympiad 177.3, or 69 BC, with the consuls given as Q. Hortensius and Q. Metellus Creticus. However, the reckonings in *AJ* 14.97, 15.180, and 20.44 with *BJ* 1.119, suggest that her death fell in 67. See Schürer (Vermes and Millar) 200-201, note 1.

73 Jos. *AJ* 13.407-408; 14.43-45.

74 Jos. *AJ* 13.409.

75 Jos. *AJ* 15.180. Cf. *AJ* 14.4-7 and *BJ* 1.120-122.

76 Jos. *AJ* 14.8-18; *BJ* 1.123-127. On this family, see Schürer (Vermes and Millar) 234 note 3. In his account of Antipater's early career, Josephus consulted Book 123 of the history written by Nicolaus of Damascus, whom he mentions in *AJ* 14.9.

77 Jos. *AJ* 14.11.

78 Jos. *AJ* 14.10-16; *BJ* 1.123-126. PETRA: Schürer (Vermes and Millar) Appendix II.

79 Jos. *AJ* 14.16-18; *BJ* 1.125-126. THE MARRIAGE: Jos. *BJ* 1.181; *AJ* 14.121; 15.184. The identity of Kypros is not explicit, but the marriage led to the friendship, according to *BJ* 1.181.

80 Jos. *AJ* 14.15-21; *BJ* 1.123-126.

81 Jos. *BJ* 1.127 characterizes the opportunity for Scaurus to invade as 'a godsend.' Pompey wintered in Asia Minor in 65/64 BC: Schürer (Vermes and Millar) 237 note 13.

82 Jos. *BJ* 1.126-129; *AJ* 14.19-32.

83 Jos. *BJ* 1.128-130; *AJ* 14.30-33. *SEG* 8 (1937) 46 should no longer be treated as a mention of this Phallion; G. Fuks, 'Antiochus Son of Phallion': *IEJ* 31 (1981) 237-238.

84 Jos. *AJ* 14.34-36 and 38-47 (63 BC); 14.37 (winter 64/63); *BJ* 1.131-132. See too Dio 37.7.5; Schürer (Vermes and Millar) 237 note 13.

85 Jos. *AJ* 14.38-47; *BJ* 1.131-132.

86 Jos. *AJ* 14.40-53; *BJ* 1.131-134; Dio 37.6-7 and 37.14-15. Eupator in 63 BC: Dio 37.10.4; Bowersock, *Roman Arabia* 31-32; above § 22.II.

87 Smallwood, *Jews* 28 f.; Schürer (Vermes and Millar) 240.

88 Details: Smallwood, *Jews* 24-26; Schürer (Vermes and Millar) 238-240. See also Jos. *AJ* 14. 54-72; *BJ* 1.138-152; Dio 37.16.

89 Dio says Hyrcanus took over 'the kingdom': 37.16.4. Josephus stresses only the high priesthood, with specific 'denial of the diadem': *BJ* 1.153; *AJ* 14.73. Cf. the summary at *AJ* 20.243-244.

90 Jos. *AJ* 20.247.

91 Jos. *AJ* 14.74; *BJ* 1.154.

92 Detailed discussion and bibliography in the edition of Josephus by R. Marcus, Vol. VII, Appendix L; Schürer (Vermes and Millar) 240-242 and 267-286; Smallwood, *Jews* 27-59. On tribute see also D. Braund, 'Gabinius, Caesar, and the *publicani of Judaea*': *Klio* 65 (1983) 241-244. KINGSHIP: Jos. *AJ* 14.78; 15.2.

93 ARMY: The four risings to come within a decade (see below) involved considerable forces of armed Jews. Glimpses of troops under the control of Hyrcanus appear during the campaign to restore Auletes to Egypt: Jos. *AJ* 14.99. A force of three thousand Jewish hoplites assisted Caesar's relief-force under Mithradates of Pergamon: Jos. *AJ* 14.91, 128; *BJ* 1.170. REGIONAL COUNCILS: Schürer (Vermes and Millar) 268-269; Smallwood, *Jews* 31-32.

94 OFFICES: Jos. *AJ* 14.103, 127, 137, 139, 143, 148, 151, 157-158, 172, 191, 194, 280, 326; *BJ* 1.178, 194, 203, 225. See also Schürer (Vermes and Millar) 244-252 and 267-275; Smallwood, *Jews* 37-39; her note 60 compares appointment of Antipater as *epitropos* with a Roman procurator's appointment for Cappadocia by Augustus (Dio 57.17.5). The ruse of Rabirius Postumus in Egypt comes also to mind (§ 23).

95 Jos. *AJ* 14.74-76 and 87-88; *BJ* 155-157; Schürer (Vermes and Millar) 240; Smallwood, *Jews* 28-29; Jones, *Cities*[2] 257-259 with 446 note 1 and 455-456 notes 42-43. DECAPOLIS: A term of convenience in the first century AD, not a 'league' a century before, despite 'Pompeian' eras on coins. So S.T. Parker, 'The Decapolis Reviewed': *JBL* 94 (1978) 437-441. Cf. Bowersock, *Roman Arabia* 30, note 11. I.W.J. Hopkins, 'The City Region in Roman Palestine': *PEQ* 112 (1980) 19-32, emphasizes the later importance of town groupings, including those around 'Scythopolis, the chief city of the Decapolis.' See also A. Spijkerman, *The Coins of the Decapolis and Provincia Arabia* (Jerusalem 1978). On its ancient, Semitic character see J. Bowsher, 'Architecture and Religion in the Decapolis: A Numismatic Survey': *PEQ* 119 (1987) 62-69.

96 Jos. *AJ* 14.74-78.

97 Schürer (Vermes and Millar) 274; Jones, *Cities*[2] 269 with 460-461 note 56; Jos. *AJ* 14.202-210. ANTIPATER'S HELP: Jos. *BJ* 1.187; *AJ* 14.130-131.
98 Jos. *AJ* 14.79, 14.194 and 82-91, 200, 209; *BJ* 1.157-158 and 160-170.
99 Jos. *BJ* 1.176-185; *AJ* 14.98-103 and 123-126.
100 Jos. *AJ* 14.84, 93, 119-121; *BJ* 1.162, 172, 180.
101 Jos. *AJ* 14.121; *BJ* 1.181. Herod to Petra: *BJ* 1.274-276; *AJ* 14.370-372.
102 On Pompey's vision of Rome's role in the east, see T. Liebmann-Frankfort, *La frontière orientale* (Bruxelles 1969) 304-311; Plut. *Pomp.* 38.4. M. Sartre, *REA* 81 (1979) 37-53, esp. 41 ff., doubts a feint by Pompey. NABATAEANS IN DAMASCUS: Jos. *AJ* 13.392; *BJ* 1.103.
103 Jos. *AJ* 14.32 and 80-81; *BJ* 1.128 and 159. For the coin, see Schürer (Vermes and Millar) 244; Meshorer 16. Pompey did not himself attack Aretas: Magie 1229 note 24. See also Bowersock, *Roman Arabia* 31-32 with § 22.II, above.
104 M. Sartre examines the question of motive in *REA* 81 (1979) 37-53.
105 App. *Syr.* 51.255-256; M. Sartre, *ibid.*, 45-46.
106 Jos. *AJ* 14.103; *BJ* 1.178.
107 *BAlex.* 1.1; Jos. *AJ* 14.128; Dio 48.41.4.
108 Dio 48.26 and 41; Jos. *AJ* 14.370-376; *BJ* 1.274-279.
109 See § 22.II. See too Jos. *BJ* 1.360-361.
110 Schürer (Vermes and Millar) 244-251; Dio 48.41.5. Josephus betrays a bias against Parthians until his account reaches Phraates IV (38-2 BC), in the view of C. Colpe, 'Die Arsakiden bei Josephus': O. Betz and others, eds., *Josephus-Studien: Untersuchungen zu Josephus, dem antiken Judentum und dem Neuen Testament, Otto Michel zum 70. Geburtstag gewidmet* (Göttingen 1974) 97-108. See also E. Täubler, *Die Parthernachrichten bei Josephus* (Berlin 1904).
111 Narrative and bibliography: Schürer (Vermes and Millar) 278-282. See also Smallwood, *Jews* 445-56. On C. Asinius Pollio, consul this year, and his 'Jewish interests,' see D. Braund in *CQ* 33 (1983) 240-241, with reply by L.H. Feldman in *CQ* 35 (1985) 240-243; cf. Braund in *TAPA* 84 (1953) 73-80. Herod had met Antony in Bithynia in 41 BC: Jos. *AJ* 14.302. Our knowledge of Herod's reign benefits greatly from the use by Josephus in *AJ* 14-17 of Nicolaus of Damascus (*FGrH* 90) and perhaps of the *Hypomnemata* of Herod (*FGrH* 236), which he mentions at *AJ* 15.174, though not asserting that he used these personally.
112 Jos. *BJ* 1.184-185; *AJ* 14.273-293 and 15.165-178; Schürer (Vermes and Millar) 279-280; Smallwood, *Jews* 54-55.
113 Jos. *AJ* 14.386.
114 KINGSHIP: Jos. *AJ* 14.381-389. Its consequences were likewise important, producing four children, among them Alexander, who sired royalty for Armenia by Glaphyra, princess of Cappadocia. Grandchildren included King Agrippa I, Herod of Chalcis, and Aristobulus, husband of Iotape IV of

Emesa. Among the great-grandchildren stood King Aristobulus of Armenia Minor, King Agrippa II, and Berenice, whose marriages included Polemo II, King of Pontus.

115 Jos. *AJ* 14.392; *BJ* 1.288.

116 Jos. *AJ* 14.403-404. Cf. Th. Fischer, 'Rom und die Hasmonäer': *Gymnasium* 88 (1981) 139-150: 'Herodes, der idumäische Abstammung, jüdisches Königtum, hellenistische Zivilisation und römisches Bürgerrecht in seiner Person vereinigt.' G.W. Bowersock, in *JRS* 65 (1975) 182, points out the imbalance of ancient and some modern accounts of Herod's background and policy.

117 Jos. *AJ* 14.399-412. Silo is mentioned in Livy, *Per.* ('Poppaedius' Silo) and in Dio 48.41.1 ('Pupedius' Silo). 'Pompaedius' has been conjectured.

118 Jos. *AJ* 14.413-420.

119 Jos. *AJ* 14.420-447; *BJ* 1.317-322; Debevoise 115-120; Dio 48.41; 49.20-22 and 32.

120 Jos. *AJ* 14.445-447; *BJ* 1.320-322; Dio 48.41 and 49.20. See also Florus 2.19-20; Orosius 6.18.23; Plut. *Ant.* 34; Magie 1281-1282 note 14.

121 Jos. *AJ* 14.447-468; *BJ* 1.323-346.

122 Jos. *AJ* 14.467; 469; 489-490; *BJ* 1.344.

123 REIGN: Jos. *AJ* 15.121 treats the reign as beginning in 37. COINS: B. Kanael in *Jewish Quarterly Review* 42 (1951/1952) 261-264; O. Edwards, 'Herodian Chronology': *PEQ* 114 (1982) 29-42, with bibliography. Jos. *AJ* 15.8-10 shows the depth of Jewish feeling for Antigonus and against Herod. DIOSCURI: David M. Jacobson, 'A New Interpretation of the Reverse of Herod's Largest Coin': *ANSMN* 31 (1986) 145-163 and Plate 32.

124 Jos. *AJ* 15.63; cf. 14.403. Herod recognized this problem: *AJ* 15.20.

125 Jos. *AJ* 14.366; 15.1-22.

126 Jos. *AJ* 15.22 and 39-40.

127 Jos. *AJ* 15.23-41.

128 Jos. *AJ* 15.25-30; 42-65; 74-76.

129 Jos. *AJ* 15.77-79; 88-96. On this region, see Schürer (Vermes and Millar) 298-300 note 36.

130 Jos. *AJ* 15.96-103.

131 Jos. *AJ* 15.106-120.

132 Jos. *AJ* 15.131.

133 Jos. *AJ* 15.110-160.

134 Jos. *AJ* 15.155-162. *BJ* 1.386 overstates this apprehension, but must rest on Octavian's assessment of matters as they stood after the battle.

135 Details in Schürer (Vermes and Millar) 302-304. Hyrcanus: Debevoise 32; 94; *PIR*^{2} H 246; G 195; Jos. *AJ* 14.342 ff.; 15.11-21 and 164-182. SALOME: For a discussion of the woman by this name (*PIR*^{2} S 76) who married Aristobulus, King of Armenia Minor, during the reign of Nero, see M. Kokkinos in *PEQ* 118 (1986) 33-50. His arguments necessitate re-examination of several

marriages as early as the reign of Herod the Great, but, for reasons that cannot be gone into here, the reconstruction has not been followed on the Judaean stemma.

136 Jos. *AJ* 15.187-196; *BJ* 1.386-393.

137 Jos. *AJ* 15.196-201; 215-218; *BJ* 1.394-400. (The incident at Ilium is related by Nicolaus of Damascus, *FGrH* 90 F 134 = *Exc. De Virtut.* I, 326, 5. See too Jos. *AJ* 16.24-26.) See also T. Africa, *Class. Ant.* 1 (1982) 1 ff.; Schürer (Vermes and Millar) §§ 15-19, 287-483; Smallwood, *Jews* 69-70. On Herod's initial building activity see M. Broshi in Y. Yadin, ed., *Jerusalem Revealed* (Jerusalem 1975) 57-60. See too A.D. Tushingham in *Levant* 19 (1987) 137-143. Herod's great building programs lie mainly outside the scope of this volume. On Judaeans in the 'dynastic network' see Ch. 10 and stemmata, and R. Sullivan in *ANRW* II 8 (Berlin 1977) 296-354. To the discussion of Julia Berenice there and *ANRW* II 8, 934-935, should be added P.M. Rogers, 'Titus, Berenice and Mucianus': *Historia* 29 (1980) 86-95 and D. Braund, 'Berenice in Rome': *Historia* 33 (1984) 120-123; 'Great Queen Iulia Berenice': *OGIS* 428; R. Jordan, *Berenice* (London 1974). Relatives of the Judaeans included the Cappadocian dynasty and they claimed mutual ties to Sparta: Ch. 6, § 17, with note 140. See also B. Cardauns, 'Juden und Spartaner': *Hermes* 95 (1967) 317-324. Bibliography and discussion: Schürer (Vermes and Millar) 184-185 with note 33. See too R. Marcus in Vol. VII of the Loeb Josephus (Harvard 1943) 769, Appendix F. I. Macc. 12 would take these ties with Sparta back to the reign of Jonathan (c. 161-142 BC). On this see Schürer (Vermes and Millar) 184 with note 31. See also below, Ch. 10, note 17. AGRIPPA I and II: Sullivan, *ANRW* II 8 321-345. The title occurs, for example, in *OGIS* 419-423; 425; *SEG* 7 (1934) 216-217 and 970. See too *IGLSyr* 2759 = *ILS* 8957; J. Meyshan in *IEJ* 4 (1954) 186-200. Agrippa II reigned still in AD 95/96: D. Barag in *NC* (ser. 7) 18 (1978) 14-23. See also H. Seyrig, *RN* (sér. 6) 6 (1964) 55-67.

Chapter 8

1 E.g., Strabo 17.1.11.796. See also Diodorus 1.83.8; Strabo 17.1.13.798, citing Cicero, probably in the speech *De rege Alexandrino*. See Plin. *N.H.* 33.47.136, for 63 BC. On the register of his regnal years: Pestman, *Chronologie* 77-83; H. Maehler, 'Egypt under the Last Ptolemies': *BICS* 30 (1983) 1-16.

2 Wealth and titles of Auletes: Pliny, *N.H.* 33.47.136; Jos. *AJ* 14.35, quoting Strabo; App. *Mith.* 114.557. Arabian Gulf: *OGIS* 186; cf. 69 and 132. Auletes: J. Tondriau in *CE* 41 (1946) 158-160; Dio Chrys. *Orat.* 32, p. 383, 22; Athen. 4.176e.

3 J. Barns and E. Reymond in *Orientalia* 46 (1977) 1-33, with J. Quaegebeur and D. Crawford in *Studies on Ptolemaic Memphis* (Leuven 1980; *Stud. Hell.* 24) 1-81, esp. 77. See Ch. 4, § 10, note 3. Cf. Maehler and Strocka (below, note 7) 158 and 239 ff. For a discussion of the imputed bastardy, see E. Bloedow, *Beiträge zur Geschichte des Ptolemaios XII.* (Würzburg 1963) 1-10. See too E. Olshausen, *Rom und Ägypten von 116 bis 51 v. Chr.* (Diss. Erlangen; Basel 1963) 30-31 note 39.

4 The work 'n'est pas un portrait d'état, c'est un portrait familier, où le prince fait place au baccant.' See H. Seyrig, 'Un petit portrait royal': *RA* 1968, Fasc. 2, 251-256 (= *Études de sculpture antique offertes à Jean Charbonneaux*, I); K. Parlasca in Maehler and Strocka (below, note 7) 27 ff. Auletes as New Dionysos, enjoying a virtual 'collège dionysiaque aulique': J. Tondriau in *CE* 41 (1946) 158-160 and in *ibid.*, 45/46 (1948) 136-139 = 50 (1952) 306-309. See also P.M. Fraser, *Ptolemaic Alexandria* Vol. I, 204 and 244, with associated notes. *SEG* 8 (1937) 468 shows the title 'New Dionysos' still in use in 59 BC.

5 Suet. *Div. Iul.* 11. See below, note 23. See too App. *Mith.* 114.557; Strabo 17.1.11.796.

6 Several papyri reflect unrest or crises in Egypt during the reign of Auletes. *BGU* IV 1185, regarding an amnesty in 59 BC; *BGU* VIII 1815: trouble from farmers in the Heracleopolite nome in 61/60; *BGU* VIII 1730, to be discussed below; *BGU* VIII 1762, 1835, 1843, 1850. See the discussion by Bloedow, 30 ff. P.M. Fraser publishes a *prostagma* of Auletes from 63 BC 'issued against a background of civil disturbances': *JEA* 56 (1970) 179-182. See below, note 29. CYRENE: Its chronology then was studied by O. Mørkholm, 'Cyrene and Ptolemy I': *Chiron* 10 (1980) 145-149; Pl. 1-2.

7 Unwarlike: E.g., Lucan 10.54: *inbellis populi.* The populace: H. Maehler and V.M. Strocka, *Das ptolemäische Ägypten* (Mainz 1978) 45-49 (W. Peremans); 239 (W. Clarysse). See also C.B. Welles, 'The Role of the Egyptians under the First Ptolemies': *Proc. XII Int. Cong. Papyrol.*, ed. D.H. Samuel (Toronto, 1970) 505 ff.; H. Braunert, *Die Binnenwanderung. Studien der Sozialgeschichte Ägyptens in der Ptolemäer-und Kaiserzeit* (Bonn 1964); J. Modrzejewski, 'Régime foncier et statut social dans l'Égypte ptolémaïque': *Terre et paysans dépendants dans les sociétés antiques* (Paris 1979) 162-188, esp. part II, 173-188; H.J. Wolff, 'Law in Ptolemaic Egypt': *Essays in Honor of C. Bradford Welles*, ed. A. Samuel (New Haven 1966) 67-77 on the 'dualistic' legal system; Cimma Ch. 3, sect. 6. In the Imperial period: J. Straus, *Historia* 26 (1977) 74-88. THEBANS: *POxy* 2820 = Sherk, *Greek East* no. 94.

8 HERACLEOPOLIS PAPYRI: W. Schubart and D. Schäfer, *Spätptolemäische*

Papyri aus amtlichen Büros des Herakleopolites (Berlin 1933; = *BGU* VIII, nos. 1730-1890). See below, notes 60, 158, and 178. ARMY: Caesar, *BCiv.* 3.110; E. Bernand, *Recueil des inscriptions grecques du Fayoum*, I, *La 'Méris' d'Hérakleidès* (Leiden 1975) 35-36 no. 9. CAVALRY: The second-century inscription from Alexandria is *SEG* 8 (1937) no. 532 = *SB* 7787. Romans, too, had long received the title of 'kinsman' in the Greek East, for instance about 196 BC at Lampsacus near Troy: *SIG*³ 591. GARRISONS: Fraser, *Ptol. Alex.* II, 195, note 107; *OGIS* 102, lines 7-8.

9 Strabo 17.1.12.797-798. See also H.I. Bell, 'Hellenic Culture in Egypt': *JEA* 8 (1922) 139-155; P.M. Fraser, *Ptolemaic Alexandria* I, 75-92; J. Barns in *Orientalia* 46 (1977) 26-28; W. Peremans in Maehler and Strocka (above, note 7) 45-48.

10 Plut. *Ant.* 27.4; J. Quaegebeur in *State and Temple Economy in the Ancient Near East*, ed. E. Lepinski (Leuven 1979) 707-729.

11 App. *BCiv.* 1.111 places it in the same year as the assumption of Bithynia. The internal situation has been studied by Stewart Oost in *CP* 58 (1963) 11-25. See also E. Badian in *JRS* 55 (1965) 118-121, with J. Reynolds in *JRS* 52 (1962) 97-103. BEQUESTS: Braund, *Friendly King* 129-164; G. Perl, *Klio* 52 (1970) 319 ff. See below, note 57. This type of claim went back to the reign of Ptolemy Euergetes in Cyrene, 155 BC: *SEG* 9 (1938) no. 7. See too É. Will, *Histoire politique du monde hellénistique*, II (Nancy 1967) 300 ff. See above, Ch. 4, § 10.

12 Cic. *De Leg. Agr.* 2.16.42: *dicitur contra nullum esse testamentum.* See too Augustus, *Res Gestae* 27.1: *Aegyptum imperio populi Romani adieci.* This claim is picked up elsewhere: *Aegypto in potestatem populi Romani redacta* (obelisk bases in Rome: *ILS* 91 = Ehrenberg-Jones nos. 14-15). See also Macrob. *Sat.* 1.12.35 (Ehrenberg-Jones no. 37); *Fontes Iuris Romani Antejustiniani* I, no. 42.

13 App. *Mith.* 114.557 on Pompey's invitation to Egypt. See also Suet. *Div. Iul.* 35.1: *veritus provinciam facere, ne quandoque violentiorem praesidem nacta novarum rerum materia esset.* See too *Res Gestae* 27.

14 Diod. 33.28a, where he is called Scipio Africanus; Plut. *Mor.* 200E-F; Athen. *Deipn.* 12.549E, with 'Africanus' for Aemilianus and 'Posidonius' for Panaetius. See also Strabo 14.5.2.669; A. Astin, *Scipio Aemilianus* (Oxford 1967) 127, 138, 177; *OGIS* 135; *P. Tebt.* I.33, with discussion by E. Olshausen, *Rom und Ägypten von 116 bis 51 v. Chr.* (Basel 1963) 6-11. Roman contacts are discussed by J.D. Ray in *The Archive of Ḥor* (London 1976) 163 ff. and elsewhere.

15 Further on Lucullus: Olshausen, *Rom und Ägypten* 12-21. See Diod. 1.83.8 on the hapless Roman.

16 Luc. 2.586 f.: *Calida medius mihi cognitus axis / Aegypto atque umbras nusquam flectente Syene.*

17 On the chronology, see R. Seager, *Pompey: A Political Biography* (Oxford 1979) 33-46. Pompey in 67: J. Reynolds in *JRS* 52 (1962) 97-103.

18 T. Rice Holmes, *The Roman Republic and the Founder of the Empire*, Vol. I (Oxford 1923) 426 ff.

19 App. *Mith.* 114.557. For argument to the contrary, see H. Heinen, *Rom und Ägypten von 51 bis 47 v. Chr.* (Diss. Tübingen 1966; publ. St. Vith, Belgium, by the author) 167-175. Suggesting the trip: A. Piganiol, 'Un épisode inconnu de la vie de Pompée': *Studi in onore di A. Calderini e R. Paribeni* I (Milan 1956) 135 ff.

20 App. *Mith.* 114.557. See T.J. Luce, 'Appian's Egyptian History': *CP* 59 (1964) 259-262.

21 *OGIS* 183-191.

22 Plut. *Crass.* 13.1; Cic. *Leg. Agr.* 2.17.44. The notice of Suet. *Div. Iul.* 11 that Caesar sought *ut sibi Aegyptus provincia plebiscito daretur* probably refers to the situation after the departure of Auletes in 58. Some are sceptical: 'neither Crassus nor any other Roman alive is likely to have thought of sending an aedile in command of a large army to Egypt in 65' (J.P.V.D. Balsdon in *CR* n.s. 16 [1966] 217). But Cicero is definite that *Alexandria petebatur ... L. Cotta L. Torquato consulibus* (65 BC).

23 For discussions of this problem, see Olshausen 34 with note 43; Bloedow 35; Seager, *Pompey* 60 note 32; A.M. Ward in *Historia* 21 (1972) 244-258; G.V. Sumner in *TAPA* 97 (1966) 569 ff. See too H. Strasburger, *Caesars Eintritt in die Geschichte* (Munich 1938) 112 ff. On the Roman domestic situation, see E.W. Gray, 'The Consular Elections Held in 65 B.C.': *Antichthon* 13 (1979) 56-65. The expulsion, if it occurred (Suet. *Iul.* 11) in 65, was brief, for no break is reflected in his reign: Pestman, *Chronologie* 79.

24 Cic. *Leg. Agr.* 1.1; 2.16.41-17.44.

25 Long debates often preceded resort to Rome by Easterners wary of the consequences: F.W. Walbank, *The Hellenistic World* (Glasgow 1981) 227-246.

26 Jos. *AJ* 14.35; App. *Mith.* 114.557; Pliny *N.H.* 33.47.136, following Varro; he notes the wealth of Auletes 'at the time' of Pompey's campaigns, but does not specifically mention the gifts. See also *FGrH* 91 (Strabo) F 14.

27 Cic. *Leg. Agr.* 2.16.43: *vendet Alexandriam, vendet Aegyptum, urbis copiosissimae pulcherrimorumque agrorum iudex, arbiter, dominus, rex denique opulentissimi regni reperietur.* Cf. 1.1 and 2.16.41. See too *De rege Alexandrino* 6. On the same group as in 65, *Leg. Agr.* 2.17.44: *an Quirites, ii qui per cursum rectum regnum tenere non potuerunt, nunc taetris tenebris et caligine se Alexandriam perventuros arbitrati sunt?*

28 Cic. *Leg. Agr.* 2.16.42: *... eum qui regnum illud teneat hoc tempore, neque genere neque animo regio esse inter omnes fere video convenire.*

29 P.M. Fraser in *JEA* 56 (1970) 179-182.

30 Seager, *Pompey* 87.

31 Suet. *Div. Iul.* 54.3: *Ptolemaeo prope sex milia talentorum ... abstulerit.* Dio 39.12.1 has him spend great sums 'on certain of the Romans' for confirmation of his rule and for the titles 'friend' and 'ally.' See also Cic. *Att.* 2.16.2: *de rege Alexandrino ... aliquando confici* (May 59 BC).

32 Dio 39.12.1; Cic. *Rab. Post.* 2.4: *huic ipsi Alexandrino grandem iam ante pecuniam credidit.*

33 Caes. *BCiv.* 3.107: *et lege et Senatus consulto societas erat facta*; Cic. *Rab. Post.* 6: *foedus ... in Capitolio.*

34 Cic. *Sest.* 26.57; Dio 39.12.1; Suet. *Div. Iul.* 11.1 and 54.3 (implied); Caes. *BCiv.* 3.107.

35 U. Wilcken in *Archiv für Papyrusforschung* VI (Berlin 1920) 404-406. But see P.M. Fraser, *Ptolemaic Alexandria* II, 222-223 note 270. See too *BGU* 1185.

36 Suet. *Div. Iul.* 54; Dio 39.12.1.

37 *BGU* 1815 (61/60 BC). See Rostovtzeff, *SEHHW* II, 908-909 on conditions. Alexandrine wrath: Dio 39.12.2; Cic. *Att.* 2.16.2; Dio Chrys. *Or.* 32.70; P.M. Fraser, *Ptol. Alex.* 90 with note 354.

38 Plut. *Caes.* 48.4.

39 Fraser, *Ptolemaic Alexandria* II, 223 note 273.

40 British Museum Stela no. 886, lines 8 ff.; E.A.E. Reymond in *Orientalia* 46 (1977) 13. See above, note 3.

41 P.M. Fraser in *JEA* 56 (1970) 179-182; *OGIS* 187 = Bernand, *Fayoum* I (above, note 8) 39 ff. no. 12. See also *SB* 6154 ff. with A.D. Nock in *HSCP* 41 (1930) 8-9.

42 *OGIS* 183-191; A. Bernand, *Les inscriptions grecques de Philae*, Tome I: *Époque ptolemaíque* (Paris 1969) nos. 50 ff. On Ptolemaic employment of ancient usages here, see L.V. Zabkar, 'Adaptation of Ancient Egyptian Texts to the Temple Ritual at Philae' in *JEA* 66 (1980) 127-136. On Auletes as 'New Osiris' at the time of his coronation, see the translation of British Museum Stela no. 886 in Bevan 347-349. On his titles *Philopator* and *Philadelphos* see *SB* I 4211; III 6309; V 8399 (= *OGIS* 185; Bernand 50a); V 8400 (*OGIS* 191; Bernand 55); *OGIS* 192; *SB* I 1569 with L. Mooren in *ZPE* 17 (1975) 199-200.

43 Bevan 354; J. Dümichen, *Zeitsch. für Ägypt. Sprache und Alterthumskunde* 8 (1870) 1-13.

44 See the comments of Bevan (357-358) and his quote of Mahaffy: 'It would seem that he desired the credit of being a temple-builder without incurring any considerable expense.' See also *Sammelbuch* 6154 ff. (69 BC) with the comments of A.D. Nock in *HSCP* 41 (1930) 8-10.

45 On the ramifications of this much-discussed and highly important event: E. Badian in *JRS* 55 (1965) 110-121; H. Volkmann in *RE* 23 (1959) 1751, s.v.

'Ptolemaios' no. 33; Samuel, *Ptol. Chron.* 155-156; Olshausen 38-44; S.I. Oost in *CP* 50 (1955) 98-112; Skeat (1969) 37-38. App. *BCiv.* 4.61 shows Cleopatra controlling Cyprus through a viceroy in 43. See below, note 224.

46 Justin, *Prol.* 40: *Ut Alexandriam post interitum Ptolomaei Lathyri substituti sint eius filii: alteri data Cypros.*

47 Full discussion by Olshausen 38-44, locating the incident in 67 on grounds not apparent from the few sources who mention it. See too App. *BCiv.* 2.23; Strabo 14.6.6.684; Dio 38.30.5. Pompey's successes against the pirates cannot furnish a *terminus ante quem* for the incident, since piracy did not disappear in 67. See Seager, *Pompey* 32-39; Badian, *JRS* 55 (1965) 110-121.

48 Amm. Marcell. 14.8.15: *Ptolomaeo ... rege foederato nobis et socio*; Fest. *Brev.* 13.

49 Cic. *Sest.* 26.57: *Rex Ptolemaeus ... nondum erat ipse a Senatu socius appellatus ... erat rex si nondum socius, at non hostis.*

50 Plut. *Cato Min.* 34.2-3. On Cato's terms of appointment – *pro quaestore pro praetore*, i.e., *quaestor pro praetore* – see E. Badian, *JRS* 55 (1965) 110-113, citing J.P.V.D. Balsdon in *JRS* 52 (1962) 134-135. See too R. Seager, *Pompey* 105. Cf. Vell. Pat. 2.45.4: *quaestor cum iure praetorio.* REVENGE: Dio 38.30.5.

51 Plut. *Cato Min.* 38.1; Vell. Pat. 2.45.5.

52 Cic. *Sest.* 26.57 (with scholion): *ab eo piratas adiuvari* against *rex amicus nulla iniuria commemorata*; Amm. Marcell. 14.8.15: *sine ulla culpa*; Vell. Pat. 2.45.4.

53 Plut. *Cato Min.* 35.1 and 36.1; Vell. Pat. 2.45.5; Amm. Marcell. 14.8.15: *voluntaria morte deleto.*

54 App. *Mith.* 95.436-437 suggests this.

55 App. *Mith.* 111.536. E. Olshausen takes the betrothal of Auletes as a marriage: *RE Suppl.* 15 (1978) 400, with vol. 15 (1932) column 2200. The date of the betrothal is hard to recover. The princes fell into the hands of Mithradates in 88 and the marriage of Auletes to Cleopatra Tryphaena had occurred by January 79. The remark that the daughters of Mithradates were still 'maidens' in 63 cannot be taken precisely for determining their ages, despite the arguments of Bloedow 18 f. Betrothal at a very young age is not impossible in the East (cf. Iotape I of Atropatene, 'still very small,' or Athenais of Pontus, age four): Sullivan, 'Commagene' 773 and 'Cappadocia' 1133 and 1137. See also Heinen 169; Bloedow 19.

56 App. *Mith.* 92.416.

57 That the motive in annexing Cyprus lay mainly in its wealth is shown by the subsequent lack of interest in it once this had been stripped. Caesar returned it to the Ptolemies in 48: Dio 42.35.5. Retained by Cleopatra: Strabo 14.6.6.685. E. Badian, *JRS* 55 (1965) 114: 'Sucked dry by the Romans, it

was an administrative liability and not worth keeping ...' Cic. *Flacc.* 13.30 shows that Ptolemy's rule was considered for the most part innocuous: ... *Syriam esse nostram, Ciliciam teneri, Cyprum per Ptolomaeum regem nihil audere.* On Cyprus later under Cleopatra, see below, note 224. See also G. Perl, 'Die römischen Provincebeamten in Cyrene und Creta zur Zeit der Republik': *Klio* 52 (1970) 319 ff. See too above, note 11. See as well I. Michaelidou-Nicolaou, *Prosopography of Ptolemaic Cyprus* (Göteborg 1976; Studies in Mediterranean Archaeology, 44), with E. Van 't Dack in *Gnomon* 51 (1979) 400-401; *SEG* XXVI 619 and 1458-61; O. Mørkholm, 'The Last Ptolemaic Silver Coinage in Cyprus': *Chiron* 13 (1983) 69 ff. with Pl. 1-4; L. Gasperini, *QAL* 5 (1967) 53 with E. Rawson, *Historia* 22 (1973) 230. See also below, note 224.

58 Dio 39.12.2 shows his departure subsequent to, and consequent upon, the loss of Cyprus.

59 Justin, *Prol.* 40: *seditione flagitatus Alexandriae Romam profugit*; App. *Syr.* 51.257; Strabo 17.1.11.796; Cic. *Rab. Post.* 4 (*pulsus ... regno*). See also Liv. *Per.* 104: *ob iniurias, quas patiebatur a suis*; Suet. *Iul.* 11.: *Alexandrini regem suum socium atque amicum a Senatu appellatum expulerant.* Suetonius appears to locate this event in 65, during the attempt on Egypt by Crassus, in which case the designation as 'friend and ally' would be anachronistic. Better to assume here a retrojection of the events of 58. See too F. Zucker, 'Simariateioi': *Philologus* 101 (1957) 164-166.

60 Dio 39.12.1-13.1. Hephaistion: see the discussion by W. Schubart in his introduction to *BGU* VIII (1932) 3. Hephaistion as *dioiketes* is also known from a marble tablet he dedicated to Auletes in 59: *SEG* 8 (1937) no. 468 = *SB* 7455.

61 Plut. *Pomp.* 49.7; Porphyry, *FGrH* 260, F 14; Plut. *Cato Min.* 35.2.

62 A. Gardner et al., *Theban Ostraca* (Oxford 1913) no. 14; Skeat 37; Samuel 155.

63 Pestman, *Chronologie* 81.

64 *OGIS* 188-189.

65 Pestman, *Chronologie* 80; Skeat 37; Samuel 155. On his return, see also Volkmann in *RE* 23 (1959) 1753, using *BGU* 1820. See also Bloedow 72 ff.

66 Plut. *Cato Min.* 35.2-4.

67 For the suggestion that he passed through Athens and that Cleopatra dwelt there for a time, see A. Wilhelm, 'Ein Grabgedicht aus Athen': *Mélanges Bidez* (Bruxelles 1934; *Annuaire de l'institut de philologie et d'histoire orientales*, II, Université Libre de Bruxelles) 1007-1020, esp. 1015-1017. Pausanias 1.9.3 mentions bronze statues of Ptolemy Lathyros and Berenice III before the Odeum.

68 Strabo 17.1.11.796; Cic. *Att.* 4.1.7. Olshausen, 49 note 66, questions this on the grounds of senatorial tradition. But the situation was, to say the least,

extraordinary, and if anyone could so breach tradition now, Pompey might, and had reason to. See also Bloedow 61-67; Seager, *Pompey* 115-120. A summary of the years to follow: Tyrrell and Purser, *The Correspondence of Cicero*, II[2] (Dublin and London, 1886 and 1906) xxix-l.

69 Plut. *Pomp.* 49.7, citing Timagenes, *FGrH* 88; cf. *Pomp.* 76.5. See also Dio 39.14.3; Strabo 17.1.11.796.

70 Dio 39.13.1; Cic. *Cael.* 10 (23-24); *Har. Resp.* 34; Olshausen 51-52. That Auletes required borrowed funds comes as no surprise: his coinage had become progressively debased throughout his reign, and now he had been cut off from Egypt's revenues. See *BMC Ptolemies* lxxx-lxxxi.

71 Cic. *Fam.* 1.1.3; 1.7.4: *Ciliciam Cyprumque teneas*; Dio 39.12.3; Cic. *Rab. Post.* 6; *Pis.* 50.

72 Plut. *Pomp.* 49.6-7.

73 *Fam.* 1.1.3; *QFr.* 2.2.3; *Cael.* 8.18; Plut. *Pomp.* 49.5-7.

74 Cic. *Fam.* 1.1-7, *passim*, esp. *Fam.* 1.1.1-3: *teneri enim res aliter non potest.* See too *QFr.* 2.2.3; Dio 39.15.2. This had occurred by 13 January 56.

75 Dio 39.14.1 and 39.55.1; Cic. *Fam.* 1.1.1.: *Regis causa, si qui sunt, qui velint, qui pauci sunt.* See also Dio 39.14.1 and 39.16.3, dating the withdrawal to 56. Fenestella, F 21, appears to locate the event in the last month of 57: *Ptolomaeo ... qui iam profectus ex urbe erat.* See H. Peter, *Historicorum Romanorum Reliquiae*, Vol. II (Leipzig 1906; repr. Stuttgart 1967) 85-86. On the activity of Ammonius, see Cic. *Fam.* 1.1.1: *Ammonius, regis legatus, aperte pecunia nos oppugnat.* Fraser, *Ptol. Alex.* II, 224, n. 275 not improbably regards *I. Didyma* 394 (= T. Wiegand, *Didyma*, II: *Die Inschriften*, A. Rehm and R. Harder [Berlin 1958] 240-241) as 'evidence for his stay in Ephesus' beginning two years before its date of 54 BC. It must at least *reflect* his stay, though Ptolemies needed no unusual reason to bestow gifts on temples. See *I. Didyma* 390 A and 217-218, with 165-166.

76 Cic. *Fam.* 1.1-7; 1.7.4. Clodius: E. Rawson, *Historia* 22 (1973) 219-239, esp. 236-237; Cic. *Att.* 4.9.

77 Cic. *Fam.* 1.7.5; cf. 1.4.2: *ne quis propter exercitus cupiditatem Alexandriam vellet ire.* See also Seager, *Pompey* 115 ff.

78 Schürer (Vermes and Millar) I, 244-246; Dio 39.55.

79 Strabo 17.1.11.796. The sons are still 'children.'

80 On her reign: Pestman, *Chronologie* 80-81; Samuel 155-156; Skeat 37-39; Bloedow 68-71 and 107-111; Olshausen 50-52 and 58-63; Macurdy, *Hellenistic Queens* 180-184. No coins of Auletes for 'year 24' have come to light, but that he was regarded as ruling for a portion at least of this period is apparent in the papyri: Skeat 37.

81 *PP* 14523; Dio 39.13.1; Strabo 17.1.11.796; Porphyry, *FGrH* 260, F 2.14; Bloedow 93-106.

82 Attested by *O. Pr. Joachim* no. 1 (= *Die Prinz-Joachim-Ostraka*, ed. F. Preisigke and W. Spiegelberg [Strassburg 1914]): 'Year 2, Tybi 8 [17 January 79] of King Ptolemy, and [the text shifts from genitive to nominative here] Queen Cleopatra who is also Tryphaena, the sister'. *P. Giss.* I 99 (= *Mitteilungen aus der Papyrussammlung der Giessener Universitätsbibliotek*, ed. H. Kling et al., Pt. I, *Griechische Papyrusurkunden aus ptolemäischer und römischer Zeit* [*P. Bibl. Univ. Giss.* 1-16], Giessen 1924) names her as queen but not sister. So does an inscription from the Faiyum in E. Bernand, *Recueil des inscriptions grecques du Fayoum*, I, *La 'méris' d'Hérakleidès* (Leiden 1975) 35-36, no. 9 = *SB* I 623.

83 *OGIS* 182 note 2; 185 notes 1 and 5; Strack, *Dynastie der Ptolemäer* 210 note 43.

84 *BGU* VIII 1762, lines 4 and 9: 'the queens' – thus probably from 58 BC, though it bears no date.

85 Published by J. Dümichen, 'Bauurkunde der Tempelanlagen von Edfu': *Zeit. für Ägyptische Sprache und Alterthumskunde* 8 (1870) 1-13: '"Ptolemaeus [XII] Neos-Dionysos mit seiner Schwester Gemahlin der Regentin Cleopatra gennant Tryphaina".' See also Bevan 357-358; Bloedow 91 ff.

86 *PP* 14524; *FGrH* 260, F 2.11-14.

87 'Year 25' also occurs in *OGIS* 188 and 189, both from Philae. Samuel 155-156 sees 'remoteness' as the cause, here and at Edfu. See also Bloedow 93-106; Skeat 37-40; G. Macurdy, *Hellenistic Queens* (Baltimore 1932) 175-184, on the two queens; *PP* 14523-24; *RE* 11 (1922) 738-790. This absence of a living queen from the documents of Auletes is not the only marital anomaly of his checkered career: *BM Stela* no. 886 mentions him entering a temple with 'his wives and royal children.' Had he instituted royal polygamy, rather than the Ptolemaic custom of one official wife and a number of concubines? See Bevan 347-349.

88 DOCUMENTS: *SEG* 8 (1937) 531. Porphyry notes the sentiment towards a husband: *FGrH* 260, F 2.14.

89 Diod. 40.1a-1b. Porphyry, *FGrH* 260, F 32 (28), here mistakenly terming Philip the son of Grypus, confusing him with his own father, Philip I Epiphanes Philadelphos. See also Bevan 355-356.

90 Porphyry, *ibid.*

91 *PP* 14567. Dio 39.57.1-2 is noncommital on his descent, saying only that he claimed to be a Seleucid. See too Strabo 17.1.11.796.

92 Suet. *Vesp.* 19.2.

93 Strabo thinks he claimed to be a son: 12.3.34-35.558. See App. *Mith.* 114.560; Sullivan, 'Cappadocia' 1149-1153; Dio 39.57-58; Strabo 17.1.11.796; *PP* 14496.

94 Dio 39.57.1-3; Strabo 17.1.11.796; 12.3.34.558.

95 On the scope of the earlier ties see J. Seibert, *Historische Beiträge zu den dynastischen Verbindungen in hellenistischer Zeit* (Wiesbaden 1967; *Historia Einzelschriften*, Heft 10) 66 note 74, 90 ff., 126 note 6. See also the stemmata herein. Others: Sullivan, *ANRW* II 7.1, 7.2, 8 (Berlin 1977-1980).

96 Livy *Per.* 105: *quem sibi regem adsciverant.* Strabo 12.3.34.558 estimates their reign together as of only six months' duration. But the last text for Berenice alone, *SB* 6156, dates to 7 March 56. See also F. Preisigke, F. Bilabel, E. Kiessling, *Sammelbuch griech. Urkunden aus Ägypten* [abbrev. *SB*] (Berlin 1915–present) no. 6156 = U. Wilcken, *Grundzüge und Chrestomathie der Papyruskunde* (Leipzig-Berlin 1912) no. 70. For 'year 25' of Auletes equated with her 'year 2,' see *P. Louvre* 3452; Pestman, *Chronologie* 81. By 16 April, Berenice is married and her new husband's status is reflected in a regnal year for him, his 'year 1' equivalent to her 'year 2': *P. Grenf.* II, 38 = B.P. Grenfell and A.S. Hunt, *New Classical Fragments and Other Greek and Latin Papyri* (Oxford 1897) 62-65, no. xxxviii. L. Ricketts seeks, in *BASP* 16 (1979) 215-216, to reassign this text to the reign of Cleopatra VII. Nothing put forward renders that suggestion any more probable than the former one, and an uncertain reading hampers the proposed reassignment. Further evidence from the period of joint rule: P. Viereck, *Ostraka aus Brüssel und Berlin* (Berlin and Leipzig 1922) no. 6179 (13 July 56) = G. Mattha, *Demotic Ostraka from the Collections at Oxford, Paris, Berlin, Vienna, and Cairo* (Cairo 1945) 193, no. 268 A: 'year 2, which makes year 1, Epēp 11,' from Thebes. See too J. Tait, *Greek Ostraca in the Bodleian Library* (London 1930) 84, Petrie no. 52; Skeat 17 and 38 ff.; Samuel 155-156. The return of Auletes occurred certainly by 24 June 55, and probably already by 22 April (*BGU* 1002 and 1820 – 'year 26'). His 'year 26' was thus shared with Berenice: Pestman, *Chronologie* 80-81; Cic. *Att.* 4.10.

97 Dio 39.55.1-4; 39.59.3; Cic. *Pis.* 21.50; *Rab. Post.* 8.20. See too Livy *Per.* 105: *A. Gabinius procos. Ptolemaeum reduxit in regnum Aegypti.* On Gabinius: Schürer (Vermes and Millar) I, 245-246. An earlier proposal that Pompey be sent without an armed force, thus averting the prohibition of the Sibyl, had borne no fruit: Plut. *Pomp.* 49.6. By the time of the restoration Pompey had no further direct intention of intervening, and had done himself political damage by getting involved so deeply. See Seager, *Pompey* 120.

98 Dio 39.58.1-2; Caes. *BCiv.* 3.110. *BAlex.* 7 terms the army *aptissimum ... ad proditionem.* See also Val. Max. 9.1, Ext. 6; W. Peremans, 'Les revolutions égyptiennes sous les Lagides' in H. Maehler and V.M. Strocka, *Das ptolemäische Ägypten* (Mainz 1976) 45-49.

99 Plut. *Ant.* 3.2-4. On the purported danger from the fleet of Archelaus: Cic. *Rab. Post.* 8.19-20.

100 Cic. *Pis.* 21.49.

101 Plut. *Ant.* 3; Dio 39.58.3; Strabo 12.3.34.558. Strabo contradicts himself at 17.1.11.796, having Auletes as the slayer of Archelaus.

102 App. *BCiv.* 5.8.

103 Dio 39.58.3; Strabo 17.1.11.796; Porphyry, *FGrH* 260, F 2.14. A receipt for chaff possibly under Auletes from 'year 27' (55/54 BC) does not bear the sovereign's name: G. Mattha (above, note 96) p. 189, no. 261. Pestman, *Chronologie* 81 cites '*Stèle Bucheum 200* (p. 68)' for year 27, the first full regnal year after the restoration of Auletes. See also Olshausen 60-62.

104 Dio 42.5.4; Heinen 55, with note 2.

105 Jos. *AJ* 14.103; *BJ* 1.177; Dio 39.59.1-2.

106 App. *BCiv.* 2.49; Caes. *BCiv.* 3.4; cf. 3.104.

107 Plut. *Cat. Min.* 43.1; Schürer (Vermes and Millar) I, 246.

108 Caes. *BCiv.* 3.103: *complures Pompei milites ... quos ... Gabinius Alexandriam traduxerat belloque confecto apud Ptolemaeum ... reliquerat.* Also *BCiv.* 3.4: *praesidii causa.* See too Dio 42.3.4.

109 Caes. *BCiv.* 3.110; 3.4; Heinen 48-52; Fraser, *Ptol. Alex.* 90, 130, 795. See also Lesquier, *L'armée romaine* 1 ff.; Graindor, *La guerre d'Alexandrie* (Cairo 1931) 42; below, notes 192, 201, 204. Alexandrines could fight well when they wished: Fraser, *ibid.*, 127 with notes 293-294.

110 Cic. *Att.* 6.1.3. The result: *Cappadocia est inanis*, Cic. *Fam.* 15.1.5-6. See also Sullivan, 'Cappadocia' 1141-1142. Deiotarus of Galatia suffered similarly, despite his loyalty: *nihil illo regno spoliatius, nihil rege egentius.* See too Strabo 17.1.13.798.

111 Cic. *Rab. Post.* 1, 4 ff., 22 ff. (*huic ipsi Alexandrino grandem iam ante pecuniam credidit*).

112 These calculations assume 1 talent = 4800 drachmas = 24,000 HS then; see Cic. *Rab. Post.* 8.21.

113 Borrowings: Suet. *Iul.* 54.3; Dio 39.12.1. Debt remaining: Plut. *Caes.* 48.4. On the financial circumstances: E. Badian, *Roman Imperialism in the Late Republic* (Ithaca, N. Y. 1968) 73-74 and 83.

114 Cic. *Rab. Post.* 8.21; 11.30; *Pis.* 21.48.

115 Cic. *Rab. Post.* 8.20.

116 Cic. *Rab. Post.* 14.39: *'Dominatus est enim' inquit 'Alexandriae.'*

117 Suet. *Claud.* 16.2: *Rabirio ... Ptolemaeum ... secuto.* See also *Inschr. Didyma* 394; Fraser, *Ptol. Alex.* II, 224, note 275; *RE* 23 (1959) 1754.

118 Cic. *Rab. Post.* 8.22-10.28.

119 Heinen 39; Bloedow 74-79; *BGU* VIII, 27 ff.

120 Cic. *Rab. Post.* 9.25: *quod suam, quod amicorum pecuniam regi crediderit.* See too *ibid.*, 11.30; 14.40.

121 Cic. *Rab. Post.* 12.34.

122 Bloedow 74-79; Heinen 39, note 2.

123 *BAlex.* 4 and 33; Dio 42.35.4.

124 Caes. *BCiv.* 3.108: *per omnes deos perque foedera, quae Romae fecisset.* See also Plut. *Caes.* 48.71; Cic. *Fam.* 8.4.5.

125 *BMC Ptolemies* lxxxi.

126 Caes. *BCiv.* 3.108: *heredes erant scripti ex duobus filiis maior et ex duabus filiabus ea, quae aetate antecedebat.* See also *BAlex.* 33; Dio 42.35.4; Lucan 10.92 ff: *Lege summa perempti verba patris*; Porphyry, *FGrH* 260, F 2.15. Arsinoe, the other daughter, is specifically termed the younger now: *minorem, Arsinoen.* See *BAlex.* 33. On one notice there had been six children born to Auletes, but by the time of the testament only these four remained. See too *OGIS* 185, note 3.

127 Dio 42.35.4.

128 No evidence remains that either Caesar or the author of the *Bell. Alex.* had seen the document; the report probably came from one who had, or from rumour.

129 Caes. *BCiv.* 3.108.

130 Dio 42.35.4: *epitropeia*; Lucan. 10.92 ff.: *tutela.* Cf. Ampelius 35.

131 *BGU* II 1002; *OGIS* 741; *BGU* VIII 1806, 1827, 1829. See comments and bibliography by H. Volkmann, *RE* 23 (1959) 1755 and in *Gnomon* 28 (1956) 67-68. The existence of several texts bearing this formula does not show association but rather succession within the same year. T.C. Skeat has been arguing this since *Mizraim* 6 (1937) 8 with note 1, the initial edition of *Reigns of the Ptolemies.* He was persuaded to drop it from the second edition (p. 2, with note 2), but, thanks to the strong argument set forth in *JEA* 46 (1960) 91-94 ('The Last Year Which Is Also the First'), the original view must be regarded as what he holds, despite the editorial concerns that prevented it from sweeping triumphantly back in the 1969 edition (Preface, with p. 2, note 2). Samuel, 157 note 53, though disagreeing on this point, has usefully collected instances of 'year 30' Auletes equalling 'year 1' Cleopatra.

132 Bevan's phrase, 357. *CIG* III 4926 mentions a *kinaidos* of his at Philae. The verb *festinare* employed for him by Lucan doubtless carries erotic overtones; see W. Lebek, 'Festinare': *ZPE* 45 (1982) 53-57.

133 Officials: see notes 8, 60, and 178. Death of Auletes from disease: Strabo 17.1.11.796.

134 His latest dated document is *OGIS* 190, 'year 30, Mecheir 21,' from Philae. *BGU* 1826 from a week earlier, and *O. Theb.* 30 (J.G. Milne, *Theban Ostraca* [London and Oxford 1913]) are also from year 30, but the reading on the ostrakon is uncertain. See Skeat 40. The first document clearly after his death is the remarkable stele showing Cleopatra and perhaps Ptolemy XIII at Thebes for the installation of a new Buchis (dated 'year 1, Phamenoth 19' or

22 March 51). See R. Mond and O. Meyers, *The Bucheum*, II (London 1934) 12 ff., no. 13, with III, Plate XLIII, no. 13. Cf. W. Tarn in *JRS* 26 (1936) 187-189. The reconstruction of H. de Meulenaere, *CE* 42 (1967) 300-305, reaches a different conclusion.

135 See previous note. On Edfu and Philae in 57, see notes 42 and 43. See Cic. *Fam.* 8.4.5: *nuntiatum nobis ... regem Alexandrinum mortuum*. See also L. Lord in *JRS* 28 (1938) 19-40 (to be used cautiously) and L. Casson in *TAPA* 81 (1950) 43-56. *BGU* 1810 has been read as 'year 30'; Professor Schubart leans towards 'year 1' after rereading it. See too Skeat 40; Samuel 156-157. Autumn of 52: *BGU* 1755.

136 Skeat (1969) 2.

137 This suggestion by A. Samuel, in *CE* 40 (1965) 391-395, was accepted by Heinen, 29 note 1, and by E. Badian, in *JRS* 58 (1968) 259.

138 Further on chronology and the succession: Samuel 156-160 and in *CE* 42 (1967) 376 ff.; H. de Meulenaere, same volume, 297 ff.; H. Volkmann, *Cleopatra* (London 1958) 11. See too Skeat 40-43; Heinen 23 ff.; Pestman, *Chronologie* 82-83.

139 No evidence exists that clearly points to association. See Heinen 24 note 1; Skeat in *JEA* 46 (1960) 91 ff.; Samuel 157-158. See also P.M. Fraser, *Ptol. Alex.* Ch. iii, note 282; W. Otto and H. Bengtson, *Zur Geschichte des Niederganges der Ptolemäerreiches* (München 1938; *Abh. Bayer. Akad.*, Neue Folge, Heft 17) 25 note 2; *BGU* 1806; Volkmann, *Cleopatra* 11, and *RE* 23 (1959) 1755; Skeat 40. For calculating these dates: Skeat 8.

140 On the interval that could occur between the death of one bull and the installation of the other: R. Mond and O. Myers, *The Bucheum*, I (London 1934) 12-13; II, 32: born 53 BC.

141 Mond and Myers, *ibid.*, 13.

142 Mond and Myers, *ibid.*, 12: the ceremony usually took place at Thebes. W.W. Tarn has pointed out the anomalous nature of the wording regarding her and thinks that she was actually present: 'The Bucheum Stele': *JRS* 26 (1936) 187-189.

143 Mond and Myers, *ibid.*, II, 11-13, no. 13.

144 Dio 42.35.4.

145 *PSI* 1098b, from 29 August 51. Cf. *P. Berol.* inv. 16277 with the discussion of Heinen 26-29.

146 *OGIS* 741; Pestman, *Chronologie* 82-85 and 129 note 55; Heinen 177-183, Anhang 2.

147 Cleopatra's birth probably fell in 69 BC: Heinen 190-191. Berenice was killed in the spring of 55 BC.

148 Plut. *Ant.* 27.3-4. T. Reinach unnecessarily questions this: *Mith. Eup.* 282 note 1.

149 Dio 42.34.4; *De Vir. Ill.* 86.2; Plut. *Ant.* 25; in 73.1, Plutarch terms her 'wondrously proud' of her beauty. A century later, Lucan (10.105) could still work himself up over her 'sinful beauty' (*facies ... incesta*). *Ibid.*, 10.69: *incestam ... Ptolemaïda.*

150 *OGIS* 741 (52 BC): *Philadelphoi.* Titles: Heinen 177-183, Anhang 2. Queens and co-regents: U. Kahrstedt in *Klio* 10 (1910) 261 ff. Rule jointly: Dio 42.35.4. See also Macurdy, *Hellenistic Queens* 184-228. A detailed treatment of the evidence in general is by F. Stähelin, 'Kleopatra' nr. 20, *RE* 11 (1921) 750-781.

151 Cic. *Fam.* 8.4.5.

152 Plut. *Caes.* 48.741.

153 Porphyry, *FGrH* 260, F 2.15.

154 Plin. *NH* 5.58. See also *BGU* VIII 1835; 1843; cf. 1730; *RE* 23 (1959) 1757.

155 *BGU* VIII 1730: 'by order of the king and queen.' The date 27 October 50 BC for this document was once thought assured by the presence of an earlier text below it naming Heliodorus, known as *strategos* of the Heracleopolite nome late in the reign of Auletes. But re-examination shows the name now unverifiable, so that an alternative possibility is year 3 of Auletes (79/78). See Bloedow 23, note 1; Fraser, *Ptol. Alex.* II, 230-231 note 298; Skeat in *JEA* 48 (1962) 104; Heinen 29-32; W. Kunkel, *Archiv* 8 (1927) 212-215, no. 15; *Select Papyri* II, no. 209.

156 Schürer (Vermes and Millar) I, 247; Cic. *Att.* 6.5.3. See also Val. Max. 4.1.15: *interfectores ad eum vinctos regina Cleopatra misit.* See too Heinen 29 ff.; 49; 57. Antiochus: Dio 49.23.

157 *PSI* 1098b; Vol. 10 (1930) 1-4. Skeat, *JEA* 48 (1962) 101, thinks this and the Bucheum text demonstrate Cleopatra 'excluding her brother from his share in the kingship.' That lays too much weight on these, and in the Bucheum text the king's role is mentioned first, as the formula would normally require.

158 Heinen 38-39 estimates April 55 to as late as December 54 for Rabirius. The notice that he 'followed' Auletes to Egypt – Suet. *Claud.* 16.2 – may preclude so early a date of inception for his term, but it probably followed soon. See too Bloedow 74-79. HEPHAISTION: *BGU* VIII, 2 ff.

159 Ptolemy's youthfulness: Plut. *Pomp.* 76.5 and 77.2. See also Dio 42.3.3; 42.43.1; App. *BCiv.* 2.71.296 and 2.84.352 ff. See too Caes. *BCiv.* 3.103 and 3.112: *puer aetate.*

160 Plut. *Pomp.* 77; App. *BCiv.* 2.84.352 ff.; Caes. *BCiv.* 3.103, 108, 112; Plut. *Caes.* 48.5. See also Heinen 29-30; 36 ff.; 40 with notes 1, 3, 4; 55 ff.; 121. See further L. Mooren, 'Über die ptolemäischen Hofrangtitel': *Antidorum W. Peremans sexagenario ab alumnis ablatune* (Louvain 1968; *Studia Hellenistica* 16, Universitaire de Louvain) 161-180; Mooren, *The Aulic Titulature in Ptolemaic Egypt: Introduction and Prosopography* (Brussels 1975)

esp. Part I, 51-80, and Part III, 216-246, for the late second century and still applicable to the court now in 51 BC. See too Caes. *BCiv.* 3.103: *per suos propinquos atque amicos.*

161 Plut. *Pomp.* 77.2; App. *BCiv.* 2.84. E. Badian suggests, in *JRS* 58 (1968) 259, that Achillas served as 'at most the superior of the *tribunus militum* Septimius who apparently commanded the Roman part of the army at Pelusium.' In general, Caesar's inquiries give us the Latin terms that he considered equivalent, but these need not be exact.

162 *PP* 14586; Plut. *Çaes.* 491. Cf. Heinen 29 with note 2.

163 Plut. *Pomp.* 77.2. Potheinos as tutor (*tithenos*): Plut. *ibid.*; App. *BCiv* 2.84.352 ff. See too Caes. *BCiv.* 3.108: *nutricius eius*; 3.112: *nutricius pueri et procurator regni.*

164 The king acts *consiliis spadonum*: Florus 2.13.52. See previous note, and bibliography in *PP* 14620, with Heinen 38-39. He was *amicus regis; procurator regni; in procuratore regni; eunuchus*; chief of the *symboloi*; *epitropos*; overseer of the finances of Ptolemy.

165 Skeat in *JEA* 48 (1962) 101.

166 See Heinen 185-187, Anhang 3; T. Skeat, 'The First Year Which Is Also the Third': *JEA* 48 (1962) 100-105. The attempt of L. Ricketts to redate *P. Bonn* 10 to this year, in *BASP* 16 (1979) 213-217, is unconvincing. It ignores the arguments of Heinen 177 ff., and relies on restoring what appear to be too many letters for the spaces indicated by the editor. It resists a straightforward restoration of the month Tybi on the grounds that Phamenoth is mentioned later in the text. Her solution also contradicts Porphyry. Better are the opposing views on *SB* IV 7419 of Bloedow 23, note 1, and Fraser, *Ptol. Alex.* II, 231, note 298. See too O. Montevecchi, *Papyri Bononienses* (Milan 1953) no. 10.

167 Thus, *SB* V 7611 and *BGU* VIII 1730 (on which see above, note 155 and Ch. 4, § 10, note 15) are both dated 'year 3' in Phaophi, or October 50 BC. *BGU* VIII 1831, dated before June 49, bears the '1 = 3' formula, but is closely followed by *P. Berol.* 13730 of 28 July 49, which uses only 'year 3.' Others from 'year 3' (*BGU* 1842-1844) lack the month; *SB* V 8754 refers to 'year 3' but was apparently written in January 48, during year 4. *BGU* VIII 1839 *may* refer to 'year 1 = 3' but has been restored as 'year 1 = 30,' though Skeat (above, note 166, 103) points out that this reverses the usual order; in any case, this text is also apparently from year 4. Finally, *SB* VI 9065 clearly does use 'year 1 = 3,' but without the month and possibly also written in year 4. Another with the formula '1 = 3,' *P. Lond.* 827 = *P.Fay.* 151, does not name the rulers.

168 *BGU* VIII 1730, 27 October 50. See also *SB* VI 9065, using '1 = 3' but without specifying the month. The arguments of Skeat for explaining away an

observed lacuna are unsatisfactory: (above, note 166) 102. See too *PSI* 1098b, 29 August 51. A demotic stele from Memphis of 'year 3' names Ptolemy only: Heinen 32, with note 1.

169 Skeat (above, note 166) 102.

170 Exile: Strabo 17.1.11.796: 'with her sister.'

171 Skeat (above, note 166, 102) thinks of 'some alternate reckoning of her own regnal years.'

172 Strabo 17.1.11.796: 'those connected with the boy.' Dio 51.5.4.: the 'first men' had 'always' disliked her. See also Caes. *BCiv.* 3.103; *RE* 11 (1921) 752; Liv. *Per.* 111; Lucan 5.49 ff.: *regnumque sorori ereptum est.*

173 Fraser, *Ptol. Alex.* note 284 to Ch. 3. See too [Aurel. Vict.] *De vir. ill.* 86: *quem fraudare regno voluerat*; Zonar. 10.10 (ii, p. 365 Dind.).

174 Plut. *Ant.* 25.3. Reconstruction by Heinen, 5-9; 29-36; 58-59. Lucan 2.636, if referring to this period, does mention both *reges.*

175 She and Ptolemy both contributed ships before Pharsalus: App. *BCiv.* 2.71.296. See also Caes. *BCiv.* 3.111. After Pharsalus, during September 48, she had been 'recently' (*arti*) expelled: App. *BCiv.* 2.84.352 ff. Caesar's arrival in Alexandria in early October 48 found her ejected 'a few months' before: *paucis ante mensibus, BCiv.* 3.103. See too Strabo 17.1.11.796; Dio 51.5.4; Liv. *Per.* 111 (48 BC): *Cleopatra ... regno pulsa est*; Ampelius 35.6; *RE* 11 (1921) 752.

176 Caes. *BCiv.* 3.111; App. *BCiv.* 2.71.296.

177 *BGU* VIII 1831.

178 THEBES: *POxy* 2820; *OGIS* 654; Strabo 17.1.53.819. See also Sherk, *Greek East* nos. 93-94; Malalas 9.279: 'into the Thebaid.' See further *OGIS* 190, from Philae; Bevan 362; Heinen 32 ff.; W. Schubart in *Klio* 10 (1910) 54-55; Strack, *Dyn.* 152 (62 BC); J.D. Thomas, *The Ptolemaic Epistrategos* (Opladen 1975) 32 ff. on this post. See above, note 8.

179 A. Brett, 'A New Cleopatra Tetradrachm of Ascalon': *AJA* 41 (1937) 452-463, esp. no. 7b, with Plate IX. See too *BMC Palestine*, pp. 107 ff.

180 Caes. *BCiv.* 3.4: *exspectabat cum Scipione ex Syria legiones II.* Exactions: *civitatibus tyrannisque magnas imperaverat pecunias.* Cf. 3.31-33; 73-83; 88. See too App. *BCiv.* 2.84.352 ff.: 'around Syria'; Strabo 17.1.11.796: 'into Syria.'

181 Parsimonious contributions from the kings: Caes. *BCiv.* 3.4. See also Caes. *BCiv.* 3.8: *magnis exercitibus Scipionis.* Parthians: *ibid.*, 3.31.

182 POMPEY: Heinen 11-23 and 57 ff. Accepted by E. Badian, *JRS* 58 (1968) 259. J. Briscoe is sceptical regarding this 'semi-legal relationship': *CR* n.s. 19 (1969) 323. Most of the Senate accompanied Pompey: Dio 41.9.7. PTOLEMY ALONE: *OGIS* 193; Lucan 5.49 ff. See also Lucan 8.448-449: *Sceptra puer Ptolemaeus habet tibi debita, Magne, tutelae commissa*

tuae; Livy *Per.* 112: *Ptolemäi regis, pupilii sui.* The guardianship claimed by Lepidus for Epiphanes even led to a coin minted in Rome by his descendant in 61 BC: Sherk, *Greek East* no. 3 A-D.

183 Allies respond: Caes. *BCiv.* 3.3.1-3.4; 3.111; App. *BCiv.* 2.71; 2.49. Friend: also Lucan 8.518-519: *nobis sceptra Senatus dedit.* See too Heinen 7-8 and 57.

184 App. *BCiv.* 2.83; Plut. *Pomp.* 76.4-6; Florus 2.13.52. See Ch. 9, § 26 note 110. PHARSALUS: J.D. Morgan, 'Palaepharsalus – The Battle and the Town': *AJA* 87 (1983) 23-54; F. Paschoud, 'La bataille de Pharsale: Quelques problèmes de detail': *Historia* 30 (1981) 178-188; Y. Béquignon in *RE Suppl.* 12 (1970) 1038-1084.

185 Dio 41.55.3-4; 42.2.5; Caes. *BCiv.* 3.82.

186 Dio 42.2-3; App. *BCiv.* 2.83.

187 App. *BCiv.* 2.83; Florus 2.13.52; Dio 42.3.

188 App. *BCiv.* 2.84-86; Plut. *Pomp.* 77-78. Cicero hardly fell prostrate with grief on receipt of the news (*Att.* 11.6.5). He had never doubted that Pompey would end thus, but *non possum eius casum non dolere.*

189 The sources contain such phrases as *perfidia Ptolomaei regis.* Florus 2.13.52 says that the murder was accomplished *imperio vilissimi regis, consiliis spadonum*; in 2.13.55 this becomes *summum civilis belli scelus.* See also Orosius 6.15.28: *Pompeius ... iussu Ptolemaei ... occisus est.* Cf. Livy, *Per.* 112; Caes. *BCiv.* 3.103-104. Lucan saw the irony of Pompey's final refuge, not Pharos but *infima ... Aegypti ... litora*: 8.464.

190 Expected to please Caesar: Orosius 6.15.28: *in gratiam Caesaris.* See also Plut. *Pomp.* 77.4, with the famous remark that a corpse doesn't bite. See too App. *BCiv.* 2.84 and 86; Fraser, *Ptol. Alex.* I, 126-127; II, 227 ff.

191 Dio 42.35.4; Caes. *BCiv.* 3.108; *BAlex.* 33. Lucan, Book X, esp. 55 ff., preserves legend and fact on this adventure. Cf. M. Schmidt, *Caesar und Cleopatra. Philol. und hist. Kommentar zu Lucan 10, 1-171* (Frankfurt am Main 1986).

192 Plut. *Caes.* 48-49. Caes. *BCiv.* 3.106-107 shows the weakness (*infirmis auxiliis*) of his forces even in his own eyes; he relied on his reputation (*fama rerum gestarum*) and soon found it insufficient. On his forces: P. Graindor, *La guerre d'Alexandrie* (Cairo 1931) 29-30 with note 5. See too Flor. *Epit.* 2.13 (4.2).

193 Dio 42.35.5, 42.39; *BAlex.* 31, 33; Livy, *Per.* 112. Ptolemy XIII allegedly drowned when his boat sank in the Nile: e.g., Orosius 6.16.2.

194 This occurred before the possible Nile cruise: J. Briscoe in *CR* n.s. 19 (1969) 322, vs. Heinen 149-150 and 154. On Cyprus: P.M. Fraser, *Ptolemaic Alexandria* (Oxford 1972) II, 228 note 288; E. Badian in *JRS* 55 (1965) 114. It may have remained in Cleopatra's possession until her sojourn in Rome,

and Antony returned it to her control. See also *BAlex.* 4 and 33 on Arsinoe; Heinen 91 and 145.

195 *BAlex.* 1, 11-15. The Rhodian commander was especially effective: *ibid.*, 25.

196 *BAlex.* 9.

197 MITHRADATES OF PERGAMON: On this man, see *RE* 15 (1932) 2205, no. 15, *RE Suppl.* 1 (1903) 10, and 7 (1940) 82-83, with the stemma in *RE Suppl.* 15 (1978) 400. See also H. Hepding in *AM* 34 (1909) 329-340; G. Hirschfeld in *Hermes* 14 (1879) 474-475. Cf. Ch. 6, § 15, note 47.

198 *BAlex.* 26: *Mithradates Pergamenus ... fidei dignitatisque in amicitia Caesaris, missus in Syriam Ciliciamque initio belli Alexandrini. Ibid.*, 78: he becomes king of Bosporus and – *iure gentis et cognationis* – ruler of Gallograecia. See also Jos. *BJ* 1.187-188; *AJ* 14.128; Strabo 13.4.3.625. See Ch. 6, § 15, notes 41, 47, 48.

199 Jos. *BJ* 1.181; *AJ* 14.121-122; *BJ* 1.187-189; *AJ* 14.127-139.

200 Jos. *AJ* 14.129; *BJ* 1.188.

201 Caes. *BCiv.* 3.112; Dio 42.39.2; Heinen 110. On the civil war in Alexandria, see esp. Graindor (above, note 192) note 204. Cf. an excellent summary in Fraser, *Ptol. Alex.* I, 126-127 with associated notes. Caesar's own account is in *BCiv.* 3.106-112 (the beginning of the war); the most detailed ancient account is the *de Bello Alexandrino*.

202 Dio 42.39.1 and 42.40.1; Heinen 115.

203 Heinen 110 ff. discusses the authority of Arsinoe and Ganymedes now. See esp. 119, note 2, on *fiduciario regno* (*BAlex.* 23).

204 The date for the battle of the Nile, 27 March 47 in the uncorrected calendar (= 14 January 47, Julian) rests on two inscriptions. The *Fasti Caeretani* (*CIL* I, 1^2, 212) read, for Martius 27, *eo die C. Caes. vicit Alexand.* The *Fasti Maffeiani* (*ibid.*, 222-223), for the same date, have *hoc die Caesar Alexand. recepit*. See also *ILS* 8744; P. Graindor, *La guerre d'Alexandrie* (Cairo 1931; *Université égyptienne, recueil de travaux publiés par la faculté des lettres*, fasc. 7) 20-23, discusses the problems of interpretation. See too Graindor, 'La date de la bataille du Nil': *Mélanges P. Thomas* (Bruges 1930) 364-368. Further bibliography: Heinen 141 note 1. Other estimates of the equivalence of the pre-Julian and Julian dates convert the date to 15 January; Balsdon, *Caesar* 141, opts for 12 January.

205 Lucan 10.520-523.

206 Dio 43.19.2-4; she was spared because of her brothers. The remark in *BAlex.* 33 – *Arsinoen ... deducere ex regno statuit* – must describe her detention, since given in a context of his departure, and followed by a remark about the danger to the rule of Cleopatra and Ptolemy XIV should she remain behind.

207 Jos. *AJ* 15.89; Jos. *Apion* 2.57-58. Dio 48.24.2 has him execute 'her brothers' there, though both were by now dead. App. *BCiv.* 5.9 has him execute

Arsinoe indirectly, and not at Ephesus but Miletus. See Heinen 143. See also below, note 261.

208 Porphyry, *FGrH* 260, F 2 (16); Samuel 158-159; Pestman 83; Skeat 41-42; Heinen 182-183.

209 L.M. Ricketts in *ZPE* 36 (1979) 65-66 and in *BASP* 16 (1979) 212-217. The texts at issue are *P. dem. Loeb* 63, with 113-116; *P.Bon.* 10; and *P.Grenf.* II 38.

210 Justin *Prol.* 40: *successit eius regno soror Cleopatra.* See also Plut. *Caes.* 49.5; Dio 42.44.3. See too App. *BCiv.* 2.90.383: Caesar set her 'to rule instead of her brother.' Further bibliography: Heinen 144 with note 1.

211 L.E. Lord, 'The Date of Julius Caesar's Departure from Alexandria': *JRS* 28 (1938) 19-40; but see Heinen 148-158. See also J.P.V.D. Balsdon in *CR* n.s. 16 (1966) 217.

212 Lucan 10.191-192: *spes sit mihi certa videndi Niliacos fontes, bellum civile relinquam.*

213 Suet. *Iul.* 52.

214 App. *BCiv.* 2.90.383.

215 Dio 42.45.1. See also J. Briscoe in *CR* n.s. 19 (1969) 322, followed by M. Grant, *Cleopatra* (London 1972) 80-81. See too J.P.V.D. Balsdon, *Julius Caesar and Rome* (New York 1967) 140-141: 'Caesar's cruise is one exploded myth.' See also his remarks in *CR* n.s. 10 (1960) 69 and 16 (1966) 217. Heinen 148-158 thoroughly examines the question of a Nile cruise and its timing. H. Volkmann, *Cleopatra* (London 1958) 73-74, accepts both the early departure and the cruise, now 'along the Nile' as part of 'the entertainment that closed the Alexandrian War.'

216 For what it is worth, *BAlex.* 33 has him leaving 'a few days' after the restoration of Cleopatra, with Ptolemy XIV her nominal co-ruler: *paucis diebus reges constituti.* STATUES: Five of these are collected in Sherk, *Greek East* no. 79.

217 Heinen 144 ff. surveys this situation and the considerations which determined attitudes on both sides now.

218 Suet. *Div. Iul.* 35.1: *veritus provinciam facere, ne quandoque violentiorem praesidem nacta novarum rerum materia esset.*

219 *Res Gest.* 27.1.

220 *BAlex.* 33; Heinen 146-147 with notes 3-4; *RE* 21 (1921) 754; Suet. *Iul.* 35.1; 49; 76.3; App. *BCiv.* 3.78; 4.59.

221 *BAlex.* 33.

222 On her loyalty: *manserat in fide praesidiisque eius.* See *BAlex.* 33. She had presumably seen to it that Caesar received the balance of the debt contracted by Auletes in 59 for recognition of him as 'friend and ally' through Caesar's agency.

223 Strabo 14.6.6.685; *BMC Ptolemies* 121, nos. 1-5, with Plate XXX.4.

224 R.S. Bagnall, *The Administration of the Ptolemaic Possessions outside Egypt* (Leiden 1976) 262 with notes 64-65. See also App. *BCiv.* 4.61 and 5.9; Dio 48.40.6; Heinen 91 with note 2, and 145; E. Badian in *JRS* 58 (1968) 259. Cleopatra and Caesarion have a coinage there too: *BMC Ptolemies* 122, nos. 2-3 with Pl. XXX.6. See above, note 57.

225 *RE* 23 (1959) 1760-1761, no. 37; Heinen 91, 145, 161-164, 183. Bibliography: M. Grant, *Cleopatra* 83 ff. with associated notes. See also *RE* 21 (1921) 754. Cic. *Att.* 14.20 need not show Caesarion unborn in 44. The passage could refer to an expected second child, or lament the existing one, or merely demonstrate Cicero's unawareness then. Further, K. Meiklejohn, *JRS* 24 (1934) 191-195.

226 Suet. *Iul.* 52.2: *M. Antonius adgnotum etiam ab eo Senatui adfirmavit. Ibid.*, 52.1: *filium ... natum appellare nomine suo passus est.* Dio 47.31.5 is sceptical. See also Plut. *Caes.* 49.5.

227 Suet. *Iul.* 52: *non esse Caesaris filium, quem Cleopatra dicat.*

228 *Stèle Sérapéum* no. 335; Pestman, *Chronologie* 82-84; 129 note 55; *O. Cairo* 30.643.4. *P. dem. Loeb* 63, as restored, mentions both Cleopatra and Caesarion on '10 Hathyr, year 8,' 5 November 45. See Otto, *P. Loeb* 115-116. This is cited by Pestman, *Chronologie* 82-84; 129 note 55. The arguments of A. Samuel, *EPap* 9 (1964) 73-79, have not proved convincing here. See Pestman, *ibid.*, and below, for the events of 37/36. See also V. and E. Revillout in *Rev. égyptol.* 7 (1896) 168 ff. Some deny unconvincingly that the birth fell even during the lifetime of Caesar. J.P.V.D. Balsdon, *Julius Caesar and Rome* (New York 1967) 141: 'It is quite certain that no child was born from her association with Caesar in winter 48/47.' See his remarks in *Historia* 7 (1958) 80-94 and in *CR* 10 (1960) 68-69. But see H. Heinen, 'Cäsar und Kaisarion': *Historia* 18 (1969) 181-203. See further L. Ricketts, 'A Note on the Dating of P. Dem. Loeb 63': *ZPE* 36 (1979) 65-66.

229 Nor did Caesar: Dio 43.27.3. See too *RE* 23 (1959) 1759. He was known *plurimas ... et illustres feminas corrupisse*: Suet. *Iul.* 50. On Caesar's extra-marital habits: R. Syme, 'No Son for Caesar?': *Historia* 29 (1980) 422-437.

230 H. Seyrig, 'Un portrait de Jules César': *RN* (sér. 6) 11 (1969) 53 ff.; Heinen 162 note 2.

231 Dio 43.27.3; 51.22.3; App. *BCiv.* 2.102; A. Nock, *HSCP* 41 (1930) 1-60. Associating her: E.W. Gray points this out, comparing Caesar's statue in the Temple of Quirinus.

232 J. Svoronos No. 1874; *BMC Ptolemies* 122 with Plate XXX.6; Kahrstedt in *Klio* 10 (1910) 261 ff.; Heinen 91 note 2 and 145 note 1.

233 A. Boëthius and J.B. Ward-Perkins, *Etruscan and Roman Architecture* (Mid-

dlesex 1970) 459-460; they take the building as 'erected by Caesar in 48-47 B.C.' See also Hercher, ed., Pseudo-Philo, *De Septem Mundi Miraculis* (1858). A detailed account: P.M. Fraser, *Ptolemaic Alexandria* 24 and II, 67-71, notes 154-162. See further Strabo 17.1.9.795; H. Heinen, 'Zur Begründung der römischen Kaiserkultes ... I, Der Kult des C. Julius Caesar': *Klio* 11 (1911) 129-137; cf. 138-177. See also Cic. *Att.* 12.45; A.D. Nock, *HSCP* 41 (1930) 1-62, esp. 1-3.

234 Cic. *Att.* 15.15: *Superbiam autem ipsius reginae, cum esset trans Tiberim in hortis, commemorare sine magno dolore non possum.*

235 Dio 43.27.3.

236 Cic. *Att.* 15.15: *Reginam odi.* Ptolemy's presence with her is noted by the sources, e.g., Dio 43.27.3. Recognized: Dio, *ibid.* Possible trip to Egypt: Suet. *Iul.* 52.1. Cic. *Att.* 15.15 shows her gone home for good by June 44.

237 Suet. *Iul.* 52: *uti uxores liberorum quaerendorum causa quas et quot vellet ducere liceret.* Cf. Dio 44.7.3.

238 Bibliography in *RE* 21 (1921) 755. Caesar as 'king': Cic. *Att.* 14.9 and 14.11; Suet. *Iul.* 79-80. See also Nic. Damasc., *FGrH* ii A, 324 and C, 229 = his *Vit. Aug.*, 28. Move to Alexandria: Suet. *Iul.* 79.3.

239 Suet. *Iul.* 79.3: ... *ut, quoniam fatalibus libris contineretur, Parthos nisi a rege non posse vinci, Caesar rex appellaretur.* See also Cic. *De div.* 2.54.110.

240 Suet. *Iul.* 80.1.

241 Virg. *Eclog.* 5.29; Grant 88 with notes 18-20; Volkmann 86-89. See also F.E. Adcock in *CAH* IX (1932) 718-735; A. Wallace-Hadrill, '*Civilis Princeps*: Between Citizen and King': *JRS* 72 (1982) 32-48. See too below, note 285.

242 *Reginae fuga*: Cic. *Att.* 14.8. Cf. the cryptic 14.20, and 15.15. *P. Oxy.* XIV 1629, from 27 Epeiph year 8 (26 July 44), still dates by her name with that of Ptolemy.

243 Porphyry, *FGrH* 260 F 2 (17): 'in seinem 4. jahre und im 8. der Kleopatra.' See too Pestman, *Chronologie* 83; Skeat, *Reigns* 42; Samuel 159.

244 Porphyry, *ibid.*; Jos. *Ap.* 2.58; *AJ* 15.89, adding that she used poison.

245 An apparent attestation for 'year 10' in *OGIS* 194 (see next note) is achieved by emendation. So is one that would mention both Cleopatra and Caesarion on '10 Hathyr, year 8' (5 November 45), while Cleopatra still abode in Rome and Ptolemy XIV yet lived. If this restoration is correct, the document should also have named Ptolemy, since he survived until July 44 or just before. The alternative is to assume that the compositor of *P. Oxy.* XIV 1629 (26 July 44) did not know of Ptolemy's death nine or more months before. A third possibility, that all three of the monarchs are in some sort of association now, but with Ptolemy not named, appears improbable, though the situation did present anomalies, with all three in Rome. See also Pestman, *Chronologie* 82-83 and 129-130, notes 55-57; *P. dem. Loeb.* 63.

246 *OGIS* 194 = Strack, *Die Dynastie der Ptolemaeer* 272, no. 157 = *Stele Turin* 1764; Pestman, *Chronologie* 130, note 56. This reads 'year 10 = 2' as restored, which Samuel terms 'restored, surely incorrectly.' The 'year 10' itself need not, however, be incorrect. At any rate, documents for both begin to appear certainly from the next year: *PSI* 549 (Oxyrhynchos); *SB* 7337 (Heracleopolis; 13 April 41); *P. Ryl.* 582. They are followed by *P. Cairo* 31.232 (see Pestman 83 and 130 note 57), from 'year 12,' and *O. Cairo* 30.643.3 (= Spiegelberg, *P. Cairo* I, 88), 'year 13, with a restoration affording a plural reference to 'the Pharaohs.' See also G. Lefebvre on *SB* 7337: *Mélanges Holleaux* (Paris 1913) 103-113; H. Volkmann, *Cleopatra* (London 1958) Appendix, pp. 223-224; A.E. Samuel, 'The Joint Regency of Cleopatra and Caesarion': *Études de Papyrologie* 9 (1964) 73-79.

247 App. *BCiv.* 5.9; Jos. *AJ* 15.89 f.; Dio 48.24.2.

248 This version turns up in unexpected places: W. Brashear, *Ptolemäische Urkunden aus Mumienkartonage* (Berlin 1980) nos. 2376-2377; E. Bernand (above, note 8) 45-46 no. 14.

249 Schürer (Vermes and Millar) 249-250; Dio 47.30-31. App. *BCiv.* 4.59-61 shows how considerable the land forces were: four legions. Stele: *OGIS* 194. See note 246.

250 App. *BCiv.* 4.58-63. Famine and pestilence: Sen. *QNat.* 4.2; Plin. *NH* 5.58; *OGIS* 194; Schürer (Vermes and Millar) 249-250.

251 App. *ibid.*, 63.

252 App. *BCiv.* 5.8.

253 App. *BCiv.* 4.61. Suppliants flee to them: *ibid.*, 5.9.

254 Sherk, *Greek East* no. 85, may refer to this journey in 41 BC. For Creticus, whose repute had to survive a defeat on Crete, see Magie 292-293 and Sherk, *ibid.*, no. 74. Antony's uncle helped in the case of Termessus (*ibid.*, 72). His grandfather fought the pirates in Cilicia (*ibid.*, 54-55). See Ch. 2, § 3, note 38; Ch. 6, § 18, note 142. See too App. *BCiv.* 5.14; 5.4; Jos. *AJ* 14.302-323; Dio 48.2.2; 48.30.2. See also Dio 48.24.; Plut. *Ant.* 24.4-6; H. Buchheim, *Die Orientpolitik des Triumvirn M. Antonius* (Heidelberg 1960; Heidelb. Akad. Wissenschaft., Philos.-Hist. Kl., Abhandlung) 11-15.

255 *Summachoi*: App. *BCiv.* 5.4 ff.; Jos. *AJ* 14.312, 317, 321.

256 App. *BCiv.* 5.6; Jos. *AJ* 14.324; Dio 48.2.2.

257 Plut. *Ant.* 24 and 54. See P. Fraser, *Ptolemaic Alexandria* I, pp. 205, 244-245, 298, 300 with associated notes. See too Socrates of Rhodes, *FGrH* 192, F 2; *IG*² ii 1043; *JRS* 47 (1957) 73 ff. Cleopatra as 'new Isis': Fraser II, 397, note 441. See too below, notes 325 and 328.

258 Plut. *Ant.* 25 ff. An enthusiastic portrait of this, with appropriate quotation of Plutarch and Shakespeare: M. Grant, *Cleopatra* 112-117. See also F. Le Corsu, 'Cléopâtre-Isis': *Bull. soc. franç. d'Égyptol.* 82 (1978) 22-33.

259 Plut. *Ant.* 26.3.

260 Plut. *Ant.* 28 ff. Revels: Livy, *Per.* 130: *M. Antonius dum cum Cleopatra luxuriatur* (36 BC).

261 Jos. *AJ* 15.89 ff. and *Ap.* 2.56-58; App. *BCiv.* 5.9; Dio 48.24.2. See also R. Rossi, *Marco Antonio nella lotta politica della tarda repubblica Romana* (Trieste 1959) Ch. IV; A. Zwaenepoel, *Ét. cl.* 18 (1950) 1-15; Buccheim 49 ff. See above, note 207.

262 Their birth: *PIR*² A 495 and C 1148. See also *PP* 14482 and 14526. The notice in Livy *Per.* 132 substitutes for Selene a second son, Philadelphos (*PP* 14563), the Ptolemy Philadelphos of Dio 49.32.4-5. See too Plut. *Ant.* 36.3; Dio 51.21.8. Regarding the children as later used in Antony's policy, see Dio 49.39-41. See further Plut. *Ant.* 53-54; Vell. Pat. 2.82.3-4. See also Dio 49.32 and Plut. *Ant.* 36.3: he acknowledged their children. Cf. W.W. Tarn in *JRS* 22 (1932) 145. The tiara of Artavasdes, prospective father-in-law of Helios, featured the sun's disc. On it, see R. Sullivan in *NC* (ser. 7) 13 (1973) 20, with note 7. Antony later employed Sol on his coins: M. Crawford, *Roman Republican Coinage*, I (Cambridge, Eng. 1974) no. 533.2. Juba: *PIR*² J 65.

263 Full citation: B. Porter, R. Moss, *Topographical Bibliography of Ancient Egyptian Hieroglyphic Texts, Reliefs, and Paintings*, V (1937) 31; 128; 133; 151; VI (1939) 79.

264 Discussion and bibliography: K. Scott in *CP* 24 (1929) 133-141; J. Tondriau, *CE* 21 (1946) 149-171, esp. 160-169; *CE* 25 (1950) 283-316, esp. 309-312. See also H. Jeanmaire, 'La politique religieuse d'Antoine et de Cléopatre': *RA* (sér. 5) 19 (1924) 241-261; Jeanmaire, *Dionysos* (Paris 1951) 464-468. See further Fraser, *Ptol. Alex.* I, 205; II, 348-349, notes 121-125; cf. 342-343, note 96; Crawford, *Roman Republican Coinage* II, 743 n. 4.

265 Vergil, *Ecl.* IV. H.B. Mattingly, *CR* 48 (1934) 161-165: written in 40, recast later. Reflected in the triumviral coinage: Crawford, *Roman Republican Coinage* II, 743 and I, 531-533, nos. 527-529. See too E. Sydenham, *The Coinage of the Roman Republic* (London 1952) 1192-1196; 1327-1328; H. Grueber, *Coins of the Roman Republic in the British Museum*, Vol. II (London 1910) 495, nos. 114-115, but with his note 1.

266 W. Tarn in *JRS* 22 (1932) 136-160.

267 Jos. *AJ* 14.330 ff.; *BJ* 1.248.

268 Jos. *BJ* 1.279; *AJ* 14.375-376.

269 Jos. *BJ* 1.359-360; *BJ* 15.93.

270 Jos. *AJ* 14.378 and 381-382; *BJ* 1.280-285 stresses his qualities, not his financial prospects. App. *BCiv.* 5.75 leaves no doubt of the required 'tribute' (*phoros*).

271 For Herod as King of the Jews: Jos. *AJ* 14.381 and 385; *BJ* 1.284-285. See also

App. *BCiv.* 5.75: 'in Idumaea and Samaria'; Strabo 16.2.46.765. Tac. *Hist.* 5.9, *Regnum ab Antonio Herodi datum victor Augustus auxit,* neatly summarizes the happy relations of Herod with these two despite their own later strife. 'King of the Jews': Jos. *BJ* 1.282. See also Jos. *BJ* 1.242; *AJ* 14.303 and 326.

272 App. *BCiv.* 5.71-76.

273 App. *BCiv.* 5.75.

274 Plut. *Ant.* 38.2; Dio 49.25.1.

275 App. *BCiv.* 5.75.

276 Plut. *Ant.* 24; Sullivan, 'Commagene' 768-769; Dio 49.20.3; Florus 4.10.28.

277 Sullivan, 'Cappadocia' 1149 ff.

278 Dio 49.32.3.

279 Hoben 195-211.

280 Zonar. 10.29; Dio 50.13.15; *PIR* P 257.

281 For detail on them: R. Sullivan in *ANRW* II 7.1, 7.2, and 8 (Berlin, 1977-1980).

282 The meeting in Syria: Dio 48.54.5, where Antony suddenly realizes, at Corcyra, that Octavia would be at risk in the Parthian War. See also Plut. *Ant.* 36; Jos. *BJ* 1.359-360; *AJ* 15.88 and 92-103; Dio 49.24; Eutrop. *Brev.* 7.6; Magie 436-437 and 1287-1288 notes 29-30. Mobilization for the campaign: H. Bengtson, *Zum Partherfeldzug des Antonius* (Munich 1974) 18-22. Discussion: Buchheim 49-83. On his legions between Philippi and Actium: W. Tarn in *CQ* 26 (1932) 75-81.

283 Dates: Buchheim 68 ff. See too Livy *Per.* 130, 131, 132; Plut. *Ant.* 36.3; *PP* 14563.

284 Plut. *Demetr. Ant. Compar.* 4.1. Livy *Per.* 131: Cleopatra, *quam uxoris loco iam pridem captus amore eius habere coeperat.* See also Plut. *Ant.* 36.3-4 and 87. Eutropius (below) does postulate divorce, *repudiata sorore Caesaris Augusti*; but this came in 32. Cf. Zonar. 10.28: 'he renounced his union with Octavia.' Volkmann, *Cleopatra* 121-122 and 235, puts the 'marriage' in 37, others in the spring of 36. Plut. *Mor.* 61 B, *Quom. Adulator* 19, has her following him about as a concubine. Many in antiquity thought that they did marry. See Sen. *Suas.* 1.6: *cum eodem tempore et Octaviam uxorem haberet et Cleopatram* (reporting a popular conviction). Eutrop. *Brev.* 7.6.2: *Antonius ... Cleopatram, reginam Aegypti duxit uxorem*; Oros. 6.19.4. See also Euseb. *Chron.* 2.14-15 Schoene; Zonar. 10.28; Syncell. 1.588.9-10; Dio 50.3.2; 50.26.2. The letter to Octavian in Suet. *Aug.* 69.2 (*uxor mea est*) used *uxor* in its usual sense if written after his divorce from Octavia in May/June 32. See K. Kraft, *Hermes* 95 (1967) 496-499 on Suet. *Aug.* 69.2. See also T. Rice Holmes, *The Architect of the Roman Empire* (Oxford 1928) 227-231 ('When did Antony marry Cleopatra?').

285 Florus, *Epit.* 2.21.3 (4.11): *diadema deerat, ut regina rex et ipse frueretur.* Cf. 2.14.4 (4.3.4) in Rossbach's Teubner ed. of 1896: *amore Cleopatrae desciscet in regem.* Bibliography in *RE* 11 (1921) 759-760. King and Emperor: A. Wallace-Hadrill, '*Civilis Princeps*: Between Citizen and King': *JRS* 72 (1982) 32-48, on convergence and distinction of the two institutions. See also above, note 241.

286 Sullivan, 'Cappadocia' 1149 ff.; 'Pontus' 915 ff.; Plut. *Ant.* 36.2; Strabo 14.5.3.669: cedar to furnish her ships. See also Strabo 14.5.6.671. Chronology and summary of the distributions: J. Dobiáš in *Mél. Bidez* (Brussels 1934) 287-314. See too Schürer (Vermes and Millar) 288-289 note 5; Buchheim 68-74; A. Schalit, *Koenig Herodes* (1969) 772 ff. and Anhang XII.

287 R. Sullivan, *NC* (ser. 7) 19 (1979) 6-20.

288 PTOLEMAIS: H. Seyrig in *RN* 4 (1962) 34 (see note 292 below). LYSANIAS: Euseb., I, 170 Schoene. H. Seyrig in *Syria* 27 (1950) 43-49 (cf. 39, note 2) shows the coinage of Chalcis resumed after Actium by Zenodorus. See also Jos. *BJ* 1.359-369; *AJ* 14.330 ff.; 15.79; 15.88-120; 132; Dio 49.32.5.; Porph. *FGrH* 260 F 2 (17).

289 Plut. *Ant.* 37.4; Livy *Per.* 130: *M. Antonius ... tarde Mediam ingressus bellum ... Parthis intulit.* For the Armenian problem resulting, see below, with Sullivan, *ANRW* II 8, 770 ff. and Magie 437. The campaign of 36: Bengtson (1974) 18-41; Buchheim 74-79; J. Kromayer, 'Der Partherzug des Antonius': *Hermes* 31 (1896) 70-104; W.W. Tarn, *CQ* 26 (1932) 75-81. Cf. Ch. 9, § 25, note 63 and Ch. 9, § 26, note 123. See also T. Rice Holmes, *The Architect of the Roman Empire* (Oxford 1928) 225-226.

290 Plut. *Ant.* 51. Dio 49.31.4 has the funds sent to Armenia.

291 Crawford, (above, note 262) no. 539 with pp. 743 and 747 note 5.

292 H. Seyrig, 'Le monnayage de Ptolémaïs de Phénicie': *RN* (sér. 6) 4 (1962) 25-50, esp. 34: 35/34, her new 'year 3' (see above, note 288, for an earlier version of this coin). See also P. Lederer, *NC* (ser. 5) 18 (1938) 65 ff.; A. Brett, *AJA* 41 (1937) 452-463, and Pl. 9; H. Seyrig, *Syria* 27 (1950) 40 ff.; Seyrig, *NNM* 19 (1950) 32 ff. See further Plut. *Ant.* 36; Jos. *AJ* 15.91-96; Svoronos I, 469 ff. (= Germ. ed. IV, 377-378).

293 Magie 439 and 1288 note 33; cf. 436-437 with 1287 note 29. The new era: Pestman, *Chronologie* 82-85. Porphyry knew of it: *FGrH* 260 F 2 (17): 'year 16 = 1, after the death of Lysimachus [Lysanias].' Thus until '22 = 7,' her final year. See too Skeat, *Reigns* 42. Samuel, *Ptol. Chron.* 159 and in 'The Joint Regency of Cleopatra and Caesarion,' *EPap* 9 (1964) 73 ff., seeks unconvincingly to demonstrate an era based on joint rule. See further H. Seyrig, 'Antiquités syriennes, 42. Sur les ères de quelques villes de Syrie; L'ère de Cléopatre': *Syria* 27 (1950) 42 ff.; 110 ff.; H. Heinen, *Historia* 18 (1969) 188-190; H. Volkmann's review in *Gnomon* 31 (1959) 178-179. THE

DOCUMENTS: *OGIS* 195: '19 = 4'; 196. See also G. Möller, *Demotische Texte aus den Königlichen Museen zu Berlin, I, Mumienschilder* (Leipzig 1913) no. 171 (= *EM. Berl.* 17.327): '20 = 5.' Cf. *P. Oxy.* 1453: '22 = 7'; H. Brugsh, *Thesaurus Inscriptionum Aegyptiacarum*, V (1891), *Historisch-biographische Inschriften altaegyptischer Denkmäler*, 931: '22 = 7' (31/30 BC). See also *P. Ryl.* II, 69.6; *P. Würzb.* 5; Tait, *Bodleian Ostr.* no. 222; *PSI* 549; *SB* 6119 and 6234. Bibliography: *RE* 11 (1921) 761; Strack 211 ff.; Svoronos (above, note 292). The discussion by Tarn, in *CAH* X 81, assumes that Cleopatra's original era began in 51/50 rather than, as it did, in 52/51. This renders impossible his suggestion that 'Antony's regnal era' furnished this date in 34.

294 Plut. *Ant.* 36.2. Dio 49.32.4 ascribes this more to the scandal over his children by Cleopatra.

295 Losses: Plut. *Ant.* 50.1. Allies: Dio 49.32-33.

296 Dio 49.31.3-4 shows the reasons he should have wintered in Armenia, as he professed himself ready to. Cf. Plut. *Ant.* 38.1; cf. 50. No one doubted that this was a defeat: e.g., App. *BCiv.* 5.134. See too Dio 50.27.5; Vell. Pat. 2.82.1.

297 Plut. *Ant.* 37.3; 39.1; 50.2; Dio 49.33.1-4.

298 Plut. *Ant.* 52-53.

299 Dio 49.33.4; Plut. *Ant.* 53.

300 Plut. *Ant.* 50 and 53; Dio 49.33.4. Octavian had withheld troops previously promised, and the effects may have been felt in 36: App. *BCiv.* 5.134.

301 App. *BCiv.* 5.133-144.

302 Jos. *AJ* 15.50-56; *BJ* 1.437; Schürer (Vermes and Millar) 287-297.

303 B. Kanael, 'The Coins of King Herod of the Third Year': *JQR* 42 (1951/1952) 261-264.

304 Jos. *AJ* 15.62-79. See also Schürer (Vermes and Millar) 287-288 with notes 3-4. The coin: *BMC Galatia* 158 no. 53; Sherk, *Greek East* no. 89.

305 Dio 49.39.2.

306 Dio 49.39; Jos. *AJ* 15.80: 'against the Parthians'; *BJ* 1.363: 'out of Parthia' – in a context confusing an Armenian captive king with a Parthian one. See too Flor. 2.21 (4.11).

307 Dio 49.40.2; Plut. *Ant.* 53.6. For some of the later dynastic uses of this princess, see Sullivan, *ANRW* II 8, 774 and 780 ff.

308 Jos. *BJ* 1.362; *AJ* 15.96-103; Plut. *Ant.* 37. On the date: Schürer (Vermes and Millar) 289 ff.

309 Jos. *AJ* 15.21-49.

310 Jos. *BJ* 1.359-362; *AJ* 15.92-103.

311 Jos. *AJ* 15.131-133; 106-107 and 92; *BJ* 1.360. Bibliography: *RE* 11 (1921) 760-761. See too Grant, *Cleopatra* 135-141 with notes; Plut. *Ant.* 36.2.

312 Crawford, *Roman Republican Coinage* I, 537 no. 539; 539 no. 543; II, 743 and 747. Campaign: Bengtson (1974) 41-46; Buchheim 90 ff.; J. Kromayer, *Hermes* 31 (1896) 70-104. See also Plut. *Ant.* 50; Dio 49.39.1-40.4. Jos. *BJ* 1.363; *AJ* 15.104-105; Tac. *Ann.* 2.3.2. (See also below, note 357.) In 34 and 33, some of the Eastern joint coinage with Cleopatra is still careful to identify Antony as Roman, with legend '*imperator* for the third time and member of the triumvirate.' Crawford (no. 543) shows this lapsing by 32; cf. II, 743. See too *RE* 11 (1921) 760; Svoronos IV 390. Octavian had been courting King Artavasdes: Dio 49.41.5; Ch. 9, § 26, note 129.

313 Dio 49.39.1-41.6; Plut. *Ant.* 54; cf. 50. See too Zonar. 10.27; Dio 49.40.

314 Dio 37.6.2; K. Meiklejohn, 'Alexander Helios and Caesarion': *JRS* 24 (1934) 191-195. W. Huss, 'Der "König der Könige" und der "Herr der Könige"': *ZPalV* 93 (1977) 131-140, shows earlier Ptolemaic restraint (Ptolemy IV). See also E.R. Bevan, *JHS* 22 (1902) 241-244. These titles in the Seleucid, Ptolemaic, and other royal houses farther east (see §§ 24-26) often reflected aspiration as much as attainment, but constituted an adjunct of policy.

315 Cf. one by no means certain restored reading: *CIL* (Suppl.) III, 7232 = Th. Homolle in *BCH* 3 (1879) 149 no. 2 = Strack, no. 158 A: *rege[M REGV]m*. Homolle's reading differs: RECV.

316 Plut. *Ant.* 54; Dio 49.41.1-3.

317 But Plut. *Ant.* 54.4 gives her Coele-Syria.

318 Crawford, *Roman Republican Coinage* I, 539 no. 543; U. Kahrsted, 'Frauen auf antiken Münzen': *Klio* 10 (1910) 276-278; Svoronos, nos. 1906 and 1897 ff.

319 Dio 49.41.3. This is given to Cleopatra in Plut. *Ant.* 54.4.

320 Plut. *Ant.* 54.6. See E. Revillout, *Précis du droit égyptien,* II (Paris 1903) 1065: 'l'an 20 de Cléopâtre unie à Amon' (33/32 BC), epitaph of Nofrého, wife of Pséamen.

321 Vell. Pat. 2.82.4: *novum ... Liberum Patrem*. Sen. *Suas.* 1.6: *cum Antonius vellet se Liberum Patrem dici. OGIS* 195 (28 Dec. 34): 'Antonius ... the God ... and Benefactor.' The reading is P.M. Fraser's, *JRS* 47 (1957) 71-73, with Plut. *Ant.* 28.2 and 71.3. Published by E. Breccia, *Cat. gen. des antiq. ég. du mus. d'Alex.* (Cairo 1911) no. 42 (10). See above, note 257.

322 Bibl.: *RE* 11 (1921) 764. On her coin portraits, see A. Mamroth in *Berl. Num. Zeitsch.* 6 (1951) 161-165 with Tafel VIII, 12-17. See also Kahrsted (above, note 318) 276 no. 3.

323 Dio 50.1.4-50.4.5; 49.41.4-5; Plut. *Ant.* 50.

324 Bibliography: *RE* 11 (1921) 765-766. See too M. Grant, *Cleopatra* 171-182; Hor. *Odes* 1.37.6-12; Flor. 2.21 (4.11); J. Dobiáš, 'La donation d'Antoine à Cléopâtre en l'an 34 av. J.-C.': *Mélanges Bidez*, II (Brussels 1934) 287-314. In *CAH* X 80, Tarn terms the donations 'a glorious house of cards.' See fur-

ther J. Geiger, 'An Overlooked Item of the War of Propaganda between Octavian and Antony': *Historia* 29 (1980) 112-114; M.P. Charlesworth, 'Some Fragments of the Propaganda of Mark Antony': *CQ* 27 (1933) 172-177, all remarks attributed to Antony; K. Scott, 'Octavian's Propaganda and Antony's *de sua ebrietate*': *CP* 24 (1929) 133-141. SPHERES OF AUTHORITY: See the examples from Aphrodisias edited by Joyce Reynolds, *Aphrodisias and Rome* (London 1982) esp. pp. 38-106, with her article in *JRS* 76 (1986) 126-127. See too Sherk, *Greek East* no. 87.

325 J. Tondriau in *CE* 41 (1946) 160-167; 45/46 (1948) 139 ff.; 50 (1950) 310 ff. See also Vell. Pat. 2.82.4; Athen. *Deipn.* 4.148 B-C; Dio 48.39.2 (39 BC); *OGIS* 195; Dio 51.15.5. See further H. Heinen in *Klio* 11 (1911) 138 and 142. 'Oriental' Portraits: K. Kraft in *Hermes* 95 (1967) 496-499; B. Holtzmann and F. Salviat, 'Les portraits sculptés de Marc-Antoine': *BCH* 105 (1981) 265-287; F. Johansen, 'Antike portraetter af Kleopatra VII og Marcus Antonius': *Meddel. Ny Carlsberg Glyptotek* 35 (1978) 55-81; H. Kyrieleis, *Bildnisse der Ptolemäer* (Berlin 1975) 70 ff.; K. Parlasca, 'Probleme der späten Ptolemäerbildnisse': Maehler and Strocka (above, note 7) 25-30, including Cleopatra's brothers and sons.

326 Dio 50.27.5; App. *Bell. Illyr.* 4.16.

327 Plut. *Ant.* 55 f.; Dio 49.44.1-4.

328 Dio 49.44.1-4; Plut. *Ant.* 56.1-5; Oros. 6.19.4. Divinities at Ephesus: G. Hölbl, *Zeugnisse Ägyptischer Religionsvorstellungen für Ephesus* (Leiden 1978; *EPRO* 73). See above, note 257.

329 *RE* 11 (1921) 766.

330 Suet. *Aug.* 69.2; Dio 50.1-4.

331 The union proved of high importance for the future of the Kingdom of Pontus. See Sullivan, *ANRW* II 8, 'Papyri' 920 note 48, and *ANRW* II 7.2, 'Pontus' 920 ff.

332 Dio 50.2.1-50.4.5; Plut. *Ant.* 60.

333 Dio *ibid.* and 50.6.1 and 26.3. See also M. Reinhold, 'The Declaration of War against Cleopatra': *CJ* 77 (1981/1982) 97-103; the charges included *maiestas* and contributions for war against Italy.

334 WAR FOR THE REPUBLIC: From the victory monument at Actium: Sherk, *Greek East* no. 92. CLEOPATRA: Eutrop. 7.7.1: *cupiditate muliebri optat etiam in urbe regnare*. Propert. 3.11.31-32: *Romana poposcit moenia*; cf. 3.11.45. Flor. 4.11.1-2: *Romanum imperium petit*. See also *Anth. Lat.* 1.462.3; Ovid *Met.* 15.826 ff.; *Eleg. in Maecen.* 1.53-54; Dio 50.5.4; 51.15.4: 'Queen of the Romans.' See too *RE* 11 (1921) 767-769. Corruptor of Antony: Dio 50.5; 50.24.1-27.1; Plut. *Ant.* 60.1-62.1. See also Zonar. 10.28-29; I. Becher, *Das Bild der Kleopatras in der griechischen und lateinischen Literatur* (Berlin 1966) 23-58, with review by B.F. McCarthy in *AJPh* 90 (1969) 252-254.

335 Dio 50.27.1; cf. 50.25.4.
336 Dio 50.5.3; B. Holtzmann and F. Salviat, *BCH* 105 (1981) 265-287.
337 Plut. *Ant.* 60.1; Horace, *Ep.* 9.13-14: *miles et spadonibus servire rugosis potest.*
338 J. Geffcken, *Oracula Sibyllina* (1902): *Sib. Or.* 3.350-380. See also W.W. Tarn in *JRS* 22 (1932) 135-160, dating the passage to 'about 33'; M.P. Charlesworth, *Cambr. Hist. Journ.* 2 (1926) 9-16.
339 *RE* 11 (1921) 766.
340 Plut. *Ant.* 59.3.
341 Jos. *BJ* 1.389.
342 *RE* 11 (1921) 767; Strabo 14.1.14.637; 13.1.30.595; *Res. Gest.* 24.
343 Dio 51.8.3.
344 Plut. *Ant.* 58.5; Zonar. 10.30; Strabo 14.1.41.648. The exactions from the cities were severe: Plut. *Ant.* 58.4-5. She had even stripped temples: Dio 51.17.6.
345 Plut. *Ant.* 61; Dio 50.6; 50.13.7-8; 50.14.1; Flor. 2.21 (4.11).
346 Jos. *AJ* 15.108-160; *BJ* 1.364-385.
347 *BMC Peloponn.* Pl. 5.9.
348 Plut. *Ant.* 61; Dio 50.6.4; 50.11.3. Others: Leucas, Patrae, Corinth: Dio 50.13.5.
349 Vell. Pat. 2.84; Plut. *Ant.* 63.2; Dio 50.13.6-8; Zonar. 10.28-29; Sen. *Suas.* 1.7: *ab Antonio transfugit ad Caesarem.* See also Plut. *Ant.* 59. But cf. 68, where some held out after Antony himself had fled.
350 Suet. *Nero* 3.2.
351 Plin. *NH* 21.9.12.
352 Hor. *Ep.* 9.17-18; Plut. *Ant.* 53.3.
353 Zonar. 10.29; Dio 50.13.5; *PIR* P 257.
354 Bibliography: *RE* 11 (1921) 771.
355 Plut. *Ant.* 67 and 69; Dio 51.5 and 17.
356 Plut. *Ant.* 69; Dio 51.6.3; Flor. 4.11.9.
357 Dio 51.5.5; Strabo 11.14.15.532; Zonar. 10.30; Tac. *Ann.* 2.3.2. See above, note 312; Ch. 9, § 24, notes 34 and 39. See too Debevoise 134.
358 Dio 51.6;. Flor. 2.21 (4.11); Oros. 6.19.3; Servius on *Aeneid* 8.713.
359 Dio 51.6.3; 51.8.5.
360 Dio 51.7.1; Plut. *Ant.* 71.1.
361 Dio 51.7.2-7 and 51.9.1.
362 Jos. *BJ* 1.392; *AJ* 15.195.
363 Jos. *AJ* 15.187-201; *BJ* 1.386-395; Plut. *Ant.* 71.1.
364 Dio 51.6.1-2; Plut. *Ant.* 71.2-3.
365 Dio 51.6.4-6; 51.8.1-7; Plut. *Ant.* 70-73; 78.2.
366 Plut. *Ant.* 74.2; Dio 51.8.5-7; 11.2.

367 *Ibid.*; Jos. *AJ* 15.196 and 199-200 (800 talents!); *BJ* 1.394-395.
368 Jos. *BJ* 1.397; *AJ* 15.217; Dio 51.9-10. Cf. Plut. *Ant.* 74.3; but see, e.g., 76.1. The 'fleet of Cleopatra' is mentioned in *POxy* 2820 = Sherk, *Greek East* no. 94.
369 Dio 51.9.5-51.10.4; Plut. *Ant.* 83.
370 Plut. *Ant.* 76-77; Dio 51.10-11.
371 Dio 51.11.1-15.4; Plut. *Ant.* 78-86; *RE* 11 (1921) 776-778. See also Hor. *Odes* 1.38.20-32; Flor. 2.21 (4.11); J. Griffiths, 'The Death of Cleopatra VII': *JEA* 47 (1961) 113-119; T.C. Skeat, 'The Last Days of Cleopatra: A Chronological Problem': *JRS* 43 (1953) 98-100.
372 Plut. *Demet. Ant. Comp.* 1.3. Early administration of Egypt: P. Brunt, *JRS* 65 (1975) 124-147; J.G. Milne, 'The Ruin of Egypt by Roman Mismanagement': *JRS* 17 (1927) 1-13.
373 Plut. *Ant.* 81-82; Dio 51.15.5. For Caesarion's claims 'as far as India' see note 316. See too K. Meiklejohn, 'Alexander Helios and Caesarion': *JRS* 24 (1934) 191-194.
374 Plut. *Ant.* 87.
375 Dio 51.15.6; Plut. *Ant.* 87; *PIR*² J 65; *RE* 11 (1921) 784-785. Coins: C. Falbe and J. Lindberg, *Numism. de l'ancienne Afrique* 3 (repr. Bologna 1964) 108-110, nos. 84-104. CLEOPATRA SELENE: *PIR*² C 1148, with Addenda to Vol. II, xxii. See also Macurdy, *Vassal Queens* 51; *Hellenistic Queens* 224-228; *Klio* 10 (1910) 301; B. Chanler, *Cleopatra's Daughter, Queen of Mauretania* (London 1936). The notion that she died 'at the lunar eclipse' of 5 BC is an obvious derivative of her epithet, Selene. Juba also married princesses from Cappadocia and Judaea.
376 *RE* 11 (1921) 780; *BGU* II 404 and 445; E. Breccia in *BSAA* n.s. 3, 1, no. 12 (1910) 87-88 (AD 4/5). As restored, this refers to a 'Great Kleopatreion' with a 'mass' of priests! Wilcken, *Chrest.* no. 115, 145-146, discusses a cult of Aphrodite and Cleopatra in the reign of Severus Alexander (222-235). See also J.H. Oliver, *GRBS* 6 (1965) 291-294.

Chapter 9

1 CLEOPATRA SELENE: Strabo 16.2.3.749; Jos. *AJ* 13.419-421 and *BJ* 1.116. See Ch. 4-5, §§ 10-11. CAMPAIGNS OF LUCULLUS: See especially the detailed study by K. Eckhardt, 'Die armenischen Feldzüge des Lukullus, I-III': *Klio* 9 (1909) 400-412 and 10 (1910) 72-115; 192-231, esp. Part II. Plut. *Luc.* 14.5 and 36.6 remind us how formidable Tigranes remained in 73-70 BC. Florus 1.40.28: Pompey *supplicem iussit regnare Tigranen*. See also H. Manandian, *Tigranes II et Rome*, trans. H. Thorossian (Lisbon 1963).
2 Plut. *Luc.* 24.1; 28.2; 29.2-6, 24.5.

3 Plut. *Luc.* 14.1. (Cf. App. *Mith.* 17.59 [88 BC] and *BCiv.* 5.17 [41 BC].) Dio 36.8.1 clearly shows the reciprocity. The area near Pontus was Armenia Minor: see 36.9.1. See too Plut. *Luc.* 25.5; 26.1-4; 21.5-7. Cf. App. *Mith.* 41.158 for similar contingents in 86 BC.

4 Dio 36.53.3-5; Strabo 11.14.6.529 and 11.14.10.530.

5 Dio 36.15.3 and 17.1; Debevoise 73-75. See also Dio 36.9.2-4; Dio 36.9.4; App. *Mith.* 109; Dio 36.2.5-3.1.

6 Magie 343-350; Dio 36.51.1-2; App. *Mith.* 97.446-101.462; 104.484-106.493. See also Plut. *Pomp.* 36.2; *Luc.* 27-29; Frontinus 2.5.33; Cic. *de Imp. Cn. Pomp. (Leg. Man.)* 52-53; Livy *Per.* 100; Vell. Pat. 2.37. See Ch. 11, § 15.

7 App. *Mith.* 87.392-393; Plut. *Luc.* 28.8 and 30.1. See also Eckhardt in *Klio* 10 (1910) 195; Debevoise 70-75; Dio 36.3.2-3; 36.1.1 and 36.1b; Vell. Pat. 2.37.2.

8 HIS KINGDOM AFTER 69: App. *Mith.* 104.484-105.496; 114.558-559. See also Strabo 16.2.10.753; Dio 36.2.5; 36.51-53; 37.7a; 37.20; 40.20-22 (53 BC: Abgar and Alchaudonius). See too Plut. *Pomp.* 67. GORDYENE AND SOPHENE: Plut. *Luc.* 19, 21, and 29; Dio 37.5.3; Strabo 11.14.15.532; App. *Mith.* 105.491. Zarbienus: See Ch. 5, § 12, note 21. See also F. Adcock in *JRS* 27 (1937) 12-17; U. Kahrstedt, *Artabanos III. und seine Erben* (Bern 1950) 58-70; Magie 343-350. On the campaigns of 69 and 68: K. Eckhardt, above, note 1; Luisa Pulci Doria Breglia, 'Tigrane il Grande di Armenia in Mosè di Corene': *DArch* 2 (1979) 95-108; B. Sabbaghian in *Haigazian Armen. Rev.* 4 (1973) 97-102.

9 DIADEM: Cic. *Sest.* 27.58. STRATEGIC POSITION: On Iberia, see the fundamental article by Cyril Toumanoff, 'Chronology of the Early Kings of Iberia': *Traditio* 25 (1969) 1-33. On Armenian geography, see R.H. Hewsen, 'Ptolemy's Chapter on Armenia: An Investigation of His Toponyms': *REArm* n.s. 16 (1982) 111-150. See too Hewsen, 'Introduction to Armenian Historical Geography': *REArm* n.s. 13 (1978-1979) 77-97, emphasizing the geopolitical complexity of the nation. PHILHELLENE: E.g., H. Seyrig, *RN* (sér. 5) 17 (1955) 85-128, esp. 87 and 121 (Nisibis). E.T. Newell, *NNM* 30 (1926) 13-14, sees in the title Parthian influence ('*more Parthico*'), but this assumption is unnecessary for the successors of Tigranes, though an interesting one for Tigranes himself.

10 CLEOPATRA: App. *Mith.* 15.54; Justin 38.3.2; Plut. *Luc.* 14; Memnon, *FGrH* no. 434, F l. 29.6 (43); Magie 1099 note 16. SONS: App. *Mith.* 104.484-105.492; Plut. *Pomp.* 33; Dio 36.50-54; 37.6.4. Head *HN*[2] 754 shows a Zariadres as ruler of Sophene about 134 BC. Artaxias, founder of the Armenian dynasty, also had a brother with this name, who ruled part of Armenia: Strabo 11.14.5.528. Strabo 11.14.15.532 records the descent of Tigranes from Artaxias.

11 Debevoise 47-48 note 70 discusses the literature and the dating – which would be 87 BC if the era used is Seleucid. For the view (as yet unproved) that the era here is the Parthian, see M. Rostovtzeff in *YCS* 2 (1936) 41 ff. and Welles, *Royal Correspondence* 302 note 8. See also *NC* (ser. 7) 5 (1965) 123 note 1, and 6 (1966) 18-20; R. Sullivan, 'Papyri Reflecting the Eastern Dynastic Network': *ANRW* II 8 (Berlin 1977) 911-916, esp. note 8. First publication was by E. Minns, 'Parchments of the Parthian Period from Avroman in Kurdistan': *JHS* 35 (1915) 22-65.

12 Dio 36.14.2. Cf. Plut. *Luc.* 35. See also *RE* 6 A (1936) 976. For more discussion on this Mithradates, see *RE* 6 A (1936) 971 and *NC* (ser. 7) 5 (1965) 123 note 1.

13 App. *Mith.* 106.497; 117.576. Relationship to Tigranes could be inferred from their common ties to the Arsacids: D.G. Sellwood in *NC* (ser. 7) 5 (1965) 113-135, esp. 128. See below, this chapter, § 25, with note 58.

14 See Sullivan, 'Thrace' and 'Pontus': *ANRW* II 7.1 and 7.2.

15 He was alive in 56: Cic. *Sest.* 27.58-59: *regnat hodie*. Dio 40.16.2 shows his son ruling in 54. Lucian, *Macrob.* 15, says that he lived till age eighty-five. The coins of Tigranes come down at least to 55/54 BC: H. Seyrig in *RN* (sér. 5) 17 (1955) 115 with 127-128 note 60; cf. 121. These dates depend, however, on regnal eras, with imprecise inception. MOSES: Luisa Breglia Pulci Doria, (above, note 8); P. Akinian in *RE Suppl.* 6 (1935) 534-541; *FGrH* 782.

16 Memnon, *FGrH* no. 434, F 1.38.5 (57); Plut. *Luc.* 28.5; App. *Mith.* 104.486-487.

17 App. *Mith.* 104.486-490; Plut. *Pomp.* 33; Dio 36.50-53; Vell. Pat. 2.37.

18 Strabo 11.14.15.532. On the relation of Sophene to Greater Armenia, see Cyril Toumanoff, *Studies in Christian Caucasian History* (Washington 1963) 285-305. See below, this chapter, § 25, note 41. YOUNGER TIGRANES: Plut. *Pomp.* 48.6; Asc. *Mil.* 47; Dio 36.53-54; 37.6.4; 38.30.1-2. App. *Mith.* 105.491-495 has him put to death after being led in Pompey's triumph (117.572), but he apparently survived at least until 58: Cic. *Att.* 3.8. A. Keaveney, *AJP* 103 (1982) 415, thinks his release now was 'part of a campaign to upset Pompey's Eastern settlement' by returning him 'to make trouble in Armenia.' See also *RE* 6A (1936) 978-979; Dobiáš 235.

19 App. *Mith.* 104.485-487; Dio 40.16.2; Cic. *Sest.* 27.58-59. The assumption that the reign of Artavasdes was now only beginning rests on identifying the 'son' mentioned in Dio 37.6.4 and Memnon, *FGrH* no. 434, F 1.38.5 (57), with Tigranes the Younger, as above, not with Artavasdes. The identification seems assured on the basis of Dio 36.51 and App. *Mith.* 104.486-487. On the numeration of Artavasdes as 'II' see Pani 17-18. Justin 42.2.6 attests the first Artaxiad of this name: *Artoadisti, Armeniorum regi.* See also Baumgartner in *RE* 2 (1896) 1308-1309.

20 Strabo 11.14.15.532. See below.

21 The passages from Memnon, *FGrH* no. 434, F 1.38.5 (57), and Plutarch, *Luc.* 28.5, if referring to Artavasdes, would show that he was associated in the rule with Tigranes as early as 69 BC. But it seems better to follow Geyer's attribution there of the passage, which gives no personal name of the son mentioned, to Tigranes the Younger: *RE* 6 A (1936) 978. A possible joint coinage of Tigranes and one of his sons was reported by Mionnet, *Supplément*, VII (Paris 1835) 725. For dates and bibliography, see Bickerman 165 and Magie 1252 note 60. GALATIA: Cic. *Att.* 5.21.2 (50 BC): *Deiotarus, cuius filio pacta est Artavasdis filia.* See the discussion by F. Stähelin, *Geschichte der kleinasiatischen Galater* (Leipzig 1907) 92, 97, 108 (stemma), and 114 (Prosopographical Appendix). For this numeration of Deiotari, Stähelin ignores the suggestion of A. Zwintscher, *De Galatarum Tetrarchis* (Leipzig 1892) 24-25, that Deiotarus I and II must have had in common a grandfather by the same name, who could have been the source of the Galatian claims upon Armenia Minor. Stähelin 97 cites Cic. *Att.* 5.17.3 in arguing that the Roman Senate had recognized his title before 51 BC. Cf. *BAlex.* 67: *rex Armeniae minoris ab Senatu appellatus.* See Ch. 6, § 16. See too *PIR*² D 36.

22 For discussion of and bibliography on the deeds of Pacorus I, see Debevoise 92-93, 97-98, 102-104, 111, and 118. See also Dio 49.20.3-4.

23 Jos. *AJ* 18.313-370; this Mithradates is *PIR* M 454, with an incorrect citation of Josephus. The account of Jewish-Parthian relations in Debevoise (93-94, 110-114, 122-123) is replaced by J. Neusner, *A History of the Jews in Babylonia*, I: *The Parthian Period* (Leiden 1965, revised 1968). See also Plut. *Crass.* 32.5 and 33; *FGrH* III C, No. 678 ('Artavasdes der Armenier'; c. 80-30 BC). Debevoise, 93, is sceptical about any conclusions from this to 'Hellenization' of Armenians. On Parthia: See below, this chapter, § 26. The Hellenization was apparent with Tigranes; Luisa Pulci Doria Breglia, 'Plutarco e Tigrane II *Philellen*': *AFLN* 16, n.s. 4 (1973-74) 37-67. Cf. note 9 above. ARCHELAUS I: *FGrH* II B, No.123.

24 CRASSUS: Discussion by A. Keaveney in *AJP* 103 (1982) 412 ff.

25 Strabo 11.14.15.532; Dio 40.16-27. On the campaign see Debevoise 78-95, with sources in note 36. See also Plut. *Crass.* 18-19, 21-22, 33; *Luc.* 36.6; *RE* 2 (1896) 1308-1309.

26 Plut. *Crass.* 33; Cic. *Fam.* 15.3.1; Strabo 16.1.23.747.

27 Cic. *Fam.* 15.2.2 and 15.3.1; Magie 1252-1253 notes 57-64.

28 Cic. *Fam.* 15.1-4, esp. 15.4.4. See above, Ch. 6, § 17.

29 TIGRANES AS *THEOS*: This can be inferred from Justin's epitome of Pompeius Trogus, Prologue to 41: *Tigranes cognomine Deus.* See J. Wolski, *Historia* 11 (1962) 144-145. The title occurs for a Tigranes on the Armenian royal coinage: H. Seyrig in *RN* (sér. 5) 17 (1955) 118; E. Babelon, *Rois de*

Syrie (Paris 1890) 216 no. 29 and Pl. 29.21. See also G. Le Rider, *RN* (sér. 6) 2 (1959/1960) 25-26 no. 32; cf. 3 (1961) 7-26. Later uses of *Theos* by successors of Tigranes: F. Taeger, *Charisma* (Stuttgart 1957) 335. See too R.N. Frye in *IA* 4 (1964) 45 ff. On the Tiara: R.D. Sullivan in *NC* (ser. 7) 13 (1973) 18-39 with Pl. 14. ARTAVASDES *THEIOS*: H. Seyrig, *RN* (sér. 6) 6 (1964) 139-140 with Fig. 1. KING OF KINGS: H. Seyrig, *RN* (sér. 5) 17 (1955) 119 (cf. 122) with Fig. 4: 'une pièce de bronze, unique, se rattache étroitement ... à l'atelier mésopotamien de Tigrane I [II].' See Babelon, *Rois de Syrie* 215 no. 25. See also T.E. Mionnet, *Description de medailles antiques, grecques et romaines*, I-VII and *Supplements* I-IX (Paris 1805-1837): IV, 456 and *Suppl.* VII, 726; Ch. Mušegjan in *Akad. Nauk Armjanskoj SSSR, Ist.-filol. zurnal* 2 (1964) 317-323; summary in *Bibl. Classica Orient.* 11 (1966) 208-209; P. Bedoukian in *ANSMusN* 14 (1968) 55.

30 PARTHIA: See below, this chapter, § 26. See also Debevoise 121-130; Dio 49.23; Plut. *Ant.* 37. On the postulate that the 'Antiochus' mentioned by Dio is the Commagenian King, see Ch. 7, § 19.

31 MURDER OF ORODES: Plut. *Ant.* 37.1 vs. Dio 49.23.3. ATROPATENE: Dio 49.25.1-2. STANDARDS OF CRASSUS: Dio 49.24.5; Plut. *Ant.* 37.

32 TROOPS OF ARTAVASDES: Strabo 11.13.4.524; 11.14.9.530; Jos. *AJ* 15.104-105; *BJ* 1.363. See also Plut. *Ant.* 37; 50.4; Tac. *Ann.* 2.3. THE CAMPAIGN: Magie 1288 note 30; J. Kromayer, 'Der Partherzug des Antonius': *Hermes* 31 (1896) 70-104; Debevoise 121-130; Buccheim 74-83, esp. 81-83. See also V. Minorsky, 'Roman and Byzantine Campaigns in Atropatene': *Bull. Sch. Orient. and Afr. Stud. (U. of London)* 11 (1943-1946) 243-265, esp. 258 ff., section 5; Sullivan, 'Commagene' 770-775; T. Rice Holmes, *The Architect of the Roman Empire* (Oxford 1928) 123-128 and 223-226. Cf. below, this chapter, § 26, notes 122-123. ARTAVASDES: Strabo 11.13.4.524; 11.14.9.530; 11.14.15.532: 'betraying Antony to the Parthians'; 16.1.28.748. See also Dio 49.25.5; 49.39.6; 51.16.2; Plut. *Ant.* 38. COINAGE: M. Crawford, *Roman Republican Coinage* I, (Cambridge, Eng. 1974) 537 no. 539, 36 BC; 539 no. 543, 32 BC; II, p. 743. See too E.S.G. Robinson, *NC* (ser. 5) 17 (1937) 250-254; E.A. Sydenham, *The Coinage of the Roman Republic* (London 1952) 194 no. 1210.

33 POLEMO: Plut. *Ant.* 38.3; Dio 49.25.4. ARTAVASDES: Dio 49.31; Livy *Per.* 130.

34 ANTONY: Strabo 11.13.4.524 and 11.14.9.530; Dio 49.25.1; 49.39-41. Cf. Magie 437 and bibliography on 1288 note 30; *RE* 18 (1949) 1996. SEIZURE: Also recorded in Jos. *AJ* 15.104, and Plut. *Ant.* 50.4. The 'Artabazes of Parthia' in Jos. *BJ* 1.363 is apparently this Artavasdes of Armenia. See also Livy *Per.* 131; *Res Gest.* 27. See Ch. 8, § 23, notes 312 and 357; below, note 39.

35 ARTAXIAS: Tac. *Ann.* 2.3.2; *PIR*² A 1167. FUSION: Debevoise Ch. 7; *RE* 18 (1979) 1997 ff. See this chapter, § 25. See also *PIR* V 671; *PIR*² A 1155.

36 ANTONY: Dio 49.32, 40, 41, 44, 49. Iotape is *PIR*² J 44. For the distributions in the decade after Actium see Dio 51.15.5-16.2; 54.9.1-4.

37 ARTAXIAS: Jos. *AJ* 15.104-105 implies that he had escaped capture entirely. See also *PIR*² A 1167; Dio 49.39-40; Magie 437, 443, 476, 1339.

38 ARTAVASDES: *PIR*² A 1162. He later furnished kings for Armenia: § 25. See also *ILS* 844; Dio 51.16.1-2.

39 DEATH OF ARTAVASDES: Dio 51.5.5; Strabo 11.14.15.532; Jos. *BJ* 1.363; *AJ* 15.104. See also Plut. *Ant.* 50; *Dem. et Ant.* 5; Tac. *Ann.* 2.3.2. The three sons are this Artaxias (*PIR*² A 1167), another Artavasdes (*PIR*² A 1163), and Tigranes III (*PIR* T 147), who was to succeed Artaxias about 20 BC. See Jos. *AJ* 15.105; Strabo 11.14.15.532; *PIR*² A 1168, son of Polemo of Pontus (*PIR*² J 472) and descendant of Antony. Perhaps he also tried to echo the founder of the Artaxiad dynasty.

40 DISCONTENTED FACTION: Dio 54.9.4. SUCCESSORS: Stemmata in R. Sullivan, *ANRW* II 8 (Berlin 1977), following 938. See also *PIR* T 147-150; *PIR*² A 1163 and 1167; E 85. Detailed study: R. Sullivan, *Some Dynastic Answers to the Armenian Question* (Diss. California 1970; publ. University Microfilms 1971). ZENO-ARTAXIAS: *PIR*² A 1168, with Sullivan, 'Pontus' 923-924; Sullivan with W. Heckel, *Ancient Coins* (Waterloo 1984) 146-147. ORONTIDS: C. Toumanoff, *Manuel de généalogie et de chronologie pour l'histoire de la Caucasie chrétienne (Arménie - Géorgie - Albanie)* (Rome 1976) 83 ff.; A. Donabedian, 'The Coins of the Last Rulers of the Artaxiad Dynasty in Armenia': *Haigazian Armen. Rev.* 1 (1970) 74-92. LATER RULERS: R.H. Hewsen, 'The Successors of Tiridates the Great: A Contribution to the History of Armenia in the Fourth Century': *REArm* n.s. 13 (1978-79) 99-126; *Cambridge Mediaeval History* IV, Part 1; C. Toumanoff, 'The Third-Century Armenian Arsacids: A Chronological and Genealogical Commentary': *REArm* n.s. 6 (1969) 233-281. PROVINCE: *Res Gestae* 27.2. ARSACIDS: The quotation is by E.W. Gray, *CR* n.s. 17 (1967) 351. PERSIA: R. Blockley discusses the fourth-century division in *Historia* 36 (1987) 222-234.

41 SOPHENE: See the remarks on this by C. Toumanoff, *Studies in Christian Caucasian History* (Washington 1963) 282-287, 294, and 300-301. Its presentation by Pompey to Tigranes the Younger merely allowed some check on Tigranes the Great; it did not follow a separate dynastic tradition. The form of its name in *-ene* shows that it had existed as a recognized region under the Seleucids, but its origins are far older, with a version of the name known from the eighth century before Christ: *RE* 3A (1929) 1015 ff. See too C. Burney and D.M. Lang, *The People of the Hills: Ancient Ararat and Caucasus* (London 1971) 192 ff.; map on 203; *RE* 3A (1929) 1015-1019 (Weissbach).

SMALLER STATES: An important monograph is that by U. Kahrstedt, *Artabanos III. und seine Erben* (Bern 1950).

42 ARMENIA A PROVINCE: *Res Gestae* 27. LOCATION: Maps in Kahrstedt following p. 89; Debevoise, endpaper.

43 SASPIRES: D. Milberg, *JNES* 28 (1969) 62 on Hdt. 1.104. KINGS OF IBERIA: C. Toumanoff, 'Chronology of the Early Kings of Iberia': *Traditio* 25 (1969) 1-33, esp. 5-7: the Georgian national era was an adaptation of the 'Era of the Romans' (elaborated in AD 363/364) and is attested from AD 897. See stemmata on p. 14 and 25. These are preferable to my version in *ANRW* II 8 (Berlin 1978) 939. See also H. Treidler in *RE Suppl.* 9 (1962) 1899-1911; J. Markwart, 'Iberer und Hyrkanier': *Caucasia* 8 (1931) 78-113.

44 Reconstruction by Toumanoff (above, note 43) 9, based on Strabo 11.14.9.529; Plin. *HN* 4.10.39. ESCAPED MACEDONIANS: Plut. *Pomp.* 34.5. TRADE AND MANNERS: Strabo 11.2.18.499-11.3.6.501; 11.14.4.528. LANCERS: Plut. *Luc.* 31.5; cf. App. *Mith.* 103.481: they are terrifying forest fighters. See also Memnon, *FGrH* 434, F 22.4 (30); Florus 1.40.21. LANGUAGE: App. *Mith.* 101.466; cf. R.N. Frye in *Archaeologica Orientalia in Memoriam E. Herzfeld* (New York 1952) 89-101. See too Strabo 11.2.19.499. COINS OF SINATRUCES: G.F. Dunda and G.A. Lordkipanidze, *NC* (ser. 7) 19 (1979) 3, with note 7.

45 TIGRANOCERTA: Plut. *Luc.* 26.4; E. Eckhardt in *Klio* 10 (1910) 103. EUPATOR: vs. IBERIANS: App. *Mith.* 101.465. POMPEY: App. *Mith.* 103.480-483; 114.556; 117.573. See also Dio 37.1-2; 37.2.7; Plut. *Pomp.* 34; cf. 36.2; Florus 1.40.28.

46 Toumanoff (above, note 43) 11. See his *Studies* 76 note 85, 81 note 103, and 111 on the Artaxiads and the later use of the name *Arsaces*. See also Dio 49.24.1; Plut. *Ant.* 34.6.

47 On these later rulers of Armenia, see C. Toumanoff (above, note 43) 11 ff.; Sullivan, *Armenian Question* sections 13-17; on Iberia, see esp. 135-144. Sullivan, stemmata following p. 938 of *ANRW* II 8, which show or list all rulers of Armenia until Sassanian times. See also M.-L. Chaumont, 'L'Arménie entre Rome et l'Iran': *ANRW* II 9.1 (Berlin 1976) §§ II-III, 91-100. Inscriptions on Iberia: M. Tod in *JRS* 33 (1943) 82-86; *SEG* 16 (1959) 781 ff.; 20 (1964) 113; *REG* 57 (1944) 237 no. 192; 61 (1948) 207 no. 251a. See too B.M. Metzger in *JNES* 15 (1956) 18-26; *IGRR* I 192; III 133 = *OGIS* 379 = *SEG* 20 (1964) 112 = G.V. Tsereseli, *VDI* 1960 (2), 123-33 = *ILS* 8795 = McCrum and Woodhead 237. See further H. Nesselhauf, *Athenaeum* n.s. 36 (1958) 219-28; J. Gagé in *RH* 221 (1959) 260; *Prosop. Late R.E.* I, 117 and 144. Further: Sullivan, *Armenian Question* 144.

48 Strabo 6.4.2.288; Tac. *Ann.* 6.34.3: *Parthus ... contra ... ignobilem Hiberum mercennario milite disserebat*. See also *Ann.* 6.36.1.

49 Toumanoff, *Traditio* 25 (1969) 12; Sullivan, *Armenian Question* 135-139; *PIR* M 457 and R 6.

50 Toumanoff, *ibid.*, 31, places the abolition of the Iberian monarchy in 580.

51 Justin 23.4.13; Plin. *HN* 6.42 f.: ... *Medorum, quorum pars sunt Atropateni.* See also Strabo 11.13.1.523; 11.13.6.524; 11.14.1-3.527; 11.14.6.529. Maps: Kahrstedt, following p. 89; *CAH* IX 612; Debevoise, endpaper. See too G. Rawlinson, *The Sixth Great Oriental Monarchy, or the Geography, History, and Antiquities of Parthia* (London 1873) map facing p. 78. See bibliography on Ptolemy's *Geography* by R.H. Hewsen, *REArm* n.s. 16 (1982) 111 f. note 2. See further Kiessling, *RE* 9.1 (1914) 454-526, 'Hyrkania'; H.C. Rawlinson, 'Memoir on the Site of the Atropatenian Ecbatana': *Journ. Royal Geographic Soc.* 10 (1941) 113 ff.

52 Persepolis reliefs: G. Walser, *Die Völkerschaften auf den Reliefs von Persepolis* (Berlin 1966) Ch. IV, Delegation I, with review by O. Muscarella in *JNES* 28 (1969) 280-285. See also Arrian, *Anabasis* 3.8.4; 3.21; 4.18.3; 6.29.3; 7.4-5; 7.13.2-6. See too Diod. 18.3.3; Justin 23.4.13; *RE* 2 (1896) 2150, 'Atropates' (Kaerst); cf. *ibid.*, 2149-2150, 'Atropatene' (Weissbach) and *Suppl.* 1 (1903), 'Atropatene' (Streck). NESAEA: Herodotus 3.106 and 7.40; Strabo 11.13.7.525; Sullivan, *Armenian Question* 29-31; 110-117.

53 Strabo 11.13.1.523; Polybius 5.54.13-5.56.1; 5.57.3. TERRITORY: This can only be Atropatene, from the geographical limits described in 5.55.2-10; cf. 5.44.3-11. The term used here, 'the people of the Satrap,' designates Media Atropatene: F.W. Walbank, *A Historical Commentary on Polybius*, 1 (Oxford 1957) 574-575 and 583, citing J. Marquart in *Gött. Abh.* 3 (1901) 3.112. DATE POLYBIUS COMPOSED: Walbank, *ibid.*, 292-297. STRABO'S TRADITION: 11.13.1.523, which claims unbroken succession, is discussed by M. Pani, *Roma e i re d'oriente da Augusto a Tiberio (Cappadocia, Armenia, Media Atropatene)* (Bari 1972) 67-89.

54 FROM THE MEDES: Strabo 11.14.5.528; cf. 11.14.15.531 f. Whether 'Artaxias took Media Atropatene' or not requires more evidence; C. Burney and D.M. Lang, *The People of the Hills: Ancient Ararat and Caucasus* (London 1971) 192. Map: E. Olshausen and J. Wagner, *TAVO* B V 6, in southern Armenia. See also Diod. 31.27a; App. *Syr.* 45.235 and 47.242. On the general situation, see Sullivan, 'Commagene' 737-742; J. Briscoe, 'Eastern Policy and Senatorial Politics, 168-146 B.C.': *Historia* 19 (1969) 49-70; Liebmann-Frankfort 99 ff. TIMARCHUS: He is usually taken as from Media Maior, e.g. Debevoise 21.

55 Strabo 11.13.1.523.

56 HYDARNES III: C. Toumanoff, *Manuel* 403-410. Cf. Terituchmes I and Artasuras, his sons, and Orontes I, son of the latter. Connections with Armenians: Strabo 11.13.3.523-524.

57 ORONTID CONNECTIONS: C. Toumanoff, *Studies* 277-305; Sullivan, 'Commagene' sections 1-2. Strabo 11.13.5.524 has Armenia Maior achieve hegemony 'of all Asia' after dismembering the Assyrian ('Syrian') Empire locally in the seventh and sixth centuries, followed by the Persian conquest. This hegemony presumably included neighbouring Atropatene. THE OTHER MITHRIDATES: Dio 36.14.2, using the Greek spelling of the name. Cf. Plut. *Luc.* 26.4. See above, note 12. OTHER NATIONS: Plut. *Luc.* 36.6, stressing Parthian inability to resist the approach of Tigranes, but not permitting precise deductions as to how far along 'the Hyrcanian sea' (the Caspian) he had conquered. See too Strabo 11.14.15.532.

58 DARIUS VS. POMPEY: App. *Mith.* 106.497; 117.576; Diod. 40.4 (Didot). See above, this chapter, § 24, with note 13. TIGRIS AND GORDYENE: Dio 37.5; Plut. *Pomp.* 36.

59 F. Justi, *Iranisches Namenbuch* (Marburg 1895) stemma on 412. AID IN 69: Plut. *Luc.* 26.4. EMBASSY: Plut. *Pomp.* 36.2.

60 ALLIES OF EUPATOR: Memnon, *FGrH* 434, F 2.22.4 (30). PHRAATES IN GORDYENE: Dio 37.5; Plut. *Pomp.* 36.

61 W. Wroth, *BMC Parthia* (1903) and *NC* (ser. 3) 20 (1900) 181; D.G. Sellwood, 'Wroth's Unknown Parthian King': *NC* (ser. 7) 5 (1965) 113-135 with Pl. 10-11; also his 'Some Politic Alterations in the Parthian Series' in R.A.G. Carson, ed., *Mints, Dies, and Currency: Essays in Memory of Albert Baldwin* (London 1971) 33-37, with Pl. 6. As pointed out by the late Otto Mørkholm in *NC* (ser. 7) 19 (1980) 33-47, esp. 46, the 'urge to provide a named King for every issue' can be misleading. See also Magie 1227-1228 notes 16 and 20; 1230 note 30.

62 U. Kahrstedt, *Artabanos III. und seine Erben* (Bern 1950) 13 note 11 suggested one of the Arabian successor-states ('einem der arabischen Nachfolgenstaaten') for the term 'Syrians,' pointing out that the Seleucid succession had been disrupted. There remains the possibility of an otherwise unattested marriage between a Seleucid and an Atropatenian before the first century, but Strabo probably had in mind the well-known ones with effects still visible when he wrote. These marriages are discussed in Ch. 7, §§ 19-20.

63 PHILIPPI: App. *BCiv.* 4.88 and 99. ARTAVASDES I OF ATROPATENE: Wilcken in *RE* 2 (1896) 1309-1311. COINS: The 'Armenian' tiara on his coinage for 36 might portray that of the Atropatenian King, which was modelled on the Armenian one adopted by Tigranes and was still used by Artavasdes II of Armenia. See M. Crawford, *Roman Republican Coinage*, I (Cambridge, Eng. 1974) 537 no. 539, from 36 BC. See also E.S.G. Robinson, *NC* (ser. 5) 17 (1937) 250-254; G. Le Rider in *RN* (sér. 6) 2 (1959/1960) 26-29, esp. no. 33. The unidentified monarch he also discusses there, with name ending *-imnalos*, 'soit aussi un souverain mède, antérieur à Artavasde' in Le

Rider's view; other traces of him are lacking, but the period is obscure. See P. Bedoukian, 'The Coinage of the Artaxiad Dynasty': *ANSMusN* 14 (1968) 41-66 with Pl. ix-xi; *BMC Galatia* xlii and 101 with Pl. 14.3. ANTONY: Dio 49.25; Plut. *Ant.* 53.6; Sullivan, 'Commagene' 772-775. CAPTIVITY OF ARTAVASDES II: See this chapter, § 24. See also Strabo 11.13.4.524; 11.14.9.530; Jos. *AJ* 15.104-105; *BJ* 1.363; Plut. *Ant.* 50.4; Dio 49.39.6; 51.16.2; Tac. *Ann.* 2.3, ANTONY'S CAMPAIGN OF 36: H. Buccheim, *Die Orientpolitik des Triumvirn M. Antonius* (Heidelberg 1960) 74-83; V. Minorsky, 'Roman and Byzantine Campaigns in Atropatene': *Bull. Sch. Orient. and Afr. Stud. (U. of London)* 11 (1943-1946) 243-265, esp. 258-262, section 5; J. Kromayer, *Hermes* 31 (1896) 70-104. See also Sullivan, 'Commagene' 770-775; Magie 1288 note 30; Debevoise 121-134. On Antony's losses now: W.W. Tarn, 'Antony's Legions': *CQ* 26 (1932) 78-79; Ch. 8, § 23, note 289; below, this chapter, § 26, note 123. The Atropatenian's alliance with Parthia: Dio 49.25. This soon broke down: Dio 49.33.

64 *PIR*[2] J 44; *PIR* M 452; Sullivan, 'Commagene' 780-783, with stemma; Dio 51.16.2.

65 Sullivan, 'Emesa' 212-216 and stemma.

66 POLEMO: Dio 49.33.2. Polemo had only recently been released after falling captive then: Dio 49.25.4. Dio 49.44 (and 49.33) and Plut. *Ant.* 53.6 omit the role of Polemo. LAND: Strabo 11.13.2.523; Dio 49.44.2. This is not the portion of Armenia Minor later ruled by Artavasdes: Dio 54.9.2, and below. SYMBACE: See F. Grosso, 'La Media Atropatene e la politica di Augusto': *Athenaeum* n.s. 35 (1957) 240 ff. He believes that the transfer of this land to Atropatene came only with the accession of Ariobarzanes II to the Armenian throne in AD 2, after ruling Atropatene since 20 BC. COINS: E.A. Sydenham, *The Coinage of the Roman Republic* (London 1952) 194 no. 1210; cf. no. 1205; H.A. Grueber, *Coins of the Roman Republic in the British Museum* (London 1910) Plate 115 no. 10; M. Crawford, *Roman Republican Coinage*, I (Cambridge, Eng. 1974) 539 no. 543; cf. 537 no. 539.

67 Tac. *Ann.* 2.3.1-2 (AD 16); Dio 49.40.1-51.16.2; Strabo 16.1.28.748. See above, this chapter, § 24.

68 See R. Sullivan, 'Diadochic Coinage in Commagene after Tigranes the Great': *NC* (ser. 7) 13 (1973) 18-39, esp. 31-32 and Plate 14.8. The issues of Artavasdes featuring the Armenian tiara in modified form were recognized by E.S.G. Robinson in *NC* (ser. 5) 17 (1937) 250-255. See also G. Le Rider in *RN* (sér. 6) 2 (1959/1960) 26-27 no. 33.

69 Dio 49.44; Plut. *Ant.* 61. See also Schur in *RE* 18 (1949) 1997 ('Parthia'): Atropatene is now 'fest im parthischen Händen'; this might have occurred indirectly, using their ally Artaxias II. ARMENIA RECEPTA: H. Mattingly, *Coins of the Roman Empire in the British Museum*, I (London 1923) 3 ff.,

nos. 10-21 and 40-44. See too Vell. Pat. 2.122.1: *Armenia recepta*; 2.94.4: *redacta ea*; Suet. *Tib.* 9. ARIOBARZANES II IN MEDIA, 20 BC: For this controversy, see Kahrstedt, *Artabonos III.* 15-16 (AD 9), with E.W. Gray in *JRS* 43 (1953) 164-165; Lily Ross Taylor, 'M. Titius and the Syrian Command': *JRS* 26 (1936) 161-173; Debevoise 140-142, using *CIL* XIV 3613 = *ILS* 918; *PIR* T 196. Another view: *CAH* X 878; cf. 264; Syme, *Roman Revolution* 398, note 1. See *Res Gestae* 32: *Ad me supplices confugerunt reges ... Medorum Artavasdes*; Dio 51.16.2. Tarn's impression in *CQ* 26 (1932) 81 that Artavasdes remained in Media to 'hold Parthia' ignores the evidence that he had by then been ejected and fled to Octavian. ARMENIA MINOR: Dio 49.33 and 49.44; 54.9.2: 'Armenia Minor he recognized for Archelaus [of Cappadocia], because the Mede [Artavasdes] who ruled it before had died' (by 20 BC). See also *CIL* VI 1798; Wilcken in *RE* 2 (1896) 1309-1311.

70 *Res Gestae* 27 and 33. See also *PIR*[2] A 1044; 1045; 1164-1165; 1155; *PIR* V 629; *AE* 1955, no. 71; *OGIS* 380-381; *IGRR* IV 149; Pani 67-89. See too A. Degrassi, 'Le dedichi di popoli e re asiatici a popolo romano e a Giove Capitolino': *BCAR* 74 (1951-1952, publ. 1954) 32-34 no. 19 = *Scritti vari di antichita* I (Rome 1962) 428 = *IG* XIV 989 = *OGIS* 381 = *IGRR* I 68 = L. Moretti, *Inscriptiones Graecae Urbis Romae* I (Rome 1968) 15. See further *BMC Galatia* xlii and 101; Head *HN*[2] 755; Magie 1345; F. Grosso, 'La Media Atropatene e la politica di Augusto': *Athenaeum* n.s. 35 (1957) 240-256. See too *OGIS* 380 = *IG* XIV 1674 = *CIL* VI 32264 = *ILS* 844 = *IGRR* I 267. Ariobarzanes II died *morte fortuita* after briefly replacing the Armenian Artavasdes, *non sine clade nostra deiectus*: Tac. *Ann.* 2.4.1. The Armenians *stirpem eius* [Ariobarzanes II] *haud toleravere*. See Sullivan, *Armenian Question* 109-117, § 14. The Arsacid succession here became 'definitive': E.W. Gray, *CR* n.s. 17 (1967) 351. See also D.G. Sellwood, 'A Die-Engraver Sequence for Later Parthian Drachms': *NC* (ser. 7) 7 (1967) 13-28: 'The new king was Artabanus ... His rejection of the Roman excesses of his predecessor was demonstrated in no uncertain manner on the coins.'

71 He is designated either the second or third of that name depending on one's view of the slender evidence for an Artabanus among the first Arsacids. Justin 42.2.6 clearly believes that the third Arsacid King, ruling about 200 BC, was named Artabanus: *In huius locum Artabanus patruus eius, rex substituitur.* Another Artabanus, father of Mithradates II, is well attested. See R.H. McDowell, *Coins from Seleucia on the Tigris* (Ann Arbor 1935) 62 ff., 187, 206-223; G. Le Rider, *Suse sous les Séleucides et les Parthes* (Paris 1965; *Mémoires de la mission archéol. en Iran*, 38: *mission de Susiane*) 391 ff.; Debevoise 16 note 66; J. Wolski, 'Arsace II et la généalogie des premiers Arsacides': *Historia* 11 (1962) 138-145, and in *Eos* 55 (1965) 152-159. See Ch. 5, § 13 and below, this chapter, § 26, note 136.

72 Strabo 11.13.1-2.523. See too *PIR* V 670-671; *PIR*² A 1044; 1155; 1164; *OGIS* 381; *AE* 1955, no. 71. See further Sullivan in *ANRW* II 8, stemma following 938.

73 Jos. *AJ* 18.48-49. See too Tac. *Ann.* 6.42.3: *materna origine Arsaciden*; cf. 2.3.1: *Artabanus, Arsacidarum e sanguine apud Dahas adultus*; 6.41.2: *Artabanum Scythas inter eductum.* See also *Ann.* 6.36.4: *Hyrcanis Carmaniisque per adfinitatem innexus erat.* As E.W. Gray has pointed out in *JRS* 43 (1953) 164-165, *affinitas* here cannot be construed as if synonymous with *vicinitas, pace* Kahrstedt, *Artabanos III.* 12-13. Cf. Frye, *Persia* 278 note 46. FLIGHT TO ATROPATENE AND ARMENIA: Jos. *AJ* 18.48-50. Artabanus regarded this as a major victory, issuing a coinage for it; his brother had done so too on the previous occasion, with an inscription reading 'King Onones [*sic*] conquering Artabanus': A. Ritter von Petrowicz, *Sammlung Petrowicz: Arsaciden-Münzen* (Wien 1904) 109-110 no. 5 with Plate 16.10. See further Kahrstedt, 11-16 with the review by E.W. Gray; Werner Schur, 'Die Orientpolitik des Kaisers Nero': *Klio* Beiheft 15 (1923) 70 ff.; E. Herzfeld, 'Sakastan': *Archaeologische Mitteilungen aus Iran* 4 (1932) 51 ff.; 61 f.; 86-87.

74 LOST: Said by Eric Gray, *JRS* 43 (1953) 165 about the Parthian reign of Artabanus III (II), and no less applicable to Atropatene. 'MEDIA' = ATROPATENE: Bibliography by Kahrstedt, *Artabanos III.* 11-12 note 5. See too Jos. *BJ* 1.476. See further *Res Gestae* 27.2: *qui erat ex regio genere Armeniorum oriundus*, with the discussion of T. Mommsen in his *Res Gestae Divi Augusti ex Monumentis Ancyrano et Apolloniensi*, 2nd ed. (Berlin 1883) 116; Sullivan, 'Cappadocia' 1161-1165.

75 LAPSE: Kahrstedt 18 with E.W. Gray, *JRS* 43 (1953) 165. LATER ATROPATENIANS: Sullivan, *Ancient Coins* (1984) 145-146 with note 13; *ILS* 844; *OGIS* 380-381; *IGRR* I 68 and 267; IV 149. See also *IG* XIV 989; Pani 68, nos. N and O.; F. Grosso, *Athenaeum* n.s. 35 (1957) 247 and 255; B. Brosset, *Collection d'historiens Arméniens*, I (St. Petersburg 1874) 45-47 (Th. Artsruni, c. AD 900).

76 See stemma, with Debevoise 270. On Sinatruces see next note, with D.G. Sellwood, 'The Parthian Coins of Gotarzes I, Orodes I, and Sinatruces': *NC* (ser. 7) 2 (1962) 73-89. See also W. Wroth, *BMC Parthia* (London 1903) xxxi and 42-55; A. von Petrowicz, *Sammlung Petrowicz: Arsaciden Münzen* (Wien 1904) 47-51, with Pl. 7-8; D. Sellwood, *An Introduction to the Coinage of Parthia* (London 1971) 83-178. Lucian, *Macrobioi* 15, has him 'in his eightieth year' at his accession and ruling for seven years. See Phlegon of Tralles, *FGrH* no. 257, F 12.6-7 (IIB, p. 1164), for the date. See the comments of O. Mørkholm in *NC* (ser. 7) 19 (1980) 42 on the relative unreliability of the 'seven years' of Lucian; Mørkholm (p. 45) sees Sinatruces as ruling

from c. 86/85 BC and association in 74. See D.G. Sellwood in *NC* (ser. 7) 2 (1962) 84. Estimates for his death vary from 71 BC to 68/67: M.-L. Chaumont, *Syria* 48 (1971) 161-162. She assumes the Nisa ostracon *Nov.* 307 and a cuneiform tablet, both from Year 180 (Arsacid), together refer to Phraates III at the inception of his reign, though neither specifies this. Both are dated to 'Year 180 [Arsacid] which is year 244 [Seleucid],' or 68/67 BC; published, respectively, by Ellis Minns, 'Parchments of the Parthian Period from Avroman in Kurdistan': *JHS* 35 (1915) 22-65, esp. 36, and Fr J.N. Strassmaier, 'Zur Chronologie der Seleuciden': *Zeitschrift für Assyriologie* 8 (1893) 106-113, esp. 112. Further discussion by A.M. Simonetta, 'Some Remarks on the Arsacid Coinage of the Period 90-57 B.C.': *NC* (ser. 7) 6 (1966) 15-40, esp. 20. As pointed out by K.W. Dobbins, 'The Successors of Mithradates II of Parthia': *NC* (ser. 7) 15 (1975) 19-45, esp. 19 and 22 (with misprint '189' for 180 on no. xxiii), Simonetta's dates are one year late. Dobbins concludes (p. 39) that we have 'the first issues of Phraates III in 68/7 B.C.' just as Chaumont would expect, though Dobbins still regards his reign as beginning in 70 or 69. Chaumont further points out (163-165) that the sources fail to specify the name of the Parthian king in 70 or 69 when referring to him, except for Memnon, whose narrative she seeks to move from 69 to 66 BC, despite its being clearly associated with the battle of Tigranocerta, when he has an embassy 'to the Parthian Phraates.' N. Waggoner (below, note 88) 19: '70 B.C., presumably the first year of Phraates' reign.' See also Memnon, *FGrH* 434, F 2.38.8 (= Müller, *FHG* III, 556-557, F 58). The 'recent' accession of Phraates noted by Dio 36.45.3 for 66 BC and App. *Mith.* 104.487 for 64 BC favour her view, though they are vague. See also her study, 'Les ostraca de Nisa. Nouvelle contribution à l'histoire des Arsacides': *Journal Asiatique* (1968) 14-19. D.G. Sellwood seeks to resolve this and other numismatic and chronological problems by postulating that Darius of Media Atropatene 'a régné entre Sinatrucès et Phraate III, c'est-à-dire vers 70': 'Deux notes sur les drachms arsacides': *RN* (sér. 6) 13 (1971) 153-160, esp. 159, citing his article, 'Wroth's Unknown Parthian King' in *NC* (ser. 7) 5 (1965) 113-135, esp. 128. But the discussion there centres on the events of 66 and 65 BC, presenting no evidence for 70. On Darius, see this chapter, § 25.

77 ALLIANCE WITH EUPATOR: App. *Mith.* 15.54; Memnon *FGrH* 434, F 2.22.3 (30). Debevoise 48 suggests that this was caused by Sulla's slight of the Parthians when in Armenia, but the treaty was apparently not concluded for some years after that, about 89 or 88 BC. TIGRANES: Plut. *Luc.* 21.4. See also G. Rawlinson, *The Sixth Great Oriental Monarchy, or the Geography, History, and Antiquities of Parthia* (London 1873) 140-142. THE LETTER: Debevoise 70-71 note 3. Bibliography and discussion: Ch. 5, § 13,

note 45; Ch. 6, § 15, note 23; Ch. 2, § 3, note 39, above. See too Sallust *Hist.* 4.69.

78 TIGRANOCERTA: The battle took place in October 69: K. Eckhardt, 'Die armenischen Feldzüge des Lukullus' I-III: *Klio* 9 (1909) 400-412; 10 (1910) 72-115 and 192-231. CAMPAIGNS IN 68: Eckhardt 192-231; App. *Mith.* 87.392-88.401. OFFER OF TIGRANES: Dio 36.1 and 3; Plut. *Luc.* 30.1; Memnon, *FGrH* 434, F. 2.38.8 (58); App. *Mith.* 87.392; Strabo 11.14.15.532. EMBASSIES: See references under OFFER OF TIGRANES. TREATIES: See Ch. 5, § 13, note 43; Plut. *Sulla* 5.7 ff. See also Florus 1.46.4-6: *percussorum cum Pompeio foederum Sullaque meminisset* (Orodes II, dealing with Crassus); 9.1.40.31. Cf. Livy *Per.* 100: *Pompeius ... cum rege Parthorum Prahate amicitiam renovavit;* cf. *Per.* 70. See too Dio 36.45.3 and 51.1; Plut. *Pomp.* 36.2; Vell. Pat. 2.24.2; Festus 15.2; Orosius 6.13.2: *contra foedus Luculli et Pompei;* Justin 42.4.6: *Parthi ... propter amicitiam cum Pompeio bello Mithridatico iunctam;* Florus 1.40.31: Parthians *foedus maluerunt.* See further J. Dobiáš, *Archiv orientální* 3 (1931) 215-256; A. Keaveney, 'Roman Treaties with Parthia, circa 95-circa 64 B.C.': *AJP* 102 (1981) 195-212; cf. 103 (1982) 412-428, and below; these do not treat the numismatic and epigraphical evidence for Parthia. LUCULLUS vs. PARTHIA: Dobiáš, 233, rightly questions this account; cf. his note 2 there.

79 MANOEUVRES: Dio 36.45.3; 36.51.1-3. Keaveney, (above, note 78, 1981) 201-202, unconvincingly adduces the first passage in suggesting that also 'Lucullus had intended the Parthians to attack Armenia.' See also App. *Mith.* 104.484-105.492. In Armenia, the forces of Pompey were inferior to those of Mithradates: Frontinus 2.5.33; this did not occasion the reverse it might have, since Mithradates fled north; Ch. 6, § 15. Then he fought and lost: Dio 36.47-49. TIGRANES THE YOUNGER: See above, this chapter, § 24, note 18; Dio 36.50.1; 36.50-54; App. *Mith.* 105.493 f.; Plut. *Pomp.* 33.5.

80 MUTUAL FEAR: Dio 37.6.3, Phraates 'fearing and paying court'; 37.7.2, Pompey 'fearing the forces of the Parthian (King).' Bibliography on their treaty: above, and Dobiáš 235 note 1. See too App. *Mith.* 106.501. 'KING OF KINGS': Dio 37.6. Pompey took to calling the younger Tigranes 'King of Kings' to further provoke Phraates. Parthian titulature now used 'King of Kings' and an assortment of ancillary terms such as 'Philhellene' or 'Great' or 'Epiphanes' or, as with Phraates, 'the God.' See also A. von Sallet, 'Beiträge zur antiken Münzkunde': *ZfN* 12 (1885) 372-375; W. Wroth, *BMC Parthia* (London 1903) xxxiv; 45-55. D.G. Sellwood, *NC* (ser. 7) 2 (1962) 81-88, regards *Nikator* ('Conqueror') as a title inappropriate for Phraates, given his relatively peaceful reign and the inconclusive nature of his Armenian campaigns. This fails to estimate his own attitudes, and some have attributed a *Nikator* series to Phraates; e.g., G. Le Rider, *Suse sous les Séleucides et les*

Parthes (Paris 1965) 394-398. But see K.W. Dobbins, 'The Successors of Mithradates II of Parthia': *NC* (ser. 7) 15 (1975) 34 ff. It is usual to assert that Arsacid kings between Mithradates II and Orodes II (e.g., Sellwood 79; J. Neusner, *IA* [1963] 46) omitted 'King of Kings' from the coinage. This view must reassign the coins bearing that title, with and without *Ktistes* ('Founder'), attributed to Phraates III in *Sammlung Petrowicz* 47-51. Whether he also used *Theopator* ('Whose Father Was a God') causes controversy as well: Dobbins 44 (it 'did not suit Phraates'); A.M. Simonetta, *NC* (ser. 7) 6 (1966) 15-40, esp. 22 ('Class F') and 39. Other kingdoms also used this range of royal formulae: e.g., Toumanoff, *Studies* 47 with note 36; 50-51 with note 44; 77; Asdourian 68-69 notes 1-2. E.T. Newell, *NNM* 30 (1926) 14, saw a reciprocity by which a king, here Tigranes III (his 'II'), could be 'forced by his jealous and more powerful neighbours' to eschew 'King of Kings.' The 'sub-kings' (a modern, not an ancient term) were full kings under this arrangement. The 'Second after the King' at an Iranian court was a separate, internal position. See H. Volkmann, 'Der Zweite nach dem König': *Philologus* 92 (1937) 285-316; E. Benveniste, *Titres et noms propre en Iran ancien* (Paris 1966) 51-65 ('le 2nd après le roi').

81 Dio 36.51.1; 37.6-7. See Keaveney 204-212; Dobiáš 235-236.

82 Dio 37.5-7. SECOND INVASION: Dio 37.6.4. Since he mentions Tigranes the Younger as taking part, this should be drawn from the account of 66 BC in 36.51. On the other hand, App. *Mith.* 105.494 has him still 'making trouble for Pompey with the Parthians,' so perhaps he was briefly freed. Ultimately, he went to Rome as a captive. See this chapter, § 24.

83 EUPHRATES: Dio 37.6.3, Phraates 'declared that he (Pompey) should not cross the Euphrates.' See Strabo 16.1.28.748; Plut. *Pomp.* 33.8; *Mor.* 2.88; *Luc.* 36.5; Oros. 6.13.2. Mithradates I: Justin 41.6.8: *imperium ... Parthorum ... usque flumen Euphraten protulit.* BOUNDARIES: Dio 37.7; Dobiáš 238-240; Rawlinson, *Sixth Monarchy* 146-147 on the moderation displayed by Phraates now; App. *Mith.* 106.501. QUIET: Dio 37.15.1.

84 MAKING TROUBLE: App. *Mith.* 105.494. FALLING INTO WAR: App. *Mith.* 106.501; Plut. *Pomp.* 39; Dio 37.7.

85 Strabo 16.1.28.748.

86 K.W. Dobbins in *NC* (ser. 7) 15 (1975) 37-39. Strabo 16.1.18.744 remarks that the King of Elymais was too powerful for subjection to Parthia. This presumably fails to hold true of the reign of Phraates as it had of Mithradates: Justin 41.6.8 says that after war with Elymais, *hanc quoque gentem regno adiecit.* CTESIPHON: Schur in *RE* 18 (1949) 1991, 'Parthia,' adducing Strabo 16.1.16.743 (a misprint gives 'VI' for 'XVI') but not why he ascribes it to Phraates. It existed already under Pacorus I: Amm. Marc. 23.6.23, who ascribes its foundation to an unknown Vardanes (not Vardanes I).

87 *THEOS*: R.N. Frye, 'The Charisma of Kingship in Ancient Iran': *IA* 4 (1964) 36-54, believes that 'Whatever the nature of Hellenistic kingship ... the Iranians did not believe in the divine character of their living Kings.' MURDER: Dio 39.56.2.

88 MITHRADATES SUCCEEDS: Dio, *ibid.*, implies that his brother came first. See, however, the numismatic articles cited by Debevoise 76 note 23, and as follows: W. Wroth, *BMC Parthia* (London 1903) xxxiv and 61 ff.; Head HN^2 820; O. Mørkholm, *NC* (ser. 7) 19 (1980) 33-47, esp. 38 and 44-46, seeing Mithradates governing Media, as in Dio, then succeeding Phraates in 58/57 BC. See D.G. Sellwood, 'Deux notes sur les drachmes arsacides': *RN* (sér. 6) 13 (1971) 154-157; D. Sellwood, *An Introduction to the Coinage of Parthia* (London 1971) 110 ff.; N. Waggoner, 'The Coinage of Phraates III of Parthia: Addenda': D.K. Kouymjian, ed., *Near Eastern Numismatics, Iconography, Epigraphy, and History. Studies in Honor of George C. Miles* (Beirut 1974) 15-26; Geyer in *RE* 15 (1932) 2211-2212, 'Mithridates' nr. 23; Rawlinson, *Sixth Monarchy* 147-148.

89 COINS: *Sammlung Petrowicz* 51-55 and 59-62 nos. 18-35; D.G. Sellwood, *NC* (ser. 7) 5 (1965) 112-135, esp. 134; Pl. 10-11.

90 Cic. *Dom.* 9.23; 23.60. GORDYENE: Rawlinson, *Sixth Monarchy* 147-148. ARMENIAN WAR: Justin 42.4.1: *Mithridates, rex Parthorum, post bellum Armeniae propter crudelitatem a Senatu Parthico regno pellitur.*

91 GABINIUS: Cic. *Dom.* 9.23-24.; 55; 23.60; 124; Schürer (Vermes and Millar) 245-246; Dobiáš 242-243; A. Keaveney, *AJP* 103 (1982) 412-428; Debevoise 77. See also App. *Syr.* 51.257; Jos. *AJ* 14.103; *BJ* 1.175 and 178; Dio 39.56. Senate disapproves: Strabo 12.3.34.558. COINS: R.H. McDowell, *Coins from Seleucia on the Tigris* (Ann Arbor 1935) 212 ff.; D. Sellwood, *An Introduction to the Coinage of Parthia* (London 1971) 41, 1-11; Geyer in *RE* 15 (1932) 2211-2212; *Sammlung Petrowicz* 56 no. 1; H. Dressel, 'Ein Tetradrachmon des Arsakiden Mithridates III' in *ZfN* 33 (1922) 156-177. OVERSTRUCK COINS: A. Simonetta, *NC* (ser. 7) 6 (1966) 23; Debevoise 77-78 with notes 30 and 33. See also Justin 42.4.4: *Orodes plus hostem quam fratrem cogitans in conspectu suo trucidari iussit.*

92 ORODES 'I': See Ch. 5, § 13; *BMC Parthia* xxxv and 68 ff. O. Mørkholm, *NC* (ser. 7) 19 (1980) 33-47, concludes that 'no coinage' in fact exists for him. See, however, A.M. Simonetta in *NAC (Quaderni Ticinesi)* 7 (1978) 95-117; Simonetta, GNS 30 (1980) 62-67; K.W. Dobbins in *NC* (ser. 7) 15 (1975) 19-45, with earlier bibliography there.

93 O. Mørkholm, *NC* (ser. 7) 19 (1980) 33 ff., esp. 38-40; D. Sellwood, *An Introduction to the Coinage of Parthia* (London 1971) nos. 41-45; *Sammlung Petrowicz: Arsaciden Münzen* (Wien 1904) 56-75 with Taf. 9-11; Tarn in *CAH* IX 602-612.

94 THE SURENA: Strabo 16.1.23.747; Florus 1.46; Plut. *Crass.* 21; Tac. *Ann.* 6.42.4: *multis coram et adprobantibus Surena patrio more Tirida[te]n insigni regio evinxit.* See also Dio 40.20-26; Herzfeld, 'Sakastan' 70-71; Rawlinson, *Sixth Monarchy* 85-86; 148 note 1; 159 note 1; Debevoise 83. Professor Toumanoff points out to me that this house began as far back as Achaemenid times and still retained its status under the Sassanids, a span of at least 550 years. Cf. A.D.H. Bivar, *JRAS* 1970, p. 65: 'the well-known family name and hereditary title.'

95 CRASSUS: Schürer (Vermes and Millar) 246. See Debevoise 78-79 for earlier bibliography. See also Rawlinson, *Sixth Monarchy* 150-177; A. Keaveney, *AJP* 103 (1982) 417-420.

96 FUNDS: Plut. *Crass.* 16 ff.; Jos. *AJ* 14.105-111; *BJ* 1.179; Oros. 6.13. GREED: This became almost legendary. E.g., Flor. 1.46.11: *cupiditas consulis Crassi, dum Parthico inhiat auro.*

97 ALCHAUDONIUS: See this chapter above, § 24; Dio 36.2.5; 37.7a; 40.20; Strabo 16.2.10.753. ABGARUS II: Dio 40.20-24; Plut. *Crass.* 21. See also A. von Gutschmid, 'Untersuchungen über die Geschichte des Königreichs Osröene': *Mémoires de l'Académie impériale des Sciences de St. Pétersbourg* (sér. 7) 35 (1887) 1-49, esp. 20-22 and 48; J. Wagner, '*Provincia Osrhoenae.* New Archaeological Finds Illustrating the Military Organisation under the Severan Dynasty': *Armies and Frontiers in Roman and Byzantine Anatolia,* ed. S. Mitchell (Oxford 1983; BAR International Series, 156) 103 ff. with 117 ff. notes 1-10; M.R. Duval, 'Histoire politique, religieuse et littéraire d'Édesse jusqu'à la Première Croisade': *JA* (ser. 8) 18 (1891) 87-133, 201-278, 381-439; 19 (1892) 5-102. See Ch. 5, § 12, note 14.

98 OSRHOENE: See Ch. 5, § 12. See also previous note, with Rawlinson, *Sixth Monarchy* 86-87 and 150-152; A.R. Bellinger and C.B. Welles, 'A Third-Century Contract of Sale from Edessa in Osrhoene': *YCS* 5 (1935) 95-154, esp. 121-125; H. Koehler, *Die Nachfolge in der Seleukidenherrschaft und die parthische Haltung im römish-pontischen Konflikt* (Bochum 1978; Bochumer Historische Studien, Alte Geschichte nr. 3) esp. 30 ff.; H.J.W. Drijvers, 'Hatra, Palmyra und Edessa. Die Städte der syrisch-mesopotamischen Wüste in politischer, kulturgeschichtlicher und religionsgeschichtlicher Beleuchtung': *ANRW* II 8 (Berlin 1978) 799-906, esp. 863-872. Roman attempts to take control of Osrhoene became more effective with the late second century, when a prefect of Mesopotamia and Osrhoene appears. See, e.g., R. Duncan-Jones, 'PRAEFECTUS MESOPOTAMIAE ET OSRHOENAE': *CP* 64 (1969) 229-233; H. Petersen, 'A Roman Prefect in Osrhoene': *TAPA* 107 (1977) 265-282. MARRIAGE ALLIANCE: See this chapter above, § 24.

99 Dio 40.16.3; Plut. *Crass.* 17-20. TREATIES: Flor. 1.46.4-6.

100 Plut. *Crass.* 16-21; Dio 40.12.1. POMPEY: The quotation comes from an address by E.W. Gray published in the *Proceedings of the African Classical*

Associations 12 (1973) 29 ff., esp. 34. CARRHAE: Debevoise 70-95; Rawlinson, *Sixth Monarchy* 155-177; D. Timpe, 'Die Bedeutung der Schlacht von Carrhae': *MH* 19 (1962) 104-129; A. von Gutschmid, *Geschichte Irans* 87-93; G. Košelenko, 'Les cavaliers parthes. Aspects de la structure sociale de la Parthie': *DHA* 6 (1980) 177-199.

101 Plut. *Crass.* 32-33; Cic. *Fam.* 15.3.1; *FGrH* III C, No. 678, 'Artavasdes der Armenier.' See below. DESIRE FOR FRIENDSHIP: Strabo 16.1.28.748.

102 Horace, *Odes* 3.5: *milesne Crassi coniuge barbara ... vixit et hostium ... consenuit socerorum in armis sub rege Medo?* Cf. 4.15: *signa ... derepta Parthorum superbis postibus*; *Ep.* 1.18.56. See also Pliny *HN* 6.47; Flor. 2.20.4: *Unus ex clade Crassiana ...*; Vell. Pat. 2.82.2: *qui clade Crassiani exercitus captus ...*; *Res Gestae* 29: *Parthos trium exercitum Romanorum spolia et signa reddere mihi ... coegi*; Dio 54.8.2.

103 HELLENISM: Plut. *Crass.* 32-33. COINS: *Sammlung Petrowicz, Arsaciden Münzen* (Wien 1904) 57-75; D.G. Sellwood, *RN* (sér. 6) 13 (1971) 157: 'Cette barbarisation de la légende se poursuit et s'aggrave sous Orode II.'

104 CITIES: Plut. *Crass.* 32. See also Strabo 11.13.1.522-523; 11.13.6.524; Dio 40.14-16. CTESIPHON: Amm. Marcell. 23.6.23; J. Wolski, 'Die Parther und ihre Beziehungen zur griechisch-römischen Kultur': *Klio* 65 (1983) 137-149. F. Cumont, 'Deux inscriptions de Suse': *CRAI* (1933) 260-268, published a text possibly from 75 BC, in the reign of Sinatruces, though this requires taking the date, 'year 173,' as of the Arsacid rather than Seleucid era. It shows one of the 'First Friends and Bodyguards' of the king serving also as *gymnasiarch*. Extremely useful for town government in the first century is the text and commentary by F. Cumont, 'Une lettre du roi Artaban III à la ville de Suse': *CRAI* (1932) 238-260 = *SEG* 7 (1934) 1 = C.B. Welles, *Royal Correspondence* 299-306, no. 75. Comments by A. Wilhelm, *AAWW* (1934) 45-66. On Susa: R. Ghirshman, *Mémoires de la Délégation archéologique française en Iran, 47: Mission de Susiane*, 13 vols., in progress (Brill). F. Cumont published one Greek inscription from Susa dated to the reign of Phraates IV: 'Nouvelles inscriptions grecques de Suse': *CRAI* (1930) 208-220. See also *SEG* 7 (1934) nos. 12-13. HYRCANIA: L. Robert, *Hellenica* XI-XII (Paris 1960) § vii, 85-91; Justin 41.4; Strabo 15.2.14.727. Jos. *BJ* 7.245 shows it under a king by about AD 73.

105 BEGINNING: Dio 40.14.1.

106 PARTHIANS AGAINST SYRIA: Debevoise Ch. 5, 95-120; Schürer (Vermes and Millar) 247; Dio 40.28.1; Tarn, *CAH* IX 612.

107 SPECIAL COINAGE: Gardner 41, with Pl. 3.29-30; B. Simonetta, 'On Some Tetradrachms of Orodes II and the Probable Issues of Pacorus I': *NC* (ser. 7) 18 (1978) 7-13, with Pl. 2; Debevoise 104 note 43; *BMC Parthia*, xxxvii and 97. OSACES: Dio 40.28-29; Frontinus 2.5.35.

108 CICERO: *Att.* 5.5, 5.11, 5.14, 5.16, 5.18, 5.20; *Fam.* 3.3; 15.1-4. See also Plut. *Cic.* 36; Debevoise 96-104. DYNASTS: Ch. 6-7, §§ 16-20. RAID: Debevoise 100.

109 PACORUS: Dio 40.30; Justin 42.4.5: *patri suspectus revocatur.* BIBULUS: Schürer (Vermes and Millar) 247; Cic. *Fam.* 12.19; *Att.* 7.2; Caes. *BCiv.* 3.31. SUMMER of 50: Debevoise 103-104 with note 39.

110 HIATUS: Debevoise 104; B. Simonetta, *NC* (ser. 7) 18 (1978) 7-13. APPREHENSIONS: Caes. *BCiv.* 3.31: *Summamque in sollicitudinem ac timorem Parthici belli provincia [Syria] cum venisset ...* (49 BC). Cf. Cic. *Fam.* 12.19.2: *de Parthici belli suspicione* (46 BC); *Att.* 14.9. Debevoise 104-105: Parthians did desire Syria. POMPEY: Plut. *Pomp.* 76.4; Dio 42.2.5; App. *BCiv.* 2.83; Florus 2.13.52; Luc. *Phars.* 8.191-330. See Ch. 8, § 23. Cf. Justin 42.4.6: *Parthi Pompeianarum partium fuere.*

111 BASSUS: Jos. *AJ* 14.268-272; Cic. *Att.* 14.9; Dio 47.27.5; App. *BCiv.* 4.58; Strabo 16.2.10.753. Bibliography: Sullivan, 'Emesa': *ANRW* II 8, 208-209. See above, Ch. 7, § 20; Schürer (Vermes and Millar) 248-249; Debevoise 106. CAESAR: J. Malitz, 'Caesars Partherkrieg': *Historia* 33 (1984) 21-59. Rawlinson, *Sixth Monarchy* 184-185, envisions possible 'subjection' of Parthia. Debevoise, 106-107, rightly scales this back to a 'very serious war with the Romans' had Caesar lived. See also Schur, *RE* 18 (1949) 1993; Dio 43.51.1; App. *BCiv.* 3.17; 4.58. From the visit of Ariarathes X of Cappadocia to Rome 'to buy some kingdom or other from Caesar' in 45 BC, Parthian control of a portion of Armenia Minor, previously assigned to him, has been inferred by some; Cic. *Att.* 13.2a.

112 PHILIPPI AND AFTER: Justin 42.4.7: *et Cassio et Bruto auxilia adversus Augustum [sic,* for Octavian] *et Antonium misere.* App. *BCiv.* 4.63 has the Parthian force arrive too late for the battle, and ravage Syria instead, but 4.88 has 'two thousand Parthian and Thessalian' cavalry and 'four thousand mounted archers, Arabs, Medes, and Parthians'; cf. 4.59 and 99. PALMYRA: App. *BCiv.* 5.9-10, connecting this action with the ensuing Parthian invasion. FUNDS FOR WAR: Plut. *Ant.* 23.1 and 25.1.

113 PACORUS: Tac. *Hist.* 5.9: *rex Parthorum Pacorus Iudaea potitus*; Justin 42.4.10: *rege ipso Pacoro*; Livy *Per.* 128: *regemque eorum occidit* (see also below); Amm. Marcell. 23.6.23: *rex Pacorus.* See also B. Simonetta, *NC* (ser. 7) 18 (1978) 7-11; *Sammlung Petrowicz* 76 with Pl. 11.28-30; Gardner 41 with Pl. 3.29-30; Rawlinson, *Sixth Monarchy* 182.

114 LABIENUS: Plut. *Ant.* 28 and 30; Dio 48.24; Livy *Per.* 127; Debevoise 108-109. ORODES INDOLENT: Schur in *RE* 18 (1949) 1992: 'Da Orodes zu bequem geworden war, um selbst ins Feld zu rücken ...' ALLIES: App. *BCiv.* 5.10.24. See too Dio 48.41.5; 49.19.2; 49.20.3; 49.22.3; 49.32.5. See above, Ch. 7, §§ 19 and 22; Buccheim 27.

115 SAXA: Schürer (Vermes and Millar) 250-251. THE CAMPAIGN: A. Bürcklein, *Quellen und Chronologie der römisch-parthischen Feldzüge in den Jahren 713-718 d. St.* [i.e., 40-35 BC] (Berlin 1879); Magie 430-432; Buccheim 75-79; Debevoise 109-110. Lydia and Ionia are mentioned by Plut. *Ant.* 30. J. Wolski dates to 39 'un tournant dans la politique des Arsacides, condamnés désormais à la défensive.': *IA* 5 (1965) 103-115, esp. 113. MYLASA: See below, note 118. POLEMO: See Ch. 6, § 15.

116 ANTIGONUS: See Ch. 7, § 22. See too Schürer (Vermes and Millar) § 14, 281-286. GAZA: B. Simonetta (above, note 107), *NC* (ser. 7) 18 (1978) 7-11. *Sammlung Petrowicz* 59, no. 17 (Sel. 273 = 40/39 BC) seems stressed rather hard here, to provide the date of May 40 BC for the fall of Gaza.

117 BASSUS: Schürer (Vermes and Millar) 251-252. DEATH OF PACORUS: Justin 42.4.10-16: *nec ullo bello Parthi umquam maius vulnus acceperunt.* See also Livy *Per.* 127-128; Vell. Pat. 2.78: *celeberrimoque iuvenum Pacoro.* Schürer (Vermes and Millar): 9 June 38. Tac. *Hist.* 5.9: *Parthi trans Euphraten redacti.* Justin provides a vivid description of the paralysing grief of Orodes, and connects his decline with it. PACORUS 'BALANCING' CRASSUS: Florus 2.19.7: *Sic Crassianam cladem Pacori caede pensavimus.* Arrian, *Parthika* F 24, Teubner (A. Roos, rev. G. Wirth) p. 233: 'The slaughter of Crassus and those around him received a counterpoise in the destruction of Pacorus with his force.' Dio 49.21.2 expresses a similar view. TRIUMPH: Plut. *Ant.* 35.5; Dio 49.21.3.

118 TRAJAN: Debevoise, 240 note 1, makes this point, thinking of 40-38 BC. ALLIES AND PACORUS: Dio 48.41; 49.19-20; 49.32.5; Justin 42.4.7-10. See also Tac. *Germ.* 37.3: *quid enim aliud nobis quam caedem Crassi, amisso et ipse Pacoro infra Ventidium deiectus Oriens obiecerit*? See further Horace, *Odes* 3.6.9-12. ARAD: Dio 48.41.6 and 49.22.3; Jones, *Cities*^{2} 260 f. PARTHIAN vs. ROMAN ADMINISTRATION: Dio 48.24.8; 49.20.4. On the situation in Cilicia: Cic. *Fam.* 15.1.3-5; 15.4.8-10. See Ch. 6, § 18, Tarcondimotus. MYLASA: J. and L. Robert in *Bull. ép.* 1976, no. 75; Chr. Habicht in *JRS* 65 (1975) 64-91, esp. 70-71; Sherk, *Documents* nos. 59-60; *Greek East* no. 91; *SIG*^{3} 768. For the inscriptions from the site, see W. Blümel, *Inschriften von Mylasa*, 1-2 (Bonn 1987; *IGSK* 35). HYRCANUS II: See Ch. 7, § 22.

119 ANTONY'S LIEUTENANT, VENTIDIUS: Frontinus 2.2.5; 2.5.36-37; Dio 48.39-41. Florus 2.19.5 sees him operating more with astonishing good fortune (*incredibili felicitate*). See also Plut. *Ant.* 33; Justin 42.4.10; Debevoise 120. EUPHRATES: Tac. *Hist.* 5.9.1: *Pacorus ... interfectus ... a P. Ventidio, et Parthi trans Euphraten redacti.* App. *BCiv.* 5.9 shows Antony regarding Palmyra as 'on the frontier between Romans and Parthians' despite its being a considerable distance west of the Euphrates. Appian terms it

'not far' from the river. Its location had kept it largely out of the conflict till now. See too Plut. *Ant.* 34.2. ANTONY'S MOTIVE: E.W. Gray, *CR* n.s. 12 (1962) 281, suggests this apprehension regarding Octavian.

120 MONAESES: Plut. *Ant.* 37. According to Horace, *Odes* 3.6.9 Monaeses had fought successfully against Rome in the recent war. See also Dio 49.23-24. TREATY: Florus 2.20.10: *Quidem ab ipso foedus Antonio cum rege percussum.* CRASSUS: Dio 49.24-25. Artavasdes is on good terms here with Antony by the time he reaches the Euphrates. See this chapter, §§ 24-25.

121 SUCCESSION AND MURDERS: Justin 42.4.11-5.1-2; Dio 49.23.3-5; Plut. *Ant.* 37; *Crass.* 33.5. The break in coinage for 38/37 BC may reflect this troubled succession. See Debevoise 121. The passage in Ovid, *Ars Am.* 1.197-198, sometimes thought to allude to the murder of Orodes II by Phraates IV has rather been ascribed to that of Phraates IV in turn by his son, Phraataces, in 2 BC: A.S. Hollis, *CR* n.s. 20 (1970) 141-142. See also *BMC Parthia* xxxviii and 99-134.

122 ROUTE: Suet. *Iul.* 44: *Parthis inferre bellum per Armeniam minorem.* See T. Rice Holmes, *The Architect of the Roman Empire* (Oxford 1928) 223 ff. on the route. Cf. above, this chapter, § 24, note 32. On the campaign: Debevoise Ch. VI, 121-142. See also H. Bengtson, 'Zum Partherfeldzug des Antonius': *SBAW* (1974, Heft 1); J. Kromayer, 'Der Partherzug des Antonius': *Hermes* 31 (1896) 70-104; Buccheim 78-79; 82-83. ARTAVASDES OF ATROPATENE: Dio 49.25, noting the hostility of the Armenian Artavasdes to him. Strabo 11.13.4.524: Antony's folly in relying on Artavasdes. ENGINES: The commander, Statianus, fell with his men. See Plut. *Ant.* 38; Livy, *Per.* 130; Dio 49.25; Vell. Pat. 2.82.2. PRAASPA: V. Minorsky, 'Roman and Byzantine Campaigns in Atropatene': *Bull. Sch. Or. Afr. Stud.* 11 (1945/1946) 243-265, esp. § 5, pp. 258 ff.; H.C. Rawlinson, 'Memoir on the Site of the Atropatenian Ecbatana': *Journ. Royal Geog. Soc.* 10 (1840/1841) 65-158. ARTAVASDES OF ARMENIA: Dio 49.25 notes that Artavasdes might have prevented the serious loss of the equipment and the men of Statianus, but did not linger. Plut. *Ant.* 39.1 is unspecific but emphasizes that Artavasdes lost confidence in the Roman force.

123 DECIMATION: Plut. *Ant.* 39.7. CASUALTIES: W.W. Tarn, 'Antony's Legions': *CQ* 26 (1932) 75-81, esp. 79. See Debevoise 125-131, with an estimate of 35,000 deaths; Plut. *Ant.* 50: 24,000. J. Kromayer, *Hermes* 33 (1898) 27, estimates that Antony lost some 37 per cent of his entire force, or 32,000 men at least. Cf. Ch. 8, § 23, note 289; above, this chapter, § 25, note 63. ANTONY'S PACE: Livy *Per.* 130. He begins *tarde* and at the end *ad Cleopatram festinat.* Broughton, *MRR* II, 396: He had lost 'the opportunity presented by a year of dynastic crisis in Parthia.' Plut. *Ant.* 51 has a picture of Antony much agitated while awaiting Cleopatra in Syria. ARTAVASDES

TO BLAME: Plut. *Ant.* 50.2; Dio 49.31.2. Strabo 16.1.28.748 has Antony 'betrayed' by Artavasdes; cf. 11.13.4.524 and 11.14.9.530. See too Dio 49.25.5. THE CAMPAIGN: Plut. *Ant.* 36-51 is the most detailed account. See also Dio 49.25-31.

124 BREAK: Plut. *Ant.* 52.1, ascribing it first to spoils and then to fear of Parthian incorporation of Atropatene. See too Dio 49.33.1. THREAT IN EAST: Debevoise 123. See Frye, *Persia* 196-201, on the Graeco-Bactrians, the Yüeh-chih, and the Sakas. See also A. von Gutschmid, *Geschichte Irans* 109-115.

125 AFTER THE CAMPAIGN: Plut. *Ant.* 50; Dio 49.33. POLEMO: Dio 49.25, 49.33, 49.44. See Ch. 6, § 15.

126 App. *BCiv.* 5.133-144; Debevoise 133 note 35; Buccheim 88-90; Broughton, *MRR* II 401 and 409. THE YEAR 35: Dio 49.33-34; 49.39.2; Plut. *Ant.* 52. ATROPATENIAN ALLIANCE: Dio 49.40-41 and 44; Plut. *Ant.* 53.6. EGYPT: E.g., Plut. *Ant.* 54.5. See also Dio 49.41. See Ch. 8, § 23; W.W. Tarn in *JRS* 22 (1932) 135 ff. and K. Meiklejohn, *JRS* 24 (1934) 191 ff.

127 PARTHIAN ARISTOCRACY: Frye, *Persia* 219; J. Wolski, 'L'aristocratie parthe et les commencements du féodalisme en Iran': *IA* 7 (1967) 133-144; Rawlinson, *Sixth Monarchy* Ch. 6, 84-95. See G. Košelenko, above note 100; M. Rostovtzeff in *CAH* XI 113-120; W.W. Tarn in *CAH* IX, Ch. XIV, § iv, pp. 588-601. See also Kahrstedt, *Artabanos III. und seine Erben* (Bern 1950) 39: '... an die mannigfachen Unruhen unter Phraates IV und V.' Plut. *Ant.* 53.6 notes an internal struggle (*stasis*) in Parthia during the winter of 35/34. Cf., later, Horace, *Odes* 3.8.19.

128 ARTAVASDES II: Dio 49.39-41; Vell. Pat. 2.82.3: *Artavasden fraude deceptum*. Artaxias is *PIR*² A 1167. See this chapter, § 24.

129 OCTAVIAN AND ARTAVASDES OF ARMENIA: Dio 49.41.5. Debevoise 134 suggests also Verg. *G.* 4.560. ANTONY'S TRIUMPH IN ALEXANDRIA: His jubilation appears in *OGIS* 195 (28 December 34 BC), republished by P.M. Fraser in *JRS* 47 (1957) 71-73 with Fig. 1.

130 ARMENIA AND ATROPATENE, 34 BC AND AFTER: Dio 49.44 and 51.16. See also this chapter, §§ 24-25; Debevoise 134-135; Buccheim 90-91.

131 JUBILATION: Rawlinson, *Sixth Monarchy* 209 note 2; Horace, *Epode* 7.9-10: *ut secundum vota Parthorum sua urbs haec periret dextera.*

132 COINS: *Sammlung Petrowicz* 49-50 nos. 12 ff.; Gardner 43 no. 13 with note; date 280 Sel. = 32/31 BC. See also R.H. McDowell, *Coins from Seleucia on the Tigris* (Ann Arbor 1935) 184-185; E.S.G. Robinson in *NC* (ser. 5) 17 (1937) 250-255: '... Nike and eagle, first introduced by Pacorus and Phraates IV.' TIRIDATES: *PIR* T 175; F. Geyer in *RE* 6A (1937) 1439-1440 ('Tiridates' nr. 4). W.W. Tarn thinks him identical with Monaeses, in *Mélanges Gustav Glotz*, 20 (Paris 1932) 831-837, a suggestion he hesitantly repeats in *CAH* X (1934) 79. Justin 42.5.6: *quendam*. ADVANCE OF TIRIDATES:

Justin 42.5.6: *Hoc [Phraate] absente regem Parthi Tiridaten quendam constituerant.* The incident of the harem would be during the second usurpation of Tiridates, if in fact there were two, since he is described by Isidore of Charax as 'being an exile' at the time of the advance. See C. Müller, *Geographici Graeci Minores*, 1 (Paris 1855) lxxx ff. and 244 ff. = *FGrH* 781 = V. Gardthausen, 'Die Parther in griechisch-römischen Inschriften': *T. Nöldeke zum siebsigsten Geburtstag – Orientalische Studien*, 2, ed. C. Bezold (Gieszen 1906) 839-859, esp. 841-842. On *two* usurpations, see Tarn in *Mél. Glotz*, *ibid.* Two embassies to Octavian need not, however, demonstrate two occupations by Tiridates. *Res Gestae* 32: *Ad me supplices confugerunt reges Parthorum Tiridates et postea Phrates regis Phratis filius.* Justin 42.5: *in exilium a populo suo pellitur.* Horace, *Odes* 3.8.19-20 may refer to later developments in this situation: *Medus infestus sibi luctuosis dissidet armis.* Dio 51.18.2: 'a certain Tiridates' arose after 'dissension among the Parthians'; 53.33.1-2. Horace plays with his topical name much as Cicero did with that of Sampsigeramus: *quid Tiridaten terreat* (*Odes* 2.26.5). He even appears in the metrical inscription mentioning Phraates, which F. Cumont published from Susa: *CRAI* (1930) 211-220. COINS: Wroth, *BMC Parthia* xxxviii-xxxix and 135; *Sammlung Petrowicz* 99; Head *HN*² 820; Gardner 44. OVERSTRUCK COINS: G.F. Hill in *NC* (ser. 5) 7 (1927) 207-208. Overstriking constituted something of a habit with Phraates, including even issues of pseudo-Philip from Antioch: G. Le Rider in *RN* (sér. 6) 2 (1959/1960) 32-33 no. 38. Cf. B. Simonetta, *GNS* 30 (1980) 62-67. The first royal Tiridates may have been a brother of Arsaces I, though the matter is disputed. See J. Wolski in *Historia* 11 (1962) 138-145 and E. Bickerman in *BO* 23 (1966) 15-17. The present king may be the Tyrydt of the Nisa Ostraca: Frye, *Persia* 76 note 11. Magie ignores Tiridates, but Anderson discusses his usefulness to Augustus in *CAH* X 261-263. A Parthian (known from *CIL* III 8746) leading a detachment of his countrymen for Rome could have been a son of this Tiridates: *C. Iul., Thiridatis f., decurio alae Parthorum* (cited by *PIR* T 175 as *prognatus* of this or some other Parthian noble). See also B. Simonetta in *RIN* 78 (1976) 19-34. Chronology of coins also in Debevoise 137 note 45. Tiridates II evidently appeared in or just before 31 BC, and can be traced intermittently through coins until 25. 'SCYTHIANS': Justin 42.5.5-6. Schur, *RE* 18 (1949) 1998, suggests Dahae and Tocharians, vs. E. Herzfeld's Sacae (*Sakastan* 74). Sacaraucae: *CAH* IX 582-587; X 79.

133 ANTONY: Florus 2.21: *cum post Parthos exosus arma in otio ageret ...* FLIGHT OF TIRIDATES: Justin 42.5.6-12, placing Octavian in Spain; Dio 51.18.1-3 has the meeting in Syria. See also Dio 53.33.1-2; Tarn, *Mél. Glotz* 831-837.

134 PHRAATES: Horace, *Odes* 2.2.17-20: *redditum ... Phraaten ... numero beatorum eximit Virtus*; Horace, *Epistles* 12. E.W. Gray, *CR* n.s. 19 (1969) 79 notes: 'The son was sent back after Augustus had finally failed to dislodge Phraates by means of the pretender Tiridates "Philoromaios".' Augustus supplies the royal title and personal name of Phraates, if *Res Gestae* 32 refers to the son of Phraates IV who accompanied Tiridates; he fled to Rome after Tiridates did (*postea*). FOUR SONS: Augustus, for domestic political reasons, describes these as 'all' of the sons of Phraates, a manifest untruth considering the large royal families in Parthia. The harem killed in 31 would have been replaced. See Strabo 16.1.28.748. Evidence on the sons and a stemma: Gardthausen in *T. Nöldecke ... Orientalische Studien*, 2 (Gieszen 1906) 844-845. Another inscription from Telmessus for a Phraates may refer to a son of the King: *ibid.*, 842-843. See also *ILS* 842; R. Syme in *AJP* 99 (1978) 55; Jos. *AJ* 18.40; Debevoise 135-142. Dio 55.10a.5, with Dindorff's emendation, would bring Ariobarzanes II of Atropatene (*PIR*² A 1944) to Rome 'along with Tiridates.'

135 ARISTOCRATS: Tac. *Ann.* 2.1.2: *haud perinde nostri metu quam fidei popularium diffisus.* STANDARDS: Aug. *Res Gestae* 29; Dio 53.33.2; 54.8.1-2. See also T. Mommsen, *Res Gestae Divi Augusti*, 2nd ed. (Berlin 1883) 110 ff.; Anderson in *CAH* X 262-266 and 877-878; R. Syme, *The Roman Revolution* (Oxford 1939) 398. See further *ILS* 918 = *CIL* XIV 3613; B. Levick, *Roman Colonies in Southern Asia Minor* (Oxford 1967) 208-209; L.R. Taylor, *JRS* 26 (1936) 161-173; T. Corbishley in *JRS* 24 (1934) 43-49. PHRAATES V: He was associated on the throne and purportedly even married his own mother, Musa (Thesmusa), the Italian previously sent by Augustus to Phraates IV. See Jos. *AJ* 18.39-44. THESMUSA: *CAH* X 265; Plates IV, 200 d. See also R. Zahn, 'Ein kleines historisches Monument': *Anatolian Studies Presented to Sir William Mitchell Ramsay*, ed. W.H. Buckler and W.M. Calder (Manchester 1923) 441-455 with Pl. 14; Sullivan, *Armenian Question* 107-108. Contrary: Debevoise 143. They ruled jointly: Head *HN*² 820. See too *PIR* P 297; cf. 295; R. MacDowell, *Coins from Seleucia on the Tigris* (Ann Arbor 1935) 147-153. FRIENDSHIP: Aug. *Res Gestae* 32: *non bello superatus, sed amicitiam nostram ... petens.* MURDER OF PHRAATES IV: A.S. Hollis, 'Ovid, *A.A.* i. 197-8: The Wrong Phraates': *CR* n.s. 20 (1970) 141-142; Jos. *AJ* 18.39 and 42; Dio 55.10a.3-4: impending war and popular disloyalty.

136 PARTHIAN EAST: Debevoise Ch. 3. Roman interest extended there too during the empire. E.g., J. Thorley, 'The Roman Empire and the Kushans': *G&R* (ser. 2) 26 (1979) 181-190. These dynasts are studied, with bibliography, in Sullivan's articles shown below (see Selected Bibliography) and in *Armenian Question*. REIGN OF ARTABANUS: See above, this chapter, § 25, notes

71-73. See too U. Kahrstedt, *Artabanos III. und seine Erben* (Bern 1950), with review by E.W. Gray in *JRS* 43 (1953) 164-165; F. Cumont, 'Un lettre du roi Artaban III': *CRAI* (1932) 238-260; Welles, *Royal Correspondence* 299-306, no. 75; M. Rostovtzeff, 'L'Hellenisme en Mésopotamie': *Scientia* 53 (1933) 120-121; Le Rider, *Suse* 35 ff.

137 CONTACT: Moses of Chorene, *Hist. Arm.* 2.69 = *FGrH* 782, Anhang, F 1. EQUALS: Justin 41.1.1: *Parthi, penes quos velut divisione orbis cum Romanis facta nunc Orientis imperium est.* Pliny *HN* 5.88 (cf. 5.25): *duo imperia summa Romanorum Parthorumque.* Jos. *AJ* 18.46: 'mightiest Empires.' Herodian 4.10.2: 'the two greatest domains.' Moses of Chorene: *FGrH* no. 782, Anhang 1 = his *Hist. Arm.* 2.69. See too Amm. Marcell. 23.6.9; Dio 40.14.3: 'considered always a match for the Romans down to the present'; Strabo 11.9.2.515: 'they have become in the mightiness of their domain a match, in a certain way, for the Romans'; Tac. *Ann.* 6.34.3: *imperium Orientis.* See further Plut. *Ant.* 34: Ventidius, who conquered Pacorus I in 38, became the only man until Plutarch's day to celebrate a triumph over the Parthians. EFFECTS: Plut. *Ant.* 34. See Ch. 7, §§ 22 and 19, Ch. 6, §§ 16 and 17, respectively. MUTUAL RECOGNITION: K.-H. Ziegler, *Die Beziehungen zwischen Rom und dem Partherreich: ein Beitrag zur Geschichte des Volkerrechts* (Wiesbaden 1964) Ch. III, Section II 82-96. Dobiáš, *Archiv orientální* 3 (1931) 215-256, questions this equivalence, partly against F. Cumont and Th. Mommsen (his p. 217, note 1). See too E. Dabrowa, *La politique de l'état parthe à l'égard de Rome, d'Artaban II. [= III] à Vologèse I (c. 11 - c. 79 de n.è.)* (Krakow 1983). EUPHRATES BORDER: Strabo 14.5.2.669; 16.1.28.748; Dio 37.6.3. See also Plut. *Pomp.* 33.8; *Mor.* 2.88; Justin 41.6.8 (c. 140 BC); Jos. *AJ* 20.87 (c. AD 51). A survey of the cultural position of Parthia in the East and with regard to Rome is in the lecture of J.B. Ward-Perkins, 'The Roman West and the Parthian East': *PBA* 51 (1965) 174-199. J. Neusner, 'Parthian Political Ideology': *IA* 3 (1963) 40-59, esp. 50 ff., points out the enduring impetus given to Parthian civilization by the victories over Rome under Mithradates III, Orodes II ('I'), and Phraates IV. For a different view of the situation created by the raids of Trajan, see Sir R. Syme, 'How Tacitus Wrote Annals I-III,' *Symbolae ... Lovaniensis*, Series A, Vol. 6 (1977): *Historiographia Antiqua* (*Commentationes ... W. Peremans*) 258-259: '... the Parthian Empire is regarded as a counterpart or rival to Rome. That situation and antithesis ceased to be valid' (Tac. *Ann.* 2.60.4).

Chapter 10

1 *Res Gestae* 27.3. In the absence of detailed argument in this chapter, citation of individual points will be omitted. These can be found in the material by

Bowersock, Braund, Eck, Halfmann, Sullivan, and Walton listed in the Selected Bibliography.

2 AUGUSTUS: Suet. *Aug.* 48. JUBA: *PIR*² J 65; Cleopatra Selene: C 1148. Bibliography and discussion on this family: D. Fishwick, 'Le culte impérial sous Juba II et Ptolémée de Maurétanie: le témoinage des monnaies': *BCTH* 6 (1984).

3 This phenomenon in the coinage: R.D. Sullivan, 'Royal Coins and Rome': *Ancient Coins of the Graeco-Roman World*, ed. W. Heckel and R.D. Sullivan (Waterloo 1984) 145-160.

4 THRACE: Sullivan, 'Thrace' 192 ff., with stemma. TRYPHAENA: Sullivan, 'Pontus' 922-923.

5 *PIR* R 41-42; 50-52; *PIR*² C 1552-54; A 900; J 517.

6 ANCESTRY OF PYTHODORIS: Sullivan, 'Papyri ... Dynastic Network': *ANRW* II 8 (Berlin 1977) 919 ff., esp. note 48 on *OGIS* 377 = *IGRR* IV 1407.

7 PONTUS: Sullivan, 'Pontus' 918 ff., with stemma. See too *PIR* P 405; 834; R 52; *PIR*² A 1197; A 1265; C 1555; J 472. On Polemo II: R.D. Sullivan, 'King Marcus Antonius Polemo': *NC* (ser. 7) 19 (1979) 6-20 with Pl. 2. Braund, *Friendly King* 49-50, questions the conclusions of this article but merely cites the passage of Magie with which it deals, and ignores the numismatic evidence (on p. 11). The papyrus in question is a copy from AD 194, valueless for onomastic evidence as to a common *gentilicium*.

8 GALATIA: See Ch. 2, § 4 and Ch. 6, § 16. See also *PIR*² A 573; D 36; R. Sherk, *ANRW* II 7.2 (Berlin 1980) 954 ff. SEVERUS: *PIR*² J 573. On the Galatian and related families in the second century, see especially the work of S. Mitchell, H. Halfmann, E. Bosch, R. Syme (on the Ummidii). Bibliography on this and discussion regarding the two men named Quadratus: Sullivan, *Festschrift Dörner* 930-937; Sullivan, *ANRW* II 8 (Berlin 1977) 935-936 with stemma on 912. See also R. Sullivan, 'Important Eastern Dynasts in the Papyri': *Proceedings of the Fourteenth International Congress of Papyrologists, Oxford 1974* (London 1975) 285-292. SEVERUS IN ARABIA: G.W. Bowersock, *Roman Arabia* (Cambridge, Mass. and London 1983) 79-85. FRUGI: B. Remy, 'Une famille de Senateurs d'Asie Mineure: Les Ti. Iulii Frugi': *Epigraphica* 45 (1983) 79-93, suggests a Galatian origin for the family.

9 CAPPADOCIA: See Ch. 2, § 5 and Ch. 6, § 17. See also Sullivan, 'Cappadocia' 1149 ff.; *PIR*² A 1023-1024; G 176. Descendants of Glaphyra: A 499-500 (J 136); J 130 and 141. See too *PIR* T 149-150. See further Gwatkin (see Selected Bibliography); T.B. Mitford, *ANRW* II 7.2, 1169-1228; P. Franke in *Chiron* 9 (1979) 377-382.

10 TARCONDIMOTIDS: See Ch. 6, § 18. See also Hoben 195-211; Dio 51.7; Tac. *Ann.* 2.42.5.

11 TRACHEIA: Strabo 14.5.6.671. On the successive kings: R. Sullivan, *NC* (ser. 7) 19 (1979) 6-20, with bibliography there. See also T. B. Mitford, 'Roman Rough Cilicia': *ANRW* II 7.2 (Berlin 1980) 1230-1261; Jones, *CERP*² Ch. 8.

12 COMMAGENE: See Ch. 7, § 19, with Sullivan, 'Commagene' 775-780.

13 Sullivan, 'Commagene' 780-798. See also *PIR* M 452; *PIR*² A 500, 741; J 44, 47-48, 136, 141, 149-151, 228, 541, 650. See too *ILS* 845; D.E.E. Kleiner, *The Monument of Philopappos in Athens* (Rome 1983).

14 Sullivan, 'Emesa' 210 ff.; *PIR*² A 497; J 7, 541.

15 SAMPSIGERAMUS II: E.g., *ILS* 8958 = *IGLSyr* 2760. TIBERIAS: Jos. *AJ* 19.338-342. See too Sullivan, 'Emesa' 213-214; 'Judaea' 324; Schürer (Vermes and Millar) 448 ff., note 34. See also *PIR*² C 1555; H 156; J 131, 149, 472, 541.

16 *PIR*² A 1051, 1693; D 195; J 45, 46, 542, 582. LATER: J 663, 678, 704; *PIR* V 184. JULIA MAESA: *RN* (sér. 6) 11 (1969) 45 ff.; Sullivan, 'Emesa': stemma.

17 JUDAEA: Sullivan, 'Judaea': *ANRW* II 8 296-354 with stemma. Bibliography as cited there. The marriages appear on the stemma following 300. See *PIR*² H 153; J 131-132. Jos. 19.338: Agrippa I was 'outstanding among the other kings.' L. Iulius Agrippa of Apamea may be a descendant of Herod, of Glaphyra (Cappadocia), and of Antiochus IV (Commagene). A series of inscriptions for him appeared in *Ann. Arch. Arabs Syr.* 23 (1973) 39-65, by J.-P. Rey-Coquais. An argument from silence questions Agrippa's royal descent. See also D. Braund in *CQ* 33 (1983) 242; *AE* 1976 nos. 677-686. See above, Ch. 7, § 21, with note 45; Ch. 7, § 22, note 137; Ch. 6, § 17, note 140.

18 SENATORS: W. Eck, *ZPE* 37 (1980) 31-68 and 45 (1982) 139-153; Eck, *Senatoren von Vespasian bis Hadrian* (Munich 1970); see Selected Bibliography. See also H. Halfmann, *Die Senatoren aus dem östlichen Teil des Imperium Romanum bis zum Ende des 2. Jhdt. n. chr.* (Göttingen 1979). Many other studies as cited there. See further M. Hammond, *JRS* 47 (1957) 74-81; C. Walton, *JRS* 19 (1929) 38-66; R. Syme, 'Greeks Invading Roman Government' (Brookline, Mass. 1982; Brademas Lecture); R. Sullivan, 'Priesthoods' (see Selected Bibliography); R. Sherk, *ANRW* II 7.2 (1980) 954-1052; cf. his *Legates* (see Selected Bibliography); C. Habicht, *MDAI(I)* 9/10 (1959/1960) 109-127.

SELECTED BIBLIOGRAPHY

These selected books and articles represent the basic materials used in this study. More specific works appear in the notes to the twenty-six sections.

Allen, R.E., *The Attalid Kingdom: A Constitutional History* (Oxford 1983).

Altheim, F., and R. Stiehl, *Die Araber in der Alten Welt*, I: *Bis zum Beginn der Kaiserzeit* (Berlin 1964).

Ameling, W., *Die Inschriften von Prusias ad Hypium* (Bonn 1985; *IGSK* 27).

Anatolian Studies Buckler: see Calder, W.M., and J. Keil, eds.

Anatolian Studies Ramsay: see Buckler, W.H., and W.M. Calder, eds.

Anokhin, V., *The Coinage of Chersonesus: IV Century B.C.–XII Century A.D.* (Oxford 1980; BAR Suppl. 69).

Applebaum, S., *Jews and Greeks in Ancient Cyrene* (Leiden 1979; Studies in Judaism in Late Antiquity, 28).

Armen, H.K., *Tigranes the Great, a Biography* (Detroit 1940).

Asdourian, P., *Armenien und Rom* (Venice 1911).

Avi-Yonah, M., *Hellenism and the East* (Ann Arbor 1978; publ. University Microfilms International).

Babelon, E., *Description historique et chronologique des monnaies de la république romaine*, 1-2 (Paris 1885-1886).

– *Inventaire de la Collection Waddington* (Paris 1897-1898).

– *Les monnaies des rois de Syrie* (Paris 1890).

– *Traité des monnaies grecques et romaines*, Iere Partie, Vol. I, *Introduction* (Paris 1901); 2e Partie, Vols. I-IV, *Description historique* (Paris 1907-1932).

Badian, E., *Foreign Clientelae (264-70 B.C.)* (Oxford 1958).

– *Roman Imperialism in the Late Republic*, 2nd ed. (Oxford and Ithaca, N.Y. 1968).

– *Studies in Greek and Roman History* (Oxford 1964).

– 'Sulla's Cilician Command': *Athenaeum* 37 (1959) 279-303.

Bagnall, R.S., *The Administration of the Ptolemaic Possessions outside Egypt* (Leiden 1976).

Balsdon, J.P.V.D., *Julius Caesar* (New York 1967).

– *Romans and Aliens* (London and Chapel Hill 1979).

Barker, G., J. Lloyd, and J. Reynolds, eds., *Cyrenaica in Antiquity* (Oxford 1985; Society for Libyan Studies, Occasional Papers, 1).

Bar-Kochva, B., *The Seleucid Army* (Cambridge, Eng. 1979).

von Barloewen, W., *Abriss der Geschichte antiker Randkulturen* (München 1961).

Bartlett, J.R., *Jews in the Hellenistic World: Josephus, Aristeas, the Sibylline Oracles, Eupolemos* (Cambridge, Eng. 1985).

Baumann, U., *Rom und die Juden. Die römisch-jüdischen Beziehungen von Pompeius bis zum Tode des Herodes (63 v. Chr.–4 v. Chr.)* (Frankfurt am Main 1983).

Bean, G., and T. Mitford, *Journeys in Rough Cilicia in 1962 and 1963* (Wien 1965; Denk. Oest. Akad. der Wissen., Phil.-Hist. Klasse, 85).

– *Journeys in Rough Cilicia 1964-1968* (Wien 1970).

Beard, M., and M. Crawford, *Rome in the Late Republic: Problems and Interpretations* (London 1985).

Becher, I., *Das Bild der Kleopatra in der griechischen und lateinischen Literatur* (Berlin 1966; Schr. der Sekt. für Altertumswiss. bei der Deut. Ak. Wiss., 51).

Bell, H.I., *Egypt from Alexander the Great to the Arab Conquest* (Oxford 1948).

Bengtson, H., *The Greeks and the Persians* (London 1969).

– *Grundriss der römischen Geschichte*, 2nd ed. (Munich 1970).

– *Marcus Antonius, Triumvir und Herrscher des Orients* (Munich 1977; Beck'sche Sonderausgaben).

– *Die Strategie in der hellenistischen Zeit. Ein Beitrag zum antiken Staatsrecht*, I-III (Munich 1937-1952; Münchener Beiträge zur Papyrusforschung und antiken Rechtsgeschichte 32).

– *Zum Partherfeldzug des Antonius* (Munich 1974).

Benoist-Méchin, J., *Kleopatra: Ihr Leben, ihre Zeit* (Frankfurt 1982).

Benveniste, E., *Titres et noms propre en Iran ancien* (Paris 1966).

Bernand, A., *Le Delta égyptienne d'après les textes grecs, 1, Les confins libyques* (Cairo 1970).

– *Les inscriptions grécques de Philae*, Tome I: *Époque ptolemaïque* (Paris 1969).

Bernand, E., *Recueil des inscriptions grecques du Fayoum*, I, *La 'méris' d'Hérakleidès* (Leiden 1975). [Cited as: Bernand, *Fayoum* I] Review: J. Bingen, *CE* 51 (1976) 213-219.

Bernand, E. and A., 'Les inscriptions grecques et latines du Colosse de Memnon': *Inst. franç. d'Archéol. orient. du Caire, Bibl. d'Étude* 31 (Paris 1960) 86-92.

Bernhardt, R., *Imperium und Eleutheria. Die römische Politik gegenüber den freien Städten des griechischen Ostens* (Diss. Hamburg 1971; publ. 1972).

Bertinelli, M.G.A., *Roma e l'oriente: Strategia, economia, societa e cultura nella relazioni politiche fra Roma, la Giudea e l'Iran* (Roma 1979; Problemi e ricerche di storia antica, 7).

Bevan, E., *The House of Seleucus* (London 1902).

– 'Antiochus III and His Title "Great King"': *JHS* 22 (1902) 241-244.

Bevan, E.R., *A History of Egypt under the Ptolemaic Dynasty* (London 1927).

Bickerman, E.J., *Chronology of the Ancient World* (London 1968; 2nd ed., 1979).

– *Institutions des Séleucides* (Paris 1938).

– *Religions and Politics in the Hellenistic and Roman Periods*, ed. E. Gabba and M. Smith (Como 1985; Biblioteca di Athenaeum, 5).

– 'The Seleucids and the Achaemenids': *La Persia e il mondo greco romano, Acad. nazionale dei Lincei* 76 (1966) 87-117.

Bingen, J., and others, *Le Monde Grec ... Hommages à Claire Préaux* (Brussels 1975).

Bloedow, E., *Beiträge zur Geschichte des Ptolemaios XII.* (Diss. Würzburg 1963).

Bohn, O., *Qua condicione iuris reges socii populi Romani fuerint* (Diss. Berlin 1876).

Bosch, E., *Quellen zur Geschichte der Stadt Ankara im Altertum* (Ankara 1967; T.T.K.Y. VII Ser., No. 46).

Bouché-Leclerq, A., *Histoire des Lagides*, I-IV (Paris 1903-1907).

– *Histoire des Séleucides (323-64 avant J.C.)*, I-II (Paris 1913-1914).

Bowersock, G.W., *Augustus and the Greek World* (Oxford 1965).

– *Greek Sophists in the Roman Empire* (Oxford 1969).

– 'A Report on Arabia Provincia': *JRS* 61 (1971) 219-242.

– *Roman Arabia* (Cambridge, Mass. and London 1983).

Bradford, A.S., *A Prosopography of Lacedaemonians from the Death of Alexander the Great, 323 B.C., to the Sack of Sparta by Alaric, A.D. 396* (Munich 1977).

Brashear, W., *Ptolemaische Urkunden aus Mummienkartonage* (Berlin 1980; = *BGU* XIV).

Braund, D., *Rome and the Friendly King: The Character of the Client Kingship* (Diss. Cambridge; publ. Beckenham, Kent 1984).

Breccia, E., *Iscrizioni greche e latine = Catalogue général des antiquités égyptiennes du musée d'Alexandrie* (Cairo 1911), nos. 1-568.

Breglia, L.P.D., 'La provincia di Cilicia e gli ordinamenti di Pompeo': *RAAN* (Naples) 47 (1972) 327-387.

Briscoe, J., *A Commentary on Livy (Books XXXI-XXXIII)* (Oxford 1973).

– 'Eastern Policy and Senatorial Politics, 168-146 B.C.': *Historia* 18 (1969) 48-70.

Broughton, T.R.S., *The Magistrates of the Roman Republic*, I-II; Supplements (Lancaster, Pa.; New York 1951-1952, 1960, 1986). [Abbreviated *MRR*]

Buccheim, H., *Die Orientpolitik des Triumvirn M. Antonius* (Heidelberg 1960).

Buckler, W.H., and W.M. Calder, eds., *Anatolian Studies Presented to Sir William Mitchell Ramsay* (Manchester 1923).

Buckler, W.H., and D.M. Robinson, *Publications of the American Society for the Excavation of Sardis*, Vol. VII, 1: *Greek & Latin Inscriptions* (Leiden 1932).

Burney, C., and D.M. Lang, *The People of the Hills: Ancient Ararat and Caucasus* (London 1971).

Burstein, S., *The Hellenistic Age from the Battle of Ipsos to the Death of Kleopatra VII* (Cambridge, Eng. 1985; Translated Documents of Greece and Rome, Vol. 3).

Cagnat, R., and others, *Inscriptiones Graecae ad Res Romanas Pertinentes*, I, III, IV (Paris 1906-1927). [Abbreviated *IGRR*]

Calder, W.M., and G.E. Bean, *A Classical Map of Asia Minor* (London 1958).

Calder, W.M., and J. Keil, eds., *Anatolian Studies Presented to William Hepburn Buckler* (Manchester 1939).

Cary, M., *The Geographic Background of Greek and Roman History* (Oxford 1949).

Chahin, M., *The Kingdom of Armenia* (Beckenham, Kent 1987).

Chitescu, M., *Numismatic Aspects of the History of the Dacian State: The Roman Republican Coinage in Dacia and Geto-Dacian Coins of Roman Type* (British Arch. Reports, Oxford 1981).

Cichorius, C., *Römische Studien: Historisches, Epigraphisches, Literargeschichtliches aus vier Jahrhunderten Roms* (Leipzig 1922).

Cimma, M.R., *Reges Socii et Amici Populi Romani* (Milan 1976; Univ. di Roma: Pubbl. dell'Istituto di Diritto Romano e dei Diritti del'Oriente Mediterraneo, 50).

Cohen, G.M., *The Seleucid Colonies: Studies in Founding, Administration and Organization* (Wiesbaden 1978).

Colledge, M.A.R., *Parthian Art* (London 1977).

– *The Parthian Period* (Leiden 1986; Iconography of Religions, XIV.3).

– *The Parthians* (London 1967; Ancient Peoples and Places). Review: E.W. Gray, *CR* n.s. 19 (1969) 77-80.

Corsten, T., *Die Inschriften von Kios* (Bonn 1985; *IGSK* 29).

Craven, L., *Antony's Oriental Policy until the Defeat of the Parthian Expedition* (St. Louis 1920; University of Missouri Studies 3).

Crawford, M., *The Roman Republic* (Glasgow 1978; Fontana History of the Ancient World series).

– *Roman Republican Coinage*, I (Cambridge, Eng. 1974).

– *Roman Republican Coin Hoards* (London 1969; Royal Numismatic Society, Special Publications No. 4).

– ed., *Sources for Ancient History* (Cambridge, Eng. 1983).

Crawford, D., with J. Quaegebeur and W. Clarysse, *Studies on Ptolemaic Memphis* (Leuven/Louvain 1980; Studia Hellenistica 24).

Cumont, F., 'L'annexion du Pont polémoniaque et de la petite Arménie': *Anatolian Studies Presented to W.M. Ramsay* (Manchester 1923) 109-119.

– *Études syriennes* (Paris 1917).
– *Fouilles de Dura Europos* (Paris 1926).
Dabrowa, E., *La politique de l'état parthe à l'égard de Rome, d'Artaban II. [*= III] à Vologèse I. (c. 11–c. 79 de n.è.) (Krakow 1983).
Dalman, G., *Palästinische Forschungen zur Archäologie und Topographie*, II, *Neue Petra-Forschungen der Heilige Felsen von Jerusalem* (Leipzig 1912).
Danov, M., *Altthrakien* (Berlin 1976).
– 'Die Thraker auf dem Ostbalkan von der hellenistischen Zeit bis zur Gründung Konstantinopels': *ANRW* II 7.1 (Berlin 1979) 21-185.
Danov, C., and T. Ivanov, *Antike Grabmäler in Bulgarien* (Berlin 1980).
Davis, N., and C.M. Kraay, *The Hellenistic Kingdoms: Portrait Coins and History* (London 1973).
Debevoise, N.C., *A Political History of Parthia* (Chicago 1938).
Degrassi, A., *Inscriptiones Latinae Liberae Rei Publicae*, I (Firenze 1957). [Abbreviated *ILLRP*]
– *Scritti vari di antichita*, I (Rome 1962).
Desideri, P., 'Posidonio e la guerra mitridatica': *Athenaeum* n.s. 51 (1973) 3-29, 237-269.
Dessau, H., *Inscriptiones Latinae Selectae*, I-III (Berlin 1892-1916). [Abbreviated *ILS*]
– 'Miscellanea Epigraphica I et II': *Ephem. Epigr.* 9 (1913) 691-705.
Dessau, H., and others, *Prosopographia Imperii Romani*, I-III (Berlin 1897-1898). [Abbreviated *PIR*]
Dittenberger, W., *Orientis Graeci Inscriptiones Selectae*, I-II (Leipzig 1903 and 1905). [Abbreviated *OGIS*]
– *Sylloge Inscriptionum Graecarum*, I-IV, 3rd ed. (Leipzig 1915-1924). [Abbreviated *SIG*^{3}]
Dobiáš, J., 'Les premiers rapports des romains avec les parthes et l'occupation de la Syrie': *Archiv orientální* 3 (1931) 215-256.
Dörner, F.K., 'Die Ahnengalerie der kommagenischen Königsdynastie': *Antike Welt* 6 (1975) 26-31, Sondernummer 'Kommagene'.
– *The Inscriptions of Nicomedia and Its Territory* (Vienna 1979; *TAM* IV.1).
– *Kommagene: Ein wiederentdecktes Königreich* (Böblingen 1971).
– 'Kommagene: Forschungsarbeiten von 1967 bis 1969': *MDAI(I)* 19/20 (1969/1970) 255-288.
– *Kommagene, Götterthrone und Königsbräber am Euphrat* (Regensberg 1981).
– 'Zur Rekonstruktion der Ahnengalerie des Königs Antiochos I. von Kommagene': *MDAI(I)* 17 (1967) 195-210.
Dörner, F., and T. Goell, *Arsameia am Nymphaios: Die Ausgrabungen im Hierothesion des Mithradates Kallinikos von 1953-1956* (Berlin 1963; Istanbuler Forschungen 23). For further work here see under Hoepfner, W.
Dörner, F., and R. Naumann, *Forschungen in Kommagene* (Berlin 1939).

Dörrie, H., *Der Königskult des Antiochus von Kommagene im Lichte neuer Inschriften-Funde* (Göttingen 1964).

Downey, G., *A History of Antioch in Syria* (Princeton, N.J. 1961).

Drijvers, H.J.W., *Cults and Beliefs at Edessa* (Leiden 1980; *EPRO* 82).

– 'Hatra, Palmyra, und Edessa. Die Städte der syrisch-mesopotamischen wüste in politischer, kulturgeschichtlicher und religionsgeschichtlicher Beleuchtung': *ANRW* II 8 (Berlin 1977) 799-906.

Droysen, J.G., *Histoire de l'Hellenisme*, I-II (Paris 1883-1885).

Dupont-Sommer, A., and L. Robert, *La déesse de Hiérapolis Castabala (Cilicie)* (Paris 1964; Bibl. arch. et hist. de l'inst. franç. d'arch. d'Istanbul, 16).

Durrbach, F., *Choix d'inscriptions de Délos* (Paris 1921-1922).

– *Inscriptions de Délos*, 1-6 (Paris and Berlin 1926 ff.), esp. Vol. V, *Dédicaces postérieures à 166 av. J.C.* (1937).

Dussaud, R., *La pénétration des Arabes en Syrie avant l'Islam* (Paris 1955; Institut français d'archéologie de Beyrouth, Bibl. Archéol. et Historique, 59).

Dyson, S., *The Creation of the Roman Frontier* (Princeton, N.J. 1985). Mainly concerned with the West.

Eckhel, J., *Catalogus Musei Caesarei Vindobonensis numorum veterum*, I, new ed. (Wien 1828).

– *Doctrina Nummorum Veterum*, I-VIII and volume of Addenda (Vienna 1792-1839).

Eck, V., *Senatoren von Vespasian bis Hadrian, Prosopographische Untersuchungen mit Einschluss der Jahres- und Provinzialfasten der Statthalter* (Munich 1970; Vestigia 13).

Eddy, S.K., *The King Is Dead: Studies in the Near-East Resistance to Hellenism* (Lincoln, Nebr. 1961).

Ehrenberg, V., and A.H.M. Jones, *Documents Illustrating the Reigns of Augustus and Tiberius*, 2nd ed. (Oxford 1955).

Ferguson, W.S., *Greek Imperialism* (New York 1963).

– *Hellenistic Athens* (London 1911).

Ferrara, J., *Poematis latini reliquiae ex volumine Herculanensi* (Pavia 1908); contains the *carmen de bello Aegyptiaco*.

Festugière, A.-J., *Antioche payenne et chrétienne* (Paris 1959).

Finley, M.I., *The Ancient Economy* (Berkeley 1973).

– *Ancient History: Evidence and Models* (London 1985).

Fischer, T., *Untersuchungen zur Partherkrieg Antiochos' VII im Rahmen der Seleukidengeschichte* (Diss. München; publ. Tübingen 1970).

– 'Zum Kult des Antiochos' I. von Kommagene für seine seleukidischen Ahnen': *MDAI(I)* 22 (1972) 141-144.

Flaceliere, R., 'Rome et ses empereurs vus par Plutarch': *AntCl* 32 (1963) 28-47.

Foraboschi, D., *Onomasticon Alterum Papyrologicum* (Milan 1967).

Franck, L., 'Sources classiques concernants la Cappadoce': *Revue Hittite et Asianique* 24 (1966) 5-122.

Frank, T., *Roman Imperialism* (New York 1914).

– ed., *An Economic Survey of Ancient Rome*, I-V (Baltimore 1933-1940). [Abbreviated *ESAR*]. Vol. IV, Part II is on Roman Syria, by F. Heichelheim; Part IV is on Roman Asia, by T.R.S. Broughton.

Fraser, P.M., *Ptolemaic Alexandria*, 1-3 (Oxford 1972). Review: E.G. Turner, *JEA* 60 (1974) 290 ff.

Frelova, N., *The Coinage of the Kingdom of the Bosporus, A.D. 69-238* (Oxford 1979; BAR Suppl. 56).

Frisch, P., *Die Inschriften von Ilium* (Bonn 1975; *IGSK* 3).

– *Die Inschriften von Lampsakos* (Bonn 1978; *IGSK* 6).

Frye, R., *The Heritage of Persia* (London 1963).

– *The History of Ancient Iran* (Munich 1984).

Fuchs, H., *Der geistige Widerstand gegen Rom in der antiken Welt* (Berlin 1938).

Gaetringen, F. Hiller von, *Die Inschriften von Priene* (Berlin 1906).

Gagé, J., *Basiléia. Les Césars. Les rois d'Orient et les 'Mages'* (Paris 1968; Budé. Coll. d'ét. anciennes).

Gajdukevič, V.F., *Das Bosporanische Reich* (Berlin 1971).

Gardner, A., and others, *Theban Ostraca* (Oxford 1913).

Gardner, P., *The Coinage of Parthia* (London 1877; repr. 1968).

Garnsey, P.D.A., and C.R. Whittaker, eds., *Imperialism in the Ancient World* (Cambridge, Eng. 1978).

Gelzer, M., *Caesar* (Berlin/Stuttgart 1921; English trans. Oxford 1968).

– *Pompeius* (Munich 1949).

Ghirshman, A., *Iran: Parthians and Sassanians* (London 1962).

Gočeva, Z., and M. Oppermann, *Monumenta orae Ponti Euxini Bulgariae* (Leiden 1979; *EPRO* 74).

Graindor, P., *Athènes de Tibère à Trajan* (Cairo 1931; Université égyptienne, recueil de travaux publiés par la faculté des lettres, 8).

– *Athènes sous Auguste* (Cairo 1927).

– *La guerre d'Alexandrie* (Cairo 1931; Université égyptienne, recueil de travaux publiés par la faculté des lettres, 7).

Grant, Michael, *Cleopatra* (London 1972).

Greene, K., *The Archaeology of the Roman Economy* (London 1986).

Griffith, G.T., *Mercenaries of the Hellenistic World* (Cambridge, Eng. 1935).

Grimal, P., and others, *Hellenism and the Rise of Rome* (London 1968).

Groag, E., A. Stein, and L. Petersen, *Prosopographia Imperii Romani*, 2nd ed. (Berlin 1933-present). [Abbreviated *PIR*²]

Grose, S.W., *Catalogue of the McClean Collection of Greek Coins, Fitzwilliam Museum*, 1-3 (Cambridge, Eng. 1923-1929).

Grueber, H., *Coins of the Roman Republic in the British Museum*, 1-3 (London 1910).

Gruen, E.S., *The Hellenistic World and the Coming of Rome*, I-II (Berkeley 1984).

– *The Last Generation of the Roman Republic* (Berkeley and Los Angeles 1974).

– ed., *Imperialism in the Roman Republic* (New York 1970).

von Gutschmid, A., *Geschichte Irans und seiner Nachbarländer von Alexander dem Grossen bis zum Untergang der Arsaciden*, ed. Th. Nöldeke (Tübingen 1888). A version appeared in the *Encyclopedia Britannica*, ninth edition, s.v. 'Persia.'

– 'Untersuchungen über die Geschichte des Königreichs Osroëne': *Mémoires de l'Académie impériale des Sciences de St.-Pétersbourg* (sér. 7) 35 (1887) 1-49.

Gwatkin, W.E., *Cappadocia as a Roman Procuratorial Province* (Princeton, N.J. 1930; University of Missouri Studies, V).

Habicht, C., *Alterümer von Pergamon*, VIII.3, *Die Inschriften des Asklepieions* (Berlin 1969).

– 'Zwei neue Inschriften aus Pergamon': *MDAI(I)* 9/10 (1959/1960) 109-127.

Halfmann, H., *Die Senatoren aus dem östlichen Teil des Imperium Romanum bis zum Ende des 2. Jhdt. n. Chr.* (Göttingen 1979; Hypomnemata, 58).

Hammond, M., 'Composition of the Senate, A.D. 68-235': *JRS* 47 (1957) 74-81.

Hammond, P.C., *The Nabataeans: Their History, Culture, and Archaeology* (Gothenburg 1973).

Hansen, E.V., *The Attalids of Pergamon*, 2nd ed. (Ithaca, N.Y. 1971; Amsterdam 1972).

Harris, W.V., *War and Imperialism in Republican Rome, 327-70 B.C.* (Oxford 1979).

Haspels, C., *The Highlands of Phrygia* (Princeton, N.J. 1971).

Head, B.V., *Historia Numorum. A Manual of Greek Numismatics*, 2nd ed. (Oxford 1911). [Abbreviated Head, HN^2]

Heberdey, R. and A. Wilhelm, *Reisen in Kilikien, ausgeführt 1891 und 1892 im Auftrage des Kaiserlichen Akademie der Wissenschaften* (Wien 1896; Denkschriften Akad. Wiss., Phil.-Hist. Kl., 44) 1-168.

Heckel, W., and R. Sullivan, eds., *Ancient Coins of the Graeco-Roman World: The Nickle Numismatic Papers* (Waterloo 1984).

Heinen, H., *Rom und Ägypten von 51 bis 47 v. Chr.: Untersuchungen zur Regierungszeit des 7. Kleopatra und des 13. Ptolemäers* (Diss. Tübingen; publ. St. Vith 1966).

Hennig, R., *Symbolae ad Asiae Minoris Reges Sacerdotes Polemonemque I. Ponti Regem* (Leipzig 1893).

Herrmann, P., *Tituli Lydiae linguis Graeca et Latina conscripti. Fasc. 1: Regis septentrionalis ad orientem vergens* (Vienna 1981; *TAM* V).

Herzfeld, E., *Am Tor von Asien* (Berlin 1920).

– *An Archaeological History of Iran* (London 1935).

– *Iran in the Ancient East* (London 1941).

– *The Persian Empire: Studies in the Geography, History, and Ethnography of the Ancient Near East*, ed. G. Walser (Wiesbaden 1968).

– 'Sakastan, Geschichtliche Untersuchungen zu den Ausgrabungen am Kūh i Khwādja': *Archaeologische Mitteilungen aus Iran* 4 (1931) 1-116; maps on pp. 24 and 116.

Hill, G.F., *Catalogue of the Greek Coins of Arabia, Mesopotamia, and Persia in the British Museum* (London 1922).

Hoben, W., *Untersuchungen zur Stellung kleinasiatischer Dynasten in den Machtkämpfen der ausgehenden römischen Republik* (Diss. Mainz 1969).

Hoepfner, W., *Arsameia am Nymphaios II. Die Hierothesion des Königs Mithradates I. Kallinikos von Kommagene nach den Ausgrabungen von 1963 bis 1967* (Tübingen 1983; Istanbuler Forschungen 33). For part I see under Dörner, F.K.

Holleaux, M., *Études d'épigraphie et d'histoire grecques*, I-VI (Paris 1938-1968).

Holmes, T.R., *The Architect of the Roman Empire*, 1-2 (Oxford 1928-1931).

Honigmann, E., *Historische Topographie von Nordsyrien im Altertum* (Leipzig 1923).

Hörig, M., and E. Schwertheim, *Corpus Cultus Iovis Dolicheni (CCID)* (Leiden 1986; *EPRO* 106).

Humann, K., and O. Puchstein, *Reisen in Kleinasien und Nordsyrien* (Berlin 1890).

Huzar, E.G., *Mark Antony: A Biography* (Minneapolis 1978; London 1986). Review: E. Gruen, *CJ* 77 (1981-1982) 63-65.

Ihnken, T., *Die Inschriften von Magnesia am Sipylos* (Bonn 1978; *IGSK* 8).

Imhoof-Blumer, F., *Kleinasiatische Münzen*, II (Wien 1902).

Instinsky, H., 'Bemerkungen über die ersten Schenkungen des Antonius an Kleopatra' in G.E. Mylonas, ed., *Studies Presented to D.M. Robinson* (St. Louis 1951-1953) 975-979.

Isaac, B., and I. Roll, *Roman Roads in Judaea I: The Legio-Scythopolis Road* (British Arch. Reports 1982).

Jacoby, F., *Die Fragmente der griechischen Historiker*, 13 vols. (Leiden 1923-1958). [Abbreviated *FGrH* or *FGrHist*]

Jalabert, L., with R. Mouterde and others, *Inscriptions grecques et latines de la Syrie*, I-XIII (Paris 1929-1982). [Abbreviated *IGLS* or *IGLSyr*]

Janke, M., *Historische Untersuchungen zu Memnon von Herakleia, Kap. 18-40, FgrHist Nr. 434* (Diss. Würzburg 1963).

Jones, A.H.M., *Augustus* (New York 1970).

– *The Cities of the Eastern Roman Provinces*, 2nd ed. (Oxford 1971). [Abbreviated Jones, *Cities*²]

– *The Herods of Judaea* (Oxford 1938).

Jones, C.P., *Plutarch and Rome* (Oxford 1971).

Justi, F., *Iranisches Namenbuch* (Marburg 1895).

Kahrstedt, U., *Artabanos III. und seine Erben* (Bern 1950).

Kajanto, I., *Supernomina: A Study in Latin Epigraphy* (Helsinki 1966).

Keaveney, A., *Sulla: The Last Republican* (London 1982).

Keil, J., and A. Wilhelm, *Denkmäler aus den Rauhen Kilikien* (Manchester 1931; = *MAMA* III).

Keller, D.R., and D.W. Rupp, eds., *Archaeological Survey in the Mediterranean Area* (Oxford 1983; British Arch. Reports).

Kennedy, D.L., *Archaeological Explorations on the Roman Frontier in North-East Jordan* (Oxford 1982).

Kindler, A., *The Coinage of Bostra* (Warminster 1983).

Kirsten, E., 'Diokaisareia und Sebaste': *AAWW* 110 (1973) 347-363.

– 'Elaiussa-Sebaste in Kilikien': *Mansel'e Armagam, Mélanges Mansel* II (Ankara 1974) 777-802.

Kleiner, D.E.E., *The Monument of Philopappus in Athens* (Rome 1983; Archaeologica 30).

Koehler, H., *Die Nachfolge in der Seleukidenherrschaft und die parthische Haltung im römisch- pontischen Konflikt* (Bochum 1978; Bochumer Historische Studien, Alte Geschichte nr. 3).

Kraay, C.M., and G.K. Jenkins, *Essays in Greek Coinage Presented to Stanley Robinson* (Oxford 1968).

Krüger, F., *Orient und Hellas in den Denkmälern und Inschriften des Königs Antiochos von Kommagene* (Greifswald 1937).

Langlois, V., *Historicorum Graecorum et Syriorum reliquiae in Armeniorum scriptis servatae* (Paris 1867) = Müller, *Fragmenta Historicorum Graecorum* V, Part 2.

– *Inscr. grecques, romaines, byzantines et arméniennes de la Cilicie* (Paris 1854).

– *Voyage dans la Cilicie et dans les montagnes du Taurus* (Paris 1861).

Latyschev, B., *Corpus Inscriptionum Regni Bosporani* (Moscow-Leningrad 1965). [Abbreviated *CIRB*]

– *Inscriptiones antiquae orae septentrionalis Ponti Euxini Graecae et Latinae*, 2nd ed. (Petersburg 1916). [Abbreviated *IOSPE*]

Launey, M., *Recherches sur les armées hellénistiques*, 1-2 (Paris 1949-1950).

Leach, J., *Pompey the Great* (1978; repr. London 1986).

Le Bas, P., and W.H. Waddington, *Voyage archéologique en Grèce et en Asie Mineure fait pendant les années 1843 et 1844*, I-VI (Paris 1853-1870).

Lenger, M.-T., *Corpus des Ordonnances des Ptolémées (C. Ord. Ptol.)* (Brussels 1964; 2nd ed., 1980).

Le Rider, G., *Suse sous les Séleucides et les Parthes: Les trouvailles monétaires et l'histoire de la ville* (Paris 1965; Mémoires de la mission archéologique en Iran, 38: Mission de Susiane).

Lesquier, J., *L'armée romaine d'Égypte d' Auguste à Diocletien* (Cairo 1918).

Levick, B., *Roman Colonies in Southern Asia Minor* (Oxford 1967).

Lewis, N., *Greeks in Ptolemaic Egypt* (Oxford 1986).
Liebmann-Frankfort, Th., *La frontière orientale dans la politique extérieure de la République romaine depuis le traité d'Apamée jusqu' à la fin des conquêtes asiatiques de Pompée (189/8-63)* (Bruxelles 1969; Académie royale de Belgique, Classe des Lettres: Mémoires, deuxième série, LIX, fasc. 5).
Lifshitz, B., 'L'hellénisation des Juifs de Palestine': *Rev. Bibl.* 72 (1965) 520-538.
– 'Inscriptions grecques du royaume du Bosphore': *Epigraphica* 32 (1970) 7-34.
Lindner, M., *Petra und das Königreich der Nabatäer* (Munich 1970).
Luce, T., 'Marius and the Mithridatic Command': *Historia* 19 (1970) 161-194.
Luttwak, E.N., *The Grand Strategy of the Roman Empire from the First Century A.D. to the Third* (Baltimore 1976).
Machatschek, A., *Die Nekropolen und Grabmäler im Gebiet von Elaiussa Sebaste und Korykos im Rauhen Kilikien* (Wien 1967; Ergänzungsbände zu den *Tituli Asiae Minoris* 2).
Macurdy, G., *Hellenistic Queens* (Baltimore 1932; Johns Hopkins Studies in Archaeology, 14).
– 'Iotape': *JRS* 26 (1936) 40-42.
– *Vassal Queens* (Baltimore 1937; Johns Hopkins Studies in Archaeology, 22).
MacAdam, H.I., *Studies in the History of the Roman Province of Arabia: The Northern Sector* (Oxford 1986; British Archaeological Reports, S295).
MacDonald, G., *Catalogue of Greek Coins in the Hunterian Collection* (Glasgow 1905).
Maehler, H., 'Egypt under the Last Ptolemies': *BICS* 30 (1983) 1-16.
Maehler, H., and V.M. Strocka, *Das ptolemäische Ägypten* (Mainz am Rhein 1976; Akten des internationalen Symposions 27).
Magie, D., *Roman Rule in Asia Minor to the End of the Third Century after Christ*, 1-2 (Princeton, N.J. 1950).
Manandian, H., *Tigrane II et Rome*, trans. H. Thorossian (Lisbon 1963).
Mansel, A.M., *Türkiyenin arkeologi, epigrafi ve tarihî coğrafyasi için bibliyografya* (Ankara 1948).
Manuwald, B., *Cassius Dio and Augustus* (Wiesbaden 1979).
Marquardt, J., *Römische Staatsverwaltung*, I-IV, 2nd ed. (Leipzig 1881-1885).
Marsh, F.B., *The Founding of the Roman Empire* (London 1927).
Mason, H.J., *Greek Terms for Roman Institutions* (Toronto 1975; American Studies in Papyrology, 13).
Matheson, S.A., *Persia: An Archaeological Guide* (London 1972).
Mattingly, H., and R.A.G. Carson, *Coins of the Roman Empire in the British Museum*, I-V (London 1923-1950).
Mattingly, H., and E.A. Sydenham, *The Roman Imperial Coinage*, I, *Augustus to Vitellius* (London 1923).
McCabe, D., and M. Plunkett, *Lists and Texts of the Inscriptions of Didyma*

(Princeton, N.J. 1985). Under a similar title, the same two authors have published texts from Teos, Colophon, Notium, Miletus, and elsewhere, beginning 1984.

McCrum, M., and A.G. Woodhead, *Select Documents of the Principates of the Flavian Emperors* (Cambridge 1966). Reviews: P.M. Fraser, *JEA* 48 (1962) 141-142, and L. Robert, *REG* (1964) 127-128.

McDowell, R., *Stamped and Inscribed Objects from Seleucia on the Tigris* (Ann Arbor 1935).

McDowell, R.H., *Coins from Seleucia on the Tigris* (Ann Arbor 1935).

McEwan, C.W., *The Oriental Origin of Hellenistic Kingship* (Chicago 1934).

McGing, B.C., *The Foreign Policy of Mithridates VI Eupator, King of Pontus* (Leiden 1986; Mnemosyne, Supplement 89).

McShane, R.B., *The Foreign Policy of the Attalids of Pergamon* (Urbana, Ill. 1964).

Mélanges Bidez, I-II (Bruxelles 1934; Annuaire de l'institut de philologie et d'histoire orientales, Université Libre de Bruxelles).

Mellor, R., *Thea Rōmē. The Worship of the Goddess Roma in the Greek World* (Göttingen 1975).

Merkelbach, R., *Die Inschriften von Chalkedon* (Bonn 1980; *IGSK* 20).

Merkelbach, R., and others, *Die Inschriften von Ephesos*, II-VII.1-2 (Bonn 1979-1981; *IGSK* 12-17.1-2). See also under Wankel, H.

Meshorer, Y., *Nabataean Coins* (Jerusalem 1975; Qedem 3: Monographs of the Institute of Archaeology, The Hebrew University of Jerusalem).

Meyer, E., *Geschichte des Königreiches Pontus* (Leipzig 1879).

Meyer, P., *Das Heerwesen der Ptolemäer und Römer in Ägypten* (Leipzig 1900).

Michaelidou-Nicolaou, I., *Prosopography of Ptolemaic Cyprus* (Göteborg 1976; Studies in Mediterranean Archaeology, 44).

Mihailov, G., *Inscriptiones Graecae, Bulgaria Repertae* I, 2nd ed. (Sophia 1970). [Abbreviated *I.G.Bulg.* or *IGBR*]

Millar, F., *The Emperor in the Roman World (31 B.C.-A.D. 337)* (London 1977).

– epigraphy: see his discussion in M. Crawford, ed., *Sources for Ancient History* (Cambridge, Eng. 1983) 80-136.

– ed. *The Roman Empire and Its Neighbours* (London 1967).

– *A Study of Cassius Dio* (Oxford 1964).

Millar, F., and G. Vermes, eds., see under Schürer, E.

Milne, J.G., *Theban Ostraca* (London and Oxford 1913).

Minns, E., 'Parchments of the Parthian Period from Avroman in Kurdistan': *JHS* 35 (1915) 22-65.

Mionnet, T., *Description de médailles antiques, grecques et romaines, avec leur degré de rareté et leur estimation*, I-VII and *Suppléments* I-IX (Paris 1805-1837; Bibliotheque du Roi).

Mitchell, S., *Armies and Frontiers in Roman and Byzantine Anatolia, Proceedings of a Colloquium Held at University College, Swansea* (British Institute of Archaeology at Ankara Monograph no. 5, Oxford 1981).

– *Regional Epigraphic Catalogues of Asia Minor II; The Ankara District: The Inscriptions of North Galatia* (British Arch. Reports, Oxford 1982).

Mitteis, L., and U. Wilcken, *Grundzüge und Chrestomathie der Papyruskunde* (Leipzig 1912).

Momigliano, A.D., *Alien Wisdom: The Limits of Hellenization* (Cambridge, Eng. 1975).

Mommsen, T., 'Die Dynastie von Kommagene': *MDAI(A)* 1 (1876) 27-39.

– 'Observationes Epigraphicae, XIII. De Titulo Reginae Pythodoridis Smyrnaeo': *Ephem. Epigr.* 1 (1876) 270-278.

– *Res Gestae Divi Augusti ex Monumentis Ancyrano et Apolloniensi*, 2nd ed. (Berlin 1883).

Mond, R., and O. Meyers, *The Bucheum*, I-III (London 1934).

Mooren, L., *La hiérarchie de cour ptolémaïque* (Leuven 1977; Studia Hellenistica 23).

– *The Aulic Titulature in Ptolemaic Egypt: Introduction and Prosopography* (Brussels 1975).

Moretti, L., *Inscriptiones Graecae Urbis Romae*, I (Rome 1968).

Mørkholm, O., *Antiochus IV of Syria* (Copenhagen 1966).

– *Sylloge Nummorum Graecorum: The Royal Collection of Coins and Medals, Danish National Museum, 39: Parthia-India* (Copenhagen 1965).

Müller, C., *Fragmenta Historicorum Graecorum*, 1-5 (Paris 1841-1870). See also under Langlois, V.

– *Geographici Graeci Minores* (Paris 1855-1861).

Münsterberg, R., *Die römischen Kaisernamen der griechische Münzen* (Vienna 1927).

Negev, A., *Nabataean Archaeology Today* (New York 1986).

– 'The Nabataeans and the Provincia Arabia': *ANRW* II 8 (Berlin 1977) 520-686; Plates I-XLVIII; maps and figures.

Neugebauer, O., and K. Van Hoesen, *Greek Horoscopes* (Philadelphia 1959).

Neusner, J., *A History of the Jews in Babylonia*, I: *The Parthian Period* (Leiden 1965, rev. 1968).

– 'The Jews East of the Euphrates': *ANRW* II 9.1 (Berlin 1976) 46-69.

Newell, E.T., *The Coinage of the Eastern Seleucid Mints = Numismatic Studies* 1 (New York 1938).

– 'The Coinage of the Parthians' in A.U. Pope, ed., *A Survey of Persian Art*, I (London and New York 1938).

– *The Coinage of the Western Seleucid Mints = Numismatic Studies* 4 (New York 1941).

– *Late Seleucid Mints in Ake-Ptolemais and Damascus* (New York 1939; *NNM* 84).

– *Mithradates of Parthia and Hyspaosines of Characene: A Numismatic Palimpsest* (New York 1925; *NNM* 26).
– *Some Unpublished Coins of Eastern Dynasts* (New York 1926; *NNM* 30).
Nicolet, C., *Rome et la conquête du monde méditerranéen, 264-27 avant J.-C.*, II (Paris 1978).
Nodelman, A., 'A Preliminary History of Characene': *Berytus* 13 (1960) 83-121.
Oates, D., *Studies in the Ancient History of Northern Iraq* (London 1968).
Oliver, J.H., *The Civic Tradition and Roman Athens* (Baltimore and London 1983).
Olsen, R.A., 'Studies in the Coinage of the Arsacid Rulers of Parthia' (Diss. U. of Minnesota, 1968; *DA* 30 [1969] 234 A).
Olshausen, E., 'Mithradates VI. und Rom': *ANRW* I 1 (Berlin-New York 1972) 806-815.
– 'Pontos': *RE Suppl.* XV (1978), cols. 396-442.
– 'Pontos und Rom (63 v. Chr.-64 n. Chr.)': *ANRW* II 7.2 (1980) 903-912.
– *Prosopographie der hellenistischen Königsgesandten*, I ff. (Louvain 1974 ff.).
– *Rom und Ägypten von 116 bis 51 v. Chr.* (Basel 1963; Diss. Erlangen-Nürnberg).
Olshausen, E., J. Biller, and J. Wagner, *Historisch-geographische Aspekte der Geschichte des Pontischen und Armenien Reiches*, I: *Untersuchungen zur historischen Geographie von Pontos unter den Mithradatiden* (Wiesbaden 1984; Beihefte zum Tübinger Atlas des Vorderen Orients [*TAVO*], Reihe B, 29).
Olshausen, E., and J. Wagner, 'Asia Minor and Black Sea Area: The Epoch of Mithradates the Great (121-63 B.C.)' = *Tübinger Atlas des Vorderen Orients* (*TAVO*) B V 6 (Wiesbaden 1981).
Ormerod, H.A., *Piracy in the Ancient World: An Essay in Mediterranean History* (Liverpool 1978).
Otto, W., and H. Bengtson, *Zur Geschichte des Niederganges des Ptolemäerreiches: Ein Beitrag zur Regierungszeit des 8. und des 9. Ptolemäers* (Munich 1938; *ABAW* N.F. 17).
Pani, M., 'Archelao II e la fine della dinastia dei Teucridi di Olba': *Athenaeum* n.s. 48 (1970) 327-334.
– *Roma e i re d'Oriente da Augusto a Tiberio (Cappadocia, Armenia, Media Atrop patene)* (Bari 1972).
Parker, H.M.D., *The Roman Legions*, 2nd ed. (Cambridge, Eng. 1958).
Pedley, J., *Studies in the History and Archaeology of Sardis* (Diss. Harvard 1965).
Peremans, W., with E. van' t Dack and others, *Prosopographia Ptolemaica* (Louvain 1950 onward), Vol. VI, *La cour, etc.* (1968), esp. nos. 14479-14636 on the Ptolemaic Court and its adherents. [Abbreviated *PP*]
Pestmann, P.W., *Chronologie égyptienne d'après les textes démotiques (332 av. J.-C.-453 ap. J.-C.)* (Leiden 1967; Papyrologica Lugduno-Batava, XV).
Peter, H., *Historicorum Romanorum Reliquiae* (Leipzig 1906; repr. Stuttgart 1967). [Abbreviated *HRR*]

Petrochilus, N., *Roman Attitudes to the Greeks* (Athens 1974).
von Petrowicz, A. Ritter, *Sammlung Petrowicz: Arsaciden Münzen* (Wien 1904).
Petzl, G., *Die Inschriften von Smyrna* (Bonn 1982; *IGSK* 23).
Pflaum, H.G., *Les carrières procuratoriennes équestres sous le Haut-Empire romain*, 1-4 (Paris 1960-1961).
Pippidi, D.M., *Parerga. Écrits de philologie, d'épigraphie, et d'histoire ancienne* (Paris and Bucharest 1984).
Poulter, A.G., *Ancient Bulgaria*, I-II (Nottingham 1981).
Prause, G., *Herodes der Grosse, König der Juden* (Hamburg 1977).
Préaux, C., *Le monde hellénistique: La Grèce et l'orient, 323-146 av. J.-C.*, 1-2 (Paris 1978).
Préaux, Hommages: see under Bingen, J.
Preisigke, F., with F. Bilabel and E. Kiessling, *Sammelbuch griechischer Urkunden aus Ägypten* (Strassburg 1915-present). [Abbreviated *SB*]
Preisigke, F., and W. Spiegelberg, *Die Prinz-Joachim Ostraka* (Strassburg 1914).
Price, M.J., and B.L. Trell, *Coins and Their Cities: Architecture on the Ancient Coins of Greece, Rome and Palestine* (Detroit 1977).
Price, M. Jessop., 'Mithradates VI Eupator, Dionysus, and the Coinages of the Black Sea': *NC* (Ser. 7) 8 (1968) 1-12.
Raillard, J., *Die Anordnungen des M. Antonius im Orient* (Diss. Zürich 1894).
Rajak, T., *Josephus: The Historian and His Society* (London 1983).
Ramsay, W.M., *The Historical Geography of Asia Minor* (London 1890; Royal Geographical Society, Supplementary Papers, 4).
– *The Social Basis of Roman Power in Asia Minor* (Aberdeen 1941).
Rawlinson, G., *The Sixth Great Oriental Monarchy, or the Geography, History, and Antiquities of Parthia* (London 1873).
Ray, J.D., *The Archive of Ḥor* (London 1976; Egypt Exploration Society, Texts from Excavations, Second Memoir).
Reinach, T., 'La dynastie de Commagène': *REG* 3 (1890) 362-380 = his *L'histoire par les monnaies* (Paris 1902) 233-248.
– *Essai sur la numismatique des rois de Cappadoce* (Paris 1887) = *RN* (sér. 3) 4 (1886) 301-355 and 452-483 = *Trois royaumes* 1-87.
– *L'histoire par les monnaies* (Paris 1902).
– *Mithridate Eupator, Roi de Pont* (Paris 1890). German edition by A. Goetz, 1895.
– 'Some Pontic Eras': *NC* (ser. 4) 2 (1902) 1-11.
– *Trois royaumes de l'Asie mineure: Cappadoce-Bithynie-Pont* (Paris 1888).
Reinhold, M., *Marcus Agrippa* (Geneva 1933).
Renan, E., 'Mémoire sur la dynastie des Lysanias d'Abilène': *MémAcInscr* 26 (1870) 49-74.
Reynolds, Joyce, *Aphrodisias and Rome* (London 1982; Society for the Promotion of Roman Studies, *JRS* Monograph I).

Rice-Holmes, T., *The Architect of the Roman Empire* (Oxford 1928). See under Holmes.

Ritter, H.W., *Diadem und Königsherrschaft* (Munich 1965; Vestigia 7).

Ritterling, E., 'Legio': *RE* 12 (1925) 1186-1328.

Robert, J. and L., *Fouilles d'Amyzon en Carie* (Paris 1983).

Robert, L., *Documents de l'Asie Mineure Méridionale: Inscriptions, monnaies et géographie* (Genève and Paris 1966).

– *Études épigraphiques et philologiques* (Paris 1938).

– *Hellenica: Recueil d'épigraphie, de numismatique, et d'antiquités grecques*, I-XIII (Paris 1940-1965).

– *Nouvelles inscriptions de Sardes*, I (Paris 1964).

– *Opera minora selecta*, 1-5 (Amsterdam 1969-1974).

Rossi, R., *Marco Antonio nella lotta politica della tarda Repubblica Romana* (Trieste 1959).

Rostovtzeff, M., *Iranians and Greeks in South Russia* (Oxford 1922).

– 'Queen Dynamis of Bosporus': *JHS* 39 (1919) 88-109.

– *The Social and Economic History of the Hellenistic World*, I-III (Oxford 1941). [Abbreviated *SEHHW*]

– *The Social and Economic History of the Roman Empire*, I-II, 2nd ed., rev. P.M. Fraser (Oxford 1957). [Abbreviated *SEHRE*]

Rostovtzeff, M., and C.B. Welles, *A Parchment Contract of Loan from Dura-Europus on the Euphrates* (New Haven 1930; = *Yale Classical Studies* 2).

Rubens-Duval, M., 'Histoire politique, religieuse et littéraire d'Édesse jusqu'à la Première Croisade': *JA* (sér. 8) 18 (1891) 87-133, 201-278, 381-439; 19 (1892) 5-102.

Şahin, S., *Die Inschriften von Stratonikaia*, 1-2 (Bonn 1981; *IGSK* 21-22).

– *Katalog der antiken Inschriften des Museums von Iznik (Nikaia)*, I and II.1-2 (Bonn 1979-1982; *IGSK* 9, 10.1-2).

Şahin, S., E. Schwertheim, and J. Wagner, eds., *Studien zur Religion und Kultur Kleinasiens: Festschrift für Friedrich Karl Dörner zum 65. Geburtstag am 28 Februar 1976*, I-II (Leiden 1978; = *EPRO* 66). [Abbreviated *Festschrift Dörner*.]

Salmon, E.T., *Roman Colonization under the Republic* (London 1969).

Sammlung Petrowicz: see under (von) Petrowicz.

Samuel, A., *Greek and Roman Chronology* (Munich 1972).

– *Ptolemaic Chronology* (Munich 1962; Münchener Beiträge zur Papyrusforschung und antiken Rechtsgeschichte 43).

Sands, P.C., *The Client Princes of the Roman Empire under the Republic* (Cambridge, Eng. 1908).

Santangelo, M., 'Il monumento di C. Julius Antiochus Philopappos in Atene': *Annuario della Scuola archeologica di Atene*, n.s. 3/5 (1941/1943) 153-253.

Sartre, M., *Bostra, des origines à l'Islam* (forthcoming; Paris, Bibliothèque archéologique et historique de l'Institut français d'archéologie du Proche-Orient).

– *Inscriptions grecques et latines de la Syrie* [*IGLSyr*], XIII, 1, *Bostra (Nos. 9001 à 9472)* (Paris 1982; Bibl. arch. et hist. de l'Inst. franç. d'arch. du Proche-Orient, 113).
– *Trois études sur l'Arabie romaine et byzantine* (Brussels 1982; Collection Latomus 178).
Schalit, A., *The Hellenistic Age* (New Brunswick, N. J. 1972; The World History of the Jewish People, Vol. VI).
– *König Herodes: Der Mann und sein Werk* (Berlin 1969; trans. J. Amix).
Schippmann, K., *Grundzüge der parthischen Geschichte* (Darmstadt 1980). Review: J. Wagner, *WdO* 14 (1983).
Schlumberger, D., *L'Orient héllenisé, l'art grec et ses héritiers dans l'Asie non méditerranéenne (L'Art du Monde)* (Paris 1970).
Schmidt, M., *Caesar und Cleopatra. Philologische und historische Kommentare zu Lucan 10, 1-171* (Frankfurt am Main 1986).
Schürer, E. (revised by G. Vermes and F. Millar), *History of the Jewish People in the Age of Jesus Christ (175 B.C.-A.D. 135)*, I-III.1 (Edinburgh 1973-1986). Abbreviated herein as Schürer (Vermes and Millar). Reviews: G.W. Bowersock, *JRS* 65 (1975) 180-185; T. Rajak, *JRS* 72 (1982) 170-175.
Schwertheim, E., *Die Inschriften von Kyzikos und Umgebung* (Bonn 1980; *IGSK* 18).
– *Die Inschriften von Miletupolis* (Bonn 1983; *IGSK* 24).
Scullard, H.H., *From the Gracchi to Nero* (London 1959; 4th ed., 1976).
Seager, R., *Pompey: A Political Biography* (Oxford 1979).
Segal, J.B., *Edessa, 'The Blessed City'* (Oxford 1970).
Seibert, J., *Historische Beiträge zu den dynastischen Verbindungen in hellenistischer Zeit* (Wiesbaden 1967; Historia Einzelschriften, Heft 10).
Sellwood, D.G., *An Introduction to the Coinage of Parthia* (London 1971).
Seltman, C., *Greek Coins. A History of Metallic Currency and Coinage down to the Fall of the Hellenistic Kingdoms*, 2nd ed. (London 1954).
Sestini, D., *Lettere e dissertazioni numismatiche*, IV (Firenze 1818).
Seyrig, H. 'Monnaies hellénistiques, XVI. Polémon II et Julia Mamaea': *RN* (sér. 6) 11 (1969) 45-47.
– 'Sur quelques ères Syriennes, 1. L'ère des rois de Commagène': *RN* (sér. 6) 6 (1964) 51-56.
– 'Trésor monétaire de Nisibe': *RN* (sér. 5) 17 (1955) 85-128.
Sherk, R.K., *Roman Documents from the Greek East: Senatus Consulta and Epistulae to the Age of Augustus* (Baltimore 1969).
– *The Legates of Galatia from Augustus to Diocletian* (Baltimore 1951).
– 'Roman Galatia: The Governors from 25 B.C. to A.D. 114': *ANRW* II 7.2 (Berlin 1980) 954-1052.
– ed., *Rome and the Greek East to the Death of Augustus* (Cambridge, Eng. 1984; Translated Documents of Greece and Rome, 4).

Sherwin-White, A.N., *The Roman Citizenship*, 2nd ed. (Oxford 1973).

– *Roman Foreign Policy in the East, 168 B.C. to A.D. 1* (London 1984).

Sidebotham, S., *Roman Economic Policy in the Erythra Thalassa, 30 B.C.-A.D. 217* (Leiden 1986; Mnemosyne, Supplement 91).

Simonetta, B., *The Coins of the Cappadocian Kings* (Fribourg 1977).

Skeat, T.C., *The Reigns of the Ptolemies* (Munich 1954; 2nd ed., 1969; Münchener Beiträge zur Papyrusforschung und antiken Rechtsgeschichte, 39). Review: H. Volkmann, *Gnomon* 28 (1956) 67-68.

Smallwood, E.M., *Documents Illustrating the Principates of Gaius, Claudius, and Nero* (Cambridge, Eng. 1967).

– *Documents Illustrating the Principates of Nerva, Trajan, and Hadrian* (Cambridge, Eng. 1966).

Smallwood, E.M., *The Jews under Roman Rule* (Leiden 1976; corr. repr. 1981). [Abbreviated Smallwood, *Jews*]

Speidel, M., *The Religion of Juppiter Dolichenus in the Roman Army* (Leiden 1978; *EPRO* 63).

Spijkerman, A., *The Coins of the Decapolis and Provincia Arabia* (Jerusalem 1978).

Stadter, P.A., *Arrian of Nicomedia* (Chapel Hill 1980).

Stähelin, F., *Geschichte der kleinasiatischen Galater*, 2nd ed. (Leipzig 1902).

Stangl, T., *Ciceronis Orationum Scholiastae* II (Vindobonae-Lipsiae 1912; repr. Hildesheim 1964).

Starcky, J., 'Petra et la Nabatène': *Dictionnaire de la Bible, Supplement* 7, Fasc. 39 (Paris 1966) cols. 886-1017.

Stark, F., *Rome on the Euphrates* (London 1966). Review: E.W. Gray, *CR* n.s. 17 (1966) 350-354.

Ste Croix, G.E.M. de, *The Class Struggle in the Ancient Greek World from the Archaic Age to the Arab Conquest* (London 1981).

Steinmann, A., *De Parthis ab Horatio memoratis: Quaestiones chronologicae* (Berlin 1892).

Stern, M., ed., *Greek and Latin Authors on Jews and Judaism*, I-III (Leiden 1974-1984).

Stevenson, G.H., *Roman Provincial Administration till the Age of the Antonines* (Oxford 1939).

Strack, M., *Die Dynastie der Ptolemäer* (Leipzig 1897, with a 'Sammlung griechischer Ptolemäer-Inschriften').

Strasburger, H., *Caesars Eintritt in die Geschichte* (Munich 1938).

Strubbe, J., 'Les Fouilles de Pessinonte', I (Diss. Bruges 1984).

Sullivan, R., in *The Anchor Bible Dictionary* (New York, forthcoming): some further detail on Armenia, Cappadocia, Commagene, Emesa, Pontus; Glaphyra, Iotape, Mariamme.

– 'Diadochic Coinage in Commagene after Tigranes the Great': *NC* (ser. 7) 13 (1973) 18-39, with Plate 14.

– 'Dynastic Propaganda in Commagene': *Proc. Tenth Int. Cong. Classical Arch.* (Ankara 1978) 295-303, with Plates 74-81.
– 'The Dynasty of Cappadocia': *ANRW* II 7.2 (Berlin 1980) 1125-1168, with stemma.
– 'The Dynasty of Commagene': *ANRW* II 8 (Berlin 1977) 732-798, with stemma.
– 'The Dynasty of Emesa': *ANRW* II 8 (Berlin 1977) 198-219, with stemma.
– 'The Dynasty of Judaea in the First Century': *ANRW* II 8 (Berlin 1977) 296-354, with stemma.
– 'Dynasts in Pontus': *ANRW* II 7.2 (Berlin 1980) 913-930, with stemma.
– 'Important Eastern Dynasts in the Papyri': *Proceedings of the Fourteenth International Congress of Papyrologists, Oxford 1974*, ed. R. Coles (London 1975) 285-292, with stemma.
– 'King Marcus Antonius Polemo': *NC* (ser. 7) 19 (1979) 6-20, with Plate 2.
– 'Near Eastern Dynasts in Athens, 100 B.C.-A.D. 100': Summarised in *Acts of the XI International Congress of Classical Archaeology* (London 1978) 250.
– 'Papyri Reflecting the Eastern Dynastic Network': *ANRW* II 8 (Berlin 1977) 908-938, with map, four stemmata.
– 'Priesthoods of the Eastern Dynastic Aristocracy': *Studien zur Religion und Kultur Kleinasiens. Festschrift für Friedrich Karl Dörner zum 65. Geburtstag*, ed. S. Şahin, E. Schwertheim, and J. Wagner (Leiden 1978; *EPRO* 66) II, 914-939.
– 'Royal Coins and Rome': *Ancient Coins of the Graeco-Roman World: The Nickle Numismatic Papers*, ed. R. Sullivan and W. Heckel (Waterloo 1984) 145-160.
– *Some Dynastic Answers to the Armenian Question* (Diss. California 1970; publ. University Microfilms 1971).
– 'Thrace in the Eastern Dynastic Network': *ANRW* II 7.1 (Berlin 1979) 186-211, with stemma.
Sullivan, R., with W. Heckel, eds., *Ancient Coins of the Graeco-Roman World: The Nickle Numismatic Papers* (Waterloo 1984).
Sutherland, C.H.V., *Roman History and Coinage, 44 B.C.-A.D. 69* (Oxford 1987).
Svoronos, J., *Ta nomismata tou kratous ton Ptolemaion*, I-III (Athens 1904); IV [German translation] (Athens 1908).
Sydenham, E.A., and others, *The Coinage of the Roman Republic* (London 1952).
Syme, Sir R., *The Augustan Aristocracy* (Oxford 1985).
– 'Greeks Invading Roman Government' (Brademas Lecture, Hellenic College Press, Brookline, Mass., 1982).
– *The Roman Revolution* (Oxford 1939).
– *Sallust* (Berkeley 1964).
– *Tacitus* (Oxford 1958).
Tachera-Hitova, M., *Eastern Cults in Moesia Inferior and Thracia (5th Century B.C.-4th Century A.D.)* (Leiden 1983; *EPRO* 95).

Taeger, F., *Charisma: Studien zur Geschichte des antiken Herrscherkultes* (Stuttgart 1957 and 1960).
Tarn, W.W., *The Greeks in Bactria and India*, 2nd ed. (Cambridge, Eng. 1951).
– 'Parthia': *CAH* IX (1932 and 1951), Ch. XIV, 574-613.
– *Seleucid-Parthian Studies* (London 1930; *PBA* 16).
Tarn, Sir W., with G.T. Griffiths, *Hellenistic Civilisation*, 3rd ed. (London 1952).
Täubler, E., *Imperium Romanum: Studien zur Entwicklungsgeschichte des römischen Reichs* (Leipzig 1913; repr. Rome 1964).
– *Die Parthernachrichten bei Josephus* (Berlin 1904).
Taylor, L.R., *Party Politics in the Age of Caesar* (Berkeley and Los Angeles 1949).
Tcherikover, V., *Hellenistic Civilization and the Jews* (Philadelphia and Jerusalem, 1959).
Teixidor, J., 'The Kingdom of Adiabene and Hatra': *Berytus* 17 (1967/1968) 1-11.
Thomas, J.D., *The Epistrategos in Ptolemaic and Roman Egypt*, Part I, *The Ptolemaic Epistrategos* (Opladen 1975; Papyrologica Coloniensia, 6). Review: L. Mooren, *CE* 51 (1976) 202-207.
Thompson, M., with O. Mørkholm and C. Kraay, *Inventory of Greek Coin Hoards* (New York 1973).
Thorossian, H., *Histoire de la littérature arménienne* (Paris 1951).
Todd, M., *The Northern Barbarians, 100 B.C.-A.D. 300* (Oxford 1975; rev. ed. 1986).
Toumanoff, C., *Manuel de généalogie et de chronologie pour l'histoire de la Caucasie chrétienne (Arménie-Géorgie-Albanie)* (Rome 1976).
– *Studies in Christian Caucasian History* (Washington 1963).
Tournebise, H.F., *Histoire politique et religieux de l'Arménie*, I (Paris 1910).
Travlos, J., *Pictorial Dictionary of Ancient Athens* (New York 1971). The Philopappus monument.
Tyrrell, R., and L. Purser, *The Correspondence of M. Tullius Cicero* (Dublin and London 1906).
Vanden Berghe, L., *Archéologie de l'Iran ancien* (Leiden 1966).
Vermes, G., and F. Millar, eds., see under Schürer, E.
Viereck, P., *Ostraka aus Brüssel und Berlin* (Leipzig 1922).
Vitucci, G., *Il regno di Bitinia* (Rome 1953).
Volkmann, H., *Cleopatra, A Study in Politics and Propaganda*, trans. T. Cadoux (London 1958). Review: Balsdon, *CR* 10 (1960) 68-71.
Waddington, W.H., *Fastes des provinces asiatiques de l'empire romain depuis leur origine jusqu' à règne de Dioclétien* (Paris 1872).
– 'Sur la chronologie des rois du Pont et du Bosphore et des princes d'Olba': *RN* (sér. 2) 11 (1866) 417-41.
Waddington, W., with E. Babelon and Th. Reinach, *Recueil général des monnaies grecques*, 2nd ed. (Paris 1925), Vol. I. [Abbreviated *Recueil* I^2]

Wagner, J., 'Dynastie und Herrscherkult in Kommagene: Forschungsgeschichte und neuere Funde': *MDAI(I)* 33 (1983) 177-224, with Taf. 45-53.

– 'Eastern Mediterranean and Mesopotamia. The Reorganization of the Orient from Pompey to Augustus (67 B.C.-14 A.D.)': *Tübinger Atlas des Vorderen Orients (TAVO)*, B V 7 (Wiesbaden 1982).

– *Seleukeia am Euphrat/Zeugma* (Wiesbaden 1976; Beihefte zum Tübinger Atlas des Vorderen Orients, [*TAVO*], Reihe B, Geisteswissenschaften, Nr. 10).

Wagner, J., and G. Petzl, 'Eine neue Temenos-Stele des Königs Antiochos I. von Kommagene': *ZPE* 20 (1976) 201-223.

Walbank, F.W., *The Hellenistic World* (Glasgow 1981).

– *A Historical Commentary on Polybius*, 1-3 (Oxford 1957-1979).

– *Polybius* (Berkeley and Los Angeles, London 1972).

Waldmann, H., *Die kommagenischen Kultreformen unter König Mithradates I. Kallinikos und seinem Sohne Antiochos I.* (Leiden 1973; *EPRO* 34). Review: R. Allison, *CP* 72 (1977) 271-275.

Walser, G., *Rom, das Reich und die fremden Völker in der Geschichtsschreibung der frühen Kaiserzeit. Studien zur Glaubwürdigkeit des Tacitus* (Basel 1951).

Walton, C., 'Oriental Senators in the Service of Rome': *JRS* 19 (1929) 38-66.

Wankel, H., *Die Inschriften von Ephesos*, Ia (Bonn 1979; *IGSK* 11). See also under Merkelbach, R., and others.

Wardman, A., *Rome's Debt to Greece* (London 1976).

Ward-Perkins, J.B., 'The Roman West and the Parthian East': *PBA* 51 (1965) 175-199.

Weinstock, S., *Divus Julius* (Oxford 1971).

Welles, C.B., *Royal Correspondence in the Hellenistic Period, A Study in Greek Epigraphy* (New Haven 1934).

– 'The Romanization of the Greek East': *BASP* 2 (1965) 42-46 and 75-77.

Wheeler, M., *Rome Beyond the Imperial Frontiers* (London 1954).

Widengren, G., *Der Feudalismus im alten Iran* (Opladen 1969).

– *Iranisch-semitische Kulturbegegnung in parthischer Zeit* (Köln and Opladen 1960).

Wiegand, T., *Didyma* II, *Die Inschriften*, ed. A. Rehm, hrsg. R. Harder (Berlin 1958).

Wiesner, J., *Die Thraker* (Stuttgart 1963).

Wilcken, U., *Grundzüge und Chrestomathie der Papyruskunde*, 2 vols. (Leipzig and Berlin 1912).

Wilhelm, A., 'Kietis, Zu Tacitus und Josephus': *Arch.-Epigr. Mitth.* 17 (1894) 1-6.

Will, É., *Histoire politique du monde hellénistique (323-30 av. J.-C.)*, I-II (Nancy 1966 and 1967).

Will, É., with C. Mossé and P. Goukowsky, *Le monde grec et l'orient*, 2, *Le IVe siècle et l'époque hellénistique* (Paris 1975).

Wirgin, W., 'Judah Maccabee's Embassy to Rome and the Jewish-Roman Treaty': *PEQ* 101 (1969) 15-20.

Wolski, J., 'Arsace II et la généalogie des premiers Arsacides': *Historia* 11 (1962) 138-145.

– 'The Decay of the Iranian Empire of the Seleucids and the Chronology of Parthian Beginnings': *Berytus* 12 (1956/1957) 35-52.

Wright, F.A., *Marcus Agrippa* (London 1937).

Wroth, Warwick, *A Catalogue of the Greek Coins in the British Museum: The Coins of Parthia* (London 1903).

Youroukova, Y., *Coins of the Ancient Thracians* (Oxford 1976; British Archaeological Reports, Supplementary Series, 4).

Zeitlin, S., *The Rise and Fall of the Judaean State*, I-II (Philadelphia 1967 and 1969).

Zgusta, L., *Anatolische Personennamensippen* (Prague 1964).

– *Kleinasiatische Ortsnamen* (Heidelberg 1984).

– *Kleinasiatische Personennamen* (Prague 1964).

Ziegler, K.-H., *Die Beziehungen zwischen Rom und dem Partherreich: Ein Beitrag zur Geschichte des Volkerrechts* (Wiesbaden 1964).

Zwintscher, A., *De Galatarum Tetrarchis et Amynta Rege Quaestiones* (Leipzig 1892).

INDEX

This Index includes all references to the persons and geographical regions mentioned in the text. In addition, it provides analytical entries for those major figures, regions, and battles that fall within the scope of the book.

Page numbers in **bold type** indicate principal discussions. Page numbers in ordinary type indicate all other references apart from principal discussions.

Roman names appear in their most familiar form.

The abbreviation [**S.**1, 2, 3, etc.] refers to the numbered stemmata at the end of the volume.

Abdagaeses, rival of Artabanus III of Parthia: 111
Abennerigus (Abinerglos) of Characene: 108, 110
Abgar II of Osrhoene: 107, 195, 282, 307
Abgar V of Osrhoene: 107
Abinerglos. *See* Abennerigus
Abrupolis, Sapaean king in Thrace: 29
Achaemenids of Persia: 9, 10, 111, 113, 161, 270, 300, 309, 312
Achillas, adviser of Ptolemy XIII of Egypt: 254, 259
Actium, Battle of: **275-279 and 443n.325-445n.376;** Amyntas of Galatia at, 173; and Antony, 313, 321; Archelaus I of Cappadocia at, 184; and Cleopatra VII of Egypt, 12, 148, 251; Deiotarus Philadelphos of Paphlagonia at, 170, 269; Dicomes of the Getae at, 148; Eastern dynasties after, 11, 11, 18, 29, 160, 163, 191, 202, 208, 209, 290, **321-328**; Eastern dynasties before, 144, 163, 171, 185, 286, 334; and Herod the Great of Judaea, 212, 213, 227, 228; and Iamblichus I of Emesa, 201, 202, 326; and the Iberians, 293; and Malichus I of the Nabataeans, 212; Mithradates II of Commagene at, 197, 326; and Octavian, 321; and the Parthians, 317, 318; and Polemo I of Pontus, 163; Rhoemetalces I of Thrace at, 150, 331; Rome and the East after, 321, 322, 323, 334; Sadalas III of Thrace at, 149; Tarcondimotus I of Cilicia at, 190, 191, 325

Adiabene (Natunia): **107-108 and 375nn.15-19;** also mentioned, 101, 102, 103, 105, 108, 110, 120, 293, 296, 301, 307. *See also* Map xxvi

Adiatorix of Galatia [**S.**3]: **171 and 393nn.87-88;** rule of Heraclea Pontica by, 169

Adobogiona [**S.**3], mother of Deiotarus Philadelphos of Paphlagonia: 170

Adobogiona [**S.**3], mother of Mithradates of Pergamon: 164

Afranius, Lucius: invasion of Gordyene by, 296, 302

Agrippa, Marcus Vipsanius: defeat of Tarcondimotus I of Cilicia by, 190; and Ilium, 228

Agrippa I of Judaea [**S.**8]: 208, 228, 322, 327

Agrippa II of Judaea [**S.**8]: 24, 63, 202, 208, 228, 321, 327

Aka [**S.**5], niece of Mithradates II of Commagene: 197

Akkadians of Mesopotamia: 10, 80

Albania: 101, 288, 293, 294. *See also* Map xxvi

Alchaedamnus, King of the Rhambaeans: 80

Alchaudonius, King of the Rhambaeans: 281, 282, 307

Alexander the Great of Macedon: 10, 23, 52, 61, 81, 90, 109, 111, 143, 205, 292, 294, 300

Alexander [**S.**8], son of Aristobulus II of Judaea: death of, 206, 222; descendants of, 222, 223; rebellion of, 219-220, 221, 243

Alexander [**S.**5, 8], son-in-law of Antiochus IV of Commagene: 173, 186, 326

Alexander of Cilicia [**S.**5-6, 8]: 18, 24, 174, 198, 202, 324, 325, 326

Alexander of Emesa [**S.**5-6]: 184, 202, 326

Alexander Helios [**S.**7], son of Antony and Cleopatra VII of Egypt: after the Battle of Actium, 279; and the 'donations' at Alexandria, 316; and dynastic plans of Antony and Cleopatra, 267, 268, 272, 273, 275, 289, 290, 297, 298, 316, 326

Alexander Jannaeus of Judaea [**S.**8]: **76-78 and 361n.25-362n.27;** and the Arabs, 221; and the Nabataeans, 73, 74, 213, 214; overthrow of coastal cities by, 74, 104, 213, 216, 218; and Parthia, 116; and Ptolemy IX Lathyros of Egypt, 73, 82; reign of, 70, 213, 330; and the Seleucids, 66, 68; and Theodore of Philadelphia, 80; and Tigranes the Great of Armenia, 104

Alexander Zebinas, murderer of Demetrius II Nicator, Seleucid: 66, 67

Alexandra [**S.**8], daughter of Aristobulus II of Judaea: 206-207

Alexandra [**S.**8], mother-in-law of Herod the Great of Judaea: 223, 225, 226, 227

Alexandra Salome of Judaea [**S.**8]: **78-79 and 362n.28;** and the Pharisees, 75, 213; and Ptolemy of the Ituraeans, 71, 75; and Tigranes the Great of Armenia, 78, 104, 213; as wife and successor of Alexander Jannaeus of Judaea, 70, 76, 213, 330

Ammonius, agent of Ptolemy XII Auletes of Egypt: 238

Amyntas of Galatia [**S.**3]: **171-174 and 393n.90-394n.98;** and Antony, 161, 169, 170, 184. 191, 207, 269, 270,

271, 290, 315; at the Battle of Actium, 276, 277; at the Battle of Philippi, 168; as last dynast of Galatia, 18, 323, 324; territory ruled by, 175, 186, 325, 331

Antigonus, general of Alexander the Great: 111

Antigonus of Judaea [**S**.8]: **223-225 and 414n.113-415n.122;** and Herod the Great of Judaea, 15, 206-207, 211, 222-223, 225, 312; and Lysanias of the Ituraeans, 207; and the Parthians, 15, 222, 312, 332; and Rome, 220, 222; as successor of Hyrcanus II, 218

Antiochis, daughter of Antiochus XII, Seleucid: 205

Antiochis [**S**.5], sister of Mithradates II of Commagene: 197

Antiochus, relative of Antiochus XIII Asiaticus, Seleucid: 241

Antiochus III, Seleucid [**S**.2, 4]: 11, 27, 32, 43, 45, 66, 67, 87, 98, 99, 111, 112, 143, 294, 295

Antiochus IV Epiphanes, Seleucid [**S**.2]: 11, 66, 111, 242

Antiochus VII Sidetes, Seleucid [**S**.7]: 11, 67, 80, 82, 85

Antiochus VIII Grypus, Seleucid [**S**.5, 7, 10]: and Antiochus IX Cyzicenus, Seleucid, 66, 67, 76, 82, 83, 85; death of, 80, 83, 116, 203; descendants of, 36, 60, 61, 65, **66-68**, 77, 103, 117, 193, 203-205, 330; and the Ptolemies, 82, 83, 85, 86, 87, 88, 92, 242, 272. *See also* Illustr. 126

Antiochus IX Cyzicenus, Seleucid [**S**.7]: and Antiochus VIII Grypus, Seleucid, 66, 67, 76, 82, 83, 85; descendants of, 117; and the Ptolemies, 66, 67, 85, 86, 88; and the sons of Antiochus VIII Grypus, 67, 77, 203

Antiochus X Eusebes, Seleucid [**S**.7]: and the last Seleucids, 61, 66, 67, 68, 77, 88, 203, 204; and the Parthians, 117; and the Ptolemies, 65, 66, 78, 83, 84, 86, 91, 94

Antiochus XI Epiphanes Philadelphos, Seleucid [**S**.7]: 68

Antiochus XII Dionysus, Seleucid [**S**.7]: control of Damascus by, 68, 71, 74; death of, 68, 71, 74, 77, 86, 103, 203; descendants of, 205

Antiochus XIII Asiaticus, Seleucid [**S**.7]: **203 and 407nn.38-39;** death of, 64, 69, 198; and the last Seleucids, 203, 204, 205; and the Ptolemies, 91, 94, 241; and Tigranes the Great of Armenia, 68, 69, 103, 104

Antiochus I of Commagene [**S**.5, 10]: **193-197 and 403n.2-405n.18;** and Antony, 269, 314, 326; and Caesar, 157; and Crassus, 306; and Darius the Mede, 296; and Deiotarus I of Galatia, 169; and Lucullus, 62, 152, 281; and the Nabataeans, 211; and the Parthians, 177, 178, 188, 189, 201, 222, 252, 310, 312; Philoromaios, 57; prosperity of Commagene under, 332; and Rome, 14; Seleucid ancestry of, 204; and the siege of Samosata, 181, 224, 312; syncretism of, 19, 60, 330; tiara of, 62, 197, 288. *See also* Illustr. 126

Antiochus 'II' of Commagene [**S**.5]: 198, 326

Antiochus III of Commagene [**S**.5]: 297, 326

Antiochus IV of Commagene [**S**.5-6, 8]: 18, 24, 162, 173, 186, 198, 270, 297, 324, 325, 326, 327

Antipater of Armenia Minor: 37

Antipater of Derbe: 172

Antipater of Idumaea [**S.**8]: and Hyrcanus II of Judaea, 209, 214, 215, 216; and the Nabataeans, 209, 211, 220, 221, 259; and the Romans, 201, 211, 219, 220, 221, 222, 223, 259, 332, 334

Antonia [**S.**1-2], daughter of Antony: marriage to Pythodorus of Tralles, 275

Antonia Tryphaena [**S.**1-2, 5-6], daughter of Polemo I of Pontus: marriage to Cotys VIII of Thrace, 151, 160, 163, 284, 323, 324, 332

Antonius, Marcus (grandfather of the triumvir): and Cilicia Tracheia, 186

Antonius, Marcus (Creticus, father of the triumvir): in the East, 266

Antony (Marcus Antonius) [**S.**1-2, 7]: and Armenia, 12, 288, 290, 298, 333; and Atropatene, 293, 294, 297, 298; and the Battle of Actium, **275-279**, 313, 321; and Cappadocia, 181, 182, 183, 184, 325; and Cilicia, 189, 190, 191; and Cleopatra VII of Egypt, 207, 243, 250, 251, 260, 262, 265, **266-279**, 332; and Commagene, 19, 62, 107, 181, 196, 197; dynastic mobilizations of, **268-270**; dynastic plans of, 322, 326; and Egypt, 243, 332; and Emesa, 201, 202, 326; and Galatia, 168, 169, 170, 171, 172, 173; and the Ituraeans, 207; and Judaea, 14, 21, 217, 222, 223, 224, 225, 226, 227, 228; and the Nabataeans, 209, 212; and the Parthians, 222, **270-273**, 288, 289, 297, 308, 311, 312, 313, 314, 315, 316, 317, 318, 333; and Pontus, 11, 18, 156, 161, 162, 163, 169, 181, 182, 183, 323, 324, 330, 331; and Thrace, 148, 149, 151; and title 'King of Kings,' **273-275**. *See also* Illustr. 137

Antyllus, son of Antony: after the Battle of Actium, 278, 279

Apollodorus, adviser to Cleopatra VII of Egypt: 254

Aquillius, Manius: in Bithynia, 34, 44-45; in Cappadocia, 44-45, 50

Arabs, Arabia: 13, 19, 20, 21, 24, 62, 63, 68, 69, 70, 71, 72, 73, 74, 75, 77, 79, 80, 102, 107, 109, 153, 198, 199, 200, 202, 207, 208, 209, 210, 211, 212, 213, 216, 217, 221, 223, 226, 227, 259, 266, 268, 280, 281, 305, 324, 327, 328. *See also* Maps xxii-xxiii, xxv

Arachosia: 113. *See also* Map xxii-xxiii

Arcathias [**S.**4], son of Mithradates Eupator of Pontus: 42

Archelaus [**S.**4], father of Archelaus I of Cappadocia: 157

Archelaus [**S.**4], general of Mithradates Eupator of Pontus: betrayal of Mithradates Eupator by, 42, 43, 46, 47; descendants of, 183; and Mithradates of Pergamon, 259

Archelaus [**S.**4, 7], grandfather of Archelaus I of Cappadocia: and Antony, 183; marriage to Berenice IV of Egypt, 54, 95, 183, 205, 241-243, 259

Archelaus I Philopatris Ktistes, of Cappadocia [**S.**1-2, 4-6, 8]: **182-185 and 397n.131-399n.141;** accession of, 11, 13; and Antony, 161, 170, 182, 207, 269, 276, 290, 325, 332; descendants of, 291, 297, 300, 322; literary work of, 286; marriage to Pythodoris I of Pontus, 324, 325; and nobles of Cappadocia, 55; rule of Cilicia by, 18, 162, 173, 187, 191, 270. *See also* Illustr. 132

Archelaus II of Cappadocia [**S.**4-6, 8]: 18, 270, 325

Ardashir (Artaxerxes) of Persis: 112

Aretas I of the Nabataeans: **72-73 and 358n.19**

Aretas II of the Nabataeans: **73-74 and 359n.21;** reign of, 70, 74, 77

Aretas III of the Nabataeans: **74-75 and 360n.23-361n.24; 209-210 and 409n.54-410n.58;** and Antiochus XII, Seleucid, 86; authority in Damascus of, 71, 72, 78; and Judaea, 77, 214, 215, 220, 221; reign of, 70, 233; and Tigranes the Great of Armenia, 104. *See also* Illustr. 142

Aretas IV of the Nabataeans [**S.**8]: 332

Ariarathes IV of Cappadocia [**S.**4]: 66

Ariarathes V of Cappadocia [**S.**4]: 49, 54

Ariarathes VI of Cappadocia [**S.**2, 4]: 32, 34, 38, 39, 53, 54, 66, 329

Ariarathes VII of Cappadocia [**S.**4]: 32, 33, 39, 53

Ariarathes VIII of Cappadocia [**S.**4]: 32, 33, 39, 53

Ariarathes IX of Cappadocia [**S.**1-2, 4, 9-10]: installation of, by Mithradates Eupator of Pontus, 17, 32, 33, 35, 41, 42, 53, 56, 58, 180; and Rome, 45, 54, 56, 58; and Tigranes the Great of Armenia, 99

Ariarathes X Eusebes Philadelphos of Cappadocia [**S.**4]: **180-182 and 397nn.124-130;** and Archelaus I of Cappadocia, 182; and Ariobarzanes III of Cappadocia, 179, 180; and Caesar, 157, 179; and Pompey, 179; and Sisines, 56

Ariarathids, Cappadocian dynasty: **52-54 and 351n.45-352n.47;** end of dynasty of, 11, 329; seat of power of, 102. *See also* Cappadocia

Ariobarzanes, Persian satrap of Cappadocia: 57

Ariobarzanes II of Atropatene [**S.**6, 9]: 299

Ariobarzanes I of Cappadocia [**S.**4]: **54-58 and 352n.48-353n.56; 174-175 and 394n.99-395n.102;** and Mithradates Eupator of Pontus, 34, 40, 46, 48, **57-58**, 88, 97, 98, 99, 330; new Cappadocian dynasty of, 11, 19, 32, 33, 40, 53; and Rome, 35, 44, 46, 50, 98, 118, 152, 153, 194, 282; successors of, 175, 176, 182, 183, 184, 332; and Tigranes the Great of Armenia, 98, 99, 153, 284. *See also* Illustr. 124

Ariobarzanes II Philopator of Cappadocia [**S.**4]: **175-177 and 395nn.103-109;** and Crassus, 306; intermarriage with Pontus, 57

Ariobarzanes III Eusebes Philoromaios of Cappadocia [**S.**4]: **177-180 and 396nn.110-123;** and Caesar, 157, 166; and Crassus, 306; death of, 332; and Deiotarus I of Galatia, 169; and the Parthians, 195, 200, 287, 310; and Pompey, 21, 244; and the Pontic faction, 58; and the priest of Comana, 183; as son of Athenais Philostorgos II, 57, 176; successors of, 181, 184

Aristarchus of Colchis: 156, 164

Aristobulus [**S.**5, 8], grandson of Herod the Great of Judaea: 297

Aristobulus [**S.**8], grandson of Hyrcanus II of Judaea: 226, 272

Aristobulus I of Judaea [**S.**8]: 71, 213

Aristobulus II of Judaea [**S.**8]: **213-217 and 412n.73-413n.91;** and Alexandra Salome of Judaea, 78, 79; descendants of, 206, 225; and Hyrcanus II of Judaea, 78, 79, 208, 209, 332; after

Pompey's conquest, 14, 219, 220, 221, 222
Armenia [**S**.9]: **96-105 and 370n.1-373n.11; 280-291 and 445n.1-450n.40;** under Artavasdes II, **285-290**; under Artaxias II, **290-291**; under Tigranes the Great, **97-105, 280-284**; and Tigranes the Younger, **284-285**; also mentioned *passim*, esp. 11-17, 20-23, 36-48, 58-66, 105-120, 143-157, 162-179, 193-206, 270-277, 291-318, 324-327, 330-333. *See also* Maps xxii-xxiii, xxvi
Armenia Minor: 18, 35, 37, 38, 63, 151, 157, 162, 163, 164, 165, 166, 179, 182, 185, 284, 286, 290, 298, 314, 315, 323, 324, 327. *See also* Maps xxii-xxiii, xxvi
'Arsaces' (Arsaces I) [**S**.10], founder of Parthian dynasty: 113
Arsaces, Parthian throne name: 113, 115, 116, 118, 120, 160, 279, 301, 302, 309, 311
Arsaces of Pontus [**S**.2]: **161 and 389n.54;** as descendant of Mithradates Eupator of Pontus, 160, 162
Arsacids, Parthian dynasty: 12, 36, 98, 103, 105, 109, 112, 288, 289, 291, 293, 294, 296, 297, 298, 299, 300, 309. *See also* Parthia
Arsinoe IV of Egypt [**S**.7]: and Caesar, 258, 259, 262; and Cleopatra VII, 254, 265, 279; death of, 250, 259, 260, 265, 267; debt to Rome of, 245
Artabanus II of Parthia [**S**.10]: 113, 115
Artabanus III of Parthia [**S**.10]: 111, 289, 293, 299, 300, 309, 318
Artabazanes of Atropatene: 294
Artabazus of Characene: 110
Artavasdes I of Armenia [**S**.9]: 97, 114, 116
Artavasdes II of Armenia [**S**.9]: **285-290 and 447n.19-450n.36;** and Antony, 269, 270, 271, 272, 273, 277, 290, 298, 314, 333; and Crassus, 306, 307, 308, 313; and Galatia, 168; literary work of, 184, 309; and Pontus, 284; as successor of Tigranes the Great, 284, 285; threat to Cappadocia by, 177, 178, 195
Artavasdes III of Armenia [**S**.9]: 291, 316
Artavasdes I of Atropatene [**S**.5-6, 9]: **297-300 and 453n.63-456n.75;** and Antony, 162, 267, 269, 271, 272, 273, 275, 276, 277, 290, 314, 315, 316; and Armenia, 333; and the Parthians, 162, 314, 315, 316, 317; as successor of Tigranes the Great of Armenia, 119; tiara of, 333. *See also* Illustr. 140
Artavasdes II of Atropatene [**S**.9]: 299
Artaxerxes II of Persia: 113
Artaxerxes of Persis. *See* Ardashir
Artaxes. *See* Artaxias II
Artaxiads, Armenian dynasty: 17, 291, 292, 293. *See also* Armenia
Artaxias I of Armenia [**S**.9]: 98, 99, 295
Artaxias II (Artaxes) of Armenia [**S**.9]: **290-291 and 450nn.37-40;** and Atropatene, 298; as successor of Artavasdes II of Armenia, 163, 273, 275, 289, 298, 316
Artoces of Iberia: 292
Aryazate-Automa [**S**.9-10], daughter of Tigranes the Great of Armenia: 47, 98, 116, 283
Arzanene: 103. *See also* Map xxvi
Asander of Bosporus [**S**.1-2]: **159-160 and 388nn.49-51;** defeat of Mithradates of Pergamon by, 159; marriage to Dynamis, 162, 324;

revolt from Pharnaces II of Pontus by, 158
Ashi'abatum [**S**.10], wife of Gotarzes I of Parthia: 116
Asia, province of: 27, 31, 45, 50, 88, 90, 157, 232, 259
Aspurgiani, Bosporan tribe: 324
Aspurgus of Bosporus [**S**.1-2]: 160, 324
Assyrians of Mesopotamia: 9, 12, 19, 61, 62, 80, 96, 102, 107, 108, 110
Astaeans, royal house of Thrace: 27, 28, 29, 147, 148. *See also* Odrysian-Astaean dynasty of Thrace. *See also* Map xxiv
Astypylaea: 27
Ateporix of Caranitis: 173
Athenais Philostorgos I of Cappadocia [**S**.4]: 57, 176
Athenais Philostorgos II of Cappadocia [**S**.4]: marriage to Ariobarzanes II of Cappadocia, 42, 46, 57, 176; Pontic influence of, in Cappadocia, 181; as regent of Ariobarzanes III of Cappadocia, 176, 177
Atropatene [**S**.9]: **293-300 and 452n.51-456n.75;** under Artavasdes I, **297-300**; also mentioned *passim*, esp. 10, 12, 15, 16, 101-120, 267-277, 282-293, 314-318, 326, 327, 333. *See also* Maps xxii-xxiii, xxvi
Atropates, founder of Atropatenian dynasty: 294, 295, 300
Attalids of Pergamon: bequest to Rome by, 11, 18, 25, 31, 32, 45, 49, 52, 54, 261; and Galatia, 165, 168, 173; intermarriage with Cappadocia, 52, 54; and Thrace, 26
Attalus II of Pergamon [**S**.3-4]: 54
Attalus III of Pergamon [**S**.4]: 45, 49
Attalus of Paphlagonia: 156, 160, 168-169
Attambelus of Characene: 110
Augustus (Gaius Iulius Caesar Octavianus Augustus), emperor: and Armenia, 290, 291, 294, 298, 299, 300, 317, 323; and Atropatene, 293, 294, 298, 299; and Cappadocia, 182, 191; and Caria, 311; and Cilicia, 191, 325; and Commagene, 191; and Eastern dynasts, 24, 321, 322; and Egypt, 232, 261; Emesa under, 191, 326; Galatia under, 173; Judaea under, 191, 332; and Parthia, 191, 291, 308, 333; and Pontus, 160, 163, 323; and Thrace, 30, 322, 323. *See also* Octavian
Aurelius, Marcus (Marcus Aurelius Antoninus), emperor: 324
Azizus, *phylarch* of the Arabs [**S**.5-6]: **63-64 and 355n.6;** and the last Seleucids, 64, 69, 80, 198, 199
Azizus of Emesa [**S**.5-6, 8]: 297

Babylonians of Mesopotamia: 9, 10, 80, 96, 107, 110, 115, 116
Bacchius Judaeus, minor dynast of the Levant: 80
Bactria: 11, 113, 114. *See also* Map xxii-xxiii
Barsabas, Thracian dynast: 27
Barzaphranes, Parthian satrap: 207
Basoropeda: 295
Bassus, Quintus Caecilius: and the Parthians, 201, 222, 310, 311
Bastarnae: 322
Berenice, daughter of Ptolemy VIII Physcon of Egypt: 83, 93
Berenice [**S**.1-2, 6, 8], great-granddaughter of Herod the Great of Judaea: 284
Berenice III of Egypt. *See* Cleopatra Berenice III of Egypt

Berenice IV of Egypt [**S**.4, 7]: **239-243 and 423n.79-426n.102;** marriage to Archelaus, Pontic noble, 17, 54, 95, 157, 183, 205, 251, 259; murder of, by Ptolemy XII Auletes of Egypt, 246, 250
Bessi, Thracian tribe: opposition to Rome by, 28, 29, 145, 146, 147, 148, 149, 150, 151, 322. *See also* Map xxiv
Bibulus, Marcus Calpurnius: as governor of Syria, 200, 252, 310
Bithynia: **30-35 and 341n.10-345n.19;** under Nicomedes III, **30-33**; under Nicomedes IV, **33-35**; also mentioned *passim*, esp. 10-13, 18, 38-55, 87-90, 149-157, 329, 333. *See also* Maps xxii-xxiv; Illustr. 122
Bocchus of Libya: 277
Bosporus: 13, 15, 16, 17, 26, 151, 158, 159, 160, 161, 162, 163, 164, 166, 174, 177, 269, 280, 284, 321, 322, 323, 324, 332. *See also* Map xxii-xxiii
Brogitarus of Galatia [**S**.3]: **164-165 and 389n.62-390n.66;** and Deiotarus I of Galatia, 331; rule in Galatia of, 18, 166, 169, 171
Brutus, Marcus Iunius: and the Cappadocians, 178, 180, 181, 332; and Cassius, 266; and Deiotarus I of Galatia, 167, 169; and the Parthians, 311; and the Thracians, 29, 148, 149
Burebistas, King of the Getae: 147, 148, 159
Byses, Thracian dynast: 27

Cadusians: 294
Caesar, Gaius Iulius [**S**.7]: Alexandrian War of, 157, 208, 219, 258, 259, 265; and the Battle of Zela, 158, 167, 171, 179; and Bithynia, 33, 34; and Cappadocia, 166, 179, 180, 182; and Cilicia, 189; and Cleopatra VII of Egypt, 250, 251, **258-262**, 262-264, 272, 332; and Commagene, 194, 196; and the East, 267, 269, 277, 321; and Emesa, 200, 201; and Galatia, 21, 160, 164, 165, 166, 167, 169, 170, 171, 324, 331; and the Ituraeans, 72; and Judaea, 201, 217, 218, 219, 220; and the Nabataeans, 208, 211; and the Parthians, 222, 264, 266, 288, 308, 310, 311, 317, 333; and Pontus, 44, 157, 158, 159, 160, 161; and Ptolemy XII Auletes of Egypt, 21, 158, 231, 232, 233, 234, 235, 243, 244, 245, 246, 247, 251, 268; and Thrace, 147, 148, 149
Caesarion. *See* Ptolemy XV
Calidius: and the Mithradatic Wars, 46
Caligula (Gaius Caesar), emperor: 322, 323, 326
Callimachus, Thebarch: 256
Calvinus, Gnaeus Domitius: as legate of Caesar in Asia, 157, 167
Campestris. *See* Cilicia Pedias
Cappadocia [**S**.4]: **51-58 and 351n.44-353n.56; 174-185 and 394n.99-399n.141;** under Archelaus I Philopatris Ktistes, **182-185**; under Ariarathes X Eusebes Philadelphos, **180-182**; under Ariobarzanes I, **54-58**; under Ariobarzanes II Philopator, **175-177**; under Ariobarzanes III Eusebes Philoromaios, **177-180**; under the last Ariarathids, **52-54**; also mentioned *passim*, esp. 9-21, 31-50, 60-69, 97-109, 152-173, 186-205, 269-310, 322-332. *See also* Maps xxii-xxiv; Illustr. 125
Caracalla (Marcus Aurelius Antoninus) [**S**.6], emperor: 63, 106, 108, 202

Caranitis: 173
Caria: 10, 44, 311. *See also* Maps xxii-xxiv
Carmania: 111, 113, 300
Carrhae, Battle of: **306-309 and 461n.96-462n.106;** and Abgar II of Osrhoene, 107, 195, 196; and Antony, 288; and Artavasdes II of Armenia, 287; and Phraates IV of Parthia, 317. *See also* Map xxvi
Caspiane: 295
Cassius, Gaius: in Bithynia and Cappadocia, 34, 44-45
Cassius (Gaius Cassius Longinus, tyrannicide): and Ariobarzanes III of Cappadocia, 180, 181, 332; and Cleopatra VII of Egypt, 265, 266; and Deiotarus I of Galatia, 168; and Judaea, 220, 223; and the Parthians, 200, 222, 309, 310, 311; and the Thracians, 146, 149
Castor II of Galatia [**S**.3]: **169-170 and 392nn.82-83;** at the Battle of Pharsalus, 171; and Deiotarus I of Galatia, 160, 167, 168, 172, 331
Castor of Phanagoria: 156
Castor Tarcondarius of Galatia [**S**.3]: 164, 167, 168, 169, 171
Cataonia: 55
Cato, Gaius Porcius (cos. 114 BC): in Thrace, 27
Cato, Gaius Porcius (tr.pl. 56 BC): opposition to Pompey by, 239
Cato, Marcus Porcius (Uticensis): and the Cappadocians, 177, 178; and Egypt, 236, 237, 238; and Galatia, 169
Catulus, Quintus Lutatius: and Egypt, 233
Celsus, Tiberius Iulius (Polemaeanus), descendant of Galatian royalty: 324
Celts: 18, 26, 48, 49, 51, 314
Chaeremon of Nysa: 43
Characene (Charax Spasinou, Mesene): **109-110 and 376nn.24-27;** also mentioned, 101, 105, 108, 110, 112, 115. *See also* Map xxv
Charax Spasinou. *See preceding entry*
Chotene: 292
Cicero, Marcus Tullius: and Armenia, 287; and Cappadocia, 39, 56, 58, 174, 175, 176, 177, 178, 179, 180, 181, 183, 332; and Cilicia, 175, 188, 189, 190; and Commagene, 195; and Egypt, 89, 90, 91, 92, 95, 234, 236, 238, 239, 242, 244, 245, 247, 248, 263; and Emesa, 199, 200; and Galatia, 165, 167, 169; and Parthia, 175, 177-178, 188, 189, 199, 201, 310, 312; and Pontus, 158; and the Thracians, 146; use of term *clientela* by, 13
Cilicia: **185-192 and 399n.142-403n.163;** under the successors of Tarcondimotus I, **191-192**; under the Tarcondimotids, **185-187**; under Tarcondimotus I, **187-191**; also mentioned *passim*, esp. 20, 21, 24, 67-69, 99-103, 151-207, 226-238, 266-297, 323-327, 332. *See also* Map xxii-xxiii; Illustr. 133
Cilicia Pedias (Campestris): **187 and 400n.143;** also mentioned, 18, 52, 65, 103, 152, 204, 325. *See also* Map xxiv
Cilicia Tracheia: **186-187 and 399n.142;** also mentioned, 18, 19, 52, 67, 68, 103, 161, 172, 173, 185, 203, 204, 270, 323-326, 331, 332. *See also* Map xxiv
Cimber, Lucius Tillius: and Deiotarus I of Galatia, 168
Cimbri: 31, 40

Cinna, Gaius Helvius: and Caesar, 264
Claudius (Appius Claudius Pulcher). *See* Pulcher, Appius Claudius
Claudius (Tiberius Claudius Drusus Nero Germanicus), emperor: 72, 208, 323, 326
Cleopatra, daughter of Antiochus XII, Seleucid: 205
Cleopatra [**S.**1-2, 4, 9-10], daughter of Mithradates Eupator of Pontus: 38, 42, 47, 282, 284
Cleopatra III of Egypt [**S.**7]: death of, 36, 85; descendants of, 60, 76, 78, 92, 330; rule of, 76, 77, 82, 84, 85, 87, 88, 89, 90, 92
Cleopatra IV of Egypt [**S.**7]: 82, 85, 88
Cleopatra V Tryphaena of Egypt [**S.**7]: 88, 92, 240-241
Cleopatra VI of Egypt [**S.**7]: 238, 240
Cleopatra VII Philopator Philadelphos of Egypt [**S.**7]: **248-279 and 427n.134-445n.376;** and Antony, 207, 243, **266-279**, 332; and Artavasdes II of Armenia, 12, 286, 290; and the Battle of Actium, 12, 148, **275-279**; and Caesar, 157, **258-262**, 332; and Caesarion, **262-264**; children of, 242, 316, 318, 322; and Cilicia Tracheia, 186, 190, 207; exile of, **255-258**; after the Ides of March, **264-266**; and the Ituraeans, 207, 212; and Judaea, 207, 212, 213, 214, 225, 226, 227, 228; and the Nabataeans, 207, 208, 209, 211, 212, 213, 227; and Ptolemy XIII, **248-251, 251-255**; rule of Egypt by, 14, 81, 321, 334; as successor of Ptolemy XII Auletes of Egypt, 92, 220, 231, 232, 236, 245, 246, 247; and title 'King of Kings,' **273-275**. *See also* Illustr. 137-139
Cleopatra Berenice III of Egypt (Berenice III of Egypt) [**S.**7]: **88-89 and 368nn.9-10;** as daughter of Ptolemy IX Lathyros of Egypt, 82, 88, 92; and Judaea, 76; marriages of, 82, 84, 90, 93; statue of, in Athens, 87, 238
Cleopatra Selene of Egypt [**S.**4, 7], daughter of Cleopatra VII of Egypt: 267, 268, 274, 279, 322
Cleopatra Selene of Egypt [**S.**7], sister-wife of Ptolemy IX Lathyros of Egypt: marriage to Ptolemy IX Lathyros of Egypt, 85, 87, 88, 92; and the Seleucids, 15, 78, 82, 83, 84, 86, 88, 90, 91, 92, 94, 95, 203, 204, 205, 241, 242, 247, 330; and Tigranes the Great of Armenia, 36, 66, 71, 78, 88, 103, 105, 203, 234, 280, 330
Cleopatra Thea [**S.**7], mother of Antiochus VIII Grypus, Seleucid: 66, 82, 87, 242, 272. *See also* Illustr. 126
Cleopatra Tryphaena of Egypt [**S.**5, 7]: 60, 82, 85, 87
'client-kings.' *See under* dynasts
Clodius. *See* Pulcher, Publius Clodius
Coele-Syria: 67, 68, 71, 74, 85, 207, 218, 221, 223, 272. *See also* Map xxvii
Colchis: 35, 37, 38, 43, 154, 155, 156, 159, 162, 164, 165. *See also* Map xxii-xxiii
Commagene [**S.**5]: **59-62 and 354n.1-355n.4; 193-198 and 403n.1-406n.21;** under Antiochus I, **193-197**; under Mithradates I Kallinikos, **60-62**; under Mithradates II, **197-198**; under Ptolemaios and Samos, **60**; also mentioned *passim*, esp. 9-11, 14-24, 51-69, 99-112, 152-162, 179-191, 199-205, 270-276, 294-314, 321-327, 330, 332. *See also* Map xxii-xxiii; Illustr. 129, 135

Costobar [**S**.8], brother-in-law of Herod the Great of Judaea: 227

Cotta, Marcus Aurelius: in Bithynia, 47

Cotys II of Thrace: 29

Cotys III of Thrace [**S**.1]: **29-30 and 340n.8-341n.9;** unification of royal houses by, 28, 329

Cotys IV of Thrace [**S**.1]: **146 and 383nn.4-6;** at the Battle of Pharsalus, 149, 150; and the Bessi, 147; regnal years of, 145, 147

Cotys V of Thrace [**S**.1]: 148, 150, 151, 322, 331

Cotys VI of Thrace [**S**.1]: **28-29 and 340n.7;** as Sapaean king, 145, 149

Cotys VII of Thrace [**S**.1]: **150-151 and 385nn.16-17;** descendants of, 322; and Sextus Pompeius, 271

Cotys VIII of Thrace [**S**.1-2, 6]: 151, 160, 323

Cotys IX of Thrace [**S**.1-2]: 163, 284, 323, 324, 327

Crassus, Marcus Licinius: defeated by the Parthians, 12, 107, 189, 191, 195, 222, 243, 252, 257, 282, 286, 287, 303, 305, 306-308, 309, 311, 312, 313, 317, 318, 333; and Egypt, 91, 233, 234, 243; and Judaea, 218

Crassus, Publius Canidius: and Armenia, 270, 289, 313; and Iberia, 288, 292, 313

Creticus, Marcus Antonius. *See* Antonius, Marcus (Creticus, father of the triumvir)

Crimea: 35, 36, 37, 42, 47, 48, 148, 154

Cyprus: **236-237 and 420n.45-422n.58;** also mentioned, 20, 36, 42, 76, 77, 83, 84, 85, 86, 87, 88, 90, 91, 92, 93, 95, 186, 203, 207, 230, 232, 234, 238, 239, 242, 247, 258, 261, 265, 267, 270, 274. *See also* Maps xxii-xxiii, xxvii

Cyrene: 11, 25, 26, 36, 82, 83, 84, 88, 90, 93, 95, 149, 186, 230, 232, 239, 246, 247, 258, 261, 274, 276, 330, 333. *See also* Map xxii-xxiii

Cyrrhestica: 189, 286

Dacians: 147, 151, 322, 323

Dahae: 299, 317. *See also* Map xxii-xxiii

Dardani: 28, 29

Darius the Great of Persia: 10, 23, 36, 52, 161, 329

Darius III of Persia: 294

Darius of Media: 101, 283, 296

Darius of Pontus [**S**.2]: **160-161 and 389nn.52-53;** and Antony, 161, 170, 268; descendants of, 158

Decapolis: 218. *See also* Map xxvii

Decidius Saxa, Lucius. *See* Saxa

Deiotarus I of Galatia [**S**.3, 9]: **51 and 350n.43; 164-169 and 389n.62-392n.81;** and Brogitarus of Galatia, **164-165**, 331; and Caesar, 21, 157, 158, 160, 179, 324, 331; establishment of monarchy by, 12, 18, 331, 334; and Mithradates of Pergamon, 173-174, 259; and Mithradates Eupator of Pontus, 38, 47, 51, 174; and the Parthians, 177, 188, 195, 310; and Pompey, 156; and Rome, **165-169**; rule of, in other regions, 156, 162, 286; successors of, 160, 169, 171, 172, 173, 174, 286; and Tigranes the Great of Armenia, 153

Deiotarus Philopator of Galatia [**S**.3], son of Castor II of Galatia: **170 and 392n.84**

Deiotarus Philopator of Galatia [**S**.3], son and successor of Deiotarus I of Galatia: 167, 168, 169

Deiotarus IV Philadelphos of Paphlagonia [**S.**3]: **170 and 392nn.84-85;** Armenian ties of, 286; at the Battle of Actium, 269, 277; rule of Paphlagonia by, 169, 173, 324

Demetrius I Poliorcetes: 72

Demetrius I, Seleucid: 54

Demetrius II Nicator, Seleucid [**S.**7, 10]: 66, 82, 111, 117

Demetrius III Eukairos, Seleucid [**S.**7]: defeat of, 80; and Mithradates II of Parthia, 68, 117; rule of Damascus by, 68, 74, 86; siege of Philip I, Seleucid by, 63, 68, 77

Dentheletae, Thracian tribe: 18, 28, 146, 149, 150, 322. *See also* Map xxiv

Dexandros, Syrian priest of imperial cult: 205

Dicomes of the Getae: 148

Didius, Quintus: and Antonian gladiators, 277-278

Didius, Titus: and Thrace, 27

Diocles, member of royal house of Mithradates Eupator of Pontus: 43, 47

Dionysius of Heracleon, minor dynast of the Levant: 80

Dionysius of Tripolis, minor dynast of the Levant: 80

Dolabella, Publius Cornelius: and Cleopatra VII of Egypt, 265, 266; and Deiotarus I of Galatia, 168

Domnilaus of Galatia [**S.**3]: **171 and 392n.86;** at the Battle of Pharsalus, 169

Dorylaus, commander under Mithradates Eupator of Pontus: 43

Drusilla, daughter of Caligula: 323

Drusilla, daughter of Juba II of Mauretania and Cleopatra Selene of Egypt: 279

Dyegilus, Thracian dynast: 27

Dynamis of Bosporus [**S.**1-2]: **159-160 and 388nn.49-51;** as descendant of Mithradates Eupator of Pontus, 44, 119, 158; marriages of, 16, 17, 158, 161, 162, 163, 283, 323, 324, 332. *See also* Illustr. 130

dynasts: as 'friends and allies,' 4-5, 14, 24; intermarriage of, **14-17**; as 'kings,' not 'client-kings,' **12-14**; as 'network' of rulers, 1-6, **321-334**

Dyteutus of Galatia [**S.**3]: **171 and 393nn.88-89;** as priest at Pontic Comana, 169

Egypt [**S.**7]: **81-95 and 363n.1-370n.15; 229-279 and 416n.1-445n.376;** under Berenice IV, **239-243**; and Caesarion, **262-264**; under Cleopatra VII Philopator Philadelphos, **248-279**; under Cleopatra Berenice III, **88-89**; under Ptolemy IX Philometor Soter II Lathyros, **84-88**; under Ptolemy X Alexander I, **82-84**; under Ptolemy XI Alexander II, **89-91**; under Ptolemy XII Theos Neos Dionysos Philopator Philadelphos Auletes, **91-95**, **229-235**, **237-239**, **243-248**; under Ptolemy XIII Theos Philadelphos, **248-255**; under Ptolemy of Cyprus, **236-237**; also mentioned *passim*, esp. 9-22, 65-78, 157-166, 200-220, 321, 325, 330-333. *See also* Maps xxii-xxiii, xxvii; Illustr. 139

Elagabalus (Marcus Aurelius Antoninus), emperor: 63, 202, 324, 327

Elam. *See next entry*

Elymais (Elam): **110-111 and 376n.28-377n.30;** also mentioned, 101, 105, 111, 112, 301, 304, 307. *See also* Map xxv

Emesa [**S.**6]: **62-64 and 355n.5-356n.8; 198-202 and 406n.22-407n.36;** under Azizus, *phylarch* of the Arabs, **63-64**; under Iamblichus I, **200-202**; under Sampsigeramus I, **64**, **199-200**; under the successors of Iamblichus I, **202**; also mentioned *passim*, esp. 15, 19, 69-72, 184-206, 297-310, 326, 327, 332. *See also* Map xxvii; Illustr. 134
Erato of Armenia [**S.**9]: 291
Eumachus, commander for Mithradates Eupator of Pontus: 47
Eumenes II of Pergamon [**S.**4]: 54

Fars. *See* Persis
Fimbria, Gaius Flavius: and the Mithradatic Wars, 43, 46
Flaccus, Lucius Valerius: and the Mithradatic Wars, 45-46
Frugi, Tiberii Iulii, descendants of Galatian royalty: 325
Fulvia, wife of Antony: commemoration of, on Galatian coin, 168; as mother of Antyllus, 278
Furnius, Gaius: and Sextus Pompeius, 271, 272

Gabinius, Aulus: and Archelaus, husband of Berenice IV of Egypt, 183, 205, 241, 242, 243; and Judaea, 218, 219, 220, 221, 243; and the Mithradatic Wars, 46; and the Nabataeans, 210, 211, 221; and the Parthians, 286, 296, 302, 303, 305, 306, 317, 333; restoration of Ptolemy XII Auletes of Egypt by, 210, 231, 239, 242, 243, 244, 245, 247, 252, 286
Gaius. *See* Caligula
Galaaditis: 77
Galatia [**S.**3]: **48-51 and 349n.40-350n.43; 163-174 and 389n.62-394n.98;** under Amyntas, **171-174**; and Brogitarus, **164-165**; under Castor II, **169-170**; under Deiotarus I, **51**, **164-169**; and Deiotarus Philadelphos and Deiotarus Philopator, **170**; and Domnilaus, Adiatorix, Dyteutus, **171**; and Mithradates Eupator of Pontus, **50-51**; under the tetrarchs, **49-50**; also mentioned *passim*, esp. 10-13, 18, 21, 31-57, 152-164, 175-195, 269-290, 323-325, 331. *See also* Maps xxii-xxiv; Illustr. 123
Galba (Servius Sulpicius Galba), emperor: 324
Galilee: 71, 77, 218, 223, 224
Gallus, Aelius: and the Nabataeans, 72
Ganymedes, Egyptian official: 245, 259
Gaulanitis: 74, 77
Gauls: 174, 244, 258
Gazelonitis: 164, 170
Gedrosia: 113. *See also* Map xxii-xxiii
geography, historical: **17-20 and 336n.6-337n.7;** of Armenia, 96-97; of Bithynia, 30; of Cappadocia, 51-52; of Cilicia, 185-187; of Commagene, 59-60; of Egypt, 81; of Emesa, 62-63; of Galatia, 48-49; of Judaea, 69-70; of Palestine, 69-70; of Parthia, 112-114; of Pontus, 35-36; of Seleucid Syria, 65-66; of Thrace, 25-26
Gepaepyris of Bosporus [**S.**1-2]: 160, 163, 323, 324
Geta (Lucius Septimius) [**S.**6], emperor: 63
Getae, Thracian tribe: 147, 148, 151, 159. *See also* Map xxii-xxiii
Glaphyra [**S.**4-6, 8], daughter of Archelaus I of Cappadocia: 185, 300, 322, 325

Glaphyra [**S.**4], mother of Archelaus I of Cappadocia: 182, 183
Gondophares, ruler in India: 111
Gordian (Marcus Antonius Gordianus), emperor: 106
Gordius, agent of Mithradates Eupator of Pontus: and Cappadocia, 32, 35, 39, 53, 58; and the Mithradatic Wars, 46
Gordyene: **108-109 and 375n.20-376n.23;** also mentioned, 10, 80, 101, 102, 103, 105, 120, 153, 175, 280, 281, 282, 285, 296, 302, 303, 305. *See also* Map xxvi
Gordys, mythological founder of Gordyene: 108
Gotarzes I Autokrator Philopator of Parthia [**S.**10]: **115-116 and 380nn.39-40;** opposition to Mithradates II of Parthia by, 97, 117, 119
Gouras [**S.**9], brother of Tigranes the Great of Armenia: 104

Hadrian (Publius Aelius Hadrianus), emperor: 109, 114, 198, 326
Hasmonaeans: expansion of, 73; in Judaean politics, 11, 21, 211, 220, 222, 223, 224, 225, 226, 227, 311, 332
Helen, wife of Monobazus Bazaeus of Adiabene: 108
Hephaistion, *dioiketes* of Ptolemy XII Auletes of Egypt: 237, 253
Heracleon, minor dynast of the Levant: 80
Herod the Great of Judaea [**S.**5-6, 8]: **223-228 and 414n.113-416n.137;** and Antigonus of Judaea, 15, 206-207, 211, 222-223, **223-225**, 312; and Antony, 14, 161, 170, 190, 191, 222, 223, 268, 272, 312; and Archelaus I of Cappadocia, 185, 187; and Augustus, 191; at the Battle of Actium, 212, 213, 227, 228, 276, 278; and Cleopatra VII of Egypt, 190, 207, 212, 222, 268, 270, 272, 273, 276, 316; descendants of, 185, 284, 291, 297, 327, 332; and Hyrcanus II, *see under* Hyrcanus II of Judaea; invasion of Arabia by, 212; and the Ituraeans, 208; and Jewish politics, 217, 218; and the Nabataeans, 211, 212, 220, 221, 222, 273, 276; and Octavian, 212, 213; and the Parthians 221-222, 223, 268; rule of Judaea by, 11, 14, 219, **225-228**; siege of Samosata by, 19, 107, 181, 196, 197, 224, 312, 313; as son of Kypros, 259
Herod of Chalcis [**S.**8]: 208, 327
Herodes Antipas [**S.**8], son of Herod the Great of Judaea: 332
Herotimus of the Nabataeans: 73
Hibrida, Gaius Antonius: in Thrace, 146
Himerus, Hyrcanian viceroy of Mesopotamia: 115
Hittites: 9, 10, 12
Homanadenses: 172, 173
Hydarnes III of Armenia: 295
Hyrcania: 105, 111, 114, 115, 289, 295, 299, 309. *See also* Map xxii-xxiii
Hyrcanus I of Judaea (John Hyrcanus) [**S.**8]: 75, 85, 213, 214, 215, 216, 218, 330
Hyrcanus II of Judaea [**S.**8]: **213-217 and 412n.73-413n.91;** and Aristobulus II, 78, 79, 208, 209, **213-217**, 332; and Herod the Great, 213, 217, 222, 223, 225, 227, 313; and the Parthians, 213, 221, 222, 306, 311, 313; after Pompey's conquest, 217, 218, 219, 220
Hyspaosines of Characene: 109, 115

Iamblichus I of Emesa [**S.**5-6]: **200-202 and 407nn.27-34;** and the Battle of Actium, 276, 326; and Caesar, 157, 259; and Cicero, 178, 310; and Deiotarus I of Galatia, 169; and the Parthians, 178, 188, 195, 306, 310, 332; as *phylarch*, 199; successors of, 202
Iamblichus II of Emesa [**S.**5-6]: 191, 202, 327
Iberia: **291-293 and 451n.42-452n.50;** also mentioned, 15, 22, 101, 105, 120, 155, 282, 288, 291, 313, 314, 318. *See also* Maps xxii-xxiii, xxvi
Iconia: 24
Idumaea: 209, 214, 218, 219, 223, 224, 225. *See also* Map xxvii
Iotape I of Atropatene [**S.**5-6, 9]: betrothal to Alexander Helios of Egypt, 267, 275, 289, 297, 298, 316, 326; marriage to Mithradates III of Commagene, 299, 326
Iotape II of Atropatene [**S.**5-6]: 297, 326
Iotape III of Atropatene [**S.**5-6]: 297, 326, 327
Iotape IV of Atropatene [**S.**5-6, 8]: 297
Iotape V of Atropatene [**S.**5-6, 8]: 297
Iotape VI Philadelphos of Atropatene [**S.**5-6]: 297, 326
Iotape VII of Atropatene [**S.**5-6, 8]: 297, 325
Iranians: 19, 21, 23, 24, 49, 51, 54, 59, 66, 80, 96, 107, 112, 113, 117, 120, 198, 205, 309, 321, 328
Isauria: 161, 172. *See also* Map xxiv
Isbubarza [**S.**10], sister-wife of Sinatruces I of Parthia: 300
Isias [**S.**5], mother of Mithradates II of Commagene: 194, 197
Ituraeans: **70-72 and 357n.16-358n.18; 206-208 and 408n.47-409n.53;** under Lysanias, **207-208**; under Ptolemy, son of Mennaeus, **70-72**, **206-207**; also mentioned, 73, 79, 212, 221, 311, 312
Izates of Adiabene: 108, 110

Jannaeus. *See* Alexander Jannaeus
Jews: 19, 63, 80, 212, 256, 266, 327. *See also* Judaea
John Hyrcanus. *See* Hyrcanus I of Judaea
Jonathon, Jewish leader: 75
Joseph [**S.**8], brother of Herod the Great of Judaea: 224
Joseph [**S.**8], brother-in-law of Herod the Great of Judaea: 227
Josephus, perhaps brother of Ptolemy of the Ituraeans: 207
Juba I of Mauretania: 257
Juba II of Mauretania [**S.**4, 7]: literary work of, 184; marriage to Cleopatra Selene, daughter of Cleopatra VII of Egypt, 267, 279, 322; marriage to Glaphyra, daughter of Archelaus I of Cappadocia, 185, 322, 325
Judaea [**S.**8]: **75-79 and 361n.25-362n.28; 213-228 and 412n.71-416n.137;** under Alexander Jannaeus, **76-78**; under Alexandra Salome, **78-79**; under Herod the Great, **225-228**; after Pompey, **217-223**; and the rivalry of Antigonus and Herod, **223-225**; and the rivalry of Aristobulus II and Hyrcanus II, **213-217**; also mentioned *passim*, esp. 11, 14-16, 19-24, 59-86, 161-173, 181-213, 268-276, 284-300, 306-318, 321, 322, 325-327, 330, 332. *See also* Maps xxii-xxiii, xxvii; Illustr. 136
Jugurtha of Numidia: 40
Julia the Younger, Queen, descendant of Tarcondimotus I of Cilicia: 192

Julia, daughter of Tarcondimotus I of Cilicia: 190, 191, 325

Julia Balbilla [**S.**5-6], granddaughter of Antiochus IV of Commagene: 198, 326

Julia Domna [**S.**6], wife of Septimius Severus, emperor: 63, 202, 327

Julia Maesa [**S.**6], sister of Julia Domna: 202, 327

Julia Mamaea [**S.**1-2, 5-6], wife of Polemo II of Pontus: 327

Kamnaskires, throne name in Elymais and Susiana: 110

Kypros [**S.**8], mother of Herod the Great of Judaea: 215, 220, 259

Labienus, Quintus: command of Parthian forces by, 170, 212, 311, 312

Lagetas, cousin of Mithradates Eupator of Pontus: 43

Lagids: 63, 92

Laodice [**S.**2], mother of Mithradates Eupator of Pontus: 36, 66, 242

Laodice [**S.**7, 10], sister of Antiochus VIII Grypus, Seleucid: 117

Laodice [**S.**5, 10], sister of Mithradates II of Commagene: 194, 197

Laodice [**S.**2, 4], sister of Mithradates Eupator of Pontus: descendants of, 33, 42; marriage to Ariarathes VI of Cappadocia, 17, 32, 39, 66, 329; marriage to Nicomedes III of Bithynia, 32, 33, 39, 53, 54, 66, 329

Laodice Thea Philadelphos [**S.**5, 7], daughter of Antiochus VIII Grypus, Seleucid: 60, 65, 66, 193. *See also* Illustr. 124

Lebanon: 19, 20, 59, 70, 80, 199, 256, 266, 268, 270. *See also* Map xxvii

Lentulus, Gnaeus Cornelius (Marcellinus): as governor of Syria, 221

Lepidus, Marcus Aemilius: and Egypt, 256

Livia, wife of Augustus: 160, 323

Longinus, Gaius Cassius. *See* Cassius (tyrannicide)

Lucullus, Lucius Licinius: campaigns against Mithradates Eupator of Pontus, 42, 46, 47, 48, 50, 51, 61, 75, 107, 108, 145, 152, 153, 154, 158, 164, 174, 177, 186, 193, 213, 257, 280, 298, 301; campaigns against Tigranes the Great of Armenia, 16, 48, 51, 58, 62, 68, 71, 75, 102, 104, 105, 107, 108, 145, 152, 153, 154, 174, 175, 177, 186, 193, 194, 203, 213, 257, 280, 281, 284, 298, 301; command in the East of, 20, 321; and Egypt, 86-87, 232; and Emesa, 198, 199

Lucullus, Marcus Terentius Varro. *See* Varro

Lycaonia: 18, 161, 170, 172, 175, 276, 287. *See also* Maps xxii-xxiv

Lycia: 89, 259. *See also* Maps xxii-xxiv

Lycomedes, priest in Pontic Comana: 161, 171, 179

Lydia: 10, 311. *See also* Maps xxii-xxiv

Lysanias of Abila: 208

Lysanias of Chalcis. *See next entry*

Lysanias of the Ituraeans (Lysanias of Chalcis): **207-208 and 408n.50-409n.53;** death of, 212, 270, 274; and the Parthians, 207, 312

Maccabaeus, Judas, Jewish leader: 73, 75

Maccabees: 215

Macedonia: 26, 27, 28, 29, 42, 106, 109, 111, 112, 145, 146, 149, 172, 230, 268, 292, 294, 307, 309. *See also* Map xxii-xxiii

Machares, son of Mithradates Eupator

of Pontus: betrayal of Mithradates Eupator by, 42, 43, 47, 48, 154, 174, 280
Malchus, murderer of Antipater of Idumaea: 222
Malchus of the Nabataeans. *See next entry*
Malichus I (Malchus) of the Nabataeans: **211-213 and 410n.60-411n.70;** accession of, 210; and the Battle of Actium, 276; and Herod the Great of Judaea, 221-222, 226, 227; and the Parthians, 201, 221, 222, 312
Ma'nu, throne name in Osrhoene: 106
Marcellinus, Gnaeus Cornelius Lentulus. *See* Lentulus
Mariamme [**S.**8], wife of Herod the Great: 223, 225, 227
Marius, Gaius: arrogance of, 43, 331; and Mithradates Eupator of Pontus, 40, 44, 45, 53, 54
Marsus, Gaius Vibius: as governor of Syria, 327
Media: 96, 101, 102, 103, 105, 107, 110, 115, 251, 272, 275, 288, 289, 292, 293, 294, 295, 296, 297, 298, 299, 300, 304, 309. *See also* Maps xxii-xxiii, xxv
Media Atropatene. *See* Atropatene
Media Maior: 101, 295, 296
Meherdates (Mithradates) of Characene: 110
Memmius, Lucius: visit to Egypt of, 83
Mennaeus of the Ituraeans: 70, 71
Mesene. *See* Characene
Mesopotamia: 9, 23, 59, 61, 96, 98, 101, 103, 105, 109, 112, 113, 114, 115, 117, 120, 194, 268, 282, 288, 291, 293, 301, 306, 311. *See also* Maps xxii-xxiii, xxv-xxvi; Illustr. 129, 131
Metellus, Quintus Caecilius (Scipio): as governor of Syria, 256
Mithradates I Kallinikos of Commagene [**S.**5]: **60-62 and 354n.2-355n.4;** descendants of, 65, 193, 330; syncretism of, 60
Mithradates II of Commagene [**S.**5]: **197-198 and 405n.19-406n.21;** and Antony, 276, 326; and the Battle of Actium, 326; inscription honouring Laodice, his sister, 194, 197
Mithradates III of Commagene [**S.**5-6, 9]: 191, 297, 299
Mithradates I of Parthia [**S.**10]: 11, 25, 111, 112, 113, 117, 303, 304
Mithradates II Euergetes Epiphanes Philhellene of Parthia [**S.**9-10], **114-116 and 379n.37-380n.40;** and Characene, 110; and Commagene, 60; empire of, 113; and Gotarzes I Autokrator Philopator of Parthia, 97, 117, 119; and Mithradates Eupator of Pontus, 101, 116, 118, 119; and Rome, 36, 100, **118-119**, 301, 303, 318; and the Seleucids, 25, 68, 87, 117; successors of, 100, 102, 119, 296, 316; and Tigranes the Great of Armenia, 14, 44, 47, 97, 98, 100, 101, 116, 118, 119, 283. *See also* Illustr. 131
Mithradates III of Parthia [**S.**10]: **304-305 and 460nn.88-91;** and Gabinius, 286; and Orodes 'II' of Parthia, 316; and title 'King of Kings,' 119
Mithradates I of Pontus: 56
Mithradates IV of Pontus [**S.**2]: 158
Mithradates V Euergetes (Mithradates Philopator and Philadelphos) of Pontus [**S.**2, 4]: 38, 49, 158

Mithradates VI Eupator Dionysus of Pontus [**S.**1-2, 4, 9-10]: **36-48 and 345n.20-349n.39; 151-155 and 385n.21-387n.34;** and Atropatene, 296; and Bithynia, 31, 32, 33, 34, 35, 101, 329; and Cappadocia, 17, 19, 21, 32, 33, 34, **38-40**, 52, 53, 54, 55, 56, **57-58**, 88, 97, 98, 101, 155, 174, 175, 176, 180, 182, 184, 329, 330; and Commagene, 193, 194; death of, 155, 216; descendants of, 155, 156, 157, 158, 159, 160, 162, 176, 177, 180, 183, 241, 242, 280, 285, 323, 330; dynastic activity of, **42-44**; and Egypt, 86, 87, 91, 92, 237, 242, 247; expansion towards empire by, **37-38**, 113, 114, 143; and Galatia, 49, 50, **50-51**, 88, 101, 169, 174, 331; and Iberia, 292; and Lucullus, *see under* Lucullus, Lucius Licinius; and Paphlagonia, 31, 34; and the Parthians, 12, 34, 116, 117, 118, 119, 120, 194, 301, 302, 303; and Phrygia Maior, 31; and Rome, 11, 14, 18, 21, 22, **40-42**, **44-48**, 93, 103, 105, 164, 280, 283, 324, 329, 333, 334, *see also* Mithradatic Wars; and the Seleucids, 66, 242; and Thrace, 27, 28, 29, 145, 146, 148, 281; and Tigranes the Great of Armenia, 14, 21, 97, 98, 99, 100, 101, 105, 281, 282, 283, 284, 285. *See also* Illustr. 122

Mithradates of Characene. *See* Meherdates of Characene

Mithradates of Iberia: 293

Mithradates of Media Atropatene [**S.**9]: 101, 283, 295

Mithradates of Pergamon [**S.**3]: **158-159 and 388nn.47-48;** and Caesar, 157, 164, 166, 167, 200, 211, 259; and Galatia, 160, 164, 166, 167, 169, 173, 259; recognition of, as king, 161

Mithradates Chrestos [**S.**2], brother of Mithradates Eupator of Pontus: 36

Mithradates Philopator and Philadelphos of Pontus. *See* Mithradates V of Pontus

Mithradates Philopator Philadelphos, son of Mithradates Eupator of Pontus: 43

Mithradatic Wars: **44-48 and 348n.33-349n.39;** and Egypt, 82, 86; and Galatia, 163, 164; and Thrace, 146. *See also* Ch. 2

Mithradatis, daughter of Mithradates Eupator of Pontus: 42

Mithrobuzanes of Sophene: 106

Moab: 77

Moaphernes, relative of Mithradates Eupator of Pontus: 43

Molon: rebellion of, against Antiochus III, Seleucid, 294

Monaeses, Parthian noble: 201, 288, 313, 314

Monikos of Chalcis: 71

Monime, wife of Mithradates Eupator of Pontus: 43

Monobazus Bazaeus of Adiabene: 108

Mostis of Thrace: **27-28 and 339n.5-340n.6**

Murena, Lucius Licinius: and the Mithradatic Wars, 46

Mygdonia: 107. *See also* Map xxvi

Mysia: 47. *See also* Maps xxii-xxiv

Nabataeans: **72-75 and 358n.19-361n.24; 208-213 and 409n.54-411n.70;** under Aretas I, **72-73**; under Aretas II, **73- 74**; under Aretas III, **74-75**, **209-210**; under Malichus I, **211-213**; under Obodas I, **74**; under

Obodas II, **210-211**; under Rabbel I, **73**; also mentioned *passim*, esp. 11, 16, 23, 65-80, 99-110, 199-207, 214-227, 273-277, 327, 332. *See also* Maps xxii-xxiii, xxvii; Illustr. 127, 142
Natunia. *See* Adiabene
Nero (Nero Claudius Caesar), emperor: 20, 23, 63, 98, 106, 114, 202, 291, 326, 332
Nicolaus of Damascus, tutor of Antony's children: 279
Nicomedes III of Bithynia [**S.**4]: **30-33 and 341n.10-342n.13;** and Cappadocia, 33, 39, 52, 53, 54, 55; marriage to Laodice, sister of Mithradates Eupator of Pontus, 39, 53, 54, 66, 329; and the partition of Paphlagonia, 38, 40, 41, 50; prosperity of Bithynia under, 87
Nicomedes IV of Bithynia [**S.**4]: **33-35 and 343n.14-345n.19;** as last dynast of Bithynia, 30, 88, 246, 329, 331; and Mithradates Eupator of Pontus, 41, 45, 46, 53
Nysa, daughter of Mithradates Eupator of Pontus: 42
Nysa, daughter of Nicomedes IV of Bithynia: 34
Nysa [**S.**4], mother of Ariarathes VI of Cappadocia: 38
Nysa [**S.**4], wife of Nicomedes IV of Bithynia: 33, 42

Obodas I of the Nabataeans: **74 and 360n.22;** and Alexander Jannaeus of Judaea, 75, 77; and Antiochus XII, Seleucid, 68, 74, 86; and the Nabataean dynasty, 70, 73, 74, 210; and Tigranes the Great of Armenia, 104
Obodas II of the Nabataeans: **210-211 and 410n.59**
Obodas III of the Nabataeans: 211
Octavia, wife of Antony: and children of Antony and Cleopatra VII, 279; divorce of, 275; in the East, 269, 271, 272
Octavian (Gaius Octavius): and Antony, 268, 275, 313, 316; and Armenia, 316; and Atropatene, 10, 297, 316; and the Battle of Actium, 275, 276, 277, 278, 279, 321; and Cappadocia, 181, 184; and Cilicia, 184, 186, 191; and Commagene, 198, 326; and the East, 274; and Egypt, 251, 266; and Emesa, 184, 191, 202; and Galatia, 168, 171, 184; and Judaea, 212, 213, 223, 227, 228; and Parthia, 317; and Pontus, 184; and Thrace, 148, 149, 151, 331. *See also* Augustus
Octavius, Gaius (father of Octavian): in Thrace, 28, 146
Odrysian-Astaean dynasty of Thrace [**S.**1]: monarchs of, 28, 29, 145, 146, 147, 148, 149, 150, 151, 322, 331
Odrysians, royal house of Thrace: 25, 27, 28, 29, 147, 322. *See also preceding entry*
Orodes I of Parthia [**S.**10]: defeat of, 119; reign of, 115, 116, 117, 119, 305; and Tigranes the Great of Armenia, 100, 117
Orodes 'II' of Parthia [**S.**5, 10]: **305-306 and 460n.92-461n.95;** and Armenia, 287, 306; and the Battle of Carrhae, 287, 307, 308; and Cappadocia, 177; Hellenization of, 304, 309; intermarriage with Armenia, 283, 286, 307, 308; intermarriage with Commagene, 194, 196, 252; and Mithradates III of Parthia, 304, 305, 316; and Pacorus I of Parthia, 309, 310, 311, 312, 313; and Rome, 257, 303,

333; successors of, 288, 313; titles of, 119, 304. *See also* Illustr. 141
Orontes I of Armenia: 295
Orontes III of Armenia: 106
Orontes of Sophene: 106
Orontids, Armenian dynasty [**S.**5, 9]: 99, 106, 295
Orxines, Persian satrap: 111
Osaces, Parthian commander: 310
Osrhoene: **106-107 and 374nn.13-14;** also mentioned, 101, 102, 105, 152, 195, 196, 282, 307, 308. *See also* Map xxvi; Illustr. 129
Oxodates, Persian ruler of Media: 294

Pacorus, father of Meherdates of Characene: 110
Pacorus I of Parthia [**S.**9-10]: **309-313 and 462n.107-465n.120;** death of, 181, 288, 313, 334; Hellenization of, 309; intermarriage of, 283, 286, 287, 290, 308; invasion of Syria, Asia Minor, and Judaea by, 188, 196, 207, 224, 288, 318; and Rome, 333. *See also* Illustr. 141
Palestine: **69-72 and 357n.16-358n.18; 205-208 and 408n.46-409n.53;** under Lysanias, **207-208**; under Ptolemy, son of Mennaeus, **70-72**, **206-207**; also mentioned, 20, 59, 72, 76, 77, 79, 80, 82, 143, 144, 209, 214, 217, 221, 222, 230, 256, 266, 268, 312. *See also* Maps xxii-xxiii, xxvii
Pamphylia: 172, 186. *See also* Map xxiv
Paphlagonia: 11, 13, 18, 31, 32, 33, 34, 35, 37, 38, 40, 41, 45, 50, 156, 160, 164, 169, 170, 173, 269, 277, 286, 324. *See also* Maps xxii-xxiv
Parsa. *See* Persis
Parthia [**S.**10]: **20-24 and 337nn.8-9; 112-120 and 377n.36-382n.45; 300-318 and 456n.76-469n.137;** and Armenia, **116-117**; and the Battle of Carrhae, **306-308**, **308-309**; and Gotarzes I Autokrator Philopator, **115-116**; under Mithradates II Euergetes Epiphanes Philhellene, **114-116**; under Mithradates III, **304-305**; under Orodes 'II,' **305-306**; under Pacorus I, **309-313**; under Phraates III, **301-304**; under Phraates IV, **313-318**; and Rome, 3-4, **20-24**, **118-119**; and the Seleucids, **117**; under Sinatruces I Theopator Euergetes Eusebes, **119-120**; also mentioned *passim*, esp. 9-24, 44-52, 61-73, 96-112, 152-225, 252-300, 322, 325-327, 330-334. *See also* Map xxii-xxiii
Peitholaus, *hypostrategos* at Jerusalem: 220
Peraea: 219
Perdiccas, general of Alexander the Great: 294
Pergamon: 11, 27, 157, 158, 159, 160, 161, 164, 166, 167, 169, 173, 200, 211, 259, 276, 286, 333
Perseus, King of Macedon: 27, 28, 29, 30, 45
Persia: 9, 10, 12, 36, 52, 56, 61, 62, 73, 79, 80, 96, 106, 110, 111, 112, 113, 115, 205, 230, 291, 292, 294, 305, 309, 312, 329, 334
Persis (Fars, Parsa): **111-112 and 377nn.31-35;** also mentioned, 101, 105, 110, 307. *See also* Map xxii-xxiii
Petubastis, high priest of Memphis under Ptolemy VIII Physcon of Egypt: 83
Petubastis, high priest of Memphis under Ptolemy IX Lathyros and Ptolemy X of Egypt: 93, 94
Peucestas, bodyguard of Alexander the Great: 111

Phallion [**S.**8], brother of Antipater of Idumaea: 215
Pharasmanes I of Iberia: 293
Pharisees: 75, 77, 78, 213, 214
Pharnabazus II of Iberia: 292, 293
Pharnaces I of Pontus [**S.**2]: 37
Pharnaces II of Pontus [**S.**1-2, 4]: **155-158 and 387n.35-388n.46;** and Caesar, 44, 159, 166, 179, 196, 261; and Cappadocia, 176, 177, 180; and Colchis, 164, 165; defeat of, 11, 18; and Deiotarus I of Galatia, 166, 169; and empire of Mithradates Eupator of Pontus, 43, 48, 174, 176, 177, 178, 216, 324, 330; successors of, 159, 160, 161, 169, 170; titles of, 44, 119, 159
Pharsalus, Battle of: Cappadocians at, 180, 181; Cilicians at, 189, 191; Commagenians at, 195; commemoration of, 261; Eastern kings at, 178; and Egyptians, 255; and Emesenes, 200, 201; Galatians at, 165, 169, 171; influence of, 321; Metellus Scipio at, 256; and Pharnaces II of Pontus, 157; Pompey's flight from, 257; and Thracians, 146, 147, 149, 150, 331
Phasael [**S.**8], brother of Herod the Great of Judaea: 211, 219, 223
Phaunene (Phauene): 295
Philip I Philadelphos, Seleucid [**S.**7]: and the last Seleucids, 63, 64, 68, 71, 74, 77, 103, 203
Philip II Barypous, Seleucid [**S.**7]: **203-204 and 407n.40-408n.42;** and the last Seleucids, 64, 68, 69, 103, 104, 199, 203, 205, 241, 242
Philippi, Battle of: Antony at, 266; Atropatenians at, 297; and Cappadocians, 180, 181; Cilicians at, 190; Galatians at, 168, 172; influence of, 321; and Parthians, 201, 311; Thracians at, 149, 150, 331
Philippion, son of Ptolemy of the Ituraeans: 206
Philippus, Lucius Marcius: as governor of Syria, 221
Philopappus (Gaius Iulius Antiochus Epiphanes Philopappus) [**S.**5-6], grandson of Antiochus IV of Commagene: 15, 65, 198, 204, 326
Philopator I of Cilicia: 191, 325
Philopator II of Cilicia: 191, 325
Philopator of Parthia, son of Gotarzes I of Parthia: 119
Philopoemen, father-in-law of Mithradates Eupator of Pontus: 43
Phoenicia: 64, 76, 77, 78, 79, 103, 104, 207, 216, 219, 222, 274, 282. *See also* Map xxii-xxiii
Phoenix, member of royal house of Mithradates Eupator of Pontus: 43, 47
Phraataces of Parthia. *See* Phraates V of Parthia
Phraates [**S.**10], youngest son of Phraates IV of Parthia: 318
Phraates I of Parthia [**S.**10]: 113
Phraates II of Parthia [**S.**10]: 113, 115, 117
Phraates III of Parthia [**S.**9-10]: **301-304 and 457n.77-460n.87;** and Elymais, 111, 301, 304; and Gordyene, 109, 296; and Mithradates Eupator of Pontus, 48, 120, 152, 153, 154; and Pompey, 118, 194, 216, 257; and Rome, 333; succeeded by Mithradates III of Parthia, 304; successor of Sinatruces I of Parthia, 48, 119, 120, 143, 300, 301; and Tigranes the Great of Armenia, 48, 100, 117, 152, 154,

281, 282, 283; and Tigranes the Younger of Armenia, 282, 283. *See also* Illustr. 141
Phraates IV of Parthia [**S.**10]: **313-318 and 465n.121-469n.137;** and Antiochus I of Commagene, 197; and Antony, 162, 201, 271, 288, 289; and Augustus, 191, 291, 325; and Rome, 333
Phraates V (Phraataces) of Parthia [**S.**10]: 318
Phriapatius of Parthia [**S.**10]: 113
Phrygia: 9, 35, 45, 47, 48, 49, 50, 172. *See also* Maps xxii-xxiv
Phrygia Maior: 31, 37, 50
Pisidia: 47, 48, 161, 170, 172, 269
Piso, Lucius Calpurnius: and Thrace, 146, 147
Polemo I of Pontus [**S.**1-2, 4-6]: **161-163 and 389nn.55-61;** accession of, 12, 161, 269; and Antony, 11, 18, 170, 172, 181, 184, 207, 228, 269, 270, 271, 276, 289, 290, 298, 299, 314, 323, 324, 330, 331; and Archelaus I of Cappadocia, 183; after the Battle of Actium, 160, 184, 321, 323, 324; and Cilicia, 186, 270; marriages of, 17, 159, 160, 185, 283, 323, 324, 332; successors of 160, 283, 323, 324. *See also* Illustr. 130
Polemo II of Pontus [**S.**1-2, 5-6, 8]: 18, 162, 163, 173, 185, 186, 270, 284, 323, 324, 325, 327, 332
Polemocratia [**S.**1], mother of Cotys V of Thrace: 148
Pollio, Gaius Asinius: and Judaea, 222
Pompeius, Sextus: and Antony, 268, 271, 272, 315; and Eastern dynasts, 271, 272, 315
Pompey (Gnaeus Pompeius Magnus): and Armenia, 155; and Armenia Minor, 164; and Atropatene, 296; and the Battle of Pharsalus, 243, 255, 256, 257; and Cappadocia, 19, 61, 174, 175, 177, 178, 179, 180, 181, 194, 244; and Cilicia, 186, 187, 188, 189, 190, 233; and Colchis, 155, 164; and Commagene, 61, 193, 194, 195, 196; dealings of, with Eastern dynasts, 14, 20, 321; death of, 257; and Egypt, 215, 231, 232, 233, 234, 235, 237, 238, 241, 242, 245, 246, 247, 251, 254, 255, 256, 257; and Elymais, 111; and Emesa, 64, 199, 201; and Galatia, 164, 166, 167, 171; and Gordyene, 109, 302, 305; and Iberia, 155, 292; and the Ituraeans, 72, 206, 208, 216; and Judaea, 79, 104, 155, 210, 213, 215, 216, 217, 228, 306; Judaea after the command of, 217-223; and Mithradates Eupator of Pontus, 154, 155, 164, 233, 257; and the minor dynasts of the Levant, 80; and the Nabataeans, 75, 210, 216, 221; and Osrhoene, 307; and Paphlagonia, 156, 164, 169; and Parthia, 117, 118, 194, 257, 301, 302, 303, 304, 307; and Pontus, 155, 156, 160, 164, 241; and Seleucid Syria, 45, 64, 69, 103, 104, 117, 155, 190, 199, 203, 204, 206, 215, 241, 261; and Sophene, 106; and Thrace, 29, 146, 147, 149; and Tigranes the Great of Armenia, 45, 117, 154, 257, 281, 282; and Tigranes the Younger of Armenia, 106, 285, 302
Pontus [**S.**2]: **35-48 and 345n.20-349n.39; 151-163 and 385n.21-389n.61;** and Arsaces, **161**; and Asander and Dynamis, **159-160**; under Darius, **160-161**; under Mithradates VI Eupator, **36-48**, **151-155**; and

Mithradates of Pergamon, **158-159**; and Pharnaces II, **155-158**; under Polemo I, **161-163**; also mentioned *passim*, esp. 9-21, 27-35, 49-57, 91-105, 113-119, 164-186, 269-276, 282-293, 311-318, 321-332. *See also* Maps xxii-xxiv
Postumus, Gaius Rabirius: and Egypt, 235, 244, 245, 246, 253
Potheinos, tutor of Ptolemy XIII of Egypt: death of, 259; power of, 251, 253, 254, 258, 262
Protarchus, *dioiketes* in Egypt: 253
Prusias II of Bithynia: 30
Psentais. *See next two entries*
Psherenptah (Psentais), high priest of Memphis (husband of Berenice, daughter of Ptolemy VIII of Egypt): 83, 93
Psherenptah (Psentais III), high priest of Memphis (grandson of Berenice): 93, 94, 95
Ptolemaios, *dioiketes* in Egypt: 253, 254
Ptolemaios of Commagene [**S**.5]: **60**
Ptolemies of Egypt [**S**.5, 7]: **81-95 and 363n.1-370n.15; 229-279 and 416n.1-445n.376;** and Commagene, 60; empire of, 12, 13, 16, 20, 22, 23, 36, 77, 78, 79, 117, 118, 330; and the Seleucids, 10, 14, 17, 25, 65, 73, 77
Ptolemy I Soter I of Egypt: 81, 84, 230
Ptolemy II of Egypt: 76
Ptolemy III Euergetes I of Egypt: 240
Ptolemy V Epiphanes of Egypt: 87, 256
Ptolemy VI Philometor of Egypt [**S**.7]: 83
Ptolemy VIII Euergetes II Physcon of Egypt [**S**.7]: 25, 60, 65, 78, 81, 83, 85, 90, 92
Ptolemy IX Philometor Soter II Lathyros of Egypt [**S**.7]: **84-88 and 366n.5-368n.8;** and Cyprus, 76, 84, 265; and Cyrene, 84; descendants of, 82, 91, 92, 229, 236, 238, 256; and Judaea, 73, 76, 77, 78, 82; and the Seleucids, 67, 68, 76, 203, 330; and Tigranes the Great of Armenia, 104
Ptolemy X Alexander I of Egypt [**S**.7]: **82-84 and 364n.2-366n.4;** and Cleopatra III of Egypt, 76, 77, 85; compared with Mithradates II of the Parthians, 119; as father of Ptolemy XI of Egypt, 87, 90; marriage to Cleopatra Berenice III of Egypt, 88; and Petubastis, high priest, 93; and Rome, 85, 89
Ptolemy XI Alexander II of Egypt [**S**.7]: **89-91 and 368n.11;** and Judaea, 76; and Mithradates Eupator of Pontus, 86, 89, 91; and Petubastis, high priest, 93; and Rome, 88, 89, 91, 92, 232, 234; successors of, 91
Ptolemy XII Theos Neos Dionysos Philopator Philadelphos Auletes of Egypt [**S**.7]: **91-95 and 369n.12-370n.15; 229-235 and 416n.1-420n.44; 237-239 and 422n.59-423n.78; 243-248 and 426n.103-427n.133;** and Ascalon, 214, 256; and Caesar, *see under* Caesar; and Cyprus, 236, 237; exile of, 205, 220, **237-239**, 240; and Judaea, 76; legitimacy of, 88, 89, 90, 239; and Mithradates Eupator of Pontus, 42, 152, 242; and Pompey, 215, 256, 257; restoration of, 210, 220, 239, 241, 242, **243-248**, 250, 286, 305; and Rome, 268, 276, 332; successors of, 19, 248-258; titles of, 275. *See also* Illustr. 128

Ptolemy XIII Theos Philadelphos of Egypt [**S.**7]: **248-255 and 427n.134-431n.173;** and Caesar, 258, 259, 260, 261, 262; and Cleopatra VII of Egypt, **248-251**, **251-255**, 262, 263, 265, 267; debt to Rome of, 245; and exile of Cleopatra VII, 255, 256, 257, 258; as successor of Ptolemy XII Auletes of Egypt, 246, 247

Ptolemy XIV of Egypt [**S.**7]: and Caesar, 157, 258, 262, 263; and Cleopatra VII of Egypt, 255, 260, 262, 263, 264, 265; debt to Rome of, 245

Ptolemy XV Caesar Theos Philopator Philometor (Caesarion) of Egypt [**S.**7]: **262-264 and 435n.225-436n.238;** after the Battle of Actium, 278, 279; co-regency of, with Cleopatra VII of Egypt, 265, 266, 271, 274; honours of, 162, 172, 250, 265, 267, 271, 274, 289. *See also* Illustr. 138

Ptolemy of Chalcis. *See* Ptolemy of the Ituraeans

Ptolemy of Cyprus [**S.**7]: **236-237 and 420n.45-422n.58;** intermarriage with Pontus, 42, 242; and Ptolemy XII Auletes of Egypt, 247

Ptolemy of the Ituraeans (Ptolemy of Chalcis) [**S.**8]: **70-72 and 357n.16-358n.18; 206-207 and 408nn.47-49;** and Aretas III of the Nabataeans, 74, 78, 209; and Pompey, 80, 208, 216

Ptolemy of Mauretania [**S.**7], son of Juba II of Mauretania and Cleopatra Selene of Egypt: 279

Ptolemy Apion of Cyrene [**S.**7]: 82, 83, 84, 95

Ptolemy Philadelphos [**S.**7], son of Antony and Cleopatra: 269, 274, 279

Pulcher, Appius Claudius: and Cappadocia, 178; and Tigranes the Great of Armenia, 47, 64, 108, 203

Pulcher, Publius Clodius: and Egypt, 236, 237, 239; and Tigranes the Younger of Armenia, 285

Pylaemenes of Paphlagonia, son of Nicomedes III of Bithynia: 31, 38

Pylaemenes of Paphlagonia, mid-first-century ruler of Paphlagonia: 156

Pythodoris I of Pontus [**S.**1-2, 4-6]: marriage to Archelaus I of Cappadocia, 185, 325; marriage to Polemo I of Pontus, 160, 163, 185, 269, 323, 324, 332

Pythodoris II of Pontus [**S.**2], granddaughter of Polemo I of Pontus: 323, 324

Pythodorus of Tralles [**S.**1-2]: 276

Quadratus, Iulius, descendant of Galatian royalty: 324

Rabbel I of the Nabataeans: **73 and 358n.20**

Rabocentus, ruler of the Bessi: 146

Radamistus of Iberia: 293

Ramses II of Egypt: 268

Rhambaeans: 80, 221, 282, 307

Rhascus [**S.**1], brother of Rhescuporis I of Thrace: 149

Rhascypolis. *See next entry*

Rhescuporis I (Rhascypolis) of Thrace [**S.**1]: **149-150 and 384nn.13-15;** and Rome, 331; as Sapaean dynast, 28, 146, 150, 151

Rhescuporis II of Thrace [**S.**1-2]: 149, 150, 151, 322

Rhescuporis III of Thrace [**S.**1]: 151, 323

Rhodogune [**S.**10], daughter of Mithradates I of Parthia: 117

Rhoemetalces, member of the Sapaean royal house in Thrace: 29
Rhoemetalces I of Thrace [**S**.1]: **151 and 385nn.18-20;** at the Battle of Actium, 150, 331; and Cotys V of Thrace, 322; as King of the Thracians, 148, 150, 323
Rhoemetalces II of Thrace [**S**.1-2]: 151, 323, 324
Rhoemetalces III of Thrace [**S**.2]: 163, 323, 324
Rufio: as legionary commander of Caesar in Egypt, 261
Rullus, Publius: and Egypt, 234

Sacesinians: 294
Sadalas I of Thrace [**S**.1]: **29-30 and 340n.8-341n.9;** as Odrysian-Astaean king, 28, 145, 329
Sadalas II of Thrace [**S**.1]: **147-149 and 383n.7-384n.12;** at the Battle of Pharsalus, 146, 150
Sadalas III of Thrace [**S**.1]: 149, 276
Sadducees: 79, 213, 214
Sakai: 114
Salome [**S**.8], sister of Herod the Great of Judaea: 227
Samaria (Samaritis): 218, 224
Samos of Commagene [**S**.5]: **60;** and Cappadocia, 53
Sampsigeramus I of Emesa [**S**.5-6]: **64 and 356nn.7-8; 199-200 and 406n.23-407n.26;** and Bassus, 201, 310; and the Battle of Carrhae, 306; establishment of monarchy by, 12; and the last Seleucids, 64, 69, 198, 241, 332
Sampsigeramus II of Emesa [**S**.5-6]: 202, 297, 326, 327
Sanatruces (Sanatruq) of Hatra: 108
Sanatruq I of Hatra. *See preceding entry*
Sapaeans [**S**.1], royal house of Thrace: monarchs of, 27, 28, 29, 145, 146, 147, 148, 149, 150, 322, 331. *See also* Map xxiv
Sardanapalus of Assyria, 229
Sasan, grandfather of Ardashir of Persis: 112
Saspires (in Herodotus): 292
Sassanids of Persia: 11, 24, 96, 110, 111, 112, 114, 318
Saxa, Lucius Decidius: and the Parthians, 308, 311
Scaurus, Marcus Aemilius: as governor of Syria, 204, 210, 215, 221
Scipio, Publius Cornelius (Publius Cornelius Scipio Aemilianus Africanus Numantinus): visit to Egypt of, 83, 232, 261
Scipio, Publius Cornelius (Publius Cornelius Scipio Nasica): as governor of Syria, 220
Scipio, Quintus Caecilius Metellus. *See* Metellus
Scordisci, Thracian tribe: 27
Scribonius of Bosporus: 160
Scythia: 42, 43, 47, 114, 156, 317
Seleucids [**S**.5, 7]: **65-69 and 356n.9-357n.15; 102-105 and 373nn.8-11; 117 and 380n.42; 202-205 and 407n.37-408n.45**; conquest of, by Tigranes the Great of Armenia, 17, 36, 45, 47, 61, **102-105**, 143, 152, 186, 199, 280, 284, 301, 330, 331; descendants of, **204-205**; and the dynasts of the Levant, 19, 25, 60, 62, 63, 69, 70, 71, 72, 73, 74, 76, 77, 78, 79, 198, 207, 209, 215, 219, 220, 332; and Egypt, 248; empire of, 11, 13, 18, 20; historical interests of, 10; intermarriage with Cappadocia, 52,

54, 57; intermarriage with Commagene, 14, 15, 17, 60, 62, 193, 224, 297, 330; intermarriage with Parthia, 14; intermarriage with Pontus, 36, 242; intermarriage with the Ptolemies, 14, 17, 76, 82, 84, 85, 86, 87, 91, 95, 230, 241, 242, 247, 272; Parthian succession to, 25, 61, 87, 113, 115, **117**, 118, 119, 309; Roman succession to, 16, 17, 19, 22, 26, 45, 64, 186, 190, 199, 261, 280, 301, 303, 331, 334; and trans-Euphrates dynasties, 106, 107, 109, 110, 111, 112, 292, 294, 297, 300. *See also* Syria

Seleucus, son of Cleopatra Selene, sister-wife of Ptolemy IX Lathyros of Egypt: 205, 241

Seleucus II, Seleucid: 11

Seleucus V, Seleucid [**S.**7]: 66

Seleucus VI Epiphanes Nicator, Seleucid [**S.**7]: 67, 203

Seleucus I of Osrhoene: 106

Semites: 24, 59, 63, 80, 96, 205, 218, 321, 328

Sentius, Gaius: as governor of Macedonia, 29

Seuthes, Thracian dynast: 27

Seven Persians, ancestors of Pontic dynasts: 36

Severus, Gaius Claudius, descendant of Galatian royalty: 324

Severus, Gaius Iulius [**S.**3], descendant of Galatian royalty: 173, 324

Severus, Lucius Septimius [**S.**6], emperor: 108, 202, 213, 307

Silas of Lysias, minor dynast of the Levant: 80

Silo, Pompaedius: and Judaea, 224

Simon, Jewish leader: 75

Sinatruces I Theopator Euergetes Eusebes of Parthia [**S.**10]: **119-120 and 382n.45;** and Iberia, 292; and Mithradates Eupator of Pontus, 34, 47; and Orodes I of Parthia, 116; strength of rule of, 331; succeeded by Phraates III, 48, 143, 285, 300, 301; and Tigranes the Great of Armenia, 100, 117, 119, 301

Sisines [**S.**3], rival of Ariarathes X of Cappadocia: 56, 182

Sittacene: 110

Socrates 'Chrestos,' brother of Nicomedes IV of Bithynia: 33, 34, 35, 42, 45

Sohaemus, Gaius Iulius, of Emesa [**S.**5-6]: 106, 162, 297, 327

Sophene: **105-106 and 374n.12;** also mentioned, 99, 101, 102, 103, 105, 106, 109, 120, 152, 153, 174, 175, 280, 282, 285, 291, 302. *See also* Map xxvi

Sosius, quaestor of Antony: and surrender of Antigonus of Judaea, 225

Spinther, Publius Lentulus: and Egypt, 238, 239

Strato, father of Tarcondimotus I of Cilicia: 187

Strato, [Gaius Jul]ius, descendant of Tarcondimotus I of Cilicia: 192

Straton of Beroea, minor dynast of the Levant: 80

Stratonice [**S.**3-4], sister of Ariarathes V of Cappadocia: 54

Styrax of Cilicia: 192

Sulla, Publius Cornelius: arrogance of, 118, 119, 331; meeting of, with Parthian envoy, 52, 61, 97, 100, 101, 115, 118, 119, 301, 318; and Mithradates Eupator of Pontus, 40, 41, 44, 45, 46, 329; and Ptolemy XI Alexander II of Egypt, 87, 89, 90, 91, 92; restoration of Ariobarzanes I of Cappadocia by, 40, 41, 44, 56, 58, 97,

100, 118; siege of Athens by, 86, 176; and the Thracians, 28, 29; and Tigranes the Great of Armenia, 100

Sumerians of Mesopotamia: 9, 10, 19, 80

'Surena,' Parthian name and title: 306, 309

Susiana: 105, 110, 111. *See also* Map xxv

Symbace: 298

Syria [**S.**7]: **65-69 and 356n.9-357n.15; 202-205 and 407n.37-408n.45;** under Antiochus XIII, **203**; and the coming of Tigranes the Great of Armenia, **68-69**; under Philip II, **203-204**; and the sons of Antiochus VIII Grypus, **66-68**; also mentioned *passim*, esp.10, 11, 15-19, 59-64, 70-105, 113-120, 185-201, 206-231, 241-288, 295-317, 327, 330-332. *See also* Seleucids. *See also* Maps xxii-xxiii, xxvii

Tarcondimotus I of Cilicia: **187-191 and 400n.144-402n.159;** and Antony, 269, 276, 277; and the Battle of Actium, 325; and the Battle of Carrhae, 306; and Caesar, 157; and Cicero, 178, 195, 200, 310; and Deiotarus I of Galatia, 169; establishment of monarchy by, 12, 19, 332; Hellenistic organization of, 205; royal title of, 162; successors of, 184, **191-192**, 325. *See also* Illustr. 132

Tarcondimotus II of Cilicia: 191, 325

Tarcondimotus Philopator of Cilicia: 192

Tectosages [**S.**3], Galatian tribe: 164, 167, 168, 171. *See also* Map xxiv

Teres, Thracian dynast: 27

Teutones: 40

Theodore of Amathus, Gadara and Philadelphia, minor dynast of the Levant: 75, 80

Theodotus, adviser of Ptolemy XIII of Egypt: 254

Theophanes, agent of Pompey: and Ptolemy XII Auletes, 237

Thrace [**S.**1]: **25-30 and 337n.1-341n.9; 145-151 and 383n.1-385n.20;** under Cotys III, **29-30**; under Cotys IV, **146**; under Cotys VI, **28-29**; under Cotys VII, **150-151**; under Mostis, **27-28**; under Rhescuporis I, **149-150**; under Rhoemetalces I, **151**; and Rome, **27**; under Sadalas I, **29-30**; under Sadalas II, **147-149**; also mentioned, 17, 18, 30, 31, 40, 42, 43, 87, 88, 159, 160, 163, 204, 271, 276, 280, 281, 284, 322, 323, 324, 327, 329, 331, 332. *See also* Maps xxii-xxiv

Tiberius (Tiberius Julius Caesar Augustus), emperor: 19, 30, 62, 185, 192, 198, 322, 325, 332

Tigranes the Great of Armenia [**S.**1-2, 4, 9-10]: **97-105 and 370n.1-373n.11; 280-284 and 445n.2-447n.15;** and Adiabene, 107; Armenian empire of, 12, 16, 113, 114, 143, 330, and Cappadocia, 46, 52, 57, 174, 175, 176, 182, 184, 330; and Characene, 110; and Commagene, 11, 60, 61, 62, 193, 194, 197, 198, 330; descendants of, 273, 285, 291, 293; and Egypt, 93, 247; and Emesa, 64; and Galatia, 331; and Gordyene, 108, 175, 302, 305; and Iberia, 292; intermarriage of, 14, 38, 42, 119, **282-284**, 295; as 'King of Kings,' 44, 47, **100-101**, 119, 143, 273, 280, 288, 297; last years of, **280-282**; and Lucullus, *see under* Lucullus, Lucius Licinius; and Mithradates Eupator of Pontus,

21, 36, 38, 40, 42, 46, 47, 48, 152, 153, 154, 155; neighbours of, **99-100**; and Parthia, 47, 113, 114, 115, 116, 117, 118, 119, 120, 154, 216, 257, 301, 302, 303, 304, 305, 318, 330; and Rome, 14, 23, 154, 331, 333, 334; and Seleucid Syria, 16, 17, 25, 45, 47, 66, 67, **68-69**, 71, 72, 75, 78, 79, 86, 88, 91, 92, 93, 94, **102-105**, 143, 190, 198, 199, 203, 204, 206, 208, 209, 234, 241, 280, 330, 331; and Sophene, 106, 152; and Thrace, 145; tiara of, 9; and Tigranes the Younger, **284-285**; and Tigranocerta, **100-102**, *see also* Tigranocerta; work of, **284**. *See also* Illustr. 128

Tigranes the Younger of Armenia [**S.**9-10]: **284-285 and 447nn.16-18;** and Gordyene, 109, 282, 302; and the Parthians, 154, 282, 283, 286, 290, 301, 302, 303; and Pompey, 282, 301, 302, 303; and Sophene, 282, 302; and Tigranes the Great, 154, 282, 283, 285, 301

Tigranes III of Armenia [**S.**9]: 261, 291, 316

Tigranes IV of Armenia [**S.**9]: 291

Tigranes V of Armenia [**S.**4-6, 8]: 162, 291, 300, 325

Tigranes VI of Armenia [**S.**4-6, 8]: 162, 291, 325

Tigranocerta: **101-102 and 372n.7;** battle near, 22, 97, 152, 204, 280, 292, 307; construction and population of, 46, 67, 99, 107, 109, 120, 174, 280; siege of, 71, 104, 108. *See also* Map xxvi

Timarchus, satrap of Media: 295

Tiridates II of Parthia [**S.**10]: 317, 318

Tiridates of Parthia [**S.**10], brother of Vologaeses I of Parthia: 20, 23

Titius, Marcus: and Archelaus I of Cappadocia, 185; and death of Sextus Pompeius, 272, 315

Tolistobogii [**S.**3], Galatian tribe: 51, 164, 168. *See also* Map xxiv

Trachonitis: 80

Trajan (Marcus Ulpius Traianus), emperor: 108, 307, 311, 312, 318

Trapezusia: 164

Triarius, Gaius, officer of Lucullus: 158

Trocmi [**S.**3], Galatian tribe: 164, 166, 167, 168. *See also* Map xxiv

Tuthmose III of Egypt: 268

Urartu, Kingdom of: 9

Valens (Flavius Valens Augustus), eastern emperor: 26

Varro, Marcus Terentius (Lucullus): in Thrace, 28

Ventidius, Publius: and the Parthians, 212, 223, 224, 312

Vespasian (Titus Flavius Vespasianus), emperor: 19, 63, 187, 198, 202, 241, 326

Vologaeses I of Parthia [**S.**10]: 20, 114

Vologaeses IV (III) of Parthia: 110

Vonones I of Parthia [**S.**10]: 299

Vonones II of Parthia [**S.**10]: 289, 299, 300

Xerxes I of Persia: 329

Zarbienus of Gordyene: and Tigranes the Great of Armenia, 80, 102, 108, 109, 153, 175, 282

Zariadras [**S.**9], father of Artaxias I of Armenia: 99

Zariadras, general of Antiochus III, Seleucid: 99, 106, 295
Zariadres [**S.**9], son of Tigranes the Great of Armenia: 283
Zeno [**S.**1-2], father of Polemo I of Pontus: 161
Zeno-Artaxias of Armenia [**S.**1-2, 5]: 16, 162, 163, 283, 291, 293, 324, 332
Zeno Cotylas of Philadelphia, minor dynast of the Levant: 75, 80
Zenobia of Palmyra: 174
Zenodorus, son of Lysanias of the Ituraeans: 208
Zober of Albania: 293
Zoilus of Dora and Straton's Tower, minor dynast of the Levant: 76, 77, 80

Phoenix Supplementary Volumes Series

1 *Studies in Honour of Gilbert Norwood* edited by Mary E. White
2 *Arbiter of Elegance: A Study of the Life and Works of C. Petronius* Gilbert Bagnani
3 *Sophocles the Playwright* S.M. Adams
4 *A Greek Critic: Demetrius on Style* G.M.A. Grube
5 *The Coastal Demes of Attica: A Study of the Policy of Kleisthenes* C.W.J. Eliot
6 *Eros and Psyche: Studies in Plato, Plotinus, and Origen* John M. Rist
7 *Pythagoras and Early Pythagoreanism* J.A. Philip
8 *Plato's Psychology* T.M. Robinson
9 *Greek Fortifications* F.E. Winter
10 *Comparative Studies in Republican Latin Imagery* Elaine Fantham
11 *Orators in Cicero's Brutus: Prosopography and Chronology* G.V. Sumner
12 *Caput and Colonate: Towards a History of Late Roman Taxation* Walter Goffart
13 *A Concordance to the Works of Ammianus Marcellinus* Geoffrey Archbold
14 *Fallax opus: Poet and Reader in the Elegies of Propertius* John Warden
15 *Pindar's 'Olympian One': A Commentary* Douglas E. Gerber
16 *Greek and Roman Mechanical Water-Lifting Devices: The History of a Technology* John Peter Oleson
17 *The Manuscript Tradition of Propertius* James L. Butrica
18 Parmenides of Elea *Fragments: A Text and Translation with Introduction* edited by David Gallop
19 *The Phonological Interpretation of Ancient Greek: A Pandialectal Analysis* Vit Bubenik
20 *Studies in the Textual Tradition of Terence* John N. Grant
21 *The Nature of Early Greek Lyric: Three Preliminary Studies* R.L. Fowler
22 Heraclitus *Fragments: A Text and Translation with a Commentary* T.M. Robinson
23 *The Historical Method of Herodotus* Donald Lateiner